ACKNOWLEDGEMENTS

Thank you first to my parents for teaching me the difference between healthy skepticism and unhealthy cynicism, and for helping me live through the trauma that defined the years from the Cuban Missile Crisis to Watergate; to Joseph Green and Faith Harper for making this book possible; to my first collaborators, Stephen Bright, Juan Garcia, David G. Armstrong, Earl Golz, Mike Blackwell, and Jay Harrison; to my co-author, Walter F. Graf; to Kathleen O'Brien for editing and proofreading; to those who published, promoted, or aided my research previously, including Jerry Rose, Andy Winiarczyk, Patrick Fourmy, Gary Rowell, Dawn Meredith, David Price, Larry Howard, Gary Shaw, Alan Kent, John Kelin, Deenie Richards, Jim DiEugenio, Lisa Pease, George Michael Evica, Charles Drago, Ian Griggs, Bill Kelly, John Judge, John Simpkin, Robert Howard, Harrison Livingstone, Noel Twyman, Barr McClellan, Linda Minor, Eric Sneary, Ed Tatro, David Denton, Judyth Baker, and Leslie Sharp; to Jeff Worcester and the founders of The Center for Deep Political Research for making our think tank a reality; and to every person named in this book, whether you told the truth or not, you ultimately contributed to the truth. Finally, I thank my wife and family for helping me know the cognitive dissonance most people have as a survival and defense mechanism in the face of the daily terror that is the Deep State in the heart of Texas.

THE DEEP STATE
IN THE
HEART OF TEXAS

RICHARD BARTHOLOMEW

ISBN: 0-9988898-3-0
ISBN-13: 978-0-9988898-3-2

CONTENTS

Foreword by Edgar Tatro
vi

Introduction by Richard Bartholomew
23

PART ONE: COINCIDENCE
(The Rifle)
27

PART TWO: HAPPENSTANCE
(The Rambler)
145

PART THREE: ENEMY ACTION
(The Media)
385

With a respectful nod to Ian Fleming.

FOREWORD
BY EDGAR F. TATRO

"A COZY LITTLE TOWN CALLED DALLAS"

Through the decades it has been my firm belief that Richard Bartholomew has essentially pursued Texas-based targets as primary suspects in the JFK assassination conspiracy. When he requested that I write an introduction for his book, it seemed appropriate that I offer an overview to support his firm belief that the so-called Texas Mafia played a dominant role in the plot.

While I have always insisted that the assassination resulted from a collaboration including the most powerful people in the country, I also believed full well that a Texas axis was instrumental in carrying out the plot and cover-up. Please consider the fact that I had befriended Madeleine Brown, Lyndon Johnson's mistress of two decades, who referred to me as her "adopted Yankee son," as well as the infamous Billie Sol Estes, the Texas wheeler dealer, a major behind-the-scenes partner in crime with LBJ, who once remarked about me, "How does that kid know so much (about the assassination) and a Yankee to boot." And yet, during my introductory statement in "The Guilty Men," part nine of Nigel Turner's *The Men Who Killed Kennedy* series broadcast on The History Channel in 2003, I clearly implicated not only Lyndon Johnson, but also Secret Service Chief James Rowley and FBI Director J. Edgar Hoover, and by insinuation, their underlings and cronies and handlers in the Dallas caper. Despite accusations to the contrary by disinformation agents and assets, I have never cited Lyndon Johnson as the mastermind of the JFK assassination conspiracy, but the evidence is overwhelmingly conclusive that the intricate plot and subsequent cover-up would have failed without his central involvement before and after the heinous crime.

With these thoughts in mind, I needed to consider how to support Richard Bartholomew's basic premise while employing brevity in doing so. I concluded that I could only accomplish my goal by criticizing, at least in part, the predominantly popular consensus of the JFK assassination research community, a term I consider an oxymoron, that "the CIA killed Kennedy," and, at the same time, try to present a brief overview of the issues implicating the Texas axis in the conspiracy.

My intention is not to exonerate the CIA, but to simply demonstrate that key conspiratorial activities, of which the CIA were not involved, were committed by others. Of course, it is impossible to offer, briefly, extensive and meticulous details establishing a "CIA DID NOT" list, but the following assertions should convince any reasonably educated person that blaming the CIA, alone, for killing JFK is an inadequate, limited hangout supposition.

Let me repeat my fair warning. Due to constrictions of brevity, the following "CIA DID NOT" list is by no means complete or thorough in rich detail, but it should be considered a significant guide to delve deeper into the issues and names delineated.

The CIA did not invite JFK to Dallas. The evidence clearly indicates that Lyndon Johnson, Jack Valenti, one of LBJ's closest henchmen, and Texas Governor John Connally, perhaps LBJ's best friend, were the key individuals who suckered JFK to Texas and subsequently Dallas.

The CIA did not set up the motorcade at 11 miles per hour down streets with right angle turns encircled by tall, insecure buildings and trees. Secret Service agents, particularly Forrest Sorrels, John Connally, and LBJ lackey Bill Moyers, were primarily responsible for the absurd motorcade route. The reader is urged to read the House Select Committee on Assassinations (HSCA) testimony of Jerry Bruno, JFK's security advance man for the Dallas trip, as well as *The Advance Man* by Jerry Bruno and Jeff Greenfield to learn the truth concerning how JFK was manipulated into the Dealey Plaza death trap by Connally and Moyers.

Even the HSCA, which resolved very little regarding the motorcade controversy, was skeptical of Moyers' responses and amnesia regarding his participation regarding the motorcade arrangements---"Moyers' recollection about these matters was less than clear. He could not recall whether it was ever questionable that a motorcade would occur in Dallas. He could not recall whether there had been a debate about the selection of the speech site. He could recall no discussion with Governor Connally about the site for the President's luncheon, but instead said his discussions involved 'who was participating and the necessity of cooperation'. In fact, he could not remember whether he had even visited Dallas."

The CIA did not remove General McHugh from the middle seat of the JFK limo which afforded conveniently more space for JFK to be a target. Likewise the CIA did not place Admiral George Burkley, the President's physician in the rear of the motorcade.

CIA did not place the press bus at position #21 so that when the assassination occurred, the professional photographers filmed none of the actual crime.

The CIA did not remove the JFK limo bubble top. The documented HSCA record includes the testimony of security official, Elizabeth Forsling Harris who stated unequivocally that Bill Moyers, one of LBJ's most loyal lieutenants, instructed her to "Get that God-damned bubble top off unless it's pouring rain."

The CIA did not reduce the number of the police motorcyclists surrounding JFK's limo nor move the remaining security escort back behind the car. (For more details of Secret Service complicity in the JFK assassination, the reader is encouraged to read *Survivor's Guilt* by Vince Palamara).

The CIA did not launder Governor John Connally's clothes, an act which destroyed crucial evidence in the case by destroying bullet traces and distorting the bullet holes which prevented any means of determining entrance or exit holes. It also eliminated a key means by which to verify or ridicule the single bullet theory which alleged one bullet hit both JFK and Connally virtually simultaneously. It is now documented that every person involved in the chain of transfer of the clothes, be it Representative Henry Gonzalez of Texas, Nellie Connally, the governor's wife, Cliff Carter, a key LBJ aide, Senator Arlen Specter of the Warren Commission or J. Edgar Hoover, Director of the FBI, were all allies of Lyndon Baines Johnson. Take your pick!

The CIA did not plant (or switch) the Parkland Hospital stretcher bullet with the controversial "bastard bullet" of single bullet theory fame with the bogus Commission Exhibit 399. The chain of transfer from Parkland Hospital orderly, Darrell Tomlinson, to O. P. Wright, a Parkland Hospital security officer, to Secret Service agent Richard Johnsen, to Secret Service Chief, James Rowley, an LBJ crony, to FBI agent Elmer Todd, to FBI ballistics expert, Robert Frazier and his FBI associates, Cortlandt Cunningham and Charles Killion includes two shocking revelations. The first one is very old. Secret Service agent Johnsen and Secret Service Chief Rowley never scratched their initials on the bullet, an act which any Oswald defense attorney at trial would have exploited to create reasonable doubt in any objective jury since the bullet was alleged to have originated from Oswald's rifle, (another accusation which is justifiably disputed and wholly rejected by researchers). The second, more contemporary shocker, resulted from the research of researcher John Hunt. The documentary record establishes that the four FBI agents all scratched their initials into CE 399, but Mr. Hunt visited the National Archives and was allowed to take high resolution photos of the bullet. Elmer Todd's initials are NOT present on the bullet. Hunt's discovery is smoking gun proof that CE399 is fraudulent as well as proof that Lee Harvey Oswald was framed! And not one CIA agent is involved in the scandal.

Likewise the CIA did not switch the three Texas School Book Depository spent shells with bogus shells. The reader is encouraged to study the research of Barry Krusch. First, Krusch has established that there are two very questionable and contradictory chains of transfer of the shells from Dallas to Washington D.C. Secondly the documented record confirms that FBI ballistics expert Robert Frazier scratched his initials on the shells, but Krusch, reminiscent of John Hunt, visited the National Archives and took high resolution photos of the shells only to find that Frazier's initials are NOT on the shells.

Virtually all of the evidence utilized in the case to incriminate Lee Harvey Oswald as the assassin is disputed and since almost all of the evidence was collected by the Secret Service before reaching the FBI and then the Warren Commission, any assertions that the evidence was planted to frame Lee Harvey Oswald cannot be employed to blame the CIA.

The CIA did not destroy the JFK limo windshield and replace it. There were at least eight credible witnesses who observed a bullet hole in the limo windshield including two respected journalists, two honest Secret Service agents, a Parkland Hospital nurse and a Dallas police officer, yet the windshield in the National Archives possesses only cracks. Thanks to the diligent research of Doug Weldon, who interviewed George Whittaker, a veteran glass expert of forty years for the company, Hess and Eisenhardt of Ohio, where the limo was rebuilt and refurbished in its entirety on orders from Lyndon Baines Johnson as suggested to him by J. Edgar Hoover, we know that there was a bullet hole in the windshield, which Whittaker insisted came from the front and that Secret Service agents ordered Whittaker to replace the original windshield which was scrapped.

Furthermore, thanks primarily to researcher Fred Newcomb, we know the windshield was switched a second time because the first fraudulent windshield was given cracks incorrectly on the inside of the glass (confirmed by Secret Service agent Roy Kellerman), to give it the impression of an impact from behind, but the unique glass of the JFK limo would have actually created cracks on the outside of the windshield. Thus a second replacement, fabricating the cracks on the outside of the glass was inserted, in order to amend the original error, and it is clear Kellerman capitulated to the fraudulent act.

The CIA did not deep-six a retrieved bullet discovered wedged in the JFK limo frame, which, typically, held the bubble top in place for the limo. A small cluster of Hess and Eisenhardt employees were aware of the discovery, two of whom were interviewed by my close friend, researcher Rick Russo, and there is little doubt that Hess executives cooperated with either Secret Service and/or FBI personnel to bury and possibly destroy the evidence. Documentation exists of one private citizen, who learned of the story from Hess employees, and tried to motivate federal law enforcement to investigate, but he was ignored.

The CIA did not deep-six a retrieved bullet found in Dealey Plaza in the 1990s which hit the JFK limo on 11/22/63. In 1998 thanks to the kindness of FBI watchdog Joe Balter, Rick Russo and I were invited to have dinner with a respected former FBI forensic expert and major whistle blower, Frederick Whitehurst, a first rate American patriot and hero, who was also a forensic chemist in the chemistry department of the FBI in Washington. A quick internet search will reveal Whitehurst's courageous battle to expose the FBI's incompetent and skewered handling of crucial evidence as a well as perjury through his lengthy tenure at the bureau. When Whitehurst presented his evidence of documented corruption allowed inside the FBI lab, the FBI opted for damage control and settled by paying Whitehurst 1.16 million dollars and his legal fees of $258.380.

At our meeting Whitehurst told me that a few years prior to 1998, he had determined that a bullet found in Dealey Plaza contained a speck of paint matching the paint from JFK's limo. My efforts to discover any documentation regarding this bullet from the National Archives and the FBI were fruitless. Another bullet fired in Dealey Plaza spells conspiracy and the CIA had nothing to do with hiding the evidence. Since this event took place in the nineties, it is also confirmation that the FBI is still obfuscating the truth regarding November 22, 1963.

The CIA did not leave James Tague's bullet-scarred curb on Main Street in Dealey Plaza unattended until August, 1964. Although FBI agents interviewed Tague in December of 1963, it was not until a Jim Lehrer article published in June of 1964 by the Dallas Times Herald that Hoover, one of LBJ's closest allies, could no longer dismiss the existence of the bullet that struck Tague, whose courage during those early years was admirable beyond words. It was an honor to know him and be trusted by him.

Since scientific tests established that no copper residue was found on the curb (the bullets allegedly employed were copper-jacketed), efforts by the Warren Commission to account for the bullet as a fragment from the JFK head shot, an impossibility considering the distance from the limo to Tague's position on Main Street near the overpass, failed. The same is true for Gerald Posner's absurd theory that the "missed shot" bullet lost its copper jacket by hitting a tree branch first, another foolish hypothesis, considering that CE 399--the bullet essential to the single bullet theory--supposedly maintained its copper jacket even after allegedly traversing two men and hitting dense bone. It is clearly evident now that at some point the curb, prior to its removal in August, 1964 by the FBI, was patched with some kind of mortar substance. The FBI's handling of this crucial piece of evidence was appalling and Hoover's specific letters citing the mark as only a smear instead of as a bullet scar are prime evidence to cover up the conspiratorial aspects of the assassination.

The CIA did not ignore the Elm Street sidewalk scar which matched perfectly as a shot fired by a grassy knoll "SOUTH" shooter. The story is an elaborate one, but succinctly, a private citizen, Eugene P. Aldredge, informed the FBI of the scar on the sidewalk adjacent to the famous grassy knoll. The FBI's examination was superficial, and even when Aldredge, just days later, told the FBI that the scar had been patched, "filled up with what appeared to be a mixture of concrete and asbestos and an attempt made to make it appear like the surrounding area," the FBI still dropped the matter.

Convinced that the scar was a bullet crease, researcher Emory Brown and I began scouring photos showing the *other* knoll, the "unfamous" grassy knoll south, in search for a shooter. Brown discovered in blow-ups of a photograph, showing the south knoll shortly after the assassination, which were taken by UPI photographer, Frank Cancellare. The photos show a human-like figure with a rifle-like object in the appropriate architectural position to cause a missed shot to the complementary sidewalk in question., and in retrospect, possibly the origin of JFK's entrance wound in the front of his throat.

In 1977 I sent copies of the figure and the details of our findings twice to the House Select Committee on Assassinations, and although they acknowledged receipt of the materials, nothing resulted. I also sent them to the National Academy of Sciences In hopes that they would consider firing test shots from the south knoll while conducting their investigation of the Dallas police acoustic tape recording, but other than acknowledging receipt of the materials, they ignored the suggestion. I even sent the materials to the television show, "That's Incredible!" to no avail. On March 24, 1995 I testified before the Assassination Records Review Board at the Boston State House, but not one member of that group wanted to look at the photos, although a Boston television news outlet briefly showed a blow up on television that night.

Researcher Harold Weisberg was unaware of our research, but he had written, "The FBI's interest was in keeping the possible point of origin inside the TSBD, where it said Oswald was, while pretending that the scar Aldredge saw and reported, was irrelevant. It does not, for example, point out that there is another knoll on the other or south side of, Dealey Plaza and that a bullet that caused that scar could have come from there."

On April 11, 1997 Weisberg and I discussed by phone the grassy knoll south figure and he was absolutely convinced that there was a sniper in the area.

Earlier, in November 1977, I was fortunate enough to meet John Kennedy's best friend, Dave Powers, at Harvard University. Mr. Powers was a guest lecturer offering anecdotes exemplifying the wit and wisdom of JFK at a course concerning the Kennedy presidency and I spoke to the same forum some weeks later about the conspiracy to assassinate the President.

Prior to his speech, we were introduced and I showed him the photos and blow ups. His eyes nearly popped. He asked calmly, but with a decidedly enthusiastic tone to his voice, "Does Congress, (the HSCA), have these?"

I answered, "Yes, I sent them myself."

He replied, "Good."

I will never forget the look of shock, but hope in his face.

The CIA did not cover up Joseph Adams Milteer's foreknowledge of the JFK assassination. This disgraceful display of FBI criminal malfeasance before and after the brutal murder of the President of the United States is also a complex trail involving conspirators and disinformation agents, initiated before the plot had occurred and carried indirectly all the way to the making of Oliver Stone's film, *JFK*. Essentially an FBI informant, Willie Somersett, tape-recorded a Dixie Klan right wing racist named Joseph Adams Milteer predicting the assassination on November 9, 1963. J. Edgar Hoover ignored the warning, even though Milteer bragged about the deed prior to the shooting on November 22, 1963 and afterward adding that Oswald had been framed for the crime. In addition, many believe a man resembling Milteer was photographed on Houston Street as the assassination occurred, but no one has yet employed computer facial recognition software to determine whether the man is Milteer or not.

Although many books, articles and documentaries discuss the Milteer saga, the most contemporary book was written by my late friend, former FBI agent Don Adams, entitled *From an Office Building with a High-Powered Rifle*. Adams detailed his nightmare ordeal of discovering that his FBI superiors had withheld the Milteer tape recording from him as well as everything else Somersett had learned implicating and incriminating Milteer in the Dallas plot so when he interviewed Milteer in person after the assassination, the young agent was flying blind.

It took decades before Adams learned that he had been exploited and manipulated into producing an empty trail in the Milteer case, which included fraudulent documents drafted by his FBI superiors to obfuscate the truth. Until he started communicating with me, Adams also had no idea that Milteer linked to another right wing member of a dangerous group called the Congress of Freedom Incorporated, Revilo Oliver, who fed massive amounts of disinformation to the Warren Commission in 1964. Likewise, Adams was unaware of another white supremacy advocate, Ned Touchstone, whose newspaper in Louisiana, *The Councilor*, published a 1949 photo allegedly of Clay Shaw and David Ferrie together. (However, the man in the photo was actually Bob Brannon, who resembled Ferrie.) In essence, it appears that right-wing disinformation agents made a concerted effort to undermine District Attorney Jim Garrison's case against Clay Shaw by enticing Garrison to place into evidence during the Shaw trial a photograph that would have falsely indicated a Shaw/Ferrie relationship. Oliver Stone's Marie Antoinette scene in the film *JFK* was based upon the inaccurate belief that the photo really depicted Shaw and Ferrie.

While it has been established by various reliable sources that Clay Shaw and David Ferrie were definitely associates of each other in the small homosexual community of New Orleans, that relationship was not provable beyond a doubt by Garrison in 1969 and the 1949 photo might have obliterated Garrison's credibility with the jury had he employed the photograph at the trial.

CIA did not lie about or ignore the Charles Bronson film taken approximately six minutes prior to the arrival of the JFK motorcade showing the TSBD windows. Given the knowledge that several witnesses insisted they had observed men in the alleged perch area prior to the assassination, the Bronson film should have received top priority during the investigation of the crime, but Dallas FBI agent Milton D. Newsom's November 25, 1963 report stated the film "failed to show the building from which the shots were fired." Rather than send Bronson's film (and other Bronson film materials) to FBI headquarters for a second opinion, the Dallas FBI office returned the materials back to Bronson.

However a quick visit to YouTube will show anyone Newsom's statement is untrue, but that document effectively terminated any interest in the film until it was brought to the attention of the House Select Committee on Assassinations on December 2, 1978. Now how's that for perfect stonewalling! Due to the late arrival of the film to the HSCA and the divided opinions of those who observed the film there, the HSCA report punted by recommending that the Department of Justice perform computer analysis to determine what it contained.

The stonewalling is evident in the bureaucratic documentation available to researchers, but the FBI and Justice Department figure heads asserted that Bronson's desire to retain his ownership rights had created an impasse. Of course, the government could have hired a private forensic firm to accommodate Bronson's wishes to avoid any Freedom of Information Act requests later or they could have forced the issue with a subpoena of the film, but instead, in one of the most disgraceful acts in American history, the Department of Justice released their final worthless report on March 20, 1988. They returned the film to Bronson and they left a crucial piece of evidence in the assassination of an American president to stay unresolved.

As we head into the sixth decade of the crime, the Bronson film has yet to be properly investigated through forensic computer analysis. Kevin Walsh, an HSCA aide and diligent researcher, concluded, "If you have film footage that bears on a murder case, you subpoena it. They didn't even consider it."

The CIA did not control or perpetrate the JFK autopsy scam. The medical aspects of this case involving the mutilation of JFK's wounds, the destruction of his brain and brain tissue slides and the insertion of fraudulent autopsy photographs and x-rays into the official record are too complex and mind boggling to report briefly, but the key suspects in the case involve Secret Service agents and Pentagon officials and possibly others, depending upon whose views one accepts, but the CIA does not appear to have any connection to JFK's corpse.

The CIA did not create two different documents about the paper bag found on the sixth floor of the Texas School Book Depository. My article, "The Paper Bag: An FBI Blueprint for Revised Documents," was originally published in *The Third Decade* in January 1985 and is available through the internet. Researcher Jack White discovered in the National Archives in two separate files, two documents purportedly the same in content except for some minor differences by FBI agent Vincent Drain about the paper bag as it compared to paper utilized in the book depository for packaging. Although the first and third paragraphs were identical, the middle sentences in the second paragraphs contradicted each other. The first Dallas FBI 89-43 document stated "This paper was examined by the FBI laboratory and found to have the same observable characteristics as the brown paper shaped like a gun case which was found near the scene of the shooting on the sixth floor in the Texas School Book Depository Building."

However the second document stated "This paper was examined by the FBI laboratory and found not to be identical with the paper gun case found at the scene of the shooting."

The subsequent response by the FBI to my request for an appropriate explanation took two attempts, but on November 27, 1984 William Baker, the Assistant Director of the Office of Congressional and Public Affairs, informed me that the document citing the paper was "not identical" to the paper gun case was inaccurate. Baker never explained how the contradiction had occurred. The elephant in the room is whether the situation indicated the fabrication of false documents to swing one way or the other or just a simple bureaucratic error, but having examined the shoddy and suspicious activities of the FBI throughout the Dallas case, it is difficult to give them the benefit of the doubt on the paper bag caper. Furthermore, the questions persist: Are other documents written by the FBI in the assassination investigation to be trusted?

Years ago, when I explained the paper bag situation to Frederick Whitehurst, the former FBI chemist who accused the FBI of utilizing tainted evidence and conducting corrupt practices during his tenure, said, "What you're telling me is that they (the FBI) were doing the same things fifteen years before I got there!"

The CIA did not destroy the lives of the whistle blowers, Don Reynolds, Bobby Baker's business partner, and my amigo, Allan Witwer, the manager of Clint Murchison's Hotel Del Charro in La Jolla, California. Both men knew too much about the Texas Mafia and the Texas axis of the Kennedy assassination conspiracy, and Lyndon Johnson and J. Edgar Hoover would make damn sure their lives were ruined.

Finally, the CIA did not select the members of the Warren Commission. Lyndon Johnson was primarily responsible for that collection of criminals to rule the labyrinth of lies, and even though the CIA-did-it pundits will be quick to point out that Allen Dulles, the former head of the CIA, who was fired by JFK after the Bay of Pigs fiasco, was a dominant member of the commission, please consider the fact that Dulles spent time in October 1963 with Lyndon Baines Johnson at the LBJ Ranch in Texas.

Hopefully my brief review stipulating that the CIA cannot be singled out as the solitary conspirators in Dealey Plaza, is convincing. It also seems relevant and appropriate to also offer a broad but distinctive overview concerning some of the Texas-based links to the conspiracy behind President Kennedy's assassination. In my unpublished manuscript, *Urgency to Kill*, there is an intriguing chapter entitled, "LBJ: The Master of Misdirection," which details specifically most of the people and organizations and agencies which Johnson, at one time or another, suggested might have killed JFK. With 20-20 hindsight, I believe his motive was simply to distract any suspicion from himself, his handlers, and his cronies.

On one occasion Johnson actually stated that JFK was killed by "divine retribution," an insinuation that Kennedy was such a despicable individual that God had eliminated him for his past misdeeds. The following excerpt offers a depressing and sobering peek at the expansive aspects of Texas-oriented motives and suspects regarding 11/22/63 in Dealey Plaza, Dallas, Texas:

Reminiscent of an omniscient pool ball, Lyndon Baines Johnson bounced one fallacious theory off another... Russian Commies... Fidel Castro... little Vietnamese assassins... the CIA... the FBI... the Secret Service... Mafia enforcers... divine retribution... with little or no substance to support his allegations, but he managed to keep most serious suspicions from his own door, and he stalled any meaningful investigations into his closest allies.

Johnson never cited the controllers of the motorcade past the Texas School Book Depository-- John Connally, Cliff Carter, Bill Moyers, J. Erk Jonsson, Eugene Locke and other Dallas Citizen Council members or Secret Service agent Forrest Sorrels. He never accused those headed for prison via the Bobby Baker-Fred Korth-Billie Sol Estes-TFX scandals. He never cited Robert Kennedy's sniffing around via the IRS of the Roy Cohn-Lionel Corporation-Pemindex-Mob linked snafu or JFK's senatorial "Stockpile Conspiracy" investigation or The Collins Radio corruption case. He never referred to the "Dump LBJ" rumors or National Security Memorandum #273 regarding Vietnam or the oil depletion allowance and diverse tax loopholes or the Federal Reserve System overhaul considerations at work. He never initiated discussions into the murders of Henry Marshall, George Krutilek, Harold Orr, Howard Pratt or Alfred Novak or the suspicious deaths of Dorothy Kilgallen, Cliff Carter, Carole Tyler, Sheila Drennan, Grant Stockdale, Mac Wallace, Josepha Johnson, (LBJ's sister), Sam Smithwick or George Parr. He never named the "Del Charro Set," the Clint Murchison-Bedford Wynne- D. H. Byrd-Gordon McLendon oil clique, which could influence any individuals, any organizations and any agencies needed to perpetrate and cover up any crime including a presidential assassination. He never pointed a finger at the specific owners of the physical evidence in the case-- James Rowley's Secret Service henchmen or J. Edgar Hoover's minions. And sadly, absolutely no one with any real authority or impact including the government, the media and the researchers, excluding a select few, perceptive, amateur sleuths, ever "followed the money," the profits gained by Johnson and his affluent cronies from 1963 and their links to the present day profiteering.

And like a ping-pong match, the critical community and the establishment have taken turns sparring with each other trying to convince the American public of their agenda, but virtually nothing concrete is accepted as a verity. Every allegation is eventually contested and every individual's credibility is undermined.

Only one undeniable factor has remained constant--- the ticking of the clock. The conspirators and their heirs and the corporate mass media propagandists have won the game of time... Prove... Disprove... Debate... Counter Attack... Misinformation... Disinformation... Instilling Doubts... Allowing controversy to stumble along... TICK TOCK... The Warren Commission... The HSCA... The National Academy of Sciences... Failure Systems Analysis... JAMA... Norman Mailer... The ARRB... Gary Mack... Dave Perry... The disgraceful tandem of David Belin and Gerald Ford against Oliver Stone... Gerald Posner... Max Holland... John McAdams... David Von Pein... Vincent Bugliosi... TICK TOCK... The infiltration of seemingly endless trolls on JFK blogs and web sites and the various ignorant prevaricators managing podcasts on the internet... TICK TOCK... The limited hangout crews, namely the self-righteous and arrogant "CIA DID IT ALONE" crowd or the shortsighted "MAFIA DID IT ALONE" supporters... TICK TOCK... all beneficiaries of the diversionary tactics of Lyndon Baines Johnson and the sleazy creeps who have followed in his footsteps through the decades of incessant deceit.

The only person who allegedly ever heard the truth from LBJ was Madeleine Brown, his mistress of twenty-one years, who heard him personally growl--- "It was Texas oil and those fucking renegade, intelligence bastards in Washington." And even then, he neglected to include himself.

Edgar Allan Poe's masterful detective, C. Auguste Dupin, in "The Murders in the Rue Morgue," said, "Truth is not always in a well. In fact, as regards the more important knowledge, I do believe that she is invariably superficial. The depth lies in the valleys where we seek her, and not upon the mountain tops where she is found."

In that context the reader is urged to examine carefully the sinister, political "mountain tops" as well as the murky valleys of Texas, Lyndon Baines Johnson, his many interlocking associations and a cozy little town called Dallas. Richard Bartholomew's research is an excellent place to continue searching for the truth.

THE DEEP STATE
IN THE
HEART OF TEXAS

"Now if the assassination of JFK was not an opportunistic event perpetrated by one assassin, but rather a carefully planned public execution, then it was absolutely imperative to fix a specific date in a specific Texas city for a motorcade to move slowly at noon through an insecure location with multiple weapon locations. With a JFK calendar filled with events to be attended in Washington, overseas and around the country, the plotters needed an extremely persuasive argument to insure that John F. Kennedy would come to Texas when they wanted him to."
—George Michael Evica, *"John Connally's Role in the Planning of the Trip"*, New Leads and Revelations Break-out Topics, Assassination Symposium on John F. Kennedy, Hyatt Regency Hotel at Reunion Square, Dallas, Texas, November 18 22, 1993.

"I assume that the President of the United States is not involved. But wouldn't it be nice to know it?"
—Jim Garrison, quoted by William Turner, *"The Garrison Commission,"* Ramparts, January 1968

"Because evil thrives in Texas."
—Joe Bob Briggs, on why Hollywood is so attracted to Texas, *"No Country for Bad Movies,"* Texas Monthly, June 2011

INTRODUCTION:
MY SMALL WORLD OF JFK CONSPIRACY

I know about vivid memory of JFK assassination-related scenes. I lived in Mesquite on 11/22/63, less than 13 miles from Dealey Plaza.

I was born in South Oak Cliff in early 1956, not far from 1026 North Beckley, where Oswald later lived, and 3126 Harlandale, a CIA safehouse used for "Operation 40" assassins at the time of the JFK assassination. Warren Commission testimony and depositions include addresses, and many are in Mesquite.

In 1964 we moved to Garland, where I graduated from Garland High School. Assassination witness Beverly Oliver graduated from GHS a decade earlier. There are many significant conspiracy links to Garland.

My dad worked at Collins Radio in Richardson, with Kenneth Porter, Marina Oswald's second husband. I married the granddaughter and niece, respectively, of Abraham Zapruder's business partners. Abe's wife, Lillian, was one of our wedding guests. Their daughter, Myrna, and her son Adam, who is a lawyer in Austin, are still family friends. My brother married the granddaughter of DPD detective B.H. Combest, the last man to talk to Oswald.

In Texas, the conspiracy is a small world, yet unknown to most.

I've been to Dealey Plaza many times since 1964. I attended several of Penn Jones' anniversary ceremonies. I was at the 20th, 30th, 40th, and many in between. I was in my second grade classroom on the day of the assassination. Our principal was there and returned to announce the bad news and dismiss class.

In a real sense, I am always in Dealey Plaza. It is the defining moment of my life.

Many of us who were college students in the late '70s, myself and *Praise from a Future Generation* author John Kelin included, saw Richard Sprague, Henry B. Gonzalez, and Mark Lane at our respective campuses during their college tour in 1976-77 at which they showed the

Zapruder film and *Rush to Judgment*. They packed auditoriums. It is a major part of our individual awakenings as researchers.

I was at the SXSW media panel, "Who Shot JFK?" in 1991. The panelists were Bob Huffacker, Earl Golz, and Gary Shaw. Joe Nick Patoski moderated. The room was filled to standing room only. It went over the scheduled time because of the flurry of questions during the Q&A. When they finally had to clear the room for the next panel, the panelists and a group of attendees continued for some time in a back hallway.

Afterward, I approached the moderator and said, "You saw what just happened in there. Nobody wanted to end it. You guys are in the conference business. What if you had a conference devoted entirely to the assassination?" I saw the wheels turning in his mind. Next thing I heard about it was when I got a call five months later from SXSW asking to get my address to send a brochure about the first "Assassination Symposium on John F. Kennedy."

I was in Dealey Plaza the day Oliver Stone filmed the assassination recreation for his film *JFK*. Larry Howard introduced me to Robert Groden and the actor who played Zapruder. I watched three takes from the sixth-floor windows. The detail was astounding, right down to the cigarette butts behind the picket fence. All the action was perfect. And I knew all the action by heart, even in the railroad yard and parking lot. When I came outside after Stone wrapped for lunch, I was surrounded by the costumed extras. It was like the Twilight Zone.

After graduating from The University of Texas at Austin, and 17 years in the graphic arts, I became an editorial cartoonist in 1995. My talent, education, training, and professional experience have been primarily in the visual arts.

My historiography and criminal investigations of the JFK assassination, began in earnest in 1988 with the realization that the U.S. was about to get its first CIA-veteran president. I was further motivated by a civic duty to report a suspicious automobile, which I spotted in 1989 on the campus of The University of Texas at Austin, fitting the description of a getaway car seen by several JFK assassination witnesses leaving Dealey Plaza in my hometown of Dallas. My police chief, Jesse Curry, went on TV the week of the assassination and asked all citizens to report anything suspicious. So I did, albeit 30 years later at Jerry Rose's Third Decade Conference in Providence Rhode Island.

My investigative work has been more in the tradition of a self-taught Sherlock Holmes than a professional Inspector Lestrade. My research of the JFK assassination includes my discovery of a 1959 Rambler station wagon possibly used in the conspiracy; a study co-authored with Walter F. Graf involving a rifle clip that contaminates the ballistic evidence; a chronological reconstruction and placement of missing movements edited out of the Zapruder film; an in-depth interview of Erwin Schwartz, with author Noel Twyman, regarding Mr. Schwartz's and Mr. Zapruder's early chain of possession of Zapruder's film; and work for author Barr McClellan resulting in my monograph establishing the methods by which the FBI and the Warren Commission concealed and obfuscated latent fingerprints from the alleged sniper's nest.

My family does not support, and strongly discourages my activism against the conspiracy, especially anything involving the Zapruders. Emotional denial and avoidance regarding the assassination have always been the overriding family dynamic. None of my family has ever encouraged, or even read my research. Except one. My wife's uncle, Erwin Schwartz, told me his story often, and allowed Noel Twyman and me to record an interview with him. He took no position on the issue of conspiracy. But he was honest and open about his personal involvement. He adamantly defended his personal story against misrepresentation.

Erwin's sister, my mother-in-law, even hated that Erwin talked about it. After his death in 1999, she was the family matriarch until her death in 2014. My sister-in-law, Allison Silberberg, was elected mayor of Alexandria, VA in 2015, which further complicates this dynamic.

Since 1990, my research has been presented at scholarly conferences, and published in books and journals on the JFK assassination. In over two decades, my findings have had no serious, negative criticism in a field rife with such.

In 2016, after years of planning, several colleagues and I founded the first think tank devoted to the honest study of deep politics, the Center for Deep Political Research. Our mission is to provide the premier venue for journalists and researchers dedicated to the dissemination of existing and new research in counter-measure to official versions of Deep State-orchestrated events.

My friend and colleague at the Center for Deep Political Research, Joseph Green, has now generously edited this selected compilation of my JFK assassination writings and published them for the first time in a single volume.

I have no illusions that yet another book will make a difference. In the very first book on this subject, *Who Killed Kennedy?* by Thomas G. Buchanan, published May 1964, Buchanan ended with these words: "The President of the United States went down to Dallas, trusting these men to protect him. But they failed him. We, the people, are the only watchmen Kennedy will ever have now. Let these watchmen, then, awaken."

But we failed him. As the Navajo saying goes, "You can't wake a person who is pretending to be asleep."

It is folly for us to dig and beg for scraps of truth for another fifty years. When we end the official propaganda of denial of these crimes, we will also end any and all corrupt justification for hiding their details. Critical mass will not come from shouting louder, as the boy did in "The Emperor's New Clothes." It will come from putting the truth on public, legal record. It was not the end of denial by the king's subjects, it was the king's own acceptance that he was naked that changed everything. Let us now force that acceptance.

COINCIDENCE
(THE RIFLE)

THE GUN THAT DIDN'T SMOKE

MY STATEMENT ABOUT WALTER F. GRAF

Walter F. Graf was born in Boston; he was raised in Martha's Vineyard and West Palm Beach, Florida. He was a graduate of West Palm Beach High and Dartmouth College, class of 1937. He was a strong swimmer and still holds the record swimming from Martha's Vineyard to the main land. He served in the United States Army Air Corp from 1939 to 1945.

He moved to Quincy, Massachusetts in 1945, where he remained for over 50 years. He worked for the New England Motor Rate Bureau until his retirement to Florida. Mr. Graf is a descendent of Francis Eaton of the Mayflower.

He served in the military during all of WWII. As we noted in endnote 174 of "The Gun That Didn't Smoke," citing his letter to me of Jul. 9, 1997: "I have not been around small arms in recent years, but was up to my ears in weapons from 1938-1950..." He mentioned to me several times that during this time he became very familiar with every small arm in the world. It was this expert knowledge of small arms that allowed Mr. Graf to be the first researcher to raise the crucial questions regarding the mechanics of the alleged JFK murder weapon, so artfully hidden in the Warren Report, as my further research proved.

Mr. Graf and I maintained a professional contact for 18 years, discussing anything directly related to our paper, and a few less-direct subjects, like the Lincoln assassination, on which he was an expert at the time of the JFK assassination, and powerhouse college football in Florida and Texas. He and I met at Jerry Rose's "Third Decade" conference June 16-19, 1993, where I delivered my research paper, "Possible Discovery of an Automobile Used in the JFK Conspiracy". He was 77 when we met, 40 years my senior.

We started corresponding because he had been trying to interest other researchers in his findings on the alleged JFK murder weapon for several years. Also, it is typical that writing and research in deep politics is rarely a collaboration, and more rarely a successful collaboration. I understood that well by 1993, having presented my first paper at the conference where we met.

When Mr. Graf wrote to me about his JFK-assassination ballistics discoveries, I was intrigued, and soon astounded. I told him he had to write about it. He said he could have as a younger man, and I understood. I could see he was just learning to use an electric typewriter when desktop publishing was the standard. I immediately offered to write it, and he accepted. We worked together easily because we were like-minded.

By the start of 2002, George Michael Evica had read our paper and offered to help expand and update it. His expert editing made the paper what it is today. Mr. Graf and I considered him an uncredited co-author ever since. It didn't surprise Mr. Graf and me that Dr. Evica immediately understood it, since we had extensively cited his groundwork in "And We Are All Mortal." As noted in the editor's note of its online publication: "George Michael Evica has characterized this study as one of the most important in the history of the case."

Mr. Graf died July 12, 2011. Dr. Evica preceded him November 10, 2007. For me, it is the honor of a lifetime to have worked with both great men.

THE GUN THAT DIDN'T SMOKE
PART 1

[Written with the late Walter F. Graf]

"ISSUES WE HAVE NOT NOW ANTICIPATED"
Privates sleep where the rain comes down
Generals have their bed in town
Hay foot, Straw foot never knows
Ifen the gun is loaded or not
So load her again and if she blows
Dead and buried and soon forgot

   -- Civil War ballad

* * *

Despite claims of prima facie evidence in the murder of John F. Kennedy, the basic issue remains, in any real sense, unresolved. Thirty years after the publication of the Warren Report, the debate over whether or not a conspiracy killed President Kennedy continues. Most people, in their day-to-day affairs, despite what they may believe, act as if the case is closed.

Journalist Robert Sam Anson once noted that "The lack of positive evidence of conspiracy surely hampers an investigation of John Kennedy's death; it need not deter it. Oftentimes negative information is almost as important. Thus, each bit of conscious disinformation that was put out after the assassination should be followed to its source. All attempts to deflect the original investigators from the truth should be rigorously followed up." University of California, Berkeley, Professor Peter Dale Scott further noted that such deflections "...should be closely examined, for in this case damage control (as well as truth) is evidence: a clue to what relevant truths are being concealed.... Just as we believe the defendant who pleads guilty more readily than the one who pleads innocent, so we will pay more attention to the official record when it raises questions about its own reliability." In 1993, former Warren

Commission Assistant Counsel Burt W. Griffin stated that rejecting the single bullet theory [a belief that one bullet caused seven wounds in two men despite its timing, flight path, points of entry and exit, and resulting condition] requires the assumption that ballistics evidence went undiscovered or was suppressed. Griffin, now Judge Griffin, is correct. He also admitted that he and other Warren Commission staff members did not believe that the Dallas Police, the FBI, the Secret Service, or the CIA, did a thorough job in investigating the crime.[1]

There are actually several conflicting single bullet theories, a good reason, among many, to reject them.[2] Rejecting them means there was more than one shooter. It also means there are problems with the ballistics evidence. This article endeavors to end assumptions about the suppression of that evidence. Notwithstanding the failure of the single bullet theories, and actually precluding them, we argue that the existence of a conspiracy is sufficiently proved by exposing two unreliable claims of the Warren Commission; by exhausting all conceivable innocent explanations for those claims; by arguing that they were instead "damage control" attempts to deflect honest inquiry; and by calling into question long-accepted theories about the alleged murder weapon and its alleged misidentification.

We demonstrate how the planting of specific evidence -- a part of the weapon -- was based on an error. The perpetrators quickly realized the mistake but not soon enough to correct it or hide it. All they could do was deflect attention from it. It was an error so obvious that it would have exposed, within hours of Lee Harvey Oswald's arrest, the conspiracy to frame him. In fact, the error has never been hidden, just confused. We therefore show that damage control was the motive for the unanticipated, but criminally necessary and deliberate, prolonged misidentification of the weapon.

Failing that proof, we further argue that there is only one other explanation for the weapon-related facts: traditional interpretations that a second reported murder weapon was deliberately replaced with one that could be traced to Oswald. If either argument is correct -- both establishing planted and suppressed ballistics evidence -- we will have sufficiently proven conspiracy.[3]

From the beginning, there has been no reason to deny the conspiracy. Four of the seven Warren Commissioners -- the majority -- including the Commission's chairman, Chief Justice Earl Warren, expressed doubts about the Commission's conclusions within a decade of their report. They were joined by a fifth Commissioner in 1978, when John J. McCloy told the House Select Committee on Assassinations (HSCA), that "I no longer feel we had no credible evidence or reliable evidence in regard to a conspiracy...." Lyndon Johnson never believed the report he commissioned. The official policy of the FBI is that the case is not closed, a policy begun by J. Edgar Hoover himself.[4] And those were the people who had supposedly found the truth.

By any standard of historiography, the lone-assassin scenario must be considered a minority opinion which is contrary to the known evidence. Yet that is not enough for a vocal minority of conspiracy deniers. Even the HSCA would go only as far as declaring a probable conspiracy. What is needed is simple evidence of conspiracy that is true, valid and sufficient at first impression. What is needed is a "smoking gun."

In a letter that remained classified until January 1993, Walt W. Rostow, advisor to Presidents Kennedy and Johnson, voiced his fear of such evidence to Secretary of State Dean Rusk in the days just before the Warren Report was made public. His main concerns were that "Overseas the report should do something to dilute the conspiracy theory of President Kennedy's assassination," that "The report does, however, blow the fact that Oswald saw a named KGB agent at the Soviet Embassy in Mexico City"; that "the major task for ourselves and the USIA will be to prevent the discussion and debate in the U.S. from projecting an image of excessive domestic disarray" and that because "As the debate unfolds, issues will arise -- almost certainly some issues we have not now anticipated...We must be a united government in this matter."[5]

That unity has never been less evident. During a 1992 campaign appearance with Bill Clinton in McKeesport, Pennsylvania, now-Vice President Albert Gore said he believed that President Kennedy was killed by a conspiracy of unknown origin and that all federal files should be opened to the public.[6] President Clinton, when asked at a thirtieth anniversary press conference whether he thought Kennedy was killed by a single assassin and whether he was satisfied with his own security arrangements, replied: "I'm satisfied with the finding that Lee Harvey Oswald acted alone. I am also very satisfied with the work done by the Secret Service in my behalf."[7] A good answer loaded with priorities perhaps, but this divided White House illustrates better than anything that, as a country, when it comes to the murder of our thirty-fifth president, believe what we might, we know no more now than we did in the waning weeks of 1963.

For more than thirty years, researchers have sought the elusive "smoking gun" -- a simple, indisputable fact that proves conspiracy in the murder of John F. Kennedy. It now appears that search may be over. This discovery is not based on new evidence. As is often the case in quests for definitive answers, it was right under our noses the whole time. It has lain dormant in the Warren Report for three decades as one of Rostow's feared "issues we have not now anticipated." Obscure and riddled with disinformation, yes, but not impossible to see.

It is well-known that the rifle allegedly used as the murder weapon was identified as a 6.5 millimeter caliber, Italian-made, bolt-action, military rifle called a Mannlicher-Carcano, after its two inventors. It is largely unknown that during WWII, it was one of only two military-use rifles in the world that fed a cartridge into the chamber from a clip. The other was the M-1 Garand. The difference between the two is that the clip on the M-1 Garand ejects when the last round is fired, while on the Carcano the clip ejects when the last round is chambered. "In the clip system, the clip remains attached to the rounds on loading and forms an essential part of the magazine system, a follower forcing the rounds out of the clip and presenting them in turn to the bolt for loading."[8]

According to the Warren Report, when the weapon allegedly used to kill the President was found on the sixth floor of the Texas School Book Depository (TSBD), one cartridge remained, and it was in the chamber.[9] Therefore, if operating properly, the rifle had automatically ejected the clip. The Warren Commission reported, however, that when the rifle was found, it contained a clip.[10] Firearms experts for the HSCA explained the discrepancy. On September 8, 1978, Monty C. Lutz of the Committee's firearms panel, was asked about this by Pennsylvania Representative Robert W. Edgar.

> Mr. Edgar. The cartridge clip was removed from CE-139 by Lieutenant Day of the Dallas Police Department on November 22, 1963 at the crime laboratory for the police department. Shouldn't a clip automatically fall out once the last cartridge has fed into the chamber?
>
> Mr. Lutz. This rifle is designed to incorporate that feature so that the last cartridge is stripped out of the clip, then that allows the clip itself to fall or to drop from the opening that you see in the bottom of the box magazine. However, in many cases, and in this particular case, where we functioned the rifle, fed cartridges through it, we found this clip to stay in the rifle after the last round had been stripped and fed into the chamber. Because the lips or the edges of the clip many times will open up, they will spring against the walls on the inside of the box magazine and it will hang up in that areaa [sic], and even though it is supposed to drop out, many times it will hang up in the box area.[11]

That explanation seems reasonable enough. But it is not. It is true that the clip must be deformed to have any chance of getting as stuck as this one. But once bent, it stays bent. Commission Exhibits (CEs) 574 and 575 are photographs of the alleged clip in its normal, unbent condition. And five years after the HSCA reported the clip deformed, Life magazine photographer Michael O'Neill photographed it in normal condition for Life's November 1983 issue.[12]

According to assassination researcher and author J.W. Hughes, who has tested this deformation over fifty times on each of his seven Mannlicher-Carcanos, "When deformed, it will not hold the rounds because the locking ridge is spread too wide to hold the round and the weapon jams."[13] The Warren Commission was apparently silent about whether expert riflemen from the U.S. Army and FBI had such difficulty firing the alleged murder weapon in 1964, and whether it was fired with its alleged clip. Whether or not those marksmen used the original clip, they were required to use any test clip in the original's apparent "found" condition, i.e., deformed. Anyone could have tested the clip by duplicating its required abnormal behavior, and can still. But CBS News, which claimed to "duplicate the conditions of the actual assassination" in its filmed rifle test in 1967, did not. According to reporter Dan Rather, "Eleven volunteer marksmen took turns firing clips of three bullets each at the moving target." They fired a total of thirty-seven three-round series, seventeen of which resulted in unfired bullets due to "trouble with the rifle." Clip problems or not, all data from those seventeen troubled series was disregarded by CBS analysts. It was the other series of shots, however, with properly emptied and ejected clips, deemed worthy of analysis by CBS, that should have been disqualified. In the CBS film, clips can be seen flying out of the gun so fast as to be a blur.[14] If a test clip is not bent, or ejects, or moves at all, Oswald's alleged feat is not duplicated, invalidating the test. The HSCA firearms panel seemed not to be interested in this phenomenon, since it did not test the clip under firing conditions. Congressman Edgar learned about the defect from Mr. Lutz when he asked for details about their firing test:

> Mr. Lutz. This was a single cartridge being inserted into the chamber and firing into a cotton waste recovery box...backing away from the box, a foot or two, and pointing the muzzle into the box and then firing into it, in order to recover the projectile.
>
> Mr. Edgar. But you weren't firing with clip -- using the clip, were you?
>
> Mr. Lutz. No sir; I did not.

Mr. Edgar. Did anyone on the panel fire with the clip in?

Mr. Lutz. I do not believe so; no, sir.

Mr. Edgar. What was the reason for that?

Mr. Lutz. There were no particular markings that we were able to identify as having come from the clip, nor were we checking for time firing or sequential firing in any way in that respect.[15]

Under the heading "Findings and Conclusions of the Firearms Panel Concerning the Kennedy Assassination," we learn that, "Two bullets were test-fired into a horizontal water recovery tank. Further tests were conducted by loading four cartridges into the CE 375 [sic] cartridge clip and inserting it into the magazine of the rifle. The cartridges were worked through the rifle's mechanism and ejected without being fired. When the last cartridge was chambered, the cartridge clip remained in the magazine instead of falling out as it is designed to do."[16] Given Mr. Lutz's "the clip many times will open up" statement, this result demands further explanation.

"Many times will" also means "many times won't." Metal expands when heated and can alter its shape. But during the HSCA tests of the loading mechanism, the rifle should have been cool. In addition, CE 541 (3), a photograph of the clip stuck in the magazine reproduced on page 83 of the Warren Report, shows it in a cool rifle. Surely the rifle had not been fired for some time before that photography session. Is Lutz suggesting that the clip's sides spring out when cool and then return to a normal shape in the heat of firing? If such a violation of the laws of physics occurs with this rifle and clip, how then could the rifle have "contained a clip" when found?

Also, the HSCA's explanation does not explain what happened after the rifle was found. Over at least the next twenty-four hours, the Dallas Police Department reported, and left uncorrected, descriptions that remain a paradox to this day. Early news reports seemed to identify the murder weapon as anything but a 6.5 mm. Mannlicher-Carcano. NBC and WBAP radio identified it as a British Enfield .303. KLIF radio said it was a 7.65 German Mauser. KRLD radio announced that the rifle was "presumed to be a .25 caliber high powered Army or Japanese rifle." Radio station KBOX reported a German Mauser or a Japanese rifle. Dallas television station WFAA described it as three different kinds of Mauser: a "German Mauser," a 6.5 "Argentine Mauser" with a four-power scope, and a 7.65 "Mauser." Dallas NBC-affiliate television station WBAP's continuous coverage between 12:56 p.m. and 5:26 p.m.

Central Standard Time (C.S.T.) reveals that the "conflicting reports" of the rifle's make evolved from the first (British .303) to the last (7.65 Mauser) in a very short time frame between 2:14 and 2:24.[17]

Despite the fact that the alleged murder weapon that allegedly belonged to Oswald reportedly was clearly stamped "Made Italy" and "Cal. 6.5," local authorities and the media seemed to finally agree that it was a 7.65 German-made Mauser. Had as few as two different descriptions continued to dominate news reports the rest of the day, one of them being an Italian, or a clip-fed weapon, an argument could be made for confusion. But that is not what happened. The supposed murder weapon was not "called...most everything," as Captain Will Fritz testified.[18] Initial descriptions quickly gave way to a short-lived consensus for a 7.65 German Mauser, not further confusion. Probably due to the earlier conflicting reports, reporters remained skeptical. But they asked if it was a Mauser, and were told, tacitly at least, that it was. As different as these early descriptions seemed from each other and from the weapon the Warren Commission finally chose, there is one difference they all have in common. It is the one difference from the Mannlicher-Carcano they all share. It is the key to the conspiracy. None of them can use an ammunition clip.

The early critics of the Warren Commission who dealt directly with the rifle descriptions and clip problems, including Mark Lane, Harold Weisberg and Sylvia Meagher, missed this particular paradox. Since the mid-seventies, most of the clip and rifle problems have been recognized by gun experts and many researchers, including Gary Shaw, Mary Ferrell, Jack White and George Michael Evica. But the fact that there is only one other clip system with which the Mannlicher-Carcano's can be confused (the significance of which is explained below), and the absolute impossibility of confusing a Mannlicher-Carcano for any rifle but that one, seem to have been completely overlooked.

In the case of Meagher, it was a near miss. She was aware of a lack of direct evidence that a clip was found at the crime scene. The Texas Department of Public Safety official "Evidence Sheet" lists the incriminating evidence against Lee Harvey Oswald in detail. The number of spent shells found at the crime scene even changed from "(2)" to an obviously distorted "(3)" by the time the Warren Commission published the list, but no clip was ever accounted for.[19]

The FBI Laboratory Report from J. Edgar Hoover to Police Chief Jesse Curry the day after the assassination itemizes and numbers everything from metal fragments to a belatedly identified rifle. But the clip is not listed or numbered. It is mentioned only in passing as part of a group of things without fingerprints.[20]

Meagher even wrote, referring to testimony about confusion over the clip, "It is another coincidence, one supposes, that someone has mistaken a six-shot clip for a clip suitable to a Mauser, just as the Carcano was taken for a Mauser."[21]

This unfortunate statement may have ended further questions before they could be asked. Mausers are loaded from a "charger" (a.k.a. "stripper clip") which must be discarded after loading. While it is sometimes called a "clip," a charger has a completely different function.

Meagher fell for FBI weapons expert Robert Frazier's subtle testimony. The question asked of Frazier was, "Is there any reason that you can think of why someone might call that a five-shot clip?" Frazier answered, "No, sir, unless they were unfamiliar with it. There is an area of confusion in that a different type of rifle shooting larger ammunition, such as a 30.06 or a German Mauser rifle, uses five-shot clips, and the five-shot clip is the common style or size of clip, whereas this one actually holds six."[22]

Frazier limited his answer to unfamiliarity with the clip itself. The full answer reveals the deception. The confusion is over the term, not the function. How could weapons expert Frazier not know this? Confusing a charger with a clip is only possible through complete and total ignorance of the way rifles are loaded. And that irrefutable fact leads, as the reader will see, to conclusive proof of conspiracy in the JFK assassination.[23]

Many questions about other rifles at the crime scene have been raised, and some of them answered conclusively, by JFK assassination researchers over the years.[24] Oswald and his fellow employees had even seen a Mauser at the TSBD in the possession of their supervisor, Roy Truly, just two days before the assassination.[25] But had the critics known about the charger-clip discrepancy, they might have asked, along with questions about other rifles, slightly different questions: Why would a description of a superficially similar but non-clip-fed rifle prevail for at least twenty-four hours (and at most three days) after a clip-fed rifle became the most important piece of evidence? Was it because it prevented questions from being asked about ammunition clips? Why avoid such questions? Was it because no clip was found with the gun? Did the crime scene investigators replace the clip? Why would the crime-scene investigators lie and fabricate evidence to hide a rifle's normal firing condition? Did they confuse the Mannlicher-Carcano's feeding system with that of the more familiar M-1 Garand, thinking it needed a clip if a round was in the chamber? Did they know, therefore, that the rifle was planted? And if they knew that, did they knowingly help frame Lee Harvey Oswald?

Things might have been very different had Mark Lane known to ask these questions when he brought the Mauser description to the Commission's attention on March 4, 1964. This analysis does not exculpate Lee Harvey Oswald. Nor does it conclusively indict other individuals. But if this analysis is correct, it does conclusively prove conspiracy. And it serves to remind us that, in this time of new evidence produced through technology and file declassification, nothing is wrong with the old evidence. A hard question we must ask -- and answer for our children -- is why it took us so long. That delay caused great damage they will have to undo.

In our search for a smoking gun, we missed the real prima facie evidence -- the gun that didn't smoke. Let us begin again.

* * *

"NO MORE SHELLS IN THE MAGAZINE"

An unlearned carpenter of my acquaintance once said in my hearing: "There is very little difference between one man and another; but what little there is, is very important." This distinction seems to me to go to the root of the matter.
-- William James, 1897

As trial jurors are reminded daily, evidence tampering can be inferred from an absence of evidence which is reasonably expected to exist, and, conversely, from the existence of evidence which is reasonably expected to be absent. Inference is the essence of circumstantial evidence, one of three major classifications of evidence. The other two major classifications are direct evidence and real evidence. The essence of direct evidence is that it directly establishes a main fact or element of the crime. It may be an actual object or an immediate experience on the part of a witness. Items of real evidence, the focus of our discussion here, are tangible objects which prove or disprove the facts at issue. Real evidence is self-explanatory. It may be either direct (e.g., an actual gun seen and collected) or circumstantial (e.g., a gun not seen or collected but inferred from established facts such as its visual and auditory effects). But real evidence needs only to be identified in court, not explained. Fingerprints and blood stains are other examples of real evidence. The most important real evidence is *corpus delicti* evidence. It consists of objects and substances which are an essential part of the body of a crime, such as a gun used to commit a murder. Investigators at a crime scene are therefore chiefly responsible for the discovery and preservation of *corpus delicti* evidence.

Those rules of evidence are among the most basic concepts used in criminal investigation. Like the basic procedures described below, they were known and used around the world at the time of Kennedy's assassination. They were studied worldwide in textbooks. One of those books, by criminologist and educator Charles E. O'Hara, *Fundamentals of Criminal Investigation*, first published in 1956, was in its third printing with 14,000 copies by 1963. Prescribed fundamentals like those in textbooks like O'Hara's were known to Dallas Police Lieutenant John Carl Day. On the day of the assassination, Day was fifty years old, had twenty-three years of experience with the Dallas Police Department, and had been the immediate supervisor of the crime-scene search section of its identification bureau for seven years.[26]

In his "shoot-out town," as Dallas was called in 1963, Lieutenant Day knew all too well that investigators of the crime of murder have the greatest responsibility for competent inquiry.[27] They face the most severe test of the full resources of the applied art of investigation. Among the most important of those investigative resources are science and prescribed methodology. In a murder involving a gun, an essential question is: "Is this the gun that fired the fatal bullet?" All the parts of the gun, including those required for its successful operation, as well as the condition of those parts, are therefore crucial pieces of *corpus delicti* evidence. Such evidence must be intelligently handled from the point of view of science and the law. Each person who handles that evidence must insure that it is accounted for at all times while in their own possession.

Fingerprints take priority during collection because they are the most fragile. But prior to submitting a gun to the crime laboratory, it should be unloaded and all parts that are removable without the aid of tools, and which may leave an imprint on the bullet or cartridge case, should be removed from the gun and properly marked or labeled for identification as they are being collected or as soon as possible thereafter. All of that information, plus any unique characteristics, such as caliber or gauge, make, lot number, and serial number, should be recorded in the investigator's notebook during or immediately after the search.

Despite those long established, most important, most fundamental procedures used throughout the world in searches of the most important of all crime-scenes -- those where murders occurred -- on November 22nd, 1963, extremely unorthodox methods and extreme neglect by experienced investigators apparently prevailed during the search of the crime scene of the murder of the President of the United States.

At 12:30 p.m. C.S.T., shots were fired at the President. Immediately,

Dallas police apparently suspected some had originated from the TSBD. According to the Warren Report, the Dallas police had two witnesses who saw from where the shots came, Howard Brennan and Amos Euins. Brennan "quickly reported his observations to police officers." And "Immediately after the assassination," Euins "reported his observations to Sgt. D. V. Harkness of the Dallas Police Department and also to James Underwood of station KRLD-TV of Dallas."[28]

Shortly before 1:03 p.m., Deputy Sheriff Luke Mooney reportedly discovered three used cartridge cases lying on the floor beneath the southeast corner window of the sixth floor.[29] Harold Weisberg observed that, "More than a half-hour elapsed before the empty shells were found, yet they were `found' at exactly the window pointed out. It was almost three-quarters of an hour before the rifle was `found,' and it was found on that very floor."[30]

Reportedly at 1:22 p.m., Deputy Sheriff Eugene Boone and Deputy Constable Seymour Weitzman discovered a bolt-action rifle with a telescopic sight attached. The Warren Commission concluded that Weitzman -- though neither man handled the rifle -- described it as a 7.65 Mauser bolt action. It was subsequently described as a 6.5 millimeter Mannlicher-Carcano Italian military rifle. It reportedly contained one round, which was a copper-jacketed military-type bullet manufactured by Western Cartridge Co.[31]

The rifle was photographed and filmed almost from the moment it was found, but the earliest known evidence of an ammunition clip was not recorded until just before 1:57 p.m. It appeared in photographs taken by William G. Allen of the Dallas Times Herald, Ira D. "Jack" Beers of the Dallas Morning News, and Daniel Owens of Fort Worth television station WBAP.[32] In his book, *Pictures of the Pain*, Richard B. Trask described the scene:

> Some time close to 1:45, Lieutenant Day left the Book
> Depository's front door carrying the rifle discovered on
> the sixth floor. Photographers swarmed around Day as
> he walked to Houston Street and crossed the street over
> to its east side and proceeded a short distance easterly on
> Elm Street to his vehicle. Day held the weapon by its
> strap and away from his body, attempting to touch it as
> little as possible to preserve any potential evidence on
> the rifle itself. The significance of the scene and the clear
> view of the presumed assassination weapon was not lost
> on any of the photographers. Allen took eight exposures
> while Beers shot at least three. By early evening the wire

services would be circulating photos of this dramatic scene. Several of these photos clearly show the end of an ammunition clip protruding from the bottom of the rifle. The brass clip held up to 6 rounds. When the final round was bolted into the rifle chamber, the clip was supposed to fall out from the bottom of its chamber. The clip, however, had a propensity to catch and not fall out.[33]

We considered three aspects of these photographs: the precise time they were taken, the clip's "propensity" to align itself in the manner shown, and the photographic authenticity of the clip's image.

Precise timing of that event can be determined because the very next photographs, taken after Lieutenant J. C. Day departed, by Allen, Beers, and a newly-arrived photographer, George Smith of the Fort Worth Star-Telegram, were of three apparent "tramps" being escorted past the TSBD by two uniformed policemen. The first of the seven known "tramp" photos, taken by Smith, shows shadows cast by the building's brickwork.[34] Shadows cast by sunlight can be read as a "sundial" by comparing the bricks' measurements to the known positions of the sun for that date. We can therefore be certain that the clip first appeared in evidence just prior to 1:57 p.m.

Using a 6.5 Mannlicher-Carcano rifle (not a carbine) in excellent working condition, two black steel clips, and one live shell with a rounded, exposed-lead tip, as opposed to a full-metal jacket, coauthor Richard Bartholomew tested Trask's claim that the clip "had a propensity to catch and not fall out."[35]

Inserting an empty clip manually from both the top and bottom resulted in the clip jamming against the clip release mechanism to its rear and against machined ridges on the sides of the magazine to its front. There were two distinctly different jamming effects, depending on which end of the magazine placement was attempted. Neither jamming effect occurred when the shell was loaded into the chamber from the clip.

First is the "bottom-placement" effect. When the clip was placed from the bottom, its posterior stayed aligned with the back of the magazine. This jamming effect could only be accomplished by manually protruding the clip partially from the bottom and turning it clockwise. Turning it counterclockwise did not produce this effect. Instead, the clip always fell out. There was an audible clicking sound when the clip's right front side jammed into place behind the machined ridge. It was stuck firmly rather than loosely. This effect visually matched what is seen in the pictures of the alleged murder weapon being carried out of the TSBD. When the clip was placed farther into the magazine, from bottom to top, the second jamming effect occurred. It was identical to the "top-placement" effect, produced by placing the clip into the magazine from the top (as described below).

Second is the "top-placement" effect. When placed from the top, the clip always fell at an anterior-posterior angle, with the bottom angling forward and the top angling rearward. This fall resulted in the clip hanging on the front edge of the magazine's opening at the bottom. Then, when aligned properly manually, the clip slid easily through the ejection port, as it is designed to. Only by engaging the clip release button was it possible to remove the clip from the top. It was loose enough to rattle, but jostling would not release the clip. During some top placement attempts, special manual alignment of the clip produced the "bottom-placement" jamming effect. The clip turned clockwise as a result of this physical handling, and holding the rifle at such an angle that the clip turned as it fell through the opening.

It is clear that there is a propensity for a normal, empty clip to stay inside the magazine when manually placed from the top. The "bottom-placement" jamming effect, which allowed partial ejection, was also reproducible when the clip was placed from the top, but it required physical manipulation to accomplish. However, neither jamming effect occurred when the shell was loaded into the chamber from the clip. The normal action of the rifle kept the clip aligned with the magazine's bottom opening, allowing it to fall out as designed.

From this experiment, experiences of others familiar with this weapon, and silence about clip-jamming frequency by official investigators who test-fired the alleged murder weapon with a clip, we concluded the clip must be deformed to jam regularly during rifle operation. A normal clip can be regularly jammed only through non-operational manipulation. The fact that no clip is seen protruding from the magazine in film taken on the sixth floor, combined with the fact that it is seen protruding from the magazine in film taken later at the front street entrance, means, at a minimum, that investigators handled the clip at the crime scene.

Therefore, the following aspects and implications of this clip's lack of an operational "propensity to catch" are discussed in this article: the clip was officially reported to have no prints; handling by investigators was never reported, nor was Captain Fritz's filmed handling of the rifle with a handkerchief; since Oswald did not take precautions against leaving prints, he either did not load the rifle, or investigators wiped his and their own prints off the clip. Given the official silence, both alternatives indicate conspiracy.

The remaining aspect of the Allen, Beers and Owens photographs, considered here, is the claim that no clip was visible to be photographed: the clip and its unusual placement are an illusion created entirely by photo-retouching. It is reasonable to consider such a forgery. It was both possible and probable with the then current state of photographic art. Photography in 1963-1964 had long been capable of altering history, and was known to have altered Russian history. The CIA's Ray Cline said, "Photography became to the fifties what code-breaking was to the forties." Code-breaking determined the outcome of WWII. During the Eisenhower administration, both C.D. Jackson, the purchaser of the Zapruder film of the assassination, and Edwin H. Land, the inventor of the Polaroid camera, worked closely with Director of Central Intelligence Allen Dulles on propaganda and U-2 photographic intelligence. While the Warren Commission was in session, Ranger 7 returned 4,308 photographs from the moon electronically.[36]

It could be argued, therefore, that the clip's image was faked because there was no evidence of a clip at the crime scene. But the plausibility of that claim ends there. Such a forgery has no other reasonable benefit to the conspirators. On the contrary, by the time the forgery could have been completed (one of the photographs was broadcast by NBC-TV News at 3:56 p.m. C.S.T.), the use of extreme confidentiality regarding the clip had become obvious.[37]

In fact, the Allen, Beers and Owens photos are among the best proof of conspiracy. As will be seen, those photos forced the bizarre, deafening silence that continues to surround the clip. Those photos forced the conspirators into a hasty cover-up of their worst mistake: thinking a clip was needed inside this rifle to satisfy its load-fire-reload characteristics. Without those photos, the conspirators could have said, "Nope, we didn't find any clip. It must have ejected normally and been ditched by the suspect." Had those photos never existed, we can be sure there would be no need for a clip in evidence, or any twenty-four-hour consensus about a Mauser.

Fifteen years later, the Allen, Beers and Owens photos forced esteemed firearms experts to tell the HSCA a ridiculous story about a clip so bent it could not move in any direction during the extensive handling of the rifle on the sixth floor. Those photos continue to force Lieutenant J.C. Day into extreme, tortured avoidance of how, where, and in what condition the clip was found. The claim least reasonably believed about the photos is the normality Trask purports in the handling of evidence at the crime scene. Would not a clip so deformed (according to the HSCA) as to stick completely inside the rifle, require extreme jarring to move it partially out of the rifle? Would the abnormality of a clip so deformed at least elicit some comment at the scene from those who described every other "normal" part of the rifle's discovery in detail?

The earliest known attempt to ask one of the crime-scene investigators for the exact location and condition of the clip when found, occurred on September 9, 1968. Dr. John K. Lattimer wrote and asked Day these questions: "Can you tell me where the empty cartridge clip was found? Was it on the floor under the window from which Oswald fired, or was it still in the rifle until Captain Fritz ejected the last round? I have not been able to find out this fact in the Warren Commission Report, and am appealing to you for clarification of this point." He gave , as a reference, Dr. Paul Peters, a member of the emergency medical team who tried to resuscitate JFK at Parkland Hospital. According to a handwritten notation, signed by Day and dated "9/16," at the bottom of Lattimer's letter, the only action taken by Day, apparently, was contacting Peters' office and learning that "Dr. Lattimer was a reputable professor." The only response to Lattimer's letter seems to have been a form-letter response, two weeks later, from Chief of Police Charles Batchelor, referring him to the Justice Department.[38]

If the clip was so deformed as to stick completely inside the rifle, unnoticed for a half hour, then stick partially outside the rifle until it was allegedly removed at the police crime lab, would not Lieutenant Day have answered Dr. Lattimer's 1968 letter that asked specifically how, where, and in what condition the clip was found? Would such a clip not elicit some comment at all, in three decades, from those who "found" it? In his 1980 book, Kennedy and Lincoln, Lattimer vaguely reported questionable results from his own experiments. He did not report his expected answers from either Day, or the Justice Department, or anyone else. Yet Lattimer declared that "the Warren Commission had been correct" that "the clip was found in Oswald's rifle...."[39] As we will see, vague and inadequate as it is, Lattimer's "proof" is vastly superior to the Warren Commission's.

JFK assassination researchers are well aware that the statements concerning the alleged murder weapon consist of a collection of information, misinformation and disinformation. In 1993, the task of citing it was greatly simplified when one author compiled most of it into a single volume, necessary in his attempt to portray the Warren Commission's unsupported minority opinions as the truth.

Gerald Posner's Case Closed includes only two direct references to the Mannlicher-Carcano's ammunition clip. Posner says that the fact that Oswald used only four bullets in a six-bullet clip is a sign of his lack of preparation.[40] With regard to the three spent cartridges ejected from the rifle, he cites Lieutenant Carl Day's Warren Commission testimony as proof that Day photographed the shells at the crime scene in their original position. He cites the photographs taken by Day and his assistant Robert Lee Studebaker, and Deputy Sheriff Luke Mooney's testimony as proof that the shells were found in a random pattern rather than in a neat row.[41] The claim that they were in a neat row was later made by Deputy Sheriff Roger Craig.[42]

Posner also refers to the so-called misidentification of the rifle reportedly found at the TSBD and the fact that it was mistaken for a Mauser.[43] The story that the Mannlicher-Carcano was planted at the Depository about twenty minutes after the assassination is "folklore," Posner claims.[44] He informs us that Mooney and Weitzman (actually, it was Boone and Weitzman) thought at first glance that the rifle was a 7.65 bolt-action Mauser. He adds that, "Although they quickly admitted their mistake, that initial misidentification led to speculation that a different gun was found on the sixth floor and that Oswald's Carcano was later swapped for the murder weapon."[45] No one "quickly admitted" any mistake. If they had, no argument would exist over the misidentification.

Posner ignores the earlier Enfield .303 identification altogether. He dismisses the Mauser identification by saying, "Firearms experts say they are easy to confuse without a proper exam (HSCA Vol. I, pp. 446-47; HSCA Vol. VII, p. 372.)" Posner gives no explanation for why, after a proper exam was made early that Friday afternoon by Lieutenant Day, the Mauser description continued uncorrected by the Dallas Police Department both internally to Police Chief Curry and public relations officer Captain Glen D. King, and externally to District Attorney Henry Wade and the press. He then ridicules Mark Lane for "trying to portray a simple mistake as evidence of conspiracy (*Rush to Judgment*, pp. 95-101)."[46]

Posner, like many conspiracy deniers who continue to assert ludicrously that Weitzman made an innocent error, is evidently unaware that his fellow denier, Commission staffer Wesley J. Liebeler, revealed a motive. Mark Lane spoke about Liebeler's June 5, 1967, remarks on Stanford radio station KZSU: "Said Liebeler, `And, of course, Mr. Weitzman is Jewish.' While the relevance of the officer's religion may not seem apparent at the outset, Liebeler's presentation of Weitzman's motive places it in context. Since `the Germans have been picking' on the Jewish people `for the last 50 years,' Weitzman reasoned, according to Liebeler, that he `got one back at them.'"[47]

An unfortunate oversight, perhaps, for someone like Mr. Posner who has studied Nazi Germany and desires to close the case based on minority opinions of the Warren Commission. Of course, given the facts, we would have to believe that the other crime scene investigators and the Dallas Police Department conspired to join Weitzman in his alleged attack on German anti-Semitism.

On pages 474-75 of *Case Closed* there is a technical illustration of the Carcano and the clip with a line drawn from the clip pointing to the area forward of the trigger, showing this position as its whereabouts when in use.

There is also a four-panel diagram illustrating the bolt action. The caption above reads, "The bolt action can easily be executed in a fraction of a second." The caption below reads, "1. Push bolt up... 2. Pull back (to eject case and position next cartridge)... 3. Push forward... 4. Push down (to lock bolt)." Posner does not point out that while the bolt action can be operated quickly, such rapid firing is only possible with the clip. Among the Warren Report's few words about the clip is the statement: "As long as there is ammunition in the clip, one need only work the bolt and pull the trigger to fire the rifle."[48] Otherwise a cartridge must be loaded after each firing.

Despite this semi-detailed look at the load-fire-reload cycle, Posner never mentions anywhere in his book the peculiarities of this rifle's feeding system. He also does not mention that there should have been some mention of discovering the clip by Boone, Weitzman, Mooney, and especially Day and Captain Will Fritz, head of the Dallas Police Department Homicide Division. The Warren Report cites Fritz's testimony[49] and Day's testimony[50] to support their statement that "When the rifle was found in the Texas School Book Depository Building it contained a clip...."[51]

Sylvia Meagher wrote: "...there is not one word on those pages about an ammunition clip, nor is there anything elsewhere in the testimony of Fritz or Day or other witnesses which establishes that an ammunition clip was found at all. The assertion in the Report that the rifle found in the Book Depository contained a clip is absolutely unsupported by direct evidence or testimony."[52]

Meagher is right. The pages cited by the Report as proof that the clip was found with the rifle say nothing about the clip. Fritz talks about Day. Day talks about Fritz. They both talk about the rifle: about finding it; photographing it; handling it; ejecting the live round; putting identifying marks on it and the live round; dusting them both for prints; and about how, when and where all of these activities were done. But nothing in this testimony indicates the existence of a clip at the crime scene.

Posner quotes the following from a January 19, 1992, interview he had with Carl Day: "I knew there could be no fingerprints on that strap, so I picked the gun up by that. The stock was pretty porous and weather-worn, so there was little chance of any prints there. Before pulling the bolt back, I satisfied myself there were no prints on the little metal lever.

Then I held the gun while Captain Fritz pulled the bolt, and a live round fell out. There were no more shells in the magazine."[53] From this statement we might be tempted to think that we now apparently have, twenty-nine years late, the first and only (and improbable) record of the clip ("magazine") being seen at the time of the discovery of the rifle. But returning to Lutz's testimony before the HSCA, aided by fellow firearms expert Donald E. Champagne, we learn otherwise:

> Mr. Edgar. ...I was interested in seeing you handle the rifle and talking about the action of the rifle. I have just a couple of questions relating to the rifle itself.
>
> Could you describe the magazine section of the rifle and how that works?
>
> Mr. Lutz. The magazine section is this attached area, a fixed box-type magazine, that is part of the trigger guard protruding from the bottom of the stock. It is the large metal object that you see on the lower silhouette. The magazine itself consists of the follower, the steel or metal arm that is inside of the receiver, that is pushed down as the cartridges are inserted into the top of the firearm, and then that steel or metal arm is on a spring that pushes on the bottom cartridge and is part of the magazine and causes the feeding of the system to operate inside of the rifle as it is loaded.
>
> Mr. Edgar. So it would be accurate to say that there isn't a portable magazine that is clipped into the rifle and clipped out again, that the magazine is part of the rifle itself.
>
> Mr. Lutz. That is correct as opposed to the detachable magazine that could be removed and taken out of the rifle....
>
> Mr. Edgar. Do the magazine follower markings found in CE-141 [the live round ejected by Fritz] indicate that the clip was used?
>
> Mr. Lutz. Could I defer that question to Mr. Champagne?
>
> Mr. Edgar. Sure.
>
> Mr. Champagne. Yes. Without the clip the weapon would not function properly. The cartridges would lie loose in the magazine.[54]

But as we have already seen, these men did not test whether the clip in evidence (as seen in CE 575) would allow the weapon to function properly. In the condition shown on page 83 of the Warren Report, given their reason for why the clip was there, it would not.

The main point here is that in Posner's book, the terms "clip" and "magazine" are used interchangeably, when, in fact, they refer to two different things. *Day was not talking about a clip.* The clip holds the cartridges. The magazine is an integral part of the rifle which, in this instance, holds both the cartridges and the clip. The clip goes into the magazine.

On Mausers, the Lee Enfield or Springfield 1903, the magazine would hold the cartridges without the clip (a.k.a. charger or stripper clip) which is thrown away when the cartridges are "thumbed" into the magazine. The term "clip" is used in this latter case commonly, but the correct term is "charger" or "stripper clip."[55]

The point is that a Mannlicher-Carcano will not function, except impossibly slowly, without a clip, and a Mauser will not function properly with one. According to J.W. Hughes, "One thing that you should be aware of is that the Mannlicher-Carcano was not designed to `single load'. If you attempt to single load the Mannlicher-Carcano, the bolt will push the round into the chamber, but will need to be forced closed. This will in most cases not properly seat the bolt behind the round and the firing pin most generally will not strike the primer with sufficient force to discharge the round. Then, in most cases, it will deform the rear of the shell as the extractor is forced around the extractor ring as the bolt is opened. I tested my Mannlicher-Carcanos again with this type of loading and 1 out of 63 rounds fired."[56] (emphasis in original) Congressman Edgar did not ask the HSCA firearms panel, and they did not volunteer, whether they had this difficulty during their firing tests conducted entirely without the clip.

Furthermore, with the Mannlicher-Carcano, we are talking about a rifle that feeds from the top. A clip feeds from the top. A detachable magazine feeds from the bottom. The magazine is temporarily attached to the bottom of the rifle and houses the cartridges. During WWII, both Mausers and Enfields were equipped with ten-round detachable magazines. These magazines were attached to the bottom. These could not have been involved in the misidentification of the Mannlicher-Carcano.

Therefore, Carl Day was still cleverly avoiding the problem of the clip after twenty-nine years. When he told Gerald Posner, "There were no more shells in the magazine," he was correct. He was not only correct, but he provided himself an avenue of escape from the glaring subject of the clip. At the moment they determined there were no more rounds in the magazine, Day and Fritz could not avoid seeing the empty clip which was supposedly stuck inside the magazine.[57]

Mr. Posner was also purposely avoiding the issue. Even if Posner and Day simply misspoke, it is still unbelievable that several witnesses to this clip-magazine, including such firearms users as Boone, Weitzman, Mooney, and Fritz, have never said a word in thirty years about finding such an essential part of the weapon. And if Posner and Day misspoke, it is still unbelievable that a description of a non-clip-fed rifle prevailed inside and outside the Dallas Police Department during that Friday afternoon, evening and night. Historian and author George Michael Evica makes a very good point about this:

> Lieutenant Day was credited by the Warren Commission with identifying the rifle in his possession as an Italian 6.5 mm. weapon. The Commission, however, supplied neither evidence nor documentation for its statement. Those references it did give to `document' the alleged Day identification were irrelevant to the Commission's assertion. And Day himself seemed to deny the Commission's statement: `I didn't describe the rifle to anyone other than [unidentified] police officers.' One of those `police officers' seems to have been public relations officer Captain Glen D. King, but if Day did describe the weapon he examined to King, and King (doing his job) passed that description on to the working press the afternoon and evening of the 22nd, either Day described the rifle as a 7.65 Mauser, or King thought Day described it as such, since that description prevailed.[58]

Day, in describing a Friday night encounter with the press, testified under oath that, "Several of the newsmen asked me various questions about what the gun was at that time. I did not give them an answer.

"When I went back to the office after Marina Oswald viewed the gun, they still were hounding me for it. I told them to check with the chief's office, he would have to give them the information, and as soon as I got back to my office I gave a complete description, and so forth, to Captain King on the gun."[59]

Day, and King in turn, should have been following the official Dallas Police Department policy on news coverage. The Warren Report states:

> Consistent with its policy of allowing news

representatives to remain within the working quarters of the Police and Courts Building, the police department made every effort to keep the press fully informed about the progress of the investigation. As a result, from Friday afternoon until after the killing of Oswald on Sunday, the press was able to publicize virtually all of the information about the case which had been gathered until that time. In the process, a great deal of misinformation [and as later discovered, disinformation] was disseminated to a worldwide audience.

As administrative assistant to Chief Curry, Captain King also handled departmental press relations and issued press releases. According to King, it was "the responsibility of each member of the department to furnish to the press information on incidents in which they, themselves, were involved, except on matters which involved...personnel policies of the department, or...unless it would obviously interfere with an investigation under way...."

...In their efforts to keep the public abreast of the investigation, the police reported hearsay items and unverified leads; further investigation proved many of these to be incorrect or inaccurate. For example, the rifle found on the sixth floor of the Texas School Book Depository Building was initially identified as a Mauser 7.65 rather than a Mannlicher-Carcano 6.5 because a deputy constable who was one of the first to see it thought it looked like a Mauser. He neither handled the weapon nor saw it at close range.[60]

Considering the number and quality of worldwide journalistic organizations represented, is it possible that not one followed Day's instruction to "check with the chief's office" (i.e., King) on the second most sought-after piece of information? For all of these professional journalists to get the name and type of murder weapon wrong is no less unbelievable than if they had gotten the name and description of the primary suspect wrong for twenty-four hours after he was in custody.

Warren Commissioner John J. McCloy asked Day: "There was never any doubt in your mind what the rifle was from the minute you saw it?" Day replied, "No, sir; It was stamped right on there, 6.5, and when en route to the office with Mr. Odum, the FBI agent who drove me in, he radioed it in, he radioed in what it was to the FBI over the air."[61] The

HSCA added that "Later that day, the rifle's six-round cartridge clip was removed by Lieutenant Day in the Dallas Police Crime Laboratory."[62]

Evica further points out that Day waited until he got to his office to dictate a detailed description of the rifle, which remained in his possession from the moment it was found. That description and four others are missing from the Commission's public record: 1) Weitzman's FBI description, 2) Day's dictated memo, 3) Day's description to FBI Special Agent Bardwell D. Odum, 4) Odum's broadcast, and 5) Dallas police Detective C.N. Dhority's description.(63) Five descriptions that would have prevented the "folklore" of a planted rifle were not made public.

* * *

Notes

1. Robert Sam Anson, *They've Killed the President!* (New York: Bantam, 1975) p. 356; hereafter cited as Anson 356. (Investigation of negative information:) Peter Dale Scott, *Deep Politics* (Berkeley, Calif.: University of California Press, 1993) pp. 58, 60-61, 69; hereafter cited as Scott 58, 60-61, 69; Charles J. Sanders and Mark S. Zaid, "The Declassification of Dealey Plaza: After Thirty Years, A New Disclosure Law At Last May Help To Clarify the Facts of the Kennedy Assassination," South Texas Law Review, Vol. 34:407, Oct. 1993; later published in "The President John F. Kennedy Assassination Records Collection Act of 1992" (ARCA), The Fourth Decade, Special Edition, 1994, pp. 411-12 n.8 (Griffin statements); hereafter cited as Sanders and Zaid 411-12 n.8.

2. Sanders and Zaid 410-12 n.8 (Warren Commission theory critique); DeLloyd J. Guth and David R. Wrone, *The Assassination of John F. Kennedy: A Comprehensive Historical and Legal Bibliography, 1963-1979* [Connecticut: Greenwood Press, 1980] pp. xxvii-xxx; hereafter cited as Guth and Wrone xxvii-xxx (House Committee theory critique); Gerald Posner, *Case Closed* (New York: Random House, 1993) p. 317, 326,-35, 474, 477, 478-79; hereafter cited as Posner with page number(s); (American Bar Association Mock Trial of Lee Harvey Oswald prosecution theory presented uncritically and without credit to A.B.A. by Posner).

3. The authors realize that the idea of proving conspiracy with finality is difficult to accept. Respected researchers have expressed aversion, on nothing more than rhetorical grounds, to our application of the notion. However, after remaining skeptical, scrutinizing our premise, relevant facts, arguments and counterarguments, and after requesting and receiving peer review, the basic premise of this article has resisted remonstration and confutation. Nevertheless, because of its awful consequences, we hope our conclusion will be quickly and rationally disproved. With regard to the identity of a possible second found murder weapon: although the alleged misidentification described a 7.65 Mauser,

and although the authors often refer to a supposed second rifle as a Mauser, that description could have been used to distract attention from a different, but completely unmarked Mannlicher-Carcano, as well as from the discrepancy over its loading mechanism; see discussion in George Michael Evica, *And We Are All Mortal* (Hartford, Conn.: University of Hartford, 1978) pp. 1-61; hereafter cited as Evica 1-61.

4. William M. Blair, "Warren Commission Will Ask Mrs. Oswald to Identify Rifle Used in the Kennedy Assassination," New York Times Feb. 5, 1964, p. 19 (Chairman Warren's doubts). This source quotes Warren's only public statement of doubt: that full disclosure was not possible for reasons of national security (Warren's statement was originally made to Dallas Morning News reporter Clint Richmond at Love Field the day Warren was in Dallas to interview Jack Ruby [Richard Bartholomew discussion with Clint Richmond, Mar. 5, 1997]). But in 1976 the extent of Warren's private doubt became publicly known. It had been confirmed in Jan. 1967, when columnist Drew Pearson told Warren about a conspiratorial lead involving CIA-Mafia assassination plots. Rather than stand by the Commission's conclusions, Warren referred the information to Secret Service Director James J. Rowley, who testified that Warren "...said he thought this was serious enough...and that the Warren Commission was finished, and he wanted the thing pursued, I suppose, by ourselves or the FBI" (Select Committee to Study Governmental Operations with respect to Intelligence Activities, The Investigation of the Assassination of President Kennedy: Performance of the Intelligence Agencies [Senate Report 94-755, 94th Cong., 2nd sess., 1976, Final Report, Book V] p. 80; cited in Bernard Fensterwald, *Coincidence or Conspiracy* [New York: Zebra Books, 1977] pp. 74-75; hereafter cited as Fensterwald 74-75). Edward Jay Epstein, *Inquest: The Warren Commission and the Establishment of Truth* (New York: Viking, Jun. 1966) pp. 149-50, (Bantam, Oct. 1966) p. 122 (doubts of Commissioners Russell, Cooper and Boggs); see also Fensterwald 86, 91, 96, 99. Hearings Before the House Select Committee on Assassinations, vol. XI (Washington D.C.: U.S. Government Printing Office, 1979) note 11 at p. 14; hereafter cited as 11 HH 14 n.11 (Commissioner McCloy's doubt); see also Fensterwald 86. Walter Cronkite interview, CBS News, broadcast on Apr. 25, 1975 (President Johnson's doubt); see also Fensterwald 76, 124. Warren Commission Hearings and Evidence (Washington D.C.: U.S. Government Printing Office, 1964, v. V) p. 99 ; cited hereafter as 5H 99 (Hoover's policy). See also discussion in Sanders and Zaid 412 n.11.

5. Letter from Walt Rostow to Dean Rusk, September 25, 1964 (LBJ Library: Papers of Walt W. Rostow, Box 14).

6. Los Angeles Times Jul. 20, 1992.

7. David E. Rosenbaum, "30-Year Commemoration In Dallas and Arlington," New York Times Nov. 23, 1993, p. A16.

8. Ian V. Hogg, "The Mannlicher Clip System," *The Encyclopedia of Infantry Weapons of World War II* (London: Bison Books, 1977, New York: Thomas Y. Crowell, Inc., 1977).

9. Warren Commission Report (Washington D.C.: U.S. Government Printing

Office, 1964) p. 555; hereafter cited as R 555.

10. R 555.

11. 1 HH 482.

12. 17H (CE 574) 258, (CE 575) 259. Life magazine, November 1983, pp. 16-17.

13. Letter from J.W. Hughes to Walter F. Graf, May 25, 1994.

14. R 193-95. "CBS News Inquiry: `The Warren Commission Report'" (4-part series produced by Leslie Midgely, narrated by Walter Cronkite) June 25-28, 1967; official transcript cited in Mark Lane, *A Citizen's Dissent* (New York: Holt, Rinehart and Winston, 1968) pp. 103, 104, 106-07; hereafter cited as Lane, Dissent 103, 104, 106-07. Anson 143. CBS rifle test film rebroadcasts: "The 20th Century" (narrated by Mike Wallace, Arts & Entertainment Cable Network, Nov. 16, 1994, 1 hr.); "Cronkite Remembers: Television and Politics" (Discovery Channel Cable Network, Jan. 23, 1997, 30 mins.).

15. 1 HH 483.

16. 7 HH 365.

17. 26 H (CE 3048) 599. Sylvia Meagher, *Accessories After the Fact* (New York: Bobbs-Merrill, 1967, Vintage Books, 1976, 1992) p. 95; hereafter cited as Meagher, Accessories 95. Sylvia Meagher, "Treasure Hunting in the National Archives," The Third Decade January 1986, p. 2; cited in Sheldon Inkol, "Other Patsies," The Third Decade May 1990, p. 8. Richard B. Trask, Pictures of the Pain (Danvers, Mass.: Yeoman Press, 1994) p. 532; hereafter cited as Trask 532. "JFK Assassination: As It Happened" (Arts & Entertainment Cable Network, Nov. 22, 1988, 6 hrs.) at 1 hr..-14 min. and 1 hr.-24 min.; hereafter cited as As It Happened 1:14, 1:24.

18. 4H 206.

19. Texas Department of Public Safety Evidence Sheet No. 443-A, and 24H (CE 2003, p. 130), reproduced in J. Gary Shaw and Larry R. Harris, *Cover-Up: The Governmental Conspiracy to Conceal the Facts About the Public Execution of John Kennedy* (Cleburne, Texas: self-published, 1976) pp. 159, 160.

20. 24 H (CE 2003 pp. 131-35) 262-64. FBI file no. PC-78243 BX, Nov. 23, 1963, p. 5; reproduced in Jesse E. Curry, *Retired Dallas Police Chief Jesse Curry Reveals his personal JFK Assassination File* (Dallas Tx.: American Poster and Printing Company, 1969) p. 94; hereafter cited as Curry 94. Suspiciously, that FBI lab report, a photo of Day with the rifle in front of the TSBD on p. 54, and a reproduction of a Klein's Sporting Goods ad on p. 99, are the only references to the essential ammunition clip in Chief Curry's 133-page book. Nowhere in his main text does Curry mention the clip.

21. Meagher, *Accessories* 119.

22. 3H 398. Meagher, *Accessories* 119.

23. The unmistakable difference between these two methods of loading a rifle (charger vs. clip) is clearly demonstrated in two adjacent film segments approximately 1 hr.-30 min. into the 1973 National General Cinema, Inc. film, Executive Action. When viewing them, keep in mind that one method is not interchangeable with the other.

24. Robert Sibley, "The Mysterious Vanishing Rifle of the JFK

Assassination," The Third Decade September, 1985; cited in Sheldon Inkol, "Other Patsies," The Third Decade May 1990, p. 8. W. Anthony Marsh, "No Mentesana Rifle," Assassination Chronicles, Mar. 1996, p. 24.

25. R 601, 612; cited in Harold Weisberg, *Whitewash: The Report on the Warren Report* (New York: Dell, 1966) p. 147; hereafter cited as Weisberg, Whitewash 147.

26. Charles E. O'Hara, *Fundamentals of Criminal Investigation* (Springfield, Ill.: Thomas Books, 1956, 1970, 2nd ed., 2nd printing) pp. 5-6, 30, 67, 69, 80, 438, 450, 493, 562, 575, 681, 684-85, 687; hereafter cited as O'Hara with page number(s). As if speaking to the crime-scene investigators at the TSBD, O'Hara wrote the following in a brief preface to his second edition: "On review, however, it would appear that insufficient attention had been given to the role of the investigator in establishing the innocence of persons falsely accused. It was thought that this aspect of investigation was too obvious to stress; that the continued insistence on objectivity and professionalism in the investigator's conduct should meet this requirement. After all, the process of establishing innocence is hardly separable from the task of detecting the guilty. One does not, that is to say, prove guilt by the method of exhaustion" (O'Hara vii). 4H 249-50 (Day's experience).

27. Garry Wills and Ovid Demaris, *Jack Ruby* (New York: New American Library, 1968, Da Capo Press edition, 1994) p. 58; hereafter cited as Wills and Demaris 58.

28. R 63-64.

29. Richard Bartholomew photogrammetric study (fig. 3) of Jim Murray photo of Gerald L. Hill in Trask 523.

30. Weisberg, *Whitewash* 190.

31. R 79. 7H 106-07. Boone statement, in 7H 106; 1 HH 442.

32. Trask 540, 549-50. Other published sources of these photographs include: Robert J. Groden, *The Killing of a President* (New York: Viking Studio Books, 1993) p. 66; Josiah Thompson, *Six Seconds in Dallas* (New York: Bernard Geis Associates [1967, p. 222] Berkley Medallion, 1976) p. 190; hereafter cited as Thompson 190; Robert J. Groden and Harrison Edward Livingstone, *High Treason* (New York: Conservatory Press, 1989) photo preceding ch. 8, p. 127; Curry 54; United Press International and American Heritage magazine, *Four Days: The Historical Record of the Death of President Kennedy* (New York: American Heritage, 1964, 1983) p. 29; hereafter cited as Four Days 29 (this photo was the first of these broadcast by NBC-TV News at 3:56 p.m. CST [As It Happened 2:56]).

33. Trask 549.

34. Trask 339, 340, 550.

35. Richard Bartholomew's contemporaneous notes on clip jamming test, Feb. 19, 1995. Thanks to Mike Blackwell for use of the test materials from his firearms collection.

36. Blanche Wiesen Cook, "C.D. Jackson: Cold War Propagandist," CovertAction Information Bulletin, No. 35, Fall 1990, pp. 33, 36. Peter Collier & David Horowitz, *The Rockefellers* (New York: Holt, Rinehart & Winston,

1976) pp. 272-73. Michael R. Beschloss, May Day (New York: Harper & Row, 1986) p. 143. William R. Corson, *The Armies of Ignorance* (New York: The Dial Press/James Wade Books, 1977) pp. 372-73. Patrick Moore & Garry Hunt, *Atlas of the Solar System* (New York: Rand McNally, 1983, third printing, 1985) p. 422.

37. As It Happened 2:56

38. Letter from John K. Lattimer, M.D. to Lieutenant J.C. Day, Sept. 9, 1968, file "DPD-1185," JFK Assassination: The Dallas Papers, CD-ROM, 1995. Letter from Charles Bachelor, Chief of Police to John K. Lattimer, M.D., Sept. 30, 1968, file "DPD-1184", op cit.

39. *John K. Lattimer, Kennedy and Lincoln: Medical & Ballistic Comparisons of Their Assassinations* (New York: Harcourt, Brace, Jovanovich, 1980) p. 299; hereafter cited as Lattimer 299. Lattimer's objectivity and credibility on the assassination have long been suspect. After Lattimer became the first private doctor to view the JFK autopsy photos and X-rays, Sylvia Meagher noted that, "Dr. Lattimer has made emphatic assertions which verge on the omniscient. He tells us that a bullet entered the back of the neck at a point even higher than ever claimed before, which happens to coincide with the point of entry on a sketch used by Dr. Lattimer in his lectures on behalf of the Warren Report as early as 1969 or some three years before he saw the autopsy photos. He does not explain how this bullet high in the neck produced holes in the coat and the shirt more than five inches below the top of the collar, except to offer the lame suggestion about the garments riding up that was discredited long ago." Seven years after Lattimer located the back wound higher, the HSCA's panel of forensic experts examined the alleged same X-rays and photos he had examined, and placed the same wound lower than the Warren Commission's placement. (Sylvia Meagher, "The case of the urologist apologist," The Texas Observer May 26, 1972, pp. 22-24. Guth and Wrone xxix, citing 7 HH).

40. Posner 263.

41. 4H 250 (Day); 3H 286-87 (Mooney).

42. Posner 269-70.

43. Posner 413.

44. Posner 446.

45. Posner 271.

46. Posner 271.

47. Lane, *Dissent* 126.

48. R 555. Any assumption that a clip was present in the manner alleged because the Carcano was rapidly fired as a "repeater" is the result of circular reasoning. In its alleged found condition, this "murder weapon" could have been used as a clip-fed repeater whether a clip had been found after the shooting or not. The clip's presence after chambering of the last round must be established independently because: 1) chambering of the last round is reason enough to expect the clip's absence, and 2) the clip's abnormal presence was too-belatedly alleged to be due to an unproven, abnormal defect. Preclusively, the claim that the alleged murder weapon was used as a repeater depends on scientific evidence chemically matching its ammunition and alleged chambered bullet to

another specific bullet and several specific bullet fragments. The likelihood of those matches, in turn, depends on the unbiased credibility of the opinions of Dr. Vincent P. Guinn who did neutron activation analysis tests of that ballistic evidence for the HSCA. Despite his oath, Guinn's testimony was not "the whole truth and nothing but...." See Guinn's oath and testimony denying he did "any work" for the FBI or Warren Commission: 1 HH 491, 557; compare with UPI's report quoting Guinn stating he did do such work: "Radioactive tests used in Oswald case," Glasgow, Scotland, Aug. 27, New York Times Aug. 28, 1964, p. 32; cited in Richard Bartholomew, "Dial `P' For Perjury," JFK/Deep Politics Quarterly Jul. 1996, pp. 7-10.

49. 4H 205.

50. 4H 258.

51. R 555.

52. Meagher, *Accessories* 117.

53. Posner 271.

54. 1 HH 481-83.

55. Charger: Ian V. Hogg, "The Mannlicher Clip System," The Encyclopedia of Infantry Weapons of World War II. Stripper clip: Interview of Mike Blackwell by Richard Bartholomew, Sept. 25, 1994. Craig Roberts (Assassination Chronicles, Dec. 1995) wrote: "A stripper clip is one in which the rounds are stripped off during mechanical operation of the bolt assembly. The Carcano, M-1, and other weapons...fall into this category." Reacting to Roberts in a letter to Richard Bartholomew, Oct. 8, 1996, Walter Graf wrote: "I always thought that a `stripper clip' was the `strip' or `charger' thrown away when the cartridge was thumbed into the Springfield, Mauser, or Enfield...Then recently I was watching an A&E documentary with top experts like Ian Hogg (English). Twice they referred to a stripper clip as the strip (charger) on the Springfield 03, etc....Somehow the usage of the term got switched over the years."

56. Letter from J.W. Hughes to Walter Graf, May 25, 1994.

57. R (17H (CE 541 [3]) 239) 83.

58. Evica 24.

59. 4H 264.

60. R 231-35.

61. 4H 264.

62. 7 HH 355.

63. Evica 25.

.

THE GUN THAT DIDN'T SMOKE
PART 2

[Written with the late Walter F. Graf]

CONFUSION OVER THE RIFLE

As out of place as a Presbyterian in Hell.
-- Mark Twain, 1912

In the main body of the Warren Report, the rifle, cartridges, cartridge cases, bullets, etc., are described under the heading, "Expert Examination," but there is not a word about the clip on the Mannlicher-Carcano despite that it would be of particular interest, since the Carcano and M-1 Garand were the only clip-fed (directly chambered from a clip) WWII military-use rifles in the world.

Turning to the Warren Report's Appendix X, we have coverage of the description and operation of the Carcano and everything associated with it in the minutest detail, but on the ejection of the clip, silence. This is the key to the operation of this weapon, because it tells the user when to reload. It is important enough to repeat that, on the M-1 Garand, the clip is ejected when the last round is fired, while on the Mannlicher system, the clip is ejected when the last round is chambered.

That was the state of the weapon left at the TSBD. Yet it is not until the Warren Report's Appendix X that, at long last, the silence is broken on the location of the clip. We read that when the rifle was found in the TSBD, it contained a clip. That was the only place in the world where the clip could not be found. It would have fallen out the bottom when the last round was chambered. The word "contained" precludes the slight possibility that the clip was stuck in the magazine.

Events at the crime scene seem to be predicated on 1) somehow a clip was involved, but 2) somehow these events were based on the misconception that the clip, as in the M-1 Garand, was ejected when the last round was fired, not chambered. See the Warren Report's Appendix X.

his latter misconception could have been the reason why Jack Ruby referred to the confusion over the rifle. For at least twenty-four hours the public was informed the weapon was a Mauser, while it was known internally at the Dallas Police Department to be a Mannlicher-Carcano. The delay could have been to allow time to locate a clip, and synchronize stories, when actually it was unnecessary. The clip would have been ejected, and the shooter could have easily pocketed it to avoid identification of fingerprints.

The most plausible explanation is that the only confusion was over when the clip ejected during the load-fire-reload cycle. Trained soldiers throughout the world have filled hundreds of thousands of graves because of failure to understand this cycle on various weapons. So it is understood that people are slow to understand the cycle of this feeding system.[64] It seems too ironic, when considering these events, that the Carcano is one of only two clip-fed WWII military-use rifles in the world, and that the misconception was based on the timing of the ejection of this only other clip-fed system, the M-1 Garand.

The facts surrounding these events cry out for explanation because of repeated indications that during the first twenty-four hours the Depository rifle was known internally to be a Mannlicher-Carcano by the Dallas Police Department. And the cry becomes deafening when we add the fact that three days after the assassination, a CIA report identified the gun as a Mauser. Dated November 25, 1963, it reads:

> The rifle he [Oswald] used was a Mauser which OSWALD had ordered (this is now known by handwriting examination) from Klein's Mail Order House, Chicago, Illinois. He had the rifle sent to a Post Office Box which Lee OSWALD had rented. In the order for the rifle, Oswald used the name Alex HIDELL. OSWALD also had in his possession at the time of his arrest (after he also killed a Texas policeman) a U.S. Selective Service Card in the name of Alex HIDELL.[65]

This seemingly authoritative report was apparently written by an analyst who had not seen the Klein's mail order form he is writing about, since it is an order form for a Mannlicher-Carcano, not a Mauser. The CIA declined to comment on the report. And a CIA-translated, Italian military report, dated six days after the assassination reads, "The weapon which appears to have been employed in this criminal attack is a Model 91 rifle,

7.35 caliber, 1938 modification...The description of a [6.5 caliber] `Mannlicher-Carcano' rifle in the Italian and foreign press is in error."[66] And then after weeks to think it over, Wade asked the Commission if a Mauser was German. This is an official who had prosecuted scores of gun shot cases.[67] The cry for answers is still deafening. The silence is still equally deafening.

During his testimony, Dallas District Attorney Henry Wade mentioned something about a "situation" and of course no one was interested in what "situation." He implied the situation was the cause of unnatural statements and events at his post-midnight press conference.

> Mr. Rankin. What did you say about it?
> Mr. Wade. I think I said I thought it was a Mauser or I thought -- was one of those things I didn't know what it was. It was an Italian gun, I think and I really thought I was giving them Italian but Mauser is a German gun, isn't it? But I think you have that -- it was a situation, I don't contend I was right on that because it was a situation somebody asked me that and that is what I thought I was telling them and I never -- all my information came from the police and actually somebody said originally it was a Mauser but it turned out it was not.[68]

All Wade had to say was, "I called it a Mauser. I was wrong." Instead, he seems to refer to "a situation" in the sense that it was a critical, trying, or unusual state of affairs -- a problem. He even passes the buck to the police. What was the problem? This "situation" was most likely the failure to understand the load-fire-reload cycle when the evidential line was being set up. There is nothing inherently sinister about an evidential line, a starting point has to be established to keep things under control. Why is he so defensive? Even if he was wrong, it should not have been a problem.

Forget where the rifle came from, forget whether Oswald ever had the rifle, rate of fire or accuracy or whether the rifle was fired that day (there appears to be no evidence it was checked for recent firing). Forget everything about the rifle except two things: 1) the Carcano was the evidence on the scene and 2) its load-fire-reload cycle in relation to the state in which the rifle was found was that the last round was chambered.

The first factor was understood on the afternoon of November 22nd. The second factor was misunderstood and may have resulted in Ruby's referral to the confusion over the rifle. This confusion governed that afternoon, evening, night and the next day. It resulted in the Warren Commission drawing a conclusion that is completely impossible. It resulted in Henry Wade being forced to make ridiculous statements.

Since there is no physical or photographic (and, as discussed below, truthful anecdotal) evidence of a Mauser or a clip at the sixth floor crime scene, the Mannlicher-Carcano was the only weapon in evidence on the sixth floor of the TSBD at 1:22 p.m., November 22nd, 1963. The evidential line therefore had to be set up. Through failure to understand the second factor above, it was mistakenly thought a clip had to be found. A clip was obtained. A period of uncertainty followed. The public had to be informed it was a Mauser (the Carcano's non-clip-fed superficial-twin). As a result, no one asked, "Where's the clip?" When the conspirators realized they must remain committed to the clip (because Day had been photographed leaving the TSBD with the rifle and the clip is shown sticking noticeably out of the bottom of the trigger guard), the cover story was explained away as Weitzman's imagination having only "glimpsed" the murder weapon of the century. This, in all likelihood, is the "situation" Wade was talking about. Neither this nor anything else, however, suggests that Wade had knowledge of what was transpiring. It suggests only that he was being given a "bum steer."[69] Why the misunderstanding? The familiar M-1 Garand, the other WWII, military-use, clip-fed rifle, during its load-fire-reload cycle, ejects the clip with a clatter when the last round is fired -- not chambered. And that, of course, is the signal to reload. Being so familiar to everyone, it was not realized the same did not apply to the Carcano feeding system.

This "misunderstanding" ruled the afternoon of November 22nd, through the next day, and when the Warren Report was issued. This "misunderstanding" was the confusion over the rifle Ruby talked about, the "situation" Henry Wade talked about.[70]

And because the weapon was apparently never tested for recent firing, a probably unfired rifle was planted supposedly in a state to suggest an actual fire. For rifle experts, the first thing they focus on in picking up the Mannlicher-Carcano is the unusual clip ejection system and the characteristic of the clip getting stuck on occasion. The silence on this subject was deafening at Dallas, and this silence continued through most of the Warren Report. Finally, in the Report's Appendix X, it was dismissed in a terse, tortured manner, dismissed with a sentence that sounds like a thunder clap: "When the rifle was found at the [TSBD] it contained a clip." "Contained" does not mean "stuck in the bottom." Had that been what was observed, it would have been among the very first observations made at the crime scene.

John K. Lattimer, author of Kennedy and Lincoln, and the man who, in 1968, asked for but reported no answer from Day about where the clip was found, dealt with this problem in his own twisted way. He explained his initial concern: "I had thought I had discovered a discrepancy in the Warren Commission report when I read that Oswald's clip was retained...." He reported that in experiments with his four Carcanos, the clip stuck on two. Instead of using the Commission's "rifle contained a clip," he used the phrases "rifles would retain the clip" and "that all these old Carcano rifles would eject the clip when it was empty...was not always so," both quite different from "contained."[71] While poetic in rhyme and synonymy, and while adequately describing the partial ejection seen rarely with Carcanos, "retain"-- to hold back -- does not describe the invisible containment of a clip necessitated by the film and testimony documenting what was actually seen and allegedly done with the Carcano in question.

But in debating details about what was or was not reported and what the rifle will or will not do, we could find it easy to lose sight of the basic problem. Either way, it is devastating to the Warren Commission's minority opinion; to those who initially conducted this investigation; and to conspiracy deniers in general.

If the clip was on the sixth floor for everyone to see, the tool mark notwithstanding, how could these men mistake a clip-fed rifle for a non-clip-fed Mauser? If the clip was there, the long-lived Mauser identification does not make sense: unless it was a deliberate lie. And since there was no reason to lie about a Mannlicher-Carcano with a clip, it either was a Mauser, quickly replaced by a Mannlicher-Carcano, or there was no clip. Those are two very good reasons to lie; but in the latter case, only if you think a clip is needed. And until there is evidence of a Mauser or a clip on the sixth floor, the latter explanation must predominate.

Therefore, if there was no clip on the sixth floor, why did the authorities say there was? If the clip was not there -- a perfectly normal situation -- the fact that they said it was does not make sense; unless they knew the rifle was planted, inserted a clip which they erroneously thought it needed, and lied to cover it up. Either way, Oswald was framed. If not for the serious implications, it would be laughable, because they did not need the clip.

As the Warren Report says, "The rifle probably was sold without a clip; however, the clip is commonly available." Given the known chain of custody of the clip, that statement incriminates Lieutenant Day as much as it does anybody. There is no evidence of clip ownership by Lee Harvey Oswald or even by his alleged paper alter ego, Alek James

Hidell. In the conflicting evidence of mail-order paperwork used to purchase the alleged murder weapon, one fact is clear: no clip was ordered or purchased. The clip was offered free with the purchase of 108 rounds of ammunition which cost $7.50. The carbine with scope was $19.95, plus $1.50 for postage and handling. The money order was in the amount of $21.45. The order form sent to Klein's Sporting Goods was for only item C20-T750 ("Carbine with brand new good quality 4X scope"). The Klein's shipping order itemized only "1 ITALIAN CARBINE 6.5 W/4X SCOPE...19.95...PP-1.50." No ammunition was ordered or purchased, and no clip was ordered or purchased.[72]

After showing the clip inside the rifle in a photograph (CE 541) on page 83, the Warren Report first mentions it on page 555 at the end of the section called "The Rifle." Here the reader learns that "As long as there is ammunition in the clip, one need only work the bolt and pull the trigger to fire the rifle." The next, and last, paragraph of this section is entirely about the clip. While this section tells how it is inserted into the rifle, no mention is made of the unique way it is ejected. Of course, if they did that they would have to open a can of threatening worms and explain why the rifle "contained a clip." FBI weapons expert Robert Frazier did testify about the ejection mechanism but said nothing about the clip remaining stuck in the weapon.[73]

The clip is not mentioned again. Even on pages 565-566, it is not mentioned as one of the "Objects in the Texas School Book Depository Building" dusted for prints. This section comes close when discussing "faint ridge formations" on the metal magazine housing in front of the trigger. (An identifiable fingerprint of Oswald's, according to the PBS Frontline television broadcast, "Who Was Lee Harvey Oswald," first aired on Nov. 16, 1993.) It comes close again when saying "No prints were developed on the cartridge found in the rifle or on the three expended cartridge cases." This statement's sources[74] are FBI fingerprint expert Sebastian Latona,[75] Lt. Carl Day,[76] and CE 2011, pp. 1, 5.

Latona testified that he dusted all parts of the weapon, and he specifically said he found no prints on the ammunition clip. His findings were even reported in an FBI report.[77] Since the Warren Report states that "There is no evidence that Oswald wore gloves or that he wiped prints off the rifle,"[78] it appears that the FBI would have been forced to explain the absence of prints on the clip had they mentioned Latona's findings.

If the clip was actually there, it is highly unusual (and therefore suspicious) for Day not to have dusted it or mentioned dusting it on the sixth floor. Unlike the cartridges, it had to be handled when it was inserted into the magazine. The absence of prints on the cartridges means that any prints made in the act of loading would most likely be found on the clip. To say there were no prints on the clip but several on the rifle is to say that Oswald was careful not to handle the clip with bare hands yet after loading, handled the rifle with bare hands. Not likely. It is more likely that no clip was found.

Austin, Texas, gunsmith Jim Westbrook, formerly of the Austin Police Department, was asked if the clip could be in the weapon during its disassembled state, thus avoiding fingerprints upon assembly. He said the clip might be loaded disassembled, but not safely. While he would not say it could not be done, he pointed out that handling the rifle would endanger the user and others. He said one could even argue that Oswald left the gun loaded after the Walker shooting, but while loaded, the weapon could not be disassembled and reassembled safely. J.W. Hughes, however, is certain that it cannot be done at all. He said a loaded clip will not stay in the ammunition "well" when the trigger guard is removed from the rifle.

Westbrook brought up another point concerning claims of Oswald assembling the rifle after he reached the TSBD. He said the rifle would need significant adjustment to align all of the parts for accurate shooting, including the seating of the action and the tension of the screws, requiring a torque wrench. Without such adjusting, even the iron sights could be misaligned. Even if it were possible, taking this kind of care during assembly would not jibe with the extremely unsafe practice of doing it while the gun was loaded.[79]

It has also been argued that the rifle was found with a clip still "attached" inside of which was that "last" round. Someone then operated the bolt so that the "last" round was chambered, followed by the clip falling out. And, afterward, it is possible that, in order to re-establish the original condition of the rifle found, the finder(s) replaced the round in the clip, or misplaced it in the chamber, and replaced the clip in the rifle.

Researcher Anthony Marsh has given this theory some thought: "The clip does not eject after the last round fired if there is still a live round in the magazine...a live round in the magazine, not chamber...if the last round was still in the magazine, then the clip would not have ejected. After someone ejected the last round to dust it, then the clip could have started falling out. The fact that it is [apparently] only partially ejected when the rifle is being carried out of the TSBD supports the idea that the clip did not fully eject as happens on most M-Cs."[80]

The clip would have "started falling out" after the last round was chambered, not ejected. And the idea that a clip does not fully eject on most Carcanos is mistaken. A normal empty clip rarely catches during operational ejection on most Carcanos. As discussed above, a clip-jamming effect can be regularly produced with most Carcanos only when an empty clip is inserted and manipulated into the relevant jammed position. Moreover, given the ejection of a last round as described by Fritz and Day, the presence of a "last" round in the clip and not in the chamber sounds impossible. Officially, Oswald had ejected three cartridge cases. Pulling the bolt back ejects the case in the chamber, and positions the next cartridge. When Oswald allegedly ejected the third cartridge, the fourth and last one remaining in the clip would have become chambered, ejecting the clip. The `03 Springfield has a cut off that enables one to work the bolt on an empty chamber and still retain rounds in the magazine. But even if the alleged JFK murder weapon has such an unreported feature, it is hard to imagine using the cut off while shooting at someone.[81] Another, more plausible, version of this un-chambered round theory will be discussed in this article. Such arguments can distract from the primary issue, however.

If the clip was found "contained" in the rifle, the argument over whether it took a blow torch to remove it or it ejected at launch velocity is irrelevant to the issue of conspiracy. Such arguments are diversions. Resolving them will not acquit the guilty parties. Their resolution will only help reveal which crime: Mauser switch; or clip replacement and Mauser lie. They claimed to have both.
By considering suppositions covering both options (clip and no clip), the truth begins to emerge: the authorities fabricated an explanation that conflicts with opposing conclusions (i.e., clip equals Mauser or Mauser fabrication, and no clip equals both clip fabrication and Mauser fabrication). Did they have a clip or did they have a Mauser? They cannot innocently have both, neither, or either, coexisting with their claims about the clip and the longevity of the Mauser identification. All options for innocence are exhausted. If the crime-scene investigators had left bad enough alone, they could have gotten away with it. Disputing the suppositions will help discover which crime took place. But the fact that these untruths concern a planted rifle, and therefore the framing of Oswald, is indisputable.

There is also the question of whether the rifle removed from the TSBD was tested for recent firing.[82] Every conceivable test of this rifle was performed repeatedly, documented, and written about exhaustively over the last thirty years -- except the most obvious one. Why was a test for recent firing not the cornerstone of the Warren Report and the FBI reports? Why was it not at least mentioned by Gerald Posner, a man who claims to have re-indexed the Warren Commission's twenty-six volumes? If Mr. Posner wishes to prove his case with finality and portray the "conspiracy buffs" as frauds, why is he not shouting such test results from the rooftops and selling poster-sized reproductions of them?

The answer, reportedly, is that there is no test for recent firing. But there is a test for whether a gun has been fired since it was last cleaned. On Tuesday, March 31, 1964, John J. McCloy fully expected such a test and asked for the result:

Mr. McCloy. Was there metal fouling in the barrel?

Mr. Frazier. I did not examine it for that.[83]

A metal fouling test, then, is more accurately a test for recent non-firing. If such a test on the Carcano had been positive, i.e., showing metal fouling in the barrel, the test would be inconclusive regarding when it was last fired. The FBI could have just gone on assuming it was the murder weapon. But if such a test on the Carcano had produced a negative result, i.e., no metal fouling in the barrel, it would have meant the rifle had not been fired since it was last cleaned. Since it had not been cleaned between the time it was allegedly used to kill President Kennedy, and the time it came into the possession of the FBI, a negative metal-fouling test result would have proven the rifle was not the murder weapon. FBI firearms expert Robert Frazier evidently was not as curious as Commissioner McCloy about the condition of this particular barrel.

Moreover, McCloy did not ask whether such a test had been performed. He asked for the result of a metal fouling test. In other words, he expected that one had been done routinely. Upon learning that the test had not been done, McCloy asked Frazier: "Could you say roughly how many rounds you think had been fired since it left the factory, with the condition of the barrel as you found it?" Frazier answered, "No, sir; I could not, because the number of rounds is not an indication of the condition of the barrel, since if a barrel is allowed to rust, one round will remove that rust and wear the barrel to the same extent as 10 or 15 or 50 rounds just fired through a clean barrel." McCloy and the other Commissioners and staff present, apparently getting the hint, abandoned that line of questioning without asking the simple question: What would it mean if this "murder weapon" had been found to have no "metal fouling in the barrel?"

As a whole then, the rifle evidence tells the following story of confusion at the crime scene. Fritz and Day, and company found the Mannlicher-Carcano on the sixth floor. It had not recently been fired but was properly set up to look as if it had (last round chambered, no clip). No other WWII military-use rifle ejects a clip upon chambering the last round.

The rifle's discoverers were not as familiar with its ammunition feeding peculiarity as the rifle's planters. Their ignorance created a "situation" (according to Wade) based on "confusion over the rifle" (according to Ruby). The discoverers thought the clip normally ejected after the last round was fired (like the only other clip-fed WWII military-use rifle, the M-1 Garand).

The way they dealt with their confusion -- their first mistake -- reveals the discoverers' roles as accomplices. Innocent, confused discoverers would have reported finding a rifle in an impossible post-firing condition, suspected it was planted, and tested it for recent firing. If it had been fired, they would have eventually realized their mistake and concluded the suspect took the clip with him (a reasonable explanation because of fingerprints). If it had not been fired they would have concluded it was planted despite their mistake. The actual discoverers did none of these things.

When we look through the eyes of persons instinctively reacting to their M-1 operation instincts, we have the reaction of 1) a person not knowing it was a plant contrasted with 2) a person knowing it was a plant. Assuming in both cases that there was no clip, based on the direct evidence and testimony about the crime scene, the first person's reaction would be that the post-firing condition was impossible and he would go from there. He would look for another weapon and check for recent firing, which is the normal, instinctive reaction in any shooting. The second person, knowing it was a plant, would say something like, "Holy S___, there has to be a clip in there!"

Therefore, the amazing fact that the rifle was never tested for recent firing reveals their knowledge that it had not been fired and was therefore planted. Since the last round was in the chamber, they thought the planters had made a mistake by not including the clip in the gun. They did two things to remedy this assumed error. They sought out an appropriate replacement clip and stalled for time until they were successful.

They purposely misidentified the rifle -- probably first as an Enfield and/or other non-clip-fed rifles -- their second mistake -- to avoid questions about clips. Then they realized there was a rifle closer in appearance to the Carcano. In an attempt to make the fake misidentification more plausible, they quickly changed it to the Carcano's superficial twin, but non-clip-fed, Mauser.

Their third mistake reveals the apparent method by which they chose the Mauser. Paul Mauser's first accepted box-magazine rifle was the 7.65 mm. Belgium 1890 Mauser. By 1963, who would be thinking any rifle was a 7.65 mm. caliber?

Gunsmith and former police officer Jim Westbrook said it was his recollection that the 7.65s were not all that plentiful even when they were the standard. He said he did not think they were much used outside of Germany and Italy. Westbrook speculated that such a number could have come from someone using the metric equivalent of the standard rifle caliber, .3006. He said it is like looking at a Chevy and knowing it is a six-cylinder because that was standard for that model year.[84] George Michael Evica, on the other hand, quoted a UPI story with a Dallas dateline, dated November 24th, 1963, which said, "...the 7.65 German-made Mauser was in big demand about two years ago....The rifle takes a 32-caliber shell and is comparable to the American 30.06."[85]

But regardless of whether 7.65s were common or rare by 1963, if a gun enthusiast had Mausers in mind when looking at the 6.5 mm. (0.26 inch) barrel, or, in this case, a rebarrelled 7.35, and thought of a .3006 inch (7.5 mm.) barrel, why would he not use the newer 7.62 mm. caliber? In 1898 Germany established the 7.92 mm. standard which lasted until the NATO standard of 7.62 mm. went into effect after 1949. The metric equivalent to .3006 inch which should have been foremost in anyone's mind by 1963 would most reasonably have been the current standard of 7.62 millimeters; or at least the previous standard for a half-century of 7.92 millimeters. Even if someone was influenced by the numbers "6.5" stamped on the Mannlicher-Carcano barrel, the moment he said "7.65" the others should have thought he was nuts. Instead, "...the police reported....a Mauser 7.65 rather than a Mannlicher-Carcano 6.5...."[86]

A surplus of 7.65 German-Mauser rifles sold recently in the Dallas firearms market would certainly explain how that caliber could be foremost in the mind of local conspirators in need of a quick distraction. Otherwise, the only way, apparently, a gun user could have reported (even by mistake) the old 7.65 caliber would be by hurriedly looking Mausers up in a reference book.[87] Mausers had been two different calibers for over a half-century -- the lifetime of those at the crime scene. Gerald Posner, inasmuch as he does not mention it in his book Case Closed, also seems to be ignorant of the oddity of the 7.65 caliber designation. Committing to a cover story involving such an old and odd caliber was obviously a horrendous mistake.

To cover that mistake, among other reasons, Deputy Sheriff Roger Craig was apparently forced by the conspirators to lie about seeing a non-existent "7.65 Mauser" tool mark stamped on the barrel, a classic misdirection strategy. Although the story meant conspiracy, it led nowhere and, because it could not be proved, weakened Craig's credibility on other events he witnessed, further protecting the actual conspirators. (See below.)

The bizarre twists in this story bring to mind a fable about an ancient land where confusion reigned. Living there was a devilish imp doing devilish things. To be effective he had to remain behind a fence so as not to be seen by the people. One day he threw a golden apple over the fence for the confused attention of the people. Attention thus diverted, he could continue his devilish ways on his side of the fence. He had an accomplice on the people's side of the fence to guide them in their confusion. He was the "confuser." In modern times, some devil threw a Mannlicher-Carcano over the fence for the world to ponder. The only flaw was that the "confuser," whose duty was to confuse the people, got confused himself over the Mannlicher feeding system. How else can it be explained that the weapon was proclaimed to the people to be a Mauser all that afternoon, after midnight and the next day? How else?

* * *

7.65 MAUSER SO STAMPED ON THE BARREL

It takes your enemy and your friend, working together, to hurt you to the heart; the one to slander you and the other to get the news to you.
-- Mark Twain, 1894

Pulitzer Prize-winning journalist Thomas Powers made two observations which students of John F. Kennedy's assassination have been slow to learn: 1) "...espionage, properly conducted, never announces itself. `Stolen' information remains in its accustomed place; the `spy' is a trusted civil servant; the spymaster betrays no sign of special knowledge; even the consumer of the purloined fact may not know whence it came." 2) "...worst of all is when an enemy gains control of your secret apparatus and begins to feed you information of his own choice. Outsiders do not quite believe in such things, but they happen." Perhaps the most difficult aspect of the conspiracy for investigators of JFK's assassination to accept is the fact that some of our most trusted sources have been used to keep us confused about the actual conspiracy.

Philadelphia attorney Vincent J. Salandria, one of the earliest critics of the Warren Commission, wrote in 1971: "I have long believed that the killers actually preempted the assassination criticism by supplying the information they wanted revealed and also by supplying the critics whom they wanted to disclose the data. Does it not make sense that if they could perpetrate a coup and could control the press, they would have endeavored to dominate likewise the assassination criticism?" The facts reveal that one of those compromised sources of information was Roger Craig.[88]

In his 1971 unpublished manuscript, *When they Kill a President*, former deputy sheriff Roger Craig revealed new details about the discovery of the rifle. On page ten of his original manuscript he wrote:

> Lt. Day inspected the rifle briefly then handed it to Capt. Fritz, who had a puzzled look on his face. Seymour Weitzman a deputy constable was standing beside me at the time. Weitzman was an expert on weapons, being in the sporting goods business for many years he was familiar with all domestic and foreign weapons. Capt. Fritz asked if anyone knew what kind of rifle it was. Weitzman asked to see it. After a close examination (much longer than Fritz or Day's examination) Weitzman declared that it was a 7.65 German Mauser, Fritz agreed with him....At that exact moment an unknown Dallas police officer came running up the stairs and advised Capt. Fritz that a Dallas policeman had been shot in the Oak Cliff area. I instictively [sic] looked at my watch and the time was 1:06 P.M. [emphasis in original]

In a 1974 videotaped interview, Craig described Weitzman as a "gun buff." Craig added that Weitzman "had a sporting goods store at one time. He was very good at -- with weapons. And he said, 'It looks like a Mauser.' And he walked over to Fritz. And Captain Fritz was holding the rifle up in the air. And I was standing next to Weitzman -- who was standing next to Fritz. And we weren't more than six to eight inches from the rifle. And stamped right on the barrel -- of the rifle -- was 7.65 Mauser. And that's when Weitzman said, 'It is a Mauser,' and pointed to the 7.65 Mauser stamp on the barrel." That interview was conducted in April 1974 by Lincoln Karle and can be seen in a videotape called Two Men in Dallas: John Kennedy and Roger Craig (Alpa Productions, 1977). In that interview, Craig speaks very slowly and deliberately when he says the words "seven-point-six-five Mauser." In the space of a few sentences the word Mauser is used four times and the caliber is given twice.

On February 8, 1975, thirteen weeks before Craig's untimely death, Massachusetts high school teacher Edgar F. Tatro wrote his first of several letters to Craig. In an article Tatro later wrote detailing that correspondence, he said, "Roger Craig's second letter to me contained a shocker, something I had never seen attributed to him in print before. He had written that the rifle was `a 7.65 Mauser so stamped on the barrel'. If this was accurate, it was new information, to my knowledge, and crucial to a new investigation."[89]

In a letter to coauthor Richard Bartholomew, Mr. Tatro updated his Craig research. He said, "...After I wrote `Roger Craig and 1984', his best friend and I corresponded for years. She was amazing! From her I learned what was true and false, who forced Roger to embellish his original story, who were disinformation agents among us....I'm afraid his Mauser identification is a lie....It's a complex and tragic story and someday I'll tell it, but several dangerous individuals are still alive and I'd rather not tangle with them."[90] While Tatro does not say it specifically, there is reason to believe Craig was forced to lie about the Mauser.

The way Craig wrote about Weitzman and the tool mark (authoritatively), and the way he spoke about it on film (slowly and deliberately) indicates that Craig's revelation -- that the stamp said "7.65 Mauser" -- could have had a sinister purpose. The tool stamp did not read "7.65 Mauser." This falsehood, therefore, smacks of setting up a straw man that can be knocked down. On these guns, the mark, if present at all, shows the caliber without the name.[91]

Coauthor Walter Graf discovered that "Mauser" existed in the tool stamp on the Chilean Mauser. He also discovered a 6.5 mm. Argentine Mauser, mentioned by Trask as one of the descriptions broadcast the day of the assassination. British researcher Chris Mills learned that the Argentine carbine has "Mauser" in its tool stamp. But these two rare tool marks are even more problematic to Craig's honesty:

M1895 rifles, short rifles and carbines known as "Boer Models" made by Loewe Co. and DWM were distributed to China, Costa Rica, El Salvador, Honduras, Luxembourg, Mexico, The Orange Free State, Persia, Paraguay, the South African Republic (Transvaal), Serbia, Sweden, Venezuela and Uruguay, as well as to Chile. Those ordered by the Orange Free State were marked "O.V.S." Those ordered by the Transvaal had no "special markings." Those ordered by Chile from the Loewe Co. had a tool stamp on the barrel which read, "MAUSER CHILENO MODELO 1895 MANUFACTURA LOEWE BERLIN."[92] This Chilean Mauser can be categorized in a Mauser group -- the M1893 and M1895, Boer, or Spanish Mauser, which was mostly 7 mm. but also 6.5 mm. and 7.65 mm. -- that definitely does not include a Carcano look alike.[93]

Chris Mills confirmed this during a visit to the "Pattern Room" at the British Royal Ordnance Factory. He examined an example of every 7.65 Mauser that has been made. He learned that there were only three that could have been remotely confused with the Carcano: the Belgian

7.65 carbine and the Argentine 7.65. Supposedly one could include the Turkish version, which is visually similar to the Argentine, but it is clearly marked in Arabic script. According to the "Pattern Room" Curator, none of the Mausers had the caliber stamped on the barrel at the point of manufacture, and none of the examples Chris saw had such. The Curator explained that it may have been possible, but rather unlikely, that the caliber was stamped on later if the guns were resold on the U.S. market. This could have been done so that 7.62 ammunition was not used by mistake. One model had the word "Mauser" in its tool stamp: the Argentine carbine. The accompanying text on the engraving, however, was obviously Spanish. Also, the sitting of the word "Mauser" on the weapon is most problematic to Craig's assertions. The weapon reportedly seen by Craig had a scope mounted. The mounting bracket of the scope would have fitted directly over the position of the "Mauser" engraving and none of the wording would have been visible until the scope was removed.[94]

Craig added "Mauser" for a reason. It could be that Craig purposely misspoke about the stamp as a subtle message to gun experts that he was lying. It may be a variation of the old trick whereby a person in danger cryptically lets someone know something is wrong.

Craig died May 15, 1975 of a rifle wound to the chest. It was ruled a suicide despite the fact that Craig did not own a rifle. A couple of weeks earlier, in an interview with author Michael Canfield, Seymour Weitzman had identified a man from a photograph as the one he saw impersonating a Secret Service agent in the parking lot north of Dealey Plaza just after the assassination.[95] On page eight of his 1971 manuscript, Craig told of a similar encounter between himself and a Secret Service impersonator. With Craig's death, these two eyewitnesses to the same and similar events that Friday afternoon never got a chance to compare their stories for the benefit of researchers.

Craig's carefully chosen words, the oddity of that particular caliber number, and his experience with guns support the idea that it was not a slip of the tongue. And if it was not a slip of the tongue, what else could it be but a lie obvious enough to be easily discredited or draw suspicion to his motive for saying it?

Given that, what then do we make of the Mauser identifications made by several others? Deputy Sheriff Boone said it appeared to be a 7.65 Mauser in two different assassination-day reports[96] because, according to his testimony, Fritz identified it to him as such just after its discovery. He said they discussed this while Day prepared to photograph it.[97] Twelve hours into the investigation, District Attorney Henry Wade told a reporter it was a Mauser because, Wade swore, the police identified it to him as such. Weitzman's sworn affidavit -- given the next day -- corroborates both Boone and Wade's police sources.

The Warren Report said Weitzman was the source of the error. They based that conclusion on absolutely nothing. Weitzman never testified before the Commission itself. Mark Lane first brought Weitzman's November 23, 1963 affidavit to the Commission's attention on March 4, 1964.[98] Nowhere in that affidavit does Weitzman say that he was Boone's source.[99] Perhaps that is why it is unmentioned in the Report.[100] The Commission called Boone twenty days later. Boone never said Weitzman was his source. After hearing Boone, all they knew was that it started with Fritz, was officially reported twice by Boone, then by the press, then by Weitzman the next day. Weitzman then gave a deposition to Staff Counsel Joseph Ball on April 1, 1964, during which he seemed to perjure himself by saying no one but him said it was a Mauser.

Mr. Ball. In the statement you made to the Dallas Police Department that afternoon, you referred to the rifle as a 7.65 Mauser bolt action?

Mr. Weitzman. In a glance, that's what it looked like.

Mr. Ball. That's what it looked like -- did you say that or someone else say that?

Mr. Weitzman. No; I said that. I thought it was one.[101]

Weitzman was not asked nor did he volunteer whether he was the source of Boone's reports dated the day before Weitzman's police affidavit. The vagueness of this exchange, as well as the question of perjury made it more important than ever for the Commission to question Weitzman -- especially if they suspected he was the original source of the Mauser identification; but they never called him to testify.

On April 22, 1964, the Commission instead questioned Curry, Fritz and Day. Strangely, Police Chief Jesse Curry and Commissioner McCloy, who with Chief Counsel J. Lee Rankin was questioning Curry, both stated they knew of no police reports or records identifying the weapon as a Mauser -- again raising the question of perjury.[102] In 1976, Curry told the Detroit News that "it's more than possible" the rifle could have been switched and that due to lack of security anyone wanting to do so "could have gotten away with it at the time."[103] Fritz denied he called it a 7.65 caliber but did not deny he called it a Mauser.[104] The November 23, 1963, New York Times, however, quoted him saying it was "of unusual, undetermined caliber."[105] That certainly applies to the ancient 7.65, Paul Mauser's original 1890s design, long replaced by the 7.92 Mauser.

Day said, "I didn't describe the rifle to anyone other than police officers." Commission Counsel David Belin's question to Day had been, "Did you ever describe the rifle as anything but a 6.5-caliber with regard to the rifle itself?" Day therefore did not answer the question. Belin pressed him: "Is the description that you used with the police officers the same that you dictated here into the record from your notes?" Day answered, "Yes, sir."[106] No such dictation was made,[107] or made public, however.

On June 8, 1964, Wade testified that, "...all my information came from the police and actually somebody said originally it was a Mauser but it turned out it was not."[108] So on June 8th the Commission knew Fritz was first with the Mauser identification; then it appeared in Boone's sheriff department reports; followed by radio and TV reports; then twelve hours after the assassination -- after Wade saw "some officer wave that gun around" and "saw somebody take it through homicide and give it to the FBI"-- Wade's police sources, who got their information from Day, told Wade it was a Mauser. Only after all this did Weitzman, knowing the penalty for perjury, make his identification in a sworn affidavit the day after the assassination; bringing the minimum time of this ludicrous misidentification to twenty-four hours.

The next and most important parts of this chronology make it impossible to deny there was a deliberate attempt to pass this rifle off as a Mauser. Three full days after the assassination, a CIA report identified the gun as a Mauser. This report did not surface until 1976.[109]

And a CIA translation of an Italian military intelligence document dated six days after the assassination, also suppressed until 1976, reads, "2. The weapon which appears to have been employed in this criminal attack is a Model 91 rifle, 7.35 caliber, 1938 modification... 3. The description of a `Mannlicher-Carcano' rifle in the Italian and foreign press is in error."[110]

This later CIA description came from the Italian Armed Forces Intelligence Service (S.I.F.A.R.). As Evica says, "...the 91 series was made up of 6.5 mm. rifles, but the original 38 model was a 7.35 mm. Encountering difficulties, the Italians `began producing many of these rifles as 6.5-millimeter caliber rifles, known as the 6.5-millimeter Model 91/38.' Warren Commission Exhibit 139 (CE 139) is one of those 91/38s, originally a 7.35 mm. rebarreled to 6.5 mm." It was the description of an originally-barreled 6.5-millimeter Mannlicher-Carcano rifle in the Italian and foreign press (and everywhere else) that was in error. The November 28, 1963, Italian S.I.F.A.R. document, shared with the FBI in Rome, ending up at CIA headquarters in the U.S. within hours, raised these important questions, posed by Evica: "If the rifle allegedly discovered by

Weitzman and Boone had a Mauser-type bolt action, and if it looked like an American caliber 30.06 or foreign 7.65 mm., why not simply say so? Why not tell the truth before the truth no longer would be believed?...a one millimeter mistake is not so bad...For almost a week, local and national papers remained confused about the precise identity of the rifle. What could have motivated the Dallas Police, the F.B.I., the Secret Service, and even the C.I.A....to keep silent through the thunder of misinformation?"[111] A one millimeter mistake is not so bad. But the original, too-prolonged mistake of a clip-fed rifle for a non-clip-fed rifle, which is unavoidable in this "7.65 Mauser" debate, is incredibly bad. To maintain the conspiracy, the clip debate must, even today, be desperately avoided, or confused.

The point of this analysis of Roger Craig's statements is that by the time Craig came around to talking about the rifle, the name Mauser and the 7.65 caliber were old news. Craig added only two new facts. First was his belated eyewitness account of Weitzman as the first person to identify the rifle. And how did Weitzman make this identification? From Craig's second new fact: the "7.65 Mauser" tool mark on the barrel. Craig's statements then became the first and only evidence supporting the Warren Report's claim that Weitzman was the original source of the Mauser misidentification. Those who forced Craig to say this probably knew that the "Mauser" tool mark never existed. Thus, since the "Commission could not accept important elements of Craig's testimony" on other matters,[112] it was again possible to prove him wrong where it counted most, and stick to their story that Weitzman was mistaken, having only glanced at the gun before it was removed from its hiding place. Craig's cryptic call for help, if that is what it was, therefore failed.

It should be reemphasized here that before Craig made his claims about the discovery of the rifle, the Commission revealed absolutely nothing to support its claim that Weitzman was the original source for the Mauser identification. The evidence showed (and still shows) that everyone took their cues first from Fritz and then from Day. (Boone did not handle the rifle and his two "Mauser" reports followed both Fritz's and Day's examination at the scene.)

J.W. Hughes did inform the authors of the eyewitness account of WFAA-TV cameraman Tom Alyea which, if true, partially corroborates Craig's and the Commission's claim that the word Mauser was first uttered by Weitzman. That is a long way, however, from a Mauser identification. And if this was the Commission's "source" evidence, they did not reveal it publicly. Perhaps that was because it did not tell exactly the story they wanted told.

According to Hughes, "The type of action `mauser' was the comment that Weitzman said he thought it was and Fritz concurred. "Tom Alyea and I have talked about this several times. Tom was standing there next to Fritz when Weitzman stated that it was a Mauser rifle and that they saw 7.65 stamped on the action.
"Mannlicher-Carcano does have a 7.35 mm. In the heat of the `find' Weitzman stated `Mauser' and everyone simply agreed. It wasn't until Day was showing the rifle off at the Police Station that it was properly identified as a 6.5 mm Mannlicher-Carcano."[113]

Although properly identified, it was officially reported to be a Mauser for the next twenty-four hours without an official correction. The point here is that this eyewitness account seems to confirm that there was no Mauser, and that Weitzman, imagining a "7" and a decimal point where there was none, somehow inspired the others present, including Fritz, the ranking officer in charge of the crime scene, to call it something it was not; and as discussed above, even something bizarre.

Given Alyea's film of this event, it seems that is probably what happened. The unnecessary complications involved in reenacting this scene make Alyea's claim even more plausible. There is no such thing as a 7.65 Mannlicher-Carcano. If "they saw 7.65 stamped on the action" it was some strange rifle. And if Weitzman misread the caliber on a 7.35 Mannlicher-Carcano, it was also another rifle. The question this raises is the same one we began with: Why in the world would the crime scene investigators enter into a criminal conspiracy to call a weapon easily linked to their suspect something else? Of course, it seems the other confirmation from Alyea's film is that there was no clip seen or handled on the sixth floor.

There is some justification that the word "Mauser," in its earliest use in Dallas, was a redundant generic term for what in effect were nearly all bolt-action rifles. Since "bolt action" would exclude just about all semi-automatic and automatic weapons, there is some justification that the redundancy was used to emphasize that very exclusion. It could even be argued that the redundant use of the word "Mauser," in addition to deflecting attention from clip-fed weapons, served the purpose of deflecting attention from early reports of automatic gunfire in Dealey Plaza. Later, Commission attorney Joseph Ball was particularly careful to refer only to "Mauser bolt action" rather than an actual Mauser rifle in his questioning of Weitzman on April 1, 1964.[114]

But within hours of the assassination, and certainly within months, the trend seemed to focus attention on an actual Mauser, a second rifle.[115] This trend was the reverse of what one would expect. One would think, at the later stage, investigators would endeavor to establish that the initial use of the word "Mauser" was one of those inadvertent, honest mistakes: that the word was used loosely. But no. The Warren Commission was, and especially Gerald Ford and staff attorneys Ball and Liebeler were, apparently trying to lend weight to the initial use of the word, even adding the word "German." Even the Commission's earliest and most vocal critic, Mark Lane, helped his professed adversary strengthen the link between "German" and "Mauser," further undermining any chance for a more correct generic interpretation of Weitzman's description.[116] Gun experts, of course, know the Mauser 7.65 was anything but solely German. One wonders if those who initiated use of that term for the rifle realized how wrong the usage was.

Two primary sources for the later references to an actual Mauser were Mark Lane and Roger Craig. It is reasonably suspected that Craig was forced to lie. Similar, and earlier, influence over Lane cannot be ruled out. It was Lane who first embellished this trend with the liberal use of the word "German."[117] An influential stockholder in Holt, Rinehart and Winston, the publisher of Lane's 1966 book, Rush To Judgment, was Dallas oilman Clint Murchison, suspected by several sober JFK researchers of being a conspirator in the assassination and coverup. Two years before Lane's book was published, Murchison helped arrange a large monetary advance and travel expenses for another author whose book on the assassination was never published. The would-be author was Dallas Judge Joe Brown, dismissed from presiding over Jack Ruby's trial because of that book deal.[118] It was not just Lane and Craig, however. Concerted effort was made in the direction of establishing an actual gun of Mauser make. But the possibly unintended result of this direction was the creation of the specter of a second rifle.

Why was attention directed down this avenue? Were they so concerned with the prolonged Mauser misidentification in connection with the clip? Were they so concerned that they were willing to sacrifice the one-assassin/one-rifle scenario by offering a second rifle as a rationalization? After all, the too-prolonged Mauser misidentification was crying for an explanation that eventually had to be met. The idea of a second rifle was therefore the apparent lesser of two evils. Conversely, feeling it necessary to go to such lengths as to entertain the idea of a second rifle, shows the seriousness they attached to the initial problem of explaining the prolonged misidentification. From the conspirators' point of view, a conspiracy that can never be proved (i.e., Mauser switch) was far safer than one that could (i.e., fake clip). The benefit to the conspirators in choosing the lesser evil can be judged by the result: a thirty-year debate over a non-existent second rifle, and no debate whatsoever over an all too real, grossly out of place clip.

FIG. 3: TEXAS SCHOOLBOOK DEPOSITORY © 1994 Richard Bartholomew
(Facing 165° South by Southeast)
Shadows Next to Southeast, Sixth Floor Window on November 22, 1963

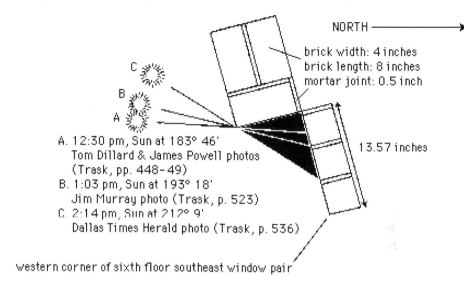

NORTH ————————→

brick width: 4 inches
brick length: 8 inches
mortar joint: 0.5 inch

13.57 inches

A. 12:30 pm, Sun at 183° 46'
Tom Dillard & James Powell photos
(Trask, pp. 448-49)
B. 1:03 pm, Sun at 193° 18'
Jim Murray photo (Trask, p. 523)
C. 2:14 pm, Sun at 212° 9'
Dallas Times Herald photo (Trask, p. 536)

western corner of sixth floor southeast window pair

With regard to another claim made by Craig, a 1:06 p.m. time for the rifle discovery, we draw the reader's attention to the diagram (fig. 3) showing the results of a photogrammetric study by Richard Bartholomew of photos of the outside of the "sniper's window" taken from the front of the TSBD just after the assassination. Reasonably, if there was no clip found with the rifle, it would take time to reach the decision to replace it, and to obtain the fake clip. The ensuing cover-up would best be served by making that extra time disappear from the chronology. One way to do that is by falsely claiming the sixth-floor investigation started at a later moment. By all accounts, the rifle was found shortly after the discovery of the three shell casings on the sixth-floor. We can substantially argue that both the shells and the rifle were found earlier than the times "established" by the Warren Commission.

The diagram shows three positions of the sun (A, B, and C) and the length of the shadow each of the positions cast on the bricks to the west of the southeast windows. The solar positions for November 22, 1963, are accurate to within a minute of the given times. They are based on astronomical tables.

The shadow corresponding to position B is seen in a photo taken by Jim Murray showing Sergeant Gerald L. Hill leaning out the arched sixth floor window, pointing to the corner window where shell casings were just found.[119] As Trask describes it, Hill responded to Luke Mooney who had just hollered his discovery of the expended shells. Seeing Sheriff Decker and others down on the street, Hill opened the sash of the east side of the arch shaped window pair and requested them to send up the crime lab people. Murray snapped his photo of Hill talking to them. The time, according to the shadow, was 1:03 p.m.

The Warren Report, citing Mooney's testimony as proof, says Mooney found the shells at approximately 1:12. But Mooney put the latest time at "1 o'clock." The Warren Report also cited "transcripts of all radio transmissions from Channel 1 and Channel 2 of the Dallas Police Department...." Between Dispatcher Henslee's announcement of the times 1:11 and 1:12 p.m., Inspector J.H. Sawyer radioed the message: "On the 3rd floor of this book company down here, we found empty rifle hulls and it looked like the man had been here for some time. We are checking it out now."[120] (emphasis added)

Sawyer may indeed have found additional shells on the third floor at 1:12 because the alleged sixth-floor shells were found ten to fifteen minutes earlier. Fritz testified that he arrived at the TSBD at 12:58, and the Warren Report agreed that he got there "Shortly before 1 p.m." Fritz said, "...it wasn't very long until someone called me and told me...they had found some empty cartridges." Those cartridges were found before 1:03. It is inconceivable that no one would have told Fritz about the shells until nearly ten minutes after Gerald Hill shouted the discovery out the window. Moreover, by the time Hill got to Mooney's location, Mooney had reportedly shouted the discovery out the window himself. Mooney said that after he squeezed behind the boxes where the shells were, he leaned out the window, "saw Sheriff Bill Decker and Captain Will Fritz standing right on the ground...And I told him to get the crime lab officers en route, that I had the location spotted." Mooney then "stood guard to see that no one disturbed anything until Captain Will Fritz approached with his group of officers, city officers." It would appear that Hill was among those city officers. When asked if he was the only officer at that corner, Mooney answered: "At that very moment I was." Although he did not check his watch, Mooney's recollection that he found the shells no later than 1 p.m. is sufficiently supported by the fact that much had happened between that moment and 1:03.[121]

Mooney testified that he left "that particular area" and joined the search for the rifle when Fritz arrived and picked up the shells. Mooney also said he stayed on the sixth floor "not over 15 or 20 minutes" after he found the location of the three cartridges.[122]

Photojournalist Tom Alyea was filming the location of the shells when Fritz arrived. Corroborating Alyea's early presence, Mooney testified that "some news reporter...was coming up with a camera" just before he found the shells. Shown in a published frame from Alyea's film are seven or eight men who initially arrived at the location. Gerald Hill appears to be among them. Most of them stayed for about one minute before continuing their search. As discussed below, Alyea said someone yelled out the discovery of the rifle just after Fritz picked up the shells. By then, according to his testimony, Mooney was "about 10 or 15 steps from Officer Boone when he [Boone] hollered, `Here is the gun.'" Strong evidence that the rifle was found much earlier is the time of its first unconfirmed report by WBAP-TV. That report was announced at 1:23, which, if the rifle was found a minute earlier, makes it the fastest report of any event that day, including the next fastest reports by NBC-correspondent Robert McNeil broadcasting live by telephone hook-up. The cartridges were not reported until 2:14. The arrest of Oswald was not reported for over an hour.[123] It is therefore likely that Craig was correct about the time the rifle was found. But whether it was found at 1:06 or 1:22, ten to fifteen minutes are unaccounted for during the sixth-floor crime scene investigation.

Trask continues the chronology beginning with Day's arrival at about 1:12 p.m. Day and Detective Robert Lee Studebaker took the elevator to the sixth floor and immediately took photographs of the shell casings. Trask is not clear on how many photos they took. But they only had one camera and Day and Studebaker took turns taking two exposures each of each scene photographed. At least six exposures are shot before Day dusted the shells for fingerprints. Four of these six exposures were taken inside the cramped "snipers lair" which took time to position the camera.

Trask continues: "The photos shot, Homicide Detective Richard M. Sims picked up the shells by their ends and gave them to Day, who then processed each one by applying black powder....[124]

"The three shells were 6.5mm and after they were dusted for prints, Day gave them to Detective Sims. Sims placed the shells in an evidence envelope and marked the envelope with his initials, the date and the time, which was now 1:23 p.m....[125]

"At just about the time Sims and Day were putting the spent rifle casings in the evidence envelope, they and Studebaker were summoned to the northwest corner of the building where a rifle had been spotted hidden among boxes. Though Studebaker would soon be released to return to the southeast corner to process the pop bottle and the stacked boxes for prints, the senior, more experienced Day would remain with the rifle -- the most important piece of evidence."[126]

The photo used to determine sun position C shows Studebaker working among the boxes in the southeast corner.[127] Since that photo was taken at 2:14 p.m., according to the shadow, it does not disprove this chronology. It also means Studebaker had begun working there well over half an hour before the photo was taken.

Trask continues his narrative describing the search for the rifle. When found, Trask writes, "Boone noted the time by his watch as being 1:22 p.m., while Weitzman, glancing at the weapon, though not able to clearly examine it, thought it to be a 7.65 Mauser bolt-action rifle."[128]

We will return to the subject of the rifle discovery. First, however, there are a couple of observations to be made. Throughout this narrative, Trask describes the movements of WFAA cameraman Tom Alyea, who was driving back to his Dallas TV station from an assignment in Fort Worth. At 12:30 p.m. he found himself in Dealey Plaza. Hearing the commotion on the police radio in his car, Alyea grabbed his camera and some film and arrived at the Depository at about 12:35. He witnessed the chaotic beginning of the search for suspects and joined in because he "wanted to record the gunfight." As things calmed down, Alyea continued filming.[129]

In describing the discovery of the shells Trask writes, "In recent years Tom Alyea recounts that `The local police were very helpful in assisting me in recording these historical events. Capt. Fritz even picked up the scattered shell casing from behind the barricade and held them in his hand for me to get a close up.' If correct, this may have been at a point following their being photographed and dusted. If not, it violated all concept of police scene documentation. This particular film scene is unfamiliar to the author."[130]

Obviously, it does much more than violate police procedures. What is of equal interest, however, is that it puts a crack in the chronology. Trask told readers that after the photos were taken, Sims picked up the shells by their ends and gave them to Day, who began dusting them. What did they do? Did they throw them back on the floor for Fritz to pick up before putting them in the evidence envelope? And if Fritz handled them, why did the FBI not report finding his fingerprints? Latona testified that he dusted the cartridge cases, "from which I got no prints."[131] This is one of several incidents where Alyea's memory, apparently supported by his film, is at odds with the sworn testimony.

Another discrepancy deserves attention: Latona reported finding no prints on the reportedly recovered clip. Recall the point made above that if the cartridges did not have prints, then the clip should have been dusted by Day, because logically it was the only thing handled by a shooter during loading. But for the clip to be apparently in the position seen in photos of Day carrying it out of the TSBD (noticeably sticking out of the bottom of the rifle), someone had to touch it.

Published frames of film and still photos of Day handling and dusting the rifle show no clip.[132] If, as the Warren Report says, "the rifle contained a clip," then someone either pulled it out enough to be seen, or took it completely out and stuck it back in partially, still noticeably exposed. None of these men were wearing gloves. If the clip was handled, it should have had prints. Fritz is seen in Alyea's film handling the rifle with a white handkerchief. He could have done the same with the clip. But why would they be handling it without dusting it? Everything from the shells to the rifle stock, and the way it was all handled, was described in detail (except for the handkerchief).[133] If there was all this handling of the clip, why did none of them mention it? Is this more proof that no clip was found?

Describing the moments right after the rifle's discovery, Trask writes, "By now most everyone on the sixth floor had congregated in the area around the discovered rifle....

"Alyea was right on the spot with the camera poised....As [Day] crouched down to pluck the rifle from its hiding place, Alyea pressed his shutter release button."[134] Trask reproduced a frame of Alyea's film in his book next to these statements. It shows Day holding the rifle for Alyea to film. There is no clip visible.

It could be argued that the clip ejected normally, and Oswald put it back in before fleeing. But the absence of fingerprints makes this scenario impossible. As much as it would have helped its case against Oswald, even the Warren Commission admitted there was no evidence Oswald wore gloves or wiped the gun clean.[135] No prints means that if Oswald did everything else the Commission claimed, he did not handle the emptied clip. The absence of prints on the clip could therefore support the argument that the clip remained stuck completely inside the magazine. If it were hidden inside the magazine, unfamiliarity with the gun would then innocently explain a failure to realize a clip existed. This argument is too short lived, however, to explain the length of time the Mauser description remained intact. And the discoverers could not have missed the clip when they checked the magazine for additional rounds.

Another innocent explanation is that the rifle's discoverers simply thought the clip had ejected and had not yet been found. Since photographs of Day leaving the building with the rifle apparently show the clip protruding from the magazine, it is reasonable to assume the clip was there but lodged firmly enough not to slip out during the operation of the bolt and subsequent handling at the scene. But as mentioned repeatedly above, when Day and Fritz determined no more rounds were in the magazine, neither man could have avoided seeing the empty clip supposedly stuck inside the magazine.[136]

If by some miniscule chance they missed seeing the clip at that moment, it could be argued that it was loosened by unreported, clumsy jarring or even dropping of the rifle on the way out of the building. The pride of a veteran evidence handler, along with the significance of this particular evidence, would reasonably explain why Day did not report such clumsiness. But even if no one saw the tool mark -- and Day and Fritz swore they did -- at the moment the clip protruded, it would have become obvious this rifle was not a Mauser. And even given some ludicrous claim he did not notice it then, the HSCA stated, "Later that day, the rifle's six-round cartridge clip was removed by Lieutenant Day in the Dallas Police Crime Laboratory."[137] Day knew the rifle was being misidentified and did nothing to correct it. This lack of action helped avoid questions about the clip. Day had an exchange with Belin about this during his testimony:

Mr. Belin. Did you ever hear this rifle referred to as a 7.65 Mauser or as any type of a Mauser?

Mr. Day. Yes, sir; it wasn't referred to as that. Some of the newsmen, when I first carried the rifle out, asked me if it was a .30-06, and at another time they asked me if it was a Mauser. I did not give them an answer.[138]

Alyea's film viewed unedited (along with the Murray photo of Hill), settles many questions about the chronology of events and confirms the fact that no Mauser was found -- only a Mannlicher-Carcano with no clip, meaning that Craig was lying about the Mauser for the reasons stated above, but not necessarily about his other sixth-floor crime scene claims: the time of the rifle discovery, and the initial closeness of the shells to each other.

Those aspects of Craig's story are corroborated by what Alyea says his film showed just prior to the rifle's discovery. Unfortunately, Alyea never saw that part of the film after the film editors finished with it at WFAA-TV.

Alyea claims he was filming the discovery of the spent shells when Fritz arrived and forbade him from squeezing behind the stack of boxes. Instead, says Alyea, Fritz picked up the shells and held them for him to film.

Alyea describes the shells' position before being picked up as being so close together, "they could be covered with a bushel basket." Just after Fritz picked them up, Alyea says, someone yelled out the discovery of the rifle and Fritz threw them onto the floor. The official Dallas police photographs, Alyea claims, show them where they landed.[139]

Had these film frames survived the editors "careless" handling, they would be proof of destruction of the crime scene by the head of Homicide Division. It would be easy to discount claims about such incriminating events were it not for the fact that Luke Mooney's testimony indicates that is just what Alyea's film showed:

Mr. Ball. Those were empty shells?

Mr. Mooney. Yes, sir.

Mr. Ball. They were turned over to Captain Fritz?

Mr. Mooney. Yes, sir; he was the first officer that picked them up as far as I know, because I stood there and watched him go over and pick them up and look at them. As far as I could tell, I couldn't even tell what caliber they were, because I didn't get down that close to them. They were brass cartridges, brass shells.[140]

According to J.W. Hughes, who has studied Alyea's film in detail, it begins with scenes of police officers searching the sixth floor, followed by footage of the sniper's nest. It then cuts to the moments after Fritz threw the shells on the floor. Fritz, at that point, is handling an unidentified rifle. The film then cuts to Fritz standing, along with some plain clothes officers, near the boxes where the Mannlicher-Carcano was found. It then cuts to Day removing the rifle from its hiding place.[141]

Another major discrepancy, however, between the crime scene testimony and Alyea's account of these events, is Alyea's claim that Lieutenant Day did not arrive until forty-five minutes after the shells were found. Day was not present, according to Alyea, when the rifle was found. He does say, however, that no one touched the rifle until Day arrived. Alyea also insists that his footage is not a reenactment. After photographing Day dusting the rifle, Alyea was ordered to leave. He left his camera with some police officers, but they did not continue filming. J.W. Hughes said the film also shows that when Day first retrieved the rifle, the bolt was open and no shells were in the ammunition well. Hughes says he cannot determine whether or not the clip was present. But the film does not show Fritz or Day operating the bolt or ejecting a live round.[142]

Was the round in the found rifle chambered? Officially, yes. Fritz said, "After the [Day-Studebaker] pictures had been made then I ejected a live shell, a live cartridge from the rifle."[143] Day said, "I picked the gun up by the wooden stock. I noted that the stock was too rough apparently to take fingerprints, so I picked it up, and Captain Fritz opened the bolt as I held the gun. A live round fell out."[144] Day also said that he was holding the rifle and examining it with his magnifying glass before Fritz touched it. Day was wrong. When asked about taking precautions against leaving his own prints on the gun, Fritz testified: "He [Day] could have taken mine [fingerprints] but I let him dust first before I ejected a shell." But Day testified that he did not dust any part of the rifle before Fritz ejected the live cartridge. Was Fritz, reportedly renowned for his photographic memory, right? The Tom Alyea film clearly shows that Fritz's hands are all over the rifle while he holds it for Day to look at. The same film shows neither Fritz nor Day operating the bolt, or ejecting a live round. In his book, Trask fudges this chronology to say that the live round was ejected after Alyea filmed Fritz and Day handling the gun and before Day dusted the rifle. Trask says the bolt-opening episode was testified to by Day as "what next transpired," after Alyea filmed "some 40-plus seconds worth of this sequence" showing Fritz holding the gun for Day to examine. Trask is wrong. Day testified, falsely, that he was the only one who had held the rifle before and during the bolt-opening episode.[145]

To believe Trask, and commercially available versions of the film, is to believe that Tom Alyea, with camera ready, inexplicably stopped filming while Fritz handed the gun to Day to examine closely, and while Day held it for Fritz to operate the bolt producing a live bullet. Only after this dramatic scene, according to Trask, did Alyea start filming again to capture Day's routine dusting for fingerprints. Given Alyea's film, neither Day nor Fritz can be believed as to what they did with the gun on the sixth floor. And given Trask's rationalized attempts to reconcile the film with Day's and Fritz's contradictory testimony, he cannot be believed.

According to Alyea himself, "Still pictures were taken of the positioning of the rifle, then Lt. Day slid it out from its hiding place and held it up for all of us to see. The world has seen my shot of this many times. Lt. Day immediately turned toward the window behind him and started dusting the weapon for fingerprints. Day was still within the enclosure formed by the surrounding boxes. I filmed him lifting prints from the rifle. He lifted them off with scotch tape and placed them on little white cards. When he had finished, he handed the rifle to Captain Fritz. Fritz pulled the bolt back and a live round ejected and landed on the boxes below. Fritz put the cartridge in his pocket. I did not see Fritz pick up anything other than the live round. If a clip ejected, I didn't notice it, nor did I see Fritz pick up a second object. I have learned that the six round clip for this rifle ejects when the last round is injected into the chamber. If this is the case, there must have been three rounds in the rifle when it was found. Fritz ejected one... another went into the chamber when the bolt was closed and one still remained in the clip. I have no idea whether the police made a notation of this, or if the rounds were dusted for fingerprints."[146] (emphasis added) So it seems that Fritz was more correct about the sequence of events. Alyea is also convincing in saying that a live round was ejected. And his account that no clip was seen, mentioned or handled, even during Fritz's rough-and-tumble working of the loading mechanism, is especially convincing given his attempt to rationalize it with a far more mundane explanation than the HSCA firearms panel's. And the reason Alyea did not film that dramatic opening of the bolt was because it followed Day dusting the rifle, which, as Alyea said, was when he was ordered to stop filming and leave.[147] However, one question remains: was the live round chambered?

As discussed above, others also claim that the last round was still in the clip, not chambered. Alyea's version of that theory ("three rounds in the rifle") is the most plausible, explaining why the clip was completely inside the magazine. Alyea's theory accounts for two additional live rounds, and, therefore, a clip originally fully loaded with six rounds. But if correct, Alyea's theory means yet another official lie about the state of the rifle when found.[148] And it does not explain why Fritz and Day lied about it. Nor does it explain why they were totally silent about the clip. Nor does it explain why the HSCA said the clip's edges were sprung against the magazine walls -- their explanation for why it remained totally stuck inside the rifle during all this handling. It is still more likely that no clip was found.

Nonetheless, since the Alyea film does not prove that the clip was present or absent, there remains the slight possibility that a bent clip was stuck in the magazine. If so, it is possible that it was put there by the rifle's planters. The clip's presence would then be the result of a mistake on the part of the planters, not the discoverers, a mistake that is only possible if the planters misunderstood the ejection mechanism, or simply did not think the clip's presence or absence was important. The Mauser cover story, though, would still have been for the purpose of hiding that mistake until it was determined how to deal with it. Obviously, the decision was to say nothing about why the clip was there.

* * *

Notes:

64. Employees of the main distributor of Carcanos in the U.S. in 1960, Folsom Arms, were so confused about how to load them, the company had to seek foreign help: "[Master Italian gunsmith Luciano Riva] went to New York in December, 1960, and found that at the Yonkers warehouse of Folsom Arms, the Folsom people had attempted to hand-load the Carcanos without success. But

the rifles 'loaded with a clip,' Riva remonstrated....Riva showed the Folsom employees how it was done..." (Evica 29).

65. CIA Document No. 1367, declassified spring 1976; cited in Fensterwald 443-44. Henry Hurt, *Reasonable Doubt* (New York: Henry Holt, 1985) pp. 102-03. Evica 23.

66. Jim Marrs, *Crossfire: The Plot that Killed Kennedy* (New York Carroll & Graf, 1989) p. 440; hereafter cited as Marrs 440. Evica 53-55.

67. Evica 23; citing 24H (CE 2169) 829.

68. 5H 250.

69. 24H (CE 2169, p. 4) 829. 5H 250.

70. Letter from Walter F. Graf to Richard Bartholomew, Dec. 17, 1996. Evica 23-24. Evica mentions Wade's amazement and disapproval over Chief Curry's Nov. 23rd TV appearance at about 2:30 p.m., during which Curry revealed details of the FBI report identifying the gun as a Mannlicher-Carcano. (5H 228) Wade testified that the report was the first evidence that Curry got directly, rather than through Captain Fritz. Wade implied that Fritz would not have revealed it to the press. Yet, Wade himself gave the false Mauser description to the press in the early hours of that same day, a description that originated with Fritz, according to the known evidence. Therefore, Wade and Fritz apparently preferred the prolonged public falsehood. J. Edgar Hoover twice singled out the FBI's "identification of the gun," to emphasize that "If the case had been in the hands of the FBI none of that information would have been given out." He even expressed regret that the gun's identity had become known before Curry "refrained from further comment" at Hoover's personal insistence. (R 235-36, 5H 115-16.)

71. Lattimer 298-99.

72. R 555 ("commonly available"). R 120 ("paperwork"). Martha Moyer, "Ordering the Rifle," Assassination Chronicles, March 1996, pp. 25-35 ("conflicting evidence"). 17H (CE 773) 635. 21H (Waldman Exhibit Nos. 7 and 8) 703, 704 ("purchase order" and "shipping order"). 17H (CE 788) 677 ("money order").

73. 3H 397-98.

74. R 855 n.132.

75. 4H 23.

76. 4H 253-258.

77. 4H 23. 24H (CE 2003 pp. 131-35) 262-64.

78. R 647.

79. Interview of Jim Westbrook by Richard Bartholomew, Sept. 1, 1994. Interview of J.W. Hughes by Richard Bartholomew, Sept. 26, 1994. Ian Griggs, "The Mannlicher-Carcano -- A Practical Experiment in its Reassembly," Dallas `63: The British Forum for Views and Research into the Assassination of President John F. Kennedy, v. 1, no. 3, August 1994, pp. 19-24.

80. E-mail from Anthony Marsh to Richard Bartholomew, "JFK_ASSN" Fidonet discussion group, posted Jul. 16, 1995.

81. Letter from Walter F. Graf to Richard Bartholomew, Feb. 5, 1996.

82. Jim Garrison, *A Heritage of Stone* (New York: G. P. Putnam's Sons, 1970, Berkley Medallion, 1975) p. 49.

83. 3H

84. Interview: Jim Westbrook by Richard Bartholomew, Sept. 12, 1994.

85. Evica 349 n.5.

86. R 235.

87. When asked how he identified the Mannlicher-Carcano sent to him from Dallas, FBI weapons expert Robert Frazier testified: "I identified it pictorially by comparing it with pictures in reference books" (3H 392).

88. Thomas Powers, *The Man Who Kept the Secrets: Richard Helms and the CIA* (New York: Knopf/Washington Square Press, 1979) pp. 26-27; hereafter cited as Powers 26-27. Vincent Salandria, "The Assassination of President John F. Kennedy: A Model of Explanation," Computers and Automation magazine, issue 20 (Dec. 1971, pp. 32-40); re-published by the Internet-based publication, Fair Play (http://rmii.com/~jkelin/fp.html, issue 16, May-June, 1997).

89. Edgar F. Tatro, "Roger Craig and 1984," The Continuing Inquiry May 1985, pp. 2-16.

90. Letter from Edgar F. Tatro to Richard Bartholomew, October 25, 1993.

91. Letter from J.W. Hughes to Walter Graf, August 22, 1994.

92. Paul Scarlata, "Classic Commando Weapon," Fighting Firearms Winter '95, pp. 56-61, p. 58: photos, p. 60 (cols. 1, 3), p. 61 (photo).

93. Letter from Walter F. Graf to Richard Bartholomew, March 1996.

94. E-mail from Chris Mills to Richard Bartholomew, 8:59 p.m., Oct. 2, 1996.

95. Michael Canfield and Alan J. Weberman, *Coup d'Etat in America: The CIA and the Assassination of John F. Kennedy* (New York: The Third Press, 1975) pp. 56-57; hereafter cited as Canfield and Weberman 56-57.

96. Decker Exhibit 5323, pp. 507-09. Meagher, Accessories 96-98.

97. 3H 295

98. Meagher, *Accessories* 96; citing 2H 46.

99. 24H (CE 2003, p. 63).

100. Weisberg, Whitewash 190.

101. 7H 108.

102. 4H 181; cited in Evica 18. Meagher, *Accessories*, 97.

103. Marrs 440.

104. 4H 206.

105. Evica 22.

106. 4H 263.

107. Michael Wiseberg, "The Rifle: Was it a Mauser or Mannlicher-Carcano?" The Third Decade Jan. 1990, p. 10.

108. 5H 250.

109. Hurt 102-03. Evica 23. Fensterwald 443-44.

110. Marrs 440. Evica 53. "Information on The Weapon Presumably Used in the Assassination of President Kennedy," CIA document, Nov. 28, 1963 (author's copy showing numbered comments 1-4, 8 and 9, from Jack White collection (created from full document acquired from Mary Ferrell collection). Letter from Jack White to Richard Bartholomew, Oct. 14, 1994.

111. Evica 4, 53-54, 55.

112. R 160.

113. Letter from J.W. Hughes to Walter Graf, August 22, 1994.

114. "Despite extensive experience with weapons he [UPI reporter Merriman Smith] had thought the sounds in the plaza were three shots from an automatic weapon, and in a subsequent [Nov. 22nd] message he identified them as 'bursts'" (William Manchester, The Death of a President [New York: Harper & Row, 1967] pp. 167-68). "Suddenly we heard three loud, almost painfully loud cracks....the second and third blasts were unmistakable. Gunfire" (Merriman Smith, UPI report, Nov. 23, 1963; Four Days 32). 7H 108, 109 (Weitzman).

115. 26H (CE 3048) 599. R 81, 235, 645-46.

116. Evica 22. Gerald R. Ford, "Piecing Together the Evidence," Life, Oct. 2, 1964, pp. 40-51; cited in Evica 48, 49. Joseph A. Ball, Statement made at Associated Press Managing Editors convention in San Diego, California, Nov. 17, 1966 (see transcript in Richmond, Virginia Times Dispatch, Nov. 27, 1966), cited in Lane, Dissent 126. See also earlier discussion of Liebeler in this article. For evidence of Ford's obfuscation of crucial aspects of the ballistics evidence, see handwritten changes to the draft chapters of the final report that were recommended by Commission member Representative Gerald Ford, Personal Files of J. Lee Rankin, General Counsel of the Warren Commission, President John F. Kennedy Assassination Records Collection housed at the National Archives facility in College Park, Maryland; cited in George Lardner, Jr. (The Washington Post), "Ford sought changes in JFK assassination report," Austin American-Statesman, July 3, 1997, p. A8.

117. 2H 46. 5H 560.

118. Wills and Demaris 79-80. Seth Kantor, Who Was Jack Ruby? (New York: Everest House, 1978); originally titled The Ruby Detail, promised by Zebra Books; later published as The Ruby Cover-up (New York: Zebra Books, 1992) p. 236. Murchison and family: Scott 73, 108, 135, 202, 205-08, 211-14, 217-22, 227, 234, 285, 286, 293, 300, 326, 345, 362, 367, 376

119. Trask 523.

120. R 79; citing 3H (CE 1974, p. 176) 285.

121. 4H 204, 205. R 8. 3H 284-85. On the flawed investigation of the shells see: Michael Wiseberg, "Three Cartridge Cases: Chain of Possession," The Third Decade, May 1990, pp. 11-17.

122. 3H 289

123. 3H 284, 289. Tom Alyea, `JFK Facts' Update, Preview Edition, 1993, p. 4; hereafter cited as Alyea 4. Planned as a monthly periodical, subsequent issues of Alyea's `JFK Facts' newsletter have not been published. This rare edition includes four never-before-published frames from his TSBD-search film. WBAP: As It Happened 0:23, 1:14, 1:41, and throughout. "Arrest Report No. 63-98115," Curry 79 (Oswald arrest at 1:40 p.m.).

124. Trask 526.

125. Trask 527. 7H 162-63, 183-86.

126. Trask 529.

127. Trask 536.

128. Trask 529.

129. Trask 520-21.

130. Trask 524. Alyea 5.

131. 4H 23. The authors are aware of the fact that fingerprints are not always left behind, as noted in the Oklahoma City bombing trial of Timothy McVeigh: "Under redirect testimony by the prosecution, however, [FBI fingerprint technician Louis] Hupp said that a person could touch something and still not leave prints. 'It's very common,' he said." But it must be noted that Hupp was a witness testifying for McVeigh's defense, and that his testimony about the absence of McVeigh's prints on key evidence "provided some of the only beneficial evidence for McVeigh," thus far in the trial. ("Expert: McVeigh's prints aren't on key evidence," Associated Press, Austin American-Statesman, May 16, 1997, p. A7.) Such testimony is only beneficial if the circumstances are such that prints can be reasonably expected on the objects in question. If the prints of Kennedy's assassin could be expected by Lt. Day on the shells, and did reportedly exist on the gun itself, the same prints and those of others could reasonably be expected on both the shells and the clip.

132. Trask 533. Alyea 5.

133. Unpublished photos of frames enclosed with letter from J.W. Hughes to Walter Graf, August 22, 1994.

134. Trask 531.

135. R 647.

136. R (17H (CE 541 [3]) 239) 83.

137. 7 HH 355.

138. 4H 263.

139. Interview of J.W. Hughes by Richard Bartholomew, Sept. 26, 1994.

140. 3H 286.

141. Interview of J.W. Hughes by Richard Bartholomew, Sept. 26, 1994.

142. Interview of J.W. Hughes by Richard Bartholomew, Sept. 26, 1994.

143. 4H 205.

144. 4H 258.

145. 4H 206, 258-59. Trask 532.

146. Connie Kritzberg, Secrets From the Sixth Floor Window (Oklahoma: Undercover Press, 1994) p. 45.

147. Alyea 5.

148. Another official lie: Letter from Jack White to Walter Graf, Aug. 3, 1995.

THE GUN THAT DIDN'T SMOKE

PART 3

[Written with the late Walter F. Graf]

"RECOGNIZING RIGHT AS WELL AS REALITY"

There is no worse lie than a truth misunderstood by those who hear it.
-- William James, 190

 A counterargument over rifles which the authors can already hear from the more zealous conspiracy deniers concerns two monstrosities: rifles designed as a hybrid between the Mauser and the Mannlicher-Carcano. The first was the 1888 Commission Rifle (a.k.a. Mauser Gewehr 88) which temporarily replaced the original Mauser used by the German army. It had the 1875 Mauser bolt with an altered locking system, and it used the Mannlicher system of clip loading.[149]

 The other was the rare and relatively unknown third modification of the Mannlicher-Carcano, the M91/38 Cal. 7.92 (the standard German caliber prior to the NATO 7.62). These modified Carcanos had an "S" stamped on the breech block to designate they accommodated the 7.92 caliber. And they were, in fact, clip-fed.[150] In 1905 when this caliber was adopted in Germany, the breech block of the Mauser 1898 was stamped with the "S" to indicate that the new standard caliber 7.92 ammunition was required. This practice was carried forward on the modified Carcano. Apparently the origin of the "S" was that it stood for "spitzer," the German word for "pointed." These new bullets were just that, rather than round-ended.

 The question could be raised, therefore, as to whether Weitzman, a small arms expert aware of the clip, mistook the 6.5 mm. Carcano for the rare 7.92 mm. Carcano. Then, through a lack of oxygen among the book boxes or something, he imagined the old clip-fed Mauser-hybrid Commission Rifle, thus calling it a "7.65 Mauser." But aside from being a worthy tribute to Rube Goldberg and Weitzman's knowledge of obscure weapons, this counterargument, like others presented here, is for a misidentification too short-lived to explain the longevity of Weitzman's "mistake."

 This Carcano that uses "spitzer" bullets might be of interest to Parkland Hospital employees Darrell Tomlinson and O.P. Wright. Students of JFK's assassination are aware of the claim that the bullet

Tomlinson found on a hospital stretcher and gave to Wright had a pointed end. In his book *Six Seconds In Dallas*, Josiah Thompson reviewed the chain of custody of this pointed bullet, which somehow became the rounded-end CE 399, the infamous "magic" bullet of the many single bullet theories.

Thompson's analysis of the evidence shows that the bullet had probably not been found on a hospital stretcher connected to the assassination. In addition, Thompson noted that "...Robert Frazier of the FBI Crime Lab received 399 on the evening of November 22 from another FBI agent, Elmer Todd (3H428, 24 412). Todd, in turn had received it a few minutes earlier from Chief Rowley of the Secret Service, who had been given it by one of his agents, Richard Johnsen (24H412)." Johnsen had attached a note to the bullet stating that he obtained it from "Mr. O.P. Wright / Personal Director of Security / Dallas County Hospital District."[151] The chain of custody was thus established as Tomlinson-Wright-Johnsen-Rowley-Todd-Frazier.

Yet, in a document released by the ARRB in January, 1996, we first learned that Gerald A. Behn, the Secret Service agent in charge of the White House detail, stated that he was in the chain of custody of CE 399. Behn claimed that he received the bullet from Special Agent Richard Johnsen then turned it over to the FBI.[152] With Behn's statement, we have Rowley evaporating from the scene. Behn's statement is a fatal conflict in the chain of custody of this crucial piece of evidence. Any break in that chain reasonably allows for the bullet's already evident, criminal transformation from pointed to rounded.

Directly related to the bullet's transformation is this statement from Trask's book (p. 532), which we previously quoted: "During the late afternoon and evening of November 22 Dallas station WFAA would variously describe the rifle as a `German Mauser' found on the sixth floor, a 6.5 `Argentine Mauser' with a four-power scope and a 7.65 `Mauser' found on the fifth floor stairway." (emphasis added) Argentine Mausers included the *Fusil Mauser modelo Argentino 1891 modificado para Bala `S' modelo* 1909. Again, the "S" probably stood for spitzer (pointed).

As noted earlier in this article, there are only three 7.65 Mausers that could have been remotely confused with the Carcano, due to their pre-1895 protruding magazine design: the Belgian carbine, the Turkish and the Argentine Mauser, which was no more than the Turkish type of 1890 with a slightly modified bolt and a stronger extractor. The Turkish type, however, is clearly marked in Arabic script. The Argentine carbine had the word "Mauser" in its tool stamp, but the rest of the text was obviously written in Spanish and the scope would have fitted directly over the position of the "Mauser" engraving, making it invisible.

Nonetheless, we cannot ignore so many coincidences involving one weapon: the 1909 modification of the 7.65 Argentine Mauser, "so stamped on the barrel," so named by WFAA, superficially similar in appearance to the Carcano, manufactured in 6.5 mm., using a pointed bullet like the one Tomlinson claimed he found on the hospital stretcher; as does the German regulation 7.92 mm. Mannlicher-Carcano Model 91/38 S T.S. Musket.

In addition to these coincidences, three men had been shot in Dealey Plaza and (1) the rifle "found" at the scene was misidentified for a prolonged period of time, and (2) there is a fatal conflict in the chain of custody of the bullet "found." These are both vital pieces of evidence needed to establish the basic, direct facts of this crime: the rifle and the bullet.

These are inconceivable mistakes in the fundamental handling of two intimately related pieces of crucial ballistics evidence. Moreover, the "mistaken" identification of the rifle matches it to the "mistaken" identification of the bullet; which leaves the reasonable impression that there was an alternative Mauser track (plan) that somehow got out of sync. If such dual tracks existed, the perpetrators had to swap both the rifle and bullet in sync. An interview of Secret Service Agent Richard Johnsen by researcher Vincent Palamara adds support to this impression:

> During an interview conducted on 9/29/92, the author learned that Johnsen did not remember having possession of CE399, the "magic" bullet that tied Oswald to the murder of JFK! In addition, although the bullet was "officially" found on a stretcher in the corridor of Parkland Hospital, the FBI reported that it was found in the emergency room.(CD 7) To compound matters, the same FBI agents bypassed Agent Johnsen and spoke to Agent Behn (who wasn't in Dallas) about "the location of a bullet which had been found on a stretcher at Parkland." (Sibert & O'Neil, 11/27/63) Finally, although two FBI agents initialed the bullet they received, Johnsen did not, breaking the chain of custody. (24 H 412) When we consider further that O.P. Wright, the man who allegedly gave the bullet to Johnsen, does not even mention this very important find in his report, and that Darrell [sic] Tomlinson, the man who found the bullet in the first place, stated that the bullet in government hands is NOT the bullet he actually found,

we have serious pause to wonder: is there more to Johnsen's present "amnesia" over this evidence than meets the eye? (Price exhibits, WC Volume XXI; 2 H 412; see also *High Treason*, page 102) O.P. Wright told CBS' Eddie Barker: "...I got hold of a Secret Service man and they (sic) didn't seem to be interested in coming and looking at the bullet in the position it was in then. So I went back to the area where Mr. Tomlinson was and picked up the bullet and put it in my pocket, and I carried it some 30 or 40 minutes. [emphasis Graf's and Bartholomew's] And I gave it to a Secret Service man that was guarding the main door into the emergency room..." Who was the first agent Wright spoke to? (*Postmortem*, page 46) [emphasis Palamara's except where indicated][153]

Agents seem to distance themselves as much as possible. Agent Johnsen did not recall the matter despite that he had written a report about it. He did not initial the bullet. An unknown Secret Service agent was disinterested in the whole thing. Josiah Thompson was told the disinterested agent was FBI (Thompson 209), which tends to remove this Secret Service agent from the entire matter of the stretcher bullet.

Johnsen indicated he received the bullet about 1:55 p.m. (Thompson 208-09), and based on that, Thompson concluded the bullet was found between 1:45 and 1:50 p.m. When we add Palamara's information, that Wright carried the bullet in his pocket for 30 or 40 minutes, we can conclude that the bullet was found around the same time as the rifle - between 1:15 and 1:25 p.m. Recall our discussion above about Roger Craig's claim that the rifle was located at 1:06 p.m. Recall also that Day was photographed carrying the rifle out of the TSBD with an exposed clip at 1:57 p.m., almost the very moment the pointed bullet was given to Johnsen. And recall that within minutes after the Carcano was seen with a clip, and the "Mauser" bullet was given to Johnsen, all of the non-clip-fed rifle descriptions, including a Mauser description and excluding an Italian or clip-fed rifle description, were reported by NBC News in rapid succession.

The point here is that there was a substantial delay in the handling of ballistics evidence at Parkland, just as there was a substantial delay in the handling of ballistics evidence at the sixth floor crime scene. And almost simultaneously with the Mauser discussion at the sixth floor crime scene, a "Mauser" bullet was found. Almost simultaneously with a non-Mauser clip appearing in evidence -- 1:55 to 1:57 p.m. -- a bullet suitable to a German regulation 7.92 Carcano, but not to an Italian 6.5 Carcano, appeared in evidence. Was the delay for the purpose of matching rifle's and bullets? Was there a switch in rifle identities with a coordinated switch in bullet identities? Was it a switch that went bad?

Were the conspirators using virtually archival rifle identifications because they were alternating descriptions of the Carcano and the old look-alike 6.5 Argentine Mauser, which also exists as a 7.65 Mauser? Why was the description "German Mauser" repeatedly and increasingly used when the 7.65 Mauser is Belgian, Turkish, Spanish and Argentine, anything but German. Was it because it further blurred reality between the non-German Mauser and the German regulation 7.92 Carcano, both of which use German "spitzer" bullets? Did the opportunistic use of a Mauser description evolve into a more elaborate Mauser plan of damage control involving the planting of a pointed bullet? Or was a Mauser track -- which was already part of the preplanned coverup, which surfaced only through a mixup in matching bullets and rifles -- opportunistically prolonged to distract attention from the Carcano clip paradox?[154] Or did Weitzman simply conclude "Mauser" because he saw an "S" on the breech block of a second rifle?

One thing is now certain. Three hours after the discovery of the rifle and bullets, the facts regarding them, which were known and no longer subject to change, were being inexplicably omitted, or were changing. And other versions of those facts were being kept viable at the highest level of the investigation. In a memorandum found in the National Archives in 1997, from J. Edgar Hoover to his subordinates, written at 5:15 p.m. E.S.T., November 22, 1963, Hoover wrote: "...we have the rifle and 3 empty shells found in the building...the rifle has been handled by dozens of people probably...by the time they got to the fifth floor, the rifle had been dropped and thrown over into a corner...and as soon as the body arrives in Washington, we will determine whether the bullets have been taken out because we will need that in the trial of the case to tie in with the empty shells found by the gun."[155] *[Editor's Note: the Belmont memo was found by researcher and author Joseph McBride, as noted in the* New York Times, *"'63 FBI Memo Ties Bush to Intelligence Agency," 7/11/1988. McBride also discussed the memo in his book* Into the Nightmare.*]*

Hoover never mentions any identifying characteristics of the rifle, nor does he mention the live shell allegedly ejected from the rifle, nor does he mention the stretcher bullet in the possession of Richard Johnsen for over two hours. Officially, the rifle had not been handled by dozens of people. The word "probably" is a qualification that let Hoover off the hook when the official story was settled. Officially, the rifle had not been dropped or thrown, nor was it on the fifth floor. Officially, the rifle had been carefully placed in an upright position between and beneath boxes on the sixth floor. However, the timing and number of reports about ballistics evidence on the fifth floor, including Hoover's own reports, indicate the likelihood of suppressed, fifth-floor ballistics evidence.

FBI Director Hoover, the one man who had access to all of the facts as they were being found, was making statements immediately after those facts were known that precluded accountability for the handling of the evidence by the crime scene investigators. In other words, while the problems with the clip, conflicting rifle descriptions and conflicting bullet descriptions were developing and evolving, J. Edgar Hoover was desperately buying time.

The facts show that the Mauser description was apparently set in stone by the time Weitzman swore to it twenty-four hours after the assassination. Weitzman was merely among the group of investigators as they "discussed" the Mauser description at the crime scene in Day's presence.[156] However, the corroborated chronology of that discussion indicates that it took place during the filmed handling of a Mannlicher-Carcano.[157] The answer to the remaining questions about the origin and purpose of the Mauser description lies in the nature of that "Mauser" discussion. As of this writing, former Dallas Police Lieutenant John Carl Day is a living participant in that discussion. The Assassination Records Review Board, an independent agency endowed by Congress with the power to "request the Attorney General to subpoena private persons to compel testimony, records, and other information relevant to its responsibilities under this Act" and "hold hearings, administer oaths, and subpoena witnesses and documents," has what is probably the last chance to be the first to learn the truth about that discussion from Lieutenant Day.[158]

Among those who know both the subjects of the JFK assassination and firearms well, there are those who stubbornly adhere to the notion that that Mauser discussion was over an innocent mistake. Those with police experience explain that there are few police officers, now or then, who know the difference between a Garand and a Mauser, a Carcano and a Berthier, or an Enfield and an Arisaka. But despite the fact that Seymour Weitzman was one of those very few who knew the difference, the general lack of knowledge among professional investigators is precisely the point. They are correct that "clip fed vs. non-clip fed" was irrelevant in the identification of the rifle. It was, however, the factor that dictated what was proclaimed to the public for a prolonged period of time. Had identification been the true objective, the "Made Italy" and "Cal. 6.5" tool stamps would have been the predominant factors.159 The sixth-floor Mauser discussion may have begun innocently enough, but by the time it ended, all semblance of straightforward, mundane, routine police work had become dishonest, secretive, devious and indirect.

Even former CIA station chief John Stockwell has told coauthor Richard Bartholomew that "Police don't know that Mauser's are non-clip fed." Stockwell said he had used many kinds of guns over the years, but had never used the Mannlicher-Carcano, and therefore never knew how it is loaded. His point was that it cannot be assumed that police know such things.160 True. Neither can it be assumed that identification of the murder weapon was being honestly pursued or reported; nor that the Mauser reports were the result of a confused atmosphere at police headquarters; nor that the reports were based on an actual found Mauser. Especially, therefore, it cannot be assumed that a deliberate, prolonged misidentification did not benefit from that very ignorance. Were it common knowledge that Carcanos use clips, and that Mausers, Enfields and Arisakas do not, Owens' news film, and Allen's and Beers' wire-service photos showing the clip in the rifle would have stopped not only the Mauser reports, but all of the earlier reports, if not prevented them. Instead, given the timing and duration of those reports on WBAP-TV, the first photographs of the clip likely necessitated the erroneous reports as a distraction. What Mr. Stockwell admitted without realizing it, however, as does anyone who argues widespread firearms ignorance, is that even if one of the conspirators was a CIA station chief, he could have found the Carcano on the sixth floor without a clip, with a round in the chamber, and assumed the clip should be there -- as with the M-1 Garand.

If such a conspirator then put a fake clip in place to "correct the error," he would have found himself in the awkward position of having to explain how a clip, with no reason for being there, magically appeared. If such a conspirator then deliberately invented the Mauser misidentification, or prolonged it opportunistically, to distract the press and the public from clips until he could plausibly comment, or, if plausibility is impossible, remain silent, on the feeding system, his actions would fit all of the known evidence of the alleged rifle discovery and alleged Mauser misidentification. The "widespread-ignorance" argument, used in defense of an innocent misidentification, does not fit.

If the arguments presented here are correct, they raise three final important questions: Why a Mannlicher-Carcano? How could conspirators allow such a blunder to happen? And, who cares anyway?

First, why, despite its too obvious paper trail leading to Oswald, would a Mannlicher-Carcano be chosen as the rifle that will live in infamy? In 1963, as head of the Senate's Juvenile Delinquency

Subcommittee, Senator Thomas Dodd of Connecticut was experimenting with ordering arms from mail order houses in an attempt to gather information allowing Congress to stem unregulated traffic. Senator Dodd instituted the program on behalf of Colt and other small firearms producers in Connecticut who complained of foreign imports.

Oswald might have participated in this program. Dodd, a former FBI agent and long-time J. Edgar Hoover loyalist,[161] was also a leading member of the Cuba Lobby (which grew out of the right-wing, red-hunting, China Lobby) through which he was in touch with some of the same Cuban-exile mercenaries as Oswald. He was also investigating the Fair Play for Cuba Committee (FPCC) in which Oswald may have been an infiltrator. Returning to the treatise of criminologist Charles O'Hara, we can see how Oswald, working in a legitimate undercover capacity for Dodd, could have easily been manipulated into simultaneous conspiracies involving a Mannlicher-Carcano: "In the investigation of subversive activities and systematic thefts undercover operations are almost indispensable.

"Undercover work is most successfully used when there is knowledge that certain persons are engaged in criminal activity, but proof which may be used as evidence is lacking...The effective undercover agent is, perhaps, the only means of obtaining detailed information concerning a subversive group or organization."[162]

Two of the gun mail-order houses Dodd's subcommittee was investigating were the ones from which Oswald allegedly ordered his Smith and Wesson .38 revolver (Seaport Traders of Los Angeles) and his Mannlicher-Carcano rifle (Klein's of Chicago). Oswald ordered his pistol two days before Dodd's subcommittee began hearings on the matter on January 29, 1963. The subcommittee's sample statistics later showed a purchase in Texas made from Seaport Traders. One of the groups being investigated for firearm purchases was one whose members Oswald had in his address book, the American Nazi Party. One of the investigators looking into interstate firearms sales at this time was Manuel Pena, the Los Angeles police lieutenant who was later one of the pivotal officers investigating Robert Kennedy's assassination. It was Pena who traced Oswald's telescopic sight to a California gun shop.[163] And one of the primary culprits, robbing domestic manufacturers of profits, was the Mannlicher-Carcano.[164]

After the assassination, Dodd, using CIA sources, helped the Senate Internal Security Subcommittee publish a story that Oswald had been trained at a KGB assassination school in Minsk. At the time, Dodd was on the payroll of the American Security Council, "the leading public group campaigning to use U.S. military force to oust Castro from Cuba, and to escalate the war in Vietnam."[165]

Along with those connections, Dodd's long tenure in the U.S. Government brought him into direct contact with, or within one degree of separation from, a statistically significant number of suspected conspirators and suspicious groups linked to the JFK assassination: the FPCC's Richard Gibson; Guy Banister, who, like Dodd, had been a member of the FBI's elite team pursuing John Dillinger; Ed Butler and his Information Council of the Americas; certain members of the Nuremberg War Crimes Tribunal; certain organized crime figures and labor racketeers; the United Fruit Company; the State Department's Office of Security; the Castillo Armas junta of Guatemala; Allen Dulles and associates, including Nazi assassination plotter Hans Bernd Gisevius and Ruth Forbes Paine's close friend Mary Bancroft; Richard Helms; the Rockefeller family and associates; the Lyndon Baines Johnson family and associates; Dutch journalist Willem Oltmans and associates, eventually including George DeMohrenschildt; the Citizens' Committee for a Free Cuba, including Clare Boothe Luce and other secret warriors against Cuba; Cord Meyer and his United World Federalists, including again, Ruth Forbes Paine; Nazi War Criminals like Alfreds Berzins; William F. Buckley, Jr. and associates, including E. Howard Hunt; expert Clay Shaw-defense witness J. Appel, Jr.; and Dodd's own son, Senator Christopher Dodd of Connecticut.

On the day Kennedy was assassinated, Dodd considered the tragedy a personal victory, bragging about his friendship with the "new" administration, grieving only over "the damage he [Kennedy] did to us in three years." But, as with Edgar Tatro's evidence of who forced Roger Craig to lie about "the Mauser," we still await George Michael Evica's proof that, "Beyond speculation...I have learned that according to two unimpeachable sources, Senator Thomas Dodd indeed caused at least one Mannlicher Carcano to be ordered in the name of Lee Harvey Oswald (or in the name of `Alek Hidell') sometime in 1963."[166]

Conspiracy investigation is never about motive, because, by definition, conspiracies involve multiple motives. Conspiracy investigation is primarily about connections. The significance of Dodd's linkage to the conspiracy lies not in the closeness of his contact to any one of these entities, but in the closeness of his contact to all of them, and the fact that the only two significant common denominators of all of these entities is the CIA and the JFK assassination conspiracy and coverup.

As O'Hara wrote, "Motive or that which induces the criminal to act must be distinguished from intent. The motive may be the desire to obtain revenge or personal gain; the intent is the accomplishment of the act. Motive need not be shown in order to obtain a conviction, but intent must always be proved where it is an element of the offense."[167]

The problem with relying on motive to identify conspirators is illustrated by the vacillating opinions of John Stockwell. In a chapter on the assassination in his 1991 book, *The Praetorian Guard*, Stockwell wrote: "In fact, there is strong evidence that both the FBI and the CIA high commands had prior knowledge of and direct involvement in the conspiracy." He cited excellent examples of that evidence, apart from motive. Two years later, for a new "Afterword" to that book, he wrote: "However, I consider the chapter on the Kennedy assassination to be substantially in error....You see, in 1963 the CIA and John Kennedy could not have been much closer....Of all the popular suspects, only the Mafia and perhaps Lyndon Johnson emerge with truly persuasive motives and opportunity to plot Kennedy['s] murder."[168] As a consequence of relying on motive, Stockwell's opinions became riddled with qualifying phrases and uncertainty.

Stockwell's vacillation seems tame, however, compared to the extremes of Evan Thomas. Addressing the subject of secrecy and oversight in a free society, during a panel discussion on the future of the CIA, Evan Thomas, "the first author or historian ever permitted to read the CIA's own secret histories," said that "eighty percent of American people believe a conspiracy killed JFK and fifty percent of the people believe the CIA was behind it." He said, "The CIA has done a lot of bad things but they did not kill JFK." He added, "I think they're nuts not to just completely open up those files." He said there will be problems with the files regarding Cuban CIA agents but the CIA will be cleared of any conspiracy to kill JFK.

The panel's moderator, ABC News Diplomatic Correspondent David Ensor, did not respond to Thomas. Neither did the other five panelists. No one at the panel discussion had mentioned the subject of JFK's assassination before Thomas, and no one addressed it after him, not even panelist Walter Pincus of the Washington Post, who had helped Thomas write a Newsweek cover story about the CIA and the JFK assassination in 1993. With a half hour left in the discussion, Thomas was the only panelist not to speak again, and the only one not asked to speak again. Silence was the least foolhardy course considering what Thomas had just said and what he has written on the subject. His Newsweek article concluded that "In the end, the story of the American government and the assassination of John F. Kennedy is a tale of human error and parochialism, not conspiracy."

Yet in his article and in his later book about the CIA, Thomas used the motives of avenging the Bay of Pigs and preserving world peace to conclude that "Slightly more plausible conspiracy theories [than those blaming Khrushchev and Castro] involve renegades and rogue agents," and that "Somewhat more plausible suspects are renegade Cuban exiles, conceivably abetted by rogue CIA agents." That is followed in his article with, "But there is no solid evidence leading to the Agency or the Cubans. There are, however, more intriguing hints of mob involvement," wrote Thomas, because "The motive was to get Bobby Kennedy off the mob's back....But, in addition to a lack of any hard evidence, there are two big problems with fingering them as the culprits."

Incredibly, Thomas' two big problems are that mobsters would be more motivated by prudence and self-preservation than by anger toward an enemy; and that they would have no motive to use an "unreliable, unlikely professional hit man" like the "paranoid loser" Oswald. Thomas cites only Gerald Posner as proof that the motiveless Oswald was the hit man, however. And he ignores the fact that "paranoid loser" perfectly describes a patsy, one who is duped or victimized -- a sucker. And he ignores the fact that patsies are essential to con-jobs perpetrated by mobsters and other swindlers.

Like the Warren Commission, Thomas thus admits to plausible evidence of conspiracy, exchanging the Warren Report's unproven qualification, "no credible evidence," for his own unproven value judgments, "no solid evidence" and "no hard evidence." In his article, Thomas wisely states that "It is impossible to prove a negative -- that someone did not plot to kill Kennedy." (Thomas' emphasis) Yet in his book, as in the panel discussion, he attempts the impossible: "The many conspiracy theories notwithstanding, there is no evidence that the CIA itself somehow became sucked into a plot to kill JFK." In other words, according to Thomas' flip-flopping, there was no conspiracy, and if we discount the CIA agents, including Cuban exiles and mobsters, who plausibly conspired to killed JFK, there is no proof that the CIA was part of the plot. This from the man who called it "an absurd leap to think the CIA would kill Kennedy."[169]

Applying Peter Dale Scott's methodology of analyzing consistently negative information, a pattern of disinformation can be seen in a preference for motive-based arguments on the part of biased media pundits and investigators. Because of its irrelevance, motive can be used either to support or to ridicule any particular conspiratorial relationship. Writing in the Los Angeles Times in the wake of Oliver Stone's film, *JFK*, former Warren Commission staff attorney Richard M. Mosk did both. He cited only the motive of going after "a fast buck" to support his theory that the publishing and entertainment industries were conspiring to "distort history for profit." Then, just before mounting a weak defense of the Commission, Mosk attempted to defend his own innocence in its coverup with the "logic and common sense" that he had no motive: "For example, why would I, a young private-sector lawyer who had just completed active military service and whose father was close to President Kennedy, participate in a cover-up?"[170]

When motive is not the focus, bias becomes obvious. Bias to the extent of bigotry revealed itself in both interviewer and interviewee when talk-show host Tom Snyder interviewed presidential candidate Arlen Specter. When "Charlie in New York City" called and asked the former Warren Commission counsel if his views had changed over the years regarding his single bullet theory, Specter failed to make any sense despite embarrassing effort. Snyder, declaring that he "truly" believed the theory, supplied his own embarrassment by attempting damage control through the next night's broadcast. He finally said, "...I'm not going to try and change your mind. Don't try and change mine."[171]

But at least Snyder figured out that the only way to be a true believer is to avoid being confused by the facts. John Stockwell's confusion only worsened. Following his epiphany about CIA innocence in JFK's death, Stockwell conducted rifle-firing tests to "debunk or verify" the ballistics claims of alleged, confessed, grassy-knoll assassin James Files.[172] By giving Files' confession a moment's thought, Stockwell compounded his motive-based flip-flop. Files claims he was a military-trained, albeit mob-connected, CIA assassin who, although he hated JFK, was just following orders from a CIA-employed mobster in a U.S. government-supported operation. Moreover, the "Files video" has been shown to be a blend of truths and untruths characteristic of classic disinformation.[173]

When hard evidence finally becomes public connecting a multipurpose Mannlicher-Carcano and the Dodds (father and son) to the JFK assassination conspiracy, the first line of defense will most likely be based on an absence of a motive.

Second, how could an obviously well-planned conspiracy such as this not have adequate communication between the rifle's planters and their accomplice rifle discoverers?[174] It is perhaps the most difficult question to answer conclusively. But, like the arguments presented here, it originates from all the known facts. The question does not eliminate the otherwise complete explanation of these facts. Without a confession from the conspirators, there remain two general, rather obvious answers.

One, non-communication was part of the plan. The planters' primary concern was to plant the rifle in a proper post-firing condition, which they did. They could not have necessarily anticipated that experienced police officers, guided by the planters' accomplice(s), would get confused over the exact configuration of that post-firing condition. Nor could they have necessarily anticipated that their accomplice(s) would take unilateral action to correct it unnecessarily. However important, it is a small detail in a complex plan that could have been easily overlooked.

Two, assuming communication was part of the plan, trained and educated military officers are well aware that, in any overt or covert operation, preplanning is only of value until the operation begins. After that, everything is in flux. Circumstances change rapidly. Things go unexpectedly right while other things go unexpectedly wrong. The failure at the Bay of Pigs is one example. That a man of Jack Ruby's background and indiscretion had to be used to kill Oswald, in the manner that he did, is another. Breakdowns in communication happen.

Those breakdowns should not be confused, however, with a complete breakdown in secure communication. Some refute the existence of large conspiracies with the simplistic argument that large numbers of people cannot keep a secret. Such arguments are intended for the naive.

Even when disclosed, mistakes and leaks can only threaten a conspiracy when they are detected at the right time by the right people. Many mistakes and leaks in the JFK assassination conspiracy, though detected, have been ignored. In most cases, the few people who did not ignore them were either silenced or rendered unworthy of serious attention through ridicule.

With the aid of coincidental timing, Tom Snyder again illustrated the folly of bigotry by using ridicule to silence debate about conspiracy. During a televised interview with writer Harlan Ellison in early February, 1997, Snyder mentioned the subject of a retrial for James Earl Ray, the accused assassin of Dr. Martin Luther King, Jr. Ellison, a Caucasian, talked of having marched with King and of having participated in the freedom rides during the 1960s. Ellison was disparaging African-American solidarity with the conspiracy theory in the O.J. Simpson civil trial by calling those who believed it "stupid" and arguing that he was "more black than O.J." Snyder expressed doubt that Ray could reveal anything that had not managed to surface in thirty years, adding his opinion that "the government can't keep a secret for fifteen minutes." Ellison agreed, saying he found conspiracy theorists entertaining. With a broad brush, he then ridiculed them (and, subtly, the espionage technique of faking one's death) by pointing out that there are those who believe actor James Dean is still alive.[175]

The next morning, The San Francisco Examiner, ran a story by Christopher Matthews revealing that newly released Nixon White House tapes confirm that Nixon himself had ordered the illegal spying that led to the Watergate scandal. Nixon's role as mastermind of those conspiracies had been kept secret for nearly twenty-five years.[176]

Less than a week later, the King family broke a thirty-year silence in support of a new trial for Ray. On that day, in stark contrast to Snyder, Dexter King stated that questions surrounding his father's assassination lack satisfactory answers, and that every effort to determine the truth can only be accomplished in a court of law. A week later, a judge ruled that new ballistics tests could and should be applied to Ray's rifle to determine whether it was the murder weapon or a "throwdown" gun.[177]

One month after that, the Liggett Tobacco Company was forced to admit that cigarette smoking causes health problems including cancer, that nicotine is addictive, and that the tobacco industry specifically markets to minors. They agreed to turn over thousands of incriminating documents about thirty years of meetings with attorneys from other tobacco companies detailing industry-wide discussions on nicotine and other subjects, including conversations among tobacco industry lawyers, and Philip Morris, R.J. Reynolds, Lorillard and Brown & Williamson. Attorney General Scott Harshbarger of Massachusetts, head of the National Association of Attorneys General, said the documents show "what big tobacco knew and when they knew it." Thus ending a conspiracy that addicts forty-six million Americans and kills 400,000 a year.[178]

Exactly three weeks after the tobacco conspiracy was confessed, after weeks of speculation in the media about a decades-long government conspiracy by Switzerland, author Tom Bower documented in his book, *Nazi Gold,* that the Swiss government had knowingly conspired to steal the assets of Jewish Holocaust victims and to cover up those anti-Semitic crimes. The Swiss had returned Nazi loot to gentiles after the war, but not to Jews. Bower emphasized that it has taken fifty years for the Swiss government to reluctantly admit to its evil. A U.S. government report by Commerce Undersecretary Stuart Eizenstat, released a few weeks later, "faulted the United States for not forcing the Swiss to come clean during and after World War II." Compounding that evil, the Swiss conspiracy was maintained for five years after Argentine authorities admitted and documented that Argentina conspired to give many Nazi war criminals, including Joseph Mengele and Walter Kutschman, safe haven in their country for forty-seven years following World War II.[179]

Three months after Snyder's conspiracy scoff, President Clinton gave a national apology to survivors of the forty-year conspiracy known as the *Tuskegee Study of Untreated Syphilis in the Negro Male,* in which poor black men were unwittingly denied treatment, starting in 1932, for the disease they were told was "bad blood." [*Editor's Note: See the fine book* Bad Blood *by James H. Jones for the full story.]* One editorial said, "Thousands of Americans and millions of Europeans died in the war to stop Hitler. And still the Tuskegee experiment went on. No, we cannot afford to `close' this chapter, ever." In February, 1997, the very same month of Snyder's self-professed belief in a fifteen-minute-maximum time limit on government conspiracies, on CBS, the very same network as Snyder's talk show, 60 Minutes first aired a report by Mike Wallace about hundreds of Nazis and Nazi collaborators hiding in Canada. Wallace noted that Canada did virtually nothing to pursue war criminals after the Nuremberg Trials. By 1997, the U.S. had deported fifty Nazis, Wallace reported, while Canada had deported only one. One of Canada's accused war criminals was even found living in the same building as an Auschwitz survivor.[180] As a veteran journalist, Tom Snyder was neither naive about, nor uninformed about such enormous, evil and long-lived government conspiracies when he spouted his conspiracy-denial nonsense.

Some 650-750,000 pages are still kept secret by the U.S. House of Representatives as part of the HSCA's investigation of King's murder in the 1970s, although tens of thousands of citizens have already signed a national petition for their release. Under House Rule thirty-six, HSCA Chairman Louis Stokes sealed those files for a period of fifty years, until 2028. Yet none of those facts prevented Ray's prosecutor, Shelby County Assistant District Attorney John Campbell, from saying, "The government can't keep anything secret." When news first broke that bullets test fired from Ray's rifle did not match the bullet that killed King, Cable News Network anchor Donna Kelley asked CNN legal correspondent, Roger Cossack, about the legality of the HSCA sealing their rifle test results for fifty years. Cossack stumbled over his answer, saying it is "just done" in "high profile cases." He concluded his answer by reminding viewers that Ray pled guilty, so there was "no reason" to release the earlier test results. Cossack failed, therefore, to report two good reasons for full disclosure: Ray quickly recanted his guilty plea and requested a trial; and Chairman Stokes stated in a Congressionally mandated report that the HSCA "intends to conclude a thorough, professional investigation of the assassinations by establishing the facts to prove or disprove, once and for all, the disparate theories that have arisen since the murders took place in Dallas and Memphis."[181]

If crucial evidence of Nixon's guilt could be kept secret for twenty-five years, so can evidence of other executive-branch conspiracies. If the King family could keep their assassination conspiracy questions secret for twenty-eight years, so can the families of other assassination victims. If crucial ballistics evidence in the King murder could be obscured, neglected and kept secret for decades, so can crucial ballistics evidence in the Kennedy murder. If the tobacco industry, the Argentine government, the Swiss government, the Canadian government and the U.S. government could keep their enormous genocidal conspiracies secret for thirty, forty and fifty years, the U.S. government and its military-industrial complex can, and does, do far more than "keep a secret for fifteen minutes."

Tom Snyder's faux erudition was directly exposed during three later broadcasts, the first of which aired just two months and eleven days after he declared long-term government secrecy impossible. Snyder listened uncritically, and seemingly in sincere sympathy, as his guest Patrick Eddington discussed his new book, *Gassed In the Gulf*. Eddington's investigation expanded and supported recent news reports of a CIA coverup of U.S. military errors during Operation Desert Storm that resulted in Gulf War Syndrome. Eddington claimed that former President George Bush, and Generals Norman Schwartzkopf and Colin Powell were continuing to deny the errors although they were knowledgeable of the coverup. Yet Snyder did not object to, nor did he ridicule, Eddington's charges.

A week after his interview of Eddington, Snyder's guest was James Sanders, who had just released his book, *The Downing of Flight 800*. Sanders told of how an unsolicited U.S. Navy source told reporter Dave Hendricks, within seventy-two hours of the crash, that TWA flight 800 had been destroyed by a direct hit from a "friendly-fire" missile. That source was corroborated by Captain Bower, an Air National Guard helicopter pilot who saw the missile travel from east to west and hit the plane. Sanders reported that the White House got radar summaries at a 2 a.m. briefing, during which the missile was discussed. He further told Snyder that the day after Hendricks' report about the missile and the radar summaries appeared in the March 10th edition of The Riverside Enterprise, the FBI seized the radar data.

Sanders' investigation had already made headlines before his book was released. He had secretly obtained samples of a residue found on some of the plane's seats. That residue, according to independent analyses, was found to be a chemical component of solid rocket fuel. The same residue was identified as glue by the official investigators. However, Sanders pointed out that modern airliner seats are glueless.

After listening to Sanders, Snyder attempted the kind of denial he had expressed over assassination conspiracies. If Sanders' reports were true, Snyder reasoned, "Someone must have talked." But this time Snyder's guest was not so accommodating. Sanders replied, "A lot of somebodys have talked." That simple, sensible answer applies equally to the conspiracies behind Kennedy's and King's unsolved murders, and many others. Snyder revealed a psychological motive behind his bigotry and denial -- a motive shared by most people, no doubt -- when he ended the interview by saying, "I hope you're wrong."

FBI Director Louis Freeh fueled Snyder's hope on NBC-TV's "Meet the Press," ten days after Sanders' television appearance. But despite headlines and sound bites trumpeting "mechanical failure," Freeh's statement was convoluted: "I think that the evidence as we have developed it to date and particularly the evidence we have not found, would lead toward the conclusion that this was a catastrophic mechanical failure." Freeh stressed that none of the investigators can state definitively that the cause of the crash was due to a mechanical problem. The headline and soundbite writers had what they needed for their preferred spin, however.

Bringing his bigotry full circle on the first day of ballistics tests on James Earl Ray's gun, and the night before Clinton's apology to the Tuskegee victims, Snyder had as his guest, Christopher Matthews, the reporter who exposed Nixon's role as Watergate mastermind. But Snyder did not ask about Nixon, even after Matthews compared the Whitewater scandal to Watergate. During the seven topics discussed, he did find time, however, to predict the end of the Kennedy political dynasty based on the latest sexual and marital problems of the Kennedys. And, in a derisive tone of voice, Snyder found time to call people who, like Dexter King, think James Earl Ray might be innocent, "Those conspiracy theory buffs...." Finally, as if to perfectly summarize his three-month folly, Snyder ended that broadcast by gushing over Christopher Anderson and his book, *An Affair to Remember*, about the long adultery between Spencer Tracy and Katherine Hepburn, which was kept totally secret by movie studios, Hollywood colleagues and the press.[182]

Media bigotry like Snyder's is not confined to his late-night broadcast, talk-show hosts or to the medium of talk shows. His behavior is symptomatic of the mainstream news media. ABC News boasts that more Americans get their news from it than from any other source. Yet one of its most visible news programs, "This Week With David Brinkley," exemplified national coverage of the August, 1996, San Jose Mercury News series called "Dark Alliance," a story by investigative reporter Gary Webb which suggested a direct connection between the start of the nation's crack epidemic and efforts to raise money in the 1980s for the CIA-organized Contra rebel force in Nicaragua.

A month after the series ran, William Bennett, former Drug Czar under President Bush, and Secretary of Education under President Reagan, appeared on "This Week With David Brinkley" and said, "I don't believe it...Investigate it and then nip it in the bud...Having people going around saying the government is killing people is a very bad thing." Nearly nine months after Webb's series ran, the show's panel of pundits was quick to declare the investigation nipped. During its May 18, 1997 broadcast, Cokie Roberts echoed many national headlines in her sound-bite announcement that the story had been "recanted" by Mercury News Executive Editor Jerry Ceppos, in an "Epilogue" he published on May 11, 1997. Roberts hammered home her sound-bite spin by lamenting that the country's state of mind was so "fraught with conspiracy." Sam Donaldson merely voiced the lame argument that the CIA was vulnerable to such accusations because of its inability to "prove a negative."

None of them quoted Ceppos, who wrote: "Our series solidly documented disturbing information: A drug ring associated with the Contras sold large quantities of cocaine in inner-city Los Angeles in the 1980s at the time of the crack explosion there. Some of the drug profits from those sales went to the Contras. Given our government's involvement with the Contras, I believe this is a major public policy issue worthy of further investigation." [Editor's Note: see Gary Webb's brilliant book, *Dark Alliance*.]

His so-called recantation consisted of admitting to giving one interpretation of evidence, not labeling a best estimate as an estimate, oversimplifying, and "Through imprecise language and graphics," creating "impressions that were open to misinterpretation" -- all of which have long happened daily in the government and major news media, especially regarding the JFK assassination. Bennett's statement, therefore, proved not only prophetic in terms of what would happen with the "Dark Alliance" story, but why it happened.[183]

As a perfect example of these broadcasters' bigotry and hypocrisy, no one associated with ABC News or "This Week With David Brinkley" recanted, or again mentioned, an incident of questionable journalism on their own program: the Sunday following John F. Kennedy, Jr.'s wedding, Brinkley and his fellow pundits ended the broadcast by laughing off tabloid reports of the marriage, arrogantly scoffing at the notion that such a thing could happen without the major media learning of it in advance. It is poetic justice, perhaps, that the son of the murdered president proved to the media that major national events can be plotted and executed in total secrecy by a large number of people.

Nonetheless, when the news reports, mentioned above, first revealed that bullets test fired from Ray's rifle did not match the bullet that killed King, CNN anchor Bill Hendricks asked news correspondent Russ Jamieson, who was at the court hearing in Memphis where the test results were announced, the following question preceded by the following editorial comment: "A lot of people in this country are conspiracy happy. Does this hearing play into that? Or will we, by the end of the day, have information that will move this case forward?" Jamieson, to his credit, simply reviewed the plating and bubbling characteristics on twelve of the test bullets which were not present on the death slug.

In another example of media bias, The Dallas Morning News, seldom outdone in its conspiracy-denial bigotry or ridicule of conspiracy realists, seized yet another opportunity for both when "shock jock" radio personality Howard Stern staged a publicity stunt in Dealey Plaza in late July, 1997, to protest his syndicated radio talk show's cancellation by Dallas station KEGL-FM. In what appeared to be an objective reporting of news, after an opening sentence describing a rare circus atmosphere at the usually solemn site of the brutal murder of the President, the News editorialized: "As if that weren't enough, a conspiracy theorist showed up." The man's conspiracy "theory," worthy of topping Howard Stern's hoopla and humbuggery, according to the News, was actually one of the most basic, solid facts disproving the many single-bullet theories: "`...you can't get a bullet to do that [which is alleged of CE 399] and stay [as] pristine,' said Greg Boatright, 28, a dental technician from Dallas." The Dallas Morning News, in its single-minded attempt to discredit Mr. Boatright's rational position, failed to do its journalistic duty and justify its ridicule by presenting history's first tenable single-bullet theory.[184]

In another example, bias against conspiracy was used by attorneys to sway a jury and repeated by the media to mislead the public about the jury's verdict. Stephen Bright, a former Texas State Treasury employee sued the former state treasurer and current state comptroller in federal district court alleging that they had him fired for writing a letter to the editor opposing their political agenda to abolish the treasury. Jury members who were interviewed by Bright's attorneys after the trial said they believed Bright was fired because he wrote the letter, but they felt they could not adequately make the causal link based solely on the evidence they were given. Jurors can vote their conscience in spite of their perceptions about the evidence they are given. But they seldom do because attorneys know how to prevent such bold actions. In closing arguments, James Todd, an assistant attorney general representing the state officials, called Bright's allegations speculation, despite the fact that Todd and his legal team failed to have the case dismissed on such grounds during the trial. He then told the jury, "Reality is not as entertaining as fantasy. We're conditioned to look for conspiracy and diabolical plots." The reporter for the local newspaper used that quote to conclude her reporting of the case without any mention of the jurors' statements or thoughts. Neither the lawyers nor the reporter pointed out that such conditioning is abundantly justified by the existence and public exposure of many high-level conspiracies over the lifetime of the jurors. Nor did they point out that being conditioned to look for such conspiracies is far less dangerous than being conditioned to ignore them.

In a final, but hardly minimal, example of media ridicule of conspiracy realists, columnist, humorist and commentator Andy Rooney reached a new low. On the subject of men's hats, during his spot at the end of CBS's 60 Minutes, Rooney noted that the most popular men's hat was the fedora, until Kennedy became president and never wore one. Rooney then joked that Oliver Stone was planning to make a movie based on the theory that hat makers killed Kennedy.[185]

The media's desperate tale that its pundits are more sane than most of its consumers, is the opposite of reality: one symptom of the public's actual fear, ignorance and gullibility, is that we believe no one has come forward with evidence of conspiracy, and that "a lot" of us are "conspiracy happy," simply because our government and media tell us so. Moreover, if the statement, "The government can't keep anything secret," is the best argument a government prosecutor can make against overwhelming evidence of conspiracy, it is proof of extreme desperation within the government to keep conspiracies secret.

* * *

Notes

149. Ian Hogg and John Weeks, "Mauser," *Military Small Arms of the Twentieth Century* (Northfield, Illinois: Digest Books, 1973).
150. Letter from J.W. Hughes to Walter Graf, June 6, 1994.
151. Thompson 207-08, 218, 228-29 n.17.
152. Document # 180-10104-10481 (HSCA seven page summary of an interview with Gerald Behn), cited in Joseph Backes, "An ARRB Update," Assassination Chronicles, Winter 1996-97, p. 29.
153. Vincent Palamara, The Third Alternative -- *Survivor's Guilt: The Secret Service and the JFK Murder* (self published, 1993), p. 43.
154. Letter from Walter Graf to Jerry Rose, Jun. 6, 1997 with attachments. Letters from Walter Graf to Richard Bartholomew, Jul. 16, 23, 1997, Aug. 16, 1997.
155. Memo from FBI Director J. Edgar Hoover to Tolson, Belmont, Mohr, Conrad, De Loach, Evans, Rosen, and Sullivan, 5:15 p.m., Nov. 22, 1963, FBI document 62-109060-57, National Archives RIF 124-10012-10168, reproduced in The Fourth Decade, Jul., 1997, p. 32.
156. Mark Lane, *Rush to Judgment* (New York: Holt, Rinehart & Winston,

1966) pp. 119-20.

157. Commercially available sources for edited versions of the Tom Alyea film include: *Four Days in November*, film documentary (David Wolper production, 1964) 2 hrs. *The Men Who Killed Kennedy*, 6-part film documentary (Nigel Turner production, 1988; part 6: 1996) 6 hrs. PBS, Frontline, "Oswald," film documentary (PBS, 1993) 3 hrs. JFK: The Case for Conspiracy, videotape (Robert Groden production, Boothwyn, PA: New Frontier Video, 1993) 1 hr., 43 min.

158. Sanders and Zaid 418, 432. ARCA, Public Law No. 102-526, 1992 U.S.C.A.N. (106 Stat.) 3443 (to be codified at 44 U.S.C. [[section]] 2107) at [[section]] 7 (j)(1)(C)(iii) and [[section]] 7 (j)(1)(F).

159. Letter from Walter Graf to Richard Bartholomew, Feb. 5, 1996 (clip fed vs. non-clip fed).

160. Richard Bartholomew's contemporaneous notes of telephone discussion with John Stockwell, 9:51 p.m. to 10:11 p.m., Feb. 9, 1995. Mr. Stockwell later wrote that "There may be some risk in y[ou]r trying to codify points I was making in our oral discussion as though they were my conclusions." (Emphasis in original: Letter from John Stockwell to Richard Bartholomew, Feb. 17, 1995.) To avoid any potential risk, we make no such codification, especially with respect to Mr. Stockwell's point of contention that he "thinks there was a conspiracy but doesn't think the issues used to support it in this paper are conclusive."

161. Curt Gentry, J. Edgar Hoover: The Man and the Secrets (New York: Penguin, 1991) p. 407; cited in Scott 249.

162. O'Hara 197, 199.

163. 22H 528.

164. Evica 252-53. Scott 249, 250, 307, 370.

165. Scott 215, 216.

166. George Michael Evica, "And We Are All Still Mortal: Thomas Dodd and Lee Harvey Oswald," Assassination Chronicles, Mar. 1996, pp. 20-24. Lisa Pease, "Thomas J. Dodd & Son: Corruption of Blood?," Probe, Jul.-Aug. 1996, pp. 18-23. Anthony Summers, *Conspiracy* (New York: McGraw-Hill, 1980) pp. 290-98, 384, 444, 489. Richard Bartholomew, "Possible Discovery of an Automobile Used In the JFK Conspiracy," Fair Play online magazine (http://rmii.com/~jkelin/fp.html, issue 17, Jul.-Aug., 1997 (and self-published manuscript, 1993, pp. 8, 31, 35-48, 50, 51, 56, 57, 59, 62, 63, 66, 68, 78, 87-89, 91, 92, 94, 96, 97, 98, 101, 102, 115, 113, 120, 124, 135, 152); hereafter cited as "Possible Discovery" with page number(s). William E. Kelly, Lines of Inquiry and The Divine Scheme (unpublished manuscript).

167. O'Hara 19.

168. John Stockwell, *The Praetorian Guard* (Boston, Mass.: South End Press, 1991) p. 125. John R. Stockwell, "Afterword," (written on his personal letterhead and inserted into later editions by his distributor, Prevailing Winds Research) Aug. 24, 1993.

169. Richard Bartholomew's contemporaneous notes from CIA Symposium: "Spying Under Siege: The Future of Covert Action," National Press Club Ball

Room, Washington D.C., Mar. 25, 1997 (broadcast live by C-SPAN2; sponsored by the Discovery Channel and held in conjunction with the CIA's 50th Anniversary and the world premiere of the mini-series, "CIA: America's Secret Warriors," Mar. 31-Apr. 2, 1997). Evan Thomas, "The Real Cover-up," Newsweek, Nov. 22, 1993, pp. 68, 92, 94, 95; and The Very Best Men: The Early Years of the CIA (New York: Simon & Schuster, 1995), pp. 308, 331, liner notes. R 374 ("no credible evidence").
170. Richard M. Mosk, "The Plot to Assassinate the Warren Commission," Los Angeles Times, Dec. 30, 1991; reprinted in Oliver Stone and Zachary Sklar, *JFK: The Book of the Film* (New York: Applause Books, 1992) pp. 333-34; hereafter cited as Stone and Sklar 333-34.
171. Richard Bartholomew, "True Believers: Tom Snyder talks to Arlen Specter," The Fourth Decade, Jul. 1995, pp. 29-32.
172. Richard Bartholomew's contemporaneous notes of phone call from John Stockwell, Feb. 7, 1995 10:48 a.m.-11:42 a.m. CST.
173. Martin Shackelford, " 'Confession of an Assassin' James E. Files, Joliet State Penitentiary, March 22, 1994: Notes on the Videotape (1996, Bob Vernon, UTL Productions/MPI Video)" JFK-Share Internet discussion group, Sept. 20, 1996 00:53:33 EDT. "Another Lone Nut? Confession of an assassin: The murder of JFK," Assassination Chronicles, Vol. 2, Issue 2, Summer 1996, p. 48.
174. As discussed earlier in this article, the fact that the alleged murder weapon was neither tested for recent firing, nor tested for recent non-firing, reveals the rifle discoverers' roles as accomplices in the conspiracy. In that discussion, the authors cited the late New Orleans District Attorney and Federal Judge, Jim Garrison, from his 1970 book, A Heritage of Stone (p. 49, Berkley Medallion edition, 1975): "Although it is possible to determine by tests whether or not a rifle has been fired recently, there is no evidence that such a test was given to the rifle which was supposed to have killed the President." The authors also briefly mentioned that there is "reportedly" no test for recent firing. Coauthor Walter Graf adds: "The qualifying term is the word 'reported'...In other words 'no test' is a claim, not a fact...I have not been around small arms in recent years, but was up to my ears in weapons from 1938-1950 and never had any trouble in 'check for recent firing' (Maybe check is a better term than test). If fired after cleaning, the barrel and chamber has that bluish-grey look. The key word is 'recent.' How many minutes is recent? I don't know if there would be that smell after three quarters of an hour or so, but the barrel and chamber would have that appearance of being fired after cleaning." (Letter from Walter F. Graf to Richard Bartholomew, Jul. 9, 1997.) See the authors' earlier discussion in this article on how their failure to conduct such tests reveals the rifle discoverers' roles as accomplices.
175. Richard Bartholomew's contemporaneous notes from "Late Late Show with Tom Snyder," CBS-TV, Feb. 6, 1997.
176. Christopher Matthews, "Tricky Dick: Tapes show Nixon ordered huge spy effort," The San Francisco Examiner, Feb. 7, 1997. The specter of Nixon's possible involvement in assassination conspiracies, including the JFK assassination, continued to haunt his own statements three years before his

death. In a 1991 interview on 60 Minutes, Nixon said that if he were still in charge he would have ordered the assassination of Saddam Hussein: "If I could find a way to get him out of there, even putting a contract out on him, if the CIA still did that sort of thing, assuming it ever did, I would be for it." ("Dubious Achievement Awards of 1991," Esquire, January, 1992, p. 98.)
177. King Family to Support Ray's Trial Request," Reuters New Media, 2:11 p.m. EST, Feb. 13, 1997 (text from Examiner and Reuters Internet World Wide Web sites). Richard Bartholomew's contemporaneous notes from Tennessee v. James Earl Ray (hearing before Judge Joseph Brown, Jr., Shelby County Criminal Court, broadcast live by Court-TV cable network, Feb. 20, 1997). On Mar. 27th, after a face-to-face meeting with Ray, Dexter King publicly stated his belief that Ray is innocent. The new ballistics tests were soon ordered and conducted. ("New tests OK'd for rifle, bullet in King's slaying," Austin American-Statesman, Apr. 10, 1997, p. A8. "Ray's rifle gets ballistics tests" Austin American-Statesman, May 15, 1997, p. A5 (from news services). According to a confidential source developed by HSCA investigator Morris Davis, on the day of the shooting, the rifle Ray had purchased "was fired once and the cartridge left in the gun. Its sole purpose was to be a throwdown gun for the coverup of the killing" (Dr. William F. Pepper, *Orders to Kill: The Truth Behind the Murder of Martin Luther King*, [New York: Carrol & Graf, 1995] pp. 128, 131). If true, Ray was framed in a manner almost identical to the framing of Oswald five years earlier. The first report on the ballistics test results, broadcast by Cable News Network (CNN, 4:41 p.m., EDT, Jul. 10, 1997), stated "Sources tell CNN that the tests will not exclude Ray." Eighteen hours later, however, Judge Brown announced that the tests revealed identifying characteristics consistent with the alleged murder weapon on each of twelve test bullets, which were not present on the death slug, indicating the tests do exclude Ray. CNN reported that the prosecution had been told before the hearing that the tests were inconclusive, and that the prosecution claimed it was shocked to hear in court that there was no match (Richard Bartholomew's contemporaneous notes from Tennessee v. James Earl Ray (hearing before Judge Joseph Brown, Jr., Shelby County Criminal Court, partially broadcast live by CNN, 10:24 a.m. to 10:58 a.m., followed by review and commentary until 11:25 a.m. EDT, Jul. 11, 1997).
178. "Liggett Tobacco Co. Admits Danger," Associated Press, 3:36 p.m. EST, Mar. 20, 1997. Five years earlier, U.S. District Judge Lee Sarokin ordered the Council for Tobacco Research to open its files to a woman suing several tobacco companies for fraud. The Council, funded by tobacco companies, was founded in 1954 as an "independent" group formed to investigate possible tobacco hazards and report their findings. Sarokin said that "All too often in the choice between the physical health of consumers and the financial well-being of business, concealment is chosen over disclosure, sales over safety, and money over morality." Citing memos from the council's files, Sarokin wrote that a jury could conclude it "was nothing but a public relations ploy -- a fraud." Tobacco company attorney William Allinder said a jury would disagree with Sarokin's conclusions. (Associated Press, "Judge: Tobacco firms lied about dangers," Austin American-Statesman, Feb. 8, 1992, p. A11.)

179. NBC News interview of Tom Bower, "Today," NBC-TV, Apr. 10, 1997.
Carol Rosenberg (The Miami Herald), "U.S. report flails Swiss for profits from
Nazis," Austin American-Statesman, May 8, 1997, p. A3. "Nazi war criminals
lived safely in Argentina, documents reveal," (New York Times News Service)
Austin American Statesman, Feb. 11, 1992, p. A5. On May 1st, the Swiss
government appointed Nobel Peace Prize laureate Elie Wiesel as honorary
chairman of a seven-member board that will administer a multi-million-dollar
fund for Holocaust victims. (Wire service reports, "Nobel winner to head panel
over Holocaust funds," Austin American-Statesman, May 2, 1997, p. A18.) For
a film documentary overview of the extent of Switzerland's crimes, see "Blood
Money: Switzerland's Nazi Gold," Investigative Reports (Arts & Entertainment
Cable Network, Jul 26, 1997, 2 hrs.).
180. "Apologize but don't forget" (editorial); Eddie Pells (Associated Press),
"Tuskegee victim tenders forgiveness in advance;" Julia Malone, "Tuskegee
survivors receive apology," Austin American-Statesman, May 16, 1997, pp.
A14, A17; May 17, 1997, p. A1. Richard Bartholomew's contemporaneous notes
from "Canada's Dark Secret," 60 Minutes (CBS-News, reported by Mike
Wallace, produced by Robert G. Anderson, Feb. 1997, rebroadcast Jul. 20, 1997,
7:37 p.m. EDT).
181. John Judge, "National Coalition Demands Release of King Assassination
Files, Public Review of Evidence: Researchers Suggest Several Ways to
Determine the Truth," Coalition on Political Assassinations Press Release, Mar.
30, 1997. Richard Bartholomew's contemporaneous notes from ABC News
interview of John Campbell by Sam Donaldson, "Prime Time Live," ABC-TV,
Apr. 2, 1997. Report of the Select Committee on Assassinations [pursuant to
mandate of H. Resolution 222]. H. Report 95-119, 95th Cong., 1st sess., Mar.
28, 1977. Committee Print. v, 14 pp. The Stokes Mandate Report; cited in Guth
and Wrone, p. 23, item no. 71.
182. Richard Bartholomew's contemporaneous notes from "Late Late Show with
Tom Snyder," CBS-TV, Apr. 17, 1997 (Patrick Eddington); Apr. 25, 1997
(James Sanders); May 15, 1997 (Christopher Matthews & Christopher
Anderson). John J. Goldman and Eric Malnic (Los Angeles Times), "FBI points
to mechanical failure in TWA crash," Austin American-Statesman, May 5, 1997,
p. A3. On the first anniversary of the downing of TWA flight 800, the
"mechanical failure" media spin continued. Introducing a story on the first
anniversary of the crash, and a follow-up story on terrorist profiling by U.S.
airlines, National Public Radio's Robert Segal said, "Investigators have turned
their attention to mechanical failure," and added that investigators are "close to
abandoning" a terrorist act as the cause. Note the inconclusive rhetoric indicative
of editorial bias. NPR failed in attempts to bolster its bias, however. The main
element of the anniversary story was an interview with crash-victim relative
Joseph Lychner. Lychner said he had accepted a supposed "spark of static
electricity" as the cause of the crash, despite finding it hard to believe that it
could cause such great loss of life. Lychner's reason for rejecting a terrorist
cause was equally inadequate: "I believe in the goodness of people," he said.
(Robert Segal, National Public Radio, Jul. 17, 1997, broadcast 5:38 to 5:51 p.m.,

CDT, on KUT, 90.5 FM, Austin, Texas.) On the subject of Gulf War illness, the Presidential Advisory Committee on Gulf War Veterans' Illnesses reported: "In the face of substantial, credible evidence to the contrary, DOD's consistent denials to June 1996 of the possibility of exposure of U.S. troops to chemical warfare agents cannot be justified." (Associated Press, "War illness panel blasts CIA, Pentagon," Austin American-Statesman, May 2, 1997, p. A2.) A later report by the General Accounting Office criticized that presidential committee for not going further. "It said Pentagon officials and the White House panel also were wrong to rule out the nerve gas sarin and other chemical weapons as a cause of the health problems because "there is substantial evidence that such compounds are associated with delayed or long-term health effects similar to those experienced by Gulf War veterans.'" (Philip Shenon [The New York Times], "Study links chemicals to Gulf War illnesses," Austin American-Statesman, Jun. 15, 1997, p. A6.)

183. Jerry Ceppos, "Epilogue: To readers of our `Dark Alliance' series" ("Dark Alliance: The Story Behind the Crack Explosion," San Jose Mercury News Internet Web site, http://www.sjmercury.com/drugs/postscriptstart.htm, May 18, 1997). "This Week With David Brinkley," ABC News, Sept. 22, 1996, May 18, 1997.

184. l Brumley, "Mourning men / Stern's buddies lament his final days in Dallas," The Dallas Morning News (online edition, dallasnews.com/arts-nf/over1-073.htm, Jul. 24, 1997).

185. Michele Kay, "Dismissed employee loses suit against Sharp, Whitehead," Austin American-Statesman, Oct. 17, 1997, pp. B1, B7. Coauthor Richard Bartholomew, a 20-year friend of Bright, personally observed the Oct. 14-16, 1997 trial and its background, and noted his observations in this text the day after the trial ended. "A Few Minutes with Andy Rooney," 60 Minutes, CBS-News, August 3, 1997.

THE GUN THAT DIDN'T SMOKE
PART 4

[Written with the late Walter F. Graf]

Two spies who were experts at keeping the biggest of government secrets were Warren Commissioner Allen Dulles and his CIA colleague, Richard Helms. Helms was the liaison between the CIA and the Warren Commission. Like his fellow OSS officers, William Colby and William Casey, Helms eventually succeeded Dulles as CIA director. Long before the Kennedy assassination, on June 6th, 1944, future JFK-assassination investigators Dulles and Helms learned that the biggest of secrets can be kept secure among the largest of groups. D-Day, the largest, most complex overt/covert operation ever known, is perhaps the best example of a successful, large, undisputed conspiracy. Over 5,000 ships landed 90,000 British, American and Canadian troops in Normandy. Around 20,000 more began landing silently by parachute and glider the night before. The planning had been under way since December, 1941. *Yet it was a successful surprise attack.* The exact time and place was known to, and kept completely secret by as many as fifty men. They struck an enemy weakened "under the combined weight of blockade, bombing, subversive activities, and propaganda."[186]

Dulles knew how to apply that example to smaller operations.

Through events that preceded and followed D-Day, Dulles became something of an expert in the secrets, successes and failures of high-level assassination conspiracies. One of the worst intra-Allied conflicts of the war was conveniently resolved when Admiral Jean Darlan, the very anti-communist, pro-Nazi, key figure in Vichy France, was assassinated allegedly by a rightist. The plotters made sure the assassination would be blamed on someone who was apparently on the same side of the political spectrum as his victim. That is not the only similarity between Darlan's and JFK's assassinations. The conspiracy behind that December 24, 1942, assassination remains a mystery to this day. However, it is known that an OSS officer was in contact with the plotters and was believed to have supplied the weapon. The man who replaced Darlan, General Henri Giraud, was principally sponsored politically and financially in Western circles by Allen Dulles.

Seven months earlier, Dulles was likely paying close attention to Operation Anthropoid: the assassination of Prague SS chief Reinhard Heydrich. That conspiracy had multiple similarities to the JFK assassination. They include: 1) a motorcade attack at a hairpin turn; 2) signals; 3) an open, virtually stopped vehicle; 4) two attacks, five seconds apart, the first inconclusive; and 5) "passers-by" directing the crowd in its confusion. And, as in Dallas, there were unanticipated mistakes in Prague.

As Alan Burgess wrote in his 1960 book, *Seven Men at Daybreak*, "The vital operational point was Heydrich's open car had to slow up here to negotiate the near-hairpin corner, and for perhaps five seconds it would provide an easy slow-moving target." And a report from the Special Operations Executive branch of the British Secret Intelligence Service reads: "The special training in the UK was based on a plan that the attack on Heydrich should be made when he was traveling by car from where he lived to his office in Prague or to any known appointment and that it must be carried out at a corner where the car would have to slow down." It is a chilling realization that one or both of those two sources were available to Kennedy's assassins during their own planning.

In fact, the other Twentieth Century assassination conspiracies involving attacks on motor vehicles, all of which would have been of interest to Dulles, had stark similarities to the Heydrich and Kennedy assassinations: the two, same-day attempts on Archduke Ferdinand (June, 1914); the assassination of Dominican Republic President Rafael Trujillo (May, 1961); and the attempt on French President Charles de Gaulle (August, 1962). Of primary interest is the fact that these assassinations were successful when the vehicle was brought to a virtual halt and unsuccessful when it was accelerated. There was no exception to this rule. The lesson to be derived by security planners is that it is not a good idea to slow or stop the vehicle in the face of an assassin. The lesson to be derived by assassination planners, however, is the opposite.[187] And Allen Dulles did have direct experience in the unsavory art assassination planning.

In his book, *Heisenburg's War*, Thomas Powers wrote about Werner Karl Heisenburg, Germany's top nuclear physicist. The OSS was nervous about Germany's atomic bomb research. Allen Dulles was the director of an OSS assassination plot against Heisenburg in the fall of 1944 -- using former major league baseball player Morris Berg as the designated assassin. It is in the context of this conspiracy that we read the only mention of OSS officer William Casey in Powers' book. Casey and Berg met to discuss that plot the night before Berg departed Britain for his abortive assassination mission in Germany. Casey, then involved in running agents into Germany, later became the CIA Director who was stricken with a seizure the day before he was to testify to the Senate about the Iran-Contra scandal. Finally, just months before directing the Heisenburg plot, Dulles had been involved in the 20th-of-July plot to assassinate Hitler. That attempt was a failure not because of the large number of conspirators, but because of an ineffective bomb. In fact, even in failure, some of its plotters and their secrets escaped detection.[188]

Those assassination plots are all examples of how, despite careful planning, anything can happen in a military-style operation. Anticipating D-Day, Field Marshal Erwin Rommel said to his aide, "Believe me, Lang, the first twenty-four hours of the invasion will be decisive...the fate of Germany depends on the outcome...for the Allies, as well as Germany, it will be the longest day."[189] And so it was from November 22nd to 23rd, 1963: in the first twenty-four hours, due to a misunderstanding about their "throwdown" gun which necessitated a hasty cover-up, the conspirators lost. They won a long battle by concealing their defeat, but they have lost the war because their worst errors on that longest day in Dallas could only be hidden for thirty years.

Third, so what? When quickly asked, this question is the most clever and effective counterargument in the conspiracy denier's arsenal: a delay tactic known as the "so what" defense. Conspiracy realists know this tactic well. Since few conspiracy realists have time to tutor deniers through their first thousand "so whats," it gives the deniers' pseudo-certainty the greatest longevity. Even after all arguments against the conspiracy have been overwhelmed, this question can still be asked in the sense: "Who cares?" We will therefore summarize the reality of our arguments, and conclude with historical examples of the consequences of not caring about right and wrong.

As with the clip, it does not matter if the Mauser was there or not. The CIA's "Mauser" report of November 25, 1963, and the silence surrounding the CIA-translated S.I.F.A.R. report of November 28, 1963, are proof that if there was no Mauser, it was not Weitzman's imagination belatedly supported by Craig's coerced embellishments, it was a high-level attempt to create the illusion of a Mauser. Such an illusion is necessary to avoid questions about a missing (or stuck) ammunition clip and the unique way it is ejected. Whether there was a clip or a Mauser or neither or both, Oswald was framed. Because in a lone-assassin scenario in which a Mauser and a Mannlicher-Carcano clip are documented in this way, you cannot have either, neither or both.

At bottom the issue is: for over thirty years the subject of the clip was treated with either silence, or, when the subject did surface it was treated in a tortured, painful manner. It should be a simple, routine matter. It is the thirty-plus years of bizarre and implausible explanations for why the clip was "stuck" and why the rifle was called a Mauser that give away the conspiracy by exposing the single most grievous error the conspirators made: not being familiar enough with the load-fire-reload cycle of the lesser known of the only two WWII clip systems in military use during their adult lives.

On one side is the claim that the Mauser and its charger are easily confused with the Carcano and its clip. On the other, the fact that the Carcano's clip is virtually the same as the M-1 Garand's, unique in its similarity and sole difference, and routinely confused.

The former, a spin of false innocence on the conspirators' biggest mistake, is like a classic Hitlerian Big Lie: psychological confabulation repeated ad nauseam by the firearms experts and trumpeted, when necessary, by government and media "public servants." The latter, the source of the conspirators' biggest mistake, is the truth: empirical evidence that explains all of the rifle-related facts, desperately avoided by those same firearms experts and public servants.

The more important expertise exhibited by such bureaucrats -- obtuseness and a cavalier attitude toward the public -- is nothing new. It can be learned from Hitler's autobiography, *Mein Kampf*: "Just as a hundred fools do not make one wise man, an heroic decision is not likely to come from a hundred cowards....All propaganda has to be popular and has to adapt its spiritual level to the perception of the least intelligent of those towards whom it intends to direct itself." (vol. I, chs. 3, 6) Nazi Germany was utterly defeated. The same does not hold true for its ideas and the effects of those ideas.

One of the biggest lies of those who desperately try to convince the public and/or themselves that the JFK murder conspiracy is a crazy notion is the one that says we are psychologically driven to invent fantastic conspiracy schemes because we cannot accept the deaths, by less significant circumstances, of our most powerful, popular leaders. The National Commission on the Causes and Prevention of Violence, appointed by LBJ after the names James Earl Ray and Sirhan Sirhan became household words, declared that doubts about lone gunmen are "a product of the primal anxieties created by the archetypal crime of parricide -- not the inadequacy of the evidence of the lone assassin." Three decades later, National Public Radio (NPR) news anchor Robert Segal retold this big lie in the form of sound bites from three writers and scholars: Columnist Robert Wilson said conspiracies are popular because people lack the education in common scientific disciplines to understand what is happening in the world today. Unintentionally undermining

Wilson's elitist view, NPR relied on a sociologist to supply the grotesque simplicity that there are no conspiracies, only people with good intentions who do bad things. Similarly, Chris Carter, producer of the popular dramatic television series, "The X-Files" (which tapped into insecurities at the end of the millennium, according to NPR), said "Confusion and failure...are things that ordinary people are sadly capable of." NPR's intended message was twofold: if we judge something a conspiracy, we are ignorant. And what we perceive as conspiracies are merely common mistakes.[190]

Whatever variation is used, the big lie of mass public retardation is another argument intended for the naive. If Americans are so emotionally and intellectually dependent on conspiratorial explanations for our leaders' questionable deaths, political and physical, we should now be inundated with national discussions about the personal tragedies, illnesses, woundings, and deaths of no less than Presidents Andrew Jackson, William Harrison, Zachary Taylor, Millard Fillmore, Abraham Lincoln, Andrew Johnson, Benjamin Harrison, Grover Cleveland, James Garfield, William McKinley, Theodore Roosevelt, Woodrow Wilson, Warren Harding, Franklin Roosevelt, John Kennedy and Lyndon Johnson (and, indeed, the famous attempts on Harry Truman and Gerald Ford).

But we are neither obsessed nor preoccupied with the misfortunes of all of those men. The problem of President Kennedy's murder is not with the psychology of the American people. The problem is with the evidence. The evidence is incongruous. Controversy and cognitive dissonance surround the subject because of 1) the reasonable conspiracy explanation, and 2) the continuing history of unreasonable dispute of that explanation.

Most Americans have, from the beginning, believed that a conspiracy was behind John F. Kennedy's murder. We are correct. Most, but not all, of that majority have also always believed that they will never really be certain in that belief. And they believe that nothing can be done to overcome that uncertainty. We all recognize that such a state of affairs is neither righteous, good, proper, nor preferable. But that pessimistic majority has resigned itself to a "reality" of hopelessness. They think they are rationally recognizing right and reality. Can they admit they are wrong? If not, the answer to Francis Scott Key's question at the end of our national anthem must be: no. Because the land of the free can only be the home of the brave.

In his book, *The Last Investigation,* HSCA investigator Gaeton Fonzi quoted his friend, Brookline, Massachusetts psychiatrist Dr. E. Martin Schotz, who made that very point: "He wrote:

`It is so important to understand that one of the primary means of immobilizing the American people politically today is to hold them in a state of confusion in which anything can be believed but nothing can be known, nothing of significance that is.

"And the American people are more than willing to be held in this state because to KNOW the truth -- as opposed to only BELIEVE the truth -- is to face an awful terror and to be no longer able to evade responsibility. It is precisely in moving from belief to knowledge that the citizen moves from irresponsibility to responsibility, from helplessness and hopelessness to action, with the ultimate aim of being empowered and confident in one's rational powers.'"[191]

Soon after Kennedy's assassination, Texas historian J. Evetts Haley, wrote that "no...prefabricated image of dynamic leadership...can substitute for a diet of truth -- for honest news....On the contrary, healthy, moral people, even when denied the facts of national life -- the truth essential to their survival -- intuitively sense that something is wrong....their confusion leads to suspicion, suspicion to distrust, and distrust to national disunity....confidence between government and governed is destroyed by mutual fear....Nor can it be cured...by any false front. The shallow deprecation of 'hate' as the cause of national tragedy; the vilification of patriots as 'extremists'...are dishonest resorts which exacerbate instead of healing the malady. Such fear cannot be banished by propaganda. It can only be restored by principle; principle based on moral character."

Ten weeks before his murder, President Kennedy pointed to progress in desegregation as an example of how such fear can be overcome: "The task was not easy....Nevertheless, as we have seen, what prevailed in these cities through the South finally was not emotion but respect for law. The courage and responsibility of those community leaders in those places provide a meaningful lesson not only for the children in those cities but for the children all over the country."[192]

Little did Kennedy know how severely tested our courage and sense of responsibility would soon be, or how badly we would fail that test, or that we would continue to fail it badly for decades to come. Perhaps those decades of disrespect for law and responsibility by cowardly leaders have so blinded most people to propriety that they ask without a qualm: "Why should I care about JFK's antiquated murder?" Instead of answering such questions, government and media leaders have encouraged apathy from the beginning.[193] Ultimately, the answer is: because murder is a crime. To ignore any murder or unduly limit the punishment of any murderer is to decriminalize the worst crime, and, by extension, all crime.

Rephrasing a famous Kennedy speech helps clarify the problem: We preach the rule of law around the world, and we use force to show we mean it, and we declare ourselves tough on crime at home; but are we to say to the world and, much more importantly, to each other that murder is wrong except for those like President Kennedy's; that all citizens have equal protection under the law except from murders like President Kennedy's; that we will not tolerate terrorist acts, government cover-ups or assassination conspiracies except for those like the one against President Kennedy? If we as Americans, because of threats of death, cannot choose our public representatives, cannot expect them to act in our best interest, cannot encourage our children to lead, if, in short, we cannot govern ourselves without fear of our own personal safety, then who among us would be content to be a responsible citizen and stand against that threat? Indeed, who has been?

Our fear, bigotry and apathy have delayed other truths. It took thirty years, and the courage and dedication of a principled few, to say with finality the simple words: "Medgar Evers was assassinated by Byron de la Beckwith." That murder teaches us that we can finish the sentence: "John F. Kennedy was assassinated by...." The choice Kennedy gave Americans the night of Medgar Evers' murder says it best: "Those who do nothing are inviting shame as well as violence. Those who act boldly are recognizing right as well as reality."[194]

Faced with the truth of conspiracy behind the JFK assassination, however, those most capable of recognizing right and reality can still be susceptible to the very bigotry they decry in others. Emory University Holocaust scholar Deborah Lipstadt, in her otherwise excellent book, *Denying the Holocaust*, wrote:

> While there is reason to question some of the
> conclusions of the Warren Commission, the theories
> regarding the killing that have increasingly gained
> acceptance border on the irrational. Notions of a
> conspiracy within the highest echelons of American
> government are readily accepted as plausible. According
> to Oliver Stone's 1991 movie *JFK*, a *coup d'état* was
> under way in the United States, with the collusion of the
> vice president, Joint Chiefs of Staff, chief justice of the

United States, FBI, CIA, members of Congress, and the
Mafia. Stone's film imposed a neat coherence on a mass
of confusing information, providing a self-contained
explanation for what still seemed to be an unbelievable
event. Many reviewers and moviegoers alike pondered
these charges with great seriousness....
...In these instances, history is rewritten for political ends
and scientific historiography is replaced, in the words of
Henry Louis Gates, Jr., professor of Afro-American
studies at Harvard, with "ideological conformity."
Scholars who might once have dismissed these
outlandish views feel compelled to treat them as having
some validity.

   These attacks on history and knowledge have the
potential to alter dramatically the way established truth
is transmitted from generation to generation. Ultimately
the climate they create is of no less importance than the
specific truth they attack--be it the Holocaust or the
assassination of President Kennedy. It is a climate that
fosters deconstructionist history at its worst. No fact, no
event, and no aspect of history has any fixed meaning or
content. Any truth can be retold. Any fact can be recast.
There is no ultimate historical reality.[195]

Dr. Lipstadt fails to understand that reasonably questioning the Warren
Commission leads most plausibly to the theory of collusion of the vice
president, at least one of the Joint Chiefs, the chief justice of the United
States, leaders and agents of the FBI and CIA, members of Congress, and
Mafia figures in JFK's murder. Where is the plausibility, never mind the
scientific historiography, in Dr. Lipstadt's implied warning that
investigating an imaginary, high-level conspiracy is a greater travesty
than ignoring any kind of real one? Oliver Stone helped influence
Congress to pass a landmark disclosure law that benefits history,
knowledge and truth. Gerald Ford, the last surviving Warren
Commissioner, was the first and only unelected president of the United
States, a president who used his pardoning power to spare Richard Nixon
from criminal prosecution, and more importantly, from further
investigation. Between Stone's *JFK* and Ford's Warren Report, only one
of them can be plausibly accused of replacing historiography with
ideological conformity for political ends. Without any stretch of the
imagination, Ford's Warren Report is the one.[196]
   Why does Dr. Lipstadt seriously ponder imagined similarities

between Oliver Stone and Holocaust deniers, but not real ones between Gerald Ford and Holocaust deniers? The ultimate historical reality of the assassination, obvious to a large majority of rational Americans long before we pondered it as "moviegoers," has been the irrational, outlandish, unacceptable, implausible, self-contained notion that the evidence of conspiracy -- evidence which even the Warren Commission admitted exists -- is not credible.[197]

That is the ideological rewriting of history that has already attacked knowledge and dramatically altered the way truth is established from generation to generation. It is the pragmatic cleaning of Augean stables -- not neurosis or psychosis -- that has kept us, in the words of Garry Wills and Ovid Demaris, "Returning to the mystery over and over, trying to `solve' it, to limit, to dispel it, poring over the volumes of clues, all the odd things that `do not fit' (not yet -- the assumption is they will fit if we only arrange them better), pinning hopes on a new book, on better photographic sleuthing, more debate, examination, science, reason...to find a simple, clear, demonstrable explanation...which can be traced with the weapons of reason, identified, pointed to, disposed of."[198] The arrangement of the facts which we have presented in this article, which does fit, is one such explanation.

If there is any doubt that such a clear and demonstrable conspiracy presents a clear and present danger, the words of Holocaust survivor Joseph Wilf dispel that doubt. Wilf was honored with the 1996 Israel Bonds Elie Wiesel Holocaust Remembrance Award, called the Crying Violin Award. In the speech he gave at his award dinner, Wilf outlined the rationalizations of the "consolers" who attempt to "reassure us" and "assuage our fear" of another government conspiracy like the Holocaust.

And yet we know that the hardest thing to predict in the 20th century is the past. Ideologues, armed to the teeth, are studiously at work rewriting history. Words foreshadow actions as lightning does thunder. When Holocaust deniers spread their venom, we survivors find ourselves again directly in the crosshairs of danger. In the 1930s, the West slumbered before the scourge. Today we must not be caught napping, even if the danger is yet relatively small. And we must stand guard against the slippery compromises that academic charlatans, clamoring to be heard, can lead an unsuspecting public to.

Survivors, as all people of conscience, must expose falsehood, catch the cunning in their craftiness. We, who have walked through the valley of death, must not be hoodwinked into silence and hurried into oblivion. We have learned the most desolate lessons that history has to offer, so horrific as to be beyond uttering. Yet we are commanded by the call of memory to speak out loudly and clearly. Not only do we owe it to ourselves, but far more importantly, we owe it to the millions of dead who can have no rest as long as the truth goes brazenly denied.[199]

But is historiographically sufficient proof of a large, high-level conspiracy behind the JFK assassination enough to overcome the "ideological conformity" that makes even Dr. Lipstadt a conspiracy denier? The opinions of Harvard-educated journalist David Plotz, Washington Bureau Chief of the on-line Slate Magazine, indicate that a new generation of journalists are no less susceptible to the big lie than previous generations. Appearing on the C-SPAN cable network, Plotz referred to Dexter King's belief in James Earl Ray's innocence, implying that King was gullible. Plotz was making the point that there is an "incredible willingness" in this country to believe things that do not exist. Yet, just before his derision of King, Plotz derided the media for its bias against the Internet in the aftermath of the "Heaven's Gate" mass suicide in Rancho Santa Fe, California.

As a writer for an Internet-based publication, Plotz was aware of how ignorance contributes to media bias against the Internet. But he cannot see how his own ignorance contributes to his own bias against investigating real assassination conspiracies. The most dangerous willingness to believe in things that do not exist is the continued, incredible willingness of journalists like Plotz to believe in the sole guilt of Ray, Sirhan and Oswald.[200]

As writer Paul William Roberts observed:

> Even George Orwell misread Adolf Hitler's intentions in his review of *Mein Kampf* for the Times Literary Supplement in 1940: `I should like to put it on record that I have never been able to dislike Hitler...The fact is that there is something deeply appealing about him...It is a pathetic, dog-like face, the face of a man suffering under intolerable wrongs...He is the martyr, the victim, Prometheus chained to the rock, the self-sacrificing hero who fights single-handed against impossible odds...One feels, as with Napoleon, that he is fighting against destiny, that he can't win, and yet that he somehow deserves to.'
> This is salutary reading, not -- I should add -- because it makes a fool of a leftist icon, but because it makes a fool of anyone who imagines he has a foolproof ability to detect those cracks through which the night gets in.

In the aftermath of the Kennedy assassination, Roberts' point about journalist Orwell is destined to become a stinging and lasting indictment of most reporters. In the words of another journalist -- trailblazing press critic George Seldes -- most reporters "know from contact with the great minds of the press lords or from the simple deduction that the bosses are in big business and the news must be slanted accordingly, or from the general intangible atmosphere which prevails everywhere, what they can do and what they must never do." Thus Roberts echoes Seldes point that "The most stupid boast in the history of present-day journalism is that of the writer who says, 'I have never been given orders; I am free to do as I like.'"[201]

Do Lipstadt and Plotz live in such a fool's paradise, populated by "academic charlatans" who, like they, are on record with their inability to see today's worst threats to domestic and world tranquility, and their inability to dislike today's true fascists? If not, then perhaps to face honestly the conspiracy that killed JFK is more terrifying than facing the Holocaust. Perhaps even Holocaust scholars like Dr. Lipstadt, and highly educated journalists like Plotz can forget the dangers in believing comforting lies.

Will they, like Orwell before them, be able to overcome their denial and write more truthfully about their times? Or are they, like President Bush, merely faking blindness? It has been proved that Bush's claim of faith in the Warren Commission's minority opinion, and his alleged memory lapse about his activities the day of the shooting, represent at best, a creative relationship with the truth.[202]

If scholars and journalists are truly blind to that which is obvious to most Americans, they need only take a wider meaning from the words of Nobel Peace Prize laureate and Nazi death camp survivor Elie Wiesel when he spoke about the Holocaust Museum -- a memorial which Dr. Lipstadt helps oversee: "To me it's very simple," he said, "If a person goes to the Washington museum and leaves saying, 'Now I don't know -- I have to learn about it,' then it's a success. If the person leaves and says, 'Now I know,' then it's a failure." Or, as Kennedy himself would have said in his undelivered speech in Dallas: "...leadership and learning are indispensable to each other."[203]

History warns us that the Nazis were democratically elected (complete with a minority of the vote and a February "October Surprise"); and history warns that Nazi Germany was a nation of judges, jurors and laws -- laws that decriminalized the murder of its "undesirable" citizens. The history of the JFK assassination warns us that the problem is not an ideological interpretation of the evidence by the American people, the problem is the ideological interpretation of the evidence by our most powerful government representatives and journalists; and, as with Germans under Nazism, the apparent cowardice of most Americans to resist that prevailing ideology.

During the fall of 1996, coauthor Richard Bartholomew guest-lectured for six weeks on the JFK assassination at a high school. On their mid-term exams, the senior honors history students were asked to discuss the controversies of the subject and their own feelings about it. All of the students recognized the reality of the conspiracy, and they all displayed a command of the evidence proving it and its continuing cover-up.

The most thoughtful of the students went beyond the evidence and struggled with their consciences. One wrote that he had learned more than he cared to know. He rationalized his preference for ignorance with two arguments: 1) that the assassination is past and should be left as such; and 2) that "all the truth in the world will not bring JFK back." Both arguments are common. The first is a disregard for history. To believe it is to fail to understand that much of what directly effects our lives was decided before we were born. To remain ignorant or indifferent about what happened before we were born is to remain forever a child. The second argument fails with a simple counterpoint: if resurrecting the dead was the justification for finding the truth, we would live in a world of lawlessness. Other students, in an example of the ineffectiveness of the Pledge of Allegiance, espoused a less egalitarian use of their knowledge. They advocated continuing the coverup because, as one said, "the truth will lead to anarchy." That is another common misconception. Such reasoning ignores the fact that anarchy is the absence of law, that a continued coverup ignores laws against murder, and that the truth will, therefore, prevent further anarchy.

James Baldwin, author of *The Fire Next Time* (1963), on racial oppression, succinctly explained the causal relationship between right and reality. He once wrote that many who live with complicity in the destruction of other human beings "do not know it and do not want to know it." He added: "But it is not permissible that the authors of devastation should also be innocent. It is the innocence which constitutes the crime."[204]

Doctrinaire rejection of this explanation of the facts surrounding the JFK "murder weapon," as sufficient proof of the clear and present danger of a conspiracy within the United States government, risks repeating the grave error of Holocaust deniers who, in the years preceding liberation of the death camps of Nazi Germany, indolently awaited too-absolute proof of that huge government conspiracy with its thousands of living witnesses, participants, documents, and millions of victims, known as the Final Solution. History and morality thus demand that we overcome the kind of "ideological conformity" that makes Dr. Lipstadt an authority on a past, enormous, high-level, foreign government conspiracy, yet unable to apply her expertise here and now. History tells us that the way to recognize right and reality is by learning everything we can about the conspiracy, and by speaking out loudly and clearly "against the slippery compromises that academic charlatans, clamoring to be heard, can lead an unsuspecting public to." History also predicts the consequences of failing to heed its warnings.

The ultimate proof of Germany's conspiracy was exacted at the cost of a long, bloody war. Starting on June 1st, 1944, the first half of a code message, comprised from the first two lines of a nineteenth-century French poem, was broadcast by the BBC to the French resistance: *"Les sanglots longs des violons de l'automne* [The long sobs of the violins of autumn]." At 10 p.m., June 5th, on orders from General Pierre Koenig, commander of Allied clandestine operations, the last half of the message was broadcast: *"Blessent mon coeur d'une languer monotone* [Wound my heart with a monotonous languor]." It meant that D-Day, the Allied invasion of Europe, the culmination of a huge conspiracy, the time and place of which had been kept totally secret by as many as fifty men, had begun. The tedious, uniform, unvarying inaction against Germany's evil conspiracy had finally ended.[205]

The history of that evil government conspiracy must not be allowed to repeat itself. The monotonous languor and banality of evil that began anew in Dallas on that longest day in the autumn of 1963 must now end. As with pre-liberation evidence of the Holocaust, or even as with modern scientific evidence for extraterrestrial life, the evidence for the conspiracy behind the assassination of John F. Kennedy is more than sufficient to justify and compel action.[206] The promise -- "Never again!"-- made to the victims of the Holocaust must be kept. Maximum resistance is essential. Failure is not an option.

The irreconcilable clip paradox and the impossible Mauser claim have long been the weakest links in the cover-up conspiracy chain. That insidious, heinous chain is now forever broken. As with the issue of conspiracy, there has been no reason to deny who is behind it. Smoking guns await public disclosure on that question too. Issues will arise -- issues we have not now anticipated. But we can now be a united people in that endeavor. "For in the final analysis," concluded Simon Wiesenthal, "the future will be determined not by how many Nazis there will be -- or fascists or extreme nationalists or white supremacists -- but how many anti-Nazis, people of goodwill, there will be to confront them."[207]

* * *

Notes:

186. Anthony Cave Brown, *The Last Hero: Wild Bill Donovan* (New York: Vintage Books, 1982) pp. 201-202, 526; hereafter cited as Brown 201-202, 526. As with Dulles, Colby and Casey, Helms' entire career at the CIA was permeated by his involvement in the most illegal acts of that secret agency, including assassinations. It is reportedly the conclusion of the Cuban government that Helms was the ultimate author of the plot behind JFK's assassination. On Mar. 30, 1997, Helms turned 84. He can be subpoenaed under ARCA. (Powers 378-79. Claudia Furiati, *ZR Rifle: The Plot to Kill Kennedy and Castro* [Melbourne, Australia: Ocean Press, 1994] p. 135.)

187. Christopher Simpson, *The Splendid Blond Beast*, (New York: Grove Press, 1993) pp. 120-21; hereafter cited as Simpson 120-21. Brown 265-73. Stephen J. Rivele, "The CIA, Assassination, and Nixon," published in Eric Hamburg, editor, *Nixon: An Oliver Stone Film,* (New York: Hyperion, 1995) p. 27 (Darlan Affair). Jan Wiener, *The Assassination of Heydrich* (New York: Grossman, 1969) pp. 86-90. Alan Burgess, *Seven Men at Daybreak*, (London: Evans Brothers Ltd., 1960) p. 142 ("near-hairpin corner"). Callum MacDonald, The Killing of SS Obergruppenführer Reinhard Heydrich, (New York: The Free Press, 1989) p. 124 (SIS-SOE report). Letter from Walter Graf to Richard Bartholomew, Nov. 2, 1993 (stopped vehicle lessons). Rumors existed that General Karl Wolff, head of the SS in Italy, was somehow behind Heydrich's murder. Wolff had the right connections and, like many of Heydrich's Nazi associates, was "in trouble." Dulles' OSS colleague and mistress, Mary Bancroft, reported to Dulles that she had asked the question of Nazi intelligence official and Hitler assassination plotter Hans Bernd Gisevius: "Did Wolff kill Heydrich?" Bancroft also revealed that while Dulles was negotiating the German mass surrender in Italy, Wolff had a friendly visit with him at his Zurich apartment. Given Bancroft's subtle, yet startling, revelations about Hans Gisevius and Ruth Paine (see below), was she trying to tell us something about a connection between Dulles, the Heydrich assassination and the JFK assassination? (*Mary Bancroft, Autobiography of a Spy* [New York: William Morrow, 1983] pp. 193, 289; hereafter cited as Bancroft 193, 289. Letters from Walter Graf to Richard Bartholomew, Jul. 13, and Aug. 2, 1993, and Mar. 3, 1997).

188. Thomas Powers, *Heisenberg's War: The History of the German Bomb*, (New York: Knopf, 1993) pp. 385-86, 388, 392. Casey, OSS chief of intelligence for the European Theater and Republican strategist since 1940, became Nixon's SEC chairman and managed Ronald Reagan's campaign in 1980. One of Casey's business partners, Carl Biehl, had been working with the criminal underworld since the early 1950s, including the Carlos Marcello crime family in New Orleans, members of which are suspected of involvement in JFK's murder. Casey's presidential campaign assistant, Max Hugel, was an executive vice-president of a company that had a consultancy contract with mobster Moe Dalitz and his Las Vegas casinos. JFK assassination suspect

Eugene Hale Brading was a charter member of Dalitz's Rancho La Costa Country Club in Rancho Santa Fe, California. The HSCA noted that the Kennedy-hating Jimmy Hoffa and other Teamsters used that club as a national mob meeting place during Kennedy's presidency. Hugel, who had known Casey for twenty years and was in charge of organizing "ethnic, nationalities," and other voting groups for Reagan, became one of Casey's deputy directors of covert operations at CIA. Another Casey protégé, Duane "Dewey Maroni" Clarridge, became Casey's division chief for Latin America who commissioned the CIA's illegal assassination manual for the Contras. (Ronnie Dugger, *On Reagan: The Man & His Presidency*, [New York:McGraw-Hill, 1983] pp. 32-33. Dan E. Moldea, *Dark Victory: Ronald Reagan, MCA, and the Mob*, [New York: Penguin, 1986, 1987] pp. 294-96. HSCA, The Final Assassinations Report, [New York: Bantam, 1979] p. 20; hereafter cited as HR 20. National Security Archive, *The Chronology: The Documented Day-by-Day Account of the Secret Military Assistance to Iran and the Contras*, [New York: Warner, 1987] pp. 8, 37, 74. Peter Dale Scott and Jonathan Marshall, *Cocaine Politics: Drugs, Armies, and the CIA in Central America*, [Berkeley, Calif.: University of California Press, 1991] p. 128. For more on Moe Dalitz and Jimmy Hoffa links to the assassination, see Evica 220, 227 30, 235 36, 244, 260 61, 276, 281, 318; and HR 217-24.) Dulles' informant within the Hitler assassination conspiracy was Hans Bernd Gisevius, one of its rare, high-level survivors. In later years, with substantial help from his friend Dulles, assassination plotter Gisevius traveled to Washington D.C., then to Texas where he became employed at Dresser Industries, the Dallas-based oil equipment company. Dulles and Gisevius were assisted in the Hitler plot by Dulles' wartime mistress, Mary Bancroft, who was Ruth Forbes Paine's close friend. Paine's son, Michael, became involved in the JFK assassination due largely to his 1963 housemate, Volkmar Schmidt. Oswald's CIA friend, George de Mohrenschildt, had introduced Oswald to Schmidt who, in turn, arranged for Oswald to meet Michael Paine and his wife, Ruth Hyde Paine. The latter Ruth Paine helped arrange Oswald's fateful employment at the TSBD. Before coming to the U.S. in the fall of 1961, Schmidt had lived in Germany. There, Schmidt had lived with and studied under another rare 20th-of-July-plot survivor, Wilhelm Kuetemeyer. From 1958 to 1967, master spy and assassination plotter Bancroft (by then the mistress of Life magazine publisher Henry Luce), "worked with JFK and RFK on campaigns and corresponded with them." Ms. Bancroft, 93, died in New York City on Jan. 10, 1997, having never been subpoenaed under ARCA (Bancroft 54, 128-31, 290. Leonard Mosley, *Dulles* [New York: Dial, 1978] pp. 247-48. Burton Hersh, *The Old Boys: The American Elite and the Origins of the CIA* [New York: Scribner's Sons, 1992] p. 367. Bruce Campbell Adamson, *Oswald's Closest Friend: The George DeMohrenschildt Story*, vol. I: "1,000 Points of Light (Public Remains in the Dark)" [unpublished manuscript, 1993 (Aptos, Calif.: self published, 1995)], p. 31; cited hereafter as Adamson, "1,000 Points of Light"; and *The JFK Assassination Timeline Chart* [Aptos, Calif.: self published, 1995] p. 80. Edward J. Epstein, *Legend: The Secret World of Lee Harvey Oswald* [New York: McGraw Hill, 1978] pp. 203-05, 213-14; hereafter cited as Epstein, Legend 203-05, 213-14. Gaeton Fonzi, *The Last Investigation* [New York: Thunder's Mouth Press, 1993] p. 419; hereafter cited as Fonzi 419. "Obituaries," New York Times, Jan. 12, 1997, p. 31; "Passages," Assassination Chronicles, Spring 1997, p. 49.). See also Bartholomew citation in note 166 above. For a history of Dresser's board of directors, which included powerful, wealthy, anti-Kennedy men, see Darwin Payne, Initiative in Energy: Dresser Industries, Inc. 1880-1978 (New York: Simon & Schuster, 1979) pp. 386-89.

189. Cornelius Ryan, *The Longest Day* (New York: Simon & Schuster, 1959) p. 8 [see also Ryan's screenplay and film adaptation of same title (Darryl F. Zanuck/20th Century Fox film production, 1962) 3 hrs]; hereafter cited as Ryan 8.

190. For an in-depth study of how pervasive ideas induced thousands of ordinary people to kill unarmed, defenseless men, women, and children by the thousands, systematically and without pity, see Daniel Jonah Goldhagen, Hitler's Willing Executioners: Ordinary Germans and the Holocaust, (New York: Alfred A. Knopf, 1996) 622 pages. For variations on the fallacious theme of mass public retardation, see: Jefferson Morley, "The Political Rorschach Test," Los Angeles Times, Dec. 8, 1991; reprinted in Stone and Sklar 231-34 (quote: 232). Andrew O'Hehir, "JFK: Tragedy into Farce," San Francisco Weekly, Dec. 18, 1991; reprinted in Stone and Sklar 269-73. George Will, "`JFK': Paranoid History," The Washington Post, Dec. 26, 1991, op-ed page. David Klinghoffer, "The Sum of All Fears," The Washington Times, Dec. 22, 1991; reprinted in Stone and Sklar 283-88. Daniel Patrick Moynihan, "The Paranoid Style," The Washington Post, Dec. 29, 1991; reprinted in Stone and Sklar 328-31. Michael Albert, "Conspiracy?...Not!," Z Magazine, Jan. 1992; reprinted in Stone and Sklar 358-64. Anthony Lewis, "JFK," The New York Times, Jan. 9, 1992; reprinted in Stone and Sklar 387-89. William Manchester, "No Evidence for a Conspiracy to Kill Kennedy," The New York Times, Feb. 5, 1992; reprinted in Stone and Sklar 451-52. Robert Segal, "Conspiracies and Coverups in Popular Culture," National Public Radio, Jun. 24, 1997, broadcast 6:53 to 6:59 p.m., CDT, on KUT, 90.5 FM, Austin, Texas.

191. Fonzi 410-11. See also Dr. E. Martin Schotz, *History Will Not Absolve Us: Orwellian control, public denial, and the murder of President Kennedy* (Brookline, Mass.: Kurtz, Ulmer and DeLucia, 1996) 326 pages.

192. J. Evetts Haley, *A Texan Looks At Lyndon: A Study In Illegitimate Power* (Canyon, Texas: Palo Duro Press, 1964) pp. 5-6. Long before the epithet "conspiracy buff," J. Edgar Hoover prejudged those who would not accept the Commission's findings as "...extremists who have very pronounced views, without any foundation for them, who will disagree violently with whatever findings the Commission makes." (5H 99) John F. Kennedy, "Southern Progress in School Desegregation," News Conference, Sept. 12, 1963, The Burden and the Glory, edited by Allan Nevins, (New York: Harper & Row, 1964) p. 185; hereafter cited as Kennedy 185.

193. Less than a month after it began in Nov. 1966, the New York Times ended its investigation of the President's murder. Assistant Managing Editor Harrison E. Salisbury explained that, "Nobody told us to stop. We just felt nobody cared."

(Rolling Stone Apr. 24, 1975) Belief in links between newsworthiness and public apathy, however, did not stop the Times from publishing in 1973, one of the early books attempting to declare victory on behalf of the Warren Commission. Its author was Commission Counsel David Belin. Salisbury who, in 1964, had authored the excessively complimentary introduction to the Warren Report's Times' edition, wrote a similarly biased introduction for Belin (Anson 139, 142, 153). Any remaining shred of credulity or sincerity left to the New York Times' investigation of the Kennedy Assassination vanished when it was revealed that their publisher, Arthur Hays Sulzberger, had cooperated with CIA Director (later Warren Commissioner) Dulles in spying on Mexico City correspondent Sydney Gruson, physically keeping him away from CIA operations and screening his articles "with a great deal more care than usual," because he "had a reputation with the CIA" for getting "in their hair." Journalist Tim Weiner, who reported those abuses 43 years after anyone could do anything about them, added that "Contacts between the CIA and the U.S. news media -- as well as far deeper relationships -- were common in the 1950s and 1960s and were reported thoroughly 20 years ago." Obviously, the thoroughness of reporting on both past and present CIA/media cooperation, is still severely inadequate. (Tim Weiner [New York Times Service], "Publisher complied with CIA," Austin American-Statesman, Jun. 7, 1997, p. A4.)
194. John F. Kennedy, "The Moral Issue of Equal Rights for All Colors," television address, June 11, 1963 (Kennedy 182, 183). Throughout his political career, Kennedy made similar statements which grow more haunting with each anniversary of his unsolved murder: "For, in a democracy, every citizen, regardless of his interest in politics, `holds office'; every one of us is in a position of responsibility; and, in the final analysis, the kind of government we get depends upon how we fulfill those responsibilities....A man does what he must -- in spite of personal consequences, in spite of obstacles and dangers and pressures -- and that is the basis of all human morality" (*Profiles in Courage* [New York: Harper & Brothers, 1956 / Pocket Books, 1957] p. 209). "The 1930s taught us a clear lesson: aggressive conduct, if allowed to grow unchecked and unchallenged, ultimately leads to war" ("Cuba Quarantined and Khrushchev Challenged," television address, Oct. 22, 1962 [Kennedy, 92]).
195. Deborah Lipstadt, *Denying the Holocaust* (New York: The Free Press, 1993) p. 19.
196. For evidence of Ford's obfuscation of key aspects of the Warren Report, see handwritten changes to the draft chapters of the final report that were recommended by Commission member Representative Gerald Ford, Personal Files of J. Lee Rankin, General Counsel of the Warren Commission, President John F. Kennedy Assassination Records Collection housed at the National Archives facility in College Park, Maryland; cited in George Lardner, Jr. (The Washington Post), "Ford sought changes in JFK assassination report," Austin American-Statesman, July 3, 1997, p. A8.
197. Paul B. Sheatsley and Jacob J. Feldman, *The Kennedy Assassination and the American Public*, National Opinion Research Center, Stanford University Press, 1965 (large majority). For sources of public opinion for the period Nov.

1963 through Feb. 1977, see: "Studies of Public Reactions," items 1673-1714, Guth and Wrone 174-77. On Sunday, Nov. 24, 1963, soon after Oswald had been shot, Gordon McClendon, owner of Dallas radio station KLIF, reported the following from Cleveland's Municipal Stadium, where 40,000 spectators were attending the Dallas Cowboys-Cleveland Browns football game: "People seem to think that the Dallas Police Department really had the wrong man, or that Oswald was being held for want of a better suspect...No one here that we've talked to -- taxi drivers, hotel employees, the various people we've had an opportunity to be around since we arrived here yesterday afternoon -- no one really thought that Oswald was the guilty party." ("The Fateful Hours: a Presentation of KLIF News in Dallas," Capitol Records, 1964; reissued on audiotape by KLIF, 1993.) For sources of public opinion just before and after the release of the Stone film, see: Kenneth Auchincloss, "Twisted History," Newsweek Dec. 23, 1991, p. 46, and Ted Gest and Joseph Shapiro, "JFK: The Untold Story of the Warren Commission," U.S. News & World Report Aug. 17, 1992, p. 29. R 374 ("no credible evidence").

198. Wills and Demaris 264.

199. Joseph Wilf, "On Holocaust Denial," The Jewish Outlook (Texas: Jewish Federation of Austin), Jan. 1997.

200. Richard Bartholomew's contemporaneous notes from "Washington Journal," with guest David Plotz (C-SPAN cable network, Mar. 29, 1997). The current state of media complacency and susceptibility to government control, seen during the U.S. invasion of Panama in 1989 and during the Persian Gulf War, was exhibited anew in the 1997 Republic of Texas standoff. Throughout the week-long siege, more than 100 reporters and photographers followed police orders to remain at a roadside rest stop about ten miles from where six members of the Republic of Texas separatist group were holed up and surrounded by Texas Rangers. Journalists could neither see nor hear what they were trying to report to the public. Press conferences by Texas officials dominated their reporting. Amy Gifford, coproducer with her husband Dan Gifford, of the documentary film "Waco: The Rules of Engagement," said "Rodney King can tell you, if there's no one there to see it, it didn't happen." "And the appearance that the government is hiding something is just as bad as hiding something," added Jess Walter, author of a book on the Ruby Ridge standoff, "Every Knee Shall Bow," a former reporter who covered the Ruby Ridge confrontation from a distance of about three miles. (Cara Tanamachi, "Critics say media should be closer to standoff," Austin American-Statesman, May 3, 1997, p. A8.)

201. Paul William Roberts, "Rage against the dying of the right" [critique of Robert H. Bork's Slouching Towards Gomorrah], The [Toronto] Globe and Mail, Nov. 16, 1996, p. D5. Norman Soloman, "Ignored Oscar Film [on George Seldes] Sets Inspiring Example," Liberal Opinion Week, Mar. 3, 1997, p. 7 (Creators Syndicate, Feb. 23, 1997). Orwell, like most people, could be fooled some of the time, but not all of the time. An essay in The Orwell Reader reveals that Orwell, had he lived to see it, might have had special insight into the JFK assassination. "Second Thoughts on James Burnham" discusses two books by the former-communist-turned-CIA-covert-action-pioneer, who eventually

became senior editor at William F. Buckley, Jr.'s National Review. E. Howard Hunt, the Watergate burglar with numerous ties to the JFK assassination, wrote in his memoirs, "I also met and frequently conferred with Dr. James Burnham, a Princeton classmate of Joe Bryan's and onetime professor of philosophy. Burnham was a consultant to OPC [Office of Policy Coordination, the first covert action group created within the CIA in 1948] on virtually every subject of interest to our organization. He had extensive contacts in Europe and, by virtue of his Trotskyite background, was something of an authority on domestic and foreign Communist parties and front organizations. Through him I was to meet a young Yale graduate, William F. Buckley, Jr...." Hunt recruited Buckley into the CIA and their first project together was opening the infamous Mexico City Station in 1950 (E. Howard Hunt, *Undercover: Memoirs of an American Secret Agent* [New York: Berkley, 1974] pp. 69-70. John B. Judis, *William F. Buckley, Jr.: Patron Saint of the Conservatives* [New York: Simon & Schuster, Touchstone ed., 1990] p. 80.). A decade earlier, in the name of strengthening communism, Burnham severely crippled the U.S. Trotskyite movement by almost single-handedly splitting it into rival factions in 1939. Burnham had shared leadership responsibilities in that movement with Michael Paine's United Fruit CIA connected father, George Lyman Paine, Jr. James P. Hosty, Jr., the FBI special agent investigating the Oswalds just before the assassination, has stated that George Paine phoned his son, Michael, from Los Angeles the night of the assassination and said, "'We all know who did this,' and told his son to be careful." If true, the Warren Commission's conflicting evidence about this phone call indicates that it was distancing George Paine's name from the one consistent fact in that evidence: the statement by the caller that someone other than Oswald was responsible for the assassination. (Epstein, *Legend* 205. Peter Dale Scott, Government Documents and the Kennedy Assassination, [self-published manuscript] ch. II, p. 4. James P. Hosty, Jr., *Assignment: Oswald* [New York: Arcade Publishing, 1996] p. 39; cited in Martha A. Moyer and R.F. Gallagher, "The Babysitters," The Fourth Decade, Sept. 1996, p. 3. See also note 188 above). After splitting the U.S. Trotskyites, the largest such organization in the world, Burnham then suddenly and mysteriously became anti-communist just in time for both assassination conspiracies against Leon Trotsky in Mexico City in 1940. The first attempt to kill Trotsky, in May, had strange links to the U.S. That conspiracy, along with the second attempt in August, which was successful, later became the focus of intense interest by JFK-assassination figures Isaac Don Levine, and Sylvia and Nathaniel Weyl (Albert Glotzer, *Trotsky* [Buffalo, New York: Prometheus, 1989] pp. 284-90. Isaac Don Levine, Mind of an Assassin [New York: Farrar, Staus and Cudahy, 1959/Signet, 1960] p. vi. Canfield and Weberman 105-06. Warren Commission Document 662 [FBI report of Mar. 5, 1964 on Nathaniel and Sylvia Weyl, John Martino, Victor Lasky and Frank Meyer]. Scott 55, 288, 289). If Burnham consulted the OPC on virtually every aspect of its operations, one aspect could have been assassinations, begun by the OSS in Algiers as early as 1942. Judging from Orwell's quotations from the two Burnham books, written in 1940 and 1942, Burnham predicted today's U.S. economy, politics and geopolitics with astonishing accuracy; as did Orwell's classic novel, 1984, begun soon after his Burnham essay (*The Orwell Reader* [New York: Harcourt, Brace, Jovanovich, 1956] pp. 335-54).

202. David Armstrong, [3-part, investigative report on George Bush] The Austin Chronicle, part 1: "Where Was George? The Answer is Blowin' in the Wind," Dec. 27, 1991, pp. 12-14; hereafter cited as Armstrong. John B. Jovich, ed., Reflections on JFK's Assassination: 250 Famous Americans Remember November 22, 1963 (Woodbine House, 1988) p. 135. David Robb, "Stone Doubts Bush's Faith in Warren Report," Daily Variety, Jan. 7, 1992; reprinted in Stone and Sklar 377-79; hereafter cited as Robb. Simpson 48. Clyde Haberman (The New York Times).

203. "Elie Wiesel's heavy burden," Austin American-Statesman, March 11, 1997, pp. E1, E8 (quote at latter page). Kennedy 271.

204. Richard Bartholomew memo to Elva Gladney: "Grade Recommendations for Mid-term Exams on the JFK Assassination," senior honors history class: "Assassinations of the 20th Century," Pflugerville High School, Oct. 10, 1996. James Baldwin quoted in Norman Soloman, "Media `Peep Show' Gawks at the Poor," Creators Syndicate, May 14, 1997.

205. William L. Shirer, The Rise and Fall of the Third Reich (1959, 1960/New York: Touchstone, 1981), p. 1037. Brown 526, 538. Paul Marie Verlaine, "Chanson d`Automne [Song of Autumn]," Poemes Saturniens, 1866; cited in Ryan 33, 84-85, 96, 97n., 146. In a worthy example of poetic justice, the title chosen by JFK-assassination activist Charles Drago for his novel about the assassination, *Autumn Too Long*, echoes the semiotic use of Verlaine's "Chanson d'Automne" as a call to arms for the French resistance. Drago further earned the Verlaine comparison in a speech to an international gathering of conspiracy resistors in Dallas during the 33rd anniversary of the assassination: "As far as the search for justice in the case of the assassination of John Fitzgerald Kennedy is concerned, there has been no progress whatsoever...Our reluctance to end formally the `conspiracy/no conspiracy' debate among ourselves amounts to an act of collective cowardice...Our fear of the truth is motivated by the unspoken realization that the death of America's moral authority as a civilized nation is depicted in Zapruder-film frame 313...The absence of moral outrage in our work (with few notable exceptions) is the death knell of our work...We are at war with the murderers of John Fitzgerald Kennedy and with their accessories after the fact; if we are to have the slightest chance of winning that war, we had better begin to think of ourselves and to act in terms of our most appropriate role models: the Viet Cong." In his "Plea For the Declaration of War," Drago wrote: "Who are we? We are the Sioux -- of AIM. We are the Jews -- of the Warsaw Ghetto uprising. We are the Viet Cong -- of Tet. We must know ourselves to be freedom fighters." The Drago-Verlaine comparison is made more poetically just by a personal revelation from former CIA Director and former U.S. President George Bush. At the end of his presidency, just prior to the Academy Awards presentation, Bush told reporters that his favorite movie was the film adaptation of Cornelius Ryan's book, *The Longest Day*, which highlights Verlaine's coded verse. That seemingly innocent choice is, at best, sardonic given Bush's strange biography regarding the JFK assassination and his odd family history regarding

fascism. "During a visit to Auschwitz in 1987," wrote Boston Globe columnist Jeff Jacoby, "what came out of Bush's mouth was, `Boy, they were big on crematoriums, weren't they?'" Since Sept., 1995, Bush has spoken at several high-profile events sponsored by the Rev. Sun Myung Moon on three continents. The former president has received speaking fees totaling in the millions from Moon's Unification Church. In Jul., 1996, in Washington, speaking at a Moon-sponsored conference, Bush praised The Washington Times, a newspaper founded by Moon, for fostering "sanity." He added that Moon's new paper in Argentina, *Tiempos del Mundo*, "is going to do the same thing." According to Frederick Clarkson's book, Eternal Hostility, Unification Church operatives "have been close to neo-fascist movements all over the world." The former president lives in Houston and can be subpoenaed under ARCA, which, ironically, Bush himself signed into law. (November In Dallas 1996 Conference Program [JFK/Lancer Productions & Publications, 1996] p. 15. Charles R. Drago, "In the Blossom of Our Sins: An Eleventh Hour Plea For War and Its Absolutions," The Fourth Decade, May, 1997, pp. 4, 6. Armstrong. Robb. Simpson 48. Adamson, "1,000 Points of Light" many references. Pete Brewton, *The Mafia, CIA & George Bush* [New York: S.P.I. Books, 1992] 70 references. John Loftus and Mark Aarons, *The Secret War Against the Jews: How Western Espionage Betrayed the Jewish People* [New York: St. Martin's Press, 1994] pp. 356-76. Bruce Campbell Adamson vs. CIA, c-95-20549 RMW, Affidavit and Motion to produce documents from the George Bush Presidential Library, U.S. District Court, Judge Ronald M. Whyte. Sarah Hornaday [Associated Press], "Governor [George W. Bush] salutes Holocaust survivors," Austin American-Statesman, May 7, 1997, p. B8. Jeff Jacoby [Boston Globe; New York Times News Service], "Want to rent an ex-president? Call George Bush," Austin American-Statesman, Jun. 7, 1997, p. A11. Norman Solomon, "How Bush Got a Golden Parachute from Moon," Creators Syndicate, Jul. 31, 1997.)

206. Robert S. Boyd (Knight-Ridder Washington Bureau), "Jupiter moon has sea and -- possibly -- life," Austin American-Statesman, Apr. 10, 1997, p. A1. Matt Crenson (Associated Press), "Pathfinder sends photos from Mars," Austin American-Statesman, Jul. 5, 1997, p. A1.

207. Yaron Svoray and Nick Taylor with an introduction by Simon Wiesenthal, *In Hitler's Shadow* (New York: Nan A. Talese/Doubleday, 1994) p. x. We began and ended "The Gun That Didn't Smoke" with reference to the words of Walt W. Rostow because he and his critique of the Warren Report best summarize and symbolize the past, present and future since the assassination of President Kennedy. The most succinct proof of that symbolism can be found in two articles by Vincent Salandria, one of the earliest critics of the Warren Commission's minority opinion of the JFK case. First is "The Assassination of President John F. Kennedy: A Model of Explanation," an insightful statement about the nature of the assassination. Second is "The Promotion of Domestic Discord," which discusses covert politics and the clandestine state. Both of these items first appeared in *Computers and Automation* magazine, issues 20 (Dec. 1971, pp. 32-40) and 21 (Jan. 1972, pp. 37-39, 40). They were re-published

together by the Internet-based publication, Fair Play Magazine (http://rmii.com/~jkelin/fp.html, issue 16, May-Jun., 1997). Salandria warned: "Chaos is required to make a people willing to accept such strong medicine as is administered by the secret police in order to restore order and to stabilize a disintegrating society. It takes an acutely sick society to be able to accept as palatable the terrible cure -- totalitarianism...We must be alert to the CIA agents who would promote the polarization of our society. We must examine the evidence which indicates that fake revolutionaries, who are inciting insurrection in our cities, have had their pockets and minds stuffed by the CIA." Salandria analyzes the role of former Kennedy-Johnson advisor McGeorge Bundy in the assassination and in social polarization. Rostow is mentioned only twice by Salandria, but in an important context. Rostow was and is the late McGeorge Bundy's alter-ego. From his three headquarters on the University of Texas at Austin campus, including the top floor of the LBJ Library, Rostow has, in recent years, launched a drive to revive the largely minority community of East Austin. The Austin Project, as the experiment is known, "...calls for a wide range of social programs allegedly aimed at improving conditions among the poor. But most East Austin activists believe Rostow's plans are misguided." (Robert Bryce, "Liberal, Conservative or Just the Right Thing to Do?" The Austin Chronicle, Sept. 25, 1992; cited in David G. Armstrong, The True Believer [unpublished manuscript], p. 51. See also: Lee Kelly, "Austinites stay up late with the Clintons," Austin American-Statesman, Sept. 19, 1993, p. F3. Debbie Graves, "Ex-UT president wins top U.S. science award," Austin American-Statesman, Sept. 29, 1993, pp. B1, B4. "UT professor, former president honored at White House ceremony," (Cox News Service) Austin American-Statesman, Oct. 1, 1993, p. B5. "Possible Discovery" 9-12, 14-20, 24, 25, 30, 31, 39, 43, 45, 51-53, 56, 59, 60, 83, 84, 96, 98, 100, 132, 144, 150, 152.) Walt Rostow lives in Austin and can be subpoenaed under ARCA.

HAPPENSTANCE
(THE RAMBLER)

BARTHOLOMEW

POSSIBLE DISCOVERY OF AN AUTOMOBILE USED IN THE JFK CONSPIRACY

Foreword

This Foreword is a proposition for those familiar with my monograph, *Possible Discovery of an Automobile Used in the JFK Conspiracy*, and a prognosticative prologue for those who are not. While based on the facts presented in the monograph, facts in its subsequent updates, and facts from research not included here, this is an interpretation of those facts, meant only as a simplified supposition, to be used as a rough guide through the complex material that follows.

In the 1930s, two anti-communist guerrillas, James Burnham and George Lyman Paine, went undercover as communists, infiltrated the leadership of the American Trotskyist movement -- the world's largest Trotskyist organization -- and helped tear it apart. In 1940, their mission ended with the assassination of Leon Trotsky in Mexico City.

One of the two anti-communist guerrillas, James Burnham, went on to teach the newly formed CIA about covert operations. He also went on to teach philosophy at Yale and recruit CIA agents from among his students.

In 1950, Burnham recruited a Yale student, William F. Buckley, Jr., and introduced him to CIA agent E. Howard Hunt. Hunt was a favorite of CIA Director Allen Dulles. Buckley's father also knew the Dulles family, having shared foreign-policy adventures in Mexico with Dulles' uncle, Robert Lansing, when Lansing was President Wilson's secretary of state.

Buckley, as Hunt's advance man, went to Mexico City to recruit informants for the CIA's soon-to-be Mexico City station. There, Buckley met and recruited a 28-year-old Spanish student from Philadelphia, George Gordon Wing, as an informant among the left-wing student groups at Mexico City College. Hunt arrived soon thereafter and arranged for Wing's CIA payment, which was disguised as a student grant. Wing was an older student because his studies had been interrupted by World War II. He served as a Naval aviation bomb-sight technician, fire controlman and ordnance specialist.

In 1952, Wing continued his Spanish studies at the University of California at Berkeley. Upon earning his Ph.D. in Spanish in 1961, Wing joined his former boss, Hunt, in Little Havana, Miami. From there, he trained with the CIA's Operation Forty assassins on No Name Key, in preparation for the Bay of Pigs invasion.

In the fall of 1962, Wing followed in James Burnham's footsteps and became a professor and CIA recruiter, but at the University of Texas at Austin. UT's past leaders had served in Wilson's cabinet with Allen Dulles' uncle, Robert Lansing. UT was also the alma mater of Lansing's friend, William F. Buckley, Sr.

Wing's association with the Dulles family became closer when John Foster Dulles' son, Jack, came to know him personally as a fellow professor in Latin American studies at UT. Professor Wing was thus in a perfect position to be useful to the plotters of President Kennedy's assassination. In fact, Wing's last name appears on the manifest of the same flight which brought the Oswalds from New York to Texas in 1962.

In early April, 1963, the date for Kennedy's trip to Texas was set for November 21st. The occasion was an appreciation dinner in Houston for Kennedy's friend, Texas Congressman Albert Thomas. On April 23rd, Lyndon Johnson made a cryptic statement at a press conference in Dallas that included a phrase about reporters figuratively shooting Kennedy during his Texas trip. The next day, April 24th, Marina Oswald moved into the home of her friend Ruth Hyde Paine. That same day, Lee Harvey Oswald departed for New Orleans, arriving on April 25th. On April 26th, George Wing acquired a used Rambler station wagon from C.B. Smith Motors, an Austin, Texas dealership owned by C.B. Smith, a life-long student of Latin America, and one of Lyndon Johnson's closest friends. The sales manager was Smith's son, C.B. Smith, Jr. The salesman, R.L. Lewis, died under unusual circumstances seven weeks after Kennedy's assassination. The senior Smith's mentor, Texas historian Walter Prescott Webb, was an intimate friend of those planning Albert Thomas' dinner. Webb died suddenly in late April, 1963, in a one-car accident near Austin.

Although Wing was a lowly associate professor whose first semester -- fall, 1962 -- was typically overburdened by the least desirable assignments and responsibilities, he was allowed to take a leave-of-absence for the entire fall semester of 1963. It was the only extended absence of his academic career. He later continued to teach without interruption, even after a heart attack in 1971.

That fall, Ruth Hyde Paine helped arrange Oswald's employment at the Texas School Book Depository. Another employee in the same building was Fronia Smith, the ex-wife of C.B. Smith, Sr. and the mother of C.B. Smith, Jr.

Wing's whereabouts and activities during that semester are unknown, but a Rambler station wagon identical to his was photographed in the parking lot of the Texas School Book Depository, within ten minutes of the shooting on November 22, 1963. And a Rambler station wagon, whose description fits Wing's car, was used to covertly extract guerrillas from Dealey Plaza immediately after they succeeded in killing John F. Kennedy.

Lee Harvey Oswald told his police interrogators that the Rambler station wagon in which he was seen leaving Dealey Plaza, "belongs to Mrs. Paine." He was referring to either Ruth Hyde Paine or Ruth Forbes Paine, the daughter-in -law and the ex-wife, respectively, of George Lyman Paine -- James Burnham's partner in the destruction of Trotskyism. Ruth Forbes Paine was also a long-time friend of Mary Bancroft, Allen Dulles' wartime lover and his chief contact with one of the leaders of the plot to assassinate Adolf Hitler.

Photographs, taken by White House photographer Cecil Stoughton of Vice-President Johnson taking the oath of office aboard Air Force One at Love Field, show President Johnson and Congressman Thomas winking and smiling at each other immediately after the grim ceremony. The original negative to that photo is the only one missing from that series of 13 exposures.

Hard to believe? Read on.

Richard Bartholomew
April 20, 1997

INTRODUCTION

Ten minutes after President Kennedy was shot, Marvin Robinson, Helen Forrest and Dallas Deputy Sheriff Roger Craig, independently of each other, reportedly saw two men leaving Dealey Plaza in a light-colored Rambler station wagon. One of them entered the car on Elm Street after running from the direction of the Texas School Book Depository (TSBD). Craig and Forrest described this man as being identical to Lee Harvey Oswald. A few minutes before this incident Richard Randolph Carr saw two of three men, who had come from behind the TSBD, enter what was apparently the same Rambler parked next to the building on Houston Street. He saw the third man enter the car seconds later on Record Street, one block east and two blocks south of the TSBD. [1]

The Warren Commission had Robinson's and Craig's reports of November 23, 1963. It also had Craig's statement to the FBI from the day before; as well as Carr's statements to the FBI and Craig's testimony. The Commission, however, apparently never knew about Mrs. Forrest and did not publish Robinson's statement.[2] It chose not to believe that Craig took part in Oswald's interrogation or that Craig identified Oswald as the man who entered the station wagon. Dallas Police Captain Will Fritz, Oswald's interrogator, denied to the Commission that Craig was present. Fritz thus never had to deal with Craig's allegation that Oswald admitted to Fritz that he had indeed left Dealey Plaza in a station wagon belonging to Ruth Paine.[3]

Despite the Robinson statement that corroborated Craig and which the Commission had; and despite other corroborating evidence such as newspaper photographs showing Craig's presence on Elm Street and at the open door of the interrogation room with Fritz during Oswald's questioning, the Commission chose to believe the contradictory and unsupported testimony of taxi driver William Whaley.[4] Whaley told the Warren Commission about two witnesses who saw Oswald enter his cab. But there is no indication that the Commission ever attempted to locate, through the simple process of examining the cab company's records, the only two people who could corroborate Whaley.[5]

With the Warren Commission's attempted classification of Marvin Robinson's statement, the death of William Whaley in 1965, and the 1975 death of Roger Craig after his many failed attempts to make his story public, the truth about this alleged getaway car has eluded the few who have tried to seek it.[6]

The House Select Committee on Assassinations (HSCA) apparently attempted but failed. It reported, "Robinson did not testify before the Warren Commission, and he has not been located by the committee." Despite this attempt, however, the House Committee, like the Warren Commission, avoided the entire matter in its report, choosing instead to repeat the Commission's conclusion that "shortly after the assassination, Oswald boarded a bus, but when the bus got caught in a traffic jam, he disembarked and took a taxicab to his rooming house." In this, as in many other areas of its investigation, the House Committee had it both ways by concluding that "The Warren Commission failed to investigate adequately the possibility of a conspiracy to assassinate the President." Thus leading to the conclusion, voiced in 1980 by DeLloyd J. Guth and David R. Wrone, "after careful study of the HSCA's Final Report, that this most recent official version does not satisfy the need for a thorough inquiry into what happened that day in Dallas."[7]

Hypothetically, if the getaway car continued to exist for the past thirty years, given the muddied trails, suspicious deaths, and failed investigations, any persons who secretly knew of the car's role in the assassination and also knew that it still existed, could safely assume it would never be identified. If one such person decided to reveal the car's secrets, however, how would he do it? Could he do it without being silenced himself? Could he do it in a way that would survive his own death?

On May 29, 1989, a Rambler station wagon was noticed on the campus of the University of Texas at Austin (UT) which fit the description of the getaway car reportedly seen by Craig, Robinson, Forrest, and Carr on November 22, 1963.[8] A cursory examination of the car revealed apparent associations between it and persons whose lives were intertwined with Lyndon Johnson's political machinery, the military-industrial- intelligence complex in the U.S., right-wing politics, and Latin American politics.

Connections between odd characteristics of the car itself and information found elsewhere on the UT campus could be interpreted as a trail of clues in the form of coded messages connecting this Rambler, its owner at the time, and its previous owner to the JFK assassination.[9] These clues appear to have been deliberately planted due to specific interrelationships in their content and the encoding technique used.

Specifically, the Rambler was found bearing a 1964 Mexico Federal Turista window sticker and displaying at least two magazines published in 1963 on its rear seat. Although this made it only a minor curiosity, it became increasingly intriguing with subsequent study.

Physical, anecdotal, and documentary evidence has revealed a mosaic of relationships extending from the car's owners to individuals who have been and are currently subjects of interest to researchers of the conspiratorial aspects of the assassination of President Kennedy.

As Dennis Ford writes in the November 1992 issue of The Third Decade, "Discovering the fate of the Rambler will go a long way toward solving this case....Whoever took or drove the car that afternoon is obviously a conspirator."[10] This paper reports on a cursory investigation and proposes a more in-depth investigation. It argues that the UT Rambler represents a possible unique opportunity to determine the fate of this alleged getaway car by investigating new leads, current clues, and fresh trails; an opportunity that should not be overlooked.

There is no intention here to implicate innocent persons in the assassination of President Kennedy. Rather, this is a presentation of circumstances which appear to support the proposed investigation.

This paper presumes, as advised by the United States Constitution, that every person referred to herein is innocent. It also presumes, as advised by Sir Arthur Conan Doyle, that, "The more outré and grotesque an incident is, the more carefully it deserves to be examined...."[11]

La Turista y los Compañeros

When first noticed, the Rambler station wagon at UT was only of interest because it was similar to the car Craig described. There was no incentive to look any closer because the odds were greatly against it being that car. Another person who had seen the car on campus mentioned the existence of the 1964 Mexican tourist sticker on its window. The inference was that if it was the getaway car it would likely have been driven to Mexico as soon as possible after the assassination and, if not destroyed, remain there during the ensuing investigation. This was judged a coincidence, however, and it seemed an easy task to find a simple fact about the car that would conclusively eliminate it from suspicion. That has not proved to be so easy.

The car was a light, warm-gray 1959 Rambler Cross Country Custom station wagon (License No. 711-TQC). The paint looked old and appeared to be original. During a two-year period of observation it was usually parked near Batts Hall which houses the university's Spanish and Portuguese Department. It had a 1964 Mexico Federal "Turista" Automobile sticker (registration no. 243495) in the right rear window and a "D" (for disabled) UT parking sticker on the windshield. In the back seat were two issues of Esquire magazine published in 1963. Only one of them still had a cover. It showed an illustration of Elizabeth Taylor and Richard Burton in the movie Cleopatra. The back seat was in disrepair but the interior upholstery appeared to be original.

The car was photographed a year later in exactly the same condition as when it was first seen. This was done because every time it was observed up to that time nothing about the car had changed, not even the identity, number, location or arrangement of the magazines;[12] despite the car's daily use. By chance, the day it was photographed, the car's driver was also captured on film driving the Rambler. This lack of change remained through the entire two-year period of observation ending in mid-1991. It was beginning to seem that there might be some significance to the display of these particular magazines in this particular Rambler station wagon with its 1964 *turista* sticker. In any event photography was the best safeguard against the car's disappearance before it could be studied further.

On November 9, 1990, a request was made to the Texas State Department of Highways and Public Transportation, Division of Motor Vehicles in Austin, for an ownership history of the Rambler. The first question to be answered was whether or not Ruth or Michael Paine had ever owned it. Unfortunately the clerk at the Division of Motor Vehicles said all of the state's ownership records prior to title numbers beginning with the digits 85 were routinely destroyed, which included those for this car.[13] Fortunately the same man had owned this car for the past twenty-seven years and his title showed up in the current computer record. A Title and Registration Verification was obtained for two dollars. It was typed like this:

NDX 239845 LIC 711TQC EXPIRES MAY/91 EWT 2800 GWT
0000 $40.80 TITLE 33883954 ISSUED 05/07/65 ODOMETER N/A
   59 RAMBLER SW D713121 REG CLASS O1
   PREVIOUS OWNER CB SMITH MOTORS AUSTIN TEX
   OWNER GEORGE GORDON WING, 2101 ROBINHOOD
TRL,AUSTIN,TX 78703 LIEN 04/13/65 UNIVERSITY FEDERAL
CREDITUNION,PO BOX 8090 U T STATIO
   N,AUSTIN TEX
   PLATE AGE: 2.

The possibility remains that the Paines owned the car prior to C.B. Smith because its ownership history during its first four years is yet to be established despite several attempts through various means. But just because Oswald was under the impression that the car belonged to Ruth Paine in 1963 does not mean that it did. Bert Sugar and Sybil Leek apparently had information that Paine borrowed such a car.[14] Nevertheless the identities of the two known owners have proven to be of potential importance to the events of November 22, 1963.

Cecil Bernard Smith, the previous owner, personally knew Lyndon Johnson. He was a major land owner in Austin who opened Austin's first Volkswagen dealership at Sixth Street and Lamar Boulevard. He was a native of Texas and a star athlete in college. He donated money to Johnson's political campaigns and to UT. During the 1980s C.B. Smith donated land to the university to endow five chairs in Mexican and Latin American Studies.[15] As a result of his generosity he served on various boards and commissions at UT.[16] Among the local citizens, however, C.B. Smith had a reputation for being an extreme right-winger who hated hippies.[17]

George Gordon Wing, the owner of the car from April 1963 until his death in December 1991, was a Ph.D. and associate professor in the Spanish and Portuguese Department.[18] Considering what he taught it is not unusual that he bought his car from C.B. Smith, a major donor to Mexican and Latin American Studies. However it must be noted, in addition to the Spanish and Latin American milieu surrounding Oswald in 1963, that Craig reportedly saw a "husky looking Latin" driving the car.[19] Both Smith and Wing will be discussed further in this paper.

In December 1990 other intriguing connections came to light. They centered once again around the Spanish and Portuguese Department and former UT President Harry Huntt Ransom, another of Lyndon Johnson's friends. Ransom had risen quickly through the UT ranks from assistant dean of the graduate school in 1951 to Chancellor of The University of Texas System by 1961. After a student career that included membership in Phi Beta Kappa, Ransom began his professional career at UT in 1935 as an instructor of English. He became an assistant professor after receiving his Ph.D. from Yale in 1938. By 1960 he had also created and was serving as editor of The Texas Quarterly, "the preeminent literary journal of Texas." This journal was highly regarded internationally as well and when Ransom died in April 1976, replacing him as editor was considered a formidable responsibility. It could not be entrusted to just anyone. The job ended up in the hands of Ransom's close associate Miguel Gonzalez-Gerth, Ph.D. and professor in the Spanish and Portuguese Department. They were reportedly close friends. Another indication of the closeness of their relationship is the fact that since Ransom's death Gonzalez-Gerth has been a constant companion to his widow, Hazel Harrod Ransom. Thus within and around the Spanish and Portuguese Department a circle of close associations began to emerge among Lyndon Johnson, Harry Ransom, C.B. Smith, Miguel Gonzalez-Gerth, and George Wing. These associations were all the more interesting considering Ransom's service in Air Force intelligence during World War II.[20]

UT, CIA, and JFK

At first, speculation about vague intelligence connections to the UT Rambler stemmed from the presumption of possible relationships between UT and U.S. intelligence agencies. It has been documented that the CIA has a long history of recruiting from, or using as cover, the foreign language departments of major universities. According to former student activist Amy Chen Mills, "With ample facilities for experimentation and an abundance of physical sites, college campuses are ideal for carrying out much larger and more insidious CIA programs. U.S. universities have housed some CIA activities that go beyond research and into active covert operations." By 1988, UT, along with the University of Miami, George Washington University, Jacksonville University, the Rochester Institute of Technology and Georgetown University were among as many as ten schools where the CIA had placed officers through its recently initiated "Officer in Residence" program.[21]

Given the massive CIA station on the campus of the University of Miami in the days of operations Zapata and Mongoose, it is not unreasonable to assume that the CIA recruited personnel from the University of Texas Spanish and Portuguese Department for those operations. In fact, anti-Castro sentiment was alive and well in Austin as of October 1, 1963 when JFK assassination figure John Martino spoke to the Austin Anti-Communist League about his arrest and imprisonment by Castro.[22] Very likely present to hear Martino was John Birch Society and Austin Anti-Communist League member Jack Nichols Payton, a friend and campaign-organizer of General Edwin Walker.[23]

Just prior to this, in September, Martino had addressed an anti-Castro meeting in Dallas. According to author Anthony Summers, "While there he mentioned that he knew Amador Odio, a wealthy Cuban then imprisoned by Castro, and that he knew one of Odio's daughters was living in exile in Dallas. This of course was Silvia Odio, the witness whose meeting with `Oswald' remains the firmest evidence of a deliberate attempt to frame the alleged assassin."[24] Evidence of Martino's Austin visit was discovered by chance while looking through local newspapers for researcher David Lifton in 1990. The visit was of interest because of a previous discovery in 1989: pages about John Martino had been cut out of the only UT copy of Anthony Summer's book, *Conspiracy*; including source notes. These were the only pages removed. Like the car itself (and by 1990, because of the car), these incidents involving Mafia associate and CIA agent Martino were a minor curiosity. Of similar interest in the same newspaper was an announcement that

William F. Buckley, Jr. would be speaking on campus in December 1963. Later however these curiosities would become integral to an understanding of other discoveries on the UT campus.

Like the university he led, Harry Ransom was no stranger to clandestine activities. Dr. Ransom, born on November 22, 1908, enlisted as a second lieutenant in the Air Corps in 1942. He was the director of the Air Force Editorial Office from 1944-46. He attained the rank of major and received the Legion of Merit in 1947 for work in "editorial intelligence." In 1945, Ransom authored "Notes for an Epitaph: Rise and Fall of the Luftwaffe" (Air Force Reprint, 32 pp.). That same year he wrote "Tactical Air Operations," with James Gould Cozzens and Brigadier General Frederic Smith (Air Force Reprint, 30 pp.). In 1946 Ransom wrote "Historical Procedures in the AAF" (Air Force Reprint, 10 pp.) and "Educational Plans of 500,000 AAF Veterans" (Higher Education, United States Office of Education.). In 1962, Dr. Ransom, while Chancellor of The University of Texas System, was elected chairman of the Advisory Panel on ROTC, Department of the Air Force, which advised the Secretary of the Air Force on ROTC programs.[25]

It must be noted here that John Stockwell, the highest-ranking CIA officer to quit and expose the truth of CIA operations to Congress, and who was an ROTC graduate of UT in the late 1950s, expressed his belief, when asked by reporter Earl Golz in 1991, that CIA associations did exist at UT within the ROTC program, the Spanish and Portuguese Department, the Institute of Latin American Studies, and with Harry Ransom.[26]

In his book, *The Praetorian Guard*, Stockwell describes his years at UT:

> At the University of Texas, I got into the elite Plan II special reading program and obtained a Naval ROTC scholarship, graduating with what the university billed as its best possible liberal arts degree. Then I took the Marine Corps option and made my way into the elite parachute- and-UDT trained 2nd Force Reconnaissance Company. Only years later did I realize that I had obtained the best half-education available. They taught me the classics; we studied philosophy and history with award-winning professors (including John Silber[27] of Boston University). But my generation didn't question. We scribbled furiously in our notebooks, trying to capture the professor's exact words so we could regurgitate them faithfully back to him (there were no

women professors in my program at that time) in the examinations. Throughout my school years, I never had a conversation with a liberal, much less a radical critic of the system, or even a serious questioner. There was one professor, Clarence Ayers, who occasionally made a suggestive comment, but he was under constant pressure from the Texas legislature, not to mention the university's regents.[28]

When asked about CIA recruiting on college campuses, Philip Agee, one of the first CIA officers to resign and tell the truth about the CIA, specifically named the Air Force and Army ROTC programs as prime sources of recruits.[29] Also, a student in the Spanish and Portuguese Department was asked if he had ever heard any rumors of CIA involvement in UT's Institute of Latin American Studies (ILAS). His response was that he had heard more than just rumors of CIA people and programs there.[30] This paper will deal further with ILAS.

Ransom's years at Yale, his past work in Air Force intelligence and his relationships with Lyndon Johnson and CIA recruiting become important when considering that Ransom was instrumental in the recruitment of two men to the faculty at UT, John W.F. Dulles and Walt Whitman Rostow.[31]

John W.F. "Jack" Dulles is the eldest son of former Secretary of State John Foster Dulles and the nephew of former Director of Central Intelligence and Warren Commissioner Allen Dulles. He has worked at UT for many years and is considered one of the world's top experts on Brazil, a Portuguese speaking country. His office is in the Harry H. Ransom Humanities Research Center, which also houses a replica of his father's office.[32] John Wheat, a former student of Wing's who has worked with Dulles, said Dulles did not have the usual academic career credentials. His interest in Northern Mexico and Brazil came from his work in the Dulles family's Hannah Mining Company. Dulles was simply made an adjunct professor and given a research position at UT.[33]

Jack Dulles' relationship with UT's Spanish and Portuguese Department goes beyond the expected professional interest in the language of Brazil however. In the mid-1960's his daughter Ellen, a great niece of Allen Dulles, attended classes in that department.[34] John Wheat said Dulles "may have" known Wing.

Walt Rostow, former Kennedy State Department counsel and President Johnson's national security advisor, had been one of President Kennedy's inner circle of advisors. He is currently the Rex G. Baker, Jr. Professor Emeritus of Political Economy at the LBJ School of Public

Affairs. His wife Elspeth is the Stiles Professor in American Studies.[35] Walt Rostow was close, socially and professionally to Allen Dulles, McGeorge Bundy, Kennedy's national security advisor, Richard Bissell, former director of all CIA covert operations, and Air Force General Charles P. Cabell, former deputy director of the CIA.[36] Like Ransom, Rostow had attained the rank of Major and won the Legion of Merit for his work with the OSS during World War II.[37] Whether or not they knew each other at Yale or during the war, Ransom and Rostow had much in common and more than a few mutual friends. It is therefore understandable that Rostow agreed to continue his career at Ransom's university.

We now see within and around UT's Spanish and Portuguese Department a circle of associations that has expanded to include not only Lyndon Johnson, Harry Ransom, C.B. Smith, Miguel Gonzalez-Gerth, and George Wing, but Walt Rostow and at least two members of the Dulles family.[38]

[OBJ]Relatively little attention has been paid to Walt Rostow in the literature of the Kennedy assassination. It seems, however, that he has several connections relevant to November 22, 1963. He and his friend McGeorge Bundy may have urged their long-time friend, Richard Bissell to establish the "Executive Action" assassination capability known as ZR/RIFLE.[39] Bissell told the Senate Church Committee on CIA assassination plots, "There is little doubt in my mind that Project RIFLE was discussed with Rostow and possibly Bundy."[40]

According to Anthony Summers, these assassination plots were being revived just when Kennedy was considering normalizing relations with Cuba. This peace move was so secret *that only six people knew about it.* Despite this tight security, Ambassador William Attwood and Arthur Schlesinger believe the secret leaked to the CIA and the Cuban exiles, possibly triggering Kennedy's assassination. Bundy was the aide most involved with the negotiations and it is very likely that Rostow was one of the six.[41]

It was these same two members of Kennedy's inner circle who advised him, on February 11, 1961, to abolish the Operations Coordination Board of the National Security Council -- the chief reason for the Bay of Pigs fiasco, according to Treasury Secretary Douglas Dillon.[42] Prior to the invasion, on April 12, Rostow was urging Kennedy to intervene militarily in Laos as well as Cuba.[43]

And on April 20, after the failure at the Bay of Pigs, along with Admiral Arleigh Burke, the Air Force, and Richard Nixon, Rostow was still pushing for a military intervention in Laos. That same day Kennedy, who still had doubts about it, ordered U.S. advisors in Laos to put on their uniforms.[44] Rostow later spearheaded U.S. intervention in Vietnam and was instrumental in initiating the stepped-up arms race of the 1960s.

The things that Rostow supported -- reduced oversight of covert operations, military intervention in Cuba, Laos, and Vietnam, policies that led to nuclear proliferation, and possibly CIA assassinations -- Kennedy later attempted to reverse. It is possible that Rostow and Bundy were not as loyal to Kennedy as he may have thought.

This disloyalty is all the more believable when considering a few more significant Rostow connections to Kennedy's assassination (aside from Rostow's long friendship with Bissell and Cabell). These connections concern his relationships with C.D. Jackson, the publisher of Life magazine who bought and suppressed the Zapruder film, Harold R. Isaacs, a research associate at MIT's Center for International Studies (CENIS) in Cambridge, Massachusetts, and Air Force Major General Edward G. Lansdale.

C.D. Jackson, former president of the CIA's National Committee for a Free Europe (NCFE), and friend of Allen Dulles, had worked closely with Walt Rostow. Among other things they co-authored Eisenhower's "Chance for Peace" address of April 16, 1953, which was "the opening gun of the post-Stalin phase of the Cold War." It is noteworthy here that the NCFE's most important operation was Radio Free Europe.[45] Jackson's connection, through Radio Free Europe, Henry Luce, and Allen Dulles, to the Paines and therefore possibly to Oswald and the Rambler will be discussed further in this paper.

In 1951 Rostow "helped launch" CENIS[46] with backing from his former OSS buddies now in the CIA. It is a think tank and well known CIA front that defended communist ideology while admitting to its industry benefactors that it was actually fighting communism.[47] For ten years at CENIS, Rostow worked closely with Isaacs. Warren Commission Document 942 says that it had been alleged that Marilyn Dorothea Murret (Oswald's cousin) was linked in some manner with the apparatus of Professor Harold Isaacs. And Warren Commission Document 1080 (CD 1080), an FBI report entitled "Marilyn Dorothea Murret," is entirely about Isaacs' background and contains no mention of Murret. This document describes Isaacs as a disillusioned leftist intellectual who had become a professional anti-communist -- which also reveals the true nature of the secret goals of CENIS. This report had been classified by the Warren Commission as a withheld file open only to the federal government and the Commission. It would probably still be secret if an assassination researcher had not discovered it misfiled in the National Archives in the mid-1970s.[48]

This report was the result, no doubt, of Isaacs' name being linked to the JFK assassination by two sources in 1964. One, according to researcher Peter R. Whitmey, was a right-wing reporter named Paul Scott who was convinced that Isaacs was a "...mastermind of the communist movement which planned to take over the government." Whitmey adds that Scott told the FBI on May 7, 1964 that Isaacs was being supported in his efforts by members of Johnson's cabinet, including Rusk, McNamara, Rostow, Cleveland and Yarmolinsky. He also accused Robert Kennedy of hiring a Communist speech writer, and linked Rusk to the British spies, Burgess and MacLean. In addition, he indicated that reliable sources had linked Prof. Isaacs and Marilyn Murret, although he did not seem to know of her relationship to Oswald; he had earlier reported in a column that she was one of the three female defectors, which, in her case was not true.

The FBI prepared a report on Murret also dated May 7, outlining her extensive travels around the world beginning in 1959, and also drew up a report on Isaacs dated May 22, entitled "Re: Marilyn Dorothea Murret", although no connection between the two was established. The first page of the six-page background report was erroneously titled "Marilyn Dorothea Murret", which created suspicion when it was found in the files at the National Archives some years later.[49]

The second source linking Isaacs' name to the assassination was Richard Giesbrecht, a Winnipeg resident who reported to the FBI that on February 12, 1964, he overheard a conversation in the Horizon Room of the Winnipeg International Airport among two men talking about the assassination. Based on what he heard he believed they were in some way involved. They were discussing how much Oswald knew about the assassination and were concerned about how much he might have told his wife. According to Peter Whitmey, the men said Isaacs "was supposed to get rid of a 1958 Dodge (later reported as a Ford.)" And according to co-authors Michael Canfield and Alan J. Weberman, Giesbrecht said that "when the first man asked the second how much Oswald knew, the second one said, `We have a film that I have seen where Issacs [sic] is near Kennedy after the landing.' The first man then mentioned something about Issacs [sic], ending the query, `Why should a person with such a good record such as Isaacs, become mixed up with a psycho?' In a November 1967 article in McCleans Magazine, Giesbrecht stated that the `psycho' referred to was Oswald."[50]

Peter Whitmey believes that, "It is abundantly clear that it [CD 1080] was classified in order to protect the good name of Professor Isaacs, who was a distinguished lecturer, researcher and writer, and a strong supporter of recognizing Red China during the 1960s." Whitmey further believes that the man being referred to in the Winnipeg airport "...is much more likely to have been Charles R. Isaacs, whose 1960 phone number was listed in Jack Ruby's notebook, and who was an airline service manager for American Airlines at Love Field." Whitmey confirmed that Charles Isaacs had known Ruby after locating and interviewing Charles' second ex-wife (of three) who had worked for Ruby "as a wardrobe designer for some time."[51]

While it is possible that the men in the airport were talking about Charles Isaacs, it is not "much more likely" that they were referring to Charles rather than Rostow's CENIS associate, Professor Harold R. Isaacs. If the men knew Charles well enough to know of links to Oswald, they must have known of his and his wife's close association with Ruby. Between the "distinguished" MIT Professor and the divorced Ruby friend, which one would most likely be talked about in terms of having "such a good record"? And of the two, which one would elicit the most incredulity over being "mixed up with a psycho"? On both counts it would more likely be the Professor. It must also be surmised that since Charles Isaacs had apparently moved to San Mateo, California by the time of the assassination, he would have about the same access to Love Field as anyone else, including Harold Isaacs.[52]

In addition, Dr. Isaacs had reportedly been a Trotskyite when he worked as a journalist in China in the 1930s.[53] As we will see in this paper, there is much evidence of a determined effort by several right-wing individuals (with links to Oswald) to blame the assassination on Communists by spreading false stories and planting false evidence linking Oswald and Ruby to Trotskyists and others. In the context of those efforts, right-wing journalist Paul Scott, the first to link Dr. Isaacs to Marilyn Murret, may very well have known that she was Oswald's cousin. After all, Paul Scott believed that Dr. Isaacs was the mastermind of a high level communist plot to take over the United States government -- a plot that had infiltrated the White House. Finding a reliable source linking his Trotskyist mastermind to the alleged Marxist Oswald, in the midst of a welter of deliberate lies about such links, would seem to have been the fulfillment of Paul Scott's greatest desire.

Neither is it "abundantly clear" that the FBI reports of investigations into the alleged links between Isaacs and Murret were classified "to protect the good name of Professor Isaacs." The FBI, who had Paul Scott's allegations, Richard Giesbrecht's allegations, and Ruby's notebooks, apparently chose only to investigate the information from Paul Scott's "reliable sources." We will see in this paper, how the FBI and CIA had a habit of cutting short investigations (and classifying reports) that threatened to reveal conspiratorial links. The investigation of Marilyn Murret not only threatened to lead to Isaacs' long-time associate Walt Rostow, who in turn had a long-time friendship with CIA assassination plotters, but to her father, Oswald's uncle and surrogate father, Charles "Dutz" Murret, who worked for New Orleans Mob boss Carlos Marcello, who in turn was also closely tied to the same CIA/Mafia assassination plots. Such an investigation would certainly have come across a report by FBI agent John William Miller stating that CIA agent William George Gaudet told him of a purchase of paintings by Jack Ruby from Lorenzo Borenstein, a close relative of Leon Trotsky.[54] Gaudet is the CIA agent who got the Mexican tourist card next to Oswald's in New Orleans in September 1963.[55] He also told attorney Bernard Fensterwald in 1975: "She [Murret] may have worked for the agency in New Orleans."[56]

With regard to Harold Isaacs' "good name" deriving from his strong support for recognizing Red China during the 1960s, consider the following. At the LBJ Library's May 1990 symposium, LBJ: The Difference He Made, journalist Tom Wicker, who was in the audience, became disturbed, during one panel discussion, that the conference was focused exclusively on domestic policy. He pointed out that the Johnson Administration has received practically no credit for being the first to develop serious arms control proposals to be taken to the Soviets. Because of the timing of the Warsaw Pact invasion of Czechoslovakia, Johnson was unable to follow through on it. The proposals survived into the Nixon Administration and were fundamentally those which Nixon took into the SALT I negotiations. Panelist Nicholas Katzenbach, the former deputy attorney general who right after the assassination was as concerned as J. Edgar Hoover about "...having something issued so we can convince the public that Oswald is the real assassin,"[57] added a historical note similar to Wicker's that had always interested him:

> ...President Nixon got so much credit for opening the door to China, and that was something that LBJ wanted to do. And indeed we developed -- the first proposals that were made by President Nixon were developed for President Johnson."
>
> And after the election, knowing Nixon was coming in, he had us go to President Nixon and say, "If you want me to start this process, I'll be happy to do it and take the political flack for doing it, which there will be from the right, but if you want to do it, I'll hold off and do nothing."
>
> And Nixon said he wanted to do it. So we did hold off, and they went down, and it was fascinating to me

because I had worked on it. They were word for word
what we had developed at the end of the
administration.[58]

The two major achievements historically credited to an otherwise
disgraced Republican administration were actually given to it by the
previous Democratic administration. And the recognition of China,
which Harold Isaacs had so strongly supported, was credited to Richard
Nixon, Kennedy's chief political nemesis (especially on such things as
arms control and *détente* with communist countries), through an under-
the- table deal between Johnson and Nixon. This paper will explore the
possible culpability of both former presidents in Kennedy's assassination
stemming from apparent ties which Johnson and Nixon had to each other
as well as to Ruby and Oswald.

Thus, considering that everything about Marilyn Murret seemed to
lead to a CIA/Mafia conspiracy and a phony Trotskyite conspiracy
(which, as we will see, may have led to the same persons), it would be a
great irony indeed if the FBI, who reportedly destroyed evidence and
threatened witnesses to hide conspiratorial leads, stopped further
investigation of Murret solely out of politeness to Harold R. Isaacs. And
although an investigation of Charles Isaacs may have led to the
conspiracy through Ruby, it is hard to imagine how he could have
provided a more direct route.

Aside from his association with Harold Isaacs, Rostow's history with
CENIS is important because of its implications regarding UT, where
Rostow has been employed since leaving the government in 1969. As
mentioned before, there are apparently more than just rumors of CIA
activities at UT's Institute of Latin American Studies, which works
closely, no doubt, with the Spanish and Portuguese Department; and has
benefited, no doubt, from the donations of C.B. Smith, who had a life-
long interest in Latin American politics and culture.[59]

Continuing in 1954 with the African-American Institute in
cooperation with a U.S.-African mining company, and in 1956 with the
Asia Foundation at Michigan State University, the CIA, from its earliest
days, has been establishing academic foreign studies institutes as part of
a larger effort to generate academic interest in a country and "spin-off"
institutes that could subsequently be tapped by the CIA and other
government agencies.[60] UT's ILAS could very well be CIA established or
a spin-off. On the other hand, ILAS's director, Richard Adams, is a harsh
critic of the right-wing government in Guatemala. He is currently
persona non grata to that government.[61] ILAS could also be similar to
CENIS in its chameleon-like ways. In fact, as we shall see, the idea of

155

ILAS was introduced to Walt Rostow by George de Mohrenschildt, Oswald's CIA friend.

Given a few more bits of information, the possible connections between CENIS, ILAS, C.B. Smith, Wing and the Rambler begin to take on ominous overtones. The first bit is only a few steps away from Walt Rostow's office on the eighth floor of the LBJ Library. According to assassination researcher Dick Russell "In 1966-67, from residences in Haiti and Dallas, de Mohrenschildt would correspond regularly with the Johnson White House. On file at the LBJ Memorial Library in Austin, Texas, the letters show high level interest in the baron's proposal for establishing an `Institute of Latin American Resources.' Replied presidential assistant Arthur C. Perry: `I feel that the President will be interested in having your views in this regard and I shall be pleased to bring them to his attention at the earliest opportunity.'...A State Department memorandum of January 14, 1967, from executive secretary Benjamin H. Read to Walt W. Rostow notes: `The Department's reply to Mr. de Mohrenschildt should be considered a *de minimus*[62] response to his letter of December 27 to the President. A lengthy file in the Office of Special Consular Services clearly indicates that de Mohrenschildt is an unstable and unreliable individual who would not hesitate to misuse or misrepresent even the slightest expression of interest.'"[63]

Russell does not tell us what "The Department's reply to Mr. de Mohrenschildt" was. It was dated the day before the memo to Rostow, January 13, 1967, from State Department Deputy Assistant Administrator Milton Barall to de Mohrenschildt: "...the United States Agency for International Development would not have an interest in supporting the creation of such an institute in Texas."

Apart from the fact that the proposal was forwarded to the CIA-backed Agency for International Development, why would Rostow be bothered with a memo about this? Despite the first expression of interest, the reply had already been sent and was final in its rejection of de Mohrenschildt's proposal. It is as if Rostow or someone else was contemplating a continued interest in the proposal and had to be warned of potential consequences.

What is also of concern here is that de Mohrenschildt's letter of December 27 proposed placing the institute at Southwest Texas State College, Lyndon Johnson's alma mater. ILAS is just such an institute that was later created at the University of Texas at Austin, in the same complex as the LBJ library and across a breezeway from Harry Ransom's posh new office. And again, the belief that CIA personnel and programs exist there was voiced to Earl Golz by John Stockwell in 1991. It is also worth noting that the golden age of collecting for UT's Latin American collection was during the reign of Harry Ransom. According to UT librarian and former Spanish student John Wheat, the Latin American collection was Ransom's favorite. Nettie Lee Benson, the collection's long-time head librarian, received major funding from and had direct access to Ransom at any time. And ILAS, as we have seen, very likely had financial support from C.B. Smith.

The close proximity to, and involvement in the creation and activities of ILAS of Rostow, de Mohrenschildt, Dulles, and Ransom, who were in just as close proximity to the CIA, is of further concern considering that the CIA had once been greatly angered by the head of Stanford's Institute of Hispanic American and Luso- Brazilian Studies. This institute was one of the first programs of inter-American studies in the U.S. It was started in 1944 by Professor Ronald Hilton, "a tough-minded liberal scholar."[64]

In October 1960, Dr. Hilton, editor of his institute's prestigious journal, the Hispanic American Report, learned of the CIA's plans to invade Cuba from Guatemala's leading newspaper, *La Hora*. He published a report that the purpose of the CIA's Retalhuleu training camp was "common knowledge". Hilton's report inspired a November 19 article in The Nation calling the invasion plans a "dangerous and hare-brained project" urging "all U.S. news media" to check the story out. The Nation made it as easy as possible by sending information about the CIA's plans to AP, UPI, and all major news media in New York, including virtually flooding the Times with copies of the reports. On November 20, more than a week after receiving the advance notice, the Times buried a story on page 32 essentially calling these reports "a lot of lies." In their Sunday edition, after the U.S. broke off relations with Cuba in January 1961, the New York Times reported that the final straw was Castro's propaganda offensive about an imminent invasion of Cuba. That same month, after the Los Angeles Times and the St. Louis Post Dispatch confirmed American funding of the base, Time magazine, apparently hedging its bets, reported that a "Mr. B." of the CIA was in charge of the whole operation.[65]

Despite this whisper of vindication, Dr. Hilton was not popular in Washington or among Stanford's trustees who represented international corporations. After Stanford received a sizable grant from the Ford Foundation, Hilton was pressured not to offend the university's powerful fund raisers -- even if it was just an opinion expressed in an editorial. In 1962, after the CIA's top Cuban invasion planners had been fired and Cuba had become a major problem for the U.S., Ford gave a grant to a Stanford committee formed to plan an international studies program. Heading the committee was Dean Carl Spaeth, former assistant to Nelson

Rockefeller in the State Department, and former director of the Ford Foundation's Division of Overseas Activities. After a year of "studies," without explanation to or input from Dr. Hilton, the Hispanic Institute was gutted and assigned mundane responsibilities. When asked how they could do such a thing, Stanford's administration told him: "The administration can do anything it pleases." Hilton resigned, his journal was suspended, and two weeks later the Ford Foundation gave Stanford $550,000 for Latin American studies to those who did not protest what had happened to Hilton and his independent, intellectually respected institute. According to Ramparts magazine, "This largesse was repeated on every campus where significant efforts on Latin America were taking place."[66] Interestingly, these Hilton controversies were taking place while George Wing was a teaching assistant and earning his PhD. In Spanish at the University of California at Berkeley.[67]

Was de Mohrenschildt's proposal the genesis of UT's institute? Was C.B. Smith involved with de Mohrenschildt in this first proposal? The last of the de Mohrenschildt-to-LBJ letters, dated June 13, 1969, adds fuel to such speculation. It reads, "You possibly remember me and we do have a lot of mutual friends, Barbara and Howard Burris, George Brown and the late Herman Brown....This summer I am not teaching at U.T.A. [The University of Texas at Arlington] and we could drive any time to visit with you." Eighteen months earlier, C.B. Smith had been named a distinguished alumnus of U.T.A.[68]

The 1969 letter is of further interest with regard to JFK assassination connections to UT. Not only was de Mohrenschildt teaching at a school which was part of the "system" that Harry Ransom oversaw, and one which had given C.B. Smith one of its highest honors, he also shared two particularly interesting mutual friends with Lyndon Johnson: Barbara and Howard Burris. Howard Burris was Vice President Johnson's military representative and an Air Force intelligence officer. His connections to UT and the assassination will be discussed further in this paper.

By 1961 Rostow was also working closely with Edward G. Lansdale. Lansdale was an Air Force Major General at the time of his retirement on November 1, 1963. He had an advertising background and extensive counter-insurgency experience in Southeast Asia. Lansdale is credited in many circles with coming up with the idea, single handed, that destroyed the Huk rebellion in the early fifties in the Philippines. The Huk were very superstitious. They believed in vampires. Lansdale got a few dead Huk bodies, put holes in their necks and hung them upside down.[69]

Like Rostow, Lansdale was a veteran of the OSS. He had served in Vietnam during the Eisenhower administration and had become a close personal friend of South Vietnamese President Ngo Dinh Diem.[70]

His advertising background blended well with his expertise: psychological warfare; or psy-ops. There are now manuals on psy-ops and Lansdale is considered the father of that type of warfare.

He was the model for the imperialistic "Colonel Hillindale" in the William Lederer/Eugene Burdick novel *The Ugly American*; the most celebrated American dark spy.[71]

During January through April of 1961, Lansdale's overriding motive was to be Ambassador to South Vietnam. Lansdale, by that time, was probably the only American advisor Diem trusted. Diem was very isolated by then. After his first White House meeting with Lansdale on Vietnam, Kennedy had decided to fire Ambassador Elbridge Durbrow. Kennedy would change his mind about this in a month or two.[72]

Following the firing of Durbrow, Kennedy appointed Frederick E. Nolting. So Lansdale sought to capture the apparatus to formulate, approve and implement Vietnam policy and be the key player in all three stages until a U.S. victory was achieved in Vietnam. It almost worked. The reason it did not, as far as military historian John Newman can tell, is because Dean Rusk threatened to resign if Lansdale got his way. Lansdale's letters from 1964 show that he found out from some of his contacts that Rusk had laid his job on the line.[73]

As the author of the book JFK and Vietnam, John M. Newman, explained: "Lansdale's a loose cannon on deck. Kennedy liked him, at least initially for a while, but he had big problems. No doubt about it. In the Pentagon, the Pentagon brass didn't like him. Secretary of State Rusk did not like him. However he did have a big patron in Kennedy's inner circle....Walt Rostow! Walt Rostow, the Vietnam guy. And I was able to track this fairly successfully I think. If it weren't for Walt Rostow, Lansdale wouldn't have had a prayer with this crazy plan of his to try and capture this emerging Vietnam policy apparatus."[74]

So in the first four months of the Kennedy Administration Lansdale sought the ambassadorship and then control of the emerging policy apparatus of Vietnam and failed at both. The only evidence of Rusk's motive is a document released in 1991 by the State Department. It is a document in which Rusk wrote about not trusting Lansdale. He was unsure of Lansdale's loyalties.[75]

Although he cannot document it, Newman is certain that Lansdale worked for the CIA while wearing an Air Force uniform. One indication of this in Lansdale's private letters and memoranda is that General Curtis Le May, the Air Chief of Staff, seemed to be unable to promote him. Allen Dulles had to be involved in getting Lansdale promoted from colonel to general. And a number of other patterns are apparent such as social events with Charles Cabell. Edward Lansdale and Charles Cabell were very close.[76]

The end result of these first few months, in essence, is that Lansdale was fired from any position on Vietnam policy. For Edward Lansdale that was a traumatic experience. Vietnam was his primary concern. South Vietnam was his creation. In his book, Newman stopped writing about Lansdale at that point although there was a lot more to him. It involved Cuba and Operation Mongoose and other matters that were not the focus of his book.[77]

Lansdale had lost something that mattered a great deal to him. In his letters he wrote about going through the experience of being relieved of these responsibilities in Vietnam. Newman describes him as a man whose heart was broken "because he could not play any more in his favorite sandbox." By the end of 1961 Kennedy had put him in charge of Operation Mongoose. He was in charge of an enormous apparatus with tremendous resources, weapons and personnel. Newman, having read the NSC meeting minutes where Kennedy announced Lansdale was now going to be in charge of Mongoose, believes that Kennedy did not appreciate the way Lansdale related to being involved in Vietnam policy.[78]

With such extreme feelings about his predicament in 1961, Lansdale might have gone any number of ways to rectify his situation. What was he thinking? In what direction and how far would he go? Newman summarized the portion of his book in which he dealt with that question:

> Lansdale was not a combat troops man, yet the very first piece of paper ever in the history of the Vietnam war where an American officer recommends a U.S. troop commitment to Vietnam, Lansdale was the one who authors it. It's right in that critical time frame right after the failure at the Bay of Pigs; right before the crucial decision Kennedy has to make on going into Laos. His Vietnam Task Force paper is coming in through the door. The night, the very night that the Joint Chiefs figure out that Kennedy is going to say no on Laos, Lansdale, late at night in the Pentagon, slips in this combat troop proposal in the Vietnam Task Force report. It's not like him. The way I interpret that -- and I may be in error -- the way I interpret that is he understands that the star rising on the horizon is U.S. intervention in Vietnam. And he understands that he has lost his position in the Kennedy administration which has a decidedly different approach. So he switches forces and

he joins forces with those planning for intervention. And
it was a good decision on his part, was it not? He was
there when they arrived. He was on the team.[79]

The Mongoose files of the Senate Church Committee reveal that they
wanted to know when and who authorized assassination. The Kennedy
Administration had supposedly gotten away from that. It was clear to the
committee, however, that they had not. There were plans and resources
being devoted to assassinate Castro. So the purpose of the questioning
was to find out who, and when it was authorized.[80]

Lansdale testified that he did it all alone. When asked why, his
answer was that during the missile crisis the Russians had changed the
terms of reference by putting missiles in Cuba. So Lansdale decided all
on his own that he was going to change things and get rid of Castro.

After reading a pre-galley copy of JFK and Vietnam, Daniel Ellsberg
called Newman one night very excitedly. Ellsberg had worked with
Lansdale and knew him extremely well. He said, "This is the first time
I've ever thought that Lansdale might have been involved in the
assassination." Ellsberg based this on Lansdale being removed from
Vietnam planning and moved to Operation Mongoose.[81]

By February 1963 Lansdale had no position in Cuban policy and was
focusing on Latin America. He was traveling to countries like Bolivia
and elsewhere. The U.S. had a lot of personnel in South America under
Kennedy. And a lot of them ended up going to Vietnam. According to
Newman there is a blind spot as to exactly what they were doing and
how many people the U.S. had in Latin America.[82]

"I can tell you," Newman said, "that in the collateral research that I
did, names that I came across, I found a correlation between -- I don't say
this is definitive but I got a lot of hits -- the same names of the guys that
were running around in Latin America, particularly in Cuban policy, end
up in the Far East Division. Very strange coincidence. There were three -
- it wasn't just one -- there were several. A neat nexus between the
Southeast Asian guys and Cuban guys."[83]

Lansdale was also spending a lot of time at air bases and other areas
in the southern United States; in Florida and in Alabama. Newman
recalled from Lansdale's travel records that one of these other areas was
some sort of a Cuban-exile camp. The record for that trip included a
cover note to the person coordinating it telling him to keep quiet.
Lansdale apparently wanted to make sure that no one knew that he was
going there.[84]

There was also an honorary graduation certificate from the sniping
school that the U.S. had in Panama. He went there, Newman recalled, in

May or April 1963. He was made an honorary graduate there. Lansdale was going to various clandestine and special forces places in the spring and summer of 1963.[85]

One more event that Newman remembered from the spring 1963 period was that Lansdale was due to retire. And he was extended by Le May, arbitrarily, for another six months or so to November 1, 1963; with no job; no real responsibilities. Fletcher Prouty claims Lansdale was just at a desk by himself.[86]

In the summer of 1963 there were two interesting events concerning Vietnam. The U.S. had a problem with Diem. The regime would not compromise at all. It went in the opposite direction. Buddhists were killed. They began immolating themselves. The regime still would not relent. The political bottom completely fell out in Saigon.[87]

Newman said he came across an intriguing article in a local, small magazine from this period. It had a picture of Lansdale and a typical title like, "America's Most Celebrated Spy." It was about a Lansdale trip to Saigon. His travel records, however, indicate that he was not supposed to be in Saigon. This was around July-August 1963.[88]

The article reported an assassination attempt on Lansdale. The assassins missed and somebody killed the alleged assassin. Then he went to a meeting with Ambassador Lodge. According to Newman, "This is clearly impossible from the record because Lansdale has no authority or position to be involved in Vietnam policy. It would make sense in terms of going back and pleading with Diem and getting Lansdale to do it. Maybe Diem would listen to Lansdale. But I did find a record. He might have been in Saigon." Newman found evidence of a six- or seven-day break in Lansdale's normal activities.[89]

Among Lansdale's contacts in the last three to four months of Kennedy's life, Newman found "a lot of Spanish names. I found names that were reminiscent of CIA type folks."[90]

In 1963, Lansdale was Fletcher Prouty's boss. Prouty insists that he was sent to the South Pole by Lansdale to get him out of the way so that he would not witness the events of November 22, 1963. Presumably this was done because if Prouty had been there he would have figured out what was going on. Prouty has claimed that in the photograph of the three tramps walking across Dealey Plaza, the man in a suit with what looks like a wire coming out of his ear and going into his suit coat is Edward Lansdale -- that he recognized the back of his head and his gate. Among Lansdale's letters, John Newman and David Lifton found a slip of paper that has "The Texas Hotel" on it and a phone number in Denton. Lansdale's letters also reveal that he was headed in the direction of Dallas in November 1963.[91]

Lansdale wrote to a number of friends and associates beginning in September 1963, of his intention to go to Texas in November. There are as many as ten letters, according to Newman, where he described this upcoming trip to two people. One was his son. The other one was General "Hangin' Sam" Williams, an old buddy and McGarr's predecessor in Vietnam. He lived in San Antonio.[92]

The last piece of paper that Newman found placing Lansdale physically in Washington is dated November 14, 1963. It concerns running errands for his wife. After that there is no record of his whereabouts except for a box of incidentals, which had this piece of paper in it. It has on it "Texas Hotel" and "Denton" and a name and phone number. As Newman said, "That might be from 1949 or it might be 1968 and again it might be November 1963. Because the Texas Hotel is where Kennedy stayed the night before he died, and Denton, Texas is just north here of Dallas, it all fits in. But it certainly is not conclusive."[93]

Lansdale dropped out of sight at this point. He resurfaced back in Washington in the Food for Peace Program and was soon given a job by Johnson back in Vietnam. He had contacts who got him interviews in the White House. In fact he would be on the ground in Vietnam when U.S. combat troops arrived.[94]

Lansdale was not the only one whose fortunes were changing now that Kennedy was dead. One of Lansdale's contacts in the White House, no doubt, was his sponsor and "big patron," Walt Rostow, who later resurfaced in a big way himself. According to Newman, "Kennedy got rid of him out of the White House after the first year; sent him packing over to the State Department."[95] Back in the White House under Kennedy's successor, Rostow moved to solidify his position. As things heated up in Vietnam, "Johnson protected himself from contrary arguments and discussions by dismissing the doubters from his staff. First McGeorge Bundy left. Then George Ball. Then Bill Moyers. The emphasis shifted to Walt Rostow, who believed that Johnson was doing the right thing in Vietnam; soon Rostow became the man who screened what the President heard and saw. Under Rostow's regime, the most optimistic news was packaged and sent to the President with covering notes which said such things as, `This will give confirmation to the statement which the President so wisely made to the Congressional leadership yesterday.'"[96] It was, most likely, only because Johnson had selected the man "who screened what the President heard and saw" that Johnson referred to Rostow as having "the most important job in the White House, aside from the President." Johnson gave credit for one crucial decision to Walt's brother, however. Eugene Victor Debs Rostow gave Johnson the idea for the Warren Commission the day Oswald died.[97]

George de Mohrenschildt's mutual friends with Lyndon Johnson, Barbara and Howard Burris, represent such significant ties between the political, economic, cultural and academic elites in Texas and the assassination of President Kennedy that they tax one's ability to call it a coincidence. The implications of their ties as they relate to the UT Rambler can be especially appreciated in their full context.

As previously mentioned, Howard Burris was Vice President Johnson's military representative and an Air Force intelligence officer. He is also much more.[98]

John Newman first learned of Howard Burris in the course of researching his book, *JFK and Vietnam*. Newman connected Burris with a pattern of gross deceptions involving battlefield statistics that took place in 1962. Kennedy and McNamara were being lied to while Johnson was being given the truth through a secret back-channel. The end point of that secret back-channel was Howard Burris. Burris would write the final memoranda that Johnson received concerning combat intelligence. Newman had discovered a foreign policy situation where the President and the Vice President were getting briefed in opposite terms. It is comparable to a hypothetical situation in which, during Operation Desert Storm, George Bush is lied to and Dan Quayle gets the truth about the status of the U.S. led coalition forces in the Persian Gulf.[99]

"I often get asked," Newman said, "about what was the exact back-channel. How did it function? How did it get there? And the best I can determine from ground zero in Vietnam all the way back to the Vice President's desk is a chain of Air Force intelligence officers all the way to Burris."[100]

In May 1961, during the Johnson trip to Vietnam, Burris was being rehearsed on how to control LBJ in the context of that trip. He was told what he could say or could not say to the vice president; which is amazing because ostensibly he works for the vice president. No one should be able to tell an Air Force colonel what he can and cannot tell to a vice president. The question is: Who is telling him? The answer is the boys in the woodwork.

There is another time period in Newman's book which deals with the back-channel to LBJ. Newman had long discussions with Burris about where he got this. "And the answer was the boys in the woodwork. And the question was: Who are the boys in the woodwork? And the answer was: 'Well I'd rather not really say and bring all of that up. You, I know, you're one of them.' Alright, I'm military, I also have an intelligence background. Peter Dale Scott and I have been working very closely on a number of issues. He's writing a book as a matter of fact. He was assuming for a while that it was military. And I said, `Peter, it may not be that. It may be Langley.' He said, `Why do you say that?' Well there's one more piece. Burris told me that later on, `McCone put a stop to what I was getting from him.' This was relating to the combat intelligence. McCone was directing CIA. And all of the clues I got out of this fellow on who his contacts were -- my own interpretation was that they were in fact CIA. I don't know that for sure."[101]

Information about Burris originally began to surface with the book *The Senator Must Die* by Robert Morrow. Morrow wrote about two colonels whom he did not name. In 1977 a young man was hitchhiking in Baltimore who had a story he wanted to tell about his father's involvement in the Kennedy assassination.

Robert Morrow happened to pick him up.[102]

The young man learned that Morrow had investigated aspects of the JFK assassination. He told Morrow a story about his father, a former Air Force intelligence officer, who was involved in the Kennedy assassination. The young man had witnessed his father, who was very close to Lyndon Johnson, taking money to Haiti during 1963. Not only did he see the money he heard the telephone conversations as well.[103]

Not really believing him, Morrow put the story out of his mind -- until the Colonel, the young man's father, went to his son's girlfriend and confessed. He said, "Everything my son told you (to the girlfriend and to Morrow) is true. Can you get me immunity from the House Select Committee?" This conversation took place in 1977.[104]

The Colonel admitted it. And this offer to testify if given immunity was given to Committee Chairman Louis Stokes in 1978. Assassination researcher Gus Russo reportedly saw the affidavit and spoke to the people involved. But when Robert Morrow gave the affidavit to the HSCA it ended there. The HSCA did not want to deal with it.[105]

The names of these colonels aren't given in the book. Morrow gives them the code names "Intellfirst" and "SIO" (First Intelligence Officer and Second Intelligence Officer). There are a few clues given in the book. He gives a couple of Air Force assignment clues in Europe; what they had done in the forties and fifties.

They are at the top of the military intelligence ladder. They are connected to the CIA.[106]

Following Morrow's clues, Russo discovered their identities. He then located one of the colonels -- the one who wanted to go to the HSCA, "Intellfirst." Russo and Jim Marrs and another researcher went to meet "Intellfirst" at his home in Florida. He is eighty years old. They said they were researching the Johnson Administration and that they knew he was on Johnson's Inaugural Committee.[107]

"Intellfirst" bought their story and invited them in. They got his whole biography from him and his military record. Russo and Marrs did not bring up the subject of Kennedy but "Intellfirst" did and he talked about how he hates the Kennedys. He gave them his whole background.[108]

The first thing he wanted to talk about was his good friend Howard Burris. They were on the Inauguration Committee together. They worked for Air Force intelligence and the CIA. He said they were CIA all the time. They ran around the world. They were friends with Charles Cabell.[109]

"Intellfirst" was air attache in Hong Kong. He was in Rumania. He was in France. He retired from the military and worked for Martin Marietta in the early sixties selling defense contracts to his former Air Force superiors. And all the while his closest buddy was Howard Burris. That is the first name he mentioned to Russo and Marrs.[110]

When he worked for Martin Marietta he was the liaison to NATO. This was during the late fifties and early sixties when they bought the Jupiter missiles to put in Turkey. Kennedy had wanted the missiles removed from Turkey. The very people who defied Kennedy's orders were this colonel's NATO clients -- the ones to whom he was selling the missiles. They were the ones who did not listen to Kennedy when he ordered them to keep these missiles out. They were all against Kennedy.[111]

When he was selling the missiles for Martin Marietta after he retired he had another buddy, a Colonel Anderson, who was with NATO in Europe. "Intellfirst" admitted that they were drinking champagne in Paris on the day Kennedy was assassinated. They were toasting Kennedy's death. He admitted all of this to Russo and Marrs. The girlfriend of the son of "Intellfirst" went to the HSCA with this story and it died there.[112]

Armed with this information Russo went back home to verify the colonel's history. Marrs did the same and they learned more about him. Russo then started reading about Howard Burris. He discovered Burris was Air Force intelligence. He is very close friends with Director of Central Intelligence Richard Helms. He is from Texas and has oil money. Russo also learned that Howard Burris is in George de Mohrenschildt's address book four times. Next to one of the entries there is a slash. It says, "Howard Burris / Haiti."[113] "Intellfirst" is so high up in intelligence that reporters refer to him for special sound bites and for blurbs for articles on occasion. His name is not commonly known but people in the business have reason to have heard of him.[114]

The critical thing for Gus Russo was that "Intellfirst" admitted what his son said was true and offered to talk to Congress. And there are other coincidences like de Mohrenschildt's phone book. Not only was de

Mohrenschildt writing to LBJ in the spring of 1963 and for years after, so was "Intellfirst." According to Russo there are many of his letters at the LBJ Library. They all knew each other. And they were all tied to this NATO network who was defying Kennedy.[115]

Russo went back to Florida to do more research into this and to look for the son. What he found instead was that the son had possibly been murdered. He was found on the streets of Florida City naked and curled up in the embryo position as if he had been tossed aside. The official medical report said his blood alcohol level was one-point-one which is not high enough to kill a man who is six-foot-four; or even enough to cause him to pass out. It was speculated that he choked on his own vomit although there was no evidence of that. At age thirty-eight he apparently just died. He was cremated two days later by his father, "Intellfirst." Although they have a family plot in Virginia he cremated his only son who was telling everybody his father killed Kennedy.[116]

Colonel Howard Burris retired in 1964 and has remained in private business and civilian life. Some personal information was learned from his resume (obtained by researcher Larry Haapanen from the LBJ Library), and a record from researcher Mary Ferrell's files. Burris was born near San Antonio on April 26, 1918 (Ferrell indicates April 18, 1926). He graduated from West Point in 1942. During World War II he commanded bomber units in England and France during two combat tours from 1943 to 1945. Ferrell lists him as "Deputy Commanding Officer" of the 386th Bombardment Bomber Group Ninth Air Force. From 1945 to 1949, Burris was Headquarters Commandant for the Continental Air Command; was assigned to staff support at the United Nations; and was involved in a "Special Mission to Government of Mexico." From 1950 to 1952 he was aide to Air Force Secretary Finletter, and became the executive officer to Air Force Secretary Talbott in 1953. From 1954 to 1957 he was attache to the U.S. Embassy in Switzerland. From 1957 to 1960 he served as International Liaison Officer, Department of the Air Force and was assigned to a special mission to Hungary, Poland, and the Soviet Union (1959). In 1961 he became Vice President Johnson's assistant for national security affairs. His foreign decorations were the *Croix de Guerre* (with Silver Star) from France; the Royal Order of the Sword from Sweden; and the Medal of Merit from Brazil.[117] According to the record from Mary Ferrell's files:

Colonel Burris was supposedly original case officer for Nosenko. When Nosenko defected, Burris was called back to Switzerland. He was intelligence officer who ran Nosenko in Switzerland in Jan. 1964.[118]

Other sources indicate that Burris was in business with Nosenko's case officer. In an article written in 1991, Robert Morrow referred to an

Air Force colonel who sounds like Intellfirst and to his "counterpart" who is also a colonel. This counterpart, after retiring, set up a firm in Paris, France as a cover for intelligence operations. In this firm, Morrow writes, "The colonel's counterpart had a partner who just so happened to be the case officer of Yuri Noshenko [sic], the famous Russian defector who, in 1964, made overtures to our embassy in Geneva, Switzerland about Lee Harvey Oswald working for the Russians." Larry Haapanen, in a letter to this author, wrote, "As far as I know, the only person who would be so described as Nosenko's case officer would be Tenant Bagley, who is mentioned in various published accounts of the Nosenko affair."[119]

For the purposes of this paper, any involvement Burris may have had with Yuri Nosenko will sufficiently speak for itself. What will be emphasized here is the possible significance of Burris' involvement with European Theater bombing, the Office of Secretary of the Air Force, and his time spent in Switzerland as it pertains to the Kennedy assassination and UT.

Walt Rostow's primary duty, as an economist in the London-based economic subdivision within the prestigious Research and Analysis Branch of the OSS, was target selection for the massive strategic bombing campaign against Germany. These economists, who called themselves the Enemy Objectives Unit (EOU), spawned a renegade group that included Rostow. They differed greatly with the others in the EOU and with their commanders over targeting strategy. Known as the "oily boys" because of their preference for petroleum, oil and lubricant (POL) targets over rail system targets, they planned and launched a covert psychological war known as "Operation Octopus" against their own commanders to force the acceptance of POL targeting.[120] The operation was a success and began a pattern of renegade behavior throughout Rostow's career as well as a long friendship between Rostow and fellow oily boy, future Deputy Director of Central Intelligence, Charles P. Cabell, Jr.[121]

As with Burris, Switzerland was a very special place for Walt Rostow. In 1947 he married Elspeth Vaughn Davies, a Barnard College girl he met in pre-war Geneva.[122] That same year he became assistant to the Executive Secretary of the Economic Commission for Europe (ECE), a U.N. agency located in Geneva Switzerland. In 1949 he left the ECE and was replaced there by his brother Eugene. It was Eugene Victor Debs Rostow to whom President Johnson credited the idea of appointing the Warren Commission.[123] Switzerland was also a special place for Allen Dulles. From December 1942 until the end of the war he was head of U.S. intelligence in Switzerland. That same month he began a long love affair and professional relationship with Mary Bancroft, who was a life-long friend of Michael Paine's parents.[124] Michael's wife is Ruth Paine, to whom Lee Oswald and Roger Craig said the Dealey Plaza Rambler belonged. This paper will further explore the Bancroft-Paine-Dulles relationship in the context of the Dealey Plaza Rambler and the UT Rambler.

As we have already seen, Harry Ransom had a special relationship with Air Force intelligence and the European Theater[125] and with the Office of Secretary of the Air Force. It is quite probable that Ransom not only knew Rostow at Yale but, during the war, provided him with editorial intelligence reports on the results of POL bombing missions undertaken by Howard Burris.

Currently Burris owns several corporations, one of which has to do with high-speed rail technology.[126] He has oil leases on two continents including leases in Iran.[127]

His son, Howard Lay Burris, Jr. was married for a while to Princess Shahrazad Pahlbod, the niece of the late Shah of Iran -- attesting to the closeness of his father's relationship with former CIA director and former ambassador to Iran Richard Helms, who himself was a life-long friend of the late Shah. When they divorced in 1982 it was reported that "Everybody's still pally, in the Royal Manner."[128]

The Shah of Iran, Muhammad Reza Pahlevi, took Iran's government back from the Iranian Nationalist Movement led by Muhammad Mussadegh in a CIA coup called Operation Ajax. "The operation was essentially formulated by the Dulles brothers, working together, on June 25, 1953, at a meeting in John Foster Dulles' office in the State Department." It was done by arranging the disappearance of Mussadegh's powerful political supporters and hiring paid demonstrators to march against Mussadegh; orchestrated by Richard Helms.[129] Chosen by the CIA to run the country for the Shah was General Fazlollah Zahedi, a suspected pro-Nazi. Mussadegh's main threat was to the profits of U.S. and British oil companies in Iran.[130]

According to Robert Morrow, "The business of putting the Shah back in power and the oil wells back into the hands of the western powers was handed over to the CIA and Kermit "Kim" Roosevelt, who headed its Middle East section. Roosevelt was to be Richard Helm's original case officer.

"Helms' career advanced rapidly. He was brought into the CIA fold to take over the Office of Strategic Operations (OSO). In those days the OSO was the group responsible for perfecting the Agency's direct espionage and other esoteric activities such as assassination. One of OSO's first assignments was to overthrow Mohammed Mossadeq....

"After Mossadeq fell from grace, Roosevelt made an enemy of OSO chief Helms. He started to feel sorry for the deposed leader after he had done a three-year stint in prison. Roosevelt arranged for Mossadeq's release with a comfortable pension! However, Mossadeq died soon afterward, a death engineered by Helms."[131]

Howard Burris, Jr. currently presides over long-held family business interests in Austin. Howard Burris, Sr. ⟨OBJ⟩⟨OBJ⟩⟨OBJ⟩⟨OBJ⟩⟨OBJ⟩⟨OBJ⟩⟨OBJ⟩⟨OBJ⟩⟨OBJ⟩⟨OBJ⟩purchased "property from Governor Beauford Jester, who died in office in 1949. The governor had planned to build a homesite on the ranch." This land is now owned by Jester Land Management (JLM) and has become the exclusive Jester residential development in northwest Austin. Howard Burris, Jr., president of Burris and Company, bought the assets of JLM in February 1988 from his father's firm, Jester Development Company.[132]

Colonel Burris' wife, Barbara J. Burris, is the daughter of Governor Jester.[133] In a news story that appeared the day after Kennedy was assassinated Texans were reminded of the late Governor's posthumous link to the assassination: Under the headline, "Gov. Connally Keeps Power" it explained, "No similar circumstance has occurred in Texas history. The only time a lieutenant governor succeeded to the governorship was on the death of Gov. Beauford A. [sic] Jester July 11, 1949. Allan Shivers, then lieutenant governor, automatically moved up to the governor's office."[134] Carl J. Eckhardt adds, "Governor Jester was the first Texas governor to die in office. He died on July 11, 1949 [at age fifty-six] while aboard a train bound for Galveston. He was interred in Oakwood Cemetery in Corsicana, Texas."[135] Few families can claim to have been as close to the deaths of two U.S. chief executives as the Burris family. And since, as John Newman and Gus Russo have shown, they possibly benefited from the death of President Kennedy, two questions are raised: How did Alan Shivers come to be lieutenant governor? And how did Governor Jester die? These questions become more important given the fact, as John Newman has reported, Burris revealed, "Johnson knew -- was sure [in 1963] -- he was going to be dropped from the ticket."[136]

In the February 9, 1993 PBS Frontline broadcast, "The Secret File on J. Edgar Hoover", eyewitness Evelyn Lincoln revealed for the first time the reason Kennedy put LBJ on the ticket at the 1960 convention: J. Edgar Hoover and Lyndon Johnson blackmailed Kennedy into doing it by threatening to reveal his sexual activities.

During the Dallas filming of the movie *JFK*, an aeronautical engineer named Ron Ellison came to the Assassination Information Center and said he had known LBJ's nephew Sam Johnson, Jr. Ellison claimed that during a meeting with Sam at a Houston hotel in October 1962, he (Ellison) criticized LBJ's political savvy for becoming vice president. Sam's response was that the reason LBJ did it was because JFK will die in office.[137]

Having been forced to take LBJ as vice president, the only recourse Kennedy may have had in removing him from the 1964 ticket, was to expose Johnson's dirty dealings with the likes of Bobby Baker and Billy Sol Estes.[138] Such exposure would prevent Johnson from assuming power even by force -- the probability of which Kennedy was well aware considering he wanted the movie *Seven Days in May* made "as a warning to the nation."[139]

A closer look at Governor Jester's daughter sheds more light on these questions. A Nexus search for the name Barbara Burris[140] revealed a Barbara J. Burris who was press secretary to Representative Dante Fascell (D, FL) of Miami. She is also a fund raiser and supporter of the Cuban American National Foundation run by Jose S. Sorzano. The chairman of the foundation is Jorge L. Mas Canosa.[141] There is also a Barbara J. Burris who was a childhood friend of famed concert pianist Van Cliburn and very involved in the Van Cliburn competition in Ft. Worth. Another "early booster and close friend" of Van Cliburn's was wealthy Dallas oil man David Harold Byrd,[142] the owner of the Texas School Book Depository Building.[143] The significance of this to UT and the JFK assassination will be explored further in this paper.

Beyond this paper, however, another matter begs to be investigated. Given the relationship between Barbara J. Burris and Brigade 2506 veteran Jorge Mas Canosa, the question arises anew concerning the origin of the name Barbara J. for the infamous Bay of Pigs troopship. As with the Burris name, perhaps the Jester name is also well known in clandestine histories.

Since Beauford Jester's appointment to the Board of Regents in 1929 the name Jester has been well known on the UT campus. According to Carl J. Eckhardt, "Beauford H. Jester spearheaded the building drive which resulted in the construction of Hogg Auditorium, Gregory Gymnasium, the Texas Union, and the Main[144] Building. ...At the time of the dedication of the Jester Center on the campus of The University of Texas, The Austin American-Statesman published the following statement: `Beauford Halbert Jester built a lot of buildings for the University of Texas, and now the University has built one for him. The Beauford Jester Center, UT's version of the resident college that was three years and $18 million in the making, was dedicated Saturday.'"[145]

Aside from having the wrong friends, Harry Ransom may have had a more direct connection to the JFK assassination. It came to light in a small circuitous story with possibly large implications. The story was a favorite of David Price's and Tom Cunningham's as an example of how "it's a small world." One detail of the story was that Harry Ransom was such a regular guest at Dallas' Adolphus Hotel he got to know a bellman there well enough to grant the bellman a special request. The bellman asked Ransom to help get his son enrolled at UT and get him a job there to help pay his tuition. Ransom was more than happy to comply.

The son, Barry Benton, left UT in 1975 and became a teacher of this paper's author at Dallas' Richland College in 1976. The job Ransom had arranged years earlier for Benton was in David Price's and Tom Cunningham's University Publications office where this author eventually worked after leaving Benton's classes at Richland in 1976 to attend UT.[146]

What is important here is that the Adolphus, according to assassination figure Jim Hicks, was the "communications center for the assassination."[147] It was across the street from Jack Ruby's Carousel Club where "Lyndon Johnson's friends" were known to frequent. Warren Commission attorneys Leon Hubert and Burt Griffin, were interested in a man named Breck Wall who "was an entertainer at the Adolphus Hotel, Dallas, at the time of President Kennedy's assassination. Ruby called him in Galveston at 11:47 p.m. Saturday, November 23, 1963. He also visited Ruby at the county jail." Hubert and Griffin requested further investigation of Mr. Wall but their request was apparently ignored by the Commission.[148]

We now begin to see a very powerful group involved with UT, the CIA and JFK, all known to each other; all with shared backgrounds and futures; shared past and future interests; anti-Kennedy people who very likely shared their grievances with each other; and all of whom have past or future, professional or personal ties to Texas, its university system, and its most notorious crime: Johnson, Dulles, Cabell, Helms, Lansdale, Burris, Rostow, Ransom, Byrd, de Mohrenschildt, and "Intellfirst." As we shall see, their ominous and dark interrelationships become even more apparent.

* * *

Notes:

1. House Select Committee on Assassinations, Vol. XII, pp. 8-9, 18, (hereafter as 12 HSCA 8-9, 18) cited in Dennis Ford, "A Conspiracy Model and a Conspirator: Predictions and Possible Refutations," The Third Decade, (Vol. 9, No. 1, Nov. 1992), p. 25; Michael L. Kurtz, Crime of The Century, (Knoxville, TN: University of Tennessee Press, 1982),p. 132; Josiah Thompson, Six Seconds in Dallas, (NY: Bernard Geis, 1967; Berkeley, 1976), pp. 303-06, 404-05.

2. Jim Marrs, *Crossfire: The Plot That Killed Kennedy*, (NY: Carroll & Graf, 1989), p. 331.

3. Warren Commission Report pp. 160-61 (hereafter as WCR 160-61); Mark Lane, *Rush to Judgment*, (NY: Holt, Rinehart & Winston, 1966) pp. 173-74; Roger Craig, *When They Kill a President*, (unpublished manuscript, 1971), pp. 14, 18; *Two Men in Dallas: John Kennedy and Roger Craig*. 60 minutes, videotape. Narrated by Mark Lane. Alpa Productions, 1977.

4. Jesse E. Curry, *Retired Dallas Police Chief Jesse Curry reveals his JFK Assassination File*, (American Poster and Printing, 1969), p. 72. Note: Craig never changed his story throughout his life, though apparently others did. This paper's author accepts Craig's own statements about the Rambler as credible and reliable. (See Two Men in Dallas, videotape.)

5. Kurtz, *Crime of the Century*, pp. 132-33; Robert Groden with Harrison Livingstone, *High Treason*, (NY: Conservatory Press, 1989) p. 162.

6. Marrs, *Crossfire*, pp. 332, 560.

7. 12 HSCA 18; U.S. Congress, House, The Final Assassinations Report: Report of the Select Committee on Assassinations, U.S. House of Representatives, (NY: Bantam, 1979), p. 56; DeLloyd J. Guth and David R. Wrone, The Assassination of John F. Kennedy: A Comprehensive Historical and Legal Bibliography, 1963- 1979, (Westport, CT: Greenwood, 1980), p. xxxiv.

8. The car's current whereabouts is known to its researchers but will not be disclosed publicly in order to protect the car from potential vandals, thieves, and publicity seekers.

9. This evidence will be presented at length in this paper.

10. Ford, p. 28.

11. As attributed to the character Sherlock Holmes in the novel *The Hound of the Baskervilles* by Sir Arthur Conan Doyle. (Orlando Park, The Sherlock Holmes Encyclopedia, (Secaucus, NJ: Citadel Press, 1981), p. 84.

12. There was a third magazine lying beneath the top two which is yet to be positively identified from the photographs.

13. This was verified by Steve Palmer (Highway Dept.) and Ken Hitchcock (Motor Vehicles Dept.) in late 1991 and again in early 1993.

14. Bert R. Sugar with Sybil Leek, The Assassination Chain, (NY: Corwin Books, 1976), p. 113.

15. Interview: Nov. 13, 1990, David Price, Director of University

Publications. Note: Price said to this author he was told this by Ross Shipman, retired oil and gas industry lobbyist and C.B. Smith's next door neighbor. Smith was in a nursing home by this time but his second wife, Austin artist Jean Andrews, still lived next door to Shipman.

16. Interview: Nov. 13, 1990, Mary Ellen Oliver, University Of Texas at Austin Visitor Center.

17. Interview: Nov. 13, 1990, Steve Bittick, University Publications staff; Jeff Kanipe, UT McDonald Observatory staff. Note: Bittick and Kanipe recalled Smith's reputation as native Austinites only; they did not know C.B. Smith personally.

18. C.B. Smith Motors Warranty Guarantee No. 64413A issued Apr., 26, 1963 to George Gordon Wing; The University of Texas at Austin, Official Directory, Students, Faculty, Staff, 1990-91, p. 561. Note: Office: Room 304, Batts Hall, phone: 471-8673, and room 112, Batts Hall, phone: 471-4936; Home: 2102 Robinhood Trail, Austin, Tx., 78703.

19. Craig, *When They Kill a President*, p. 9.

20. Carl J. Eckhardt, *One Hundred Faithful to The University of Texas at Austin*, (self published after 1976) p. 80; Interview: Dec. 7, 1990, David Price and Thomas G. Cunningham, Assistant Director of University Publications. Note: Price often told this author that Ransom was fond enough of former UT art student Price to give him a job in the Office of Coordinator of University Publications in 1960 where he began working closely with Ransom designing and printing The Texas Quarterly. In 1969 Ransom appointed Price director of the department where he remained until his death in July 1991. Cunningham often told this author that had been a Specialist Fourth-Class in the U.S. Army Counter Intelligence Corps in Korea in the late 1950s after receiving training at Ft. Holabird, Maryland. Before joining David Price at UT Publications, Cunningham said he had worked at Chance Vought Aircraft near Dallas, Tx. (See Maxine Price letter to the editor, Austin American-Statesman, May 12, 1993, p. A18.)

21. Ami Chen Mills, *CIA Off Campus*, (Chicago, IL: Bill of Rights Foundation, 1990), pp. 22, 23.

22. Marj Wightman, "Cuban Revolt Devours Own, Ex-Prisoner Says," Austin American, Oct. 2, 1963, p. 29, col. 6.

23. Warren Commission Exhibit (CE) 2094, Warren Commission Hearings and Exhibits, Vol. 24, p. 528 (hereafter as CE 2094, 24 H 528), cited in Peter Dale Scott, The Dallas Conspiracy, (unpublished manuscript, 1971), ch. III, p. 15n.

24. Anthony Summers, *Conspiracy*, (NY: McGraw-Hill, 1980), pp. 450-52. 25.

26. John Stockwell, *The Praetorian Guard*, (South End Press, Boston, MA: 1991), p. 32; Interview: May 29, 1991, Earl Golz.

27. Silber was fired as dean of UT's College of Arts and Sciences in 1970. In a surprise resignation, C.B. Smith left his position as chairman of the Arts and Sciences Foundation, a major private fund-raising organization at UT. "Several members of the foundation committee, composed of 27 widely-known and

mostly wealthy Texans, were known to be opposed to the dismissal of former A&S Dean John R. Silber and the division of the college into three separate units." (See Sandra Goertz, "A&S Foundation Chairman Steps Down as Panel Head," The Daily Texan, Sept. 30, 1970.)

28. Stockwell, *The Praetorian Guard*, pp. 32-33.

29. Interview: Apr. 27, 1991, Philip Agee.

30. This student, who wishes to remain anonymous, was interviewed in late April 1991 by John Garcia, one of the primary researchers for this paper.

31. Interview: Mar. 22, 1991, David Price.

32. Interview: Mar. 22, 1991, David Price.

33. Interview: Jun. 29, 1993, John Wheat.

34. Interview: Feb. 25, 1993, a source who requested anonymity. Note: This source had personally known Ellen Dulles when they were both students at the UT Spanish and Portuguese Department.

35. The University of Texas at Austin, Official Directory, Students, Faculty, Staff, 1990-91, p. 518.

36. Peter Wyden, *Bay of Pigs*, (NY: Simon & Schuster, 1979), p.266. Note: At the time of the assassination Charles' brother Earle Cabell was mayor of Dallas. The Cabell family owned the Minit Mart chain of curbside convenience stores which had been bought by Dallas oil man Clint Murchison when another Cabell brother, Ben, became mayor. Murchison sold them to Joe C. Thompson who turned them into 7-Eleven. (See Jane Wolfe, The Murchisons: The Rise and Fall of a Texas Dynasty, [NY: St. Martin's, 1989], pp. 172-73.)

37. William J. Gill, *The Ordeal of Otto Otepka*, (New Rochelle, NY: Arlington House, 1969), p. 92.

38. According to John Wheat, a former student of Dr. Wing's, another daughter, Edith Dulles, was a student in UT's Spanish and Portuguese Department. (Interview: Jun. 29, 1993, John Wheat.)

39. Church Committee, Alleged Assassination Plots Involving Foreign Leaders, (NY: W.W. Norton, 1974), p. 181-187, cited in John Ranelagh, The Agency: The Rise and Decline of the CIA, (NY: Simon & Schuster, Touchstone ed., 1987), p. 358.

40. Church Committee, Alleged Assassination Plots, p. 184.

41. Summers, *Conspiracy*, pp. 425-426.

42. Trumbull Higgins, *The Perfect Failure: Kennedy, Eisenhower, and the CIA at the Bay of Pigs*, (NY: Norton, 1987), pp. 85, 86.

43. Higgins, *The Perfect Failure*, p. 121; ; Edward B. Claflin, ed., JFK Wants to Know: Memos from the President's Office, 1961-1963, (NY: William Morrow, 1991), p. 58.

44. Higgins, *The Perfect Failure*, p. 151.

45. Blanche Wiesen Cook, "C.D. Jackson: Cold War Propagandist," CovertAction Information Bulletin, No. 35, Fall 1990, pp. 33, 36.

46. Some sources describe Rostow simply as a staff member of CENIS while others have him co-founding it with economist and former CIA Office of National Estimates Director Max F. Millikan. David Wise in his book The Invisible Government, reported that Rostow founded CENIS on his own and

was joined by Millikan in 1952.

47. Gill, *The Ordeal of Otto Otepka*, pp. 94-98; David Wise with Thomas B. Ross, *The Invisible Government*, (NY: Bantam Books, 1965), p. 260.

48. Michael Canfield with Alan J. Weberman, *Coup d'état in America*, (NY: The Third Press, 1975), p. 21; Dick Russell, *The Man Who Knew Too Much*, (NY: Carroll & Graf, 1992), p. 120.

49. Peter R. Whitmey, Letter to the Editor, The Third Decade, (Vol. 9, No. 5, Jul. 1993), pp. 13-14.

50. Canfield with Weberman, *Coup d'état in America*, p. 22; Russell, *The Man Who Knew Too Much*, p. 121; Whitmey, pp. 13-14.

51. Whitmey, pp. 13-14.

52. Whitmey, p. 13.

53. Whitmey, p. 13; Russell, *The Man Who Knew Too Much*, p. 121.

54. Peter Dale Scott, *Crime and Cover-Up: the CIA, the Mafia, and the Dallas-Watergate Connection*, (Berkeley, CA: Westworks, 1977), p. 54, n. 34; republished in Santa Barbara, CA: Open Archive Press, 1993.

55. Russell, *The Man Who Knew Too Much*, p. 30.

56. Russell, *The Man Who Knew Too Much*, pp. 120-21. See also: Bernard Fensterwald, Jr., *Coincidence or Conspiracy*, (NY: Zebra, 1977), pp. 38, 217-218, 228-230, 470.

57. Church Committee, Alleged Assassination Plots, p. 33, cited in Bernard Fensterwald, Jr., Coincidence or Conspiracy, (NY: Zebra, 1977), p. 251.

58. The University of Texas at Austin with The Lyndon Baines Johnson Library, LBJ: The Difference He Made, 25th Anniversary Symposium, May 3-5, 1990, unpublished complete transcript, (Austin, TX: Kennedy Reporting Service, 1990), pp. 321-25.

[OBJ]59. The University of Texas at Arlington, "C.B. Smith, Sr., October 24, 1967," (Galleys of biography prepared for annual homecoming ceremonies honoring outstanding alumni), photocopy from Austin American-Statesman files.

60. Ken Lawrence, "Academics: An Overview," Dirty Work II: The CIA in Africa, eds. Ellen Ray, et. al., (Secaucus NJ: Lyle Stuart, 1980) p. 80, cited in Mills, CIA Off Campus, pp. 17, 18.

61. Interview: Mar. 1991, John Garcia.

62. Part of a Latin phrase meaning "unconcerned with this trivial matter."

63. "De Mohrenschildt -- LBJ White House letters: December 27, 1966, and January 6, 1967" respectively, cited in Russell, The Man Who Knew Too Much, pp. 271, 759.

64. Warren Hinckle with William Turner, *The Fish is Red*, (NY: Harper & Row, 1981), pp. 67-69; republished as *Deadly Secrets*, Thunder's Mouth Press, 1992; David Horowitz, Ramparts magazine, Oct. 1969, pp. 39- 40.

65. Hinckle with Turner, *The Fish is Red*, pp. 67-69.

66. David Horowitz, Ramparts, Oct. 1969, pp. 39-40.

67. George Gordon Wing, *Octavio Paz: Poetry, Politics, and the Myth of the Mexican*, doctoral dissertation, University of California at Berkeley, Mar. 3, 1961, p. 3; Biographical information obtained from UT's Spanish and

Portuguese Department.

68. The University of Texas at Arlington, "C.B. Smith, Sr., October 24, 1967."

69. Unpublished Transcript: John M. Newman with Gus Russo, "Unscheduled Workshop on Major General Edward G. Lansdale, Colonel Howard L. Burris and Air Force Intelligence Connections to the Kennedy Assassination," Second Annual Assassination Symposium on John F. Kennedy, Hyatt Regency Hotel at Reunion Square, Dallas, Tx., Oct. 24, 1992, p. 1.

70. John M. Newman, JFK and Vietnam, (NY: Warner Books, 1992), p. 3.

71. Unpublished Transcript: Newman with Russo, p. 1.

72. Unpublished Transcript: Newman with Russo, p. 3.

73. Unpublished Transcript: Newman with Russo, p. 3.

74. Unpublished Transcript: Newman with Russo, p. 14.

75. Unpublished Transcript: Newman with Russo, p. 3.

76. Unpublished Transcript: Newman with Russo, pp. 3-4. 77. Unpublished Transcript: Newman with Russo, p. 4.

78. Unpublished Transcript: Newman with Russo, p. 4.

79. Unpublished Transcript: Newman with Russo, pp. 13-14.

80. Unpublished Transcript: Newman with Russo, p. 5.

81. Unpublished Transcript: Newman with Russo, pp. 4-5.

82. Unpublished Transcript: Newman with Russo, p. 5.

83. Unpublished Transcript: Newman with Russo, p. 27.

84. Unpublished Transcript: Newman with Russo, p. 8.

85. Unpublished Transcript: Newman with Russo, p. 8.

86. Unpublished Transcript: Newman with Russo, p. 8.

87. Unpublished Transcript: Newman with Russo, p. 8.

88. Unpublished Transcript: Newman with Russo, p. 9.

89. Unpublished Transcript: Newman with Russo, pp. 9-10.

90. Unpublished Transcript: Newman with Russo, p. 10.

91. Unpublished Transcript: Newman with Russo, p. 2; Stone, JFK: The Book of the Film, pp. 182-183.

92. Unpublished Transcript: Newman with Russo, p. 11; Stone, JFK: The Book of the Film, p. 183.

93. Unpublished Transcript: Newman with Russo, pp. 11-12.

94. Unpublished Transcript: Newman with Russo, p. 12.

95. Unpublished Transcript: Newman with Russo, p. 32; David Halberstam, The Best and the Brightest, (NY: Penguin, 1972), pp. 159-99; Edward B. Claflin, ed., JFK Wants to Know: Memos from the President's Office, 1961-1963, (NY: William Morrow, 1991), p. 58; Cecil B. Currey, Edward Lansdale: The Unquiet American, (Boston: Houghton Mifflin, 1988), p. 395, 14n.

96. Doris Kearns, Lyndon Johnson and the American Dream, (NY: Harper & Row, 1976), p. 320.

97. "Scholar Who's No. 2 at the White House," Business Week, Feb. 25, 1967, cited in Gill, The Ordeal of Otto Otepka, p. 21; Lyndon Baines Johnson, The Vantage Point: Perspectives of the Presidency, 1963-1969, (NY: Holt, Rinehart & Winston, 1971), p. 26.

98. Unpublished Transcript: Newman with Russo, pp. 1, 14.
99. Unpublished Transcript: Newman with Russo, p. 15.
100. Unpublished Transcript: Newman with Russo, p. 26.
101. Unpublished Transcript: Newman with Russo, pp. 24-25.
102. Unpublished Transcript: Newman with Russo, pp. 15-16.
103. Unpublished Transcript: Newman with Russo, p. 16.
104. Unpublished Transcript: Newman with Russo, p. 16.
105. Unpublished Transcript: Newman with Russo, p. 16.
106. Unpublished Transcript: Newman with Russo, pp. 16-17
107. Unpublished Transcript: Newman with Russo, p. 17.
108. Unpublished Transcript: Newman with Russo, pp. 17-19.
109. Unpublished Transcript: Newman with Russo, pp. 17-19.
110. Unpublished Transcript: Newman with Russo, pp. 17-19.
111. Unpublished Transcript: Newman with Russo, pp. 17-19.
112. Unpublished Transcript: Newman with Russo, pp. 17-19.
113. Unpublished Transcript: Newman with Russo, p. 19.
114. Unpublished Transcript: Newman with Russo, p. 21.
115. Unpublished Transcript: Newman with Russo, p. 21.
116. Unpublished Transcript: Newman with Russo, pp. 21-22.
117. Unpublished Transcript: Newman with Russo, pp. 32-33; Biographic Data, Howard Lay Burris, LBJ Library; Mary Ferrell Database record, "Howard Lay Burris," obtained by this author from Gordon Winslow.
118. Mary Ferrell Database record, "Howard Lay Burris,".
119. Robert Morrow, "The Kennedy Cover Up Continued," EastSide Weekend newsmagazine, Apr. 25-May 1, 1991, pp. 1-3; Larry Haapanen, Letter to Richard Bartholomew, Jul. 27, 1993.
120. Barry M. Katz, *Foreign Intelligence*, (Cambridge, MA: Harvard University, 1989), p. 97-115, 120.
121. Walt W. Rostow, *Pre-invasion Bombing Strategy: General Eisenhower's Decision of March 25, 1944*, (Austin, TX: The University of Texas Press, 1981), pp. 32, 45.
122. Gill, p. 92.
123. Gill, pp. 92-98; Johnson, *The Vantage Point*, p. 26.
124. Mary Bancroft, *Autobiography of a Spy*, (NY: William Morrow, 1983), pp. 54, 128-31.
125. Harry Huntt Ransom, "Notes for an Epitaph: Rise and Fall of the Luftwaffe" (Air Force Reprint, 32 pp.), cited in "Bibliography of Harry Huntt Ransom," p. 1.
126. A Texas grassroots organization called DERAIL is currently fighting powerful interests which has included John Connally and Ben Barnes. These special interests would use the idea of high-speed rail to create a boondoggle to enrich themselves at taxpayers' expense.
127. Unpublished Transcript: Newman with Russo, p. 33.
128. Style section, The Washington Post, Mar. 17, 1982; Princess Ashraf Pahlavi, *Faces in a Mirror*, (NY: Prentice Hall, 1989), cited in Robert Morrow, *The Senator Must Die*, (Santa Monica, CA: Roundtable, 1988), p. 11n.

129. Morrow, *The Senator Must Die*, p. 10.

130. Ranelagh, *The Agency*, p. 261-62.

131. Morrow, *The Senator Must Die*, p. 10.

132. John MacDougall, "Not Jester Estates", Austin Business Journal, Jun. 26, 1989.

133. Unpublished Transcript: Newman with Russo, p. 33.

134. San Antonio Express News, Nov. 23, 1963, p. 16A, col. 4.

135. Eckhardt, *One Hundred Faithful...*, p. 51.

136. Unpublished Transcript: Newman with Russo, p. 33.

137. Interview: Sept. 20, 1991. Daryl Howard, Assassination Information Center.

138. Kirk Wilson, *Texas Unsolved Mysteries*, (NY: Carroll & Graf, 1990), p. 99.

139. Arthur Schlesinger, *The Imperial Presidency*, pp. 198, 417, cited in Robert Sam Anson, *They've Killed the President*, (NY: Bantam, 1975), p. 280.

140. In January 1993, while going through old notes, this paper's author noticed a coincidence involving an incident that meant nothing at the time it occurred. A resume that came to UT Publications on April 16, 1991, long before this author had ever heard of the name Burris, included the reference, "Barbara Burris/de la Burdé Partnerships-Strategic Land Investments. Roger de la Burdé, Investor/Collector, Windsor, Powhatan, VA 23139. (804) 379-3674." A quick search of Nexis led to the belief that this Barbara Burris was either the wife or a daughter of Colonel Howard Burris. Nexis also revealed that Roger de la Burdé was murdered in March 1992. Charged with the crime was his girlfriend, Beverly Ann Monroe. The resume was that of a woman in her early thirties who had relatives in Austin and was checking the job market there. No notation of her name was made by this author, however.

141. "Jorge Mas still says that the man he hates most after Fidel Castro is John F. Kennedy." For more on Mas Canosa, his links to Operation 40 veterans Felix Rodriguez and Luis Posada, and his relationship with Dante Fascell, see "Who is Jorge Mas Canosa?", Esquire, Jan. 1993, pp. 86-89, 119-122. Its author is former HSCA investigator Gaeton Fonzi. Operation 40 was under the CIA's ZR/RIFLE assassination project umbrella.

142. David Harold Byrd, *I'm an Endangered Species*, (Houston, TX: Pacesetter, 1978), p. 39.

143. Conover Hunt, *The Sixth Floor: John F. Kennedy and the Memory of a Nation*, (Dallas TX: Dallas County Historical Foundation, 1989), p. 5. Note: Another Byrd property, Temco, Inc., played a role in the murder of Henry Marshall which has political overtones involving LBJ (See section on Byrd in this paper).

144. Most people know the Main Building as the infamous "Deadly Tower" from which Charles Whitman shot and killed sixteen people in August 1966. Ron Ellison (mentioned earlier in this paper) claimed that the full truth about the Whitman shooting was suppressed by LBJ and his friends. He also claimed Whitman had been in a building overlooking Dealey Plaza shortly before the UT incident. Whitman researcher John Slate, however, says that his gasoline

receipts do not place him in Dallas prior to the tower shooting.

145. Eckhardt, *One Hundred Faithful...*, p. 51.

146. This paper's author first realized this coincidental story along with Price and Cunningham soon after becoming employed by them in 1981.

147. Jim Hicks affidavit to New Orleans District Attorney Jim Garrison, cited in Gary Shaw with Larry Harris, *Cover-Up*, (Cleburn, TX: Self Published, 1976) p. 118, cited in Groden with Livingstone, *High Treason*, p. 213, photo with caption 14 pp. after p. 180.

148. Beverly Oliver recollections, cited in Oliver Stone with Zachary Sklar, *JFK: The Book of the Film*, (NY: Applause Books, 1992), p. 120; HSCA, JFK Exhibit F-591, p. 8. Exes and Texas

PART TWO

Mary Bancroft (M.B.) was born on October 29, 1903. She was Allen Dulles' mistress. She was also his primary OSS contact with the "20th of July" assassination plotters against Hitler. And she was a close friend of Michael Paine's parents. According to researcher Gus Russo, FBI and ONI documents reveal that Michael Paine's wife, Ruth, was making inquiries about Lee Harvey Oswald in 1957 -- six years before the Warren Commission claimed they had met.[149] To see how all of this came about and how it relates to UT and the Rambler, we must backtrack and explore seemingly unrelated matters. We are able to do this because Ms. Bancroft wrote a book about her life which was published twenty years after Kennedy's death and which seems to speak directly to assassination researchers.

Mary's father, Hugh Bancroft, married as his second wife, the stepdaughter of Clarence Walker Barron (C.W.), publisher of The Wall Street Journal. (M.B.'s mother died in childbirth.)

Barron seems to have had foreknowledge of President Warren G. Harding's death. During a bridge game at his home one evening with M.B., C.W. had his secretary phone his office every ten minutes until news came across the wire that Harding had a stomach ache from eating crab. C.W. then exclaimed, "That's it! Get me the Vice President!" Vice President Coolidge was spending that evening visiting his father. With them that evening was a good friend of C.W.'s.[150]

Depending on which history book is consulted, the cause of Harding's death was either from a heart attack that was misdiagnosed as ptomaine poisoning by the so-called "incompetent crony whom he had made surgeon general," or to an apoplectic stroke (a blood clot in the brain), or is left entirely to the reader's imagination. Barron's anticipation of and reaction to Harding's stomach ache would seem to corroborate poisoning as the cause of death.[151]

Now almost lost to history is the fact that poisoning was indeed suspected by the American people for many years after Harding's death, much in the same way that suspicions linger in President Kennedy's death. Like Kennedy's, Harding's was one of the few presidential deaths deeply mourned by the American people. Shortly before he died, Harding had been asking Commerce Secretary Herbert Hoover's advice on publicly exposing "a great scandal in our administration." Hoover advised disclosure, but Harding died before taking his advice. Mrs. Harding permitted no autopsy and destroyed her late husband's private papers.[152] Scandals surfaced which tended to be more damaging to Harding's reputation than to what he called his "goddamn friends" who kept him "walking the floors nights." Even in the worst of these scandals, known as Teapot Dome, the culprits escaped conviction on the charge of conspiring to defraud the government. Barron also knew, before any other journalist, the exact moment of the Supreme Court's Teapot Dome decision (not expected for several months). M.B. called this "a nose for news."[153]

Upon Harding's death in August 1923, Vice President Coolidge became president and was himself succeeded by Hoover in 1928. Coolidge had "cryptically" removed his name from consideration allowing Hoover, whom he detested, to easily win the Republican nomination.[154] It is interesting to note, as will continue to be evident in this paper, the similarities in this to Johnson's succession, subsequent surprise withdrawal in 1968, and Nixon's succession to the presidency. To paraphrase Napoleon: It is not necessary to bury the truth. It is sufficient merely to delay it until nobody cares.

M.B.'s first husband, Sherwin Badger, had a job lined up at United Fruit prior to his June 1923 graduation from Harvard. Sherwin's job was in the head office. The manager of the company's sugar mill town of Banes, Cuba, where M.B. and Sherwin requested to be transferred, was David Armstrong a man who had devoted his life to United Fruit. Sherwin did not share his devotion.[155]

After a year at United Fruit, Sherwin quit and went to work for the Boston News Bureau. He later transferred to The Wall Street Journal and eventually became editor of Barron's.[156] Their son, Sherwin Badger, Jr. was born on July, 26, 1928.[157]

Mary's and Sherwin's Boston friends, the Paines, moved to New York and were there when Mary and Sherwin moved back to the city after living in the suburbs of Scarsdale for most of 1929. [George] Lyman Paine was an architect and Ruth [Forbes] Paine was a painter. M.B. had her first love affair with a friend of the Paines. He was Leopold Mannes, a pianist/composer who helped perfect Kodachrome color processing. The affair began at the end of the summer of 1930 while M.B. was visiting Ruth Paine at her family summer home on Naushon Island off the coast of Massachusetts. Because of anti-Semitism in M.B.'s family and the disapproval of Leopold's mother, the affair ended. Still, M.B. and Sherwin decided to divorce in the summer of 1933. M.B. then took a trip to France with Ruth Paine by ship. On this trip M.B. met her next husband, Jean Rufenacht.[158] She and Leopold were still in love, however.[159]

At this point in the chronology, around the time of the birth of the

Paines' son Michael, it is important to look at an overview of the Paine family for insight into M.B.'s past history with them as well as an understanding of their impact on her future. It is equally important here not to ignore the dominating dynamics in the U.S. of the so called "Old Boy Network."

Michael Paine...was sixth in descent from Robert Treat Paine the signer of the Declaration of Independence. His mother Ruth Forbes was a great-granddaughter of Emerson and a granddaughter of William Hathaway Forbes, founder and first president of the American Bell Telephone Company. Her father, Ralph Emerson Forbes, left an estate of $2.5 million when he died in 1937. Her uncle, W. Cameron Forbes, a former Ambassador to Japan, had been until his recent demise a director of United Fruit....Michael's great-great-great-uncle, Robert Bennet Forbes, is said by the Dictionary of American Biography to have played "a prominent role in the outbreak of the Chinese Opium War." Robert's mother was a Perkins, of a family who were partners in the "most powerful American house in China." ...Michael Paine was descended from the Cabots on both his father's and his mother's side; he was thus a second cousin once removed of Thomas Dudley Cabot, the former President of United Fruit who offered another of his companies, Gibralter Steamship, as a "cover" for the CIA during the Bay of Pigs adventure. He was also a cousin of Cabot's partner, Alexander Cochrane Forbes, a director of United Fruit and trustee of Cabot, Cabot and Forbes. Paul F. Hellmuth vice-president of Cabot, Cabot and Forbes, was a trustee of the J. Frederick Brown Foundation, a CIA "conduit", along with G.C. Cabot. Thus the Paine family [had] links with the blue-blood intelligence circles of the "Oh So Social" OSS and CIA, though one would not guess this from their description in the Warren Report....In the summer of 1963 it was Ruth [Michael's wife], rather than Michael, who maintained close relations with the patrician Paine and Forbes families, traveling east in July to stay with her mother-in-law at the traditional Forbes clan retreat of Naushon Island near Wood's

Hole, Massachusetts (CE 416, 17 H 119).[160]

..Michael Paine...had an uncle, Eric Schroeder, who was a friend and investment associate of [Dallas oil man Everette Lee] deGolyer;[161] his cousin Alexander "Sandy" Forbes, a former director of United fruit, belonged to the elite Tryall Golf Club retreat in Jamaica with former deGolyer associate Paul Raigorodsky, a financial patron of the St. Nicholas Parish.[162]

With that history in mind, it must be noted that Allen Dulles and his brother John Foster had, and profited from, extensive conflicts of interest between their government positions and the United Fruit Company.[163]

Between the fall of 1933 and the end of June 1934, M.B. moved to
Zurich; married Jean, returned to the U.S. to get custody of her daughter,
Mary Jane (born May 15, 1930), and returned to Zurich on a steamship
of the Italian Line called Rex.[164] She and Mary Jane lived for a while in
the village of *Les Geneveys-sur-Coffrane* in the *Val de Ruz* above the city
of Neuchâtel in the Swiss canton of the same name; visited on weekends
by Jean. He had inherited the Villa Joliette from his father. Eventually,
feeling like a hermit, M.B. moved back to Zurich. Mary Jane had started
school at this time. M.B. joined the "American Women's Club, a
flourishing organization in those days. There were a surprising number
of American women married to Swiss in Zurich, as well as American
Businessmen and their wives and a large consular corps."[165] Did Elspeth
or Walt Rostow participate in the American Women's Club while in
Switzerland? If so they probably met Mary Bancroft by 1937 and were
among her mutual friends with Allen Dulles, whom she met in 1942.

Some weeks after "The Night of Long Knives," June 30, 1934, M.B.
and Jean went to Germany on a business trip. On the eve of their
departure King Alexander of Yugoslavia and Louis Barthou, the French
foreign Minister, were assassinated in Marseilles [by a Croatian gunman
named Petrus Kalemen on Oct. 9, 1934]. Mary discovered in Germany
that this assassination was blacked-out in the German press and that it
was known about but never discussed by the Germans with whom she
and Jean socialized. The Germans felt that discussing politics would lead
to speculation about the true meaning of events -- something they did not
want to know.[166] It was a lesson in mass psychology that was valuable in
the world of assassination plotting and cover-up.

She had also prepared herself psychologically for her future work
with Allen Dulles: "For if there was one thing my work during the war
convinced me of, it was essential to have a very clear-cut idea of your
own moral values, so that if you were forced by necessity to break them,
you were fully conscious of what you were doing and why....In short, I
personally would be incapable of engaging in intelligence work in the
service of an idea. But when war broke out and my own country was
under attack, that solved the problem for me."[167] Did Bancroft consider
Kennedy a threat to her country after the Bay of Pigs? If so, she probably
shared that opinion with mutual United Fruit friends of Allen Dulles and
the Paines.

She shared another interest with Dulles as well: "I also developed an
interest in Yugoslavia, which was to continue all during the war, until my
file on Yugoslavia actually became second in size only to my file on
Germany. I noted with interest that the grandmother of the new, eleven-
year-old King Peter of Yugoslavia was Grandpa Barron's friend, Queen

Marie, now the Dowager Queen of Rumania...."[168]

Bancroft spent the next four years getting to know the famous Swiss psychiatrist Carl Gustav Jung and developing a lifelong interest in his work.[169] She also made friends at this time with two American Women: Mary Briner and Carly Goetze.[170]

Mary and Jean went to Venice, Italy in early summer 1938, staying until early August 1938. During their absence the Queen of Rumania had died. "I would eventually become much more familiar with her country and her people because of Jean's many trips to Rumania during the war, as well as by meeting his Rumanian friends who came to visit us on their way to Paris or other European capitals."[171]

After Pearl Harbor, Bancroft, through her friend Don Bigelow, the First Secretary at the American Legation, met and began writing articles on Switzerland and Germany for Gerald Mayer, a representative of the Office of Coordinator of Information[172] [predecessor to the OSS].[173] Through Mayer, after working for him for several months, M.B. met Allen Dulles, who was posing as assistant to the American Minister, in early December, 1942. Mayer was actually an OSS recruiter and Dulles was head of U.S. intelligence in Switzerland. A few days later over dinner at Dulles' apartment in Bern, they "...discovered [they] had many mutual friends and talked about them for a while." Prior to this meeting M.B. had learned that Dulles had held various positions in the State Department and that his uncle, Robert Lansing, had been Wilson's Secretary of State.[174]

Wilson also had several powerful University of Texas personalities in his cabinet: Colonel Edward M. House, David Franklyn Houston, Albert Sidney Burleson, and Thomas Watt Gregory. House, then a kingmaker in Texas politics was the man principally responsible for Wilson being nominated for and elected President.[175]

Dulles asked M.B. to continue to analyze the speeches of Hitler, Goering, and Goebels and send them to him rather than Gerald Mayer. "He'd also like me to see some people coming from adjacent countries who had to be careful where they went and whom they saw because they would be returning to occupied territories. Switzerland was riddled with enemy agents. Officially, mine was a Swiss household where such people could visit with a minimum of risk. Or, if I had to meet them in public, I was a journalist and that was an excellent cover.... Useful was a word that was constantly on his [Dulles'] lips. He judged everyone and everything by the yardstick of its usefulness in the war effort...."[176] It is speculated that such techniques and personality traits would also have been useful if Bancroft had to relay information from Dulles to Ruth and Michael Paine in 1963.

Dulles said of Howard Burris' close friend, Richard Helms, that he was "useful," and he "knew how to keep his mouth shut." According to Helms biographer Thomas Powers, "When Dulles undertook the delicate job of getting a Postmaster General's okay for an illegal mail-opening program, it was Helms he picked to go with him."[177]

Considering that Helms "had a certain slippery ability to avoid crisis situations in which failure might wreck a career..." and considering "...his skepticism of covert action," the reason he worked on this delicate job might have been due to another trait of Allen Dulles. As Bancroft describes it: "One of his greatest strengths was the devotion he was able to evoke in those who worked for him and this kind of devotion on my part began on that very first evening in Bern."[178]

Mary Bancroft and Allen Dulles fell in love. For M.B. it was much deeper than her feeling for Leopold had been. M.B. did not like Allen's attitude toward John Foster, however. When their father was dying he told all his children to regard Foster as the head of the family. M.B. thought the American people should have made more of a fuss "over the constellation of power resulting from Foster at State and Allen at the CIA."[179] She probably knew about their conflicts of interest with the United Fruit Company.

M.B. noticed that Dulles was annoyed with the wrongness of facts in Hitler's speeches and found herself having to explain the Nazi theory of propaganda, "how it had nothing to do with presenting facts accurately but solely with an appeal to the emotions of the German people."[180] To do this she translated passages on the subject from Mein Kampf for Dulles. M.B.'s work included comparing articles in the most respected German newspaper with the contents of Goebbel's weekly and issues of the Nazi party paper. She summarized significant articles in each "and also reported on the obituaries -- how many deaths were of the military or seemed significant in connection with specific bombings."[181]

While she never mentions the term "editorial intelligence" in her book, Bancroft, nevertheless, gives a good definition of it: "But intelligence is a mosaic. General material about background and people's interrelationships can be both illuminating and important. Quite often missing pieces of the mosaic emerge that make a previously incomprehensible picture unexpectedly clear."[182] Indeed.

Toward the end of May, 1943, M.B. was asked by Dulles to translate a book on the Third Reich by Hans Bernd Gisevius, a member of the Canaris organization -- the *Abwehr* -- stationed under the diplomatic cover of vice-consul at the German consulate in Zurich. His book was about the July 20 plot against Hitler, being coordinated by Admiral Canaris' subordinate, Colonel Hans Oster. M.B. reported: "I told Allen it all made sense to me. Difficult as it might be to believe, the conspirators actually hoped that if they got rid of Hitler they would be able to take over the whole country and to negotiate peace with the Anglo-Americans. Their hopes went even further: They envisaged the western Allies joining them in a crusade against Russia -- and communism. Gisevius had been sent to Switzerland to get in touch with the western Allies. Other emissaries were making similar contacts in Sweden and elsewhere."[183]

Bancroft reveals more about Dulles' background: "In addition to Rumanians, I was also meeting with a considerable number of Yugoslavs....Allen was already thoroughly familiar with both the history and present conditions in Yugoslavia, having at one point in his State Department career been in charge of the desk that dealt with the affairs of that part of the world. He apparently knew the names of every city, town, river, bridge, railway line, and personality in the entire country."[184]

Gisevius told M.B. that the Rumanians, Bulgarians, and Hungarians were watching how the U.S. treated Italy after the fall of Mussolini in the summer of 1943. He said we should have made peace with them and followed it with peace offers to the Balkan countries, who would have jumped at the chance. This, he said would have destroyed German morale enough that Germany would have collapsed "within seventy-two hours."[185]

Gisevius claimed that the Allies behavior in Italy was proof they were not interested in fighting fascism. He also felt that Allied bombing strategy and the demand for an unconditional surrender would drive the German's toward "an eastern solution" being offered by the Russians and their *Freies Deutschland* ("Free Germany") committee established in Moscow after Stalingrad and headed by Field Marshal Friedrich von Paulus and General von Seydlitz. "This was causing difficulties for the conspiracy of civilians and officers who wanted to get rid of Hitler -- particularly the older men who, like Gisevius himself, favored `a western solution.'" Gisevius felt that if we "disappointed" the Germans "they might well fling themselves in the arms of the Russians, and the resultant terror would mean `the end of Western Civilization.'" M.B. felt this phrase was overused to promote ones menace of choice -- in this case the menace of Russian communism. The July 20 plotters were both anti-Nazi and anti-communist, but not necessarily anti-fascist.[186]

Concerning intelligence which would have been of certain interest to Rostow, Mary tells us, "Allen had been beside himself with eagerness for Jean's return. On August 1, Allied planes had raided the Rumanian oil fields at Ploesti, and Allen, realizing that the railroad ran by these fields, knew Jean would be able to give him a firsthand report of the damage caused by the raid....The Rumanians were greatly upset by the bombing of Sofia. They couldn't understand why Sofia had been bombed and not Bucharest. Their pride had been hurt!" Although the Rumanians loved the Americans and hated the Germans, they preferred German over Russian occupation.[187]

In early July, 1944, Gisevius left for Germany to prepare for the coup. M.B. and Mary Jane left for Ascona for six weeks. Gisevius' friend and Abwehr colleague, Eddie Waetjen, also attached to the German consulate in Zurich, also spent the summer in Ascona with his family. On July 20, the coup failed. M.B. and Mary Jane returned to Zurich on September 1, 1944. Jean spent the summer traveling.[188]

In late January, 1945, Gisevius returned to Zurich and eventually moved to a rented house on Lake Geneva.

In the weeks preceding July 20, Gisevius had been constantly on the move between Basel, Bern, Geneva, the Grisons, and Zurich.[189]

On July 13, Gisevius met with General Beck who wanted to put the whole plan down on paper. "Men of Beck's generation had no conception of how, under a terror, everyone, including one's own children, must be regarded as potentially dangerous spies. Nor did it occur to such old school gentlemen that any slip of paper, even if only written for ones own private information, might find its way into the hands of the Gestapo with devastating results for all concerned. Gisevius was only too aware of this problem." One detail of the putsch was that "Immediately after the bomb exploded, the headquarters' communications center would be put out of commission. This would insure that headquarters would be cut off from the outside world for several hours and prevent the issuance of counter-orders should there be any survivor with the authority to issue them." This never happened and allowed not only counter-orders but verification of Hitler's survival.[190]

It is recalled here that Kennedy's entire cabinet was out of the country at the time he was killed. Also, for an hour after the JFK assassination, phone service in Washington was sporadic at best.[191] Whether or not this was due to deliberate tampering can be researched by checking the memories of people in other cities with large populations about whether their phone system was having problems during that hour.

By July 23 Gisevius had managed to find a hiding place where he waited for Dulles to smuggle false papers to him. On January 20, 1945 the papers mysteriously appeared at the house where he was staying. "The papers included a special pass and a letter from Gestapo headquarters signed by Himmler (a perfect forgery), instructing all government officials to assist said Hoffman [his new identity] on an important secret mission to Switzerland." Still, he was lucky to make it back.[192]

After analyzing Gisevius, Carl Jung told M.B., "`Of course, he still has rather grandiose ideas, and if he goes to the United States, he might attach himself to some current of power there that would permit him to realize at least some of them.'"[193] Prior to this comment, the only contact Bancroft had established between Gisevius and the United States was with Dulles through Bancroft herself. Did Gisevius wish to continue his work in anti-communist assassination plots? As we shall see, Gisevius did go to the U.S. He "spent some time in Texas, then returned to Germany...."

[OBJ]In another statement that overlaps with the interests of Ransom and Rostow M.B. writes that among Dulles' achievements cited in his Medal for Merit is "...his reports on damage inflicted by the Allied Air Forces as a result of raids on Berlin and other German, Italian, and Balkan cities, which were forwarded within two or three days of the operations."[194]

On her relationship with Dulles, M.B. says, "He knew that there was nothing he could say or do that would affect in the slightest my deep affection for him. He was also aware that I knew his dark side and that it didn't bother me in the least." Again we see personality traits that were and would remain useful in the business of assassination plotting.

Dulles went to Germany in the spring of 1945 to head the OSS mission there.[195] When the Russians learned of the secret negotiations for the first great German surrender, from which they were excluded, they protested to Washington. "So Allen withdrew personally from the negotiations, but indicated, without saying so in so many words, that it would be quite all right for others to proceed as long as he didn't know anything about what they were doing. This was an old trick, similar to the one practiced by Admiral Canaris in connection with the July 20 conspiracy."[196] And again we see techniques that were and would remain useful in the business of assassination plotting.

According to Robert Morrow, it was Tracy Barnes, second in command of the Bay of Pigs operation under Rostow's friend Richard Bissell, who was the recipient of Lee Harvey Oswald's information from Minsk. Barnes went on to head the CIA's super secret Domestic Operations Division (DOD); and was therefore the boss for whom J. Walton Moore was working in Dallas in 1962 when he initiated de Mohrenschildt's relationship with Oswald. Though fired from the CIA by Kennedy, Dulles was still considered "the Director" by some who had worked under him.[197] One of them was very likely Tracy Barnes. Barnes was disliked at CIA but got top jobs because Dulles liked him. E. Howard Hunt, a mutual friend of Barnes and Dulles, was Barnes' covert action chief at DOD.[198]

In early summer 1952, M.B. and Mary Jane "again returned to the States, and she and Horace Taft announced their engagement at the Republican Convention in Chicago, where Horace's father, Senator Robert A. Taft, was contending with General Dwight D. Eisenhower for the presidential nomination. Mary Jane and Horace were married that September in Washington, where we made our headquarters with Clover [Allen's wife] and Allen. Sherwin [Jr.] could not make the wedding because by then he was a lieutenant in the United States Navy serving off Korea. Clover and Allen's son was also in Korea serving as an officer in the US marines." In the fall of 1953, M.B. moved back to the States permanently and Sherwin, Jr. started working for Time magazine. Of particular interest, Bancroft reveals that "Gisevius married his Fräulein Braut, spent some time in Texas, then returned to Germany where he published several more

books; he finally settled on the Lake of Geneva near Vevey. We kept in touch until his death in 1974."[199]

When Allen Dulles retired in 1961 he took M.B.'s wartime reports home with him. Despite his urging, M.B. procrastinated on writing her war memoirs (Allen wanted to "go over them" with her). After his death, in 1969, she asked Clover for the reports. Richard Helms had them by then and took two years to return them to her.[200]

With all of her references to Kennedy assassination-related persons and subjects, Bancroft could scarcely have overlooked another detail of her life that was not in her book. Perhaps Bancroft is purposely making it conspicuous by its absence -- a possible coding technique.[201] It is in Leonard Mosley's 1978 book, *Dulles*. Mosley says that in 1948, a year after her divorce from Jean Rufenacht, "Mary Bancroft was still a friend of Allen Dulles, as she would continue to be until his death, but the intimacy they had achieved in wartime Switzerland had now gone out of their relationship. Mrs. Bancroft had turned her strong personality in other directions and lighted upon Henry M. Luce, president and editor-in-chief of Time magazine, whom she set out to "convert" from his right-wing ways to her more liberal philosophy."[202]

Also in a description, that researchers of the JFK assassination will find intriguing, Mosley says about Allen Dulles: "He had periods when he was out on the tennis courts owned by his rich friends, the Belins, challenging and beating Bill Bundy, Jim Angleton, and Bob Amory, or other members of the Agency's top echelon bold enough to take him on." Whether or not this is the family of Warren Commission attorney David Belin, or the family of Gaspard d'Andelot Belin, acting Secretary of the Treasury at the time of the assassination (making him the ultimate head of the Secret Service because Treasury Secretary C. Douglas Dillon was out of the country) and husband of Harriet Lowell Bundy, niece of Kennedy's National Security Advisor, Frederick McGeorge Bundy, this reference has probably been overlooked all these years because the name Belin is *not* in Mosley's index.[203]

Clover Dulles and M.B. continued to be close friends until her death in 1974. Mary Bancroft continued to keep in touch with her daughter, Joan. Her book ends with a quote from C.W. Barron, which M.B. used in other parts of her book: "But remember that facts are not the truth. They only indicate where the truth may lie."[204]

This comment, along with Bancroft's statement about knowledge of "interrelationships" which "make a previously incomprehensible picture unexpectedly clear"; her experience with codes (she used a different verbal and written code with each of her contacts and informants); the importance of the Paines in her life: the mutual ties to United Fruit, their involvement with her meeting her first love and her second husband, and their possible mutual friendship with Dulles -- who also had close ties to United Fruit; her knowledge and understanding of "the Nazi theory of propaganda"; the fact that she was Dulles' secret contact with a group planning to take over a government by assassination, using techniques of forgery and plausible deniability, so they could wage "a crusade against Russia -- and communism"; all of these facts leave no doubt that she would have followed the events following, if not leading up to, the Kennedy assassination and would realize the importance of revealing these "interrelationships" in 1983.

Can there be any doubt that Bancroft asked, if she did not know first hand, how her close friend's son and daughter-in-law, Ruth and Michael Paine, came to know Lee Harvey Oswald? If she did, she would have learned that George de Mohrenschildt, who in 1940 worked briefly for his distant cousin, Baron Constantine Maydell, then the top German Abwehr agent in the U.S., had introduced Oswald to Volkmar Schmidt, whohad lived and studied with one of the July 20 plotters.[205]

She would have learned that after talking to Oswald, Schmidt particularly wanted him to meet Michael Paine. Schmidt arranged the party where, allegedly, Oswald and Ruth Paine met. And Paine eventually got him the job in the School Book Depository.[206] Oswald also met, at that party, a man whose father had worked for C.D. Jackson's Radio Free Europe. Jackson, along with being the man who bought the Zapruder film for Bancroft's lover Henry Luce's Life magazine, was the CIA's propaganda mastermind.[207]

What did Mary Bancroft think of all this? Did she know Michael's friend, Volkmar? Did she know Volkmar's former professor and housemate, Dr. Wilhelm Kuetemeyer?[208] Did she know de

Mohrenschildt?

While in Yugoslavia in 1957 de Mohrenschildt was accused by the authorities of making drawings of military fortifications. At this time de Mohrenschildt was working for a subsidiary of the CIA funded Agency for International Development.[209] Upon returning to the U.S. he met with a CIA representative who "obtained foreign intelligence which was promptly disseminated to other federal agencies in ten separate reports" according to a CIA report.[210] Whether or not Bancroft knew Oswald's CIA friend, Dulles surely must have known him, being one of the CIA's top experts on Germany and Yugoslavia.[211] De Mohrenschildt had applied to the OSS in late 1942 (about the time Bancroft and Dulles met) and was rejected because of FBI reports that he had done undercover work in the U.S. for Nazi Germany.[212]

And just what is the rest of the story of Gisevius' grandios ideas that required currents of power in the United States? Was this his motivation for a trip to Texas?[213] Researcher Bruce Campbell Adamson discovered that, by 1953, Hans Gisevius was working for Dresser Industries, a Dallas-based oil equipment company. Adamson's research, for a book he is writing about George de Mohrenschildt, revealed that Dresser's long-time chairman of the board, Henry Neil Mallon and newly appointed CIA Director Allen Dulles were mutual friends of Gisevius. He was "handling" one of Mallon's prized projects -- a worldwide economic development program called the "Institute on Technical Cooperation."[214]

The "current of power" to which Gisevius had attached himself in the United States did not stop there. Prescott Bush, the father of former U.S. President George Bush, had just ended a record setting twenty-two year stint on Dresser's board to take his seat in the U.S. Senate in 1952. The senior Bush, who had been inducted into Yale's secret Order of the Skull and Bones with Mallon in 1917, used his financial expertise to reorganize his friend's company in 1928 and 1929.[215]

As Adamson points out, "It was at a Dresser subsidiary, International Derrick and Equipment Company (IDECO), where young George [Bush] would get his first start in 1948." And "For clear evidence of George Bush's admiration for Mr. Mallon, one need look no further than the birth certificate of Bush's third son. Neil Mallon Bush was born on January 22, 1955, in Midland, Texas. In fact it was Mallon who personally offered George Bush the IDECO job." Like his father, the future president would form a close personal friendship with Mallon, "the man who used his company, friends and business contacts as cover for CIA-sponsored projects."[216]

Adamson's research also indicates that Mallon and Dulles also formed a close friendship. They visited each other in Washington and Dallas, exchanged gifts, and noted significant family anniversaries. Bruce Adamson notes that, "it was Neil Mallon who helped introduce Allen Dulles to the wealthy and influential in Dallas society." He further notes that when George Bush was founding Zapata Oil (which later explored for oil near a Carribean base used for CIA raids against Cuba), Prescott Bush and Neil Mallon were meeting in Washington, D.C. with CIA Director Dulles to discuss a "Pilot Project" in the Carribean.[217]

Adamson also discovered that George Bush offered more pay to Wayne H. Dean, a top engineer at Kerr & McGee Oil, to come work for him as one of Zapata's first drilling superintendents. Adamson learned from another engineer who worked at Kerr & McGee in 1952, that "Wayne Dean and de Mohrenschildt were very good friends." Dean went on to become a top executive at Zapata.[218]

According to Zapata's 1960 annual report, "In September, Mr. Wayne Dean resigned his position as executive vice president and director in order to go into the drilling business in Mexico. Mr. G.H. Walker, managing partner of G.H. Walker and Co., New York City, has been elected to fill the vacancy on the board." As we will see, in 1934, a shipping line established at the end of World War I in a deal arranged for Brown Brothers, Harriman by Prescott Bush's partner and father-in-law, G.H. Walker, was found by Congress to be subsidizing "a wide range of pro-Nazi propaganda efforts both in Germany and the United States."[219]

In other Bush-de Mohrenschildt links, Adamson notes that wealthy oilman Edwin Wendell Pauley, with whom Bush and others at Zapata formed the Permargo drilling company in Mexico, is listed in de Mohrenschildt's phone book four times. An employee at Mexico's Pemex Oil Company, Antonio J. Bermudez, is also in de Mohrenschildt's phone book. Bermudez was "a very close friend to Everette DeGolyer, owner of DeGolyer & MacNaughton and father-in-law of one of LBJ's right-hand men, George Crew McGhee."[220]

Of all of the possible implications of Mary Bancroft's cryptic reference to a post-war trip to Texas by Hans Gisevius, it turns out that Dulles' and Bancroft's fellow expert on political assassination continued to stay in close proximity to the places and people whose names would one day be linked to the Kennedy assassination. Considering Gisevius' "rather grandios ideas" that this current of power in the U.S. "would permit him to realize," two questions are raised: what were these ideas, and did he realize them? Given the truth behind Mary Bancroft's seemingly mild statement that Gisevius "spent some time in Texas," this more severe but equally cryptic statement takes on greater importance.

All of this makes crucial the need for research into the possible relationship between George Lyman Paine and CIA covert action pioneer, James Burnham. Both had been leaders in the Trotskyist movement in the U.S. Burnham is responsible for introducing William F. Buckley, Jr. to E. Howard Hunt in June 1950.[221] Hunt then hired Buckley to work with him at the infamous Mexico City station. Paine and Burnham would certainly have shared a common interest in one of Stalin's most successful covert operations – the assassination of Trotsky in Mexico City.[222]

After a failed attempt in May 1940, Stalin and his secret police, the GPU, succeeded three months later, in assassinating the anti-Stalinist Leon Trotsky, who was living in exile in Mexico. It was accomplished by Spanish Communist Ramon Mercader, a trained agent of the secret police, who cunningly, over a period of several weeks, used unwitting Trotsky loyalists to penetrate Trotsky's guarded and fortified house in Mexico City. Mercader struck the fatal blow with an alpenstock (an iron staff used in mountain climbing) into Trotsky's head during a private, unguarded meeting in the exiled leader's workroom.[223] The Burnham-Paine link is one of at least nine Trotskyite connections to Oswald:

1. Harry L. Power, an Army veteran and "Trotskyist or Maoist type" from San Antonio was an associate of Oswald, according to undercover intelligence operative Richard Case Nagell. On Nov. 23, 1963, a 7.65 German Mauser rifle (the type of rifle Roger Craig and others identified as the murder weapon on the sixth floor of the TSBD) was found in his Indiana hotel room. Another San Antonio man who professed knowledge of Power, John Robert Glenn, an Air Force intelligence operative whose life story was strikingly similar to Oswald's, also professed to be a Trotskyist.[224]

2. Oswald is holding the Trotskyite newspaper The Militant in the backyard photos;[225]

3. Michael Paine's father (a friend of Mary Bancroft) was a leader of the movement;[226] as was

4. James Burnham, the CIA covert-action chief who introduced William F. Buckley, Jr. to E. Howard Hunt.[227]

This connects to Oswald not only because Burnham may have known Paine but because Hunt had just become chief of the Mexico City station when he and Tracy Barnes became involved with David Atlee Phillips (Maurice Bishop?) in the 1954 overthrow of Arbenz in Guatemala for United Fruit[228] -- the Paine-Dulles connected business.

Also, Hunt hired Buckley to work at his Mexico City station. De Mohrenschildt had worked at Buckley's parent's oil company, Pantipec, with his future business partner, Pantipec's president, Warren Smith;[229]

5. On New Year's Day 1963, Oswald ordered several political pamphlets from the Trotskyite Pioneer Press and soon began checking

out books about Marxism, Trotskyism, and American imperialism in Latin America, especially Cuba;[230]

6. Vaughn Marlowe, the executive officer of the Los Angeles chapter of the Fair Play for Cuba Committee (FPCC) whom Leopoldo and Angel almost recruited to be the shooter in the June 1963 plot against

JFK, had been associated with "Trotskyists";[231]

7. Harold R. Isaacs (Rostow's co-worker at CENIS) is referred to as a "Trotskyist" in two books about the Far East;[232]

8. FBI agent John William Miller reported that CIA agent William George Gaudet told him of a purchase of paintings by Jack Ruby from Lorenzo Borenstein, a close relative of Leon Trotsky.[233] Gaudet is the

CIA agent who got the Mexican tourist card next to Oswald's in New Orleans in September 1963.[234] He also told attorney Bernard Fensterwald in 1975: "She [Dorothea Murret, Oswald's cousin linked to

Rostow's associate Harold Isaacs] may have worked for the agency in New Orleans."[235]

9. Felipe Alvahuete, a secretary and aide of the late Leon Trotsky and a leader of the Fourth Internationale, accused the Communist Party of complicity in the Kennedy assassination a few days after the murder.[236]

There are at least three possible explanations for this Trotsky business. First, Burnham and Paine may have been plants in the movement (Richard Gibson, one of FPCC's founders was suspected of being CIA),[237] or they may have been rightists who sought to use Trotsky as the best hope for overthrowing Stalin; a sort of "Trotsky-right." Since Burnham and Paine had close ties to Oswald by the time of the assassination, Trotskyism may have been part of his intelligence cover as well -- a link that made him a prime candidate as a patsy for those wishing to blame the assassination on the Communists.

Second, Leopoldo and Angel, the two unknown, shadowy figures who were reportedly posing as pro-Castro agents around Oswald in 1963, were apparently thinking of recruiting Marlowe, a real leftist with a Trotskyite background, to shoot Kennedy in Los Angeles in June 1963. They may have been working in league with Burnham and Paine in efforts to set up several Trotskyists as patsies.

And third, since Oswald was either becoming a Trotskyite, or it was part of his sheepdipping as a leftist, and since he told Volkmar Schmidt that he thought the U.S. was becoming fascist,[238] he may have suspected that a Trotsky-right, foiled by the GPU in its attempt to overthrow Stalin, was now conspiring to assassinate JFK and blame it on the KGB for revenge (among other motives).

Recall that Oswald was reading Trotskyite literature, books on U.S. imperialism in Cuba and Latin America, and checking out library books on Kennedy simultaneously with books on the assassination of Huey Long. Oswald may have been the original assassination researcher, studying aspects of the conspiracy in advance that other researchers would be examining thirty years hence. The GPU's assassination of Trotsky in Mexico City, while not as sophisticated, had its similarities to the conspiracy involving Oswald. Maybe Paine and certainly Burnham were inspired by the KGB's institutionalized assassination program; especially given the infamous William Pawley- and Allen Dulles-assisted Doolittle Report of 1954 which urged the CIA to think more like the KGB.[239]

It has been said that neither Rostow nor his father had ever been leftists but actually avowed Mensheviks (anti-communists).[240] This fact may shed light on Isaacs' Trotskyite past and on Rostow; especially since Oswald's cousin and Isaacs' associate Marilyn Dorothea Murret may have worked for the Agency in New Orleans with William George Gaudet.

Many researchers still think of Rostow as a reformed leftist and still others think he continued to be a leftist and a victim of the extreme right. This type of confusion has served the cover-up well. Dick Russell himself seems to be confused by all of these Trotsky goings-on when he says of Michael Paine that "...interestingly enough, his father, George Lyman Paine, was one of the leaders of the American Trotskyite movement."[241] While having obviously read Scott's manuscripts, Russell overlooked the Paines' extensive ties to the national security establishment.

Also needed is a close look at how and when Foster Dulles' son, John W.F. "Jack" Dulles, expert on Brazil, came to be employed at George de Mohrenschildt's alma mater, The University of Texas at Austin. Foster's and Allen's uncle, Robert Lansing, after all, had several powerful friends there, some of whom were fellow cabinet members in the administration of Woodrow Wilson, Harding's predecessor.[242]

Perhaps the more fitting question is how de Mohrenschildt came to attend the academic halls of Lansing's fellow cabinet members. Keeping in mind the earlier discussion of Harding's death which ultimately resulted in the presidency of his "detested" commerce secretary, Herbert Hoover, it is worth noting that Harding's secretary of state was Charles Evans Hughs, who narrowly missed becoming president in 1916 when Woodrow Wilson was elected. Wilson suffered a stroke in 1919 while on a countrywide speaking tour to gain support for ratification of the League of Nations. He was trying to overcome the protests of the Republican controlled Congress.[243] Harding, who won the nomination in 1920 because his "...lack of strong convictions made him attractive to many of the politicos after eight years of the headstrong Wilson,"[244] also became "determined that America should join the League of Nations' World Court despite Congressional disapproval...." Like Wilson, he went on a cross-country tour to take the issue to the people -- the tour on which he, again like Wilson, suffered his so called stroke.[245] As will be seen in this paper, the fact that President Wilson had several powerful University of Texas personalities in his cabinet, as well as Allen Dulles' uncle, Robert Lansing, has potentially major implications concerning links between the UT Rambler and the JFK assassination. For now, however, we will take a closer look at these Texan cabinet members.

Colonel Edward M. House, a kingmaker in Texas politics and an advisor to four Texas governors, was the man principally responsible for Wilson being nominated for and elected President. He was not elected or appointed to any office. "He was, simply, President Wilson's friend and adviser."[246]

David Franklyn Houston, UT's president in 1905, had as three of his closest friends in Austin, Colonel House, Albert Sidney Burleson, and Thomas Watt Gregory. He served Wilson as agriculture secretary and later as treasury secretary. His first jobs after leaving Washington, were as vice president of AT&T and then president of Bell Telephone Securities of New York; linking him to associates of Michael Paine's maternal great grandfather, William Hathaway Forbes, founder and first President of the American Bell Telephone Company. Houston died in 1940 after directing Mutual of New York through the Depression; earning twice the salary of the President of the United States.[247]

Albert Sidney Burleson, descendant of soldiers in the Texas Revolution, Mexican War, Civil War and American Revolution, was one of UT's first students. Later as a Texas congressman he was generous in matters where his alma mater was concerned. He served Wilson as postmaster general for eight years establishing the first air mail service; which no doubt led to associations with aviation pioneers. In 1918 Burleson became chairman of the U.S. Telegraph and Telephone Administration, a capacity in which he could have also known members and associates of the Paine family.[248]

Wilson's attorney general, Thomas Watt Gregory, was admitted to the bar in 1885 after earning his law degree at UT in only one year. After eight years on the Board of Regents, he worked with Colonel House to secure Wilson's nomination in 1912. As attorney general he concentrated on anti-trust violations, creating the War Emergency Division, and enlarging the FBI.[249]

These were the men who were fellow cabinet members of Allen Dulles' uncle, Robert Lansing. It appears Wilson fared no better with his

Texans and Dulles family member than did Kennedy with his. And like Kennedy, Wilson was well aware of the dangers. "`Remember,' Woodrow Wilson warned his daughter when his first administration was sailing smoothly, `the pack is always waiting to tear one to pieces.'"[250] According to Wilson biographer Arthur S. Link:

> Wilson's greatest problem was Robert Lansing, Secretary of State from 1915 to 1920. Lansing, who looked every inch the statesman, was brilliant while executing routine business and often bungling while conducting important negotiations. A very bad blunder by Lansing in a controversy over armed ships in January 1916 first revealed the Secretary of State's ineptitude to Wilson and was one reason why Wilson increasingly refused to permit him to make any important decisions on his own. Worse still, the discussions over policy toward German submarine warfare in the spring of 1916 first made it apparent to Wilson that Lansing was trying to lead him into war. Lansing revealed this purpose even more clearly in the following autumn and winter. Since Wilson did not want to go to war, his distrust of Lansing naturally increased. Finally, Wilson lost all confidence in his Secretary of State when he tried to sabotage Wilson's efforts to end the war through mediations in December 1916 and January 1917. Unable to find a good replacement or dismiss Lansing in the midst of various crises, Wilson thought that he had no recourse but to conduct all important negotiations himself. This isolation only increased Lansing's bitterness and tendency toward disloyalty, particularly during the peace conference and afterward. There is some evidence that Lansing contemplated a coup that would put him in the White House after Wilson's breakdown in October 1919. There is good evidence that Lansingtried to provoke a war with Mexico about this same time.[251]

Wilson's critics have suggested a final reason for his techniques as a diplomatist -- his personal egotism, jealousy of others, and inability ever to delegate authority. A search of the record does not yield much evidence to support these charges. A fairer conclusion would be that Wilson was generous in dealing with subordinates, welcomed and took advise, and often changed his mind. Indeed, Wilson's chief weakness as a diplomatist was his soft heart and unwillingness to dismiss incompetent and even disloyal subordinates. He could not do anything to embarrass or hurt another person. He finally dismissed Lansing in January 1920, but Lansing had done irreparable damage by then. Even though Wilson had good proof of House's disloyalty at Paris during the early stages of the peace negotiations, Wilson appointed the Colonel as his chief spokesman when he, Wilson, left the conference for a visit to the United States. House gave away most of Wilson's positions during the President's absence.[252]

Thus Wilson's cabinet members were anti-Wilson and Wilson's successor, Warren G. Harding, had anti- Wilson cabinet members. Both presidents were stricken with a "stroke" when they pushed for participation in the League of Nations. Harding died of his stroke/heart attack/poisoning and was replaced by Coolidge who was immediately (if not sooner) informed of Harding's anticipated stomach ache by Bancroft's step-grandfather. Coolidge, with his "genius for inactivity,"[253] withdrew from the election in 1928 allowing Herbert Hoover to win. Hoover had been the member of the anti-Wilson cabinet in whom Harding (just prior to his death) confided about publicizing a "great scandal" in his administration which was rumored never to have surfaced.

In light of Bancroft's revelations about "old-boy" Dulles-UT connections, it might be worthwhile for researchers of the JFK assassinating to take a closer look, in the future, at two other past and present members of UT's power structure, Harry Huntt Ransom and Walt Whitman Rostow. As discussed earlier, Rostow, who selected bombing targets as a major in the OSS, went on to a dubious career guiding Vietnam policy with the advice of his close friends Allen Dulles, Charles Cabell, Richard Bissell, and Edward G. Lansdale. Ransom, as we have seen, was head of Air Force editorial intelligence during World War II, and went on to become Chancellor of the University of Texas System from 1962 until his death in 1976. He had been instrumental in the recruitment of professors Walt Rostow and Jack Dulles.

In Mary Bancroft's book about facts, truth, interrelationships, the Paines, and the Warren Commission's most active member, Allen Dulles,[254] it is apparent that Bancroft is deliberately telling the true story of one assassination conspiracy while telling us "where the truth may lie" in others. And perhaps most disturbing of all, as we shall see next, are the implications of a Navy Department document which reports that Ruth Paine was requesting information about the family of Lee Harvey Oswald in 1957. Schmidt's party was in late February 1963.[255]

George de Mohrenschildt, born in 1911, served in the Polish military and government throughout the 1930s and worked for French counterintelligence in the U.S. after 1938. In this latter capacity he recruited agents to gather intelligence about oil exports to Europe.[256]

This activity certainly brought him into contact with the OSS considering the fact that the British and American commanders planning the European invasion did not trust the French resistance. Even when Churchill decided to aid the French in 1944, the U.S. Army Air Force refused to cooperate. Through the persistence of the OSS' William "Wild Bill" Donovan, however, most of the war material dropped into France in 1944 came from the United States.[257]

By 1941 de Mohrenschildt was involved with German and Japanese intelligence, the OSS, and Nelson Rockefeller, who was then coordinator of information for Latin America. After the war de Mohrenschildt got a degree in petroleum engineering at UT and entered the joint worlds of oil exploration and the CIA; working for William F. Buckley, Sr. along the way, while E. Howard Hunt was getting to know William F. Buckley, Jr.[258]

By 1962 Allen Dulles' friend, Tracy Barnes was head of the CIA's mysterious Domestic Operations Division (DOD). That same year J. Walton Moore was head of the DOD's Domestic Contact Service in Dallas when he encouraged de Mohrenschildt to pursue a relationship with Oswald. E. Howard Hunt, a mutual friend of Barnes and Dulles, was Barnes' covert action man at DOD.[259]

During 1962 Lee and Marina were "befriended" by de Mohrenschildt's associates in the small, wealthy, heavily petroleum-connected and U.S. intelligence-connected Russian exile community in Dallas. According to Peter Dale Scott, "One of the chief Russian guardians, George Bouhe, was a sixty-year old personal accountant for Lewis MacNaughton of the famous oil exploration consulting service DeGolyer and MacNaughton, a man with numerous CIA contacts. Bouhe was said actually to have been `rather mad at Marina for taking an apartment at Oak Cliff because it was rather too far for him to drive and help her when she needed help with the baby.'"[260]

In April 1963, despite that kind of intimacy among the Oswalds and their Russian "babysitters" there was an apparent change in the people with whom the Oswalds associated. Marina moved in with Michael's wife, Ruth Hyde Paine, and Lee left for New Orleans. Although they would never see or hear from de Morhrenschildt again, neither Lee nor Marina had "escaped from the United Fruit-CIA sphere of influence." With regard to Marina, we have already explored the Paines' CIA connections. Most of Lee's known political connections "after April 1963 in New Orleans and Dallas were with right-wing anti-Castro Cubans and their contacts, many of whom (possibly including an Army Intelligence Officer) were also bitterly hostile to John F. Kennedy."[261]

As mentioned earlier, the Oswalds, according to the Warren Commission, first made contact with the Paines at a party in Dallas. Considering the Navy Department report mentioned earlier, however, indicating that Ruth Paine was aware of Lee Oswald in 1957, it must at least be said that this introduction was anticipated. This "initial meeting" between the Paines and the Oswalds was also strange in other ways.

It seems that almost everyone at the party was connected to an oil company in Dallas called Magnolia. While that alone is not unusual, these particular party guests, as we will see, had other associations that were.

Not only were these Magnolia employees now in contact with Oswald, but another man with older and just as dubious links to the company happened to be connected to Jack Ruby and David Ferrie.[262] And like Oswald, this man ended up in Dealey Plaza.

This strange party came about because in February 1963 de Mohrenschildt introduced Oswald to Volkmar Schmidt. In Germany several years earlier Schmidt lived with and studied under a professor at the University of Heidelberg who had been involved in the plot to assassinate Hitler. After meeting Oswald, Schmidt "particularly wanted him to meet Michael Paine...."[263]

Volkmar Schmidt had come to Dallas from Germany in the fall of 1961 to do geological research for the Magnolia Laboratories in Duncanville, Texas. Schmidt's teacher and housemate in Germany had been Dr. Wilhelm Kuetemeyer, professor of psychosomatic medicine and religious philosophy at the University of Heidelberg. His work involved conducting experiments on a group of schizophrenics until Kuetemeyer became involved in the "20th of July" plot against Hitler and had to go into hiding -- like Gisevius. When Schmidt first met Oswald he brought up the subject of General Walker and Hitler. As Schmidt told Edward J. Epstein, "Oswald instantly seized on the analogy...to argue that America was moving toward fascism. As he spoke, he seemed to grow more and more excited about the subject."[264]

Schmidt's two housemates, geologist Richard Pierce and chemist Everett Glover, who owned the house, also worked at Magnolia.[265] Glover arranged the February 22 party at which the Oswalds met Ruth Paine and Pierce also attended. Michael wasn't able to come. This would be the first of an apparent pattern of incidents whereby Ruth would have closer contact with the Oswalds than Michael. However, as we have seen, it was Ruth, not Michael, who was in contact with Michael's CIA-United Fruit relatives during the same period as her contacts with the

Oswalds. Two other guests at the party, Pierce's girlfriend Betty MacDonald and geologist Norman Fredricksen were also Magnolia employees.[266]

Fredricksen, was invited because he had been studying Russian with Schmidt and Pierce. Fredricksen's father, it turns out, had been director of Radio Free Europe. RFE was the main project begun by Life magazine's purchaser of the Zapruder film, C.D. Jackson, when he was president of the CIA's National Committee for a Free Europe.[267]

Schmidt, Fredricksen and Paine represent many overlapping connections between this party and Allen Dulles. Schmidt had been closely associated in Heidelberg with a man who was involved in one of Allen Dulles' and Mary Bancroft's most important wartime exploits. Frederickson's father had directed the CIA project created by C.D. Jackson, friend and co-worker of Walt Rostow and of Bancroft's two lovers, Allen Dulles and Henry Luce. Furthermore, "Fredricksen had been hired by [Magnolia][268] to come to Dallas after studying Russian with the U.S. Army in Heidelberg."[269] And Ruth Hyde Paine probably knew Mary Bancroft, Allen Dulles' former lover and Henry Luce's current lover, and may have visited with her in July 1963 when she was at Ruth Forbes Paine's home on Naushon Island, Massachusetts.

In 1975 Dick Russell got an anonymous letter telling him that the mastermind of the JFK assassination was one Tscheppe Weidenbach, a famous American general who was born in Heidelberg Germany in 1892. Years later Russell discovered in a history of General MacArthur's era, "that Adolf Tscheppe-Weidenbach of Heidelberg, Germany, had changed his name, upon arrival in the United States shortly before World War I, to Charles Willoughby." Willoughby was MacArthur's radical right-wing chief of intelligence.[270]

Schmidt, Pierce and Fredricksen were taking scientific Russian classes at Magnolia from Ilya Mamantov who, after the assassination, would become Marina's interpreter by arrangement of Jack Alston Crichton. According to Peter Dale Scott, "Crichton of Army Reserve Intelligence Service, was the apparent outsider who arranged for Marina Oswald to have the "excessive rightist" Ilya Mamantov as her interpreter."[271] Scott adds, "There is an Army Intelligence Reserve Office under the Army's Director of Combat Intelligence (along with the Special Warfare Branch)."[272] As discussed earlier in this paper, Vice President Johnson's military aid, Colonel Howard Burris, was the end point of a treasonous secret back-channel of information to Johnson concerning combat intelligence; Edward G. Lansdale was visiting special forces bases in the spring and summer of 1963; Lansdale, "Intellfirst" and Burris were friends with Rostow's long-time friend, General Charles P.

Cabell (Lansdale and Cabell were very close); and Rostow was Lansdale's sponsor and "big patron" in the White House.

A fellow director of Crichton's firm, Dorchester Gas Producing, was D.H. Byrd, close friend of Barbara J. Burris' father, and owner of the Texas School Book Depository building in which Ruth Paine helped arrange a job for Oswald.[273] Paine herself was tutoring a "boy astronomer" at Dallas' St. Marks School in scientific Russian.[274] As Peter Dale Scott points out, "The task of keeping abreast of Soviet science and technology is of course an intelligence responsibility, albeit a perfectly legitimate one without "black" overtones, for which an overall coordinating responsibility is assumed by the CIA."[275]

If that is not strange enough, Eugene Hale Brading, who was arrested and released in Dealey Plaza because his new alias, "Jim Braden" was not yet known to local authorities, had a connection to Magnolia Oil. Brading had travelled to Dallas the day before the assassination and stayed at the infamous Cabana Motel with his friend Victor Periera and other traveling companions. The Cabana is where Jack Ruby met with friends from Chicago in the Bon Vivant Club on the evening of November 21.[276]

Brading and Periera had a long history of marrying rich widows and embezzling from them. In a much publicized vagrancy arrest by Sheriff Bill Decker in Dallas in 1952, Brading's fifty-dollar fine was paid by Periera. "The vagrancy rap stemmed from Brading's lingering presence, without any apparent effort to earn his take, at the Dallas area mansion of D.A. Little, president of Magnolia Oil Co. Little had died and Mrs. Little had become Periera's sixth wife after a whirlwind courtship."[277]

In Texas, a "community property" state, married couples equally own each other's assets. Therefore, Periera could have owned an interest in Magnolia Oil at the time of Schmidt's party.

Brading told the sheriff's department, after his arrest in Dealey Plaza, that he was in Dallas on "oil business." Only four years out of prison, Brading had checked with the U.S. Probation Office in Dallas when he arrived, as was required for his out of state travels. Had the deputy sheriffs checked his name with that office they would have gotten negative results because Brading had given chief probation officer Roger Carroll only his real name. In the early 1970s Brading was investigated by federal authorities for an alleged role as courier for laundering the mob's illegitimate money in Amsterdam and Zurich.[278]

Brading and Periera may have visited the offices of Lamar Hunt the day before the assassination on "oil business." The Dallas probation office's report of his visit to Dallas states Brading "advised that he planned to see Lamar Hunt and other oil speculators while here." Years later Brading reportedly told an official of the Los Angeles Police Department that he did not go to the Hunt offices on November 21 because of his criminal record. He said one of his traveling companions, Morgan H. Brown of Los Angeles, did go however. Brown, who had signed the Cabana register for the travellers' third floor suite, has since served time in a California prison. According to Earl Golz, "An old friend of the Hunt brothers who first met Brading almost 20 years ago said Brown, Brading's traveling partner, `knew the Hunts very well -- knew Lamar and Bunker and all of them.' Brown and his wife and other couples played `mixed poker' in Dallas with the Hunts about 25 years ago,' he said." Jack Ruby also admitted being at the Hunt office building that day but claimed he was just dropping someone off there.[279]

H.L. Hunt's security chief, Paul Rothermel, told researcher Peter Noyes that he is sure Brading visited the Hunt offices (of Lamar and Nelson Bunker) on Nov. 21, 1963.[280] If so, this is very likely a right-wing/Orlando Bosch/Paine/CIA link given Brading's fellow Hunt visitor and Magnolia Oil friend Periera, and the Magnolia sponsored party where the Oswalds met Ruth Paine.

Bosch comes into the linkage because Hinkle and Turner raised the question of where Orlando Bosch got the massive funding he needed to continue his raids on Cuba after splitting from the CIA. Bosch rebelled against U.S. government backing in 1963 after an FBI informant foiled his Violynn III raid (involving Frank Sturgis, Alex Rorke, and the Minutemen) and brought twin FBI raids against his Florida airfield and Lake Pontchartrain training camp. The answer to the funding question came when "During a 1968 trial of Bosch's group in Miami, a telephone tape transcript was introduced in which Bosch indicated that a Mr. Hunt -- `the one with the wells' -- was providing backing."[281] These raids were in July 1963, the same month Ruth Hyde Paine was visiting her mother-in-law, Ruth Forbes Paine (Mary Bancroft's long-time friend).

During 1963 in New Orleans, Brading frequented an office in the Pere Marquette building down the hall from an office frequented by David Ferrie. In a building across the street were the New Orleans offices of (H.L.) Hunt Foods and Zapata Off-Shore; as well as both of Oswald's employment agencies, and many other intriguing companies and individuals.[282]

Zapata Off-Shore was the oil company owned by former President George Bush after he split it off from Zapata Oil partner Hugh Liedtke in 1954.[283] Beginning in 1957 Zapata Off-Shore's rig was drilling on the Cay Sal Bank.[284] These islands had been leased to Nixon supporter and CIA contractor Howard Hughes the previous year and were later used as a base for CIA raids on Cuba.[285] In 1969, Zapata bought the United Fruit

Company of Boston.[286]

Bush, like Harry Ransom, is a Phi Beta Kappa and graduate from Yale. Liedtke was a graduate of the UT Law School.[287] Former FBI agent and Magnolia Oil employee, W. Dewey Presley, was director, president and CEO of First International Bank Ltd. when George Bush became a director there after leaving the CIA in 1977.[288]

Not only did Bush's father, former U.S. Senator Prescott Sheldon Bush, have post-war ties to Hitler assassination plotters Dulles, Bancroft, and Gisevius, through Dresser Industries, he had been deeply involved in companies used to finance Adolf Hitler's rise to power. In 1942, Prescott was the senior managing partner of Brown Brothers, Harriman. That year, "the Union Banking Corp., an affiliate of Brown Brothers, Harriman, was seized by the U.S. government as a front for German nationals who had helped bankroll Hitler since the early 1920s." In 1934, a shipping line established at the end of World War I in a deal arranged for Harriman by Prescott's partner and father-in-law, G.H. Walker, was found by Congress to be subsidizing "a wide range of pro-Nazi propaganda efforts both in Germany and the United States."[289] Bush's close friend and confidant, William "Will" Stamps Farish III, also has family ties to companies that helped sponsor the Nazis. In 1937, William Stamps Farish, Sr., became chief executive and president of Standard Oil of New Jersey after merging his own company, Humble Oil, with John D. Rockefeller, Jr.'s. In 1942, a Senate committee headed by Harry S Truman found that Standard had extensive secret relations with both Germany and Japan; including close relations with Hitler's government and a virtual cartel with "Germany's giant I.G. Farben chemical complex, manufacturers of Zyklon B, the nerve gas used in the Nazi death camps to exterminate `undesirables.'" Bush made a habit of going quail hunting annually on Farish's Lazy F Ranch near Beeville, Texas.[290]

Another Beeville rancher is James R. Dougherty, former resident of UT's "politically correct" upperclassman dormitory, "Old B Hall"; an honor shared with William F. Buckley, Sr., Rex G. and Hines Baker (top executives at Humble Oil), Senator Richard Kleberg (LBJ's former Capitol Hill boss), William B. Bates (founder of the law firm Fulbright and Jaworski), D.H. Byrd, and C.B. Smith. The Dougherty clan produced right-wing Dallas oilman Dudley Dougherty, who brought Madam Ngo Dinh Nhu to Dallas in October 1963 to be honored at General Walker's "U.S. Day" rally attended by Lee Harvey Oswald. Walker's aid, Robert Surrey, author of the infamous "Wanted for Treason" poster attacking JFK, was rumored to be a member of a Minuteman group, training at the ranch of Dudley Dougherty.[291] Brading's proximity to Magnolia, Hunt, Zapata, and David Ferrie, and his arrest and release in Dealey Plaza, make it well worth examining a similar incident in Dealey Plaza.

According to researcher Dennis Ford, someone may have helped in the release from custody of the Rambler's driver. Ford stated that Roger Craig saw the Rambler driver in the custody of the Dallas Police briefly and that "the release was facilitated by a man Craig later identified as Edgar Eugene [Bradley]. ([Bradley] was carrying fake Secret Service credentials.)"[292]

The source Ford cited for this is Henry Hurt's *Reasonable Doubt* which says only that "According to Craig, the Latin man was released when he indicated he could not speak English." Hurt does not say whether or not the release was aided. Hurt cites Gary Shaw with Larry Harris (*Cover-Up*, p. 88).

Shaw says in his book that Craig, in a taped interview, stated the Latin man was released. But Shaw also does not say whether or not the release was aided. Perhaps the 1971 taped interview with Craig gives more information. Simply from the books referenced, however, the Bradley claim cannot be documented.

Groden and Livingstone (*High Treason*, p. 162) cite Penn Jones (*Forgive My Grief, Vol. III*, p. 29) saying that Craig claimed the Rambler driver was released by a man posing as a Secret Service agent and that Craig later identified Bradley as the man who was doing this.

Whether or not there is a Magnolia Oil connection between Brading and the Paines, it is essential to find out if this story is true; and if so who, if anyone, helped release the Rambler driver.

When Jim Garrison charged Edgar Eugene Bradley (who like Brading was from California), with conspiracy to kill the President, Ronald Reagan, then Governor of California, refused to extradite him.[293] Although a Democrat in 1962, Reagan probably became anti-Kennedy. Bobby Kennedy subpoenaed his tax records in 1962 as part of a major Justice Department investigation which implicated him in MCA's anti-trust activities. After President Kennedy's assassination, Reagan became a Republican, an overnight multimillionaire, a governor, and proceeded to make executive decisions that were greatly beneficial to MCA and other corporations with motion picture studio interests.[294]

In his 1971 book manuscript, written the same year as the taped interview, Craig wrote about his encounter with and later identification of Bradley:

> I ran to the front of the Texas School Book
> Depository where I asked for anyone involved in the
> investigation. There was a man standing on the steps of
> the Book Depository Building and he turned to me and

said, "I'm with the Secret Service." This man was about 40 years old, sandy- haired with a distinct cleft in his chin. He was well-dressed in a gray business suit. I was naive enough at the time to believe that the only people there were actually officers -- after all, this was the command post. I gave him the information. He showed little interest in the persons leaving. However, he seemed extremely interested in the description of the Rambler. This was the only part of my statement which he wrote down in his little pad he was holding. Point: Mrs. Ruth Paine, the woman Marina Oswald lived with in Irving, Texas, owned a Rambler station wagon, at that time, of this same color.

I learned nothing of this "Secret Service Agent's" identity until December 22, 1967 while we were living in New Orleans. The television was on as I came home from work one night and there on the screen was a picture of this man. I did not know what it was all about until my wife told me that Jim Garrison had charged him with being a part of the assassination plot. I called Jim Garrison then and told him that this was the man I had seen in Dallas on November 22, 1963. Jim then sent one of his investigators to see me with a better picture which I identified. I then learned that this man's name was EDGAR EUGENE BRADLEY. It was a relief to me to know his name for I had been bothered by the fact that I had failed to get his namewhen he had told me he was a Secret Service Agent and I had given him my information.[295]

If Craig had witnessed the driver in custody it seems incredible, given his persistence during his lifetime to tell his story and tell every detail accurately, that he would leave such a significant event as that out of his manuscript; especially given the fact that he included such trivia as going out in the rain and sleet years later to feed the cows.[296]

According to Dick Russell, in September 1963, Richard Case Nagell attempted to convince Oswald that he was being set up as a "patsy" in the assassination conspiracy by the mysterious Cubans Angel and Leopoldo. At this meeting in Jackson Square in New Orleans, Nagell told Oswald he was being "used by fascist elements."[297]

That statement rings true considering the Trotsky-right/Paine link, the Brading-Hunt/Magnolia-Paine links, the Bancroft-Dulles/Hitler plot/Paine links, and the Bush-Farish/Hunt-Zapata/Ferrie-Brading links in New Orleans.

* * *

Notes:

149. Bancroft, Autobiography..., pp. 50, 54, passim; Unpublished Transcript: Newman with Russo, pp. 31.

150. Bancroft, Autobiography..., pp. 24-27.

151. Clifton Daniel, ed., *Chronicle of the 20th Century*, (Mount Kisco, NY: Chronicle publications, 1987), p. 304; John A. Garraty, *The American Nation: A History of the United States Since 1865*, Third ed., (NY: Harper & Row, 1975), p.702; Frank Freidel, *The Presidents of the United States of America*, (Washington DC: White House Historical Association / National Geographic, 10th ed., 1985), p. 62.

152. Garraty, *The American Nation*, p.702; Poisoning: Interview: Mar. 10, 1993, Mabel Green Beckham, 95 years old; Don Bauer, "The Secret lives of Ohio's Presidents", The Plain Dealer Magazine, Apr. 27, 1986, p. 24; (Scandal:) Freidel, The Presidents of the United States of America, p. 62.

OBJ OBJ OBJ OBJ OBJ OBJ OBJ OBJ OBJ OBJ OBJ OBJ OBJ OBJ OBJ OBJ OBJ 153. Bancroft, Autobiography..., pp. 24-27.

154. Garraty, *The American Nation*, p.709-10.

155. Bancroft, Autobiography..., pp. 34-39.

156. Bancroft, Autobiography..., pp. 45-48.

157. Bancroft, Autobiography..., p. 52.

158. Bancroft, Autobiography..., pp. 54-61.

159. Bancroft, Autobiography..., p. 62.

160. Scott, *The Dallas Conspiracy*, ch. IV, pp. 2-4.

161. DeGolyer was an advisor to UT and Harry Huntt Ransom, and a business partner of Lewis MacNaughton in the Dallas oil exploration firm DeGolyer and MacNaughton. MacNaughton had many CIA contacts and his personal accountant, George Bouhe, was one of Oswald's chief Russian guardians in Dallas in 1962. See Lon Tinkle, *Mr. De: A Biography of Everette Lee DeGolyer*, (Boston, MA: Little, Brown, 1970), pp. 224, 239 and Scott, *The Dallas Conspiracy*, ch. III, p. 6.

162. Peter Dale Scott, Government Documents and the Kennedy Assassination, (unpublished manuscript), ch. II, p. 4. Note: The St. Nicholas Parish was a CIA-subsidized Russian Orthodox church outside Russia, restricted to aristocratic anti-Bolshevik Russians who had been "checked, rechecked, and double checked" by the CIA-subsidized Tolstoy Foundation. (9 H 5, 7, cited in Scott, Government Documents..., ch. II, p. 1.)

163. Stephen Schlesinger with Stephen Kinzer, *Bitter Fruit: The Untold Story of the American Coup in Guatemala,* (NY: Doubleday, 1982/Anchor ed., 1990), p. 106.

164. This may be a veiled reference to the CIA Cuba raider ship Rex leased by the Collins Radio Co., commanded by Eugenio Martinez, and which possibly included Frank Sturgis as a crewman. Bancroft names none of the other ships mentioned in her book.

165. Bancroft, Autobiography..., pp. 65-83. Note: Bancroft's time in Switzerland overlapped with Elspeth Vaughn Davies, the future Mrs. Rostow, who, like Mary was from New England.

166. Bancroft, Autobiography..., pp. 84, 86.

167. Bancroft, Autobiography..., p. 89.

168. Bancroft, Autobiography..., p. 90.

169. It is worth noting here that it was Burris' close friend Richard Helms who first proposed to Allen Dulles the creation of the CIA's mind control program, MK/ULTRA, in 1953. (See Russell, *The Man Who Knew Too Much*, pp. 30, 381.)

170. Bancroft, Autobiography..., pp. 91-97.

171. Bancroft, Autobiography..., pp. 104-05.

172. It is scarcely a coincidence that the formal name given to the UT Publications office by Harry Ransom was "Office of Coordinator of University Publications."

173. Ranelagh, *The Agency*, p. 36.

174. Bancroft, Autobiography..., pp. 128-31.

⌂175. Joe B. Frantz, The Forty Acre Follies, (Austin, TX: Texas Monthly Press, 1983) pp. 28, 36.

176. Bancroft, Autobiography..., p. 134.

177. Thomas Powers, *The Man Who Kept the Secrets: Richard Helms and the CIA*, (NY: Washington Square Press, 1979; Pocket Books ed., 1981), p. 41.

178. Bancroft, Autobiography..., p. 135; Powers, *The Man Who Kept the Secrets*, p. 42.

179. Bancroft, Autobiography..., pp. 138-39.

180. Perhaps this is what Dulles was thinking when he told the Warren Commission on July 9, 1964, "But nobody reads. Don't believe people read in this country. There will be a few professors that will read the record...the public will read very little." (Mark Lane, *Plausible Denial*, NY: Thunder's Mouth Press, 1991), p. 53.

181. Bancroft, Autobiography..., p. 144. Note: Is this "editorial intelligence"? Would her work concerning "specific bombings" be of interest to the Air Force Editorial Office, headed by Harry Huntt Ransom from 1944-46 and who won the Legion of Merit for his work in editorial intelligence? Would it be of interest to Walt Rostow, the OSS bombing target expert? Were Ransom and Rostow among the "mutual friends" of Mary Bancroft and Allen Dulles?

182. Bancroft, Autobiography..., p. 150.

183. Bancroft, Autobiography..., pp. 161, 168-170.

184. Bancroft, Autobiography..., pp. 185-86.

185. Bancroft, Autobiography..., p. 187.

186. Bancroft, Autobiography..., pp. 187-88.

187. Bancroft, Autobiography..., pp. 196-97.

188. Bancroft, Autobiography..., pp. 202-05.

189. Bancroft, Autobiography..., pp. 206-08.

190. Bancroft, Autobiography..., p. 214.

191. William Manchester, *The Death of a President*, (NY: Harper & Row,

1967), pp. 193, 206, cited in Stone with Sklar, *JFK: The Book of the Film*, p. 109.

192. Bancroft, Autobiography..., pp. 235-36.

193. Bancroft, Autobiography..., p. 240.

194. Bancroft, Autobiography..., p. 243.

195. Bancroft, Autobiography..., p. 264.

196. Bancroft, Autobiography..., p. 289.

197. This dangerous attitude also seems to be a problem in the FBI among zealous "Hooverites." (See Jan Jarboe, "Wanted by the FBI," Texas Monthly, May 1993.) Note: Alice Sessions, wife of Bush appointed FBI director, William Sessions, is another Texas friend of Barbara J. Burris. (See Susan Katz Keating, "Alice Sessions' friends stand up in time of need," The Washington Times, Feb. 23, 1993, paragraphs 7, 24, 27, 28, 34.)

[OBJOB]198. Russell, *The Man Who Knew Too Much*, pp. 180, 274, 407, 473-75; Ranelagh, The Agency, p. 359.

199. Bancroft, Autobiography..., p. 290.

200. Bancroft, Autobiography..., p. 291.

201. While not sure such a technique exists, considering the long history, extreme sophistication, and massive efforts of cryptology, it stands to reason that this paper's author has not inadvertently imagined a totally new form of code-making.

202. Leonard Mosley, *Dulles: A Biography of Eleanor, Allen, and John Foster Dulles and their Family Network*, (NY: Dial Press, 1978.): pp. 247-48. Note: For Luce's connection to other subjects in this paper see Warren Hinckle with William Turner, *The Fish is Red*, (NY: Harper & Row, 1981), pp. 164-68; republished as *Deadly Secrets*, Thunder's Mouth Press, 1992.

203. Mosley, Dulles, p. 287. (Acting Treasury Secretary G. d'Andelot Belin:) Vincent Palamara, "Anonymous No Longer -- The Secret Service Detail of November 22, 1963," The Investigator, Jun.-Jul., 1993, pp. 14, 15; CE 1026 (18H 810-815), "Secret Service Memorandum, dated March 19, 1964, re Secret Service Report on the Assassination of President Kennedy," Secret Service doc. no. CO-2-34,030, James J. Rowley, Chief of the Secret Service, to G. d'Andelot Belin, Gen. Counsel to the Secret Service, naming all Secret Service personnel assignments and duties in Dallas the day of the assassination.

204. Bancroft, Autobiography..., p. 292.

205. 24 H, CE 2124; Edward J. Epstein, *Legend: The Secret World of Lee Harvey Oswald*, (NY: McGraw Hill, 1978), pp. 203-05.

206. WCR 738, cited in Scott, *The Dallas Conspiracy*, ch. IV, p. 4.

207. Epstein, *Legend...*, p. 206; Cook.

208. Epstein, *Legend...*, p. 206.

209. Twelve years later this same agency would reject his proposal for an "Institute of Latin American Resources" at LBJ's alma mater, Southwest Texas College. One was eventually established at his own alma mater, UT. Rostow was informed of these communications at the time. (See earlier discussion of this in this paper.)

210. Summers, *Conspiracy*, pp. 225, 226-27.

211. Bancroft, Autobiography..., pp. 185-86.

212. Epstein, *Legend*..., p. 180; Summers, *Conspiracy*, p. 224.

213. Bancroft, Autobiography..., p. 290.

214. Bruce Campbell Adamson with Steve Perez, Oswald's Closest Friend, The George De Mohrenschildt Story, (unpublished manuscript, 1993), Bush ch., p. 31.

215. Adamson with Perez, Oswald's Closest Friend..., pp. 29, 30.

216. Adamson with Perez, Oswald's Closest Friend..., pp. 30, 37.

217. Adamson with Perez, Oswald's Closest Friend..., pp. 18-21, 31.

218. Adamson with Perez, Oswald's Closest Friend..., pp. 32-33.

219. David G. Armstrong, "Sins of the Fathers," The Austin Chronicle, Apr. 10, 1992, pp. 14, 16.

220. Adamson with Perez, Oswald's Closest Friend..., pp. 34-36.

221. As mentioned earlier, in the same newspaper reporting John Martino's speaking engagement in Austin in October 1963 was an advertisement announcing that Buckley would speak on the UT campus in December.

222. Epstein, *Legend*..., p. 205; John B. Judis, *William F. Buckley, Jr.: Patron Saint of the Conservatives*, (NY: Simon & Schuster, Touchstone ed., 1990), p. 80. Note: Although Stalin's widely accepted role as the force behind Trotsky's assassin is given brief rhetorical credit in this paper, even a cursory review of the facts of Trotsky's assassination indicates that such a conclusion may have been arrived at naively.

223. Albert Glotzer, *Trotsky: Memoir and Critique*, (Buffalo, NY: Prometheus, 1989), pp. 284, 293; Spies, "License to Kill", 30 minutes, Produced by Anthony Potter with Arts and Entertainment Network, Columbia House, 1992.

224. Russell, *The Man Who Knew Too Much*, pp. 28, 585; Sheldon Inkol, "The Indiana Rifle," (The Third Decade, Jul. 1993), pp. 4, 5-6, 8n. 42.

225. *Who Didn't Kill JFK* (later distributed under the title: Fake), video tape, 60 minutes, Produced by Jack White with Jim Marrs, JFK Video Group, 1990, Third Coast Productions, 3-G Video Group 1992.

226 Epstein, *Legend*..., p. 205.

227. Judis, *William F. Buckley, Jr.*, p. 80.

228. David Atlee Phillips, *The Night Watch*, (NY: Atheneum, 1977), pp. 34, 35; Schlesinger with Kinzer, *Bitter Fruit*, p. 167; Bishop: Gaeton Fonzi, "Keynote Address," Addendum to Proceedings of the Second Research Conference of the Third Decade, (Fredonia, NY: The Third Decade, 1993), p. 42; Russell, *The Man Who Knew Too Much*, p. 31; Donald Freed, *Death in Washington*, (Westport, CT: Lawrence Hill, 1980), pp. 41, 47. Note: At the time of the assassination Phillips was chief of covert action in the CIA's Mexico City station. Henry Luce's wife, Clare Boothe Luce became one of the first directors and active members, in 1975, of Philips' extreme right-wing Association of Former Intelligence Officers, composed of lobbyists for "the military right." (Freed, pp. 124, 138.)

229. Canfield with Weberman, *Coup d'état in America*, p. 29.

230. Russell, *The Man Who Knew Too Much*, p. 162.

231. Russell, *The Man Who Knew Too Much*, p. 334.

232. Russell, *The Man Who Knew Too Much*, p. 121.

233. Peter Dale Scott, *Crime and Cover-Up*, p. 54, n. 34.

234. Russell, *The Man Who Knew Too Much*, p. 30.

235. Russell, *The Man Who Knew Too Much*, pp. 120-21.

236. "Trotsky Comparison Made," New York Times, Nov. 27, 1963, cited in Inkol, "The Indiana Rifle," p. 8n. 42.

237. Russell, *The Man Who Knew Too Much*, p. 188.

238. Epstein, *Legend...*, p. 205.

239. Hinckle with Turner, *The Fish is Red*, p. 45; Ranelagh, *The Agency*, p. 276.

240. J. Robert Moskin, "The Dangerous World of Walt Rostow," Look magazine, Dec. 12, 1967.

241. Russell, *The Man Who Knew Too Much*, pp. 312-13.

242. Frantz, *The Forty Acre Follies*, pp. 28, 36.

243. Robert A. Rosenbaum, ed., *The New American Desk Encyclopedia*, (NY: Signet, 1984), pp. 516, 560, 1274-75.

244. Garraty, *The American Nation*, p. 699.

245. Rosenbaum, *The New American Desk Encyclopedia*, p. 516.

246. Frantz, *The Forty Acre Follies*, pp. 28, 36; Alexander L. George and Juliette L. George, *Woodrow Wilson and Colonel House: A Personality Study*, (NY: Dover, 1964), p. xviii.

247. Frantz, *The Forty Acre Follies*, pp. 27, 28, 32, 36, 39-40.

248. Eckhardt, *One Hundred Faithful...*, pp. 12-13.

249. Eckhardt, *One Hundred Faithful...*, pp. 38-39.

250. Manchester, *Death of a President*, p. 46.

251. Also involved in these provocations was none other than William F. Buckley, Sr., who in 1919 helped Tampico General Manuel Pelaez organize an abortive coup against the bourgeois nationalist Carranza, whom he accused of being a Bolshevic when testifying before the Senate Foreign Relations Committee. (See Judis, *William F. Buckley, Jr.,* p. 22.)

252. Arthur S. Link, *Woodrow Wilson: Revolution, War, and Peace*, (Arlington Heights, IL: AHM, 1917), pp. 16-17.

253. Garraty, *The American Nation*, p. 699.

254. Lane, *Plausible Denial*, p. 363.

255. Epstein, *Legend...*, p. 206; James Di Eugenio, *Destiny Betrayed*, (NY: Sheridan Square, 1992), pp. 342-43 n.22.

256. Epstein, *Legend...*, pp. 177-83.

257. William Casey, *The Secret War Against Hitler*, (NY: Berkeley, 1989) pp. 82-87.

258. Epstein, *Legend...*, pp. 177-83; Canfield with Weberman, *Coup d'état in America*, p. 29; Judis, *William F. Buckley, Jr.*, p. 80.

259. Russell, *The Man Who Knew Too Much*, pp. 180, 274, 407, 473-75; Ranelagh, *The Agency*, p. 359.

260. Scott, *The Dallas Conspiracy*, ch. III, pp. 1-6; 2 H 304, Mrs. Ford, cited in Scott, ch. III, p. 6.

261. Scott, ch. IV, pp. 1, 5.

262. Earl Golz, "Did the Mafia kill JFK?" The Texas Observer, Nov. 30, 1973, pp. 7-10; hereafter as Golz.

263. Epstein, *Legend*, pp. 203-05, 213-14. Note: Michael's father, George Lyman Paine, as discussed in this paper, had been one of the leaders of the Trotskyite movement in the United States.

264. Epstein, *Legend*, pp. 203-05, 213-14; Russell, *The Man Who Knew Too Much*, p. 310.

265. Magnolia was bought by the Mobil Oil Company. The famous Mobil "Pegasus" logo sits atop the old Magnolia building as one of the oldest landmarks of the downtown Dallas skyline.

266. Epstein, *Legend*, pp. 203-05, 213-14.

267. Cook, p. 36; Russell, *The Man Who Knew Too Much*, p. 583.

268 Scott refers to this facility by its parent company's name, Socony Mobil, while Epstein more correctly calls it Magnolia Laboratories. Scott is excused, however, because he makes crucial connections, in his manuscript, between Socony Mobil and anti-Kennedy Vietnam policies.

269. 9 H 129, cited in Scott, ch. IV, p. 1.

270. Russell, *The Man Who Knew Too Much*, pp. 691-92.

271. 9 H 106, 107 cited in Scott, *The Dallas Conspiracy*, ch. III, pp. 16, 37. Note: After the assassination, accompanied by Ruth Paine, Marina Oswald was secretly taken by the Secret Service to the Inn of the Six Flags in Arlington, Texas. According to Peter Dale Scott, this motel was owned by the Great Southwest Corporation, a company jointly owned and controlled by Murchison and Rockefeller interests. The motel manager there, James Herbert Martin, soon became Marina's business manager and lodged her in his home. He also negotiated the sale to the world press of the dubious photograph of Oswald posing with a rifle and a Trotskyite newspaper, which ended up on the cover of Henry Luce's and C.D. Jackson's Life magazine. Mamantov conspiratorially altered Marina's statements in a way that connected Lee Oswald to the rifle in that photograph. (See Scott, *The Dallas Conspiracy*, ch. III.)

272. H.H. Ransom, *The Intelligence Establishment* , (Cambridge, MA: Harvard, 1970), p. 112, cited in Scott, ch. III, p. 17n. Note: This Ransom is Harry Howe and not Harry Huntt of UT, although Walt Rostow knew them both.

273. Scott, *The Dallas Conspiracy*, ch. IX, pp. 20-21; Byrd, I'm an Endangered Species, p. 78.

274. Scott, *The Dallas Conspiracy*, ch. IV, p. 1.

275. Scott, *The Dallas Conspiracy*, ch. IV, pp. 1-2.

276. Golz.

277. Golz.

278. Golz.

279. Golz.

280. Russell, *The Man Who Knew Too Much*, p. 593.

281. Hinckle with Turner, *The Fish is Red*, p. 202.

282. Summers, *Conspiracy*, p. 447; Polk's New Orleans City Directories,

1962-65; Epstein, *Legend*, pp. 348- 49.

283. "Zapata Petroleum Corp.," Fortune magazine, Apr. 1958, p. 248.

284. "Zapata Petroleum Corp.," Fortune.

285. Hinckle with Turner, *The Fish is Red*, pp. 279-80.

286. Prospectuses of sale, Louisiana Collection, Univ. of New Orleans Library.

287. "Zapata Petroleum Corp.," Fortune.

288. The Wall Street Journal, Feb. 23, 1977; FIB, Inc. Annual Reports, 1977-79; Julius Mader, *Who's Who in CIA*, (Berlin: Self-published, 1968), p. 420.

289. David G. Armstrong, "Sins of the Fathers," The Austin Chronicle, Apr. 10, 1992, pp. 14, 16; hereafter as Armstrong.

290. Armstrong; Note: Christopher Simpson, author of the 1988 book, *Blowback: America's Recruitment of Nazis and Its Effects on the Cold War*, has written a book which sheds considerably more light on the past Nazi ties of both the Bush family and the Dulles family. The revelations in Simpson's new book, *The Splendid Blond Beast*, (Grove Atlantic, 1993), are too recent to include in this paper. Nevertheless, it is highly recommended for further insight into the interrelationships discussed here.

291. Frantz, *The Forty Acre Follies*, pp. 97-100; Byrd, *I'm an Endangered Species*, p. 17; Scott, Government Documents..., ch. II, pp. 18-21; WCR, p. 298.)

292. Ford, p. 26.

293. Penn Jones, *Forgive My Grief III*, (Midlothian, TX: Self published, 1969; revised ed. 1976), photo caption;

294. Dan E. Moldea, *Dark Victory: Ronald Reagan, MCA, and the Mob*, (NY: Penguin, 1987), pp. 6-7.

295. Craig, *When They Kill a President*, pp. 10, 11.

296. Craig, *When They Kill a President*, p. 34.

297. Russell, p. 673.

[OBJ]

PART THREE: Byrds, Planes, and an Automobile

One of the men with whom the truth may lie, concerning the JFK assassination's links to the University of Texas, was one of UT's most ardent supporters who happened to own the building that has become synonymous with the assassination. His ties to UT are well known. His numerous ties to the assassination are lesser known. One of his least known ties, it appears, is to the UT Rambler.

Somewhat like the plot to assassinate Trotsky and most unlike the failed assassination conspiracy against Hitler in which Allen Dulles and Mary Bancroft participated, the plot to assassinate President Kennedy seems to have been sophisticated, intricate, and meticulously planned. It can be presumed therefore that, as researcher William Weston has written, "One of the most critical elements of this plot was the Texas School Book Depository." In addition to both the circumstances of Oswald's employment at the TSBD, and the routing of the motorcade by the building, Weston points out that there would have been a need for a team of plotters to make detailed plans inside the building well in advance of November 22, including firing angles, planting of false evidence, and getaway plans. This could have been done, Weston says, by six TSBD employees assigned to lay new flooring on the fifth and sixth floors from late October until November 22.[298] It is a plausible argument, which brings up the concern that any long-term improvement to the property such as a flooring project would have to have been of interest to, if not directly initiated and contracted by, the building's owner.

Roy Truly, the "superintendent" who hired Oswald was "a building manager."[299] In a story published the day after the assassination, Dallas Morning News reporter Kent Biffle referred to Roy Truly as "Superintendent of the textbook building...."[300] The floor crew was supervised directly by William Shelly, "the assistant manager who was in charge of the floor laying project."[301] These titles imply that they were building managers more closely associated with the landlord than with the private textbook brokerage firm which leased the building.[302] The employment of these individuals would seem to be a relatively easy fact for researchers verify.

Weston writes, "The electrical power for the whole building and even the telephone stopped working about five minutes prior to the assassination.[303] How two such entirely different systems as the electricity and the phones could go out simultaneously is beyond explanation, unless one can assume that the interruption was deliberate."[304] Although this claim is currently in dispute, it cannot be denied that the conspiracy to assassinate President Kennedy would have involved intimate knowledge of the TSBD building. Truly and Shelly were possibly employed to some extent by the building's landlord, David Harold Byrd.

Dallas oilman David Harold Byrd, born April 24, 1900, was the cousin of Admiral Richard E. Byrd and his brother, Senator Harry F. Byrd, "the leader of conservative opinion in the United States."[305] D.H. Byrd owned the Texas School Book Depository building from the 1930s to the 1970s. In May 1964, he had the "Oswald window" removed and kept it as part of his estate.[306] In 1972, after Byrd sold the building to Mr. Aubrey Mayhew, an arsonist set it on fire. It was saved, however. Shortly thereafter Mayhew defaulted on his payments to Republic National Bank of Dallas[307] and the property reverted to the Byrd family.[308] In 1975 Byrd sold it again.[309]

Byrd had a close relationship with both Lyndon Johnson and John Connally. Evidently not satisfied with being the cousin of a powerful and respected U.S. senator,[310] for D.H. Byrd, "Another goal was to reach a rapport with the politicians who ran things, especially at the seat of state government in Austin....Sam Rayburn, Morrie Sheppard, John Connally, and Lyndon Johnson on the national scene were to become men I could go to any time that I wanted action, and so were a succession of Texas governors. Among the ablest was John Connally...who says he's in my debt for pleading his cause... with...Ida Nell (Nellie) Brill, Sweetheart of The University of Texas in 1940...."[311]

Byrd probably also knew George de Mohrenschildt, David Atlee Phillips and George Bush through the Dallas Petroleum Club.[312] In 1945, future club member de Mohrenschildt obtained a masters degree in petroleum engineering after eighteen months at the University of Texas at Austin.[313] During that year he was investigated by the FBI and ONI.

That same year he worked under Warren W. Smith, president of Pantipec Oil, owned by the parents of William F. Buckley, Jr. Smith and de Mohrenschildt soon quit and formed the Cuban-Venezuelan Oil Voting Trust Company. When Castro took over, this company forfeited oil leases covering about half of Cuba. Jack Crichton of Army Intelligence Reserve Service, mentioned earlier, had also worked under Warren Smith at Pantipec, which sells to Sun Oil.314 By 1957, George de Mohrenschildt had established himself in oil ventures ranging from wildcat drilling to aerial surveillance and had begun working for the CIA.[315]

It is probable that Byrd knew David Ferrie and he definitely knew the very top Air Force brass through Civil Air Patrol (CAP). CAP Captain David Ferrie was CAP cadet Lee Harvey Oswald's trainer.[316]

Byrd was a co-founder of Civil Air Patrol. Displayed in his office, at 1110 Tower Petroleum Building in Dallas, were many pictures of himself in uniform with aviation dignitaries and Air Force Generals.[317] He was an aviation buff but could not become a fighter pilot because his eyesight was bad.[318] He co-founded CAP six days before Pearl Harbor.[319] After World War II he spearheaded the establishment of the Cadet Program in CAP and contributed many scholarships to its cadets.[320] In Dallas on May 24, 1963, the U.S. Air Force presented to Byrd its Scroll of Appreciation, which reads:

> For rendering meritorious service to the United States Air Force from Dec. 1941 to April, 1960. Motivated by a strong sense of patriotism, Mr. Byrd played a major part in the successful operation of the Texas Wing, Civil Air Patrol, throughout World War II. After the war he assisted in the incorporation of the Civil Air Patrol and its designation as an Auxiliary of the Air Force. Mr. Byrd helped initiate the International Air Cadet Exchange and worked closely with the Air Cadet League of Canada. The many scholarships established or supported by Mr. Byrd have aided countless cadets in the attainment of additional training and higher education. His contributions of material and personal aircraft to the use of Civil Air Patrol materially aided in the performance of its mission.. The distinctive accomplishments of Mr. Byrd have earned for him the sincere gratitude of the United States Air Force.
> (Signed) - Curtis E. Le May Chief of Staff
> (Signed) - Eugene M. Zuckert
> Secretary of the Air Force[321]

D.H. Byrd counted among his close friends one of the most famous aviators, General Jimmy Doolittle.[322] Byrd and Doolittle were hunting buddies. Of Doolittle he wrote, "Having a fondness for being Number One in all my undertakings, it doesn't come naturally for me to confess that Doolittle is the one man whom I would gladly serve in any venture as Number Two."[323] On one intriguing trip without Doolittle, Byrd went hunting in central Africa in November and December 1963. It was his first such trip of five during his lifetime outside of the U.S., Mexico, and

Canada.[324]

Byrd prepared well for the trip: Temco, Inc. was an aircraft company founded by D.H. Byrd and which later merged with his friend James Ling's electronics company (1960), and aircraft manufacturer Chance Vought Corporation (1961) to form Ling-Temco-Vought (LTV). Byrd became a director[325] of LTV and bought, along with Ling, 132,000 shares of LTV in November 1963.[326] Byrd then left the country to go on his two-month safari in central Africa. He returned in January to find his good friend Lyndon Johnson president of the United States, his building famous, and a large defense contract awarded to LTV to build fighter planes -- to be paid for out of the 1965 budget which had not yet been approved by Congress.[327]

Mac Wallace, who received a five-year suspended sentence in the shooting death of John Douglas Kiner in Austin on October 22, 1951, went to work for Temco, Inc. of Garland, Texas five months after his trial. He remained in that position until February 1961, four months before Henry Marshall's mysterious death on June 3, 1961, when he transferred to the Anaheim, California offices of LTV.[328]

The transfer required a background check by the Navy. "The most intriguing part of the Wallace case was how a convicted murderer was able to get a job with defense contractors. Better yet, how was he able to get a security clearance? Clinton Peoples [the Texas Ranger Captain who investigated the Marshall and Kiner murders][329] reported that when the original security clearance was granted, he asked the Naval intelligence officer handling the case how such a person could get the clearance. `Politics,' the man replied. When Peoples asked who would have that much power, the simple answer was, `the vice president,' who at the time was Lyndon Johnson. Years later, after the story broke [of Billie Sol Estes' March 20, 1984 testimony that implicated Lyndon Johnson, Malcom Wallace, and Clifton Carter in the death of Henry Marshall], that investigator could not recall the conversation with Peoples but he did say no one forced him to write a favorable report. He also added that he wasn't the one that made the decision to grant the clearance. The whole matter might have been solved with a peek at that original report but unfortunately, when the files were checked, that particular report was suspiciously missing. It has never been seen since."[330]

Wallace was transferred and given clearance in February 1961. "In January 1961, the very month Johnson was sworn in as vice president, and the month Henry Marshall was in Dallas discussing how to combat Estes-like scams, Billie Sol Estes learned through his contacts that the USDA was investigating the allotment scheme and that Henry Marshall might end up testifying. The situation was supposedly discussed by

Estes, Johnson, and Carter in the backyard of LBJ's Washington home. Johnson was, according to Estes, alarmed that if Marshall started talking it might result in an investigation that would implicate the vice president. At first it was decided to have Marshall transferred to Washington, but when told Marshall had already refused such a relocation, LBJ, according to Estes, said simply, `Then we'll have to get rid of him.'"[331]

According to Craig Zirbel, author of *The Texas Connection*, in May 1962, "...Johnson flew to Dallas aboard a military jet to privately meet with Estes and his lawyers on a plane parked away from the terminal....This incident would probably have remained secret except that LBJ's plane suffered a mishap in landing at Dallas. When investigative reporters attempted to obtain the tower records for the flight mishap the records were "sealed by government order."[332]

Still more LTV intrigues were revealed by Peter Dale Scott: "A fellow-director of [Jack Alston] Crichton's[333] firm of Dorchester Gas Producing was D.H. Byrd, an oil associate of Sid Richardson and Clint Murchison, and the LTV director who teamed up with James Ling to buy 132,000 shares of LTV in November 1963. While waiting to be sworn in as President in Dallas on November 22, Johnson spoke by telephone with J.W. Bullion, a member of the Dallas law firm (Thompson, Wright, Knight, and Simmons) which had the legal account for Dorchester Gas Producing and was represented on its board. The senior partner of the law firm, Dwight L. Simmons, had until 1960 sat on the board of Chance Vought Aircraft, a predecessor of Ling-Temco-Vought. One week after the assassination, Johnson named Bullion, who has been described as his `business friend and lawyer,' to be one of the two trustees handling the affairs of the former LBJ Co. while its owner was President."[334]

Another appreciative friend of Byrd's was Arthur Andrew Collins, the founder of the Collins Radio Company.

Byrd, along with John D. Rockefeller, Jr., was a financier of his cousin Admiral Richard E. Byrd's polar expeditions by air. A mountain range at the South Pole is named the Harold Byrd Mountains in his honor.[335] Some of that money went for the purchase of radio equipment and technical support from Arthur Collins.

The 1933 expedition was the first big break for the young Collins Radio Company of Cedar Rapids Iowa.[336] In May 1951 Collins began an expansion program to build a one-million dollar plant near the Dallas suburb of Richardson. A hanger was leased at nearby Red Bird Airport to install and repair airborne equipment. The move was due to a decentralization plan urged by the Defense Department for security reasons.[337]

According to Dick Russell, "At about 1:OO p.m. on the afternoon of

November 22, half an hour after the president was shot, neighbors who lived along the road that runs by the little Redbird [sic] private airport began calling police. A twin-engine plane, they reported, was out there behaving very peculiarly. For an [OBJ.OBJ]hour it had been revving its engines, not on the runway but parked at the end of the airstrip on a grassy area next to the fence. The noise prevented nearby residents from hearing their TVs, as news came over about the terrible events in downtown Dallas. But the police were too busy to check it out, and shortly thereafter the plane took off....

"Louis Gaudin, the government's air traffic control specialist at Redbird [sic] airport...recalled observing three men in business suits board a Comanche-type aircraft at about 2:00 p.m. on November 22, head north, then return with only two occupants, where they were met by a Dallas policeman named Haake."[338]

In August 1978, former Dallas Assistant District Attorney Bill Alexander and author Anthony Summers were retracing Oswald's movements. According to Summers, Alexander told him that the spot where Tippit was killed was near R.L. Thornton Freeway, the route to Red Bird airport. Alexander speculated that Oswald may have expected to be picked up and taken to the airport.[339]

In 1963, Wayne January rented planes at Red Bird Airport. He told researcher Jones Harris in 1966 and Summers in 1978 that before the assassination he was approached by two men and a woman, who inquired about renting an aircraft on November 22, to go to Mexico. After the assassination he thought that Oswald strongly resembled one of the men he had encountered.[340]

On November 24, 1963, FBI Special Agent Norman W. Propst was in Witchita Falls, Texas inquiring whether a South Texas pilot named Chuck Rogers or anyone from South Texas had been in contact with anyone at an aircraft plant in Olney, Texas or the crop dusting industry in North Texas in recent months.[341] In 1991, Houston Police Department Forensic Artist Lois Gibson concluded, after photographic studies, that one of the Dealey Plaza tramps was either Charles Frederick Rogers, the CIA pilot and CAP member from Houston, "or a dead ringer close enough to be an identical twin."[342]

Rogers joined CAP in the early 1950s to learn to fly. "During his spare time, he participated in various CAP activities, including searches for downed pilots, which brought him into contact with other CAP leaders and cadets in the Texas-Louisiana region."[343]

Raymond Broshears, the former roommate of Oswald's Louisiana CAP unit captain, David Ferrie, told Dick Russell in 1975, that the purpose of Ferrie's sudden trip to Houston on the night of November 22,

1963, "was to meet a plane. He was going to fly these people on to Mexico, and eventually to South Africa, which did not have an extradition treaty with the United States. They had left from some little airfield between Dallas and Fort Worth, and David had a twin-engine plane ready for them, and that was the purpose of his

mad dash through a driving rainstorm from New Orleans."[344] Ferrie told New Orleans D.A. Jim Garrison that the purpose of his "mad dash" was to go goose hunting. Perhaps D.H. Byrd also had reasons other than hunting for his first trip to Africa in November 1963.

A vice president at Collins Radio in Richardson knew George de Mohrenschildt and Oswald. Throughout the summer of 1962, de Mohrenschildt and his wife, Jean, made almost daily visits to the home of Admiral Henry C. Bruton. De Mohrenschildt introduced the Brutons to Lee and Marina and solicited the Brutons' help in his attempts to arrange and rearrange the Oswalds' lives.[345]

De Mohrenschildt was not only friends with Bruton, a former director of top secret Naval communications, he was also a friend of Colonel David L. Schurger, a Czech-born engineer who had served in Air Force intelligence. De Mohrenschildt was a frequent guest at this same house when it was owned by Schurger from 1954 to 1958.[346]

Carl Mather of Garland, Texas, a twenty-one year employee of Collins radio at the time of the assassination, had security clearance for electronics work and had done work on Johnson's airplane, Air Force Two. At about 2:00 p.m. on the day of the assassination a mechanic saw a man who looked like Oswald sitting in a red 1957 Plymouth in the parking lot of El Chico restaurant. The license number of the car (Texas PP 4537) was the same number issued to Mather's blue 1957 Plymouth. Mather was a close friend of J.D. Tippit's.[347]

Within the first year after the assassination, Kenneth Porter quit his job at Collins Radio. Soon thereafter articles began to appear in the Dallas papers about his dating Marina Oswald. J.H. "Bart" Bartholomew, an employee at Collins' Richardson plant since 1955, reported that after Porter had been working there for a while he quit "all of a sudden." Fellow workers wondered why he quit so suddenly. According to Bartholomew, Porter got along with everyone at the plant. No one knew any reason why he would quit. Then the news media reported that Kenneth and Marina were engaged. He had divorced his wife just prior to the engagement announcement. Porter also had children and had not mentioned any domestic problems. When news of the engagement broke, rumors began at Collins that he was marrying Marina for her money. Bartholomew said the talk around the plant was that the quitting, divorce and engagement all happened very quickly in that order within a year of the assassination.[348]

Bartholomew's job at Collins was inspecting work done on two-man communications "Huts" used in Korea and Vietnam. Collins also equipped military aircraft and ships with sophisticated top secret electronic gear. In March 1963, Collins was awarded a two-million-dollar-plus contract from the CIA connected United States Information Agency (USIA) to build nine short-wave transmitters to be used in Southeast Asia. Two weeks later, however, the work had to be postponed when President Kennedy requested a cut in USIA funds. By October, it appears, the contract had turned into a scandal. Assistant Secretary of Defense BeLieu was charged with giving false data to the House Human Resources subcommittee on a "sole source" contract awarded to Collins. Despite his denials, subcommittee members urged that BeLieu be dismissed if he did not give a satisfactory explanation. One week later, however, this heated debate would be eclipsed by a bigger scandal involving Collins Radio and the CIA.[349] It also involved a ship with sophisticated electronics -- installed while Ken BeLieu was Assistant Navy Secretary for Installations and Logistics under Navy Secretary John Connally.[350]

On Halloween night 1963, Castro's soldiers captured four CIA agents attempting to infiltrate Cuba from a 174-foot ship called the Rex that was based in the Port of Palm Beach, flew a Nicaraguan flag and was being leased to the Collins Radio Company of Dallas by J.A. Belcher, a Miami oilman. The four agents confessed on Cuban television. One of those captured, Montero Carranzana, said he had "once landed twelve infiltrators on the north coast of Matazzas Province from a yacht that had a crew of American CIA agents." The U.S. government did not deny Castro's charges. The Rex mission was not the first time Collins had provided cover for CIA operations. Two weeks after Kennedy's death, the Rex and another mystery ship called Leda, again left their Florida ports.[351] This paper will further explore several apparent connections between the Rex and the UT Rambler.

Byrd was able to give Arthur Collins his "big break" in 1933 because he had made his fortune by 1931. When he mapped out his goals he decided, "High on my list was the University of Texas. Despite my enforced drop-out after two years, I have nursed an abiding affection for the "Forty Acres" and its fortunes, especially on the football field...."[352] D. Harold Byrd, as he is known on campus, donated large sums of money to the University of Texas and its Longhorn Marching Band. Among the things this money helped purchase was "Big Bertha," the largest bass drum in the world, and the construction of the Music Building East, in which a lounge is named the "Byrd Room" in his honor.

Each year three band members receive the "Harold Byrd Awards" for leadership.[353]

As mentioned earlier, D.H. Byrd knew Barbara J. Burris, a mutual close friend and supporter of pianist Van Cliburn. "I wanted to be a welcome member of Dallas Society." Byrd wrote, "I was an early booster and close friend of pianists Van Cliburn and Jose Iturbi...."[354] Barbara J. is the wife of Air Force intelligence Colonel Howard L. Burris, Vice President Johnson's military representative, discussed earlier in this paper.

Her father, Texas Governor Beauford Jester was a "dear friend" of D.H. Byrd's.[355]

Thus the story of Byrds and planes comes full circle to our mysterious automobile. Through his enthusiastic patronage of The University of Texas, as well as through their mutual political and Air Force friends, and mutual contacts at DeGolyer and MacNaughton Byrd knew Harry Huntt Ransom. Ransom and UT are the key to Byrd's association with Cecil Bernard Smith, who had sold the mysterious UT Rambler to George Gordon Wing two years earlier. D.H. Byrd and C.B. Smith became founding members, in 1965, of UT's Chancellor's Council created by Harry Ransom.[356]

The interrelationships previously discussed and yet to be discussed in this paper were not the result of unaided insights on the part of this paper's author or researchers. They were ascertained by studying what at first appeared to be a professor's eccentric collection of old magazines carried in his old car, and random mutilations of books on the JFK assassination and one rather obscure reference book in the UT libraries. Upon closer examination, however, patterns began to emerge.

For reasons to be discussed, the mutilations are believed to have been done by a single individual whom this paper's researchers have dubbed the "Red Ripper." This section will deal with an apparent combined purpose behind the eccentricities of George Wing and the mutilations of the Red Ripper.

To be explored, in this and later sections, are the probable identification of Wing's Rambler by an eyewitness who seems to corroborate Wing's background in Florida as predicted by a significant detail of the mutilations; the probable identity of the Red Ripper; and possible interpretations of the magazines and books as evidence.

In September 1988, this author began a daily reading program on the JFK assassination in preparation for the inevitable misinformation that would dominate media coverage of the twenty-fifth anniversary of that event. Despite having sporadically kept up with the subject over the years, large gaps in personal knowledge of the findings of researchers over the previous ten years was quickly realized. The reading continued past the anniversary and a learning curve began, resulting in a progressively greater understanding of the facts and history of the assassination.

By May 1989, this author was familiar enough with the Roger Craig story and its implications to take more than a passing glance at George Wing's old Rambler parked among the late model Honda's and Toyota's.

Another direct result of the reading program was the attention given, in the summer of 1989, to the mutilations of Anthony Summers' 1980 edition of Conspiracy. The annoyance of this led to a determined effort to find what was written on those missing pages.

As mentioned at the beginning of this paper, the missing "John Martino" pages in Anthony Summers' book were only a minor curiosity even in 1990 after the discovery of Martino's pre-assassination visit to Austin. This book was the 1980 edition, which was UT's only copy prior to the release of the 1989 edition. It was still missing the pages dealing with Martino in May 1991, despite the fact that these pages were reported missing in April 1990 and new pages had been "on order" since May, 9 1990.

When the second mutilation was found (Anson's 1975 book, *They've Killed the President*) it was still only a bothersome inconvenience. UT card catalog records showed a second copy in the Flawn Academic Center, UT's undergraduate library. That copy of the book was missing, however, and according to the librarian, had never been checked out. That indicated it was probably stolen just after being purchased.

It was only with the discovery of a third mutilation, the testimony of Santos Trafficante in a volume of hearings of the House Select Committee on Assassinations, that a pattern began to emerge.

The HSCA pages were removed in a way that left marks from a red ball point pen. The pen had been repeatedly stroked along the gutter of the book until the page could be easily ripped out. This was the same technique used in Anson's book and, in blue ink, in the fourth book discovered: an obscure biographical reference work called The Directory of American Scholars.

The only reason this book was consulted was because of attempts to find biographical information about Professor Wing. Wing's name was not listed, but near where his name would have been was a rectangular hole in the page that had been cut out using a blue ball point pen.

After consulting an older edition of this same directory it was suspected that the biography removed from this page (p. 672, sixth ed., 1974) was that of Nathaniel Weyl, the former OSS operative who helped expose Alger Hiss.[357] Weyl was friends with John Martino[358] (subject of the Summers missing pages and a [359] [360] "close friend" of Santos Trafficante), Frank Meyer (friend of William F. Buckley, Jr. and subject of Warren Commission Document 662), and William Pawley,[361] who, aside from being a missing pages subject himself, wrote a letter to the editor of Esquire defending the planners of the Bay of Pigs invasion.[362]

That letter was published in George Wing's most prominently displayed back seat magazine. After receiving an intact copy of the sixth edition of the directory through an interlibrary loan, the suspicion that Weyl's biography was the one removed was confirmed.

The next book found was Peter Dale Scott's *Crime and Cover-Up*. Prior to discovery of *The Fish is Red*, Scott's was the most mutilated book. Once again a red ball point pen had been used.

The sixth book is perhaps the most unusual. It is the only known foreign language book to be mutilated, Wim J.F. Meiners' *De Moordfabriek: Tussen Dallas En Watergate*. Little is known about this book due to lack of access to Dutch translation services. It was determined much later that its missing pages included a photo section. No major significance between the photos and other aspects of the UT mysteries has been found. However, there are portraits of the Watergate burglars, who seem to have been of special interest to the Red Ripper. But still, this book may not be related to the others since there was no red ink. And the book was poorly bound which could have easily resulted in the loss of pages. There is one fact that makes it worth considering. The Dutch journalist, Willem Oltmans, who is referred to on one of this book's missing pages, had not only visited de Mohrenschildt just prior to his death, but was also talking to Manuel Artime and William Pawley at the time of their deaths. Artime and Pawley are prime subjects of other missing pages.[363]

Missing pages from *The Fish is Red*, again with traces of red ink along the gutter, also included the photo section. Since it was not known at this time that De Moordfabriek had a photo section, this was considered the first photo section removed. It was predicted, therefore, that there might be a significant photograph removed from this book. A second, intact, copy of this book was soon obtained from UT's Benson Latin American Collection. A quick perusal of the photos revealed no obvious connection to UT, or to George Wing and his station wagon.

A closer look, however, revealed what may be the most significant link of all between Wing and the JFK assassination: a 1961 photo of a man wearing a turtle-neck shirt, in Little Havana, Miami who looks like a young George Gordon Wing. He is pictured with a group of men being recruited by E. Howard Hunt for the Bay of Pigs invasion. Attempts were made to obtain an enlarged print of this photograph from its photographer, Andrew St. George. He has not responded to this author's request to purchase his photographs.

With the chilling discoveries of the Weyl biography and possible Wing photo mutilations, an effort began not only to analyze the known missing pages but to search the campus libraries for others. This led to the first indications of patterns in the contents of the various books as well as the discovery of the remaining books.

The study and analysis of the missing pages has proven to be a lengthy and time-consuming project. The findings concerning them are beyond the scope this paper. A thorough analysis of the missing pages would require another paper of considerable length. For researchers who would like to attempt their own analysis and critique, however, a complete list of the books, their missing pages and their discovery dates, as well as the back seat magazines, can be found in this paper's appendix. This paper will deal with some significant aspects of the missing pages that led to a greater understanding of the interrelationships previously discussed and yet to be discussed.

One of the initial themes to emerge in the missing pages subsequently took on greater importance. It was the first section missing from Anson (197-98). According to the index, it was about Loran Eugene Hall. On these pages Anson tells a story derived from Warren Commission Documents 1563 and 1179.

On September 18, 1963, Hall, "Frank" [possibly Sturgis], Celio Castro and Gerry Patrick Hemming (Oswald's Marine buddy) arrived in Los Angeles from Miami where Hall retrieved a rifle that he had pawned a year before to private eye Richard Hathcock.

After picking up a trailer of arms they all headed back to Miami with a stop in Dallas. "Frank" did not make the return trip with them. Frank Sturgis turned up in Fort Lauderdale, Florida on September 24 to orchestrate the mysterious Beech Travel-Air flight of September 25 by Alex Rorke, Geoffery Sullivan and a mystery passenger.

According to Sid Marks, a witness to the retrieval in Hathcock's office, the rifle was identical to the one shown on television on Nov. 23, 1963 as being used in the assassination. The FBI ended this investigation on Hathcock's word that it was not the same rifle.

This activity took place just prior to Oswald's Austin visit (September 25), the "Odio incident" (September 26) and Martino's Austin visit (October 1). The FBI later got Hall to confess to being one of Odio's mysterious visitors -- a story that satisfied the Warren Commission and proved to be a complete fabrication after the Warren Commission Report went to press.

As we will see, this Loran Eugene Hall story in Anson's book is a major link between the missing pages and the story of Miami Rambler eyewitness Michael Kensington. Kensington's story also has intriguing links to George Wing's Rambler.

The other missing pages from Anson provide a good introduction to the similarities in content of the missing pages in all of the mutilated books. The next set of missing pages (255-58) are in Anson's chapter nine, "The Cuban Connection." The source notes for chapter nine (notes 1-123), are also missing. These pages discuss Gilberto Alvarado ("D"), Jack Anderson (also missing from Scott's *Crime and Cover-Up*), Manuel Artime (Artime and "D" are also subjects of missing pages from the other books), Carlos Bringuier, Rolando Cubela (a.k.a. AM/LASH, another prime target of the Red Ripper), Allen Dulles, Peter Edelman, Richard Helms, E. Howard Hunt, James McCord, Sixto Mesa (also missing from Scott, Crime and Cover-Up, p. 52, n. 20), and the Nicaragua intelligence Service.

The missing pages after these (267-68) are also in chapter nine. They deal with the CIA raider ship, Rex, discussed earlier in this paper. The story of the Rex is also missing from *Crime and Cover-Up*. These missing pages led this paper's author to the interrelationships discussed earlier concerning D.H. Byrd and Collins Radio.

The next missing pages (275-76) are the first two of chapter ten, "The Gentlemen from Langley." These pages refer to the Rockefeller Commission Report pages 254-57, and a story from the New York Daily News of April 23, 1975, concerning E. Howard Hunt's possible presence in Dealey Plaza on November 22, 1963. According to Marita Lorenz, the group who drove from a Miami safehouse in a station wagon "to kill Kennedy" rendezvoused with Hunt in Dallas.[364]

Chapter eleven, "The Organization Men," contains missing pages 307-14. They concern links between Trafficante, Meyer Lansky, Carlos Marcello, Jack Ruby and the Mannarino brothers of Pittsburgh, (Philadelphia was the hometown of Frank Sturgis and George Wing.) Missing page 331 is the last of this chapter and contains only one footnote (147) which refers to the Warren Commission Report (Bantam, 1964), page 707, and its vague reference to "gambling acquaintances" which eluded the Commission's attention at every turn.

Chapter twelve, "Toward a New Investigation" contains missing pages 332-34 concerning omissions by the Rockefeller Commission. Of particular note on page 334 is "data on Sylvia Odio's father (he had been imprisoned by Castro because he harbored two fugitives in an assassination plot; moreover, Manuel Rodriguez, the Oswald look-alike and Dallas Alpha 66 leader [C.D. 23.4], belonged to the same group as Odio's father), and the Agency's apparent lie to the FBI the day of the assassination that it had no CIA- originated material in its file on Oswald."

Due to skepticism and perhaps some denial on the part of this paper's researchers, the back seat magazines which were known about since 1989, were first examined closely in 1993. Once again their content proved to be more than mildly intriguing.

A study of microfilm of the most prominent Rambler-back seat magazine (Esquire, August 1963, Vol. LX, No.2, whole No. 357) revealed an obvious connection to the missing pages.

The first letter to the editor on page twelve is from William D. Pawley, Miami Florida. Pawley, Eisenhower's ambassador to Brazil and Peru, and co-founder of the Flying Tigers, was a friend of both John Martino and Nathaniel Weyl (subjects of missing pages). Weyl ghost wrote autobiographies for both men. He wrote the very book John Martino was plugging during his October 1, 1963 speech to the Austin Anti-Communist League. Pawley himself is a subject of missing pages from The Fish Is Red. The letter is entitled "The Cuban Story."

In the letter Pawley disputes the facts of a story about the Bay of Pigs which appeared in the June issue: "How I Signed Up at $250 a Month for the Big Parade Through Havana Bla-Bla-Bla" by Terry Southern. Pawley calls it a "beatnik story" and blames the failure at the Bay of Pigs on the Kennedy Administration's "terrible mistake of judgment in cancelling the bomber strike on the Havana airport...", and defends those who prepared the plans for the invasion.

He calls the publicity given the article by Esquire "a great tragedy." He enclosed a copy of an ad "that appeared in the Miami Herald a few days ago." He accuses Esquire of inserting it. Southern's article is an interview of Boris Grgurevich concerning events he experienced prior to the invasion. Pawley's letter is the longest of four in this issue.

On the cover of the June 1963 Esquire is a photograph satirizing James Montgomery Flagg's "I want you for U.S. Army" poster from World War I. The satirical caption reads "The CIA wants you. Join up for the march through Havana."

On page sixteen of the August issue is the regular column by Norman Mailer called "The Big Bite." Continuing on page eighteen, Mailer writes, "Given his [JFK's] virtues, suffering his huge vice, his emptiness, his human emptiness, we have moved as a nation under his regime, deeper into totalitarianism, far deeper than his predecessors could have dreamed, and have been granted (by the cavalier style of his personal life and the wistfulness of his appreciation for the arts) the possible beginnings of a resistance to the American totalitarianism."

A study of microfilm of the second most prominent Rambler-back-seat magazine (Esquire January 1964, Vol. LXI, No.1, whole No. 362) revealed no obvious connections to the Rambler or the missing pages. However the cover is devoted to Esquire's annual "Dubious Achievement Awards."

One photograph has become an icon in this annual humorous look at the previous year due to its repeated appearances. This feature, which began in 1962, has traditionally used a photograph of Richard Nixon with his mouth wide open in laughter and the caption, "Why is this man laughing?" This photo with this caption was displayed by George Wing as part of a photo montage assembled on the door of his office. Also displayed on Wing's door were four items arranged in a vertical group in the following sequence: An old newspaper advertisement, written in Portuguese, with the headline, *"Cursos De Detetive"*, for a detective school in Sao Paulo, Brazil (*Academia Paulista de Investigacoes*).

A handwritten notation on the ad reads "*Podares Psiodicos*," which is Portuguese for "crazy powerful people." Below the ad was a cut-out newspaper headline which read, "A four-letter word: work." Below it was the word "Pain," cut from another source, in bold white letters on a red background. Directly below that was a bumper sticker bearing the AAA logo of the American Automobile Association.

Since many former Nazis reportedly settled in Sao Paulo after the war and were involved in U.S. intelligence activities in Latin America; and since Oswald's "work" in the School Book Depository was obtained with the help of Ruth Paine (Pain) who, allegedly, had an automobile (AAA) which fit the description of George Wing's Rambler; and since Wing's Rambler carried on its back seat, one of the first publications of the Nixon "Why is this man laughing?" photographs, associations can be made between Wing's photo montage, his car, Ruth Paine, Richard Nixon, and Allen Dulles. Of course, the fact that such an interpretation of this photo montage in UT's Spanish and Portuguese Department is possible could also be a coincidence.

Also of possible significance in the January 1964 Esquire are the first two of twelve letters to the editor.

They are both critical of an article appearing in the November 1963 issue entitled "Apocalypse at Dresden" by R.H.S. Crossman. The letters, by Ronald L. Richter of Philadelphia and "Cleaver Matwaen (Don Eyles)" defend the military necessity of the bombing against Crossman's moral and strategic condemnation. Is this a reference by Wing to Rostow?

While a complete analysis of Crossman's article, as with most aspects of the back seat magazines and mutilated books, must await the results of future detailed studies, the question of whether there is any relevance to

Walt Whitman Rostow should be given a brief examination here; especially given Rostow's previously discussed relationships.

Crossman's article does not mention Rostow despite the fact that, as Crossman wrote, "Unexpectedly I found myself recruited to a secret department attached to the Foreign Office, with the title `Director of Psychological Warfare against Germany.' My main task was to plan the overt and subvert propaganda which we hoped would rouse occupied Europe against Hitler. But I soon found myself caught up in a bitter top-secret controversy about the role of bomber offensive in breaking of German morale."[365]

Later transferred to Eisenhower's staff, one of Crossman's "pleasantest memories" was "the attitude of General Walter Bedell Smith displayed a few weeks after the Dresden raid." According to Crossman, Smith countermanded direct orders to prevent the realization of Churchill's desire "to use terror tactics in order to panic them out of their homes and onto the roads, and so to block the German retreat."[366]

Rostow, it seems, displayed no such remorse with regard to Dresden or the tactics of area bombing. While presenting the facade of a purely objective approach to the subject, Rostow nevertheless displayed hints of a lack of compassion toward Dresden's civilian destruction, which was "far more devastating than either of the two atomic raids against Japan that were to follow it two months later."[367]

In a 1943 memo to an advocate of the policy, Rostow wrote, "I see no evidence or reason to believe that area bombing, whatever its great virtues as a generalized drain on the structure of Germany and its military potential, is capable of precipitating a decisive crisis" (emphasis added).[368] Even while writing in 1981, that "EOU opposed the bombing of Dresden and Chemnitz,"[369] Rostow does not give an opinion of Berlin or Leipzig. His feelings are again hinted, however, in his 1943 memo: "it is my private view that the rest of Germany would take some modest pleasure in Berlin getting it."[370]

There is no indication in the available record that Rostow expressed any moral objections to a target that, weeks prior to its total destruction, "had been considered so famous a cultural monument and so futile a military target that even the Commander in Chief of Bomber Command, Air Marshal Sir Arthur Harris, had given it hardly a thought."[371]

Also of possible relevance in the January 1964 issue is the article, "Our Man In Saigon" by George J.W. Goodman. The deck reads, "Since September, 1962, David Halberstam has been in the middle of the mess in Vietnam, winning enemies and influencing America."

On page fifty-seven Goodman writes, "Now a military junta has deposed the regime of Ngo Dinh Diem; as turbulence grows over the destiny of South Vietnam, Halberstam and the U.S. press in Saigon almost surely will be charged as participants and not merely observers by those who felt the best bet for the United States was the status quo. Frank Conniff, the Hearst columnist, has written that Halberstam's reporting has misled the President and `is a political time bomb' like the Times' coverage of the Cuban revolution: `Well, the good grey Times has decreed the Diem government in Vietnam has got to go, so...brace yourself for the emergence of an Asian Fidel Castro.'"

There may also be some significance found in the Reese Cleghorn article on page seventy-one of the January 1964 Esquire. It is an article in which "Five of the South's leading Segregationists speak for themselves."

One of the most memorable moments during the study of the UT connections to the assassination came on May 13, 1991. It was the chance discovery of the removal of Nathaniel Weyl's biography from the obscure reference book, the Directory of American Scholars. Four days earlier the pages missing from the HSCA volumes had been found. The first suspicions were already being entertained that one individual, using, in most cases, a red ball point pen, was guilty of the vandalism.

Nothing detailed was known at this time about the contents of the missing pages except that one mutilation was entirely about John Martino and the rest were about the assassination. It was known that Martino was a friend of Nathaniel Weyl and that he claimed to know much about Oswald's actual role in the conspiracy. It was also clear that if the odd aspects of George Wing's car related to anything concerning the assassination, it would have to be Oswald. Wing, therefore became the prime "Red Ripper" suspect.

It was therefore decided to indirectly learn more about Dr. Wing. That is the only reason this author has ever consulted the Directory of American Scholars. And it was only the fact that it was necessary to look in the "W" section, that the discovery was made. In the location of Weyl's biography on page 672 was a rectangular hole cut out using a dark blue ball point pen.

This was the first indication that there may be substantial similarities between the missing pages; similarities which were sought out by the Red Ripper either for the purpose of censoring the material or allowing its discovery by others. Either way, the possibility existed that the pages communicated something of importance to the Red Ripper. The next step was to learn as much as possible about John Martino and Nathaniel Weyl. The following was learned about these men and their connections.

According to an FBI report cited by Canfield and Weberman, a few days after the assassination, "James Buchanan, had written an article for the Pompano Beach Sun Sentinel which quoted [Frank] Sturgis as saying that `...Oswald had telephone conversations with the Cuban Government G-2 Intelligence Service during (a) November 1962 visit to Miami. He also contacted `Miami-based supporters of Fidel Castro...,' gave out his famous leaflets and tried to infiltrate a Cuban anti-Castro group which turned out to be the International Anti-communist Brigade [IAB]. He failed because he was outsmarted by their leader, Frank Sturgis. When questioned about this by the FBI, Sturgis said it was just speculation."[372]

An informant told the FBI that Buchanan, who according to Sturgis was Director of Propaganda for the IAB, was trying to incite the U.S. government to take action against Cuba. During their investigation, the FBI learned about a fight between Oswald and members of IAB in Miami in October 1962. The source of the alleged fight was John Martino and Nathaniel Weyl. In October 1962 Martino and Weyl were writing Martino's book *I Was Castro's Prisoner*.[373]

Because of this book, Martino, a "Florida electronics manufacturer," became "the nation's most famous former Castro prisoner." Martino claimed he flew into Cuba by Pan-American Airways in July 1959 on "a routine vacation and business trip...." He said he was framed by Castro's secret police as a member of the anti-Castro underground and accused of hauling guns in his own plane and burning sugar cane fields. During his trial, witnesses "said he had landed a light aircraft on a highway in the course of clandestinely entering Cuba." Martino said, "Well, this was ridiculous."[374]

Martino's denials did not ring true, however, because he was a friend of Captain William Morgan. Morgan was an early supporter of Castro but was exposed by Cuban Military Intelligence in 1960 as an anti-Castro triple agent. He was executed by firing squad in Havana, and became an instant anti-Castro martyr.[375]

After the assassination Martino was actively spreading several false stories that Oswald was paid by Castro to kill Kennedy.[376] These false stories and especially the story of "D" (Gilberto Alvarado) are the subject of many of the missing pages.

Nathaniel Weyl testified before the Senate Internal Security Committee on February 19, 1952 that he had been a member of the same Communist "cell" as Alger Hiss. His testimony was "the only outside support [Whittaker] Chambers' story ever received." By the time he testified, Weyl, a freelance writer, had authored several books about treason and espionage. Also at this time Hiss was in jail and public support was building for a new trial.[377] Even without vindication, a new trial for Alger Hiss would have been a blow to the political career of then Vice President Richard Nixon.

[OBJ]Another bit of information about Weyl, revealed by Canfield and

Webberman, was that Frank Meyer was cited as a reference for the Weyls in CD 662. This FBI report of March 5, 1964, says that informant "T-1" was a house guest at the Weyls' home in Florida and had long conversations there with John Martino about Oswald's links to Castro. At the end of the report its author added, "Frank Meyer, Woodstock, New York, a self-admitted former member of the CP [Communist Party], was interviewed as a reference in 1953, and stated that the Weyls broke with the CP sometime between 1937-1939. He indicated the Weyls have made public statements concerning their past activities and present feelings and he feels they are both strongly, clearly and deeply anti-Communist." This eventually became a major UT connection because Meyer "often wrote for the National Review, the editor of which was [E. Howard] Hunt's confidante William Buckley."[378] Actually, Meyer was more than just a writer for National Review. He became senior editor in 1957.[379]

According to Canfield and Weberman, "...William F. Buckley's column of March 26, 1964...ponders the possibility that Oswald was a Soviet agent by citing the hypothesis of a `recently retired member of the CIA.' This `friend,' who was `extensively schooled in espionage,' told him that before Oswald left Russia he was recruited as an agent. Hunt had `recently retired' from the CIA to become a `contract agent' around this time, and was very close to Buckley. Jack Anderson reported that William F. Buckley was `behind a defense fund to pay Hunt's lawyers what the secret Watergate hush funds didn't cover.'"[380]

The possibility of a domestic right-wing conspiracy was not unknown to Buckley but he apparently only gave serious consideration to a foreign communist conspiracy. Soon after the assassination Buckley left the country. He went to Switzerland to write a book that never materialized. While there, a friend arranged a dinner party for the Buckleys with Mr. and Mrs. Charlie Chaplin. According to Buckley biographer John B. Judis, "Chaplin was preoccupied with the assassination of President Kennedy...and he suggested to his guests that it had been a plot by the CIA or Texas John Birchers.

"`I don't trust the FBI. Do you, Mr. Buckley?' Chaplin asked.

"`No,' Buckley replied. `After all, they let you get out of the country without paying your income tax.'"[381]

As discussed earlier in this paper, Buckley was recruited into the CIA and introduced to Hunt by James Burnham who could have known Michael Paine's father as a fellow leader of the U.S. Trotskyist movement. Buckley himself could have known de Mohrenschildt who had worked for his parent's oil company, Pantipec. De Mohrenschildt later entered the oil business in Cuba with Pantipec's president Warren W. Smith and several Cubans who were to become involved in anti-

Castro activities that included Oswald. Army Intelligence reservist Jack Crichton, who was a mutual friend of Ilya Mamantov with Ruth Paine, had also worked for Warren Smith at Pantipec. Buckley's good friend, Hunt, was a favorite CIA employee of Allen Dulles. Hunt worked for Dulles' other favorite agent, Tracy Barnes, as covert action chief of Barnes' mysterious Domestic Operations Division. It was another agent of Barnes' division, J. Walton Moore, who encouraged de Mohrenschildt to get to know Oswald in Dallas.

Allen Dulles, the CIA's expert on Yugoslavia, "having at one point in his State Department career been in charge of the desk that dealt with the affairs of that part of the world" and "apparently knew the names of every city, town, river, bridge, railway line, and personality in the entire country,"[382] very likely knew de Mohrenschildt at least through his CIA reports on Yugoslavia in 1957; if not through his cousin Baron Constantine Maydell, the top German *Abwehr* agent in the U.S. when Dulles began working with members of the *Abwehr* in attempts to assassinate Hitler along with the Paines' close friend, Mary Bancroft.

Moreover, Dulles' uncle, Robert Lansing, "contemplated a coup that would put him in the White House after Wilson's breakdown in October 1919" and "tried to provoke a war with Mexico about this same time."[383]

Another man who was intimately involved in these 1919 provocations was William F. Buckley, Sr.[384] Lansing's fellow cabinet members were at the top of UT's power structure. Two of them were involved in businesses that linked directly to the Paine family interests in the American Bell Telephone Company. Buckley, Sr. was a former resident of UT's "Old B Hall" dormitory and shared that distinction with Rex G. and Hines Baker (top executives at Humble Oil with Nazi supporter William Stamps Farish, Sr.), Senator Richard Kleberg (who launched LBJ's political career), William B. Bates (founder of the law firm Fulbright and Jaworski), D.H. Byrd, C.B. Smith, and Jack R. Dougherty, Farish III's fellow Beeville rancher whose clan produced right-wing Dallas oilman Dudley Dougherty.

It was Dougherty who brought Madam Ngo Dinh Nhu to Dallas in October 1963 to be honored at General Walker's "U.S. Day" rally attended by Lee Harvey Oswald. These Beeville connections became the most unexpected UT-JFK assassination link to George Wing's Rambler. The only thing about Wing's Rambler that did not seem to hint at a right-wing/UT-connected conspiracy was an unusual bumper sticker on the rear bumper. It was from the 1964 gubernatorial campaign of progressive Democrat Frances "Sissy" Farenthold.

Amazingly, despite her political leanings, she turned out to be one of the Beeville Doughertys.[385]

It was rare to see this particular piece of political ephemera anywhere by the 1980s -- let alone still on a car's bumper. But then everything about Wing's Rambler, except the required license and registration, screamed "1964" (a look that would seem to have taken some effort to maintain some twenty-five years later). Added to that effort is the fact that each anachronism, including the car itself, whispered "JFK assassination."

These were not the only revelations that resulted from the Red Ripper's removal of Weyl's biography. One of the connections that leads directly back to George Wing's Rambler station wagon, is the fact that William Pawley, whose letter was featured in the most prominent back seat magazine, also knew Nathaniel Weyl. According to Hinckle and Turner, in 1963, "The aging millionaire was working on his memoirs with author Nathaniel Weyl, the right-wing ghostwriter whose books in his own name included Red Star Over China and Red Star Over Cuba. At the same time the prolific Weyl was commissioned to ghostwrite John Martino's account of his three years in a Cuban prison entitled I Was Castro's Prisoner."[386] Through Weyl, Martino arranged for two ex-CIA agents on Pawley's payroll to attend a meeting in Fort Lauderdale of anti-Castro leaders designed to "find out what the CIA was doing" and report back to President Kennedy who "didn't trust the agency and felt he was receiving bad information." An initial meeting had already brought Martino together with fellow anti-Castro loose cannons Howard Davis, Eddie Bayo, and Gerry Patrick Hemming (Oswald's Marine buddy), in the office of Miami News editor Bill Boggs, a Kennedy confidant.[387]

The anti-Castro leaders did not trust the CIA either. They were using the meeting to solicit support from Florida conservative leaders to back a mission to smuggle two Soviet Army colonels out of Cuba who knew where the Russians had hidden offensive missiles in violation of the Missile Crisis settlement.[388]

One of the solicitors was Hemming, who would later travel to California with Loran Eugene Hall to retrieve a special rifle. It was Hemming's right-hand man, Howard Davis who had gotten word to Kennedy about the Russian colonels through New York financier Theodore Racoosin. As a result of the meeting, Senator James O. Eastland of the Senate Internal Security Subcommittee urged Pawley to help Martino arrange the secret mission. It was called Operation Red Cross.[389]

Life magazine's Dick Billings accompanied Pawley, Martino, William "Rip" Robertson, and the exile guerrillas, led by Bayo, on the mission.[390] Billings would soon be stationed at Life's temporary bureau at the Adolphus Hotel in Dallas covering the Kennedy assassination, where he would aid Richard B. Stolley and C.D. Jackson in the negotiations to buy the Zapruder film.[391] Rip Robertson, the former World War II Marine frogman from Texas who helped overthrow Arbenz for United Fruit, was the commander of the Barbara J. and one of the first two men ashore at the Bay of Pigs.[392]

Former Ambassador Pawley, who founded General Chenault's Flying Tigers, had also participated in the Guatemala coup, had co-authored the infamous Doolittle Report with his friend Allen Dulles, had pressured Eisenhower to give American support to the first anti-Castro exiles, and had persuaded Clare Booth Luce to finance anti-Castro guerrilla operations. An FBI report written years before the assassination described Martino as a "close friend" of Santos Trafficante.[393] Bayo was reportedly involved in the July 1961 double assassination plot against Fidel and Raúl Castro run out of the Guantánamo Naval base. He later joined Alpha 66.[394]

Hinkle and Turner described the meetings that led to Operation Red Cross this way: "It was through these show-and-tell meetings about the CIA that the matter of the Russian missile officers would pass from the hands of Kennedy's friends to those of his foes."[395]

Indeed. Snubbed by the CIA, Hemming formed his own group, Interpen, "a kind of Dirty dozen times two." With him was Robert K. Brown, a graduate of the counterintelligence school at Fort Holabird, Maryland. Hemming funded Interpen with support from right-wing Dallas oilman Clint Murchison, who was a close associate of the Cabell brothers, Lyndon Johnson and J. Edgar Hoover.[396] Additional funding came from Howard Hughes associate C. Osmet Moody, who owned the Cay Sal Bank islands where George Bush's rig was drilling from 1957-1963.[397] Funding also came from H.L.'s son Nelson Bunker Hunt, and right-wing radio station magnate Gordon McLendon.[398]

McLendon owned the Dallas top-40 station, KLIF. Jack Ruby had a close relationship with McLendon and other staff at KLIF and visited the station several times during the weekend of the assassination.[399] On the back of an envelope found in Ruby's pocket when he shot Oswald was the phone number (DA1-0467) of his friend, KLIF disc jockey, Russ "Weird Beard" Knight. Ruby had even called McLendon's home the night of the assassination.[400] The high-risk Operation Red Cross, launched in June 1963, failed when Bayo and his guerrillas disappeared in Cuba.[401]

In 1975, Martino confided to his close Texas business associate Fred Claasen that he had been a CIA contract agent and had personal knowledge of the conspiracy behind the Kennedy assassination. He told Claasen:

The anti-Castro people put Oswald together. Oswald
didn't know who he was working for -- he was just
ignorant of who was really putting him together. Oswald
was to meet his contact at the Texas Theater. They were
to meet Oswald in the theater, and get him out of the
country, then eliminate him. Oswald made a
mistake....There was no way we could get to him. They
had Ruby kill him.

Martino died soon after he talked to Classen. His widow said, "the
Company or the government picked up his body."[402]

Technically, Operation Red Cross could be considered part of a larger
effort underway in 1963 to once again invade Cuba. In January 1963,
Manuel Artime, "the CIA's `Golden Boy' of Brigade 2506," met with
Robert Kennedy and soon began receiving funding for Operation Second
Naval Guerrilla (SNG), the third Cuba invasion attempt after Mongoose
fizzled.[403] Artime, like Buckley, would later organize a defense fund for
his friend E. Howard Hunt and the other Watergate defendants.[404]

SNG would depend on one of the previously mentioned assassination
plots (the AM/LASH plot) being revived just when President Kennedy
was considering normalizing relations with Cuba. Why then would
Bobby Kennedy go along? As Hinckle and Turner explained,
"...underlying RFK's genuine sympathy for the exiles was the slight edge
of extortion, for Artime knew things about the invasion that were better
left unsaid."[405]

Second Naval Guerrilla involved not only Artime and the CIA, but
General Edward Lansdale; General Samoza of Nicaragua; Rolando
Cubela alias AM/LASH;[406] E. Howard Hunt;[407] Cubela's close friend
Jose Aleman, Jr.; Haiti/Nicaragua lobbyist I. Irving Davidson; Cuba
raider Orlando Bosch; Aleman-ally and SNG- Somoza liaison Carlos
Prio Socarras; Artime's Somoza liaison Miguel de Leon; CIA/Somoza
linked United Fruit and Steamship of New Orleans; and the Lake
Pontchartrain training camp, which had Somoza's blessing and whose
graduates would be sent on to Nicaragua.[408]

Involved in the Lake Pontchartrain training camp were camp member
Carlos Bringuier; camp dynamite supplier and life-long friend of Cubela,
Victor Espinosa Hernandez alias "A"; camp arms cache holders Sam
Benton, Mike McLaney and his brother William McLaney; camp
manager and former leader of Sturgis' Cuban underground, Victor
Paneque Batista and his alleged uncles, camp head, Laureano Batista and
his brother Augustin Batista, who was one of several real estate investors
calling themselves the Ansan Group.[409]

The Ansan group laundered millions of dollars in Cuban money into Key Biscayne real estate deals involving the Teamsters and Richard Nixon. A principal of the Ansan group was Jose Aleman, Sr., the father of Cubela's close friend. Aleman, Sr. was a former Cuban minister under President Carlos Prio Socarras.[410]

These were the most direct participants in Second Naval Guerrilla. And just as the Ansan Group members had links to Nixon, I. Irving Davidson had connections through Clint Murchison, for whom he lobbied in Washington, to Lyndon Johnson and J. Edgar Hoover. Davidson had earlier been intimately involved in the Bobby Baker scandal which implicated Johnson. He would later mobilize Teamster political influence to prevent the anti-Kennedy Jimmy Hoffa from going to prison.[411]

The Lake Pontchartrain training camp, as Scott said, "in short, was part of he CIA-Artime-Cubela-Somoza plan [SNG]." SNG activities had twice, despite warnings, "violated President Kennedy's ban on U.S.-based guerrilla operations, and one if not both of these incidents involved the future burglars of Watergate."[412]

One of these incidents was the October 1963 raid on Cuba "from a Florida-based ship of the Somozas called the Rex, [involving] both [Eugenio] Martinez as skipper (according to Sturgis) and very probably Sturgis himself as well." According to Scott, "...at least four (perhaps six) of those associated at this time with the Artime-Nicaragua plan [SNG] disseminated similar stories [to the story of "D"] linking Oswald (or Ruby) to Fidel Castro."[413]

Simply put, the missing pages appear to tell the story of Operation Second Naval Guerrilla, participants of which were closely involved with the activities of Lee Harvey Oswald prior to the assassination and Marina Oswald after the assassination.

A major part of that story, involving many of the same participants, concerns the planting of false stories linking Jack Ruby and Lee Oswald to both Fidel Castro and the Soviet Union. Among those behind the false stories were James Buchanan, Frank Sturgis, John Martino, Nathaniel Weyl, William F. Buckley, Jr., Miguel de Leon, and Carlos Bringuier, who together with his close friend Ed Butler, debated Oswald on WDSU radio in New Orleans, exposed his defection to Russia, and publicly released a "truth tape" of the debate right after the assassination.[414]

Bringuier had been the Press and Propaganda Secretary of the CIA-sponsored Cuban Revolutionary Council (CRC) in New Orleans located at 544 Camp Street -- the address of Guy Banister's office that was stamped on leaflets distributed by Oswald in front of Clay Shaw's International Trade Mart.[415]

Butler was head of the Information Council of the Americas (INCA). He conceived of the propaganda activity he called "truth tapes" while serving in a special Army Unit in Alexandria Virginia. After 1963 he sat on the Planning Committee for the Freedom Studies Center of the American Security Council with Edward Lansdale. INCA's production manager, Manuel Gil, was a member of Bringuier's CRC at 544 Camp Street. Gil would later become involved with SNG's Orlando Bosch whose anti-Castro raids included Frank Sturgis and James Buchanan's brother Jerry Buchanan.[416]

Along with Lansdale, Nelson Rockefeller may have also had an interest in INCA's pre- and post- assassination activities concerning Oswald. In 1941, Rockefeller, apparently arranged letters of credit from the Rockefeller family's Chase Manhattan Bank for de Mohrenschildt and his *Abwehr* cousin Konstantin Maydell. At that time Rockefeller was coordinator of information for Latin America.[417]

Shortly after Castro's takeover, Nelson's brother David became president of Chase which had controlled Cuba's credit for half a century. David was also director of Punta Allegre Sugar Corporation, the second largest producer of Cuba's primary export. Rockefeller family advisor A.A. Berle, Jr. was chairman of SuCrest, the largest sugar refiner on the East Coast. According to biographers Peter Collier and David Horowitz, "When the National Security Council made its decision to invade Cuba, five of those present were David's close friends or associates (Secretary of State Rusk, Secretary of the Treasury Dillon, CIA chief Allen Dulles, Presidential Assistant McGeorge Bundy, and Berle)." While president of Chase, David Rockefeller shared CEO responsibilities with George Champion, who had succeed future Warren Commissioner John J. McCloy as chairman of the board. Another of Nelson's brothers, John, Jr., had helped D.H. Byrd buy Collins radios for Admiral Byrd's polar expeditions.[418]

Nelson Rockefeller's influence in the White House improved greatly when his family's candidates Eisenhower and Nixon took office in 1953. He was "charged with sweeping away the administrative debris of twenty years of Democratic rule." He swept three New Deal programs under the new Department of Health, Education and Welfare. He was then named Undersecretary of HEW to Texan Oveta Culp Hobby, publisher of the Houston Post and wife of Texas Governor William P. Hobby.[419]

Mrs. Hobby would occasionally socialize with Houston's ultra powerful in Suite 8F of the Lamar Hotel in downtown Houston. According to author Pete Brewton, former reporter for the Houston Post and Houston Chronicle, "In 8F were the Brown brothers, George and Herman, the financial backers of LBJ who owned the giant construction firm Brown & Root; Gus Wortham, the insurance king of American General Insurance Co.; Jesse Jones, `Mr. Houston,' lumber man, banker and publisher of the Houston Chronicle who headed the Reconstruction Finance Corp. for Franklin D. Roosevelt; Judge James Elkins, who founded the law firm of Vinson & Elkins and First City Bank in Houston...."[420] Hobby's fellow Houston newspaper publisher, Jesse H. Jones, had been yet another Texan in Woodrow Wilson's cabinet. His Houston Endowment, Inc., founded in 1937, is a primary beneficiary of the University of Texas at Austin.[421]

George Brown, George de Mohrenschildt's mutual friend with Howard Burris and Lyndon Johnson, was president of the CIA-conduit Brown Foundation. A director of Brown's firm Texas Eastern Transmission, George A. Butler, was trustee of the CIA-conduit Hobby Foundation with Mrs. Hobby. Hobby also sat on the CIA's Cuban Freedom Committee, which was set up for the CIA by E. Howard Hunt's future employer, the Robert R. Mullen Agency. A supporter of the Cuban Freedom Committee was INCA's president, Dr. Alton Ochsner who, like Harry Ransom, was a consultant to the U.S. Air Force. Ochsner was also a director of Latin American Reports, whose editor was William G. Gaudet the CIA agent who was issued the Mexican travel permit immediately preceding Oswald's. Gaudet, it is recalled, was the source of the Trotskyite link to Ruby, and had hinted that Oswald's cousin and Rostow/Isaacs (?) associate, Marilyn Dorothea Murret, was a CIA agent in New Orleans. In May 1963, the similar but more paramilitary minded Committee for a Free Cuba was formed. Its membership included Clare Booth Luce.[422]

Despite Nelson Rockefeller's UT/Texas connections through Oveta Culp Hobby, this route from George Wing's Rambler to Pawley to Operation Red Cross to SNG to the false stories about Oswald to Rockefeller's interest in these matters, may seem to be somewhat distant from the subject of this paper. However, these "Free Cuba" groups bring us once again back to the story of Loran Eugene Hall's retrieval of the rifle as told in CD 1179, a story which is a subject of missing pages. And it is also a story which, as we will see, has an apparently direct connection to George Wing's Rambler. Canfield and Webberman noted that "Hathcock volunteered the information that Hall paid for the rifle with a check drawn on `The Committee To Free Cuba.'" They go on to explain that, The Committee To Free Cuba, like the Free Cuba Committee, Citizens for a Free Cuba, Crusade to Free Cuba, Crusade to Free Cuba Committee, Cuban Freedom Committee, and the Committee for Free Cuba, was merely a CIA front group established in order to account for funds the CIA was pumping into various exile groups. Either directly or indirectly, they could all be traced back to Watergate mastermind, Everette Howard Hunt.[423]

Furthermore, the Free Cuba Committee was headed by David Ferrie's friend, Eladio Del Valle, and Citizens for a Free Cuba was founded by Guy Banister. Canfield and Webberman, bringing all of this to a focus, point out that, "Loran Hall was an officer of the Committee to Free Cuba -- also known as the Free Cuba Committee. So what we have here is a CIA front group taking a rifle `out of pawn' that looked like Oswald's a month before the assassination."[424]

Several officials of these groups disseminated false stories tying Oswald and Ruby to Castro, and Castro to plots against other U.S. officials. One of the stories was given to the Free Cuba Committee by Andrew St. George -- the photographer who took the picture apparently showing George Wing with E. Howard Hunt's men in Miami.[425] This SNG/false story connection to Wing will take on even greater importance when we explore the significance of CD 1179 to Wing's Rambler. But first, we will return to Nelson Rockefeller's connections to see where else they lead.

Oveta Culp Hobby sat on the Cuban Freedom Committee with Peter O'Donnell, Jr. who was president of Harry Ransom friend Karl Hoblitzelle's Foundation and a member of the right-wing National Advisory Council of Young American's for Freedom (NAC-YAF) with Robert Morris. Morris was Otto Otepka's defense attorney, General Walker's attorney, H.L. Hunt's attorney, a John Bircher, and a Naval intelligence officer.[426]

Young American's for Freedom was founded in September 1960 by William F. Buckley, Jr. "One of the YAF's leading board members by 1963," wrote Dick Russell, "was retired major general Charles Willoughby, who had a daughter living in Texas."[427]

A Dr. Stubblefield of Parkland Hospital had helped Robert Morris get General Walker released from the mental hospital to which Bobby Kennedy had him committed in 1962. It was through the offices of Dr. Stubblefield that Sylvia Odio's psychiatrist was later obtained.[428] On the NAC-YAF with O'Donnell and Morris was Russian Prince Igor Cassini who with Bobby Baker tried to intervene in the the Kennedy sanctioned overthrow of Trujillo -- a coup that resulted in Mafia financial losses.[429]

Even if Rockefeller had known de Mohrenschildt since the war, and created Hobby's historic governmental position and served under her, and had extensive family ties to Cuba's economy, the Bay of Pigs invasion, and the Collins Radio Company, are there any indications that he would have a more direct interest in CIA- sponsored stories linking Oswald to Castro? The answer may lie in Rockefeller's next position in the

Eisenhower administration.

Eighteen months after Nelson's appointment to HEW, C.D. Jackson (friend and co-worker of Walt Rostow, Allen Dulles, and later Henry Luce), resigned his post as Special Assistant to the President for Psychological Strategy (the position which gave him the authority to create Radio Free Europe, whose director was Norman Fredricksen's father). Rockefeller replaced Jackson and changed his title to Presidential Coordinator for the CIA. In that capacity he served as the first head of a secret unit called the Planning Coordination Group,[430] a subcommittee of the Operations Coordination Board that was abolished by Kennedy on the advise of Rostow and Bundy. After the Bay of Pigs, Kennedy gave its oversight responsibilities to the President's Foreign Intelligence Advisory Board (PFIAB).[431]

The little known PFIAB is currently composed of fourteen members drawn from "outside government." It reviews all intelligence operations and activities and reports to the president at least semiannually.432 Texas Senator John Tower, also a YAF board member, had personally interceded in 1962 with the Immigration and Naturalization Service in the case of Marina Oswald. Tower was chairman of Bush's PFIAB when he died in a plane crash in April 1991. Two long-time members of the PFIAB were Edwin H. Land of the Polaroid Corporation, and William O. Baker of Bell Telephone Laboratories.[433] Recall that Mary Bancroft's first love affair was with Leopold Mannes, who was helping to perfect color photography -- a man she met through the Paines. Recall also that the Paine family and two of President Wilson's UT cabinet members were closely associated with Bell Telephone.

Rockefeller then, was obviously working closely with Allen Dulles and was also interacting with C.D. Jackson during the Eisenhower-Nixon administration. It seems, therefore, that Nelson Rockefeller "an expert on Latin America and psychological warfare,"[434] had many connections and motives indicating access to information about, if not direct participation in, the events and propaganda preceding and following Kennedy's assassination.

Most ominously, however, the essential theme of the false stories spread by INCA and others, predates the assassination. The false stories are prima facie evidence of a conspiracy to cover up the assassination. And the fact that they predate the assassination is prima facie evidence of the conspiracy to assassinate Kennedy. According to Scott, "Beginning in October 1963 the CIA disseminated to other agencies a series of CIA messages about `a man who identified himself as Lee Oswald, [who] may be identical to Lee Henry Oswald' who had `contacted the Soviet Embassy in Mexico City.'" These messages alleged that Oswald was in contact with the KGB assassination department. There is substantial evidence that Oswald was being impersonated in this incident. Meticulous research by Paul L. Hoch clearly shows that the CIA was devoting considerable energy to obstructing a public resolution of this matter by the Warren Commission.

Spearheading that effort was Deputy Director of Central Intelligence Richard Helms[435] -- Howard Burris' close friend.

As of late 1992, evidence of this alleged impersonator was actively being kept secret. Among the files yet to be released on the assassination is a lengthy report by HSCA investigator Edwin Lopez which reportedly shows that Oswald was being impersonated in Mexico City. The "President John F. Kennedy Assassination Records Collection Act of 1992" specifically excluded the Lopez report. The act began as a bill jointly sponsored by former Warren Commission attorney Arlen Specter, former HSCA Chairman Louis Stokes, and Chairman of the Senate Intelligence Committee David Boren.

At the same time Helms was reportedly obstructing the truth about an Oswald impersonator in Mexico City, he was leading the Warren Commission on a wild goose chase. The story of "D" -- a prime target of the Red Ripper -- alleged that Oswald was paid $6,500 by a "a tall, thin Negro" in Mexico City to kill Kennedy. After the story failed to hold water, "D" retracted his claim, then recanted the retraction, then failed a polygraph test. The story first came to the Commission's attention in a memo from Richard Helms, who never identified "D". The FBI later discovered he was Gilberto Alvarado, an agent of Nicaraguan intelligence -- another link to Second Naval Guerrilla and its leading participants, future Watergate figures Bernard Barker, James McCord, and E. Howard Hunt.[436]

In an incident similar to the "D" story, Miguel de Leon and Sixto Mesa, both associated with Hunt's friend Artime, got Fernando Penabaz, a friend of Bringuier's, to spread a story that Oswald had contacted Cuban intelligence in Nicaragua.[437] DeLeon, Mesa, and Penabaz are also subjects of missing pages.

Thus, a cursory analysis of the missing pages seems to indicate that an apparent purpose behind the mutilations of the Red Ripper was to either censor facts about, or bring attention to the persons involved in both Second Naval Guerrilla and the false stories. One particularly noteworthy SNG/false stories connection to the UT Rambler is that some of these individuals were closely associated with Allen Dulles, Walt Rostow, William F. Buckley, Sr., Lyndon Johnson, and Howard Burris; who in turn had close UT ties to Harry Ransom, D. Harold Byrd, C.B. Smith, and the Spanish and Portuguese Department. As we will see next, there are even stronger connections between people involved in Second Naval Guerrilla, the false stories, and the Rambler.

Why is this Man Laughing?

It was apparently important to the Red Ripper that Watergate burglars Frank Sturgis, E. Howard Hunt, Eugenio Martinez, Bernard Barker, and James McCord were principal players in Second Naval Guerrilla and/or the false stories about Oswald and Ruby. We have seen that these persons had overlapping relationships with Lyndon Johnson and Allen Dulles; and they in turn had links not only to Ruth Paine and her alleged Rambler but to the UT Rambler as well.

One of them, Bernard Barker, may have been indirectly involved with the Dealey Plaza Rambler on the day of the assassination. Whether or not a man carrying fake Secret Service credentials aided in the release of the Rambler's driver (a story attributed to Roger Craig), Craig did say he reported his sighting of the Rambler to a fake Secret Service man, who was only interested in Craig's description of the car. Craig identified the man as Edgar Eugene Bradley.

Patrolman J.M. Smith and Deputy Constable Seymour Weitzman also reported an encounter with a fake Secret Service agent behind the infamous grassy knoll picket fence immediately after the shooting, while the smell of gunpowder was still in the air. In April 1975, one month before Roger Craig died of a rifle wound to the chest, Weitzman identified Bernard Barker, the leader of the Watergate burglary team, as the man who produced the fake Secret Service credentials.

Barker was E. Howard Hunt's top deputy during the Bay of Pigs, the CIA's chief liaison to the various Cuban exile groups, and was "paymaster" for all exile work for the Agency. Barker is also solidly linked to Santos Trafficante (Martino's friend), and the Cuban Revolutionary Council (whose New Orleans address was stamped on Oswald's leaflets). Barker has admitted, as has Frank Sturgis, to being close to Carlos Prio Socarras, the wealthy financier of Cuban exile activities. Prio Socarras was once arrested in a gunrunning conspiracy with Robert Ray McKeown. McKeown had been involved with Jack Ruby in "running jeeps to Cuba" and other smuggling schemes. As we will see, McKeown may be a key link between not only Ruby and Oswald, but Ruby, Oswald, George Wing, and C.B. Smith. Thus Barker has many ties to SNG (not the least of which is the fact that it was he who exfiltrated Artime out of Castro's Cuba) and apparent ties to our anachronistic Rambler.[438]

We have seen through examining the missing pages that SNG players

Jose Aleman, Sr. and Augustin Batista had financial ties to Richard Nixon. Ten years after SNG they would all be embroiled in the Watergate scandal, and Hunt's friends, false story propagator William F. Buckley, Jr. and SNG principal Manuel Artime would raise funds to try to get them out of their Watergate mess.

Assuming that the Red Ripper was trying to communicate something important relating to George Wing's Rambler, are there more direct or more significant links from SNG and the Watergaters to the Rambler and the person to whom Oswald thought it belonged, Ruth Paine? It seems there are.

Although Nixon's ties to SNG's Ansan Group members are somewhat indirect, they take on greater importance given indications that he had closer ties to other SNG players who were directly involved with Jack Ruby and Lee Harvey Oswald. To examine those ties we must first return to Ruth Paine's July 1963 trip to Naushon Island to visit her mother-in-law -- a trip about which some still classified Warren Commission documents may shed light;[439] and we must also explore Ruth's mutual Dallas friends with the Oswalds.

As we have seen with the close ties of Allen Dulles and Hans Gisevius at Dresser Industries, Ruth and Michael Paine were not the Massachusetts Paine family's only link with the city of Dallas. They had other possibly conspiratorial associations in that city as well. Michael's cousin Sandy Forbes belonged to an exclusive golf club with former deGolyer associate Paul Raigorodsky, the unofficial leader of the close knit Russian exile community in Dallas as well as a financial patron of that community's CIA-sponsored St. Nicholas Parish. Ruth, who spoke Russian well enough to tutor a student in scientific Russian at an exclusive private Dallas school, interacted with this same community. She was even a friend of Ilya Mamantov, who co-founded the St. Nicholas Parish. Mamantov was teaching the same subject as Ruth (scientific Russian) to a group of employees at Magnolia Laboratories. Therefore, cousin Sandy could have had an interest in Ruth's friend Marina, the newest darling of the Dallas Russian community.

Likewise, Michael's uncle, Eric Schroeder, had been a friend and investment associate of Everette deGolyer, who died in 1956, and whose "very close friend," Antonio J. Bermudez, was listed in George de Mohrenschildt's phone book. Even if Schroeder did not know deGolyer's partner Lewis MacNaughton, he would have been familiar enough with him to be interested in Ruth's new friend Marina Oswald. Marina had been in close contact with MacNaughton's personal accountant George Bouhe. Although he felt it was too far to drive, Bouhe would make the trip to Oak Cliff when Marina "needed help with the baby." That insight into the relationship between Marina and Bouhe came from Mrs. Declan Ford (another of Marina's Dallas friends) when she testified before the Warren Commission.[440] Uncle Eric had even lived in the Dallas area for many years, where he came to know deGolyer. As Scott says, it is "thus worth learning whether Schroeder had anything to do with his niece's assumption of the babysitting role formerly exercised by MacNaughton's personal accountant, George Bouhe."[441]

Peter Dale Scott tells us more about Bouhe and notes the strange and complete withdrawal of Bouhe's attention to Marina:

> "George Bouhe testified before the Commission that while Raigorodsky was the `godfather' of the group, he himself `did the organization work' (8 H 358); others testified that he `even kept files on new arrivals' (8 H 453). From the fact that all members of the Russian Community were `well acquainted...with each other'. Commission counsel Jenner elicited testimony that it was `perfectly normal' (9 H 7) for the community to have lavished such care on the Oswalds.
>
> "Nevertheless, from April to November 1963, the Russian community severed all contact with the Oswalds (even when Marina was separated and more helpless than before), and their baby- sitting role was now temporarily assumed by the Russian-speaking American Ruth Paine, a Quaker. Ruth Paine had her own contacts with the Russian community (9 H 107, 133), but had `accidentally' met the Oswalds through one Russian she did not know -- Count de Mohrenschildt (R 722)."[442]

Along with her husband, Mrs. Declan Ford (who revealed Bouhe's babysitting role) took care of Marina after the assassination. Mr. Ford had worked many years at DeGolyer and MacNaughton (2 H 323, 336), the former employer of Jack Crichton.[443]

As Scott reminds us, "...Crichton was simultaneously an Army Reserve Intelligence officer and an employee of Empire Trust, one of whose directors was Bouhe's and Ford's employer, Lewis W. MacNaughton. (Crichton himself had been a Vice-President of DeGolyer and MacNaughton, from 1946 to 1950). Crichton moreover had not only intelligence but political connections: in 1964, still an army reserve intelligence officer, he ran unsuccessfully against John Connally as Republican candidate for Governor of Texas."[444]

We will return to Mr. and Mrs. Ford, but first we will turn to the research of Peter Dale Scott to become acquainted with Mr. and Mrs. Max Clark and some of Marina's other Dallas friends through transcripts of tapes of her interrogations. These transcripts are intriguing because at the November 24 questioning Marina's translator, Peter Gregory, left out one name repeatedly. The transcriber noted these omissions along with Gregory's deliberate changing of many of Marina's statements. The transcriber also noted that the omitted name Marina kept saying was unintelligible. The names which Peter Gregory did translate on the 24th were Anna Meller, George Bouhe, and his own.

From this Scott deduces: "The first Russians mentioned by Marina in her next substantive interview of November 28 were the Gregorys, George Bouhe, Anna Meller, and Mr. and Mrs. Clark (CE 1792, 23 H 406- 07). To the Commission she listed Gregory, Mrs. Clark, Elenor Hall, Bouhe, and Ann Meller (1 H 7). The first four names (Meller, Bouhe, de Mohrenschildt, Clark) supplied by Alexander Kleinlerer, another member of the group, also suggest that the missing name, which may or may not have been deliberately erased from the tape, may have been Gregory's friend Max Clark, the former security officer of General Dynamics (11 H 119)."[445]

What reason would there be to erase any mention of the Clarks from the tape? Why would Peter Gregory avoid translating Marina's repeated mention of them? And why was Mrs. Clark also left off of the Warren Commission's list of thirty-four persons with whom Lee Harvey Oswald may have had contact? Many of those listed had met Oswald for only a single evening; while Mrs. Clark was the second Russian, after Gregory himself, whom Oswald had met in Fort Worth. In fact, she was apparently the first Russian with whom Oswald made telephone contact in "attempts to arrange a prompt visit" (R 281) after obtaining the names of two Russian speaking persons in Fort Worth from the local office of the Texas Employment Commission.[446] A close look at Mr. and Mrs. Clark may provide answers to these and other questions in this paper.

According to Scott, "There were many leads -- some obvious, some not so obvious -- linking Lee Harvey Oswald to Peter Gregory's friend Max Clark, former security officer for the Fort Worth plant of General Dynamics and Jack Ruby to the milieu of General Dynamics' controlling stockholder Henry Crown and his friend Jake Arvey."[447] (There is also a CIA connection: General Dynamics' president, Frank Pace was one of the nine members of JFK's President's Foreign Intelligence Advisory Board.)[448]

Max Clark was interviewed by the FBI after the assassination. He was on a first name basis with the Fort Worth FBI agent who interviewed him (Earl Haley, 8 H 349). This may be because, along with having been a security officer for the Convair Division of General Dynamics (8 H 352), he was, according to one witness, connected with the FBI (9 H 235). In these capacities he was not far removed from a major political scandal. Up to the time of the JFK assassination, Convair was being investigated by a senate committee concerning the controversial contract award to build the TFX experimental fighter plane. Deputy Defence Secretary Roswell Gilpatric and resigned Navy Secretary Fred Korth were under particular scrutiny in this matter. Korth resigned because he had used his office in favor of his own Continental National Bank of Fort Worth, which had made loans to General Dynamics. Korth also had several Fort Worth business ties to the Oswald family.[449]

Henry Crown, a director of the Hilton Hotel chain, major Democratic contributor and the leading shareholder of General Dynamics in 1963, was a friend and allegedly an associate in corrupt land deals, with Jack Ruby's old political boss Jake Arvey of Chicago's 24th Ward.[450] In addition to that, Crown's dealings, through the Havana Hilton, would come to encompass individuals close to Ruby, Oswald, Syvia Odio, Second Naval Guerrilla, CIA/Mafia assassination plotters, and possibly George Wing.

Former Marine intelligence officer John W. Houser, who became a fellow director with Henry Crown of Hilton Hotels International, had negotiated with a pro-Batista Cuban faction for the casino in the new Havana Hilton. The fact that mobster Albert Anastasia had met with this same group, and was Meyer Lansky's rival in Cuba, may have been one reason Anastasia was executed by the Mafia on October 25, 1957. The hit was allegedly a consensus between Lansky and Santos Trafficante (CIA/Mafia assassination plotter and close friend of John Martino). Trafficante had dinner with Anastasia and then stayed in his hotel room the day before the hit. Shortly after Anastasia's death, Trafficante attended the Apalachin meeting with Pennsylvania mobster Gabriel Mannarino.[451]

From 1952 to 1954, Pittsburgh's Mannarino brothers (Samuel and Gabriel) were part-owners, with Trafficante of Havana's San Souci Hotel, managed by Norman "Rough-house" Rothman, a syndicate figure in both Miami and Havana. Rothman co-owned the nearby Tropicana with Meyer and Jake Lansky. The man they hired to be their casino boss was Lewis J. McWillie -- Jack Ruby's friend and idol.[452]

In 1959 Rothman and Sam Mannarino were arrested in connection with a Canadian bank hiest -- the "biggest burglary in the world," according to the FBI. Two years later, when the CIA decided to approach the Mafia about killing Castro, Rothman, according to the New York Times, was the go-between who contacted Trafficante, Sam Mannarino, and John Roselli.[453]

Ten years after that, in 1971, Gabriel Mannarino was on trial in federal court in New York along with John Sebastian La Rocca, boss of the Pittsburgh organized crime family. They were charged in connection with a Teamsters-connected kickback scheme. A star witness in their defense was the head of the local CIA.[454]

Both Mannarino brothers are said to have participated in Syndicate gun-smuggling to Castro in 1958, along with Vito Genovese's son Michael. The Warren Commission mentions Ruby's role as middleman in the sale of jeeps to Cuba and the release of prisoners from a Cuban prison (R 369). But the Commission ignored testimony by Nancy Perrin Rich that she had witnessed Ruby in gunrunning negotiations with her husband, a colonel, a Cuban, and "unless I am very much mistaken...Vito Genovese's son." (14 H 353). Ruby's contact in these ventures (on behalf of "a person in Las Vegas, Nevada") was Robert Ray McKeown, "convicted in February 1958 of conspiracy to smuggle guns to the Castro forces in Cuba (CE 1689, 23 H 159). Ruby himself was linked by Harry Hall to the movement of `contraband' from Florida to Cuba (23 H 363); the same activity has been attributed to Meyer Lansky. Ruby also had numerous high-level contacts in the Teamsters in Miami (Dave Yaras, 22 H 372, cf. 25 H 295), Dallas (Dusty Miller, 25 H 244, 5 H 200), and Chicago (Barny Baker, 25 H 244); and Teamsters Pension Fund finances were said to have played a role in financing the attempted smuggling of planes and arms (perhaps the Mannarino arms) to the Dominican Republic."[455]

Andrew St. George, the man who may have captured George Wing in his 1961 photograph of E. Howard Hunt's men in Miami, was reportedly heavily involved with two men who were in turn connected to the Mannarino brothers and the Havana Hilton. St. George was named by informed witnesses before the Senate Internal Security Subcommittee as one of three Americans who were prominent in Castro's campaign against Batista, along with James Gentry and "gunrunning pilot Frank Fiorini [Sturgis]." Subcommittee Counsel Sourwine described St. George as an American double agent. According to Scott, "...U.S. intelligence agents such as Jules Dubois of Army Intelligence and Andrew St. George were allied with Syndicate figures such as Norman Rothman [the close associate of the Mannarino brothers] in efforts which supported Castro in 1958 but swiftly turned against him [by September 1959]." As mentioned earlier, St. George, after the assassination, had given a false story -- about Castro plots against U.S. ambassadors -- to the Free Cuba Committee, headed by Eladio Del Valle and Loran Eugene Hall. By 1965, St. George was serving as a publicity agent for Manolo Ray, "the engineer in charge of the Havana Hilton, co-conspirator with Dubois against Batista, and personal friend of Sylvia Odio."[456]

Considering the small world which closely links photographer Andrew St. George to these subjects of missing pages; the Mannarino brothers' proximity to Wing in his home state of Philadelphia; close links yet to be discussed between Del Valle, Loran Hall, a Miami Rambler which sounds identical to Wing's, possible Jules Dubois links to C.B. Smith and the Miami Rambler, apparent ties between McKeown, Smith, and Wing; and the way it all stems from Ruth Paine's mutual friends with the Oswalds (including persons closely tied to UT's oil advisors DeGolyer and MacNaughton) preceding and following the assassination; it seems likely that the man in the St. George photo (which is itself on a missing page) is indeed George Wing.

The Warren Commission avoided the subject of Oswald's initial contact with the Clarks, as did Peter Gregory -- Max Clark's friend. The one man on the Commission's staff who would have easily seen the red flags in a General Dynamics employee introducing Oswald to the CIA connected Russian community in Dallas, was assistant Counsel Albert E. Jenner. Jenner was put in charge of investigating the possibility of a conspiracy in the assassination. He was also Henry Crown's attorney in 1964. Considering this inexcusable conflict of interest, his conclusion comes as no surprise. He wrote that, "Review of Oswald's life and activities since 1959...did not produce any meaningful evidence of a conspiracy...." Nor did the Commission's investigation of Jack Ruby "produce any grounds for believing that Ruby's killing of Oswald was part of a conspiracy" (R 374, emphasis added). Jenner, who carefully chose the Warren Report's wording as one of its key authors, was sitting on the board of directors of General Dynamics by 1970 with his former client Henry Crown. In 1974, Nixon approved the appointment of Mr. Jenner as minority counsel for the House Judiciary's investigation into his impeachment.[457]

Whatever meaning Jenner gave to his evidence of conspiracy, and whether or not any grounds were produced that would have changed Jenner's beliefs about Ruby's killing of Oswald, the Warren Commission had ample opportunity to investigate the conspiracy both through Mr. and Mrs. Clark, and through Mr. and Mrs. Ford, who seemed to know Lewis MacNaughton's personal accountant, George Bouhe, well enough to know his complaints about having to babysit for Marina Oswald. As Peter Dale Scott tells us, "Mrs. Katya Ford, who after the assassination took Marina into her house and became her business agent, is of the Oswalds' four Russian patrons the only one alleged to be linked to Jack Ruby."[458]

She and her first husband, Stanley Skotnicki, were listed as persons "supposed to be associates or friends of people that Mr. Ruby knew and associated with closely" (1 H 239, 436). Mrs. de Mohrenschildt told the Commission that Skotnicki "was too anxious to make too much money" (9 H 306). Katya denied knowing Ruby but she and her husband Declan Ford, "an employee of DeGolyer and MacNaughton until October 1962," (about the time Oswald met Ford and moved to Dallas) suggested that a friend and neighbor of theirs, John M. Grizzaffi, did know Ruby (2 H 296, 323). Grizzaffi, who was also a friend of Stanley Skotnicki, may be the reason the Skotnickis made it onto the list of Ruby associates. He may have been "Little Johnny Grissaffi," the hit man hired by mobster Benny Binion to kill his Dallas gambling rival, Herbert Noble, in 1946.[459]

The importance of the Fords' friend having such a relationship with Binion is that Ruby's idol, Lewis J. McWillie, had worked for Binion and his gambling associates Earl Dalton, Ivy Miller and J.C. Adams, whose name was also found among Ruby's effects. McWillie had worked for Dalton and Miller at a club in Arlington, Texas in the forties. (Arlington is located between Dallas and Fort Worth.) Another Ruby friend, Ralph Paul, had formerly run a bar for J.C. Adams. Paul was a financial backer of Ruby's Carousel Club, and also owned a restaurant in Arlington. In addition to his restaurant, Paul ran an ice cream parlor at the Wynnwood Shopping Center in the Oak Cliff section of Dallas with Ruby's brother Sam. Sam Ruby was in Army Intelligence during World War II. And as discussed earlier, McWillie had been close to the CIA/Mafia plots as Norman Rothman's casino boss at the Tropicana in Havana. Rothman, Trafficante, Roselli, and the Mannarino brothers were among the first CIA contacts in the Castro assassination plots.[460]

So it appears that Marina Oswald's post assassination hosts, the Fords, were friends and neighbors of a Ruby associate tied to Mafia hits and CIA assassination plots. It is also worth noting that Benny Binion, Ralph Paul, and Lewis McWillie had such a long history in the city of Arlington. As we will see, C.B. Smith not only made a name for himself in Arlington, but may have had links to the ordnance smuggling operations of Ruby, McWillie, and Robert Ray McKeown. Smith served with the Chief of Staff, Army Ordnance, during World War II. George Wing had also been involved in ordnance during World War II in Florida. And as we have seen, Andrew St. George, the man who possibly photographed Wing with E. Howard Hunt's men in Miami, was also allied with Rothman, Frank Sturgis, and Jules Dubois of Army Intelligence, in these same Cuban gunrunning activities. Later we will explore how Jules Dubois may be a key person linking C.B. Smith and a

Rambler station wagon to a CIA safehouse in Miami.

It is likely that the Fords' friend, John M. Grizzaffi, was "Little Johnny Grissaffi" and that the Warren Commission knew it. One of Grissaffi's accomplices in the Herb Noble hit was a man named Hollis DeLois Green, who went by the name of Lois Green. He was "...the most desperate, the most depraved thug that ever operated in this section," according to a retired Dallas police captain who was active during the Binion era. Peter Dale Scott noted that, "The Commission went out of its way to hear from Ruby's sister that she did not know Lois Green personally, only by reputation (`The conversation was great about him...he was with the rough element,' 14 H 452-53)." Apparently Ruby himself was never asked about Grizzaffi.[461]

On February 24, 1964, Marina spent the day at the Declan Ford home with the Fords, two FBI agents, her new attorney, William A. McKenzie, and McKenzie's law partner, Henry Baer. Baer was also the secretary of the Reliance Life and Accident Insurance Company, owned by Maurice Carlson, "a close friend of Richard Nixon." Two directors of Reliance Life were the brothers Bedford and Angus Wynne, of the law firm, Wynne, Jaffe and Tinsley (and the Wynnwood Shopping Center). Law partner Morris Jaffe was George de Mohrenschildt's attorney.

The Reliance Life building also housed the Dallas office of the Secret Service. The building was owned by the Great Southwest Corporation (GSW), a real estate investment group based in Arlington. GSW's investors included Dallas oil man Clint Murchison and the Rockefellers. The group owned Arlington's Inn of the Six Flags, where Marina was taken on November 24, 1963 by Peter Gregory and his friend, Mike Howard of the Secret Service. They, along with another Secret Service agent named Charles Kunkel hid her there from all authorities, including the FBI. (The name Kunkel with telephone numbers was found in Ruby's notebook.) Wynne, Jaffe and Tinsley, who represented GSW and LTV, were also the Washington oil lobbyists named in connection with the Bobby Baker scandals. Bedford Wynne was the oil pay-off man to Bobby Baker and the Democrats.

Marina's new attorneys who were at the Ford home with her that February day in 1964 had taken over her business affairs a week earlier from James Herbert Martin. This appeared to be a change, but Martin had been employed by GSW as the manager of the Inn of the Six Flags. And Baer and McKenzie had recently left the law firm of GSW (Wynne, Jaffe and Tinsley).[462]

With this background in mind, stemming as it does from the Fords' relationship with Marina, we now turn to Nixon's stay in Dallas from November 20 to 22, 1963. Nixon's odd memory of this trip seems to explain the presence of Baer and McKenzie at the Ford home. It also shows that the Fords may represent, in addition to links between Oswald and Ruby, ominous links between Oswald, Ruby, and Richard Nixon. In fact many things about this trip to Dallas seem to shed light on the subjects discussed in this paper.

Nixon went to Dallas on legal business for Pepsi-Cola (now Pepsico). When Nixon's political career seemed to die after he lost his bid for governor of California in 1962, Pepsi came to his rescue by offering to give their account to the New York law firm of Mudge, Stern if they took Nixon on as a senior partner. According to Peter Dale Scott:

> This political favor by Donald Kendall, who became president of Pepsi in September 1963, has been viewed as a quid pro quo: Kendall is said to owe his presidency of Pepsico in part to his success (through the good offices of Richard Nixon) in having Khrushchev pose with a Pepsi bottle at the 1959 American exhibition in Moscow. But Kendall's success can also be attributed to his marriage with the daughter of Admiral Edward Orrick McDonnell, the veteran of Wilson's Vera Cruz expedition and a former director of Pepsi, of Pan Am, and (with Henry Crown and FrankManheim of Lehman Brothers) of the Hertz Corp.[463]

Kendall was very involved in Loeb Rhoades, Empire Trust, and General Dynamics investments with close associates of Jack Crichton, Joseph Walker (Air America), Toddie Lee Wynne (cousin of Bedford and director of GSW), and Robert Bernard Anderson.

Anderson, a long-time associate of LBJ and Fort Worth oil man Sid Richardson, had been appointed, in the fifties, to the Special Committee to Investigate Crude Oil Imports, which resulted in mandatory oil import quotas designed by Anderson, LBJ, and Senator Kerr of Oklahoma (of the Kerr-McGee Oil Co., from which George Bush hired a close friend of de Mohrenschildt). Reportedly, Anderson's reward was a phony deal concocted by Richardson in June 1957. In this scheme Anderson would buy oil stock for one dollar, then sell it to Toddie Lee Wynne's Dalada Corp. for $900,000. In September 1963, Richardson's nephew Perry Bass bought Dalada, thus reacquiring the stock for Richardson's estate. Today, Bass is a major financial contributor to the University of Texas at Austin. Anderson's other investment partner, Carl M. Loeb Rhoades, was described by Walter Winchell as LBJ's top financial advisor.[464]

Anderson was also involved in deals with a man closer to the subject of this paper. According to Scott, "In February 1964 Anderson's World Banking Corp. in the Bahamas brought in the Belgian Banque Lambert, along with Augustin Batista of Loeb-linked former Cuba Trust Company in Havana."[465]

As we have seen, Augustin Batista was a member, with Jose Aleman, Sr., of the Anson Group, which was closely tied to Second Naval Guerrilla and to Richard Nixon. As we will soon see, Augustin Batista's Cuban Trust Company employed a director of de Mohrenschildt's Cuban oil company -- a company with close ties to William F. Buckley Sr. and possibly to C.B. Smith and a familiar sounding Rambler station wagon in Miami.

Like Anderson, Robert H. Stewart III had financial ties to both LBJ and Nixon. And as a prominent Dallas Republican fund raiser, director of GSW, Braniff and Lone Star Steel (all close to LBJ), president in 1963 of First National Bank, Dallas (FNBD), and future director of Pepsico (1964), and LTV (1970), Stewart, too, had financial ties to the apparent conspiracy to manipulate Marina Oswald's testimony.

On November 15, 1963, Nixon petitioned to join the New York Bar. Then on November 20 he flew, with Donald Kendall in a Pepsi plane, to a bottler's convention in Dallas. Ten months later Pepsi announced plans to build a multi-million dollar plant in Arlington -- thus enhancing the value of GSW. This project must have been related to Pepsi's intended merger with Frito Lay of Dallas (which interlocked with James Ling's Electro-Science Investors).

This merger between Pepsi and Frito Lay was objected to by the Federal Trade Commission in a complaint filed November 19, 1963 -- the day before Nixon flew to Dallas. It was a complaint that must have been of great concern that week to Wynne, Jaffe and Tinsley (GSW's law firm), Nixon, (Pepsi's lawyer), Robert H. Stewart (director of GSW and FNBD), and Herman Lay (of Frito Lay and director of FNBD). If these men met that week, the meeting represented links to de Mohrenschildt (through Morris Jaffe), post assassination links to Marina Oswald (through William A. McKenzie and James H. Martin), the Bobby Baker payoffs (through Bedford Wynne and Robert H. Stewart), and CIA/Cuba connections (through Nixon).[466]

It was Robert H. Stewart who hired George Bush in 1977 (after President Carter replaced him as CIA director) to be director of First International Bankshares, Inc. (FIB, Inc.) of Dallas.[467]

Bush was also named a director of First International Bankshares, Ltd. (FIB, Ltd.), FIB, Inc.'s London Merchant bank. Another FIB, Ltd. director was W. Dewey Presley, the president and chairman of FIB, Inc.'s executive committee.[468] He is also listed in the book Who's Who in CIA (the acronym CIA is used loosely here to mean any intelligence related work). Presley's entry reads:

b.: 26.5.1918;
1939-42 in Magnolia Oil and Pipe Line Companies; 1942-52 Special
Agent of FBI; from 1960 Vice President of First National Bank, Dallas;
    OpA [area of operation]: Dallas[469]

We have already explored the presence of Magnolia Oil around Oswald, Ruth Paine, and Eugene Hale Brading. There is, however, another intriguing individual at FIB with connections to Magnolia, George Bush, and others discussed in this paper. He is J. Rawles Fulgham Jr., president of FIB, Inc. and chairman of FIB, Ltd. Fulgham was identified in a 1982 news report as a director of Dorchester Gas Corp. (see Nexis). Dorchester Gas was the company owned by Jack Alston Crichton, which had D.H. Byrd as a director. It was Crichton who selected his and Ruth Paine's friend, Ilya Mamantov to be Marina's interpreter. And as we have seen, Mamantov was teaching scientific Russian to the Magnolia employees who met the Oswalds at the party discussed earlier.

It will be recalled that one of the three Mamantov students living at the house where the party took place, Volkmar Schmidt, had lived and studied with one of the survivors of the failed plot to assassinate Hitler -- a fact which brings us to another intriguing connection of FIB's president and chairman. Fulgham was identified as a director of Dresser Industries (see Nexis), where Bush's father had been a director and Bush himself got his first job. It is recalled that Dresser is also where Hans Gisevius, another survivor of the Hitler plot, friend of Allen Dulles and Ruth Paine's friend Mary Bancroft, "spent some time in Texas."[470] Given all of this, we can perhaps agree with Professor Scott that:

> Mr. Nixon should be asked whether his legal efforts
> helped to block this complaint [against the Pepsi merger
> with Frito Lay]; and if so, with whom and how he
> handled it in Dallas. For it was this merger that brought
> to the Pepsico board Robert H. Stewart III...for fifteen
> years an acquaintance and backer of James Ling (who
> [with D.H. Byrd] bought heavily into LTV and Electro-
> Science Investors in October and November 1963).
> Robert Stewart and his bank were named in the Bobby
> Baker Hearings for the $250,000 loan Stewart had
> advanced to Baker and his friends in 1961, for an

insurance stock purchase which looked to many like a
political reward.

    Stewart, like his "very good friend" Senator John
Tower, and Tower's campaign manager Peter O'Donnell,
was powerful among the conservative Republicans of
Texas....In 1970 he became one of three new
directors...of LTV, along with Ling's old backer Troy
Post...and William H.

    Tinsley who by now was the senior partner of
Wynne, Jaffe and Tinsley.[471]

Nixon's flurry of activity the week of November 15 to 22, 1963,
during which he worked so intently on behalf of his rich and powerful
political allies in Dallas, would seem to have been quite memorable to
him; and even more so given the fact that the week ended with the world
shattering assassination (in that very city) of the man to whom he lost the
U.S. presidency three years earlier by the closest margin in American
history. After all, even those who were children (including this author)
have remembered that day with unusual clarity for their entire lives. But
for Kennedy's historic rival, Richard Nixon, that seems not to be the
case. Only three months after the assassination, Nixon did not remember
that he was in Dallas almost up until the time of the assassination;
despite the fact that during this incredible lapse of memory, he did
remember being invited to Dallas in April 1963; he did remember that
the purpose of that trip "never materialized"; and he did remember not
giving any consideration to going (CE 1973, 23 H 831).[472] And despite
remembering these details, Nixon called his memory of this invitation
vague. Most unusual of all is that the story of the invitation was
completely false.

    Let us review this. Richard Nixon's three month old memory of being
in Dallas on the most memorable day in the history of that city; the most
memorable day of their lives for most people in the world; and what
should have been, for Nixon, the most memorable day of his life, was
vague. Yet his ten month old memory of a forgettable invitation to come
to Dallas for a forgettable event which never transpired, and about which
he gave no consideration, was relatively detailed; even though there had
never been any such invitation. And Nixon called his relatively detailed
memory of this non-invitation vague.

    This raises the question: who was the source of this falsehood? It
turns out that it was started on February 19, 1964 by Maurice Carlson of
Reliance Life and Accident Insurance (23 H 414, 416); a man described
by the FBI as "a close friend of Richard Nixon" (23 H 414). The

chairman of Mr. Carlson's insurance company was a man named James H. Bond, who was also with James Ling's Electro-Science Investors (and later with LTV). And we must not forget that the secretary of Mr. Carlson's insurance company was Henry Baer (formerly of the Wynne law firm which represented de Mohrenschildt, LTV, and GSW), the man who was at the Ford home on February 24 with Marina Oswald. The interesting thing about Mr. Baer being there that particular day is that it was the very next day that Maurice Carlson retracted his story about the Nixon invitation to Dallas.[473]

Joining Carlson in the denial of his own story was Peter O'Donnell, the campaign manager for Robert H. Stewart's "very good friend" Senator John Tower. It is recalled that O'Donnell is also the man who sat on the Cuban Freedom Committee with Oveta Culp Hobby; was president of Harry Ransom friend Karl Hoblitzelle's Foundation; and who was a member of William F. Buckley, Jr.'s National Advisory Council of Young Americans for Freedom with Robert Morris. Morris, it is recalled, was Otto Otepka's defense attorney, General Walker's attorney, H.L. Hunt's attorney, a John Bircher, and a Naval intelligence officer.[474]

Why then would Richard Nixon come along three days after the denial of this story (February 28) and seem to corroborate it with his "vague" yet detailed memory of it? Two days before Carlson's February 19 telling of the false story, Baer and McKenzie replaced Martin as Marina's attorneys. The false story, had it been true, would have corroborated an equally incredible story that Marina was reportedly telling. On the same day Carlson told his story, Robert Oswald said that "Marina had locked Lee Harvey Oswald in the bathroom the entire day" (of Nixon's alleged April visit) to prevent him from going to shoot Nixon (22 H 596). By February 24, it had been established that the bathroom locked from the inside. Marina changed her story that day saying she had held onto the doorknob and braced her feet against the wall for three hours (23 H 511-12). When time came to testify under oath, however, she changed her story again and said she and her husband struggled inside the bathroom (R 188).[475]

Unless something came along very quickly to back up this bizarre bathroom story, it could have cast doubt on all of Marina's testimony which was essentially all the Commission had to convince the public that Oswald was guilty. And more importantly, if Marina's bathroom story had been proved false, it could have implicated a number of people in its creation; including Henry Baer, William McKenzie, two FBI agents, and the Fords, who were all with her the day her story first changed to accommodate the facts about the door lock. It could have also implicated

Carlson who withdrew his invitation story the very next day, and Robert Oswald who first reported Marina's bathroom story. The reason her story was not proved false was because Richard Nixon came to everyone's rescue by "vaguely" remembering the "invitation" on February 28, three days after the whole matter self-destructed.[476] Had these people been investigated honestly, it is extremely likely it would have led to the connections discussed in this paper.

There are indications that the Warren Commission came quite close to investigating those very connections. In February 1964, the same month these desperate falsehoods about Nixon were being spread, LTV won the Navy contract to build limited war fighter planes which resulted in huge returns on the insightful investments of James Ling, D.H. Byrd and others in November 1963. Also in February 1964, the Joint Chiefs began calling for "intensified operations against North Vietnam", and Ling was charged with misconduct by the Security and Exchange Commission. And the Warren Commission, on February 24 (the day Marina's story began to change), wrote a memorandum to the CIA raising promising questions about Ruby's links to Lewis J. McWillie, Barney Baker, Thomas Hill of the John Birch Society head office (who was in Ruby's notebook), and "Leopold Ramos Ducos," who with Mike Singer (both subjects of missing pages) was linked to Bobby Baker and the teamsters (CE 2980, 26 H 467-73).[477]

The fact that these individuals came so close to being investigated yet were not (because of Nixon's vague remembrance), would seem to be reason enough for Richard Nixon to have a good laugh. He laughed all the way to Asia twice in 1964, where he spoke to South Vietnamese officials and Chiang Kai-shek. When he returned in April 1964 he lobbied hard for carrying the war to North Vietnam. His second trip to Taiwan on Pepsi business enabled him to address the National Toilers Alliance-National Alliance of Solidarists (NTS), the Anti-Bolshevik Nations (ABN), and assorted German right-wingers and ex-Nazis at the Asian Peoples' Anti-Communist League (APACL) -- the colleagues of Oswald's contact Spas T. Raikin.[478]

As Dr. Scott tells us, the NTS and ABN collaborated closely with the APACL in Taipeh to establish the proposed World Anti-Communist Conference for Freedom and Liberation. "This makes it likely," Scott writes, "that the NTS was also in contact in Texas with the allies of the APACL and through them with the John Birch Society and the supporters of General Walker." Thus, these Nixon/Pepsi intrigues hit close to home when we recall that "Jack Nichols Payton, a friend and campaign-organizer of General Walker, described himself in Commission Exhibit 2094 (24 H 528) as a member of both the John

Birch Society and the Austin Anti-Communist League."[479] It is also recalled that SNG veteran John Martino, who claimed to have knowledge of the conspiratorial manipulation of Oswald, spoke at a meeting of the Austin Anti- Communist League on October 1, 1963 -- one week after Oswald was in Austin.

Considering these Nixon ties to the Watergaters of Second Naval Guerrilla, Ruth Paine, Jack Ruby, and Lee Harvey Oswald, it no longer seems as much a stretch that the Red Ripper was trying to communicate something important about George Wing's Rambler and the JFK assassination. But could Wing's car be an actual car used by the conspirators? We will next explore some indications that it could. They show that George Wing may have had good reason to pose the question (on his office door and in his anachronistic car) of why Richard Nixon was laughing.

* * *

Notes:

298. William Weston, "Collaborators of the Conspiracy", The Third Decade, Nov., 1992, pp. 5, 10.

299. Weston, p. 6; Warren Commission Hearings, Vol. 3, p. 249, cited in Weston, p. 10. Note: This is how Truly referred to himself.

300. Dallas Morning News, Nov. 23, 1963, section 4, p. 1.

301. Weston, p. 13.

302. Hunt, The Sixth Floor..., p. 5.

303. Warren Commission Hearings, Vol. 6, pp. 391, 395, 396, cited in Weston, p. 11. Note: It was pointed out in the March 1993 Third Decade (pp. 22-23) that the testimony cited by Weston referring to "lights all went out and phones became dead" has two different interpretations. While that is true, there is ample evidence that commission attorneys altered testimony and chose language very carefully. Weston believes "that the Warren Commission was trying to avoid the subject." In a cover-up, this matter would be a prime target for obfuscation.

304. Weston, p. 11.

305. Alden Hatch, The Byrds of Virginia: An American Dynasty, 1670 to the Present, (NY: Holt Rinehart Winston, 1969.), p. xv; Byrd, I'm an Endangered Species, p. 3.

306. Austin American-Statesman, Nov. 15, 1988, p. A5.

307. It is suspicious that this building was set on fire while this bank carried the lien because one of the numerous CIA contacts of Lewis MacNaughton, mentioned earlier, is that he was a director of Republic National Gas and Republic National Bank of Dallas with Karl Hoblitzelle, who set up the CIA-conduit Hoblitzelle Foundation. A theater magnate and Ransom friend,

Hoblitzelle donated to UT the core of its theater collection. (Newsweek, Feb. 27, 1967, p. 26, cited in Scott, *The Dallas Conspiracy*, ch. III, p. 6; Frantz, p. 25.)

308. Hunt, The Sixth Floor... p. 5.

309. New York Times, Sept. 22, 1975, p. 36.

310. The esteem Lyndon Johnson held for Senator Harry Byrd of Virginia can be seen in a 1964 photo of Lyndon Johnson kissing his hand "in a gesture of condolence and respect...." (Hatch, The Byrds of Virginia, photograph.) The Nov. 16, 1963 Dallas Morning News mentions Senator Harry Byrd of Virginia, head of the Senate Finance Committee, and his opposition to a proposed Kennedy tax cut of $11 billion, passed by the House, while increasing spending for a proposed deficit increase to $334 billion over the next two-and-a- half years.

311. Byrd, *I'm an Endangered Species*, pp. 37-40.

312. Byrd, *I'm an Endangered Species*, p. 108; Jim Garrison, On the Trail of the Assassins, (NY: Sheridan Square Press, 1989), pp. 51, 53, 286.

313. The University of Texas at Austin, Permanent Record Card, "de Mohrenschildt, George Serguis."

314. 9 H 202, cited in Scott, *The Dallas Conspiracy*, ch. VI, pp. 32-33; Canfield with Weberman, *Coup d'état in America*, p. 29. Note: Ilya Mamantov, whom Crichton selected as Marina's interpreter after the assassination, was a friend of de Mohrenschildt and a Sun Oil employee. Mamantov, with his friend Peter Gregory, altered Marina's testimony in order to connect Lee with the alleged murder weapon. (See Scott, *The Dallas Conspiracy*, ch. III.)

315. Summers, *Conspiracy*, pp. 223-25; Epstein, *Legend*, pp. 175-77, 180-82.

316. Hinckle with Turner, *The Fish is Red*, p. 206; *Beyond JFK: The Question of Conspiracy*, 90 minutes, Produced by Danny Schechter & Rory O'Connor with Globalvision, Warner Home Video, 1992.

317. Byrd, *I'm an Endangered Species*, p. 105; David Nevin. *The Texans*, (NY: Bonanza, 1968), p. 150. Note: Amazingly Nevin even had a role in the assassination. (See Curtis Prendergast with Geoffrey Colvin, *The World of Time Inc.*, NY: Atheneum, 1986, p.121.)

318. Byrd, *I'm an Endangered Species*, p. 53.

319. Byrd, *I'm an Endangered Species*, p. 98.

320. Byrd, *I'm an Endangered Species*, pp. 99, 100.

321. Byrd, *I'm an Endangered Species*, pp. 101-02.

322. General Jimmy Doolittle co-authored, with Allen Dulles and William Pawley of Flying Tigers fame, the infamous Doolittle Report of 1954 which greatly empowered the CIA. (See Hinckle with Turner, *The Fish is Red*, p. 45; Ranelagh, *The Agency*, p. 276.)

323. Byrd, *I'm an Endangered Species*, p. 41.

324. Byrd, *I'm an Endangered Species*, pp. 105-06.

325. A fellow director of LTV was R.B. Gilmore, the president of DeGolyer and MacNaughton, the oil firm mentioned earlier in this paper. (See Scott, *The Dallas Conspiracy*, ch. IX, p. 20.)

326. Scott, *The Dallas Conspiracy*, ch. III, p. 37; Byrd, *I'm an Endangered*

Species, pp. 68-69.

327. Aviation Week, Jan. 27, 1964, p. 21, cited in Scott, *The Dallas Conspiracy*, ch. IX, p. 20. Note: The question is raised of the role in this budget process of D.H. Byrd's cousin Sen. Harry Byrd, head of the Senate Finance Committee.

328. Wilson, *Texas Unsolved Mysteries*, p. 115. Note: Marshall had been a key figure in the investigation into the cotton allotment dealings of Billie Sol Estes, a scandal implicating Lyndon Johnson. Marshall died from five rifle wounds in what was ruled a suicide. "Wallace was supposedly friendly with the Johnson family to the point of dating Josefa, Lyndon's sister. During his trial, Wallace was represented by John Cofer, the same attorney who had represented Johnson in the famous `Ballot Box 13' voter fraud case in 1948..."

329. Captain Peoples reportedly died in a one-car accident in early 1993 after announcing he was going to retire soon and tell all about the Marshall and Kiner murders. (Interview: Mar. 7, 1993, Resident of Franklyn, Texas, site of the Marshall murder, who whishes anonymity.)

330. Wilson, *Texas Unsolved Mysteries*, p. 123.

331. Wilson, *Texas Unsolved Mysteries*, p. 118.

332. Craig I. Zirbel, *The Texas Connection*, (Scottsdale, AZ: The Texas Connection Co., 1991), p. 159, n. 17.

333. "Crichton of Army Reserve Intelligence Service, was the apparent outsider who arranged for Marina Oswald to have the "excessive rightist" Ilya Mamantov as her interpreter." (See Scott, The Dallas Conspiracy, ch. III, p. 37.)

334. Steinberg, *Sam Johnson's Boy*, pp. 667, 626, cited in Scott, *The Dallas Conspiracy,* ch. IX pp. 20-21.

335. Byrd, *I'm an Endangered Species*, pp. 3, 96; Peter Collier with David Horowitz, *The Rockefellers*, (NY: Holt, Rinehart & Winston, 1976), p. 193.

336. Ken C. Braband, *The First 50 Years: A History of Collins Radio Company and the Collins Divisions of Rockwell International*, (Cedar Rapids, IA: Rockwell International, 1983), p.14-15.

337. Braband, *The First 50 Years: A History of Collins Radio...*, p. 95. Note: Red Bird Airport is twenty-three miles south of Collins' Richardson plant and just over five miles south of Tenth Street and Patton where Officer J.D. Tippit was murdered.

338. Russell interview: May 12, 1992 with Mary Ferrell, FBI report of Mar. 10, 1967, cited in Russell, The Man Who Knew Too Much, pp. 576, 788 n.42.

339. Summers, *Conspiracy*, p. 545 n. 33.

340. Summers, *Conspiracy*, p. 545 n. 33.

341. FBI Field Report No. DL 89-43, Nov. 24, 1963, cited in John R. Craig with Philip A. Rogers, *The Man on the Grassy Knoll*, (NY: Avon, 1992), pp. 275-76.

342. Craig with Rogers, *The Man on the Grassy Knoll*, p. 273. Note: It is recalled here that Col. Fletcher Prouty identified his boss, Gen. Edward G. Lansdale, in a photo of these tramps. Lansdale's "big patron" was Walt Rostow, a mutual friend of LBJ and Ransom with Byrd, Burris, CIA asset Karl Hoblitzelle, and Paine family friend Everette deGolyer.

343. Craig with Rogers, *The Man on the Grassy Knoll*, pp. 116-17.

344. Russell, *The Man Who Knew Too Much*, pp. 475-76.

345. Epstein, *Legend*, pp. 175-77, 183-85.

346. Epstein, *Legend*, pp. 175-77, 183-85.

347. 12 HSCA 40, 41, cited in Groden with Livingstone. *High Treason*, pp. 238-39.

348. Interview: Mar. 30, 1991, Evelyn Bartholomew, widow of J.H. Bartholomew. (Note: James Hayes Bartholomew, Sr., was the author's father.)

349. New York Times, Mar. 19, 1963, p. 4; NYT, Apr. 2, 1963, p. 22; NYT, Oct. 25, 1963, p. 14; NYT, Oct. 26, 1963, p. 10.

350. Scott, *The Dallas Conspiracy*, ch. IX, p. 30.

351. "Castro Says CIA Uses Raider Ship," New York Times, Nov. 1, 1963, pp. 1, 15; "Alleged CIA Men Talk on Havana TV," NYT, Nov. 3, 1963, p. 40, Nov. 20, 1963, p. 42, Dec. 6, 1963, p. 41; Hinckle with Turner, The Fish is Red, p. 138.

352. Byrd, *I'm an Endangered Species*, p. 37.

353. Byrd, *I'm an Endangered Species*, pp. 48, 103.

354. Byrd, *I'm an Endangered Species*, p. 39, with photo of Van Cliburn, age 7, with Byrd's parents and Martha Byrd, Harold's wife.

355. Byrd, *I'm an Endangered Species*, p. 78.

356. Byrd, *I'm an Endangered Species*, p. 104; The University of Texas at Arlington, "C.B. Smith, Sr., October 24, 1967." Note: Smith and Byrd were also both residents, during their college years, at UT's "Old B Hall" upperclassmen dormitory, a place with strong fraternal ties and traditions which outlasted its fifty- year existence. Smith and Byrd had at least one overlapping year there. (See Frantz, pp. 95-109; Byrd, p. 18, 22.) Both the timing and transaction of the sale of the Rambler from Smith to Wing have implications concerning the JFK assassination and will be explored further in this paper.

357. Canfield with Webberman, *Coup d'état in America*, p. 107; John Chabot Smith, *Alger Hiss: The True Story*, (NY: Holt, Rinehart, Winston, 1976), p. 143n.

358. Canfield with Webberman, *Coup d'état in America*, pp. 105-06.

359. Summers, *Conspiracy*, p. 149.

360. Canfield with Webberman, *Coup d'état in America*, p. 107.

361. Hinkle with Turner, *The Fish is Red,* p. 170.

362. Those planners were Richard Bissell, Tracy Barnes, Charles Cabell, and Allen Dulles. On the eve of the invasion, Kennedy asked one man to look over the plan for final approval: Walt Rostow, the close friend of Bissell, Cabell and Dulles.

363. Gaeton Fonzi, statement made at the Second Research Conference of The Third Decade, Jun., 20, 1993.

364. Lane, *Plausible Denial*, pp. 295-301

365. R.H.S. Crossman, "Apocalypse at Dresden," Esquire, Nov. 1963, p. 149.

366. Crossman, p. 149-50. Note: In 1953, Allen Dulles succeeded Walter Bedell Smith as CIA director. (Collier with Horowitz, *The Rockefellers*, p. 271.)

367. Crossman, p. 149.

368. Rostow, Memo on Area Bombing, 1943.

369. Rostow, Pre-Invasion Bombing Strategy, p. 70.

370. Rostow, Memo on Area Bombing, 1943.

371. Crossman, p. 150.

372. CD 59, cited in Canfield with Weberman, *Coup d'état in America*, p. 104.

373. Canfield with Webberman, *Coup d'état in America*, pp. 104-05.

374. Canfield with Webberman, *Coup d'état in America*, p. 106; Austin American-Statesman, Oct. 2, 1963, p. 29.

375. CD 657; New York Times, Sept. 27 and Oct. 22, 1960, Mar. 11 and 12, 1961, cited in Canfield with Webberman, *Coup d'état in America*, p. 106.

376. Canfield with Webberman, *Coup d'état in America*, p. 107.

377. John Chabot Smith, *Alger Hiss: The True Story*, (NY: Holt, Rinehart, Winston, 1976), p. 143n.

378. Canfield with Webberman, *Coup d'état in America*, p. 107.

379. Judis, *William F. Buckley, Jr.*, p. 130.

380. Canfield with Webberman, *Coup d'état in America*, p. 143.

381. Judis, *William F. Buckley, Jr.*, pp. 215-16.

382. Bancroft, Autobiography..., pp. 185-86.

383. Link, *Woodrow Wilson*, pp. 16-17.

384. Judis, *William F. Buckley, Jr.*, p. 22.

385. Frantz, *The Forty Acre Follies,* pp. 97-100.

386. Hinckle with Turner, *The Fish is Red,* pp. 168-173.

387. Hinckle with Turner, *The Fish is Red*, p. 169.

388. Hinckle with Turner, *The Fish is Red*, p. 169.

389. Hinckle with Turner, *The Fish is Red*, pp. 161, 169-70.

390. Hinckle with Turner, *The Fish is Red*, p. 172.

391. Curtis Prendergast with Geoffrey Colvin, *The World of Time Inc.*, (NY: Atheneum, 1986), p. 125; Richard B. Stolley, "Four Days in Dallas: 25 Years Later," Columbia [University] magazine, Oct. 1988, p. 58.

392. Peter Wyden, *Bay of Pigs*, (NY: Simon & Schuster, 1979), pp. 84-86.

393. Summers, *Conspiracy*, pp. 449-50. Note: Loran Eugene Hall and Santos Trafficante had been in jail at the same time in Cuba and were released together in July 1959. In 1963 Hall was working with Eladio del Valle's Committee to Free Cuba. Del Valle had been a smuggling partner of Trafficante and was also a close friend and associate of David Ferrie. (See Summers, *Conspiracy*, p. 346; *Anson, They've Killed the President, p. 197; Hinckle with Turner, The* Fish is Red, p. 230.)

394. Hinckle with Turner, *The Fish is Red*, p. 169.

395. Hinckle with Turner, *The Fish is Red*, p. 169.

396. Hinckle with Turner, *The Fish is Red*, p. 160; Wolfe, *The Murchisons*, pp. 172-73; Scott, *Crime and Cover-Up*, p. 11.

397. Hinckle with Turner, *The Fish is Red*, p. 160; Interview: C. Osmet Moody by David G. Armstrong, Mar. 23, 1992.

398. Hinckle with Turner, *The Fish is Red*, pp. 160-61.

399. David E. Scheim, *Contract on America*, (NY: Shapolsky, 1988), p. 130. Note: One of Ruby's visits was right after the midnight press conference where Ruby corrected Dallas D.A. Henry Wade's apparent mistake that Oswald was a member of the Free Cuba Committee. Aside from the fact that Ruby knew it was the Fair Play for Cuba Committee, the Committee to Free Cuba was headed by David Ferrie's close friend Eladio del Valle. (See Scheim, p. 126; Summers, *Conspiracy*, p. 346; Anson, *They've Killed the President*, p. 197; Hinckle with Turner, *The Fish is Red*, p. 230.)

400. CE 1322, p. 730; 5 H 188, cited in Scheim, *Contract on America*, p. 424, n. 66; Increase Records INCM-2007: Cruisin' 1962, long-play recording "Featuring Russ `Weird Beard' Knight KLIF Dallas, Texas," 1984. Note: McLendon was later named by Marcello associate D' Alton Smith as someone lined up to assist the Mob's spring-Hoffa campaign (Scheim, *Contract on America*, p. 424, n. 66).

401. Hinckle with Turner, *The Fish is Red*, p. 173.

402. Claasen interview with Earl Golz of The Dallas Morning News, 1978, cited in Summers, *Conspiracy*, pp. 451-52.

403. Hinckle with Turner, *The Fish is Red*, p. 148.

404. Anson, *They've Killed the President*, p. 256.

405. Hinckle with Turner, *The Fish is Red*, p. 148.

406. Hinckle with Turner, *The Fish is Red*, p. 148-49; Scott, *Crime and Cover-Up*, p. 10.

407. Tad Szulc, *Compulsive Spy: The Strange Career of E. Howard Hunt*, (NY: Viking, 1974), pp. 96-97, Church Committee, Alleged Assassination Plots, p. 89-90, cited in Scott, *Crime and Cover-Up*, pp. 10-11, 52, n. 18.

408. Scott, *Crime and Cover-Up*, pp. 12, 15, 17, 18.

409. Scott, *Crime and Cover-Up*, pp. 17-18.

410. Scott, *Crime and Cover-Up*, pp. 17-18.

411. Scott, *Crime and Cover-Up*, pp. 11-12.

412. Scott, *Crime and Cover-Up*, p. 11.

413. Scott, *Crime and Cover-Up*, pp. 11, 20.

414. Scott, *Crime and Cover-Up*, pp. 13-14.

415. Scott, *Crime and Cover-Up*, pp. 13-14.

416. Scott, *Crime and Cover-Up*, pp. 14, 56, n. 52a; Scott, *The Dallas Conspiracy*, ch. IV, p. 10.

417. Summers, *Conspiracy*, p. 224; Epstein, *Legend*, p. 179.

418. Peter Collier with David Horowitz, *The Rockefellers*, (NY: Holt, Rinehart & Winston, 1976), pp. 193, 408, 414.

419. Collier with Horowitz, *The Rockefellers*, p. 271-72; Pete Brewton, *The Mafia, CIA & George Bush*, (NY: S.P.I. Books, 1992), p. 101.

420. Brewton, *The Mafia, CIA & George Bush*, p. 101.

421. The University of Texas at Austin College of Communication, Ceremony To Name The Communication Complex The Jesse H. Jones Communication Center, Program, April 30, 1982.

422. Scott, *The Dallas Conspiracy*, ch. III, p. 7, ch. VIII, p. 15-16; Scott, *Crime and Cover-Up*, pp. 14-16, 53, n. 33-34.

423. Canfield with Webberman, *Coup d'état in America*, p. 138.

424. Canfield with Webberman, *Coup d'état in America*, p. 139.

425. Canfield with Webberman, *Coup d'état in America*, p. 141.

426. Scott, *The Dallas Conspiracy*, ch. II, pp. 21-22.

427. Russell, *The Man Who Knew Too Much*, pp. 191, 321; Judis, *William F. Buckley, Jr.*, p. 188.

428. Scott, *The Dallas Conspiracy*, ch. IV, p. 18.

429. Scott, *The Dallas Conspiracy*, ch. VII, p. 5.

430. Collier with Horowitz, *The Rockefellers*, p. 272-73.

431. Ranelagh, *The Agency*, p. 280; William R. Corson, *The Armies of Ignorance*, (NY: Dial, 1977), pp. 372- 73, 382n.

432. Amos A. Jordan with William J. Taylor and Lawrence J. Korb, American National Security: Policy and Process, (Baltimore, MD: Johns Hopkins University Press, third ed., 1989) p. 141.

433. Paul Brancato, *Coup d'état: The Assassination of John F. Kennedy*, illustrated cards, (Forestville, CA: Eclipse, 1990), p. 25; Austin American-Stateman, Sept. 1989; Linda Latham Welch, "A Towering Task," Austin American-Stateman, Sept. 3, 1992, "Neighbor" Section; Land and Baker: Corson, *The Armies of Ignorance*, p. 373.

434. Ranelagh, *The Agency*, p. 280.

435. Scott, *Crime and Cover-Up*, pp. 12-13.

436. Anson, *They've Killed the President*, pp. 255-56.

437. Anson, *They've Killed the President*, p. 256.

438. Bernard Fensterwald Jr., *Coincidence or Conspiracy?*, (NY: Zebra, 1977), pp. 511-13; Canfield with Weberman, *Coup d'état in America*, pp. 56-57, 74, 76.

439. Garrison, *On the Trail of the Assassins*, p. 63.

440. 2 H 304, cited in Scott, Government Documents..., ch. II, p. 3.

441. Scott, *The Dallas Conspiracy*, ch. IV, p. 3.

442. Scott, *The Dallas Conspiracy*, ch. III, pp. 10-11.

443. Scott, Government Documents..., ch. II, p. 4.

444. Scott, *The Dallas Conspiracy*, ch. III, p. 17.

445. Scott, *The Dallas Conspiracy*, ch. III, p. 22 n.

446. CE 3116, 26 H 760, cited in Scott, *The Dallas Conspiracy*, ch. III, pp. 1-2.

447. Scott, Government Documents..., ch. III, pp. 20, 21.

448. Scott, *The Dallas Conspiracy*, ch. VII, p. 18.

449. Scott, *The Dallas Conspiracy*, ch. III, pp. 3, 4, 5, 44, 45. Note: Scott suggests that Gilpatric and Korth, along with the former assistant Navy secretary for installations and logistics (under Connally), Ken BeLieu, should have been questioned about the contracts for installing sophisticated electronics aboard the Collins Radio ship Rex and another ship, the Maddox, of Tonkin Gulf infamy. (see Scott, *The Dallas Conspiracy*, ch. XI, pp. 30-31)

450. Ovid Demaris, *Captive City*, p. 230, Kenneth Lamott, *The Moneymakers*, (Boston, MA: Little Brown, 1969), p. 65, cited in Scott, *The Dallas Conspiracy*, ch. VII, p. 17.

451. Hank Messick, *Lansky*, p. 212, Ed Reid, *The Grim Reapers*, p. 94, cited in Scott, *The Dallas Conspiracy*, ch. VI, pp. 24, 25, 26.

452. Scott, *The Dallas Conspiracy*, ch. VI, pp. 25, 28; Anson, *They've Killed the President*, p. 309.

453. Anson, *They've Killed the President*, pp. 299, 309.

454. Anson, *They've Killed the President*, p. 296.

455. Scott, *The Dallas Conspiracy*, ch. VI, pp. 25, 28.

456. Scott, *The Dallas Conspiracy*, ch. VI, p. 35, ch. VII, p. 4; Canfield with Webberman, *Coup d'état in America*, p. 138, 141.

457. Scott, *The Dallas Conspiracy*, ch. VII, pp. 25, 26; Fensterwald, *Coincidence or Conspiracy?,* pp. 549- 50.

458. Scott, *The Dallas Conspiracy*, ch. III, pp. 7, 8.

459. Ed Reid with Ovid Demaris, *The Green Felt Jungle*, (NY: Trident Press, 1963), p. 191, cited in Scott, *The Dallas Conspiracy*, ch. III, p. 8; moved to Dallas: Scott, ch. IX, p. 20.

460. Scott, *The Dallas Conspiracy*, ch. V, pp. 24-27, ch. VI, p. 25; Anson, *They've Killed the President*, pp. 299, 309.

461. Scott, *The Dallas Conspiracy*, ch. V, pp. 26, 27; Reid with Demaris, *The Green Felt Jungle*, (NY: Pocket Books, 1964), p. 158.

462. Scott, *The Dallas Conspiracy*, ch. III, pp. 3-6, 7, 21, 30, ch. IX, pp. 23, 27, ch. X, pp. 16-21.

463. Scott, Government Documents..., ch. X, p. 11.

464. Scott, *The Dallas Conspiracy*, ch. IX, pp. 10-33.

465. New York Times, Feb., 9, 1964, 111, 6, cited in Scott, Government Documents..., ch. X, p. 13.

466. Scott, Government Documents..., ch. X, pp. 13-15, 21.

467. Wall Street Journal, Feb. 23, 1977.

468. FIB, Inc. Annual Reports, 1977-79.

469. Julius Mader, *Who's Who in CIA*, (Berlin: Self-published, 1968), p. 420.

470. FIB, Inc. Annual Reports, 1977-79.

471. Scott, Government Documents..., ch. X, p. 15.

472. Scott, Government Documents..., ch. X, p. 16.

473. Scott, Government Documents..., ch. X, pp. 16-17.

474. Scott, *The Dallas Conspiracy*, ch. II, pp. 21-22.

475 . Scott, Government Documents..., ch. X, p. 18.

476. Scott, Government Documents..., ch. X, p. 20.

477. Scott, Government Documents..., ch. X, p. 18, 19.

478. New York Times, Apr. 17, 1964, p. 1, Apr. 19, 1964, p. 82, cited in Scott, Government Documents..., ch. X, p. 13.

479. Scott, *The Dallas Conspiracy*, ch. III, p. 15.

PART FOUR

Smiths, Wings, and Ramblers

As mentioned earlier, a major link between the UT Rambler, the mutilated books, and the JFK assassination is the story of Miami Rambler eyewitness Michael Kensington. In his September 1992 Third Decade article he stated that the Dealey Plaza Rambler was "the same make and model as ours, and a similar car was seen often in the driveway of the CIA's Cuban exile safehouse in Miami [known as Hernando's Hideaway]."[480] When he first saw the car, Kensington did a "double-take" thinking his father had come home too early.[481]

He then wrote about the Loran Eugene Hall story (subject of missing pages) because it is the subject of an FBI report (CD 1179) on which there is an address that is about half a mile from Hernando's Hideaway. The address on the FBI report is also "only a mile or so from the Central Shopping center where del Valle met his untimely demise." Kensington and his father reportedly overheard an assassination plot against President Kennedy at Hernando's Hideaway days prior to November 22, 1963.[482]

In December 1992, Michael Kensington was shown two color slides of Wing's Rambler. As anyone who has seen the slides can attest, the color of the car is nondescript. There are three significant results from Kensington's comparison of George Wing's car to the one he saw:

First, the colors match. Kensington said he could not make out the hue in the slides of Wing's Rambler but stated that his father's car was "Pepto-Bismol" colored, or light-pink, as was the Hernando's Hideaway Rambler. That is the color, although faded, of George Wing's Rambler station wagon.[483]

Second, Kensington could not have done his double-take prior to 1959. His family bought their 1956 Rambler in 1959. When he stated this he did not yet know Wing's car is a 1959.

Third, there is a visual similarity to the 1950s styling. Upon comparison of the pertinent body styles Kensington determined he could not have confused a 1960, 1961 or 1962 model with their family's 1956 Rambler. Therefore the car he saw could not have been later than a 1959. And although Kensington could not rule out the 1958 model, the possibilities are substantially narrowed.[484]

Kensington looked up Rambler styles and determined that the pronounced rear fins he remembers are on both the 1958 and 1959 models. The 1960 and 1961 models had much less pronounced "shark fins". He remembers doing his double-take near the end of the ownership of their 1956 Rambler. His father sold it when they bought a 1960 Corvair in 1961 or 1962, according to one of his parents. Kensington added that he was not a teenager in 1959 but he was a teen when he did the double-take. This means that a 1959 Rambler cannot be ruled out based on the timing of Kensintgton's observations. Only if he had done his double-take prior to the fall of 1958 would it rule out Wing's car. Kensington also said he was interested in C.B. Smith's possible Jules Dubois connection because it was David Salvador, a friend of Dubois, who started the 30th of November movement.[485] The significance of this connection requires a detailed look at Cecil Bernard Smith, Sr. George's widow, Lucila Lopez Wing, believes the car was C.B. Smith's personal automobile and not just a car from his used car lot.[486] Even if Smith was the original owner of the car he had enough right-wing, military-industrial, LBJ, and Latin American connections to make his ownership important.

If Lucila Wing is correct, the car's owner could still have been either C.B. Smith, Sr. or his son, C.B. Smith, Jr. It is much more likely that it was the elder Smith's car, however, since Rambler reportedly went out of business because of their inability to appeal to younger drivers. It is also known that Smith, Jr. had a preference for Porches, making it unlikely he would own a Rambler wagon.[487]

Smith, Jr. was sales manager of C.B. Smith Motors by October, 1964. The son's ownership of the car would not make much difference with regard to links to the assassination since Smith, Sr. still owned the dealership as late as 1967 and his son (born 1923) was more military than his father. Smith, Jr. was a dive bomber pilot when he was a Marine Air Corps first lieutenant in the Pacific during World War II. In Korea he was promoted to captain and served with the First Marine Division.[488]

C.B. Smith, Sr., was born in West, Texas, to a farm and ranching family, and graduated from Rotan high school in 1920. He was a captain in the College Cadet Corps at Grubbs Vocational College from 1920-22 (Grubbs became the University of Texas at Arlington which named Smith an outstanding alumnus in 1967 -- mentioned earlier in reference to de Mohrenschildt). He didn't do anything else militarily until World War II when he was Chairman of the United States-Canadian War Production Committee and served with the Chief of Staff, Army Ordinance, in Washington and Detroit, as Director of Tools and Equipment.[489]

It would be interesting to learn, though, the nature of his work just prior to the war. After Grubbs, Smith, Sr. got his BA and MA at the University of Texas at Austin where he continued to be quite a frat, scholar and athlete until 1928. He then became athletic director and professor of government at Houston Junior College (now the University of Houston). While in Houston he considered joining the diplomatic corps but opted to join the Universal Credit Company instead, spending two years with that organization in Mexico.[490] Could that have been some kind of intelligence work?

After the war Smith, Sr. spent ten years with the Chevrolet Division of General Motors (GM) as an executive in Detroit, Chicago, Minneapolis and Houston. This raises the question of whether Smith, with his intense interest in Latin American politics, ever became associated with Amadeo Barletta.

Barletta was a director of Cuban-Venezuelan Oil Voting Trust (CVOVT), the company started by George de Mohrenschildt and former Pantipec Oil president, Warren Smith (Canfield and Webberman, Coup de Etat in America). Barletta was also the Cuban representative of General Motors and a close associate of Batista and Trujillo. Pantipec Oil was owned by William F. Buckley, Jr.'s parents.[491] De Mohrenschildt, in what had to have been one of his first jobs upon graduating from UT, worked at Pantipec under Warren W. Smith in 1945. The question of a possible family relationship between C.B. Smith and Warren Smith should also be a focus of future research.

If C.B. Smith knew Barletta it would not only be a link to de Mohrenschildt but to another director of his company, Jose M. Bosch Lamarque. Bosch Lamarque supported Castro then turned against him in 1959. He was Castro's chief contact with Jules Dubois, a journalist and Army intelligence vet who helped engineer the Guatemala coup in 1954. Dubois' old underground contract, David Salvador, founded the anti-communist 30th of November Movement. A Cuban, identified by the Secret Service as belonging to 30th of November, said during an arms deal on November 21, 1963 that the financial backers of his group would soon "take care of Kennedy."[492]

A national 30th of November leader, Jesus Fernandez Hernandez, was the resident, in 1962 and 1963, of Hernando's Hideaway. He was leasing the house from the Keys Realty Company. Rolando Cubella's co-plotter in the AM/LASH plot was Eugenio Rolando Martinez, the owner of the CIA front, Keys Realty, which owned Hernando's Hideaway where Kensington witnessed the Rambler similar to George Gordon Wing's. Martinez was also the skipper of the Collins Radio ship Rex during its ill-fated raid on Cuba in late October 1963 -- a fact attributed to Frank Sturgis by Peter Dale Scott in Crime and Cover-Up. Scott adds that Sturgis was probably involved with this raid as well. Sturgis was a long-time associate of Eugenio Martinez.[493]

Bosch Lamarque was an original supporter of Carlos Bringuier's Directorial Revolucionario Estudiantil (DRE) and Alpha 66 which was linked to three attempts on Castro including the attempt involving the Odios.494 DRE and Alpha 66 grew out of the group originally funded by Bosch Lamarque, and DRE had overlapping goals and personnel with 30th of November.495 It is therefore probable that de Mohrenschildt's fellow oil company employee Bosch Lamarque was one of the financial backers who would soon "take care of Kennedy."

Yet another director of CVOVT, Jose I. de la Camara, was an employee of Augustin Batista Falla's Trust Company of Cuba. The Batista Falla family was behind the Lake Pontchartrain training camp where Loran Hall and Gerry Patrick Hemming were training Cuban exiles.[496] Bringuier accused Oswald of attempting to infiltrate this very camp after Oswald allegedly went there with David Ferrie.[497] And of course Hall and Hemming bring us full circle back to Hernando's Hideaway. The FBI report, which Michael Kensington wrote about (CD 1179) links Hall and Hemming to Dick Whatley, a former Brigade 2506 trainer in Guatemala, whose address on that report was near Hernando's Hideaway. Also, according to Marita Lorenz, Hemming was among those who left from a Miami safehouse and drove to Dallas in a station wagon to kill Kennedy.[498]

Aside from the fact that these people were primary players in Second Naval Guerrilla and the false stories about Oswald (subjects of missing pages), these associations would sufficiently link Smith to the conspirators and go a long way toward proving this car to be the infamous Hernando's Hideaway/Dealey Plaza Rambler. The possibility that C.B. Smith did not know this Cuban GM representative, during a time when even the average American was riveted by the events in Cuba, would be incredible.

More direct links between C.B. Smith, Warren W. Smith, and George de Mohrenschildt are also likely. Although older, William F. Buckley, Sr., like Smith, had resided at UT's very fraternal upperclassmen dormitory, "Old B Hall." By the time C.B. Smith was at UT (1922), Buckley had been expelled from Mexico for his counterrevolutionary activities (no doubt in league with Allen Dulles' uncle, Robert Lansing) and had begun lecturing on Mexican politics.[499] During his years at UT, C.B. Smith "was a member of the Friar's Senior Honor Society; president of the International Relations Society, President of Student Graduate School, Pi Sigma Alpha Honorary Government Society; Manager, University Men's Dormitory." Smith was an avid student of Southwest and Latin American history and government and after graduating remained a "great friend and admirer of Walter Prescott Webb," his professor of Southwestern history. Smith also spent "as much time as possible in research on these subjects."[500] It is therefore likely that Smith and Buckley came to share their mutual interests in UT and Mexico long before 1963. The question of a family relationship between C.B. Smith and Warren Smith should also be a focus of future research.

In addition to Smith's former ownership of the Rambler station wagon, several questions remain concerning its ownership prior to Smith, and during George Wing's ownership. Two questions to be answered are: who, if anyone, owned the car prior to C.B. Smith?; and to whom was the "turista" sticker registered in 1964?

The first question is important because Oswald was under the impression that he left Dealey Plaza in "Mrs. Paine's" station wagon. If, as indicated by Navy Department documents, Ruth Paine knew Oswald as early as 1957[501] then it could be that the Paines originally owned the car and sold it to Smith who in turn sold it to Wing in an attempt to "launder" the car.

While we do not know when or from whom Smith bought the car, we do know he "delivered" the car to Wing on April 26, 1963 (this date was on a warranty card in the glove compartment). This was possibly a very significant time in the conspiracy.

On April 24, Marina moved in with Ruth Paine, and Oswald left for New Orleans. On April 25, Oswald arrived in New Orleans to begin his infamous summer there. And before any of these things happened, LBJ arrived at Love Field shortly before noon on Tuesday, April 23, for a busy day of two luncheons, two private conferences at both Dallas newspapers' offices, a large banquet, and an address to a meeting of scientists. During the one-hour conference at the Dallas Times Herald, he said that Kennedy may visit Dallas "on a one-day visit to Texas in the near future." According to some news accounts, Johnson referred to Kennedy using the analogy of a pilot. He reportedly told the press not to shoot Kennedy down now but wait until his visit to shoot him down.[502] It sounds like a "go" signal.

The second question is about the turista sticker. It will be difficult to answer but it is still important. Either Wing took the car to Mexico or someone else did. If Wing made the trip it was either a vacation or UT business. Both of these reasons can be verified through Wing's UT personnel records. If there is no record of Wing being away from UT during that period then things get strange again. If someone else took the car, who was it? Did Wing let him use the car or was it stolen (and was it reported stolen)? Did the borrower or thief have any links to the assassination?

Unfortunately the most detailed information we have on Wing, aside from photographs of a most interesting montage on his office door, comes from his obituary:

> Mr. George Gordon Wing, born August 31, 1922, in Philadelphia, Pennsylvania, died at his home in Austin on Thursday, December 19, 1991.
> He was preceded in death by his father, George Wing, his mother, Geraldine Gordon Wing, and his brother William.
> He served in the United States Navy during World War II. He graduated from Temple University in Philadelphia, attended Mexico City College and received a doctorate from the University of California at Berkeley.
> He was a professor in the Department of Spanish and Portuguese at the University of Texas at Austin from 1962 to the time of his death.
> He is survived by his wife, Lucila Lopez Wing and her four children, Adriana Rodriguez Conchola, Esteban Rodriguez, Carlos Rodriguez, and Sergio Rodriguez, and by a nephew and a niece from Philadelphia, Terence Wing and Susan Wing.
> A memorial mass will be held on Tuesday, December 24 at 10:00 AM, at the University Catholic Student Center.
> Services under the direction of the Angel Funeral Home, 1811 South Congress Avenue, 441- 9738.

Other known pieces of significant personal information are his Social Security number, 187-18-5710; his UT employee number, 96139; and his 1972 Texas Driver's License index number, 2398458. We know that in 1963 he lived at 717 Landon Lane, Austin, Texas. From as early as September 13, 1967 to as late as June 6, 1977 he lived at 2102 Marquette Lane, Austin, Texas (phone: GL-27210). And as early as October 30, 1982 he lived at 2102 Robinhood (phone: 476-1630). In 1966 his license plate number was BGS839; in 1967 it was BTD307; in 1971 it was BJY237; in 1972 it was BKN46; in 1975 it was BKN973; and in 1977 it was AGQ821. The mileage on the car on September 1, 1966 was 68162; on September 13, 1967 it was 73525; and on February 19, 1975 it was 79930. Finally, his insurance agent at one time was "M.E. Luper, State Farm Insurance Co's, Tex. Pub. Employees Assoc. Bldg., 311 East 14th Street, Austin 1, Texas, Ph. GR 8-8545."

The final coincidences of his life were that he died the day the movie *JFK* premiered. And his funeral was at the "Angel" Funeral Home. (This latter coincidence will become apparent in this paper.) In addition, it is recalled that Philadelphia is the hometown of Frank Fiorini Sturgis and is near Pittsburgh, hometown of the Mannarino brothers -- all subjects of missing pages.

A page of biographical information included with Wing's 1961 doctoral dissertation states that he was at Mexico City College from 1949 to 1950. The next listing puts him at the University of California beginning in 1952. This two-year gap following his stay at Mexico City College is intriguing for several reasons. 1950 was the year Hunt hired Buckley to work with him at the CIA's Mexico City station. Hunt hired him because, as he recalled, "I knew the student situation in Mexico City was crying out for some corrective attention, and I thought here was a young man just out of college. I was going to be in the embassy myself, and I needed somebody on the outside who could make contacts and deal with the younger people." Besides Wing, another student who was reportedly at Mexico City College in 1950 was Fidel Castro.[503]

Military personnel records of George Wing's Naval career include a photograph taken of Wing in the early 1940s. All of the facial features closely resemble those of the "turtleneck" man in the missing photo from The Fish is Red. It is inconclusive however since neither it nor the reproduction of the St. George photo show his left ear's anatomy with sufficient clarity.[504]

[OBJ]Wing's service record was the first document found which linked Wing to Florida. Also intriguing is Wing's heavy involvement with ordnance (weapons, ammunition, combat vehicles, tools and equipment) and naval aviation. During World War II, C.B. Smith served as Director of Tools and Equipment for the Chief of Staff, Army Ordnance. In 1940 D.H. Byrd made a successful bid for the location of Hensley Field, U.S. Naval Air Base in Grand Prairie, Texas, near Dallas.

In July 1962, while he was Secretary of the Navy, Fred Korth awarded Byrd a plaque calling him a "Long- time friend of the Navy -- and particularly of Naval aviation..." for his role with Hensley field and for supporting the expeditions of his cousin Rear Admiral Richard E. Byrd, a pioneer of naval aviation.[505]

It is rumored Wing was not tenured despite his being an associate professor. Dr. Wing, who earned a Bachelor of Science from Temple University in Philadelphia in 1949 and a Ph.D. at the University of California at Berkeley in 1961, was a specialist in Latin American literature for almost thirty years at UT. This is unusual for two reasons. First, it is extremely rare in academia to be anywhere that long without tenure.

Second, Wing has apparently published very little. The following articles are all that have been located by this paper's researchers: "Trilce I: A Second Look," (Austin, TX: ILAS, 1972); "Octavio Paz: Or The Revolution in Search of an Actor," (Austin, TX: ILAS, 1973); "Some Remarks on the Literary Criticism of Carlos Fuentes," (in Rob Brody with Charles Roseman [eds.] Carlos Fuentes: A Critical View, The University of Texas Press, 1982, pp. 200-215); "A Gallery of Women in Carlos Fuentes's *Cantar de ciegos*," (in Review of Contemporary Fiction, Vol. 8, Summer 1988, pp. 217-224); and his 1961 doctoral dissertation, *Octavio Paz: Poetry, Politics, and the Myth of the Mexican*. It thus appears Wing violated the "publish or perish" rule.

An associate who had worked with Wing considered him to be a "very weird person." She said that during the period she worked with him he drank heavily and wore disheveled clothing. She also spoke negatively about his personal hygiene.[506] In a similar description, Chuck Bradshaw, described Wing as "an odd fellow."[507] Bradshaw is a former employee of C.B. Smith, Sr. who also knew George Wing. His observations about Smith will be discussed further.

John Wheat, a former student of George Wing's, found Wing to be very intelligent and to have a sarcastic wit. He said Wing would stand under a "no smoking" sign, light up a cigarette, and make a point about literature. He was never cruel, John said, but he enjoyed playing around.

John said Wing was primarily interested in the psychological and political aspects of literature. That is also evident from Wing's scarce writings. John said Wing was liberal and progressive much in the same way as Carlos Fuentes and Gabriel Garcia Marquez. On the subject of tenure, John said that Wing must have been tenured because it comes with being an associate professor.[508]

In his writings, Wing comes across as an intelligent and insightful literary critic. Former students have described him as politically to the left. One former student said he was "obsessed with Pablo Neruda." In the first posthumous anthology of the work of this Nobel Prize winning Argentine poet, editor and translator Ben Belitt described Neruda as prophetic, adding, "The vision of things to come -- as cancer, as coup d'état, as assassination -- is there." In this same volume, *Pablo Neruda, Five Decades: A Selection* (Poems: 1925-1970), is a poem entitled The United Fruit Company.[509]

On October 28, 1992, researcher John Garcia had a short conversation with UT Spanish professor Miguel Gonzalez-Gerth (the close friend of Harry Ransom) about the late George Gordon Wing. Gonzalez-Gerth said he thinks Wing came to UT in 1960-61 (actually Wing began teaching at UT in the fall of 1962). John asked if it is possible that Wing was involved with Cuban exiles in Florida. Gonzalez-Gerth said Wing was very progressive and involved in civil rights. He said he did not think Wing would have had much to do with right-wing anti-Castro Cubans. Finally, Gonzalez-Gerth said, "What if all this time the George Wing that we knew was disguised?" Gonzalez-Gerth was in a hurry to get to his office and the conversation rested there.[510]

[OBJ][OBJ][OBJ][OBJ][OBJ][OBJ][OBJ]This conversation took place on the elevator at the Harry Ransom Humanities Research Center. While talking to Gonzalez-Gerth, Garcia had an odd sense that Gonzalez-Gerth and Wing had not been very close. The tone was that Gonzalez-Gerth had not known Wing that intimately.

Auto records kept by George Wing during his lifetime reveal that R.L. Lewis, a salesman at C.B. Smith Motors, handled the sale of the Rambler from Smith to Wing. It was learned that Lewis died of a heart attack on January 11, 1964.[511] This was only seven weeks after the assassination.

Wilma Johnson of Manor, Texas, the former office manager at C.B. Smith Motors, said that all the old records were lost in "the flood." She said they had been stored down on Lamar. She was referring to the Memorial Day Flood of 1981 which severely damaged businesses along Lamar Blvd. from about twelfth street down to the river. The auto dealerships at Sixth Street and Lamar were especially hard hit since they are right next to Shoal Creek.512 Other records still to be sought are those for P.K. Williams Rambler, Austin's dealership at the time, to see if Smith bought the car there and whether or not it was bought new.[513]

Chuck Bradshaw, born 1937, became C.B. Smith, Sr.'s garage manager in 1962. Chuck told a story about how he and C.B. Smith, Jr., who became his father's sales manager, built three racing cars in Smith's shop while Smith, Sr. was in Japan for a year partly to see the Olympics. Upon his return, Smith, who was not a race car enthusiast, ordered Chuck to get rid of the cars immediately.[514] The XVIII Summer Games were held in Tokyo October 10 to 24, 1964. In light of D.H. Byrd's late 1963 hunting trip, it is noteworthy that Smith left on his year-long trip to Japan one year prior to the Olympics and returned in late October 1964 - - one month after the Warren Commission Report was issued. The U.S. and Japan did not have an extradition treaty in effect at that time, as the current treaty began in 1980.[515]

C.B. Smith, Sr. always drove Chryslers, according to Bradshaw, and Smith, Jr. always drove Porsches. Chuck said that Smith Jr.'s son David is a helicopter pilot. He also said that Smith was so tight with money "He could take a nickel and squeeze a dime out of it." Smith owned only three suits, black, brown, and blue.[516]

Despite his frugality, Smith financially supported Lyndon Johnson's campaigns. When asked about this Chuck said, "Oh yes, C.B. Smith and Johnson were very close. We would often hear him on the phone with Lady Bird." Chuck said one of C.B. Smith Motors' Christmas parties (he thinks 1965) was held at the LBJ Ranch. One of Chuck's mechanics got drunk at this party and shot Smith's van full of holes with a shotgun.[517]

Smith, Jr. took over the business, according to Chuck, around 1968, about the time Chuck left, and sold it to Chuck Nash's Pontiac dealership in the 1970s. Bradshaw described Smith, Sr. as "military" in the way he ran his business with a clear chain of command.[518]

These bits of personal information about Smith and Wing have proven and may continue to prove useful in analyzing the missing pages. The more that is learned about these men and about the assassination, the more intertwined they seem to become.

Red Ripper Reprise

In Dick Russell's book *The Man Who Knew Too Much*, many names, places, dates, events, and themes are identical to the same information that reoccurs throughout missing pages in all of the mutilated books, including the Odio incident; false stories planted about Oswald in Mexico City and their cover-up by CIA; Oswald's leafleting in New Orleans; the raid on the Lake Pontchartrain camp; John Martino; Loran Eugene Hall; Rolando Cubela and the AM/LASH plot; Manuel Artime; Carlos Bringuier; Santos Trafficante; Little Havana, Miami; JFK's secret negotiations with Castro; September 1963; Alpha 66; and the Cuban Freedom Committee.

Of interest from Russell's references to "Angel" are the following: "Of Angel, Nagell wrote to Fensterwald in 1975: `A friend out here, formerly connected with Alpha 66, advises that an Angel was apprehended in Cuba while on ice, possibly in 1965 or 1966. This Angel was found in possession of .45 calibre ammunition containing (?) or coated with cyanide....He is said to have copped out that he and several cohorts were on a CIA-sponsored mission to assassinate Fidel.'

"In 1984, Nagell hinted to me that Angel might have been among forty-eight political prisoners released by Castro that June, in what was termed by the Cuban premier as a `personal gesture' triggered by a visit from Jesse Jackson."[519]

This indicates that Angel could not be Wing. The thought was entertained because a "war name" is, in many cases, a whimsical reference to one's real name. George Wing's only UT yearbook photos appear in the Cactus Yearbook for 1964 (p. 48) and 1967 (p. 549).

A list of the forty-eight former prisoners, however, might reveal a name of someone currently suspected of being Angel and a check could be made for associations to Wing; especially since the yearbook photos do not rule out the possibility that the St. George photo in *The Fish is Red* is Wing.

"Nagell has said that he `complained' to Desmond FitzGerald on August 27, 1963, apparently about the Oswald-related operation having gone out of control." This date is one day before Wing put new tires on the Rambler, and in the same time frame that Oswald visited Ruby's friend Robert Ray McKeown in Bay Cliff, Texas; having been driven there by "Hernandez" in a "light-colored car."[520]

As discussed earlier, Watergate burglar Bernard Barker has admitted, as has Frank Sturgis, to being close to Carlos Prio Socarras, the wealthy financier of Cuban exile activities. Prio Socarras was once arrested in a gun-running conspiracy with Robert Ray McKeown. McKeown had been involved with Jack Ruby in "running jeeps to Cuba" and other smuggling schemes. The point of these relationships in connection with McKeown's "light-colored car" is that Barker was the man identified by Deputy Constable Seymour Weitzman as one of the fake Secret Service agents in Dealey Plaza. Another fake Secret Service man, identified by Roger Craig as Edgar Eugene Bradley, only made a note of Craig's description of the Rambler - - not the men who were escaping in it. It is possible, as we will see, that C.B. Smith was also in contact with Prio Socarras and his gun-running activities through a fellow Texan and financial supporter of LBJ.

As with the story of the arrest and release of the Rambler driver in Dealey Plaza, this story of "Bay Cliff, Texas" should be double-checked by researchers. A search for "Bay Cliff" using maps adapted from the county maps issued by the Texas Department of Highways and Public Transportation and prepared by the Texas A & M University Cartographics Laboratory, reveal no such city. There are the cities of Bacliff, Bay City, Bayside, Baytown, and Bayview, all in far South Texas, not between Dallas and Houston where Dick Russell said Bay Cliff is supposed to be.[521]

Most likely the correct city is Bacliff, just south of Houston off of Interstate Highway 45 which runs between Dallas and Houston. It is also near Beaumont, where Ruby's other gun-running associate, Thomas Eli Davis III, lived. Author Henry Hurt says that Beaumont is "not far from where McKeown had his headquarters." Making matters worse, reporter and author Seth Kantor (whom Hurt cites) places McKeown in "Bashore, Texas" -- another non-existent town.[522] If this geography lesson seems a bit trivial, it will become more important when we discuss an incident in another Texas town that took place around the same time. If the two incidents are related, the traveling required could have been the motivation behind putting new tires on Wing's Rambler on August 28, 1963.

Russell points out that "[Victor Espinosa] Hernandez -- identified only as `A' in the congressional investigation's reports -- was involved `with anti-Castro exiles and underworld figures who were operating the guerrilla training camp in New Orleans in July, 1963,' according to CIA files. [He] purchased twenty-four hundred pounds of dynamite and twenty bomb casings meant to be dropped on Cuban targets. His contact was Richard Lauchli, a co-founder of the paramilitary Minutemen group.[523] After Hernandez transported the matériel to the New Orleans camp, it was seized on July 31, 1963 in an FBI raid. Hernandez, Lauchli, and nine other men were temporarily detained." The raid on the Lake Pontchartrain camp and specifically the story of "A" are subjects of many missing pages in the mutilated copies of *Crime and Cover-Up* and *The Fish is Red*.

It is essential to note here, in thinking about the Rambler, that Victor Espinosa Hernandez was a lifelong friend of Rolando Cubela and that Cubella's co-plotter in the AM/LASH plot was Eugenio Rolando Martinez, the owner of the CIA front, Keys Realty Company, which owned Hernando's Hideaway where Kensington witnessed the Rambler similar to George Gordon Wing's.

Martinez was also the skipper of the Collins Radio ship Rex during its ill-fated raid on Cuba in late October 1963 -- a fact attributed to Frank Sturgis by Peter Dale Scott in *Crime and Cover-Up*. Scott adds that Sturgis was probably involved with this raid as well. Sturgis was a long-time associate of Eugenio Martinez.[524]

Robert Sam Anson, in his book, *They've Killed the President!*, uses the Rex as an example of a violation of Kennedy's warning to six Americans to stop their anti-Castro activities -- namely Sturgis. The above information was a specific target for censorship (or discovery) in these mutilated books.

However, in the most mutilated book found to date, *The Fish is Red*, the entire story of the Rex survived. The only difference between it and the accounts in Scott and Anson is Hinckle/Turner's failure to mention the roles of Martinez and Sturgis[525] -- roles that link them to Collins Radio and ultimately to de Mohrenschildt, Oswald, and D.H. Byrd.

In bringing to a full circle the McKeown story, the missing pages mystery, the many UT connections to the assassination, and Mike Kensington's near identification of George Wing's Rambler, it is of interest that some researchers are looking for a man named Hernandez in their search for "Angel."

One suspect is Jesus Fernandez Hernandez, the Cuban who was leasing Hernando's Hideaway from Eugenio Martinez in 1962 and 1963. However, considering the coincidences seen in the combined discoveries of Wing's car and the mutilated books, another candidate is Victor Espinosa Hernandez. Completing the circle could depend on the declassification of the only classified document in the three boxes comprising Lyndon Johnson's pre-presidential office diary.

The only known information about what is contained in this document is its description on the pink "removed" form filed chronologically in its place. This pink form shows that the document is a Secret Service report about an incident in Graham, Texas on August 31, 1963 and that the report was given to LBJ's aid Walter Jenkins.

This date is within the time frame of Oswald's visit to McKeown in a light-colored car driven by "Hernandez," four days after Nagell's report to Desmond FitzGerald about the Oswald-related operation having gone out of control, and three days after George Wing put two new tires on his Rambler.[526] Records exist of several tire purchase dates, including August 28, 1963, (2 tires/27 mo. guarantee), and November 20, 1964, (2 tires/30 mo. guarantee).[527] They place the Rambler in Austin on these dates.

Graham, Texas is in the southeast corner of Lee County, just west of Fort Worth. It is a fairly direct route between Graham and Bacliff -- a trip that could be made in a day. Thus the earlier of the two dates may be significant with regard to an anti-Castro Cuban/ Minuteman/ Oswald/Ruby connection discovered by Warren Commission attorneys Hubert and Griffin but not investigated by the FBI or CIA. It involves Robert Ray McKeown and the fact that Ruby associate Bertha Cheek was the sister of Earlene Roberts, the housekeeper at Oswald's rooming house. The Hubert/Griffin leads will be discussed further in this paper.

A declassification request was filed for this Secret Service report on November 21, 1991. On Oct. 21, 1992, it was learned that declassification requests are sent to the agency where they originated for approval and that it is not unusual for the process to take as long as two years. However, it is likely that one other person will make the final decision: the man who watches over the research and researchers in the LBJ Library reading room and who compiled Johnson's national security file at the Library, Walt Whitman Rostow.

Considering the possible importance of missing pages subject "A" to the McKeown affair, a check was made of the other missing pages for McKeown. The following was found:

[OBJ]*Crime and Cover-Up* (p. 44): Here Scott discusses links between Ruby, Roselli, and Ramsey Clark. "One of Ruby's...`close personal friends' and character witnesses for his liquor license was Hal Collins (22 H 928), brother-in-law of prominent local attorney Robert L. Clark, the brother and uncle respectively of U.S. Attorneys General Tom and Ramsey Clark (CD 4.371)....Robert L. Clark and his law partner Maury Hughes... arranged the...parole in 1947 of John Roselli....It is probably irrelevant that Robert Clark also served as general counsel for an airline originally organized in part by Houston syndicate pay-off connection Jack Harold Halfen, who channeled money from the Dallas-Chicago mob's slot machines in Houston to Texas politicians as high (he claimed) as Lyndon Johnson. But Halfen also `smuggled guns and surplus American bombers to Fidel Castro,' in a deal which apparently involved Carlos Prio Socarras and his Texas associate, Ruby's Cuban business contact, Robert R. McKeown."

In another possible example of purpose behind the mutilations, two McKeown pages in Anson survived (239-40). Anson discusses McKeown's gun running to Castro, Ruby seeking McKeown's help in a sale of surplus Jeeps to Castro, and Ruby seeking McKeown's help in getting three people out of Cuba. This standard McKeown-Ruby story, devoid of details, survived. However, it seems the "irrelevant" McKeown- Prio-Halfen-Houston-LBJ-Clark-Roselli links had to disappear.

LBJ's financial supporters Halfen and C.B. Smith both had experience in military ordnance and shared an interest in Cuba. Could Smith have been involved with Halfen and McKeown in Cuban gun running? If so, it would be a Smith-Ruby link reminiscent of the possible Carousel Club link of Smith's friend Harry Ransom. Leon Hubert, the Warren Commission's attorney in charge of investigating Ruby, found significance in "Ruby's admission that in 1959 he was interested in selling jeeps to Cuba and other reports that persons interested in Cuban arms sales were responsible for the assassination of President Kennedy."[528]

George Michael Evica writes about memoranda written by Leon Hubert and Bert Griffin indicating they were investigating an anti-Castro

Cuban/Minutemen/Oswald/Ruby connection. It says, "We have...suggested the theory that Ruby and Mrs. [Bertha] Cheek could have been involved in Cuban arms sales of which Oswald gained knowledge through his efforts to infiltrate the anti-Castro Cubans."[529] Mrs. Cheek was the sister of Earlene Roberts, housekeeper at 1026 N. Beckley, where Oswald was living at the time of the assassination.[530]

The CIA and FBI failed to follow up on these leads. They seem to corroborate the McKeown-Hernandez- Lauchli-Oswald connection and the Ruby-Periera-Magnolia-Paine connection. Given those connections, the Hubert/Griffin leads may still trace back to the Dealey Plaza Rambler in a way that substantiates the possibility that the light-colored car used for Oswald's visit to McKeown was that very Rambler station wagon. That possibility involves the fundamental question of how Oswald could claim that the Rambler "belongs" to Ruth Paine when she apparently did not own such a car.

Earlier in this paper, it was mentioned that Bert Sugar and Sybil Leek apparently had information that Paine borrowed a car similar to the one seen in Dealey Plaza. What was not mentioned, however, was that they claimed she "sometimes borrowed" the car from Jack Ruby.[531] Whatever the vices of Sugar's and Leek's book, to make a claim that Ruth Paine borrowed anything from Jack Ruby must be based on something. If they invented the claim out of nothing it is certainly odd that a possible Ruby-Oswald-Paine link through Bertha Cheek and her sister Earlene Roberts seems to corroborate it. If true, this is the second possible Paine-Ruby link after the Paine-Magnolia-Periera-Ruby connection.

There is also a third scenario which, as we have seen, brings together the Miami Rambler, the Dealey Plaza Rambler, Wing's Rambler, Ruth Paine, Jack Ruby, and Oswald. In his manuscript, Peter Dale Scott mentions Jesus Fernandez Hernandez, the leaseholder of Hernando's Hideaway. He says he is a leader of the "30th of November Movement (founded by Dubois' old underground contact David Salvador)...."[532] That is why Kensington found the possible connection between C.B. Smith and Jules Dubois interesting.

Jose M. Bosch Lamarque, the director of de Mohrenschildt's Cuban-Venezuelan Oil Trust, was Castro's chief contact with Dubois.[533] Bosch Lamarque, Barletta, and de la Camara (all on de Mohrenschildt's board) are collectively tied to the Castro assassination attempt involving the Odios, General Motors, Batista, Trujillo, and the Lake Pontchartrain training camp -- the camp where Bringuier, Hall, Hemming, Victor Espinosa Hernandez ("A"), and Lauchli are all tied together.

Scott's research ties all of this to Marina's interrogators, the Abwehr,

Reinhard Gehlen, the Paines, General Walker, Operation Second Naval Guerrilla, the false Oswald stories (specifically "D"), Martino, Weyl, Andrew St. George, Haiti, DIA, Vietnam withdrawal, Charles Willoughby, the Minutemen, Dudley Dougherty, the Hunts, and Pennsylvania[534] -- the home state of Frank Sturgis, the Mannarino brothers, and George Wing.

Furthermore, before Batista's fall at the hands of Castro, DeGolyer and MacNaughton had been active exploring for oil in Cuba, on behalf of a closely linked company which later (as Panoil) had Jack Alston Crichton as director. De Mohrenschildt's Cuban-Venezuelan Oil Voting Trust, an "interlocking" company with DeGolyer and MacNaughton, also explored in Cuba at this time.[535] DeGolyer and MacNaughton advised Harry Ransom's university about its most important asset -- oil.[536]

Crichton, head of a local Army Intelligence Unit, former employee of DeGolyer and MacNaughton,[537] and trustee of the H.L. Hunt Foundation,[538] had D.H. Byrd as a director of his own company,[539] arranged for Marina Oswald to have his, George Bouhe's and Ruth Paine's friend Ilya Mamantov as her interpreter,[540] had worked under Warren Smith at Pantipec,[541] and was John Connally's Republican opponent in the 1964 governor's race.[542]

Mamantov (the mutual friend of Paine, Crichton and de Mohrenschildt),[543] from whom Schmidt, Pierce, and Fredricksen were taking scientific Russian classes at Magnolia Laboratories,544 co-founded the CIA-backed St. Nicholas Parish,[545] which had as a financial patron former deGolyer associate Paul Raigorodsky, who belonged to the elite Tryall Golf Club retreat in Jamaica with Michael Paine's cousin Alexander "Sandy" Forbes, a former director of United fruit.[546]

All of these connections together account for the Rambler, the missing pages, Bancroft, Burris, Byrd, Ransom, Angel, and Leopoldo. Are the Rambler and C.B. Smith tied to Hernando's Hideaway through de Mohrenschildt's Cuban Oil Trust? Are the Rambler and Wing tied to Angel (a.k.a. Hernandez?) through the St. George photo in The Fish is Red and the fact that the Esquire magazine displayed most prominently in Wing's back seat was the August 1963 issue -- the month the "Oswald operation" went out of control, and possibly the month Oswald was driven to McKeown's by "Hernandez"?

A reference to *The Fish is Red* in *JFK: The Book of the Film* led to more insights into these questions:

"H.L. Hunt backs anti-Castro Cubans [Hinkle and Turner, The Fish Is Red, P. 202]. Hunt voices his concerns about the threat of a Kennedy dynasty in a July 11, 1963 letter to Senator Harry Byrd: `The stake is the entire future of the nation' [Letter to Senator Byrd, Box 270, Byrd

Papers, University of Virginia Library].

Hunt is trying to persuade Southern Democrats to switch affiliation to the Republican Party."[547]

Page 202 *of The Fish Is Red* is not a missing page but pages 203 through 206 were removed. On page 202, as discussed earlier, Hinkle and Turner raise the question of where Orlando Bosch got the massive funding he needed to continue his raids on Cuba after splitting from the CIA. Bosch rebelled against U.S. government backing in 1963 after an FBI informant foiled his Violynn III raid (involving Sturgis, Rorke, and the Minutemen) and brought twin FBI raids against his Florida airfield and Lake Pontchartrain training camp.

The answer to the funding question came when "During a 1968 trial of Bosch's group in Miami, a telephone tape transcript was introduced in which Bosch indicated that a Mr. Hunt -- `the one with the wells' -- was providing backing."

Page 202 also ties Bosch to the Rorke/Sullivan flight in a discussion that is continued on missing page 203. Allowed to remain is the fact that Rorke was an early associate of Bosch. Deleted was the fact that Rorke was once an FBI employee and may have been suspected by Bosch of being the informer who tipped the FBI about the Violynn III mission, the bombing run from the Florida airstrip, and the bomb cache at Lake Pontchartrain; a suspicion that led Bosch to set up the flight to get rid of Rorke.

Two other theories about this flight are also presented on page 203. Hemming says the mystery passenger was a Cuban double agent who hijacked the plane to Cuba. Sturgis says the plane was shot down by Castro.

Since the missing section (203-06) is primarily about Guy Banister's connections to Friends of Democratic Cuba (linked by Dick Russell to Angel and Leopoldo), the Santa Ana mission (which also involved Gordon Novel), the Anti-Communist League of the Caribbean (linked to Nixon and the China Lobby), and Ferrie and Oswald, formerly of Civil Air Patrol, there are many connections to UT and Wing's Rambler.

Why then focus on the deletion of only part of the story of the Rorke/Sullivan flight? That flight began on September 25, 1963, the day Oswald was in Austin.[548] The Beech Travelair's whereabouts between taking off from Fort Lauderdale at 8:00 a.m. and its "non-refueling" thirty miles away in Hollywood Florida five hours later are a complete mystery.[549]

Due to evidence which cannot yet be fully disclosed, this paper's author believes this flight may have had something to do with Oswald's trip to Austin. That evidence may be related to the fact that Lyndon

Johnson arrived in Austin that night. Three times that day Johnson talked by phone to the East Coast representative of Beech Aircraft, Darrell Schneider. They spoke twice in Washington D.C. and later that night by long distance after Johnson arrived at his ranch. It was the last call Johnson made before going to bed.[550]

They spoke to each other many times between late 1963 and 1968 but apparently never again did they speak three different times in one day or at odd hours. The other calls between them in 1963 appear to coincide with major moves by Oswald leading up to and including his employment at the Texas Schoolbook Depository.[551] According to Hinkle and Turner, Bosch used H.L. Hunt's money for pilots and twin engine planes for his raids.

This reference in *JFK: The Book of the Film* not only shows H.L. Hunt complaining about a Kennedy dynasty at the same time he is funding Bosch, he is complaining to Senator Harry Byrd of Virginia, the cousin of D.H. Byrd.

Since Sturgis and Hemming were trainers at the Lake Pontchartrain camp, and since Sturgis arranged the Rorke/Sullivan flight, their theories about the flight must remain suspect. All three theories conflict with Marita Lorenz's claim that Rorke, Sturgis, Bosch and Hemming were with the group that drove from a CIA safehouse in Miami to Dallas in November 1963 to kill Kennedy.[552] Casting doubt on Lorenz, however, Gus Russo said:

> I know Marita and a lot of work was done on her by various people. John Stockwell -- to put it in a nutshell -- had made a deal with Marita Lorenz to write her biography.
>
> He spent two years of his time with no income researching, working with her, writing this biography. He wrote this thing then went around to try to fact check all the stuff that she had given him. It was all lies. And he wasted two years of his life.
>
> And he told me specifically where it was all lies. The Castro story is to an extent true but nowhere near as big as she makes it out to be. There was never a child by Castro, which she claims. He went down to Havana and checked all the hospitals.
>
> I mean he really tried to push this thing. He's spoken to all of the people who were supposedly in the motorcade going to Dallas. Nothing clicks. There's a lot more to it than that but I don't know what her motivation

is. I don't want to get into that, you know, kind of thing. But I just don't believe her for a lot of reasons.[553]

The fact that the Beech Travelair attracted so much attention to itself with its odd takeoffs, landings, flightplans, and final disappearance may have been intentional. The purpose would be to distract attention from its actual flight plans that day. If Rorke took part in the drive to Dallas with Sturgis and Bosch two months later it is highly unlikely that he was the FBI informant Bosch suspected.

It is interesting to note, however, that Oswald was suspected both of being an FBI informant and (by Hemming and others) of infiltrating the anti-Castro Cubans and the Lake Pontchartrain training camp. Rorke, Sturgis, Hemming, and Bosch may have found their infiltrator, he may have been the mystery passenger on that flight, and they may have gotten their revenge by framing him for the assassination of President Kennedy.

Another event that helped shed light on the missing pages (especially those dealing with Sylvia Odio) was when in early 1993 author Pete Brewton spoke about his book *The Mafia, CIA, and George Bush* to a crowd of about fifty people in Austin. Some of what he said adds to information concerning the Rambler's possible connection to the Odio incident.

In 1985 Walter Mischer, Sr., friend and fund raiser for LBJ, Lloyd Bentsen, Ronald Reagan, and George Bush, bought 12,000 acres in Belize near Guatemala for the CIA. Mischer's son-in-law, Robert Corson, was a CIA asset. The land has not been used for anything. Belize is an English speaking country. The Coca-Cola Company had land there. It is primarily a trans-shipment point for Columbian cocaine and an area for marijuana crops.[554]

Belize was where Geoffrey Sullivan was seen days after his Sturgis-arranged flight with Alex Rorke and their mysterious passenger reportedly crashed at sea soon after September 25, 1963.

Corson, scheduled for trial in December 1992, was found dead in El Paso the day after the presidential election. Brewton got a note that said, "How does it feel to be a murderer.-- Corson" No drugs were found in his body although pills were strewn around his room. The cause of death was determined to be heart blockage. His face was cyanotic.

Corson had decided to turn states evidence against someone high up. The Justice Department, however, denied he was turning states evidence. County Judge John Lindsey of Houston could have been greatly damaged by Corson. Lindsey is a powerful Republican and is close to a lot of Republican officials.

Corson was basically a money-launderer. His mother tried to

convince Brewton, after Corson died, that her son was not a CIA contract agent. Brewton thinks she was put up to this because of a subsequent event which he could not talk about.

During the question and answer period journalist David Armstrong said that George Bush's Zapata Oil Company leased land from E. Trine Starnes' preacher father. E.T. Starnes declared bankruptcy in 1976 after borrowing money from Mischer's Continental Bank in Houston. Brewton did not know this. Starnes was also the second largest borrower at Silverado Savings and one of the biggest private donors to the Contras.

Brewton said Bush and Bentsen are the main movers of a group of businessmen in Houston who were behind the S&L scandal. "The point," Brewton said, "is who got the money. These Houston guys probably got it. We may never find out. It can be done however but the Justice Department is not doing it. Justice has stopped subpoenas to banks in the Grand Cayman Islands."

The Parvus Company, according to Brewton, is a security-investigations company which has Richard Helms as its board chairman. "The only guy there who is not a former member of the intelligence community," Brewton said, "is Theodore Dimitry of the Vinson & Elkins law firm." Judge James Elkins was especially close to Walter Mischer.

Brewton reported that another Houston law firm, Fulbright and Jaworski, stopped Brewton's stories in the Houston Post. They are the libel lawyers for the paper. They had conflicts of interest with Mischer that they did not reveal to the Post. They had represented many of Mischer's companies.

Jaworski is indirectly related to the missing pages. Canfield and Weberman referenced Julius Mader's *Who's Who in CIA* about Texas Attorney General Waggoner Carr's CIA connections (*Coup d'Etat in America*, pages 577-578). The pages to which Canfield and Weberman referred were found missing from UT's only copy of Mader's book.

Pages 577-78 of *Who's Who in CIA* include both of Canfield's and Weberman's only citations from this book. The first concerns Carr's board membership at the M.D. Anderson Foundation. The second regards Robert Gerald Storey's CIA connection as a board member of the International Education Exchange, a part of the CIA's Institute of International Education.

The "Texas Court of Inquiry" into the Kennedy assassination consisted of only three men: Carr, Storey, and Jaworski. Peter Dale Scott adds that Storey is a former Army intelligence colonel and a member in 1946 of the U.S. legal team at Nuremberg along with Leon Jaworski.555

Dallas D.A. Henry Wade, Carr, Storey and Jaworski met with the Warren Commission in January 1964 to discuss allegations that Oswald had been an informant for either the FBI or CIA. Scott also cites Harold Weisberg's observation that Jaworski himself sat on the board of the M.D. Anderson Foundation, "a CIA conduit." Scott also notes many other connections between these three men and the financial backers of Second Naval Guerrilla and those involved with Lee and Marina Oswald.[556]

The Mader pages had been torn out leaving a single dot of red ink on the edge of the tear -- a red ball point pen had been used to remove many of the other missing pages. This book was kept in a locked "cage" and had to be requested at the circulation desk.

It is understandable that UT's protectors would be sensitive about these particular Mader pages. In 1941, the Texas legislature provided funds for a state cancer research hospital to be administered by UT. The newly formed M.D. Anderson Foundation, in its first major project, provided matching funds and a site in downtown Houston. For over thirty years, the M.D. Anderson Hospital for Cancer Research was directed by Dr. R. Lee Clark. He was succeeded in 1978 by Dr. Charles A. LeMaistre, who by the time of Harry Ransom's death two years earlier had become UT's system chancellor.[557]

At the time of Kennedy's assassination, LeMaistre was the director of Woodlawn Hospital and an associate professor at the University of Texas Southwestern Medical School in Dallas. The Dallas County Hospital District was comprised of Parkland Memorial Hospital and Woodlawn Hospital. Among his fellow teachers at Southwestern Medical School were the doctors who treated Kennedy, Connally, Tippit, and Oswald. Two months earlier Governor Connally had appointed LeMaistre to chair the state committee on tuberculosis. Dr. LeMaistre's counterpart at Parkland Hospital was its administrator, Dr. Charles Jack Price. It was C.J. Price who was asked by Secret Service agent Clint Hill to help in obtaining a casket for the President. And it was Price's assistant, Steve Landregan, who called Vernon O'Neal's funeral home.[558]

In the late 1980s, the M.D. Anderson Hospital was the focus of a bizarre homicide case (see Nexis). A staff member was charged with attempted murder when it was determined he was trying to kill a co-worker by injecting him with cancer cells -- despite the fact that this is supposed to be impossible. In 1982, Dallas Deputy Sheriff Al Maddox told researchers that a phony doctor had been assigned to Ruby while he was in jail by "...whoever supplied the county at that time with doctors....And one day I went in and Ruby told me, he said, `Well, they injected me for a cold.' He said it was cancer cells. That's what he told me, Ruby did. I said you don't believe that shit. He said, `I damn sure do!'"

Police officer Tom Tilson has told researchers, "It was the opinion of a number of other Dallas police officers that Ruby had received injections of cancer while he was incarcerated in the Dallas County Jail following the shooting of Lee Harvey Oswald." After Ruby's death in January 1967, an autopsy determined that there were traces of white cancerous tumors throughout his body. The Dallas County medical examiner who performed the autopsy, Dr. Earl Rose, was asked by the House Assassinations Committee if Ruby could have known about his cancer in November 1963. He said no. Ruby died after a three week stay at Parkland Hospital -- having been admitted two days after his new trial site had been announced.[559]

Pete Brewton's statements overlapped with a few other subjects discussed in this paper. "The Tower ⊙⊡⊙⊡⊙⊡⊙⊡Commission never did their job," Brewton said, "They never looked for any of this." There are some "deepthroats" coming out of the woodwork now, but they believe their lives are in danger. In making the point that major political scandals do go undetected, Pete said that James McCord wrote to Judge John Sirica and kept Watergate alive after everyone had dropped it, including Woodward and Bernstein. McCord had been closely involved with E. Howard Hunt, Bernard Barker, Frank Sturgis, and Eugenio Martinez in Second Naval Guerrilla and the AM/LASH plot.

With regard to Austin, Pete did not know much about Austin's Lamar Savings, he writes about Austin's Creditbanc in his book. Brewton does know, however, that Adnan Khashoggi, Lamar's largest borrower, borrowed money from Continental Savings a week before he did the first arms for hostages deal.

In August 1990 Lamar Savings owner Stanley Adams, Jr. was being deposed for the civil lawsuit against him over the collapse of his savings and loan.[560] The deposition was stopped on August 1 when he became emotionally upset. The U.S. District Judge who presided over the case had appointed a special court master to prepare the case for trial. The man he appointed was Waggoner Carr. The case was settled December 4, 1990 when Adams agreed to pay the government $1.9 million. The lawsuit sought $92 million in damages and a maximum sentence of seventy years in prison. Other charges against Adams involving another savings and loan were dropped entirely.[561]

The Judge was James Nowlin, the same judge who had presided over the July 1990 airliner hijacking trial of Jose Manuel Gonzalez-Gonzalez. This defendant, who was eventually convicted of the hijacking, made statements in that trial indicating that he may be the son of Reinaldo Gonzalez.[562] Reinaldo Gonzalez was Antonio Veciana's gunman in the October 24, 1961 CIA attempt to assassinate Castro. After the plot failed he hid at the Odios' house before being captured by Castro and imprisoned along with Amador Odio. Robert Morrow, in his book, *The Senator Must Die*, refers to a document published in his appendix to show that Jose Miro Cardona, the first head of the Cuban Revolutionary Council, had been Castro's prime minister. This same document lists, "In Charge of Foreign Relations: Reinol Gonzáles Gonzáles" -- who may be the same person as Veciana's gunman.[563]

During his trial, Jose said his father had been a political prisoner of Castro and had died in prison. Born in Cuba on January 3, 1951, Jose testified that he and his brother (age ten) emigrated to the U.S. in 1962. They arrived in Miami leaving their mother and father in Cuba. His mother later went to Spain where her family owned property. She came to the U.S. in 1966. Until then, he and his brother lived with friends of his father and family in Florida City and in Opalaca for a year. Because they did not get along with their surrogate family they were put into a Jesuit school until their mother arrived in Miami.[564]

Their mother then took them to New Orleans where she worked as a housekeeper. Jose dropped out of high school and took electrical engineering classes at Control Data Institute in Virginia. He soon returned to New Orleans and was working in the restaurant-bar-hotel business by age seventeen. He was heard to say, while on the witness stand, that he was working at the Habana Bar when he met his future wife, Helen Virginia Masferrer. This intriguing statement could not be varified due to the unavailability of transcripts for this trial (none was made because there was no appeal).[565]

Had Jose been questioned about any of this, we might have learned whether this was the same Habana Bar owned by Orest Pena, the FBI informant who had worked closely with Sergio Arcacha Smith and David Ferrie at the Cuban Revolutionary Council in New Orleans, and who claimed that Oswald met with several men in his bar on many occasions in the summer of 1963. In an interview for CBS News, broadcast on November 26, 1975, Pena said that his FBI contact, Warren deBrueys, had also been in contact with Oswald that summer. Pena stated that deBrueys came to him about ten days before Pena testified before the Warren Commission and said, "If you ever talk anything about me, I will get rid -- get rid of your ass."[566]

If Gonzalez-Gonzalez had been asked about his wife, we might have learned whether she was related to Rolando "El Tigre" Masferrer, the old hand at gunrunning and "hatchet man" during the Batista dictatorship. According to Robert Morrow, Masferrer convinced Batista to go along with Meyer Lansky's post war gambling and narcotics plans for Cuba. As a Cuban senator with his own private army, Masferrer protected the

Mafia's interests, becoming friends with Santos Trafficante, Jr. in the process. Morrow says that "Richard Nixon was among Batista's frequent and well received guests" during this period.[567]

The friendship between Masferrer and Trafficante continued in the U.S. after Castro took control. Masferrer escaped from Cuba with Cuban congressman Eladio del Valle. Masferrer's anti-Castro mercenaries (training on Howard Hughes' island, No Name Key) had been the ones approved by Rostow's friend Richard Bissell to assassinate Castro. They were the core group of Operation Forty. The future leader of Masferrer's anti- Castro mercenaries in Florida was Loran Eugene Hall. Gerry Patrick Hemming, who was a member of the group, claimed Oswald had tried to join after leaving the Marines in 1959 but was turned down by Masferrer's men in Los Angeles.[568]

When Howard Burris' good friend Richard Helms took over Bissell's job as the CIA's Deputy Director of Plans with the blessing of the just fired Allen Dulles and Charles Cabell, he decided, despite a CIA internal memo to the contrary, to continue the assassination plots against Castro using Trafficante's and Masferrer's men. He worked directly with John Roselli as his sole contact with Trafficante. By February 1962, J. Edgar Hoover had struck a deal with Helms to jointly cover up their agencies' criminal activities. By May 1962, Dulles favorite Tracy Barnes had established his super-secret Domestic Operations Division, hiring Dulles loyalist E. Howard Hunt as its covert action chief.[569]

After the missile crisis, Kennedy declared a "hands-of Cuba" policy. Antonio Veciana, the head of Alpha 66, defied the Kennedy brothers with a March 17, 1963 attack against a Soviet military post and two Soviet freighters. The Kennedys cracked down against the anti-Castro raiders on March 30. The next day, Oscar del Valle Garcia, the organizer of Operation Forty, used Masferrer's men to blow up a Soviet ship. The sole American on board the raider ship was Jerry Buchanan, protege of Frank Sturgis, Orlando Bosch, and INCA's Manuel Gil -- whose boss, Ed Butler (Oswald's radio debate opponent), later sat on the American Security Council with Rostow favorite Ed Lansdale; the same Jerry Buchanan whose brother James Buchanan became the propagator of Frank Sturgis' false Oswald stories in the Pompano Beach Sun Sentinel.[570]

The Kennedys cracked down harder. The anti-Castro groups intensified their raids. In May, Masferrer's men raided a Cuban militia camp near Havana. American right-wing groups, angered by the Kennedy crack- down, threw their support behind the raiders. Miro Cardona resigned as head of the CRC, declaring Kennedy a Russian-led traitor against Second Naval Guerrilla. Mario Garcia Kohly, the former

Cuban businessman, picked by conservatives in Eisenhower's administration (like Nixon), to replace Castro, united the anti-Castro leaders, including former Cuban president Carlos Prio Socarras, Masferrer's group in Miami (who merged with Alpha 66 and 30th of November), and David Ferrie's Lake Pontchartrain group in Louisiana. The assassination teams were chosen from these groups, according to Morrow, to shoot Kennedy. Meanwhile, Trafficante had Masferrer set up a phony CIA team to kill Castro, making sure they would be caught, provoking anti-Kennedy statements from Cuba's leaders. He arranged for a Cuban lawyer, Carlos Garcia Bongo (subject of missing HSCA pages) to leak the plot to Castro. Concurrently, the CIA had Rolando Cubela and Manuel Artime begin the real AM/LASH plot against Castro. Finally, it was Masferrer, according to Morrow, who coordinated the plan to give Ferrie's old Civil Air Patrol cadet, Lee Oswald, a high profile as the lone Castro-affiliated gunman.[571]

Peter Dale Scott notes that, "Whatever their shortcomings, the FBI and the Warren Commission between them meticulously demolished the prima facie case that Oswald and Ruby were agents of Castro and the Fair Play for Cuba Committee."[572]

Perhaps it was his failure to blame the assassination on Castro that Masferrer was killed in a car bombing in 1975 for his "systematic work in the destruction of the anti-Communist struggle." Thirty years later the exiles still sit in Florida and wait to return to Cuba. There is one other connection to Nixon: Masferrer's nephew, Rolandito, had been employed with SNG veteran Gerry Hemming at Parabellum, a subsidiary of gunrunner Mitchell WerBell's arms manufacturing company headed by Anselmo Alliegro, Jr., "an heir to the shadowy Anson millions."[573]

While testifying in his own defense, Jose Manuel Gonzalez-Gonzalez claimed he hijacked the plane in an attempt to seek political protection in Cuba because he was being pursued by federal agents and Cuban exiles. He said they were after him because he had learned of a plot to assassinate former mayor Morial of New Orleans, who was seeking reelection. Morial died under uncertain circumstances after a party. He had apparently collapsed next to his car where his body was found the next morning.[574]

Neither the prosecutor, nor his court appointed defense attorney, nor Judge Nowlin asked Gonzalez- Gonzalez any questions about any of this. Gonzalez-Gonzalez's attorney was pleading insanity for his client. It was an ongoing joke among trial spectators, however, that the defense was not providing any proof of this. Jose was calm and focused on the witness stand. The prosecution provided two expert witnesses to show Gonzalez-Gonzalez was sane.[575]

The first, Dr. Richard Coons, stated he was an Austin criminal forensic psychiatrist who graduated from a Virginia college, UT Law School, and UT's Southwestern Medical School in 1964. He said he served at Fort Sam Houston in the Army Medical Corps from 1971 to 1972. The second was Dr. James Fredrickson, who said he graduated from UT's Southwestern Medical School in Dallas, and Baylor University in Waco before practicing at Dallas' Timberlawn and Parkland Hospitals. He has done work for the Marines, Army, Navy, and State Department, mostly as an expert witness in Texas.[576]

The reporter who covered this trial for the Austin-American Statesman told this author during a trial recess that one of the jurors had been on a jury in Nowlin's court the previous month. The reporter said she was surprised that this juror was not disqualified. One other juror, who had an extensive military background, produced the same reaction. The reporter said she thought the military nature of the airline business should have been reason enough for disqualification.

Both the Gonzalez-Gonzalez trial and the Adams trial were potentially damaging to the CIA. In 1992, Nowlin was at the center of a political scandal involving secret consultations with Republicans while overseeing the redrawing of Texas congressional districts.

There are two final items relating to these topics worth noting here. First, Robert Sam Anson revealed in his book, They've Killed the President, a claim by researcher Richard Sprague that CBS has film of the Rambler leaving the crime scene.[577] If true, this film is crucial to the identification of Wing's Rambler.[578] And second, the book *Government by Gunplay* revealed that George Wallace's accused, would-be, assassin, Arthur Bremer, drove a Rambler. Considering his role in the Bremer case, this may be another example of E. Howard Hunt's involvement with an assassin with a Rambler.[579]

Conclusion

Many researchers of the JFK assassination eventually pass a difficult psychological threshold. When confronted with the first evidence of conspiracy, most rational people have no doubt responded, "so what?" The circumstantial evidence presented here is far from immune from such skepticism. The threshold is different for each person because it is defined by the individual's tolerance for the number of times they can say "so what" before skepticism becomes denial. And denial is perfectly understandable because the alternative leads to frightening speculation about the true meaning of events in the recent history of the United States.

One of the researchers for this paper has been extremely valuable in the role of devil's advocate. His arguments on occasion become circular, however, when he insists that because no hard evidence has been found, none should be sought. "Pursue the UT connections," he said, "and leave George Wing and his Rambler out of it." But, if nothing else, the evidence presented here, stemming directly from Wing's outré and grotesque station wagon, is a map possibly leading to several "smoking guns."

Sincere effort has been made here to avoid direct claims of involvement by individuals mentioned in this paper in any conspiracy to assassinate President Kennedy. The implications, however, are unavoidable. It must be noted, therefore, that any implied conspiracy presented in this limited context does not pass the "so what" test. Too many fundamental questions are left unanswered. Taken in the context of the research of others over the past thirty years, however, this evidence can be viewed as part of a substantive circumstantial case which begins to define the conspiracy.

Ironically, the fact that the available record indicates that Ruth Paine did not own a Rambler station wagon at the time of the assassination makes relevant one of the most fundamental questions: was George Wing's car the one seen in Dealey Plaza and the one believed by Oswald and Craig to belong to Ruth Paine? The answer might be found among available information.

Gary Shaw's original seven slides of Elm Street traffic are labeled in other than chronological sequence. The photo used in his book *Cover-Up*, to show the Rambler, is the fifth in the chronological sequence.[580]

This photo shows a car that is darker in color and a later model than Wing's. In the seventh slide, however, there are two light-colored cars crossing the intersection at Houston Street. This photo was first published on the cover of Penn Jones, Jr.'s book, *Forgive My Grief III*. The car in front does not match the 1959 Rambler's grill or headlight design. The one behind it, sitting in the intersection has similar grill, headlight, hood, and wheel well characteristics to Wing's Rambler. The image is outside the camera's depth of field and only the front half of the car is visible. Perhaps computer expert Tom Wilson can enhance it. The Hertz clock still reads 12:40 in the seventh photo.

Film of this scene taken at 12:40, however, would be ideal for answering this question, and seems to actually exist. Not only does Richard E. Sprague (the researcher not the HSCA counsel) believe that CBS has such a film, he claims it shows exactly what Roger Craig, Marvin Robinson, and Mrs. James (Helen) Forrest all independently described.[581]

FBI document 5920 is a letter with enclosures which Sprague sent to Senator Robert Kennedy in 1967. It was forwarded to J. Edgar Hoover by RFK's secretary, Miss Polly Busselle. A researcher at UT found it among microfilm of FBI documents in the summer of 1992.

Of particular use to Rambler identification efforts in Sprague's list of photos are numbers 32-35, 41-46, 58, 59, 66, 130, 131, 233-35, 246-58, 337, and 342; as well as some of the Gene Daniels photos. The CBS film Sprague spoke of may actually be one of these.

The most important point, which certainly should not be overlooked here, is that if there is film of the Rambler incident it would show Oswald or "his identical twin" getting into the car, thus proving the existence of a conspiracy! Only this fact makes the identification of Wing's Rambler less important. If it then turns out to be Wing's car, living conspirators may have already been found.

It is obvious that finding this film is of supreme importance. If the CBS film exists, however, it is not naively suggested that they will simply hand it over. But of all the lawsuits that could be brought against CBS, none could be more important than a suit for the release of such a film.

Perhaps attempts to identify Wing's Rambler in Dealey Plaza are premature, however. If in fact Ruth Paine did own a light-colored Rambler station wagon in 1963, it would be a major step toward eliminating Wing's car from suspicion. It will be interesting to see how the evidence manipulators (see below) deal with this dilemma. Should evidence of a Paine Rambler suddenly appear, it would further corroborate Oswald and Craig, casting further suspicion on Paine.

Despite Dallas County Deputy Sheriff Roger Craig's published Warren Commission testimony which, according to Craig, had fourteen changes from his original testimony, Craig is certain he saw a Rambler station wagon with a luggage rack on top. Craig also maintained his certainty that the Rambler was light- green although the Commission changed it to white. Craig was also certain that "Mrs. Ruth Paine, the woman Marina Oswald lived with in Irving, Texas, owned a Rambler station wagon, at that time, of this same color."[582] Craig does not say in his autobiography how he knew this.

When asked if he had anything to add to his Warren Commission testimony Craig said, "No; except -- uh -- except for the fact that it came out later that Mrs. Paine does own a station wagon and -- uh -- it has a luggage rack on top. And this came out, of course, later after I got back to the office. I didn't know about this. Buddy Walthers brought it up. I believe they went by the house and the car was parked in the driveway."[583] Craig apparently told Jim Garrison that "Deputy Sheriff

Buddy Walthers drove out to the Paine residence in the suburb of Irving and confirmed that Mrs. Ruth Paine did have a Nash Rambler station wagon with a luggage rack on top."[584]

The FBI, however, apparently established that Ruth Paine owned a green, 1955 Chevrolet station wagon with a luggage rack on top. But since the agent conducting the investigation was James P. Hosty, who admitted destroying evidence under orders,[585] and since he did not see the car until three months after the assassination, the "evidence" of this car could have been altered or fabricated.[586] Another possible explanation for why Oswald said it was Ruth Paine's Rambler stems from something Oswald said at his interrogation. According to Captain Fritz's report Oswald said, "No. I don't own a car but the Paines have two cars."[587]

It seems Craig is the only witness in Dealey Plaza to describe the hue of the car. The others described it as light-colored or light-gray, possibly having been uncertain of the hue. Because of this, it is important to establish whether or not Craig was color-blind since light-pink would appear light-green to a color-blind person. Another explanation for the color discrepancy is that this was a similar situation to Carl Mather's car being seen with a different color but having the same license plates.[588] Neither case rules out the possibility that a car the color of the UT Rambler was used in some way by the conspirators.

If the UT Rambler was used by the conspirators in the JFK assassination, then it was in Mexico in 1964, ended up back in the United States as some sort of souvenir, and stayed near a circle of friends that included Lyndon Johnson, Walt Rostow, Jack Dulles, Harry Ransom, C.B. Smith, and two professors of Spanish and Portuguese at the University of Texas at Austin.

According to the rule of falsifiability, if this car was not involved in the assassination, the evidence will prove the claim (that it was involved) false. If the claim is true, the evidence will not disprove it. So far none of the evidence disproves that George Wing's station wagon was the car seen by Michael Kensington, Roger Craig, Marvin Robinson, Helen Forrest, and Richard Carr.[589] Neither does it disprove Wing's Rambler was the one known to Oswald as the car that took him from Dealey Plaza. The search for evidence continues however. Help in that search is both needed and requested from the research community.

But perhaps this car had nothing to do with the assassination. Perhaps like the back seat magazines and the missing pages, it too was just a sign or a signal, something that would attract the attention of someone knowledgeable about the JFK assassination, something which would help put the other clues into perspective and lead to previously unseen relationships in the mosaic of the Kennedy assassination.

That being the case then perhaps too the whole thing is an elaborate hoax. If so, assurance is given here that no such hoax originated with this author or others whose research contributed to this paper. It cannot as yet be conclusively ruled out, though, that such a hoax originated with George Wing or someone who knew him. Those who have made these findings, with the exception of those wishing anonymity, are willing to undergo polygraph examination, voice stress analysis, brain wave scanning, or other physically non- intrusive methods of varifying truthfulness, relative to any and all statements made herein.

Then again maybe all of this is just one of the most amazing coincidences that has ever existed. Whether real, coincidence, or hoax however, the evidence of the UT Rambler is similar to and predates the evidence of Ricky White, which was first made public in August 1990, concerning his father Rosco White's role in the assassination. By the time White's story broke in the Austin American-Statesman, the Rambler, the magazines, and the first of the missing pages had already been discovered. In fact it was the similarities between the story of the Rambler and the story of Rosco White -- the idea of leaving artifacts, clues, and documents where they could be found -- that led to sufficient curiosity to start the first hard research into the Rambler in November 1990.

In the search for truth about the Kennedy assassination, rife as it is with disinformation in the accepted areas of learning, we cannot be blinded to the possibility that the truth can still be found or that it may be in some rather unorthodox places. This paper's author and researchers understand the damage that continues to be done by those who introduce red herrings, intentionally or not, into the investigation of President Kennedy's murder. As a group, we decided in January 1993 that the public release of our findings would help in the search for the truth more than hurt it. After nearly four years of justifiable caution we felt that at least some of what we had found pointed in the direction of what had actually happened to President Kennedy. In the months that followed, leading up to the presentation of this paper at the Second Research Conference of The Third Decade in June 1993, that decision was reinforced by subsequent findings.

Whether real, coincidence, or hoax, the Rambler has led to a new look at those with well known roles in the story of the assassination like the Paines, Dulles, Brading, Johnson, and de Mohrenschildt, those with lesser known roles like Martino, Burris, Byrd, Bancroft, Lansdale, Bush, Nixon, and Rostow, and a first look at those with as yet unknown possible roles like Harry Huntt Ransom, George Gordon Wing and Cecil Bernard Smith.

To quote Wing himself, from an article he wrote in 1982, in which he examines "...a brilliant analysis [by Carlos Fuentes] of *Moby Dick* in terms of its profound meanings,..."

> ...Fuentes gives us a Melville who is not only a
> subverter of the established order but also a prophet
> whose prognostications gain validity in our own time.
> Melville could not accept the idea of the United States
> held by his fellow countrymen -- God's chosen people, a
> nation that had never experienced defeat and felt itself
> heir to the future. Melville had a vision, Fuentes says, of
> the excesses to which all of these certainties could lead:
> to the imposition of false ends and private fetishes; to the
> sacrifice of the collective good on the alter of an abstract
> freedom of the individual, to the simplistic division of
> history into a Manichean struggle between the good --
> the United States -- and the evil -- those who oppose the
> United States, to manifest destiny, to "the lonely crowd,"
> inorganic atomism; to the confusion between private
> opinion and general truth; to the radical lack of
> comprehension of the truth of others whenever it does
> not correspond to the particular vision of things held by
> a North American: as a consequence, the truth of others
> is suspect and must be destroyed. Indeed, Fuentes
> concludes, in our time, Captain Ahab still lives, and his
> name is MacArthur and Dulles, Joe McCarthy and
> Johnson, the white whale is in Cuba, in China, in
> Vietnam, in Santo Domingo, in a film, in a book....[590]

Wing ends this same article with a statement which can be applied to other aspects of his life -- a statement which may one day prove to be very revealing about what had once been viewed as his eccentricities:

"In this essay, I have of necessity treated a complex subject in a somewhat fragmentary and incomplete fashion. Nevertheless, I hope to have awakened some interest in pursuing further any of the topics I have deliberately left truncated."

APPENDIX

The Mutilated UT Library Books and Rambler Back seat Magazines

The following are the nine books discovered missing or with pages removed at the Perry-Casteñeda and Benson Libraries on the campus of the University of Texas at Austin. The first was discovered in June 1989; the rest in May-June 1991 when only the author and one other person knew all of the facts about what was being found. No books were found after these; but books with missing pages yet to be found, now that word of them is more widespread, are less credible. Following the nine books are the only two back seat magazines to be positively identified of at least four that are visible in photographs of George Wing's Rambler station wagon. The identity of the third is at present only tentative, but the visible elements on its cover do appear to be an identifiable match.

1. Anthony Summers, *Conspiracy,* (NY: McGraw Hill, 1980), pp. 125-26, 447-52, 545-46, 593-94; discovered June 1989.

2. Robert Sam Anson, *They've Killed the President*, (NY: Bantam, 1975), pp. 197-98, 255-58, 267-68, 275-76, 297-300, 307-14, 331-34, 387-88; discovered May 1, 1991.

3. HSCA Volume V: Trafficante testimony, pp. 363-68, 373-76; discovered May 9, 1991.

4. Jaques Cattel, ed., *Directory of American Scholars, Vol. I,* (NY: R.R. Bowker Co. sixth ed. 1974), p. 672 (only the Nathaniel Weyl biography was removed, the rest of the page remains intact); discovered May 13, 1991.

5. Peter Dale Scott, *Crime and Cover-Up,* (Berkeley, CA: Westworks, 1977), pp. 7-22, 27-28, 31-38, 41- 44, 51-56, 61-62, 65-66; discovered May 13, 1991.

6. Wim J. Meiners, *De Moordfabriek: Tussen Dallas En Watergate*, (NY: Ace; Bussum: Centripress, 1974), pp. 42-64, photos 4 pp.; discovered May 23, 1991. Note: An intact copy of this book was obtained through an interlibrary loan from the University of Kansas Libraries; E / 842.9 /.M43.

7. Warren Hinckle with William Turner, *The Fish is Red*, (NY: Harper and Row, 1981), pp. 31-40, 43-46, 53-54, 101-04, 111-26, 131-34, 155-74, 203-06, photo section: 8 pp., 215-18, 223-24, 335-38, 349- 52; discovered May 24, 1991.

8. Michael Canfield with Alan J. Weberman, *Coup d'Etat in America*, (NY: Third Press, 1975); confirmed missing May 24, 1991.

9. Julius Mader, *Who's Who in CIA*, (Berlin: Self-published, 1968), pp. 577-78; discovered June 1, 1991.

1. Esquire, August 1963, Vol. LX, No. 2, whole No. 357.

2. Esquire, January 1964, Vol. LXI, No. 1, whole No. 362.

3. Life, June 7, 1963, Vol. 54, No. 23.

Notes:

480. Michael Kensington, "The Miami Connection to the JFK Assassination," The Third Decade, Sept., 1992, pp. 26-31.

481. Interview: Jan. 3, 1993, Michael Kensington.

482. Kensington.

483. A discussion of the implications of this fact with regard to Craig's description of "light-green" can be found in the conclusion of this paper.

484. Interview: Jan. 3, 1993, Michael Kensington.

485. Interview: Jan. 16, 1993, Michael Kensington.

486. Interview: Mar. 1992, Lucila Lopez Wing, widow of George Gordon Wing. Note: Mrs. Wing has not been interviewed extensively about the subjects dealt with in this paper. She was sent a polite letter in March 1993 asking for any information she could provide concerning her husband's interest in his Rambler.

487. Interview: May 6, 1993, Chuck Bradshaw by researcher Stephen Bright.

488. "C.B. Smith Handed Festival Task," The Austin American, Oct. 16, 1964.

489. The University of Texas at Arlington, "C.B. Smith, Sr., October 24, 1967."

490. The University of Texas at Arlington, "C.B. Smith, Sr., October 24, 1967."

491. Scott, Government Documents..., ch. II, p. 4. Note: Buckley, Sr. and Smith, Sr. were former residents of UT's "Old B Hall" upperclassmen dormitory. Also recall the newspaper announcement dated Oct. 2, 1963, mentioned earlier in this paper, which says that Buckley will speak at UT Austin from Dec. 8-14, 1963; Martino gave his talk in Austin on Oct. 1, and Oswald was in Austin on Sept. 25, the day before the Odio incident.

492. Scott, Government Documents..., ch. II, pp. 4, 8-9. Note: Dubois continued to be an important CIA "asset" to David Atlee Phillips throughout the 1960s. (See Freed, Death in Washington, p. 50.)

493. Scott, Crime and Cover-Up, p. 20; interview: Jan. 3, 1993, Michael Kensington.

494. Scott, Government Documents..., ch. II, pp. 5, 7; Hinkle with Turner, The Fish is Red, p. 106-07. Note: Hinkle and Turner put the date of that attempt in October 1961, while Scott places it in October 1962. There is a story, to be discussed in this paper, about a trial here in Austin in 1990 involving the son of the man who hid at the Odios' house after fleeing that failed attempt. (See Summers, Conspiracy, pp. 417-18.)

495. Scott, Government Documents..., ch. II, pp. 7-10.

496. Scott, Government Documents..., ch. II, pp. 5-6; Scott, Crime and Cover-Up, pp. 17-18, 34-35; Summers, Conspiracy, p. 417.

497. Scott, Government Documents..., ch. II, p. 5; Summers, Conspiracy, p.

417.

498. Lane, *Plausible Denial*, pp. 300-01.

499. Frantz, *The Forty Acre Follies*, p. 98; Judis, *William F. Buckley, Jr.,* p. 22; Link, *Woodrow Wilson*, p. 16-17.

500. The University of Texas at Arlington, "C.B. Smith, Sr., October 24, 1967."

501. Di Eugenio, *Destiny Betrayed*, pp. 342-43 n.22.

502. "A Busy Day in Dallas for LBJ -- Thousands Welcome Johnson," The Dallas Times Herald, Apr. 24, 1963; "Continued Cuba Watch Revealed By Vice President," The Dallas Times Herald, Apr. 24, 1963; Interview: Feb. 2, 1993, David Lifton.

503. George Gordon Wing, *Octavio Paz: Poetry, Politics, and the Myth of the Mexican*, doctoral dissertation, University of California at Berkeley, Mar. 3, 1961, p. 3; E. Howard Hunt, *Undercover*, (NY: Berkeley, 1974), p. 69, cited in Judis, *William F. Buckley, Jr.,* p. 80; Interview: Jun. 7, 1993, with an individual wishing anonymity, who told this paper's researchers that Castro used to try to get dates with his Spanish teacher at Mexico City College in 1950.

504. The author's chance photo of Wing driving his Rambler in 1990 is a left profile. No two ears are alike and a match is reportedly as good as a fingerprint.

505. Byrd, *I'm an Endangered Species*, pp. 94, 97.

506. Bill Christensen, a student in the UT Spanish and Portuguese Department, learned this from his girlfriend, Jean Miller, who used to work with Wing.

507. Interview: May 4, 1993, Chuck Bradshaw.

508. Interview: Jun. 29, and Aug. 10, 1993, John Wheat.

509. Ben Belitt, ed., *Pablo Neruda, Five Decades: A Selection* (Poems: 1925-1970), (NY: Grove Weidenfeld, 1974), pp. xvii, 78, 79.

510. Interview: Oct. 28, 1992, Migel Gonzalez-Gerth by John Garcia. Note: According to Donald Freed, "Good old David [Atlee] Phillips...passed among his liberal friends as a McGovern Democrat" while setting up his extreme right-wing Association of Retired Intelligence Officers. (See Freed, *Death in Washington*, p. 124.)

511. C.B. Smith Motors Warranty Guarantee No. 64413A issued Apr., 26, 1963 to George Gordon Wing; Interview: Jan., 8, 1993, a close relative of R.L. Lewis, who wishes anonymity.

512. Interview: Jan. 13, 1993, a secretary for C.B. Smith Investments, by researcher David G. Armstrong.

513. P.K. Williams Motors repair receipt nos. 8494 (Sept. 1, 1966) and 14693 (Sept. 13, 1967) were found in Wing's Rambler's glove compartment.

514. Interview: Feb. 17, 1993, Chuck Bradshaw, former C.B. Smith employee who knew Wing and later worked on his car at P.K. Williams Motors.

515. Interview: May 4, 1993, Chuck Bradshaw.

516. Interview: Feb. 17, 1993, Chuck Bradshaw.

517. Interview: Feb. 17, 1993, Chuck Bradshaw.

518. Interview: Feb. 17, 1993, Chuck Bradshaw.

519. Russell, *The Man Who Knew Too Much*, p. 581.

520. Russell, *The Man Who Knew Too Much*, pp. 431-32, 701.

521. *The Roads of Texas*, (Fredericksburg, TX: Shearer Publishing, 1988), pp. 52-53, 68-69, 88-107, 120- 23, 161. Note: These maps include places considered to be ghost towns with populations as small as five people.

522. Henry Hurt, *Reasonable Doubt*, (NY: Henry Holt, 1985), p. 402; Seth Kantor, *The Ruby Cover-Up*, (NY: Zebra, 1978), pp. 43, 249-50.

523. Russell, *The Man Who Knew Too Much*, p. 432.

524. Scott, *Crime and Cover-Up*, p. 20; Interview: Jan. 3, 1993, Michael Kensington.

525. Hinckle with Turner, *The Fish is Red*, pp. 137-42, 144-46.

526. Graham, Texas is in eastern Young County, which would put it less than two-hundred miles from "Bay Cliff" if Bay Cliff actually existed and was where it was reported to be, half-way between Dallas and Houston.

527. Montgomery Ward tire warranty forms 27420-4 and 27420-6 found in Wing's Rambler's glove compartment.

528. CD 205, p. 453-62; Hubert Memos, Mar. 6 and 19, 1964, cited in Canfield with Weberman, *Coup d'état in America*, p. 51.

529. CD 23, CE 2694, CD 853, cited in George Michael Evica, *And We Are All Mortal: New Evidence and Analysis in the John F. Kennedy Assassination*, (West Hartford, CT: University of Hartford, 1978), p. 112.

530. Canfield with Weberman, *Coup d'état in America*, pp. 50-52.

531. Sugar with Leek, *The Assassination Chain*, p. 113.

532. Scott, Government Documents..., ch. II, p. 9.

533. Scott, Government Documents..., ch. II, p. 4.

534. Scott, Government Documents..., ch. II, passim.

535. Scott, Government Documents..., ch. II, pp. 3-4.

536. Tinkle, *Mr. De,* pp. 224, 239.

537. Scott, Government Documents..., ch. I, p. 11; Scott, *The Dallas Conspiracy*, ch. IX, p. 20.

538. Scott, Government Documents..., ch. II, p. 19.

539. Scott, *The Dallas Conspiracy*, ch. IX, pp. 20-21.

540. 9 H 106, 107 cited in Scott, *The Dallas Conspiracy*, ch. III, pp. 16, 37, ch. VII, p. 17, ch. IX, p. 27. Note: "After the assassination there were repeated conspiratorial efforts to extract from Marina Oswald false evidence against her late husband. Those involved in these efforts included Jack Crichton of Army Reserve Intelligence Service, at least one Russian "interpreter" [Mamantov] from Oswald's restricted circle of contacts in the oil industry, and at least four apparently unrelated persons linked to Marina's post- assassination hosts (the Great Southwest Corporation) and their lawyers (Wynne, Jaffe and Tinsley). Bedford Wynne of this law firm, a prominent oil lobbyist in Washington for the Murchisons, was investigated for his role in a Murchison kickback to [LBJ friend] Bobby Baker." (See Scott, *The Dallas Conspiracy*, ch. III.)

541. 9 H 202, cited in Scott, *The Dallas Conspiracy*, ch. VI, pp. 32-33.

542. Scott, *The Dallas Conspiracy*, ch. X, p. 4.

543. Scott, *The Dallas Conspiracy*, ch. VI, p. 32.

544. 9 H 106, 107 cited in Scott, *The Dallas Conspiracy*, ch. III, pp. 16, 37.

545. Scott, Government Documents..., ch. II, p. 1.

546. Scott, Government Documents..., ch. II, p. 4.

547. Stone with Sklar, *JFK: The Book of the Film*, p. 92.

548. "Oswald in Austin," The Texas Observer, Dec. 27, 1963, pp. 4-5.

549. Unsolved Mysteries, "Rorke-Sullivan Flight", 60 minutes, NBC Television Network, Dec. 19, 1990.

550. "Pre-presidential Office Diary, Sept. 25, 1963," LBJ Library, Box 3.

[OBJ]551. "Pre-presidential Office Diary, Sept. 25, 1963," LBJ Library, Box 3.

552. Lane, *Plausible Denial*, pp. 300-01.

553. Unpublished Transcript: Newman with Russo, pp. 28-29.

554. Pete Brewton, Speech, Unitarian Church in Austin, Feb. 10, 1993.

555. Scott, Government Documents..., ch. III, pp. 29-31.

556. Scott, Government Documents..., ch. III, pp. 29-31.

557. Clyde W. Burleson, *A Guide to the Texas Medical Center*, (Austin, TX: University of Texas Press, 1987), p. 104; Eckhardt, *One Hundred Faithful...*, p. 81.

558. Austin American-Statesman, "Governor Appoints TB Group," Sept. 26, 1963, p. AA-14; 6 H 1-152; David Lifton, Best Evidence, (NY: Macmillan, 1980), p. 673.

559. Marrs, *Crossfire*, pp. 431-33.

560. Kim Tyson, "Fatigued Adams to be examined," Austin American-Statesman, Aug. 11, 1990, pp. D1, D3.

561. Kirk Ladendorf, "Adams case settled for $1.9 million," Austin American-Statesman, Dec. 5, 1990, pp. D1, D10.

562. Brian Builta, "Gonzalez-Gonzalez convicted in hijacking," The Daily Texan, Jul. 19, 1990, p. 1; Morrow, The Senator Must Die, p. 245.

563. Hinckle with Turner, *The Fish is Red*, p. 106-07; Exhibit 28 of the Senate Select Committee on Internal Security, Jan. 23, 1959, cited in Morrow, The Senator Must Die, pp. 244-45.

564. Author's notes from Gonzalez-Gonzalez trial, Jul., 17, 1990.

565. Author's notes from Gonzalez-Gonzalez trial, Jul., 17, 1990.

566. Fensterwald, *Coincidence or Conspiracy*, pp. 257-58.

567. Hinckle with Turner, *The Fish is Red*, pp. 232-33; Morrow, *The Senator Must Die*, pp. 14-17.

568. Morrow, *The Senator Must Die*, pp. 14-17, 25, 31, 39, 82.

569. Morrow, *The Senator Must Die*, pp. 58-61, 80.

570. Morrow, *The Senator Must Die*, pp. 39, 71, 72; Canfield with Webberman, *Coup d'état in America*, pp. 104-05; Scott, *Crime and Cover-Up*, pp. 14, 56, n. 52a; Scott, *The Dallas Conspiracy*, ch. IV, p. 10.

571. Morrow, *The Senator Must Die*, pp. 72-75, 88, 107.

572. Scott, *The Dallas Conspiracy*, ch. II, p. 2.

573. Hinckle with Turner, *The Fish is Red*, pp. 317, 320, 321.

574. Interview: Apr. 1991, Aug. 11, 1993, Aletha Reppel, a New Orleans native, who was told this by her family who are long-time residents of New Orleans.

575. Author's notes from Gonzalez-Gonzalez trial, Jul., 17, 1990.

576. Author's notes from Gonzalez-Gonzalez trial, Jul., 17, 1990.

577. Anson, *They've Killed the President*, p. 360.

578. A study of the catalog of the Sprague collection reveals several color and black-and-white films and still photos which may show the Dealey Plaza Rambler.

579. William Turner, "The Shooting of George Wallace," Sid Blumenthal with Harvey Yazijian, eds., *Government by Gunplay: Assassination Conspiracy Theories from Dallas to Today*, (NY: Signet, 1976), p. 64; Hunt: Senate Watergate Committee Report, GPO ed., p. 129, cited in Fensterwald, Coincidence or Conspiracy, p. 523.

580. For researchers who have access to Gary Shaw's original slides, the chronological order and their labels are as follows: 1) 220 JAN 75; 2) 23 FEB 75; 3) 22 FEB 75; 4) 21 FEB 75; 5) 334 JAN 75; 6) 199 JAN 75; 7) 188 JAN 75.

581. Anson, *They've Killed the President*, p. 360.

582. Craig, *When They Kill a President*, pp. 10, 16, 18; *Two Men in Dallas: John Kennedy and Roger Craig,* 60 minutes, videotape. Narrated by Mark Lane. Alpa Productions, 1977.

583. 6 H 271.

584. Jim Garrison, *On the Trail of the Assassins*, p. 95n.

585. Hurt, *Reasonable Doubt*, p. 253.

586. Warren Commission Exhibit (CE) 1875, Vol. 23, p. 681, paragraph 5; CE 2125, 24 H 697. Note: a strange coincidence about this motel registration card is that it is from the "Rambler Motel" in Wa-Kom Texas.

587. Sylvia Meagher, *Accessories After the Fact*, (NY: Bobs-Merrill, 1967; Random House, 1976; Vintage, 1992), p. 232.

588. Groden with Livingstone, *High Treason*, p. 238-39.

589. Carr described it as a "1961 or 1962 Grey Rambler Station Wagon...which had Texas license...." Craig described it as light-green and wrote in 1971, "I said the license plates on the Rambler were not the same color as Texas plates. The Warren Commission: Omitted the not -- omitted but one word, an important one, so that it appeared that the license plates were the same color as Texas plates." In a cover-up, this matter would be a prime target for obfuscation. Therefore, the consistencies in the descriptions of the car -- that it was a light color, a Rambler station wagon, driven by a man with a dark complexion, and a white male identical to Oswald entered it -- carry the greater weight as evidence. (See Thompson, *Six Seconds in Dallas*, pp. 303-06, 404-05. Craig, *When They Kill a President*, p. 18; Kurtz, *Crime of The Century*, p. 132.)

590. George Gordon Wing, "Some Remarks on the Literary Criticism of Carlos Fuentes," Rob Brody with Charles Ruseman, eds., *Carlos Fuentes: A Critical View*, (Austin, TX: The University of Texas Press, 1982), pp. 210, 211.

1994 UPDATE

The following is in addition to the joint articles by myself and Jack White published in The Investigator, (issue no. 10, Aug.-Sept. 1994). Robert Groden, who was there when I found the No Name Key photo mentioned in my Investigator article, told me that he thinks Dick Sprague may have identified this man during the HSCA days. I need to send a copy to him and ask about it. Larry Haapanen has told me that he believes the collection of No Name Key photos were originally from Garrison's files. Since he has copies of some of those, I plan to send him a copy of this one to see if he recognizes it.

In the mean time, I am pursuing other documents based on the assumption that the photo is of Wing. My Texas Open Records Act request to UT, and Dave Armstrong's FOIA request to the CIA for records on Wing were accepted. The CIA couldn't find anything on Wing (no surprise). I have already received the UT files on Wing (more on them below). I still need to request files from the FBI, State Dept., and anyplace else I can think of.

Also, the Weaver Polaroid which was printed in Josiah Thompson's book years ago and more recently in Richard Trask's Pictures of the Pain (Yeoman Press, 1994, p. 243), will hopefully be found and studied soon. It may reveal a Rambler identical to Wing's sitting exactly where Richard Carr said it was. Regardless of an exact match, however, any degree of similarity between Wing's car and the getaway car continues to relate to Wing's enigma. More on this below.

Carol Hewett informed me that Anna Marie Kuhns Walko has found a Dillard photo showing a light-colored station wagon at the intersection of Elm and Houston. Dillard was certainly there at the right time to make this worth pursuing. The CBS film I referred to in my manuscript will hopefully turn up if the Tunheim Committee (ARRB) succeeds in getting their archives on the assassination released. Also, there are witness statements to be examined and witnesses to be interviewed. Helen Forrest and James Pennington, a largely unknown witness to the Rambler incident, are still being sought. I heard that Marvin C. Robinson has been located and wants to talk.

Wing's UT records:

I received 734 pages of personnel files on Wing through the Texas Open Records Act. These documents confirm some long-held suspicions. Listed on a 1962 biographical data form was the answer to what Wing was doing after he left Mexico City College in 1950 and before he entered UC Berkeley in 1952 (see my manuscript p.124). He received a 1951 "travel grant" from the "International Institute of Education." To my utter astonishment I found that, according to the page ripped out of UT's copy of Who's Who in CIA, "Institute of International Education" received money from the J.M. Kaplan Fund.

This same source also financed the CIA's Institute of International Labor Research. That missing page is the one showing a chart of CIA cover organizations and their private funding conduits. The National Student Association is also listed. See John Ranelagh's The Agency, the "Students and Labor" section in chapter 9, and its footnote on Jack Kaplan's nephew (p. 252, paperback ed.). Larry Haapanen suggested that I talk to Bill Turner about Kaplan, since he has done some writing on him.

E. Howard Hunt says in his memoirs (*Undercover*, pp. 68-69) that this secret funding was directed by the International Organizations Division within the Office of Policy Coordination under the direction of Tom Braden and his assistant Cord Meyer, who took over the division in 1954. Hunt volunteered to set up the Mexico City station for OPC -- their first fully staffed station in Latin America. He arrived December 13, 1950; three-and-a-half months after Wing married his first wife, Margarita Silvia Fuentes, on August 22, 1950 and left Mexico City College. John B. Judis says in his biography of William F. Buckley, Jr. that Buckley arrived in early September and began his CIA work for Hunt "learning about the Mexican student movement." Hunt's mission in Mexico was to "encourage anti-Communists to challenge Communists for leadership in the trade unions, professional and artistic organizations, and student organizations."-- exactly the same mission as Braden's and Meyer's IOD (*Judis,* pp. 90-91).

Given that missing page (the CIA chart), the other mutilated pages, Wing's Rambler and his interest in Pablo Neruda, the amazing thing here is that there are three significant connections to the Paines:

1) Hunt, who was being closely advised by James Burnham at this time, infiltrated agents into Mexico's Trotskyite organization. Burnham, who almost single-handedly killed the U.S. Trotskyite movement, had shared leadership responsibilities in that movement with Michael Paine's United Fruit/CIA-connected father, George Lyman Paine (more on this below);

2) Burton Hersh writes in his 1992 book, *The Old Boys: The American Elite and the Origins of the CIA*, that, "Old chums from Bern had no trouble finding Dulles. By 1950 the hulking Hans Bernd Gisevius had lurched into Washington, where Tom Braden and his wife looked

after him for some months as a favor to Dulles. Already something of a hardship case, Gisevius would stultify Allen with long stories about his efforts in the interests of the Lutheran Synod. Nevertheless, Dulles retained `a great fondness for him,' Braden says, and throughout this period `Allen was feeding him money, I know that Allen was signing chits for $5,000 at a time for Gisevius."'

And 3) Michael Paine's Dulles/Bancroft-connected mother, Ruth Forbes Paine, apparently later married Arthur Middleton Young, one of the inventors of the helicopter. Ruth Forbes Paine was an active member, in Paoli, Pa., of the United World Federalists, founded by Cord Meyer. After selling his helicopter ideas to Bell Aviation in 1942, Young settled in Berkeley, founded the Institute for the Study of Consciousness, and wrote about metaphysics. He is now in his 80s and back in Pa. Bill Kelly has spoken to him and will be interviewing him soon.

Now, I wonder, from whom could a student at Mexico City College have heard about CIA/OPC/IOD money (whether he knew that's what it was or not) in late 1950? At this very same time, Tom Braden and Cord Meyer, both with close contact with the Dulles/Bancroft/Paine circle, controlled the money Wing received!! Both the nature and duration of Wing's travel fellowship now seem to be the crucial questions surrounding the two years prior to his beginning a six-year stay at UC Berkeley in August, 1952. We need to get similar documents from UC Berkeley to see what Wing told them about his travel fellowship.

Now more on that first Paine connection. Recently, Carol Hewett sent me a list of books published by right-wing publisher Arlington House. She circled some authors and subjects which I had already come to know in connection with the assassination, namely William F. Buckley, Jr., Frank Meyer, William J. Gill, Paul Bethel, James Burnham and Nathaniel Weyl.

The only two things I had known about Arlington House before seeing her list was that they published two of the books listed in the Nathaniel Weyl biography removed from The Directory of American Scholars (see my manuscript, pp. 77-79) and a book by William J. Gill that's not on her list. By the time I discovered that Weyl mutilation I had read about John Martino in Coup d'état in America and learned of his relationship with Weyl and Frank Meyer. Also from Canfield's and Weberman's Coup d'état In America, I learned of Commission Document 662 which is an FBI report on all three of them. I'll say more about CD 662 in a moment.

From the Summers missing pages, I already knew about Martino's relationship with Trafficante and Pawley. I had also been reading about Rostow in Gill's The Ordeal of Otto Otepka (Arlington House, 1969). I later learned from the biography of Buckley by John B. Judis that James Burnham (not circled but on her list) had introduced Buckley to E. Howard Hunt. Judis' book also taught me about the close relationship between Buckley and Meyer. All of these people, with the possible exception of Rostow, were spreading phase-one (communist conspiracy) stories about Oswald and Ruby after the assassination, including their apparent ties to Trotskyism.

Rostow, I learned, was on the phase-two (Oswald as lone assassin) bandwagon prior to the public release of the Warren Report. But his main concerns were not over whether Oswald had acted alone, rather they were that "Overseas the report should do something to dilute the conspiracy theory of President Kennedy's assassination;" that "The report does, however, blow the fact that Oswald saw a named KGB agent at the Soviet Embassy in Mexico City;" that "the major task for ourselves [State Dept.] and the USIA will be to prevent the discussion and debate in the U.S. from projecting an image of excessive domestic disarray;" and that because "As the debate unfolds, issues will arise -- almost certainly some issues we have not now anticipated," State, Treasury, Justice, and the White House "must be a united government in this matter."

Even Paul Bethel, also on the Arlington House list, was a member of the Free Cuba Committee (headed by Eladio del Valle) and was helping disseminate a phase-one story that an "admitted Castro agent" had been arrested a week before the assassination for plotting to kill Kennedy. The fact that this motley crew is represented among the books in print at Arlington House is reason enough to suspect them of being a CIA publisher.

The most interesting individual on the list, however, is James Burnham. A suggestion from Jeff Pascal to read an essay about Burnham in *The Orwell Reader* led to some intriguing revelations about him. He may be a key to Wing's interest in the assassination and the Rambler. According to a former Wing student, Wing was "obsessed" with Chilean poet and politician Pablo Neruda. It is therefore interesting that Neruda, who is mentioned in David Atlee Phillips' *Night Watch* (Atheneum, 1977), wrote poetry about coups, assassinations and the United Fruit Company. Neruda was also a diplomat in the Allende government, "accompanying [Allende] in his concerns and sharing that whole turbid atmosphere with its noxious plots and intrigues orchestrated from afar." (Volodia Teitelboim, Neruda, University of Texas Press, Austin, 1991, p. 424.)

Most interesting, however, is the fact that Neruda spirited one David Siqueiros out of Mexico. Siqueiros was awaiting trial as the leader of the first abortive assassination attempt on Leon Trotsky. I learned this fascinating tidbit from a little known book on the Trotsky assassination by CIA publicist Isaac Don Levine (see Scott, *Deep Politics*, Univ. of Calif. Press, 1993, pp. 55, 288, 289). In the acknowledgments of that book, *The Mind of an Assassin* (Farrar, Straus and Cudahy, 1959; Signet, 1960), Levine writes, "To Sylvia and Nathaniel Weyl, who lived in Mexico and wrote the first biography of President Cardenas, I am indebted for translating from the Spanish the voluminous official and documentary reports on the assassin and his crime, and for their collaboration in digesting the material for publication."

E. Howard Hunt says in his memoirs, "I also met and frequently conferred with Dr. James Burnham, a Princeton classmate of Joe Bryan's and onetime professor of philosophy. Burnham was a consultant to OPC [Office of Policy Coordination, the first covert action group created within CIA in 1948] on virtually every subject of interest to our organization. He had extensive contacts in Europe and, by virtue of his Trotskyite background, was something of an authority on domestic and foreign Communist parties and front organizations. Through him I was to meet a young Yale graduate, William F. Buckley, Jr...."

The fact that this former communist was friends with Hunt and Buckley and ended up as a pioneer of CIA covert operations is even more intriguing considering Burnham was not your ordinary Trotskyite. In 1938, as a leader of the American Trotskyists on the National and Political Committees of the Socialist Workers Party (SWP), Burnham introduced a resolution declaring the USSR was no longer a workers' state but had become, as exhibited by the Hitler-Stalin Pact, totalitarian and its leaders Fascist (Albert Glotzer, *Trotsky*, Buffalo, NY: Prometheus, 1989, p. 284-90).

This caused such a bitter debate that Trotsky attempted to defend the movement against the "revisionists" led by Burnham. Trotsky labeled him an enemy of the dialectic and argued that Burnham "was using the Hitler-Stalin Pact and the Finnish invasions merely as vehicles for developing what he regarded as untenable theoretical views." Despite Trotsky's hope that the movement remain united in case the impending world war caused the political destruction of Stalin, a formal split occurred in April 1940 -- one month before the Siqueiros led assault on Trotsky's life.

By this time, interestingly enough, despite the fact that Burnham was to address the new Minority faction's Workers' Party at their first convention, he was nowhere to be found and had in fact deserted leftist politics. A few weeks later Siqueiros gained entry to Trotsky's fortified compound because a guard simply let him in. The guard, who had been a

Trotskyite for only six months, was an American named Sheldon Harte, the 23-year-old son of a wealthy New York businessman. After spraying the compound with machine gun fire, the gunmen took Harte with them. He was later found dead and thus forever silent about his strange actions on the night of the attack. But, as Trotsky's friend and biographer Albert Glotzer points out, "What is certain is that it was most unusual for the SWP to send a guard to Mexico, especially someone who was in the organization for so short a time." After Harte's death, his father said he was surprised Sheldon was a Trotskyist because he knew he had a picture of Stalin in his room and assumed Sheldon supported the Kremlin.

With the split of the American Party (the largest organized Trotskyist group), and the successful assassination of Trotsky in August 1940, Trotskyism essentially died out, but not before one last small triumph. The Workers' Party and its successor, the Independent Socialist League, were placed on the Attorney General's List of Subversive Organizations alongside the Communist Party and similar organizations. The Trotskyist groups successfully sued the government and were removed from the list. Despite long efforts to obtain witnesses against the Trotskyists, the government was only able to find two -- a Russian expert from Columbia University, and their former leader James Burnham.

After leaving Trotskyism Burnham wrote two books on his political views, *The Managerial Revolution* (1940) and *The Machiavellians* (1942). In 1946, two years before publishing his prophetic masterpiece, 1984 George Orwell was giving a lot of thought to, and wrote his essay about these two books called "Second Thoughts on James Burnham" (*The Orwell Reader,* NY: Harcourt, Brace, Jovanovich, 1956, pp. 335-54). According to Orwell, Burnham's view was that,

"Capitalism is disappearing, but socialism is not replacing it. What is now arising is a new kind of planned, centralized society which will be neither capitalist nor, in any accepted sense of the word, democratic. The rulers of this new society will be the people who effectively control the means of production: that is, business executives, technicians, bureaucrats, and soldiers, lumped together by Burnham under the name of "managers." These people will eliminate the old capitalistic class, crush the working class, and so organize society that all power and economic privilege remain in their own hands. Private property rights will be abolished, but common ownership will not be established. The new "managerial" societies will not consist of a patchwork of small, independent states, but of great super-states grouped round the main industrial centers in Europe, Asia, and America. These super-states will fight among themselves for possession of the remaining uncaptured portions of the earth, but will probably be unable to conquer one another completely. Internally, each society will be hierarchical, with an aristocracy of talent at the top and a mass of semi-slaves at the bottom."

In *The Machiavellians*, Orwell tells us, Burnham adds that, "Society is of its nature oligarchical, and the power of the oligarchy always rests upon force and fraud. Burnham does not deny that `good' motives may operate in private life, but he maintains that politics consists of the struggle for power, and nothing else. All historical changes finally boil down to the replacement of one ruling class by another....Power can sometimes be won without violence, but never without fraud, because it is necessary to make use of the masses, and the masses would not co-operate if they knew that they were simply serving the purposes of a minority." I have never read a more true and concise description of the U.S. military-industrial complex and its rise to world domination over the last 45 years.

I suspect that Burnham was a plant in the Trotskyite movement with a mission to do as much damage to it as possible in order to prevent Trotsky from taking the USSR back from Stalin and spreading Communism beyond its borders with greater skill and commitment than Stalin. I also suspect that Burnham's fellow plants in the movement, if not Burnham himself, were the actual murderers of Trotsky. How else could Burnham have the experience to advise the Office of Policy Coordination on every aspect of its operations, which included assassinations begun by the OSS in Algiers as early as 1942.

Burnham wasn't the only future Arlington House associate making 180 degree turns in his politics in the late 1930s. According to CD 662, mentioned above, the FBI investigated Sylvia Weyl in 1953 and determined that she had been a member of the Communist Party (CP) of the United States from 1931 to 1937. The report adds,

"She stated she became disillusioned because of the increasing awareness of Russian control and broke definitely with the Party in 1939.

"Frank Meyer, Woodstock, New York, a self-admitted former member of the CP, was interviewed as a reference in 1953, and stated that the Weyls broke with the CP sometime between 1937-1939. He indicated the Weyls have made public statements concerning their past activities and present feelings and he feels they are both strongly, clearly and deeply anti-Communist."

Meyer's own political transformation was seemingly so drastic that he joined the staff of Buckley's National Review in 1956 and later became a senior editor along with former Trotskyist James Burnham.

And finally, with his probable background in deep cover operations and assassinations, ties to E. Howard Hunt, William F. Buckley, Jr., and other Kennedy assassination figures published by Arlington House, it is most interesting that Burnham shared leadership responsibilities in the American Trotskyist movement with none other than George Lyman Paine, Michael Paine's CIA/United Fruit-connected father.

When we add to all of this the existence of two images in George Wing's office door montage that appear to be a photograph of Trotsky next to a photograph of his assassin, Ramon Mercader (a drinking buddy of Sheldon Harte), the implication that Wing is hinting at a connection between his Rambler and the Paine family becomes more compelling than ever.

Another discovery in the UT files on Wing has to do with his activities in 1963. Despite documented plans to the contrary, Wing missed two fall semesters during his career. His 1991 absence is accounted for by his grave illness prior to his death. The other -- long predicted through supposition -- is the fall semester of 1963 -- no explanation. In 29 years of scheduled teaching, he apparently missed only these two semesters. He even taught a reduced load in 1971 after a severe heart attack in December, 1970. Yet with increasing workloads all around, Wing, a lowly assistant professor, was apparently allowed to skip what was only the second fall semester of his new employment at UT.

Also, a new name has come up. A June 5, 1967 letter from then Spanish & Portuguese Chairman Theodore Andersson (the man who hired Wing in 1962) suggests Mafia links to a man known to Wing and Andersson as "Jack." The letter reads:

"Jack has mentioned to me a playwright and novelist named Jorge Ibarguengortia as somebody you might be interested in getting acquainted with if you don't already know him. Jack thinks he is connected with the National University, says his English is perfect and that he is not part of the Maffia [sic]. Would you be able to look him up when you go down to Mexico City?"

Wing was beginning to research literary developments in the Mexican theater around this time so this is partly innocent. But four questions immediately come to mind: 1) Who is Jack? 2) How does Jack know who is or is not part of the Mafia? 3) Who is Jorge Ibargüengortia? and 4) Why would Jorge's non-affiliation with the Mafia be of concern to Wing? Also, after re-reading Philip Agee's *Inside the Company: A CIA Diary,* I am wondering if the misspelling "Maffia" is a deliberate code. CIA cadets using Air Force officer school as cover were only identifiable by an "xxx" after their names on Air Force documents.

If "Jack" is Jack Dulles, the adjunct UT professor and expert on Brazil, this gets quite interesting considering Greg Doyle's latest findings on "Honest Joe" (The Fourth Decade, vol. 1, no. 5, July 1994, pp. 13-16).

I accept, based on John Franklyn Elrod and other evidence, that Ruby and Oswald were involved in gun running together. Given that, it is not a stretch to accept a Paine-Ruby link through Oswald. There are also the likely Paine-Ruby links through her friend Mamantov and Ruby's buddy Periera -- both of Magnolia Laboratories. Now we learn from Doyle that Julius Schepps, associate and financier of Ruby's closest friends, was friendly with Benjamin H. Stephens, one of the organizers of Magnolia Oil, a director of Standard Oil, and an advisor to Harold Ickes, FDR's interior secretary. There are several Ruby-Dulles connections suggested by this.

Ickes, according to Emanuel Josephson's 1948 book, *The Strange Death of Franklin D. Roosevelt*, was an attorney for the Rockefeller-Standard Oil interests in the Chicago area (p. 231). Josephson also connects Ickes to the "Union Now" conspiracy to return the U.S. to the British Empire as a secret colony (p. 225). That conspiracy is a major part of the writings of Carroll Quigley and Anthony Sutton, from whom we learned of similar conspiratorial intrigues involving the Wall Street law firm of Weinburg and Posner (relation to Gerald suspected but not yet known). This firm was tied to the whole Skull & Bones crowd in the 1910-20 era.

Those activities (creating the German/Russian conflict), and that crowd, included friends and members of the Dulles and Bush families. In Sutton's *America's Secret Establishment*, we find, on page 146, that this Posner firm was also tied to Colonel Edward Mandell House, the man who put Wilson and his cabinet from the University of Texas in the White House with Allen Dulles' treasonous uncle, Robert Lansing. Also, Lansing was stirring up trouble in Mexico at the same time as William F. Buckley, Sr. With that in mind, look at page 615 of Dick Russell's book, *The Man Who Knew Too Much* (paperback ed.). Mamantov and Bush knew each other "very well." All of this makes me really want to read *The Secret Diary of Harold L. Ickes* (Simon & Schuster, New York, 1959). I'm becoming more and more interested in "interior departments" and "commerce departments." Mexico's DFS (see below) was part of that country's Interior Ministry. A look at interior and commerce officials in this and other countries reveals a motley cast of characters.

A further motivation to study Ickes is the fact that Schepps and Stephens were prominent personalities at Mercantile National Bank, in whose building was the H.L. Hunt family offices where Ruby dropped off a young woman named Connie Trammel for a job interview the day before the assassination. According to Peter Noyes, Connie told the FBI that she was a graduate of UT in 1963, the year Wing skipped a fall semester. She also told them she met Ruby while still a student when she and some girlfriends visited Dallas and stayed at Harry Ransom's old haunt, the Adolphus Hotel. Bill Kelly and I are trying to locate her.

This becomes more significant when we include a fact from the chronology section of Gaeton Fonzi's book: Michael Paine was a resident at Everett Glover's house at the time of the "Strange Magnolia" party. Of the four house mates (Schmidt, Pierce, Glover and Paine), only Paine did not work at Magnolia Labs. But Paine must have known his wife's friend Mamantov who was teaching Russian to Schmidt, Pierce and Fredricksen at Magnolia. Here are some other related items from Fonzi's book: Four days prior to Oswald beginning his job at Jaggars-Chiles-Stovall (a job arranged by de Mohrenschildt according to Marguerite), de Mohrenschildt attended a party at the Oswalds' apartment after having just left the Van Cliburn Piano Competition! Recall Van Cliburn's long time friends and supporters Barbara J. Burris and D.H. Byrd. Fonzi also reveals that John Martino was a relative of Philadelphia Mafia boss Angelo Bruno! This may be where Wing's suspected interest in both Martino and the Mafia originated.

Byrd's powerful cousin, Sen. Harry Byrd, had dealings, naturally, with Ickes. And in early 1941, Byrd wrestled control of the Lend-Lease program from Roosevelt. Eugene Rostow's first Washington post was in the Lend-Lease program. (Richard Bissell's, by the way, was in the Commerce Dept.)

According to Josephson (p. 226), Lend-Lease was a slick way around the law. The Johnson Act forbade loans to countries who had defaulted on their WWI debts. It also pulled the U.S. further into the War despite the strong isolationist sentiment in the country and in Congress. Then, according to Josephson, the Rockefeller-Standard Oil interests ordered their creature, Hitler, to attack Russia rather than England, pulling the U.S. farther into the conflict. The move that finally worked, however, was Rockefeller-Standard Oil's arming of Japan and Roosevelt's goading them to attack. (An example of this, not mentioned by Josephson, was revealed in an A&E documentary on Yamamoto. In 1938, he was an invited foreign guest at U.S. Naval maneuvers showing off the effectiveness of aircraft carriers. The maneuver chosen by the Navy to do this was a mock bombing of Pearl Harbor!)

Now here's something even more intriguing: In *Deep Politics*, Scott tells about Mexico's DFS Chief, Miguel Nazar Haro (a close friend of Winston Scott) who "was secretly indicted by a U.S. grand jury in San Diego for his participation in North America's largest stolen-car ring, the CIA blocked the indictment because of Nazar Haro's `indispensability as a source of intelligence in Mexico and Central America.'" (Scott, p. 105) The footnote for that statement tells us, "Others who have been linked to trafficking in stolen cars across the U.S.-Mexican border include Frank Sturgis and Richmond Harper (see Chapter 5), as well as the major Nicaraguan drug trafficker Norwin Meneses Canterero."

Moving on to chapter 5 we learn that Richmond Harper is the brother of Tito Harper at whose ranch George and Jeanne de Mohrenschildt stayed as the first stop of their walking trip from Mexico to the Panama Canal. Richmond was also involved with Herman Beebe, drugs and arms smuggling, Barry Seal, the Gambino crime family (Ruby was involved with the Genovese family in Cuban gun running according to Ruby employee Nancy Perrin Rich whose husband, Robert, owned a Rambler), and deeply tied to the Nixon White House. De Mohrenschildt reported back to the CIA after that walking trip.

Based on this, de Mohrenschildt is very likely another Oswald-Ruby-Paine connection -- with the addition of stolen cars. This strengthens the likelihood that the third Oswald-Ruby-Paine-Rambler connection I noted in my manuscript, involving de Mohrenschildt's Cuban-Venezuelan Oil Trust and its ties to 30th of November gun running and the assassination, also involved a Rambler wagon like Wings. Why? Because of C.B. Smith's ties to de Mohrenschildt's former employer Buckley Sr. (Pantipec Oil) and General Motors (whose Cuban representative was on de Mohrenschildt's Oil Trust board; see p. 134 of my manuscript.) I strongly suspect that somewhere there is a Smith connection to Nazar Haro's stolen-car ring also. And let's not forget Jack Lawrence's background in auto dealerships in Florida.

Even the Warren Commission, in its February 24, 1964 memo to Richard Helms noted, based on a Chicago informant connecting 30th of November arms sales to the Kennedy assassination, that Ruby could have been motivated by involvement with such a group.

And I'll bet that when I take a look I find a C.B. Smith link to Jack Valenti's Al Thomas Appreciation Dinner committee in Houston; on which sat Jack Halfen (another gun runner involved with Ruby). Of course it was that dinner (the November 21, 1963 date of which was set just prior to April 23, 1963 and never changed) that brought Kennedy to Texas. Recall that the UT Rambler switched ownership from Smith to Wing on April 26, 1963 -- two days after LBJ announced the Texas trip to the press in Dallas, Marina moved in with Ruth, and Oswald left for New Orleans.

"Wing" and the Secret Service:

In WC Vol. 26 there is a Secret Service report (CE 3075) with attachments. One of the attachments is the manifest for Delta 821, the flight the Oswalds took from New York to Dallas on June 14, 1962. At the bottom of the alphabetized list is the name "Wing".

George Wing was in Berkeley around this time finalizing his employment plans with the spook-schooled Theodore Andersson (Yale, Wells College, American University, State Dept.), and preparing for his trip to Austin to start his new job at UT. But of course he could have been anywhere. I'd sure like to learn as much as possible about this manifest. And if that is George on that flight, I'd like to find out who "Smith" and "White" are. The Secret Service obviously wanted to know who flew with the Oswalds. Now, so do I.

Craig Coverup?:

I received from Walter Graf pages that appear to be copied from Roger Craig's 1971 manuscript. I was worried by differences between some of the statements in those pages and slightly different statements in a copy of Craig's manuscript I received in March 1993 from Michael Murphy of Fort Lauderdale. Mr. Murphy sent his copy to me via computer linkup, but I trusted it was faithful to Craig's original work. If Mr. Graf's excerpts from the manuscript are verbatim, then those in Murphy's copy are not.

Another thing that bothered me was that I based an erroneous conclusion on one of those differences (see my manuscript pp. 64-67). A notation about "Page 22 - Par. 5" in Mr. Graf's copy made me realize I had completely missed Craig's reference to the release of this prisoner. I falsely accused Craig of omitting it from his manuscript. The relevant passage from my copy reads:

"I had several meetings with Jim Garrison. He showed me numerous pictures taken in Dealey Plaza on November 22, 1963. Among them was a picture of a Latin male. I recognized him as being the same man I had seen driving the Rambler station wagon in which I had seen Oswald leave the Book Depository area. I was surprised and I asked Jim who the man was. Jim did not know but he did say this man was arrested in Dealey Plaza immediately after the assassination but was released by Dallas Police because he could not speak English! This was, to me, highly unusual. In my experience as a police officer I had never known of a person (or prisoner) being released because of a language barrier. Interpreters were, of course, always available."

Had I noticed this it would have answered all my questions about it and possibly also about the Rambler. Dennis Ford erroneously stated that Craig saw the driver in custody because of Henry Hurt's statement that "According to Craig, the Latin man was released...." It was according to Craig, but Hurt left out the fact that Craig's source was Garrison.

That's because Hurt's source (Gary Shaw's *Cover-Up*) also failed to credit it to Garrison. Shaw's source, an interview with Craig taped the same year he wrote his manuscript, has Craig stating that the Latin man was released. True enough, but Craig didn't see it happen. This led Prof. Ford to credit it to a nonexistent eyewitness account by Craig. Craig only learned of the release from Garrison.

Making matters worse, Ford blended this photo identification with an entirely separate photo which Craig identified for Garrison -- that of Edgar Eugene Bradley. This blending of facts led Ford to state that Craig saw the driver released by Edgar Eugene Bradley. Amazing! Dennis Ford has been the leader in warning researchers against such inaccuracies based on unreliable memories.

Ford's problem may well have come from his own vague memory of two poorly written sentences in Penn Jones' *Forgive My Grief III*. Those sentences, in which the same facts are blended, reads: "The driver of the station wagon, according to Craig, was a Latin who had been arrested minutes before and immediately released by a man posing as a Secret Service agent. In October 1967 when Craig was shown a picture of Edgar Eugene Bradley he identified Bradley as the man who posed as a Secret Service agent that day."

Whether or not a fake Secret Service man was involved (Garrison only said the "Dallas Police" released him), that does not mean it was the same one Craig encountered. Maybe Garrison told Craig that Bradley got the driver released. Maybe Craig said this on that tape Gary Shaw has. But if that is so, why did Craig not put it in his manuscript? In any event, the important thing here is that we can now track down that photo Garrison showed to Craig and see if the Latin man is Eladio del Valle. That is who Cuban Intelligence identified as the Rambler driver based on witness descriptions (see Claudia Furiati's recent book, *ZR Rifle*, Ocean Press, 1994, p. 130).

William F. Buckley, Sr.:

On August 26, 1994, Bill Kelly told me an amazing fact he found in a biography of the Buckley family: William F. Buckley, Sr. taught Spanish at the University of Texas at Austin! That makes it all but certain that C.B. Smith was a student of Buckley's. I plan to request Buckley's UT personnel file. Someone also needs to look into an incident that has been a curiosity to me for years: The April 1963 death of Walter Prescott Webb in a car accident in Austin. Webb was Smith's mentor and a close friend of LBJ (see my manuscript, p. 122). Webb was also the type of person who could put two and two together, and who would not tolerate a conspiracy to assassinate the President.

Back Seat Magazines:

Bill Kelly made a fascinating connection regarding the June 7, 1963 Life magazine (see my appendix). I looked through it in vain for anything as obviously JFK connected as in the Esquires. Bill called on

May 14, 1994 and said it is obvious if you are familiar with a little-known story among the Kennedy assassination lore. In the magazine is a small story about dredging the underwater debris field of a nuclear sub that sank the previous April, the Thresher.

As I have recently learned, only a handful of researchers -- Bill Turner, Kenneth Formet and Larry Haapanen among them -- know anything about this aspect of the assassination. According to Kelly and Haapanen, no one has ever published a word about it; a fact that is most intriguing with regard to Wing's back seat magazines. It is the Bray-Thresher story. I first read about it in Bill Kelly's excellent unpublished manuscript.

In brief, Edward F. Bray sent Governor Connally a warning letter on August 12, 1963. It said that, "a plot is underway to assassinate you." Bray, who worked for the Bendix Corporation, claimed he had been visited by some men who said they were investigating the sinking of the Thresher. They said they were members of an organization known as Justice for the Crew of the Thresher (JFCOTT).

The men claimed its members were planning to assassinate John B. Connally and another former Secretary of the Navy, Fred Korth. Bray reported this to the authorities three months before the assassination. He also predicted, based on what he had learned from the men, that Connally would be shot by a disgruntled ex-serviceman with a high powered rifle while riding in an open car during a parade in Dallas.

The men later returned, according to Bray, and left him an 8mm film of the assassination, taken from the vantage point of the alleged assassin's lair on the sixth floor of the Texas School Book Depository. Bray claimed that stills from the film were received by Chief Justice Earl Warren.

The Bendix Corp. was the plaintiff and Bray was the defendant in a trial that took place in Natrona County, Wyoming in March, 1965. Court documents obtained by researcher Kenneth Forment indicate that Bray tried, unsuccessfully, to have the film entered into evidence.

Bray claimed he later showed the film to former Presidential assistant Theodore Sorensen, at a banquet in Portland, Oregon in 1966. when contacted by Formet, however, Sorensen's office, declined to comment on anything involving the assassination of President Kennedy.

Bill Kelly speculates that alternative motives were being set up for Oswald in case the `lone-nut' scenario did not hold up. The JFCOTT motive, according to Kelly, "was predicated upon Oswald's dissatisfaction with his `undesirable' military discharge."

Kelly also points out that during World War II, George DeMohrenschildt lived in Washington D.C. with two men, one a British

MI6 agent, and the other a U.S. Naval officer named Hall, who was later a skipper of the Thresher, but not at the time of its accident.

Kelly also notes that "DeMohrenschildt also went out of his way to introduce Oswald to retired Admiral Chester `Henri' Bruton, a former nuclear sub commander who was a senior executive at Collins Radio. Burton's [sic] last job for the Navy was to redesign the Navy's communications systems with its nuclear submarine fleet."

On May 21, I talked with David Gage, whom I've known for several years through local politics. He joined the Navy in 1970, was in underwater demolitions, attended Marine sniper school, and spent most of his Navy career serving submarine duty. For many years he's been involved in high-level sonar research at the University of Texas.

When I mentioned the June 7, 1963 Life pictorial about the dredging operations, he surprised me by saying, "Yeah, the one showing the O-rings." I asked how he knew that. He said everyone in the submarine fraternity knows about the Thresher. He had never heard of JFCOTT or the Bray incident, however -- a fact also intriguing with regard to Wing.

According to Gage, the common opinion among submarine crews is that the official story is wrong. Thresher, he said, could not have been crushed due to a failure of its pressure gauges. Subs have several backup systems and the engineers even have non-technical means of sensing depth.

Gage's theory, shared by other submarine crewmen, is that Thresher was involved in an unauthorized search and destroy bluff of a Soviet sub. It is a game he admitted being involved in often. They would carry the bluff as far as opening the torpedo doors -- which can be heard by the enemy sub. When I asked if they always stopped short of firing, he said, "If they fired, no one ever admitted it."

He described a tricky maneuver that Hunter class subs use in this game to position themselves behind the enemy. It causes a period of blindness of the surrounding terrain. He suspects Thresher clipped a mountain during one of these maneuvers. A coverup could have simply been to keep the Soviets from making political hay out of it. But David said those who knew anything could have kept it from ONI investigators without all that much difficulty.

I asked him about Collins Radio equipment on board and he said he didn't know of any used for navigation, which is what he did. He added that they could have been used in communications but subs never transmitted, they only received. He encouraged me to keep digging and said if he comes across anyone with knowledge of the Thresher he would put me in touch with them. I also intend to contact a former next door neighbor, Eric Copt, who is now an executive with Chevron Oil in

Denver, Colorado. He was serving on a sub in 1963 which was later in the Tonkin Gulf during the "attack" on the Maddox.

I also need to see if another fellow I know, Gerrell Moore, can shed any light on this. He's currently the comptroller of the Pflugerville Independent School District. He was the chief intelligence officer (NSA) aboard the Maddox during the Tonkin Gulf incidents. He's been telling what he knows about that period for years but none of the "authors" who have interviewed him, including one from U.S. News and World Report, have every published his more incriminating observations. He may at least know someone equally willing to talk about the Thresher. The fundamental question, though, is: What, if any, was George Wing's interest in the subject?

Smith-Wing-Rogers Nexus:

There seems to be a promising line of inquiry concerning C.B. Smith and Charles Frederick Rogers. Keep in mind that any truthful part of the assassination must necessarily connect to other truthful parts.

It began with new information related to the January 1964 Esquire back-seat magazine. At the very least, this issue refers back to Wing's office door montage (see my manuscript pp. 82-83). I'd like to hear someone argue that none of this could be considered cryptic. It would have to be someone with quite a high tolerance for coincidence.

Consider this piece of the puzzle: R.H.S. Crossman (whose article on Dresden appears in that issue of Esquire) has also written about the psychological warfare aspects of the Darlan affair. Admiral Jean Darlan was a key figure in Vichy France who led that collaborationist government's negotiations with Hitler. The U.S. made a deal with him allowing them to land in North Africa without French resistance and allowing the very anti-communist Darlan to be military governor of North Africa with assurances that he would have U.S. support as a senior leader in postwar France. Moscow was of course very upset about this and it was quickly turning into another Hess situation.

The intra-Allied conflict was conveniently put on ice when Darlan was assassinated allegedly by a rightist! The strongly suspected conspiracy behind the assassin remains a mystery to this day. Sound familiar? The man who replaced Darlan was his political twin General Henri Giraud. There was one difference, however. Giraud was principally sponsored politically and financially in Western circles by Allen Dulles. This was prior to Dulles becoming involved in the Hitler plot with Ruth Paine's friend! (See Christopher Simpson, *The Splendid Blond Beast*, Grove Press, 1993, pp. 120-21.)

While we are in this era, let's not forget the similarities between the fatal Kennedy motorcade and the motorcade that resulted in the assassination of Reinhard Heydrich. There are also indications (from Mary Bancroft no less) that Dulles may have been involved in that assassination.

I found something related to this while thumbing through Thomas Powers' new book, Heisenburg's War. Werner Karl Heisenburg was Germany's Robert Oppenheimer. The OSS was very nervous about Germany's atomic bomb research. I looked up Dulles in the index and to my amazement discovered that Powers wrote about Dulles as the manager of an OSS assassination plot against Heisenburg -- using as the assassin, a former major league baseball player.

Meanwhile, back in the states, C.B. Smith's work overlapped with the War Production Board whose vice chairman was Ferdinand Eberstadt, formerly a central figure in Dillon, Read & Company's financing of Aryanized German industrialists, and later a central figure in the creation of the CIA. Eberstadt sat on this board with John J. McCloy.

After the war, C.B. Smith went to work for GM, whose pre- to post-war German plant managers benefited greatly from Nazi prisoner/slave laborers, and who, according to a 1936 report from Ambassador William Dodd to President Roosevelt, had become deeply involved in German weapons production. Smith was an executive in the company's most prestigious division, Chevrolet. He was GM's Chevrolet man in Houston, where he had already made a big name for himself as a professor and athletic director at the University of Houston.

Add to this the fact that in Houston, directly after the war, Charles Frederick Rogers, CIA/CAP pilot, cold blooded killer, and identical twin of "Frenchie," lived with his Marcello-bookie father, next door to a Chevrolet dealership while attending the University of Houston. Rogers spent the war as a carrier and destroyer radio man (read cryptographer) for ONI in the South Pacific stomping grounds of Navy Secretary James Vincent Forrestal (former president at Dillon, Read with his good friend Eberstadt). Spanish student Wing was an aviation fire controlman and ordnance specialist (and according to his UT files, worked on bomb sights) in the Navy during the exact same period that fluently Spanish speaking Rogers was enlisted. Forrestal's Navy legal aide was John B. Connally. This most definitely suggests the pre-history of a Smith-Wing-Rogers nexus.

These same South Pacific islands were the testing grounds (using allied prisoners as guinea pigs) of the germ warfare experiments whose Japanese perpetrators were given immunity by General Charles Willoughby in exchange for their test data. This data, no doubt, later found a home in Richard Helms' brainchild, MK/ULTRA. Serving directly under Willoughby, of course, was Colonel William Potter Gale,

who directed the anti-Japanese guerrilla operations in the Philippines --
the same operations that later made Edward G. Lansdale's name
legendary. (See the November 1993 *High Times* magazine.)

These same germ warfare experiments were allegedly the target of
photo-reconnaissance by the ill-fated Earhart-Noonan flight. If so,
Forrestal could have given it his blessing. Interestingly, Earhart often
visited, as a nurses aide, the same airfield in Toronto where Forrestal had
trained as a pilot. More interestingly, Richard E. Byrd, pioneer of naval
photo-reconnaissance, helped finance the Earhart-Noonan flight.

I recently learned from Richard Ryckoff in Maui that, according to
John Judge, Forrestal debriefed Byrd after a post war trip to the South
Pole. Byrd then gave several public speeches about how WWII was not
over because there were Nazi camps operating at the South Pole.

Forrestal, who returned to Dillon, Read after the war and later became
the nations first secretary of defense, died in 1949 after being sacked by
Truman for plotting against him in the 1948 presidential election.

He allegedly committed suicide after telling his friend Ferdinand
Eberstadt that certain people in the White House were out to get him.
Eberstadt sent him to visit Robert Lovett in Florida where things got
worse. He was admitted to Bethesda Hospital where on May 22, he fell
sixteen floors to his death when a pajama cord he was hanged by,
snapped outside a storeroom window. No one of Forrestal's stature in
Washington hierarchy has committed suicide since then until very
recently -- Clinton's friend Vince Foster. There was, however, the 1987
attempted suicide by then private citizen, former National Security
Advisor Robert McFarlane, one of the original planners of the Contra
war against Nicaragua and a central figure in the Iran-Contra scandal.

Forrestal was not only the man who directed Eberstadt to put in
writing his ideas that created the CIA, he urged and co-planned, with
CIA Director Hillenkoetter, the first political covert action by the agency,
and he was the one who originally had George Kennan put his ideas on
containment in writing -- thus becoming arguably the father of the
modern military-industrial-intelligence establishment and all it wrought.
(Kennan's brother, Kent W. Kennan, is a professor emeritus at UT.) The
icing on this cake is the fact that the Dillon of Dillon, Read & Company
was Douglas Dillon, the man ultimately in charge of JFK's Secret
Service.

It's becoming more and more unlikely that the January 1964 Esquire
magazine, with its references to R.H.S. Crossman, just found its way into
the back seat of Wing's unusual car with at least one other highly
intriguing magazine and remained there for at least two years by a
normal run-of-the-mill coincidence. Can the argument that there is

nothing whatsoever cryptic about this magazine be made beyond any reasonable doubt?

When thinking about this, I consider the concepts of cryptology and advertising. Wing, it seems, was engaged in both. On the one hand he had to advertise the existence of his car and its strange holdings. On the other he had to disguise the ultimate message being advertised. Put another way, he had to draw attention to a mystery.

Perhaps he knew human nature well enough to realize that there are people who cannot ignore a mystery, whereas there are lots of people who will ignore, and in this case perhaps discredit, advertising. Also there is the possibility that if he were too obvious, depending on how long he had been engaged in this activity, his attempted communication could have been directly noticed by Gonzalez-Gerth, Ransom, Dulles, Smith, Rostow, Kennan, Kozmetzky, Gemberling, Burris, LBJ, D.H. Byrd, Dr. Oscar W. Reinmuth (reportedly Ransom's closest friend and OSS office mate who was head of the UT Classics Dept.), Charles Kunkel (the Secret Service man who interrogated Marina, was possibly listed in Ruby's notebook, and later became Austin's SAIC), or any number of other possible informants.

Sugar and Leek:

These authors of *The Assassination Chain* (Corwin Books, 1976), were among the first, if not the first to point out the strangeness at the party where Oswald "met" Ruth Paine. Having not read their book, I had to figure all of that out on my own. Their book was the last place I expected to find a prior study of it. Sybil is dead but I would like to locate Burt Sugar and ask him some questions about his Paine-Ruby claim.

Links between persons A, B and C:

A common counter-argument against my manuscript is that it is merely guilt by association. But when person A is accused of killing the president of the United States from a building he was working in due to help from person B, and person C kills person A in police custody, and persons A, B and C all have past and present links to political assassination conspiracies, and there is an additional mountainous preponderance of circumstantial evidence (e.g. Ruth Paine, Arthur Young and the Catherwood Foundation), the probability of linkage extends well beyond a reasonable doubt. In the U.S. legal system a preponderance of circumstantial evidence is equal to hard evidence. Ruth Paine could have borrowed a Rambler station wagon from Jack Ruby.

Another counter-argument is: Because there is no hard evidence, none should be sought. Mine is: There is plenty of evidence to make it worth asking Burt Sugar what he knows and how he knows it. A good case in point is the Phillips/Bishop situation. There is not a shred of hard evidence that they are one person, but the circumstantial evidence is conclusive. As Fonzi says, "'Maurice Bishop' was David Atlee Phillips. I state that unequivocally....In addition to the abundance of evidence...believe me, I know that he was. And Bob Blakey and the House Assassinations Committee knew that he was, although its report did not admit that." (Fonzi p. 408) That also applies to the evidence suggesting the pre-history of a Wing-Rogers-Smith nexus.

Jane Robertson:

I give her full credit for anything that results from our Rambler research. After telling her about Wing's car briefly during ASK `92, she made me aware, two months later, of the Ruby-Cheek connection and Kensington's and Ford's articles referring to the Dealey Plaza Rambler. That, in turn, led directly to my paper. Prior to her interest I thought the Rambler was a dead issue despite my curiosity about Wing. Ironically, the reason we had our initial conversation was because she vaguely remembered reading about a Paine-Rambler-Ruby link. She was most disappointed when she rediscovered it in Sugar and Leek. She then attempted, without success, to locate Sugar.

Dave Reinmuth:

On July 25, 1993, I got a call from researcher Dave Reinmuth of Irving, Texas. He was one of Jim Marrs' students and had a friend, John Armstrong, who had helped Craig Roberts with his book, *Kill Zone: A Sniper Looks at Dealey Plaza*, (Typhoon Press, 1994).

Reinmuth had just read my Providence paper and wanted to tell me that his maternal grandmother was a member of the Byrd family and, more importantly, that his paternal grandfather was Dr. Oscar W. Reinmuth, former chairman of the UT Classics Department. Dr. Reinmuth was Harry Ransom's best friend and former office mate when Reinmuth was serving in the OSS. This was the first direct connection between Ransom and the OSS.

Dave Reinmuth said he had many of his grandfather's letters in his attic and would read them for more information on Ransom. He also said he had Ruth Paine's phone number and would call her and attempt to get her on record regarding any contact at any time with a Rambler station wagon or the owner of such a car.

Dave Perry suggested that I do that myself and gave me Ruth Paines address and phone number. But I think that's a bit naive considering Paine's connections to the CIA and Allen Dulles. I also must assume that Ruth Paine is aware of my research and its incriminating nature to her and her family. I would rather see her under oath before the Tunheim Committee.

Reinmuth also told me his grandfather and Ransom took road trips together in 1963.

Bernard Barker:

Two Dallas lawmen at the scene of the crime encountered and later identified one fake Secret Service man each. These incidents are therefore related. Craig's encounter dealt with a Rambler directly, and Weitzman's encounter later dealt with Barker directly, and the Red Ripper dealt with a Rambler and Barker directly. As for Craig's and Weitzman's sightings, the only possibilities are 1) they were both wrong, 2) one of them was wrong, and 3) they were both right (the most dangerous possibility for all concerned). Ed Tatro says, from a position of authority, only that Craig's "identification of Edgar Eugene Bradley is suspect." Apparently both Weitzman and Craig lied about the Mauser so they may have both been engaging in disinformation here too. But the circumstances of Weitzman's identification (*Coup d'état*, pp. 56-57) suggest he was telling the truth. (I don't know, but would like to learn, whether Patrolman Joe Marshall Smith was ever shown Barker's photo for ID purposes.)

Since Weitzman feared for his life and may have suffered a nervous breakdown as a result of his identification, it raises further suspicions in Craig's death which occurred only a couple of weeks later. Ed Tatro also accepts Craig's death as a suicide, but Ed's source close to Craig's circle of friends does not. The jury is still out. Whatever the truth, the relationship of Weitzman's Secret Service man ID to Craig's and Wing's Rambler is obvious and had to be included in my study.

Paine-Oswald relationship:

Bill Kelly said he would try to get copies of the 1957 ONI Paine-Oswald documents from Gus Russo but he said Russo is pretty secretive these days since his book is about to be published.

Roger Craig's Rambler allegations:

The following is an analysis of Dave Perry's 1992-1993 unpublished articles "Men of Zeal" and "The Rambler Man". Some researchers have privately distrubuted copies of these. In both articles, which are nearly identical, Perry tried to debunk Roger Craig's eyewitness account of the Rambler incident.

In the later article, "The Rambler Man", he refined his argument so that an apparent error was less obvious. He then sent a copy to Ruth Paine, who was very complimentary of it! On the other hand, Dave has done some excellent debunking of his friend Gerald Posner.

Garrison says matter of factly on page 95 of *On the Trail of the Assassins* that, "Walthers drove out to the Paine residence...and confirmed that Mrs. Ruth Paine did have a Nash Rambler station wagon with a luggage rack on top, as Craig had observed." Rather than speculate about what Walthers reported to Craig, I would like to see if Walthers' investigation of the car was ever verified. How was Garrison so sure? Was Walthers interviewed? Hopefully someone can find the answer in Garrison's files. It would settle the issue of Craig's and Garrison's credibility on that point.

As for Oswald's thought process during the interrogation, I will address Sheldon Inkol's "simplest explanation" (i.e., that Oswald was lying about the car belonging to an innocent Mrs. Paine to make his getaway appear innocent) as well as Dave Perry's "miscommunication" hypothesis. Perry, at least, does not ignore the important fact that Oswald's statement was an excited utterance, which is frequently considered inherently truthful by our legal system.

Dave Perry makes an argument for a communication problem in "The Rambler Man." He claims it stems from Fritz's question to LHO, as quoted in Craig's testimony to Belin (6H 270): "What about this station wagon?" Dave writes, "Perhaps when Oswald heard the words station wagon, he immediately thought of Ruth Paine's Chevrolet station wagon. His response to Fritz could then be predicated by the fact Mrs. Paine had given him driving lessons in the Chevy a few short weeks before. Craig and Oswald would then be referring to different station wagons!" To make these suppositions Dave depended on a prior conclusion that he drew in error.

Referring to the above quotation of Fritz in Craig's testimony Perry writes, "Wait a minute! Craig never charged the Warren Commission altered this portion of his testimony. He also claimed Fritz never mentioned the station wagon. The cracks in the `story' began to appear."

The only cracks apparent here are in Dave's comprehension. In fact, Craig did charge the Warren Commission with altering this portion of his testimony. The "charge" and the "claim" that Fritz never mentioned the station wagon are one and the same. Perry's error occurred by taking Craig's single statement about this in his autobiography completely out of context, allowing him to see it falsely as a claim unrelated to altered testimony.

In his 1992 version of this paper titled "Men of Zeal," Dave makes the same error. But in this earlier paper he follows his error with a long quote from the very portion of Craig's manuscript which is about altered testimony. Yet he ends the last paragraph after the first two sentences -- exactly where Craig makes the charge Dave says he "never" made. The complete paragraph in Craig's manuscript, cut short by Dave reads:

*I said that I got a good look at the driver of the Rambler. The Warren Commission: I did not get a good look at the Rambler. (In

Captain Fritz's office) I had said that Fritz had said to Oswald, "This man saw you leave" (indicating me). Oswald said, "I told you people I did." Fritz then said, "Now take it easy, son, we're just trying to find out what happened", and then (to Oswald), "What about the car?" to which Oswald replied, "That station wagon belongs to Mrs. Paine. Don't try to drag her into this." Fritz said car -- station wagon was not mentioned by anyone but Oswald. (I had told Fritz over the telephone that I saw a man get into a station wagon, before I went to the Dallas Police Department and I had also described the man. This is when Fritz asked me to come there). Oswald then said, "Everybody will know who I am now;" the Warren Commission: Stated that the last statement by Oswald was made in a dramatic tone. This was not so. The Warren Commission also printed, "NOW everybody will know who I am", transposing the now. Oswald's tone and attitude was one of disappointment. If someone were attempting to conceal his identity as Deputy and he was found out, exposed--his cover blown, his reaction would be dismay and disappointment. This was Oswald's tone and attitude--disappointment at being exposed!

This asterisked paragraph is the last of five such itemized paragraphs prefaced with, "The following are some of the changes in my testimony:". Also noteworthy is the fact that the "station wagon" charge is sandwiched between two other examples of changes in his testimony. Taken in context then, Craig did indeed charged that the Warren Commission altered this portion of his testimony.

Revisionist delusions aside, the correct supposition is that Oswald understood the question about "what happened," with "the car," when "this man saw you leave." His answer was: "I told you people I did [leave]," adding that he left via "that station wagon" which "belongs to Mrs. Paine" but despite that, "don't try to drag her into this."

Furthermore, Oswald claimed he had left work that day because there would be no more work that day because the President had been shot that day. He also knew he was accused of shooting a police officer that day. Oswald's interrogation session began at about 4:20 p.m. on Friday. Craig says he arrived at Fritz's office shortly after 4:30 p.m. The primary focus of the questioning that early was most likely about Oswald's whereabouts that day after leaving work. Under those circumstances, even if he had driven the station wagon himself, it is not likely his thoughts drifted to driving lessons in the previous weeks. If anything, he wondered how he got into this fix.

Sheldon Inkol's "innocent-looking pick-up" explanation is interesting, but it's not all that simple. What he is saying is that the lie backfired. Oswald was trying to ride the coattails of an "innocent" Mrs. Paine. But in Craig's mind it linked Paine to the "guilty" Oswald. The first problem is that this does not explain Oswald's very next statement: "Everyone will know who I am now."

Along with being an excited utterance, maybe that is why that explanation did not occur to Belin during Craig's testimony. I wonder if it ever crossed the minds of the Commission's staff attorneys. They certainly gave the issue enough thought to obstruct justice by burying Robinson's statement, fabricating Oswald's escape route and altering Craig's testimony and reports. Apparently, if they had explained it that way they could have accepted the facts as Craig stated them, and decided Fritz was mistaken about Craig (or allowed Fritz to corroborate Craig). They could also explain Oswald getting to the Tippit murder scene in the allotted time. The only down side would be coming up with an innocent driver who knew nothing about what had happened. But even that seems easier that the way they handle it.

In telling this lie Oswald would be gambling that Craig didn't get a good enough look at the license plate. Also, if Oswald knew it was not a car the Paines owned, he was gambling that Craig did not notice the model. We can be sure that Oswald left in a Rambler. The lie would be exposed as soon as it was determined the Paines did not own a Rambler.

For those reasons Oswald's self-serving lie would be very flimsy to begin with. And I do not see Craig taking Oswald's word for anything. Craig apparently did withhold judgment until Walthers reported his trip to the Paine residence. Even in Craig's mind, such a lie could only backfire if it checked out. Craig was so adamant that the Paines had a Rambler, I cannot believe he did not at least hear that fact from Walthers. If Craig was lying he was also purposely making a fool of himself. He knew how easily a lie about such a thing could be exposed. It is highly unlikely he would do that voluntarily. Most importantly, the Commission's Rube Goldberg way of covering it up seems to make sense only if they knew Paine had some connection to the Rambler.

For Oswald to make an attempt to look innocent, it also follows that Oswald himself did not have any suspicions of the Paines. Oswald knew he was falsely accused and had in fact been framed. If Oswald was lying about the car belonging to Mrs. Paine the question arises: Was Oswald himself trying to drag her into it? And if so, why? In thinking about how he ended up "a patsy," did he see her role in getting him the job in that building (among other things) as a major part of the set up? More complex scenarios are figured out every day the moment anyone is confronted with a surprise party. Both his mother and brother implicated the Paines even in their Warren Commission testimony. If Oswald was prepared to show how the backyard photos had been faked, I do not think he would hesitate to point out the Paines role in setting him up.

On the other hand, if Oswald was responding honestly to the question, he was under the impression that the Rambler station wagon, in which he left Dealey Plaza that day, belonged to (but was not necessarily owned by) Mrs. Paine. In that case, the question to be answered is: how did he get that impression? Using either supposition (i.e. truthful answer or false answer), it follows that Oswald alone connected "Mrs. Paine" to a conspiracy; because the truthful answer implicates at least Oswald, the Rambler's driver and Mrs. Paine in the assassination. And the false answer implicates at least Oswald and the Rambler's driver. However, Mrs. Paine's involvement is implied in Oswald's most reasonable motive for lying. Either way "Mrs. Paine" is involved.

Something I had not considered until recently is the possibility that we have been wrong about the identity of "Mrs. Paine." There are two Mrs. Paines in this story: Ruth Hyde Paine of Irving, and her mother-in-law, Ruth Forbes Paine, who is the one with more direct Dulles/CIA connections. A possible third Mrs. Paine might even be a possible wife of Secret Service Agent William Paine, the Austin based agent whom Bill Moyers has characterized as the man in charge of JFK's Dallas itinerary.

Was Oswald saying the Rambler station wagon belonged to Ruth Forbes Paine? There is an indication, based on a new piece of the puzzle, that this is something George Wing was trying to tell us. Researcher Bruce Adamson found that Ruth Forbes Paine had married a man named Arthur Young from Philadelphia. He also found correspondence between Allen Dulles and an Arthur Nichols Young, an international economist who served as financial adviser to the Chinese Nationalist Government and represented the U.S. after WWII in missions to the Middle East and Latin America.

The connection to Wing is a reference I came upon indicating that an Arthur Young was involved with Esquire magazine in some major way. I cannot find the reference now, but the connection can still be verified through research. Adamson also sent me copies of HSCA pages concerning their staff's (Fonzi's?) interview of Palm Beach stock broker Joseph Dryer, who knew de Mohrenschildt in Haiti. Dryer remembered an association between de Mohrenschildt and William Avery Hyde, Ruth Hyde Paine's father.

John Martino:

I spoke to Earl Golz on May 26, 1994. He said he couldn't remember if he ever knew the name of Martino's electronics company. Earl was more familiar with the bullet proof vest business in which Klassen and Martino were later partners. Fortunately there is another, and seemingly more promising, route to the answer. Bill Kelly told me that Robin Summers (Anthony's wife) has located Klassen and made plans to talk to him. Even more promising is that Bill Kelly has located Martino's four brothers and sister in Atlantic City, New Jersey. I think he said some of them are in the phone book.

Beverly Ann Monroe and related incidents:

She is added to my list of things to check on (see my manuscript, footnote 136), but for now it's a lower priority than getting harder evidence that Wing actually knew something. If the "No Name Key" photo is Wing, I think we can safely take Monroe out of the coincidence category. Scary thought.

Such incidents have caused me to give a lot of thought to the word "paranoia." Knowing what we know, I think researchers experience the opposite of paranoia -- rational fear. For those of us involved with the Rambler here locally, it stems from knowledge of several highly coincidental incidents which may indicate an interest in our efforts by intelligence operatives. I recently wrote about it to Sheldon Inkol, Carol Hewett, Cindy McNeill, Lou Sproesser and Bill Kelly. Before that, most of this was known only to the few of us researching the car here in Austin.

In August 1993, a man had just moved into a house down the street from where the car is kept, and said he was inquiring about the car on behalf of another man who had just moved into some apartments nearby. He did not mention it, but my friend knew that those apartments were rented on a weekly basis. As an isolated incident, of course, this is no problem.

The only one of these incidents in my manuscript is the one about Beverly Ann Monroe in footnote 136. I only wrote about it because it led to the discovery of Barbara J. Burris. That incident alone was strange enough but it may not have been isolated. Something else strange had happened three weeks prior to that. Of course I was oblivious to this connection until January 1993 when I realized the significance of the Monroe incident.

At around 4:40 p.m. on March 21, 1991, I ended a long phone call to Earl Golz. I had been telling him about meeting a woman at a party a few days earlier. The woman, Victoria S. Bacon (maiden name Gibbons or something similar), had worked in the office of security at the State Department from 1960-1964. She said she typed many documents dealing with security approvals within the State Department. We talked about Otto Otepka, Rostow, Rusk, Harold R. Isaacs and Oswald. It is too involved to go into here but our discussion of that aspect of the assassination ended when I brought up CD 1080 which seems to link

Isaacs to Oswald. She said she remembers things about Isaacs that she probably should not talk about. She had learned only recently that Rostow lived in Austin.

This phone call to Earl was also the first time I had told him about George Wing and the Rambler. These were the weeks when I was beginning to see a method to Wing's madness possibly leading to Rostow. Twenty minutes after we hung up I answered a call from a woman who identified herself as Dawn Owens, a special agent for the Defense Department. She wanted to speak to my boss, David Price. I told her he was not in, and she left her local number, 834-8617. David returned to the office after a while and I gave him the message. He and I were usually the only ones who stayed late after work. He looked puzzled. He picked up his other messages from the secretary's desk and before calling her back he called his close friend Paul Burns at 5:45.

Burns is a career Secret Service agent who served on Truman's and Kennedy's White House details. As recently noted in one of Vincent Palamara's Investigator articles, Burns was on the Fort Worth leg of Kennedy's fateful Texas trip. I've known a bit more about him for several years now. At the Austin Bureau he served as the number two man under Charles E. Kunkel for many years (I have the obituary and article in my files).

I must continue to regress for a moment to pick up a crucial detail of this story. After I wrote down Dawn's message I took it to the secretary's desk where David's phone messages were kept. I noticed that several messages had been left in the twenty minutes between my hanging up with Earl and answering Dawn's call. Thumbing through them I was shocked to see that there had been a call from someone with the CIA in Houston. There was also a call from Burns and one from Hazel Ransom. Hazel's office was on the floor below ours. Earl and I had discussed her husband's possible CIA connections.

When David went to his desk with his messages he closed both doors to his office. This prompted me to eaves drop. That's how I know he called Burns first. He asked Burns about Dawn and what she might want. Burns didn't seem to have any answers. The phone rang again at 5:49 and David answered on the first ring. He talked for one minute and then left for the day. I stayed until about 8 p.m. then went to a researcher friend's house to tell him about this and attempt to calm down. It did not help when a helicopter flew over and shined a bright light in his front yard.

I got to work an hour early the next morning so I wouldn't miss anything. Finally at 9:05 a.m. he called Dawn Owens and left a message. He then came into the office where we made coffee and I asked him if he knew what she wanted. He said Burns had told him that someone must be getting checked out. He then told me about other Secret Service men he had known in the last twenty years. He mentioned Jim Rose, Cecil Calvin and the current Austin chief, Steve Beecham.

At 10:48 a.m. Dawn returned his call. I listened discreetly and learned that they were checking out the son of a close friend of David's, Michael Brewer, whose father Dave Brewer was the former head of purchasing for the university. David speculated that he was applying for a sensitive job. At the time, this explanation seemed innocent enough. But I never heard any more about the CIA man in Houston or what Hazel Ransom had called about. And as I discovered by chance two years after this, it occurred only three weeks before the "Barbara Burris" incident.

By that time (January 1993) other stranger things had happened. On July 31, 1991, at the age of 55, David died of a previously undetected aortal aneurysm while being prepped for an angioplasty operation at Seton Memorial Hospital in Austin. He had been admitted to emergency the day before when his blood pressure soared high enough to turn his face red. He had been undergoing medical tests and experiments of blood pressure medication levels for months.

After his death a vice president who had never liked David temporarily took over our office and ended many of David's easy-going policies, including one allowing us to freelance on our own time. This was clearly aimed at me since I was the only one taking advantage of the policy at that time. I was also having a successful and highly publicized one-man show of my art work. The show was in Harry Ransom's former office near the LBJ Library.

I resigned over that and a few other changes which had made my future at UT impossible. I gave seven days notice, was locked out of my office the next day, and was eventually replaced by a man named Joe London. London, I came to learn, is reportedly a former Army Intelligence assassin who was stationed in Vietnam. He was also overqualified for my former position and apparently did not need the job since he was a partner in his own business with another man I knew, Jay Lake.

They operate a graphic design studio called "The Good Art Company" which is in a part of downtown devoid of art studios but surrounded by high-power law firms, temporary state Senate offices and a state police organization. It is also a short walk from where Rachel Oswald worked at the time. And where, according to a guy who dated her, "she feels safe." London has another business doing digital scanning of artwork called "Honest Joe's Scans." So much for zero-tolerance of outside artwork. I only had a couple of freelance clients.

Since February 1992, London has been in a position to learn a great deal about what I knew, up to the time I left, about the Rambler. I had given copies of my file memos to a former friend and co-worker who got his job there on my recommendation ten years earlier. He repaid the favor by lying about his participation with me in an effort to blow the whistle on government waste in our office. He kissed up to the vice president who was calling the shots because he and his wife had four kids to support. His own occasional freelancing was overlooked and he was appointed the new head of the department. It was under those circumstance that he hired London.

I also knew some interesting things about London's business partner, Jay Lake. I had met Jay a couple of years earlier when we tried to start a Macintosh users group. I knew that Jay's father was Joe Lake, the number three man in the Bush State Department under Baker and Eagleburger.

That is, until President Bush appointed him ambassador to Mongolia very quietly during the Gulf War. I also knew that many of Jay's relatives were CIA employees. Even today Mongolia is a likely launching ground for covert operations aimed at China and the former Soviet Union. Lake must have accomplished his mission there because he was recently appointed by President Clinton as ambassador to Albania.

A March 1994 development to all of this involves John Palese, the Nash Car Club of America chapter president. He is the first and only NCCA person to call me after a year of membership. A membership that had lapsed I might add. Naturally he asked about our Rambler. Keep in mind that he was visiting his son who is a local graphic designer -- like me, Joe London, Jay Lake, and my friend who has the car in his driveway.

The same morning Palese called I received a call to do an illustration for 3M's local ad agency, Kamstra Communications. Jay Lake had recently become employed there as their computer expert. When I arrived at Kamstra that afternoon to pick up a file of photos, the art director who hired me "lost" the file and kept me waiting in the lobby while he looked for it.

While I was waiting, Jay came out and sat in the chair next to mine and started making small talk while looking at The Wall Street Journal. We had not talked in years. That's when I learned about his dad's recent job change. The art director came out shortly and we had our meeting. He said the "lost" file had been on his desk the whole time.

This illustration job was the latest of a spate of recent jobs from this agency. These two calls also came the morning after I had called John Judge late the previous night to confirm that I was coming to the COPA meeting.

There are some other interesting stories to tell about incidents during this period. One happened the night after our small group of researchers met in January 1993 to decide whether to present our findings at Providence. One member of our group (who must remain anonymous) was given a message at a local restaurant. The maitre d' came to his table and said that the gentleman across the room said to say hello and that he sees him everywhere he goes. Our member did not recognize the man but discovered the next day that he was a member of his downtown social club. He recognized the man's name though. He was Howard Burris, Jr.! A couple of days later we confirmed that he is the Howard Lay Burris, Jr.! For obvious reasons this researcher has stayed in touch with Burris but we do not know who is spying on whom.

There is also reason to believe that LBJ loyalists who now protect Lady Bird are aware of our research. Near the end of February I got a call from my former college illustration instructor about a job he had recommended me for. He had been approached by Liz Carpenter who wanted an authentic Texas artist to illustrate her new book being published by Random House. He turned down the job because he felt his style was not humorous enough for the book's subject matter. He thought mine was.

I contacted Ms. Carpenter's secretary who recognized my name and said I had come highly recommended. She asked me to fax some samples of my work. I sent them along with a resume and the Austin paper's review of my 1991 art show. The reviewer pointed out that I was probably the only artist anywhere specializing in caricatures of famous Texans.

After a few days I called to verify that the materials had been received. The secretary said they had and were being discussed. That is the last I heard about it. It is unusual to be left hanging like that. The secretary was very happy when I first called because they were "desperate" to find an artist.

Knowing Ms. Carpenter's long career in journalism I knew from the beginning that it was likely she would check further into my background. It would not have been difficult for her to come across Earl Golz's November 22, 1993 Austin American-Statesman article about me and the Rambler. Basically that is why we pay attention to anyone asking about the Rambler. And that is why we think its theft would not have a totally innocent meaning. And that is also why we are fatalistic about security.

- END OF 1994 UPDATE -

1996 UPDATE

In my 1994 update, I noted: "Robert Groden, who was there when I found the No Name Key photo mentioned in my Investigator article, told me that he thinks Dick Sprague may have identified this man during the HSCA days. I need to send a copy to him and ask about it. Larry Haapanen has told me that he believes the collection of No Name Key photos were originally from Garrison's files. Since he has copies of some of those, I plan to send him a copy of this one to see if he recognizes it." Long-time JFK-assassination photographic researcher Richard Sprague died before I was able to contact him about this. And I have not yet followed-up with Larry Haapanen. However, I am no longer sure if Groden meant the now-deceased Richard E. Sprague, or Richard A. Sprague of Pennsylvania, the former chief counsel to the HSCA.

There have been some significant developments involving photographs, however. The two photos Tom Dillard took at 12:35 p.m. in the rail yard parking area show a 1959 Rambler station wagon that is all but identical to George Wing's Rambler. In a development that brings further importance to that Rambler's similarities to Wing's, we have confirmed that C.B. Smith's first wife, Fronia Ellen S. Smith, the mother of C.B. Smith, Jr. (the sales manager at the time of the April 1963 Rambler sale to George Wing), was working in the third floor, TSBD office of Macmillan Publishing Co. at the time of the assassination. The Dallas Police questioned at least one of her coworkers, Mrs. Edna Case, about conspiratorial links to the principal suspects. File "DPD-101," on the CD-ROM, "JFK Assassination: The Dallas Papers," is a digitized copy of a Dallas Police report. It reads as follows:

[Begin Document]
February 18, 1964
Captain W. P. Gannaway
Special Service Bureau
Dallas Police Department
Thru:
Lieutenant Jack Revill
Criminal Intelligence Section
Special Service Bureau
Dallas Police Department
SUBJECT: MRS. EDNA CASE (6)
1703 So. Vernon
WH 6-3077
Sir:

Pursuant to the instructions of Captain W. P. Gannaway, the SUBJECT was interviewed relevant to the assassination of J. F. Kennedy.

The SUBJECT stated that on November 22, 1963 she was in the office of the Mcmillan Publishing Company on the third floor of the Texas Book Depository Building at the time the Presidential Motorcade was passing the building. She stated that she had only heard of the shooting after it occured. She stated that she did not know Lee Harvey Oswald and that as far as she knew, she had never seen him around the building.

Respectfully submitted,

[signed]

O. J. Tarver, Detective

[signed]

L. D. Stringfellow, Detective

Criminal Intelligence Section

OFFICER'S COMMENT: This SUBJECT stated that she did not know Jack Ruby.

[longhand:] 66

[stamped:] 151 [longhand:] C-37

[End Document]

Based on the minutes of a meeting of an organization called The Sons of San Jacinto, held in April, 1963, we have learned that the senior Smith's mentor, Walter Prescott Webb, was indeed in on the plan to bring JFK to Texas. Webb and the minutes mention the beginning of the planning for Congressman Albert Thomas' appreciation dinner in Houston on Nov. 21, 1963. *[This was a mistaken reference to the Knights of the Order of San Jacinto, a subgroup of the Sons of the Republic of the Republic of Texas. – ed.'s note.]*

As noted in my Rambler manuscript, just prior to Webb's premature death, in late April 1963, LBJ had made a cryptic remark to reporters in Dallas about shooting Kennedy when he comes to Texas. Immediately after LBJ's remark, Lee and Marina Oswald began their intimate involvement with the Paines, and their involvement in the summer intrigues in New Orleans. And the day after Oswald arrived in New Orleans following LBJ's remark, George Wing acquired his Rambler from C.B. Smith Motors. More coincidence?

Six months before Allen Dulles became the lover, spy master and fellow Hitler-assassination plotter of Ruth Forbes Paine's close friend Mary Bancroft, and discovered that he and Bancroft "had many mutual friends..." (Bancroft, Autobiography of a Spy, pp. 54-61, 129-31, 161-62), Dulles was likely paying attention to Operation Anthropoid: the

May 29, 1942, assassination of Prague SS chief Reinhard Heydrich. That conspiracy had multiple similarities to the JFK assassination. They include: 1) a motorcade attack at a hairpin turn; 2) signals; 3) an open, virtually stopped vehicle; 4) two attacks, five seconds apart, the first inconclusive; and 5) "passers-by" directing the crowd in its confusion. And, as in Dallas, there were unanticipated mistakes in Prague.

As Alan Burgess wrote in his 1960 book, *Seven Men at Daybreak*, "The vital operational point was Heydrich's open car had to slow up here to negotiate the near-hairpin corner, and for perhaps five seconds it would provide an easy slow-moving target." And a report from the Special Operations Executive branch of the British Secret Intelligence Service reads: "The special training in the UK was based on a plan that the attack on Heydrich should be made when he was traveling by car from where he lived to his office in Prague or to any known appointment and that it must be carried out at a corner where the car would have to slow down." (Jan Wiener, *The Assassination of Heydrich* [New York: Grossman, 1969] pp. 86-90. Alan Burgess, *Seven Men at Daybreak*, [London: Evans Brothers Ltd., 1960] p. 142 ["near-hairpin corner"]. Callum MacDonald, *The Killing of SS Obergruppenführer Reinhard Heydrich*, [New York: The Free Press, 1989] p. 124 [SIS-SOE report].)

It is a chilling realization that one or both of those two sources (Burgess' book and SIS-SOE's report) were available to Kennedy's assassins during their own planning.

Another new photographic discovery increases the likelihood that their planning included George Wing and his Rambler:

Researcher Greg Jaynes discovered that there is a Rambler station wagon visible in the Paschall film. He does not know if it is the one that Roger Craig described seeing. But he is convinced that it is the one that Richard Carr described to Gary Shaw.

Greg reported that in 1963, Record Street ran on the east side of the Dallas County Criminal Courts/Records Building grounds, as well as the east side of the courthouse. Today, Record Street on the east side of the courthouse has been blocked off and is part of the plaza that is the John F. Kennedy memorial. Record Street, where it ran on the east side of the DCCC/RB grounds is now part of the Dallas County Historical plaza.

Greg said he has done a descriptive analysis of the Paschall film, using a VHS video tape that was copied from a Betacam SP broadcast quality video tape that was produced from the original Paschall film, not the partial copy multi-generation video that Robert Groden has shown.

The following excerpt from his report explains this segment of the film, which is three and three fifteenths of a second in length:

"From tower, a shot to her right, aimed at the corner of Record and

Main streets. (Record street is now blocked off and has been made into a plaza both on the east side of the Records building and east side of the old red courthouse. Also the buildings that were on the east side of Record street directly east of the two mentioned buildings have been torn down and the land they were built on is part of the plaza. The plaza on the east side of the old red courthouse is where the John F. Kennedy memorial is located today. And the plaza on the east side of the Records building is now called Dallas County Historical plaza.)

"A dark car is in the shadow of the old red courthouse on Main street. A police motorcycle is following at it's right rear.

"Parked at the near corner of Record and Main, on Record street facing south (the motorcade is passing directly in front of it) is a light colored Rambler station wagon. To the rear of the Rambler station wagon and parked bumper to bumper, a dark colored sedan the model is unrecognizable on video. Perhaps an examination of the film itself could reveal more.

"Back to the motorcade, a dark convertible then two white convertibles pass by on Main street as they approach the intersection at Houston street."

Greg Jaynes' discovery appears to be an important find. I have not yet seen this film segment myself.

Greg and I met briefly after Patsy's presentation at the 1995 COPA meeting in Dallas. I asked him about whether Patsy's film showed anything relating to Craig's sighting. My question and his answer were both focused on the 12:40 incident on Elm Street, however. He said he didn't see anything. That was understandable since she was filming intermittently at that moment.

Greg learned of my interest in the Rambler from my article in Assassination Chronicles, which was a combination of a speech I gave in 1993 and introductory material from my 174-page manuscript on the Rambler. The published article is really about my entry into the world of JFK research more than about what I learned about the Rambler itself.

As for whether the Rambler Patsy filmed on Record Street is the one Craig saw, I do not know either. But I think the question is answerable. Greg's sighting has already answered some questions. We can now be sure enough that this is one of the Ramblers Richard Carr described. That alone makes it suspicious.

We can also be sure that it is not the same Rambler Carr saw parked on Houston Street facing north against the east curb next to the TSBD. That car too is suspicious. I am quite sure it is visible in the Weaver Polaroid. See page 243 of Richard Trask's book, Pictures of the Pain. Follow the dark edge of the TSBD's north corner down to street level and there it sits, just as Carr described it.

Given Greg's discovery, three questions come to mind:

1.   Is the identical Rambler seen in the railroad yard in Murray 5 and 6 (Trask 494) and the Bell Film (Groden, TKOAP 68) either the Record-St. Rambler or the Houston-St. Rambler?

2.   Is the seemingly identical Rambler (?) at the Elm-Houston intersection in Murray's last photo (Trask 499) the same one as either the Record-St., Houston-St. or RR-yard Ramblers?

3.   Is the identical Rambler seen in the documentary film, "Four Days in November," stopped in traffic as the camera is panning the ambulance leaving Parkland on its way to Love Field, the same one as any of the above?

The Elm-Houston Rambler (?) is most likely the one Craig saw due to the timing of the sighting described by Craig and the timing of Murray's last photo. They are all worthy of suspicion and investigation.

Researcher Michael Swanson brought to my attention an HSCA document referring to investigations of some of these very Ramblers. It also refers to some that are unknown to us. The HSCA document links the unknown Rambler(s) to David Ferrie and Gen. Edwin Walker from April 8-10, 1963 -- significant dates in the timeline of our Austin Rambler, and in timelines of JFK research by others.

This HSCA Rambler document now carries the National Archives Record Number: 1801007610360; Agency File Number: 006795. According to the Archives' Record Identification Form (RIF), it is a one-page document that originated with the FAA. It is dated "04/08/63." The Archives filed it with the following subject key word: FAA.

Although the document itself is only one page long, it has an internal HSCA "JFK Routing Slip" attached displaying the stamped number: "006795," and dated "3/31/78." It has a handwritten heading: "Contact Report & Documents." Handwritten on the slip are the following "Index" items: Comstock, Raymond; Parker, Mrs Jessie Affidavit; Ferrie, David - flight plan; Hardeman, James Affidavit; Habighorst, Aloysius Affidavit; Gunn, Wm - Affidavit.

None of the typed, HSCA staff names, to which copies of the document were to be routed, are initialed. Below the column of staff names there is a column listing "Team #1" through "Team #5." Only "Team #3" is circled by hand.

The flight plan itself contains the following information:

Filing time: "4-4-8-'63"

[?]essees and/or Originato[?]: "N63"

Type of flight plan: "VFR"

Type of aircraft: "Cessna 37"

Proposed/Actual Time of Departure: "1300"
Aerodrome of Departure: "Hammond, LA"
True Airspeed(s): "160 K"
Cruising Level(s): "7500"
ETE for Route Segment: "Direct"
Aerodrome of Intended Landing: "Garland, Tex"
Alternate Aerodrome: "Dallas"
ETE to Aerodrome of 1st Intended Landing: "3-20"
Fuel: Hours: "5" Minutes: "30"
Total Number Persons Aboard: "4"
Name of Pilot in Command: "D. Ferrie"
Color of Aircraft: "Red - W"
Address of Pilot in Command or Aircraft Home Base: "NOLA"
Miscellaneous (For Station Use): [three names stacked top to bottom and bracketed "}":] "Hidell Lambert Diaz" [bracket "}" label:] "Pasg"

Typed on a separate sheet of paper above the flight plan is the following HSCA "Contact Report":

"Here is flight plan. Check light colored station wagon bought in Houston, Texas in Feb. or Mar. (Wagon was 1959 model) of 1963. Check this wagon at Walkers on April 10th 1963 and at Garland Texas airport and on railroad parking lot behind book depository. (See Hollands testimony to Commission on this wagon."

I lived in Garland, Texas for most of my youth (1964-1976), and I am not aware of any "airport" in Garland. However, there was reportedly an airstrip at a Garland company called E Systems, Inc. It is an electronics firm and major defense contractor which is still in the same location. Aerial photos taken of Garland in 1963 would verify the existence of that airstrip and reveal the locations of any other airstrips.

I am not aware of any further HSCA investigation of a Rambler "wagon at Walkers on April 10th 1963 and at Garland Texas airport." Nor am I aware of any further HSCA investigation of a 1959 "light colored station wagon bought in Houston, Texas in Feb. or Mar. (Wagon was 1959 model) of 1963."

I am positive, however, that the Ramblers in "Four Days," the Murray photos, the Bell Film and the Weaver Polaroid are the same year, model, and color value as the one we have been investigating in Austin, which fits the HSCA's description. I believe studies of the best sources of the Murray, Bell and Weaver photos will reveal legible license plate numbers. To date, unfortunately, no one has accessed or studied such sources. The Murray negatives are in the Sprague collection. I have not yet tracked down original sources for the others. Nonetheless, research of these photos could lead to a momentous discovery.

Roger Craig's Rambler allegations:

Another document brought to my attention by Michael Swanson further corroborates Roger Craig's account of the Dealey Plaza Rambler getaway car. This document now carries the National Archives Record Number: 124-10005-10159; Agency File Number: 89-43-581. According to the Archives' RIF, it is a two-page document that originated with the FBI, from "SAC, SF" [Special Agent in Charge, San Francisco] to SAC, DL," [Special Agent in Charge, Dallas]. It is dated "11/26/63." The Archives filed it with the following subject key words: JFK, Motorcade, White Station Wagon, Deuel, Norman.

The document is marked "URGENT," and its text is typed in uppercase characters. It reads as follows:

Assassination of President Kennedy, Dallas, Texas, November two two, last. AFO.

Norman Deuel, four two two five Telegraph Avenue, Oakland, California, retired inspector of Oakland Police Department, who is considered a reliable individual, advised that on Friday last just after assassination of President he was watching TV showing first rerun photos of motorcade and distinctly heard a male voice in audio background comment about a white station wagon speeding from the area after the shooting. Deuel does not know what station he was tuned to at the time. In subsequent TV news reports Deuel heard mention made that a white station wagon with Texas license had been identified as moving Oswald when he left his residence without paying rent and moved to another. Foregoing submitted for information Dallas.

End and ACK PLS.

Greg Jaynes and I exchanged views on Dave Perry's attempt to debunk Roger Craig's Rambler allegations.

In light of Greg's Paschall-film discovery regarding the Rambler, Greg noted the irony in the following quote from Dave Perry's unpublished article, "The Rambler Man":

"We are left with another story we thought had possibilities, turned sour. At one point I thought there was independent corroboration of Craig's Nash Rambler story in High Treason. The Groden/Livingstone book describes the episode on pages 161 and 162. Imagine my disappointment when I discovered the authors were merely rehashing Penn Jones' 'investigation.'"

If Craig's allegations were not credible, and if Oswald did not admit to the Dallas Police that he left Dealey Plaza in a Rambler station wagon which he believed belonged to "Mrs. Paine," it is difficult to explain how the subject of vehicles owned by the Paines came up during Oswald's interrogation ("Report of Captain J.W. Fritz, Dallas Police Department,"

p. 7; "Reports of Inspector Thomas J. Kelley, U.S. Secret Service," Warren Report, pp. 605, 626).

And if Oswald's interrogators were quickly satisfied that he had not left Dealey Plaza in a station wagon, or in any vehicle belonging to the Paines ("Report of U.S. Postal Inspector H.D. Holmes," p. 4, Warren Report, p. 636), it is even more difficult to explain why the Dallas Police would be filing surveillance reports on station wagons observed at a new Paine residence nearly four years after the assassination. File "DPD-671," on the CD-ROM, "JFK Assassination: The Dallas Papers," is a digitized copy of a Dallas Police report. It reads as follows:

[Begin document]

8 June 1967

Captain W. F. Dyson

Administrative Services Bureau

Dallas Police Department

SUBJECT: Criminal Intelligence (4)

MICHAEL R. PAYNE [sic]

Sir:

SUBJECT and his wife, RUTH PAYNE, [sic] were associates of LEE HARVEY and MARINA OSWALD.

The undersigned officers observed the following vehicle parked in the driveway of SUBJECT'S residence, 1028 WOODLEIGH, IRVING, TEXAS, on June 7, 1967.

KGE-237 1959 Plymouth, four door, color green and white, station wagon registered to: GENS CONDEN WALKER, 4610 BLUFFVIEW BOULEVARD.

Respectfully submitted,

[signed]

A. J. Carroll, Jr., Patrolman

Criminal Intelligence Section

[signed]

R. W. Westphal, Detective

Criminal Intelligence Section

OFFICERS COMMENTS: The indices of the Criminal Intelligence Section were searched with negative results regarding WALKER.

[longhand:] Correct Lic # is KGX-237 on a 1959 Plymouth belonging to Ruth Payne [sic] 10[?]1 Woodleigh, Irving Texas 1-25-68 [illegible longhand initials and numbers] 104 6-12-67

[End Document]

As noted in my 1994 update, I acquired two different versions of Dave Perry's "The Rambler Man" article from two different sources. I have since heard that he had stopped distributing them. I have also heard that would-be conspiracy debunker John McAdams has posted the Perry article on the Internet many times, and even has it on his web page.

McAdams notwithstanding, Perry may have stopped his own distribution because of the critique I wrote for Sheldon Inkol, concerning apparent discrepancies he had edited out of his second version. At the very least, I proved Perry's reasoning to be faulty in both versions. Also, Ruth Hyde Paine's favorable review of Perry's faulty analysis, which was solicited from her by Perry, has become more curious.

Perry's "disappointment" upon "discovering" alleged problems with Craig's sighting strikes me as crocodile tears. If not, such disappointment is very strange. Personally, I would like nothing better than to prove Craig wrong. If Craig is right, and Oswald left Dealey Plaza in a car which he believed belonged to "Mrs. Paine," the official version of modern U.S. history is wrong. The consequences of Craig's story being true are horrifying. I can't imagine Perry's disappointment over proving Craig wrong. But I can imagine Perry's disappointment in himself if he discovered my critique of his Craig analysis.

Disposition of the D713121 Rambler:

A documentary filmmaker, Reg Reynolds, filmed George Wing's car on Saturday, May 18, 1996, and offered to buy it. He apparently appreciated its curious value and said he can and will restore it mechanically and preserve it cosmetically. He saw its potential for exhibition and film use (reenactments, etc.). He told me his wife would love having it too.

As if there weren't enough coincidences surrounding this car, on Wednesday, May 15th, the day after Reg and I confirmed the filming schedule via long-distance phone, the City of Austin tagged it as a junk car and served notice to remove it within 10 days. I decided it would be a good time to find another storage location and I began polling everyone concerned about our options. Then along came Reg Reynolds' offer to buy it.

I asked all concerned about whether to sell, and if so, on what terms. I currently have what amounts to power of attorney over the car, even though my name has never been on the title. My main questions were: Should I maintain a financial interest? Should I require that my name be added to his on the title to maintain a minimum legal interest even if that means my own financial liability?

I could think of nothing else to do with the car, physically, to obtain useful data, except perhaps to disassemble it. We have all the numbers, everything it contained, including dirt, and photos and video of the car. We do not prefer to give it up, but our current storage options are increasingly limited -- unless someone takes storage responsibility.

My reason for agreeing to the filming and interview was consistent with all of my actions since noticing the car in 1989; to push the investigation of it and the Dealey Plaza Rambler incident forward.

As with most everything concerning this car, Reg Reynolds is unusual. His father was Harold Reynolds (see Anthony Summers citation below). Despite what he told me when setting up our meeting, he is not a graduate film student. Reg Reynolds' son, who accompanied him, is actually the student at Stephen F. Austin State University (SFA). Reg Reynolds, the father, however, was running the show completely during the filming. Reynolds is also head of military police for his National Guard unit in Lufkin, Texas.

Reynolds called after he saw the raw footage to say he thought it was great, and that he would send me a video of it as documentation. That dispelled my fears that he might abuse the footage. I think that offer was very professional of him. But as of late April, 1997, his promise has not been kept.

He also mentioned that he teaches at a community college in Lufkin. He said he earned an MFA in Art History in 1989 from SFA. His graduate work was in recreating period pieces. What he wants to do with the Rambler is what I have often thought about doing -- use the car in filmed recreations. As a film project Reynolds said he can generate investment money to restore it. He was also forthcoming about his father, despite the fact that everything he said meant his father was a spook, trained at the original "Farm." Reynolds also promised to send me further information on his father's LHO sighting. That promise has not been kept either.

Reynolds said he has no problems at all with my name on the title. I offered a token purchase price in exchange for his future financial investment in the preservation of the car as evidence. He volunteered percentage points in the car's future income. I told him that a continuing financial interest would be part of having one of our names on the title but that my main concern was having a say in protecting the car from abuse. However, I am concerned about maintaining any personal liability in the car. A life-limb-property lawsuit could be disastrous. I told Reynolds that if a permanent storage option came along before the end of May, the sale was off. He was agreeable to that.

By the deadline, however, the need to move the car became less crucial because we learned that the city's removal notice was more of a warning than a demand. Through the end of 1996, the D713121 Rambler remained in the same location where it has been since three months after its purchase from Lucila "Luchi" Lopez Wing on March 27, 1992.

Anthony Summers, Conspiracy, New York: McGraw-Hill, 1980, pp. 406-07, 588. Relevant text quoted as follows:

Five Days before the assassination a citizen of Abilene, two hundred miles west of Dallas, picked up a note left for one of his neighbors. It was an urgent request to call one of two Dallas telephone numbers, and the signature read "Lee Oswald." After the assassination the citizen, Harold Reynolds, twice tried and failed to arouse FBI interest. The neighbor, it turns out, was Pedro Gonzalez, president of a local anti-Castro group called the Cuban Liberation Committee. Gonzalez became noticeably nervous when he was handed the note and minutes later was seen phoning from a public telephone. Reynolds says he had previously seen a man who closely resembled Oswald attending a meeting at Gonzalez' apartment along with a second and older American from New Orleans. Gonzalez is remembered for extreme anti-Kennedy sentiments and was known as a friend of Antonio de Varona, leader of the CIA-backed Cuban Revolutionary Council. [95] He left Abilene soon after the assassination and was last heard of in Venezuela.

Sources and Notes, Summers, Conspiracy, p. 588:

Abilene incident: article by Earl Golz, Dallas Morning News, June 10, 1979.

Note 95: On November 15, 1963, one week before the assassination, de Varona attended a Cuban Revolutionary Council meeting in New Orleans. It is of note that he stayed at the home of Agustin Guitart, the uncle of Silvia Odio. Odio, as discussed in the latter part of this chapter, was visited in September 1963 by men claiming to be anti-Castro fighters. One of their number looked exactly like Oswald and was introduced as "Leon Oswald." One of the party later called Odio and made comments apparently designed to ensure that she remembered "Oswald." The caller said that Oswald thought the President should have been shot (see this chapter and HSCA X.62).

Joe London and Jay Lake:

Joe London and I have never met (see "Beverly Ann Monroe" section of 1994 update). I know of him only because his name was mentioned to me by mutual acquaintances in 1992. We were all in the same occupation (graphic design), and London had just been hired in my former department at UT, from which I had just resigned after ten years. My interest in London continued because of my suspicions, upon learning of his reported military background in assassination, that he may have had a possible covert interest in my Rambler investigation.

Even now, London could only know of me in any detailed way through my former co-workers with whom he has worked since 1992.

Since I severed all contact with those former co-workers in September 1991, his knowledge of me after that date would be limited. My suspicions regarding his possible covert interest in me and in the D713121 Rambler have not been minimized by subsequently learning the following information about Mr. London.

Since writing my 1994 update, I have been told that London owns a sizable yacht which he has sailed to South America on more than a few occasions. I noted in my 1994 update that London, who was reportedly an Army Intelligence assassin during the Vietnam war, had been hired in early 1992 to replace me in my former, low-paying, staff-artist position at the University of Texas. He was hired despite being overqualified for the position, and despite his ownership of two graphic design businesses, one of which was called Honest Joe's Scans. A new office policy had been in effect at the time of my departure, September 1991, forbidding "moonlighting" by doing graphic design work.

On December 8, 1996, I was told of a chance meeting resulting in information about Joe London, which all but confirmed my suspicions about him. My source for that meeting requires anonymity. The meeting took place at a black-tie, political fund-raiser in Austin, Texas on December 7th. It was at the home of a local business man who owns a clothing store called The Texas Clothier.

Just after arriving at the party, my informant met a man who introduced himself as Joe London. The informant reported the following conversation:

INFORMANT: "Yeah, I know you."

LONDON: "I know you too."

INFORMANT: "You have a business called Honest Joe's Scans."

LONDON: "Yeah, that turned into a really successful business."

INFORMANT: "I'm interested in the Kennedy assassination and there was a truck in Dealey Plaza with the name Honest Joe's on it."

LONDON: "Yeah, Honest Joe's Pawn Shop. I know a lot about the Kennedy assassination."

INFORMANT: "You know Richard Bartholomew don't you?"

LONDON: "Yeah, I know Richard."

Joe London and I do not "know" each another in any traditional sense. Beyond any supposed innocent interest on his part in the JFK assassination, any indication that London knows about my Rambler research raises a relevant question with sinister implications. London's reported military background, the timing and circumstances of his employment in my former position at UT, and his business partner Jay Lake's CIA connections add to those sinister implications.

Although he does not "know" me, whether or not London personally knows someone else named "Richard Bartholomew" is also open to question -- perhaps even another relevant question with sinister implications: assassination suspect Larry Florer reported in his sworn statement on Nov. 22, 1963 that, just before the assassination and his own arrest in Dealey Plaza, he had been having lunch at a barbecue restaurant on Pacific Avenue with a friend, a bank employee named Richard Bartholomew. That Richard Bartholomew is not me, but he is the only namesake that makes sense in the context of my informant's question to Joe London. My informant reported that London had not been drinking, and that he drank no alcohol at the party at all; only ginger ale.

During their brief conversation, my informant also mentioned Jay Lake, London's partner in an Austin graphic design business called The Good Art Company. According to the informant, London responded to the mention of Lake's name with: "Yeah, he's with Questar Communications now."

The following report about Jay Lake, along with his photo, appeared in the Austin Business Journal in September, 1996:

"JAY LAKE has joined QuestLink Technology Inc., an Austin-based on-line publisher of technical information for design engineers, as emerging technologies strategist. His Responsibilities will include surveying and evaluating new Internet technologies and processes as well as supporting the development of QuestLink services. Lake formerly worked for Kamstra Communications as the interactive communications manager. He holds bachelor's degree from the University of Texas at Austin."

Since writing my 1994 update, Albania has become a hot-spot of geopolitical conflict and intrigue. It is also the country where Jay's father, Joseph Edward Lake, is U.S. ambassador.("Texan nominated as ambassador to Albania," Associated Press, Austin American-Statesman, Apr. 13, 1994, p. B6.) In all of the reporting regarding the war in Bosnia and its aftermath, including the role of Albania as a center for U.S. military involvement in that conflict, and including the subsequent criminal activity and anarchy in Albania, I am aware of no mention of Joe Lake's role as the U.S. ambassador to that country.

These new facts, along with those reported in the earlier update, continue to give me reason to suspect that London, and possibly his CIA-connected business partner, Jay Lake, may have a covert interest in my investigation of George Wing's Rambler.

Paul Galmor's Rambler Investigation:

After reading Earl Golz's 30th anniversary article on the state of JFK-assassination research, which mentioned my Rambler investigation and the basic facts surrounding George Wing's Rambler (Austin American-Statesman, Nov. 22, 1993), Paul Galmor, a salesman for a local automobile dealership, called me and requested a copy of my manuscript. I sent it to him on Nov. 29th. On December 2nd, he called to discuss some ideas about furthering the Rambler investigation.

Galmor wrote a letter to the Chrysler Corporation's Historical Antique Collection (12000 Chrysler Dr., Highland Park, MI 48288), requesting information on tracing the ownership history of the D713121 Rambler. Chrysler had merged with the American Motors Company, which had acquired the Nash motor company in the mid-fifties and continued producing "Nash" Ramblers as "AMC" Ramblers. Galmor received the following reply:

[Begin document]
[logo] CHRYSLER
MOTORS
Chrysler Corporation
Chrysler Center
December 15, 1993
Mr. Paul Galmor
Route 1 54 C-2
Dale, TX 78616
Dear Mr. Galmor:

The Chrysler Historical Collection exists to collect and preserve all information deemed pertinent to the history of the Chrysler Corporation. While our main objective is the retention and organization of this information, we also offer, on a limited basis, assistance to persons seeking information on Chrysler products. This assistance is offered in a number of ways, including provision of photographs, service manuals, a Restorer's Guide, and a video history of the Chrysler Corporation. We are also able to direct persons to other sources of information.

Enclosed are several order forms that you may find helpful. If any of these services interest you, please contact us in the future.

Yours truly,
[signed]
Brandt Rosenbusch
Corporate Archivist
BJR/fq
12000 Chrysler Drive
Highland Park, MI 48288-1919
[End Document]

Chrysler's historical information services proved to be inadequate for our purpose, however. We still need to learn the name of the original dealership to which the D713121 Rambler may have been shipped.

Paul Galmor's next project, in early 1994, was to have his friend, Jack Prurier, scan my slide copy of one of the relevant Dealey Plaza photos and digitally enlarge it. It was the last exposure of the Jim Murray sequence taken from 12:39 to 12:40, his storm sewer cover frames, 13-19 on his #1 roll. The right-hand-most car seen in the Elm-Houston intersection in frame 19 of that sequence (cover of FMG III; and Trask 499) is the one I suspect to be the getaway Rambler described by Roger Craig, Marvin Robinson and others. My slide -- a copy of Gary Shaw's slide of a print from the original negative -- proved to be inadequate, however, for discerning any new information.

A year later, on Jan. 31, 1995, after I obtained new information about George Wing from his UT personnel records and passed some of it on to Galmor, he reported that he had asked a Spanish-speaking friend, Linda Cantu, to place an international phone call to George Wing's first wife at her residence in Mexico in attempt to interview her:

Margarita Silvia Fuentes (married 08-22-50 to G. Wing; still married as of 11-06-61, but apparently divorced soon thereafter)

Now going by the name Marguerite Wing, she was reached at a phone number, known to be current as of Jan. 1992, by Ms. Cantu. She told Mrs. Wing that she had located her for the purpose of writing a possible biography of George Wing. When asked to verify the above address, Mrs. Wing volunteered that she had lived at that address for the last 14 years.

Cantu asked about "Curt Blalock." Mrs. Wing did not recognize Curt Blalock's name. Nonetheless, determining his identity and relationship to Wing is justified.

According to a 1961 letter to George Wing from Theodore Andersson, then Spanish & Portuguese chairman (the man who hired Wing in 1962), Curt Blalock had recommended Wing for his future job at UT. The name Blalock is of further interest because of its difference from the more common spelling, "Blaylock," and because of a Warren Commission witness whose name had the same, less common spelling.

On April 7-8, 1964, the Warren Commission took the testimony of Vance Douglas Blalock, a 16 year old boy who was accompanied by his unnamed parents at his hearing. Vance testified about his and his friend's encounter with Lee Harvey Oswald and Carlos Bringuier during the summer of 1963 in New Orleans (10H 81-82). Vance's friend, Philip Geraci III, who testified on April 7, 1964, was asked for, and gave, his birth date and address (10H 74). Vance was not asked, nor did he volunteer such basic identifying information.

A later letter from Andersson to Wing justifies a continued interest in any relationship between Vance Blalock and Curt Blalock. The June 5, 1967 letter suggests Mafia links to a man known to Wing and Andersson as "Jack." The letter reads:

"Jack has mentioned to me a playwright and novelist named Jorge Ibarguengortia as somebody you might be interested in getting acquainted with if you don't already know him. Jack thinks he is connected with the National University, says his English is perfect and that he is not part of the Maffia [sic]. Would you be able to look him up when you go down to Mexico City?"

As mentioned in my 1994 update, "Jack" could very well be John W.F. "Jack" Dulles, the son of John Foster Dulles, and the fellow professor of Wing's in Latin-American studies at UT. Related to Andersson's odd "Maffia" statement is a key piece of information in the testimonies of Geraci and Blalock. It is a question the two boys heard Oswald ask of Bringuier:

Mr. GERACI. Well, Carlos and me and Vance were kind of talking among ourselves, and he came in and said, "Excuse me," and, you know, he acted a little nervous and things like that. He asked, "Is this the Cuban headquarters, Cuban exile headquarters?" And, "Are you a Cuban exile?" You know, the way I acted when I first went in there. Just asked him a few questions, was he a Cuban exile, and Carlos said yes. He asked him some questions like was he connected with the Cosa Nostra, La Cosi Nostra.

Mr. LIEBELER. Who asked that?

Mr. GERACI. Oswald; he asked that.

Mr. LIEBELER. Of Carlos?

Mr. GERACI. Yes; and Carlos said no, he wasn't....(10H 77)

Mr. LIEBELER. Well, the report that I have here says that you seemed to remember Oswald mentioning something about having recently visited something called the Casa Nostra, C-a-s-a N-o-s-t-r-a. Do you remember saying anything about that to the FBI man?

Mr. BLALOCK. Yes, sir; I remember mentioning the organization, but I couldn't remember the name. That organization was mentioned in the conversation with Carlos Bringuier and Harvey Oswald.

Mr. LIEBELER. It was?

Mr. BLALOCK. I believe so.

Mr. LIEBELER. Do you remember that it was Oswald who mentioned it?

Mr. BLALOCK. I don't remember which one mentioned it first.

Mr. LIEBELER. And it was mentioned as being a Cuban organization in Florida? Is that your recollection?

Mr. BLALOCK. Yes, sir; I think that is the name they mentioned. It could be something similar. I know I got this Mafia name mixed up with a Cuban organization name.

Mr. LIEBELER. Well, you know that that name that I just mentioned, Casa Nostra, is very similar to the Cosa Nostra. Do you think you may have been confused at the time you talked with him?

Mr. BLALOCK. Well, I meant the Cuban organization. I may have said the Mafia, the Cosa Nostra.

Mr. LIEBELER. You may have used that name?

Mr. BLALOCK. But I meant the Cuban --

Mr. LIEBELER. You meant some Anti-Castro Cuban organization?

Mr. BLALOCK. Yes, sir.

Mr. LIEBELER. So the best you can recall, Oswald didn't say that he had recently visited someone in the Cosa Nostra?

Mr. BLALOCK. No, sir. Yes, sir. (10H 84-85)

Another oddity in Blalock's and Geraci's testimonies is worth noting. Geraci told Liebeler that his and Blalock's meeting with Oswald was their first and last. Liebeler then asked if Geraci saw Bringuier after that:

Mr. GERACI: Yes. That time when we found out that it was Oswald who killed him. well, then I went there, you know, to get things straightened out and talk with Carlos a little about him, you know.

Mr. LIEBELER: You went back and talked with Carlos, about this meeting with Oswald, after the assassination? Is that right?

Mr. GERACI: Yes.

Near the end of his testimony, however, Philip's mother said, "When I found out he met Oswald, I nearly died. The week this happened he was camping with the Boy Scouts and gone Friday, Saturday, and Sunday when the stuff was on TV." Philip then corrected his mother:

Mr. GERACI. I was in school when he got shot.

Mrs. GERACI. But you were in camp, but you didn't see a lot of the funeral and all that stuff showing Oswald's picture.

Mr. LIEBELER. How did you first become aware that Oswald was the fellow you met? Did Vance talk to you about it? Do you remember?

Mr. GERACI. The first time was when the FBI agent came to my house and asked did I see an ex-marine and showed a picture and all that. I didn't even know it before that. It was just then that I realized.

Mr. LIEBELER. Did the FBI man tell you how he --

Mr. GERACI. Got my name?

Mr. LIEBELER. What prompted him, why did he come to your house? Did he tell you?

Mr. GERACI. Well, he said he couldn't tell me that. I asked him, and he said, well, he couldn't tell me. (10H 81)

The date and time of this FBI agent's visit is not mentioned, but

Blalock's testimony helps pinpoint the timing of the post-assassination FBI visit to the Geraci home:

Mr. LIEBELER. You must have talked to Philip abut Oswald after the assassination.

Mr. BLALOCK. Yes.

Mr. LIEBELER. Did you recall to each other and discuss with each other the meeting that you had with Oswald in the store on Decatur Street at that time?

Mr. BLALOCK. I think I was the one that recognized him. I called it to Philip's attention, and the next day at school he said, "Yes, that is the man we met at the store," I recognized Oswald late one night when I was just about going to bed. I told my Daddy, "I went uptown and met that man up there."

Mr. LIEBELER. This was shortly after the assassination?

Mr. BLALOCK. Yes; during the time they didn't have any shows but the funeral....

Therefore, the FBI interviewed Geraci and his mother at their home sometime between Friday and Monday, Nov. 22-25, 1963. The "next day at school," therefore, when Philip and Vance discussed their meeting with Oswald, could only have been Tuesday, Nov. 26th. Philip said, "I didn't even know it before that," meaning he only realized they had met Oswald when the FBI agent showed him a picture of Oswald. Since Vance "called it to Philip's attention" the day before school "during the time they didn't have any shows but the funeral," Philip either learned it from the FBI man and from Vance on Monday, or Philip was lying.

Philip's discussion with Bringuier about Oswald at "That time when we found out that it was Oswald who killed him," was most likely during the week after the assassination.

Moreover, such early FBI interest in Blalock's and Geraci's encounter with Oswald indicates some hidden importance to it. Liebeler stated that the FBI agent who interviewed Blalock after the assassination was named Kevin J. Herrigan. Blalock testified that the timing of that interview was "during the Christmas Holidays" (10H 84). It seems unlikely that the FBI would interview Geraci on Monday, Nov. 25th, then wait a month to interview Blalock. If they were lying or hiding something about the timing of those interviews, it only increases their hidden importance.

Such a lie would also support the already grossly apparent attempt to hide the fact that Oswald had asked Bringuier if he was connected to the Mafia. When we add to this the fact that Bringuier testified to the presence of mysterious Mexicans in Oswald's company during this same time period (10H 45-46), more potential connections to George Wing emerge.

According to Michael Benson's Who's Who in the JFK Assassination (NY: Citadel Press, 1993), Geraci was a friend of Perry Russo, and Geraci died in Aug. 1968 by electrocution. The fate of Geraci's friend, Vance Blalock, is not yet known, as is any relationship between Vance and George Wing's friend Curt Blalock. Such questions are well worth pursuing, however.

Marguerite Wing may have stumbled, according to Galmor and Cantu, on the next name mentioned to her: "Buckley." But she did not say anything further about recognizing the name.

When the subject of Wing's activities at the University of Mexico was mentioned, Mrs. Wing started to say something, then interrupted herself to say she did not know anything about it "anymore." She said, "It's been a long time," then avoided the subject.

Galmor and Cantu did not ask Mrs. Wing about the International Institute of Education. Galmor reported that no further information was obtained from Mrs. Wing.

"Ruth and Michael Pentz":

Beginning on Oct. 17, 1994, I received the following information in a series of letters, the first dated Oct. 8, 1994, from Robert E. Doran, a student of the JFK assassination, and possible witness to a "Paine" Rambler station wagon: Robert Edwin Doran.

Mr. Doran wrote that he had just completed a cursory reading of my Rambler manuscript. He had obtained it the day before from Prevailing Winds Research. Doran said he may have one small piece of the puzzle concerning the "Paine / Rambler" that was seen in Dealey Plaza.

He said that in the early 1960's he was stationed at Carswell AFB, at Fort Worth, Texas. He was assigned to a Heavy Bomb Wing and worked in an Armaments & Electronics Squadron. This was a maintenance support squadron for SAC nuclear bombers. The primary aircraft was the Boeing B-52. Doran said this assignment required a "Secret" level of security clearance for flight line access. For approximately eighteen months, Doran claims, he worked with an individual that he now believes to have been Michael Paine. Doran was his immediate supervisor.

Doran said the individual in question at that time used another name. These events occurred in 1960 and early 1961, ending when Doran received an Honorable Discharge after completion of a four-year enlistment. He said he now feels that events he witnessed, involving "Michael Paine," were a part of a "security program" that was connected with military intelligence.

Doran said he had recently seen a PBS TV special that included an interview with Michael & Ruth Paine. This reinforced his past associations with them, he said. Doran and his wife had spent some time in their house after duty hours. "The similarities between the 'Air Force couple' and the historic Paines are remarkable," Doran wrote.

He said that I might be interested in "the fact that the Air Force couple owned a Rambler station wagon! It was about three to five years old and in very good condition. I remember this very well because of the kidding that we gave this individual about such a non-cool car."

Doran said he had previously read about the Dealey Plaza Rambler. But he had always considered it to be one of those "tangents" that the JFK study takes at times. Doran said he never gave it much credence until he read my "thesis about the Paine / Rambler connection."

He said he thought that I might be interested in pursuing this "if possible at this point in time." Despite my interest, and the impossibility of devoting sufficient time to it over the last two-and-a-half years, I still believe Mr. Doran when he said: "I promise you that this is not a 'crack pot' thing."

There are aspects to his story that either test my belief in his honesty, or speak to the ultimate importance of investigating his allegations further. Doran added that another possible historical JFK figure was also assigned to his "shop." "His military record name," said Doran, "was Charles Melvin Coffey! Another of the "Spooks" as we refereed [sic] to them."

A number of months before Doran's release date, several new "recruits" suddenly appeared in his work station. "These very young 'enlisted men' did not have the typical entry background into the USAF. Neither did the individual that I now consider to be Michael Paine. One of these 'new' individuals may have been Kerry Thornley!"

Doran volunteered the following information about himself:

Birth date: Jul. 4, 1937

Place of Birth: Oakmont, Delaware County, Pa.

USAF Enlistment: Mar. 1, 1957; sworn in at Frankfort Arsenal recruiting center, Philadelphia, Pa.

USAF Serial Number: AF13608965 (later corrected as 13607965)

Basic Training: Lackland AFB, Texas

Technical Training: June 1957, Sheppard AFB, Wichita Falls, Texas

AFSC: 4732, "Aircraft Electrical Systems Repairman" (specialist in auto pilot / compass systems)

Clearance Rating: Secret (allowed flight line access)

Permanent Assignment: Nov. 1957, Carswell AFB, Ft. Worth, Texas

Work Assignment: 7th Field Maintenance Squadron Electric Shop

Transfer: Dec. 1958, 7th Armaments & Electronics Squadron Auto

Pilot / Compass Systems Shop

Doran reported that his duties were to bench test aircraft components for acceptance and serviceability. His shop had five people assigned to it in 1959. In mid-summer, 1960, his shop's assignments were combined with those of "flight line only," "Auto Pilot" personnel working in another building. They were housed in one work area in a different building which had much higher security.

In about August 1959, according to Doran, a man named Michael David Pentz was assigned to the 7th A&E Squadron Auto Pilot shop. Doran claimed Pentz did not have a "normal entry" into the Air Force. "He had not been through the Lackland Air Force Basic Training center nor a USAF Technical Training school, as far as I could determine."

Bob Doran described Pentz, who preferred to be called David, as about 27 to 30 years old (which he later changed to "mid-twenties), Caucasian, small build, about five feet, six inches tall (later changed to 5'-7"), 140 lbs, with light brown hair. He did not smoke. He was from the Northeast, but never indicated to Doran exactly where. "He was a very tight lipped individual," Doran said, "especially about personal information." The only exception to this, according to Doran, was a personal conversation in which Pentz confided to Doran that he and his wife "were having deep sexual problems...."

According to Pentz's wife, "Ruth Pentz," he had some previous "engineering" courses in college. They had two pre-school children, according to Doran, "ages about 2 & 4 years old." (Doran later wrote that his own wife remembers "Ruth" Pentz as "Katie, as in Kathryn" Pentz. He admitted that his wife's memory is better than his, but Bob Doran still remembers the name as "Ruth.")

Doran described Katie/Ruth as "about 30 years" old, "slender build and perhaps 5'-7" [later changed to 5'-8"], being somewhat taller" than Michael. "She wore horn rimmed glasses that made her look older," said Doran. "She said that she was a registered nurse and was working at a hospital/clinic in Fort Worth. She was from the southeast area of Pennsylvania, again only vague references as to where. She was self described as belonging to some kind of 'Friends' organization [Doran later changed this to 'The Brethren' religious organization"]. She described this as being similar to the 'Quakers.'"

Doran later said Katie/Ruth was an RN, requiring a Texas nursing license, and that she "worked the floor" at "All-Saints Hospital, in Fort Worth," during 1960-61. He also said his own wife received her original LVN nurses training there in 1959, and worked in the "OR (surgery) at the same period" that Katie/Ruth Pentz was there.

Bob Doran and his wife visited the Pentzes at their "rental" house, "in the River Oaks area," on several occasions. The Dorans "did not socialize with them," however, because of "differences in background and having no children...."

Doran described their Rambler as a "station wagon style with a factory chrome luggage rack on the top rear of the roof. It was a 'light off colored Green', that looked a dirty grey in poor light. The car was about five years old but looked in excellent shape." Doran, in a later correction, said he only saw the car in the dark on a few occasions, was uncertain about the hue and concluded, "I will have to settle for 'a light grey'."

Doran said he saw Ruth and Michael Paine in separate interviews on the PBS Frontline program titled "Who Was Lee Harvey Oswald," which aired on Nov. 17, 1993. In the 1970s, Doran had seen a picture which he described as showing Michael Paine "leaving the 1964 Warren Commission...." "But after seeing both, although thirty three years older," said Doran , "I am absolutely convinced that they are the same Air Force 'odd couple' that I knew in 1959 -1961."

Bob Doran later found and sent me his military service record, which corroborated his military background as presented in his letters.

I have omitted many other verifiable details of Bob Doran's story for the purpose of future identification of any misinformation or disinformation pertaining to his allegations. I have also omitted some promising leads and many of his thoughts which, as Doran himself readily admits, are "rambling," speculation and "personal diatribe."

None of Mr. Doran's basic, concrete information has been followed up by myself or, to my knowledge, anyone else, except for a cursory check of Fort Worth telephone directories for the name Pentz during the years 1960-61. That brief check, though inconclusive, was negative.

Nonetheless, I feel that Mr. Doran and his allegations deserve to be investigated at greater length. My impression is that he is honest and has witnessed potentially astounding and crucial details of the assassination conspiracy. It is also apparent to me that his intense curiosity and interest in solving the assassination have cluttered his story with information of varying quality from secondary sources which will take time, but perhaps not great effort, for an erudite researcher to sift through.

I strongly sense that Bob Doran, like most witnesses from that time and place, has answers to questions he does not know are being asked, and answers to questions which are not yet being asked.

---END 1996 UPDATE---

Here is a brief summary of my last direct interactions with the car:

I lost track of the D713121 Rambler when Jay Harrison moved it in late 2000 (without my knowledge). I went to check on it a year later, shortly after 9/11, and got the update from the property owner. I've since been given photos and other leads to its location, which I will give to a grand jury when one is formed.

None of the Rambler research was ever done by Jay. I could never get Jay to research the car beyond a thorough forensic search on November 12, 1994 (recorded on VHS - all found material in my possession). Beyond that search, Jay was too busy with his own research. Jay helped us continue to store the car when we were forced to move it from the original hiding place five years after we bought it in 1992. He arranged storage with a friend who owned a junkyard.

That move was preceded by some suspicious events. In 1996, a strange fellow named Reg Reynolds contacted us about doing a documentary about the car. We showed him the car and he filmed it and interviewed us on film. Reynolds also offered to buy it. We declined. We never heard from him again or heard anything about his film. Around the same time, right before Reynolds appeared, the City of Austin tagged the car as violating city ordinances for storing cars, motivating us to move it from the residential driveway where we placed it in 1992.

Jay was homeless, living in his step van parked in the same driveway. I arranged with my friend Stephen Bright to let Jay stay in his driveway after Jay was forced to move his van from a previous property: an empty lot next to a business owned by one of Jay's friends. That was where he was living when I first met him in 1994. In late 1997, Jay arranged to move into a mobile home that had belonged to another friend of his. I helped him move some very, very heavy furniture from storage that winter.

Jay was never one of the original partners who chipped in financially to buy the Rambler from Lucila Lopez Wing, the widow of George Gordon Wing. I think all three of my partners are mentioned in my Rambler paper's end notes: John Garcia, Stephen Bright, and Ronan Lynch (whose name is on the last title). The original idea to contact Ms. Wing about the car, and try to buy it, came from Earl Golz in March 1992.

Jay and I thoroughly searched the car at 3304-A Robinson Avenue and documented its contents on November 12, 1994. Stephen Bright videotaped the search.

Suspected spook Reg Reynolds filmed Wing's car on May 18, 1996, interviewed Stephen Bright, Jay and myself on film, and offered to buy it. Despite his promise to send me a video of the footage, I never heard from him again. More details about the Reg Reynolds episode are in my "1996 Update."

Jay confirmed that C.B. Smith's first wife, Fronia Ellen S. Smith, the mother of C.B. Smith, Jr. (the sales manager at the time of the April 1963 Rambler sale to George Wing), was working in the third floor, TSBD office of Macmillan Publishing Co. at the time of the assassination.

In 1997, Jay arranged for the Rambler to be stored at Del Valle Imports, a junk yard at 3501 Darby St., Austin, TX 78721 (now Vanoye's Auto Sales) after it had been tagged by the City of Austin for removal from 3304-A Robinson Avenue.

Jay moved the car from Del Valle Imports without my knowledge or permission in December 2000 and gave it to Tosh Plumlee. I learned about the move from the junk yard's owner a year later when I went to check on the Rambler. Bill Kelly told Dawn Meredith and me that it was scrapped in a junk yard on Airport Blvd. in Austin around 2009, presumably by Plumlee.

Lee Harvey Oswald's interrogation statement, as reported by Deputy Sheriff Roger Craig, that the station belongs to Mrs. Paine, always raises the question of Ruth Hyde Paine's car. The question is simple, but the answer is a little more complicated. I cover all of the facets at length in the monograph and its updates. One example is the fact that there are three Mrs. Paines involved: Ruth Hyde Paine of Irving, and her mother-in-law, Ruth Forbes Paine, who is the one with more direct Dulles/CIA connections. A third Mrs. Paine might be a possible wife of Secret Service Agent William Paine, the Austin based agent whom Bill Moyers has characterized as the man in charge of JFK's Dallas itinerary (discussed in the Evica-Connally Transcript).

Ownership of the D713121 Rambler prior to C.B. Smith is still an open question. But I think I've answered it as well as it can be without judicial power. I never contacted Lucila Lopez Wing after buying the car from her, and amazingly neither has anyone else to my knowledge. Nor have she or her son and daughter (both last known living in Pittsburgh, PA) contacted me. Feel free, but be warned. Ms. Wing was employed in some very powerful areas of UT. And around the time of the assassination of Luis Donaldo Colosio Murrieta, the a Mexican PRI presidential candidate who was assassinated (March 23, 1994) at a campaign rally in Tijuana during the Mexican Presidential campaign of 1994, I noted some spooky-looking cars at her house with Mexican plates. I was contacted by the grandson of C.B. Smith and offered to meet with him. I told him I was no longer actively investigating, but would talk to him if he wanted. He never contacted me again.

Based on what Gerry Patrick Hemming told me about Howard K. Davis' identical Rambler, I think it was the car he loaned to two gunrunners. They were arrested in Mexico and the car was impounded in Houston. The guy who had the Texas region's federal contract for auctioning impounded cars was a man named "Boots" Trousdale. His daughter, my neighbor Michelle Sheehan still has the federal contract and runs the auction house in Pflugerville. They famously auctioned Madalyn Murray O'Hair's estate after her death. I interviewed her mother, Mrs. Trousdale. He and C.B. Smith were close friends. Trousdale's junkyard was just up the same street from Smith's dealership. Davis' car was impounded, according to Hemming, in late '62. The Rambler was sold to Wing April 26, 1963. The timing works.

The evidence I found and analyzed regarding Wing's Rambler failed to rule it out, amazingly, as one of several suspicious identical Ramblers photographed and witnessed in Dealey Plaza. I discuss most of the photographic aspects of the Rambler in my monograph and it's updates. The captions and comments throughout my restricted Facebook "Rambler" photo album give further updates.

I've never known Tosh Plumlee. Jay reportedly knew him well for decades, but never mentioned him to me. Jay compartmentalized everything and everyone. Dawn got to know Tosh through Jay. I've kept a healthy distance. I have a simple rule: once CIA, always CIA. Actions speak louder than words, and Tosh is no Philip Agee. Whatever else he is, Tosh will always be an accessory to Jay's theft of Wing's Rambler, and the one who scrapped it.

Could Jay be trusted and can Tosh be trusted? No. Jay once showed me his service revolver and threatened to shoot me with it. Despite that, I stayed with the fingerprint investigation because the evidence was worth the risk. Jay's unilateral decision not to name Asa Nathan Darby as the CLPE at the press conference ended the best legal breakthrough in the case since Garrison. Jay unilaterally decided to take the Rambler from those who had protected and treated it as criminal evidence of a CIA-backed conspiracy and gave it to a known CIA agent who scrapped it. We are all judged by our actions.

Here are the circumstances of Jay's threat to shoot me. Jay and I were in personal contact nearly every day for three-and-a-half years. He confided a lot in me. One afternoon in September 1997 he brought me fully into the Wallace fingerprint investigation and showed me the documents. After briefing me on them and confiding other important matters, he pulled out his gun and showed it to me. He said, "This is my service revolver. If you ever reveal any of my secrets, I will shoot you with it." He had never said anything like that to me. Up until then, we had a fairly trusting relationship. We had tested each other many times and passed. So this was a surprise to me. But I knew the stakes were high, and I knew the details of at least one attempt by someone to sabotage his car to make it lose control while he was driving. He narrowly survived that attempt. Privately, I seriously considered severing our relationship. I finally decided that the fingerprint evidence was worth the risk. After the press conference debacle and Jay's misplaced and foolhardy hatred of me, I was forced to avoid him. He stalked me for a while, but I survived it. Ironically, it was Jay himself who leaked the fingerprint-investigation secrets in April 1998. His mobile home (which was a free gift to him from an old friend, and which I helped him move into during that winter) had become a Fellini film. Strange characters were coming and going all the time. For all of his secrecy and compartmentalization of everyone and everything, Jay naively put too much trust in these flatterers and sycophants

How does Walt fit into Jay's fingerprint investigation and how did he come to get the Harrison archives?

Since Jay's death, Walt has been hoarding and gatekeeping Jay's files. I was not around after the failed press conference to see how Walt became so close to Jay and inherited them. But I personally saw those files in Jay's possession and saw him work with them and compile them. Except for hard-copy documents he obtained from outside sources, everything Jay documented began digitally on his self-built computer. His computer system took up a wall of his van next to the bed. Until we moved them to his mobile home in early 1998, the file cabinets full of hard copies were in a storage unit on North Lamar Blvd. The biggest mystery to me about Walt's possession of the files, is that he has never mentioned, to my knowledge, Jay's digital files. Everything Jay had in hard copy, was entered digitally. Jay was meticulous about that. Everything Jay showed me in his files, he first showed me the computer entry version.

In focusing on the prints, history will always demand an accounting for how and why the May 29, 1998 press conference self-destructed solely at the hands of Walt and Jay.

Jay trusted Barr and Walt. Barr trusted Jay and Walt. They trusted Darby and Darby unfortunately trusted them, at first. I never trusted Jay, Walt, or Barr. I later came to trust Darby and he me, because he and I did our own studying/thinking based on the facts.

In September 1997 Jay threatened to shoot me with his service pistol. After that threat, I wanted to end our relationship, but chose not to solely because I knew the potential importance of the print evidence and believed it was worth dying for.

As soon as Jay revealed Barr's name to me in October 1997, I knew him as the former husband of Carol Keeton, former mayor of Austin and daughter of the powerful Dean Keeton of the UT law school. I knew better than Jay that we were in the lions' den of conspirators.

In January 1998, Jay asked me to contact Walt Brown and see if he would be willing to act as a possible spokesperson for him and Barr McClellan. I warned Jay that Walt had a huge ego and could not be trusted, but Jay insisted. I called Walt and recorded the conversation for Jay's benefit. After that, Jay and Walt contacted each other directly. What I did not anticipate was how Walt's and Jay's egos would fuel each other to the detriment of the fingerprint investigation.

Jay and Barr were collaborating long before I knew. Jay's ego was immense and he couldn't help teasing me with hints that he was working with someone important. When he finally told me it was Barr, all of my own suspicions were triggered. Jay, on the other hand, always seemed completely convinced that Barr's story was true. The dynamic I witnessed between them was not a struggle for control, it was mutual admiration between two huge egos. I witnessed the exact same dynamic between Jay and Walt.

The purpose of the press conference was to reveal the fingerprint match evidence, which could only be done by naming the CLPE who made the matches. All of our plans were for that purpose, and never changed, except secretly and apparently unilaterally by Jay and Walt, seemingly at the last minute.

Walt and Jay fooled me only by going incognito the day before the press conference, changing the plans secretly, then springing the surprise anonymity of Darby on everyone.

It was Walt's and Jay's subterfuge that was at work at the time of the press conference, and only theirs. I knew from the beginning that Barr's book would need a lot of peer review and editing to be worth anything. I wasn't concerned about Barr's book after we agreed to treat the print evidence legally and respectfully. Had the press conference been handled legally and professionally, the conspiracy would be proved, regardless of anything Barr did after that. It's not about Barr, it's all about the press conference. Barr was nowhere near the press conference, and Walt claims Jay ordered him not to name Darby.

I had been working with Jay on a daily basis by phone and at least one meeting per week from when we met September 1, 1994 until the day after the failed press conference, May 30, 1998. That whole time he appeared in excellent health for a man in his early 60s. He was active, and mentally sharp. He certainly could not be categorized as having an "illness." I later realized that the stomach cancer that killed him in 2005 was probably caused by his daily diet of processed meats, which are now known to cause that very cancer. Whenever I visited him, he was often eating a baloney sandwich. It was the simplest meal he could prepare in his van.

And even if Jay was having some kind of mental lapse, why would Walt go along with him at the press conference, and continue to defend the disastrous decision years later? If I had caught wind of any attempt to keep Darby's name from the press, I'd have raised hell. And I did with Barr immediately following the debacle. Why wasn't I told of this poorly judged, destructive, major change in plans? Naming Darby had always been the whole purpose for the press conference. It was the only way to prove a match. Even if there had been a legitimate reason not to name Darby but continue with the press conference, as I pointed out at the time, copies of Darby's affidavits were in the press kit with his initials and signature on them, and Darby's name was listed in the Austin phone book. A cub reporter could have figured out who the CLPE was. If you can't name Darby, you cancel the press conference. You don't give the press another reason to call it another unproven conspiracy theory.

One final note: Walt must have Jay's entire computer system, along with any and all backups up to 2005. Walt knew Jay from right after New Year's Day 1998, after my initial contact on Jay's behalf, to Jay's death, May 25, 2005. Walt's silence on all of that computer data is deafening!

ENEMY ACTION
(THE MEDIA)

THE GORDIAN KNOT: WHY 54 YEARS OF REVELATIONS HAVE FAILED TO MAKE A DIFFERENCE

We all know that the ancient legend of the Gordian knot represents a no-win situation, a seemingly intractable obstacle. In the legend, it was a strand of many knots tied by King Gordius, the father of future King Midas, designed as an intricate puzzle which, if solved, would transfer his power to whomever solved it. After a great many failed attempts to untie it by many contestants, Alexander the Great succeeded by reimagining the problem. He cut it with his sword in the best known version of the legend, and pulled the linchpin of the yoke it was tied to in another version, allowing it to unravel itself.

For those of us who study seriously and honestly the assassination of President Kennedy and other deep political conspiracies, we eventually see them for what they are, modern-day, darker versions of the Gordian knot. We have spent decades trying and failing to untie it when the solution is as simple as refusing to play the game.

Chris Hedges said, "You don't fight tyrants because you are going to win. You fight tyrants because they are tyrants." But our 54-year fight has been ineffective. We must to do something different and better.

What is the goal of assassination research?

Many who study American Deep State assassinations and other deep political events believe the goal is to "solve the case." They are wrongheaded.

They have been duped in large part by one of the conspiracy's longtime tricks. It is essential conspiracy propaganda to parse the theory; to call its different segments different theories. Using the plural, "theories," is a thought-terminating cliché. The counter-propaganda antidote to this is to point out that there is only the conspiracy theory, the one to which the Warren Commission Report refers. Then point out that there are at least half-a-dozen single-bullet theories.

The short answer to who the conspirators are is, basically, the same ones who were trying to kill Castro. It is the same variety of groups with the same leaders and hierarchy, and it is mainstream history since the Church Committee reports in 1975-1976. That is mainstream history, and it is never parsed. We have for too long allowed the propagandists to parse the one and only conspiracy theory.

(https://en.wikipedia.org/wiki/Church_Committee)

Putting great effort into finding the minutia of the conspiracy is counterproductive, and has been for a long time. There is a lack of a realpolitik goal by conspiracy realists, due to the wrongheaded belief that redoubling our efforts to debate, discuss, release more files, or publish will bring us any closer to justice, or change anything.

One of the reasons I accepted an invitation to speak at the JFK Historical Group conference in Alexandria, Virginia in 2014 was that it was the 20th anniversary of my trip to Washington DC to the organizational meeting of the Coalition On Political Assassination (COPA). I planted the seed in 1991 at the South By Southwest conference that led to the Assassination Symposium on John F. Kennedy (ASK) conferences, which in turn led to Lancer and COPA, and now the first post-COPA conferences.

I saw long ago that while COPA became the only one to attempt and achieve any gravitas or integrity, the conferences became big-tent revivals inside the bubble of assassination research. As a result, these conferences have outlived their usefulness.

We need a new paradigm, like a think tank, to replace the status quo of a precarious, loose, ragtag public resistance which, seen from outside our bubble, is a total half-century failure.

What is the problem with assassination research?

Martin Schotz defined the problem in his 1998 COPA speech, "The Waters of Knowledge versus the Waters of Uncertainty: Mass Denial in the Assassination of President Kennedy," especially in reference to "pseudo-debate."

He said, "The lie is that there is a mystery to debate. And so we have pseudo-debates. Debates about meaningless disputes, based on assumptions which are obviously false. This is the form that Orwell's crimestop has taken in the matter of the President's murder. I am talking about the pseudo-debate over whether the Warren Report is true when it is obviously and undebatably false. …there is no mystery except in the minds of those who are willing to drink this premise. The premise is a lie, and a society which agrees to drink such a lie ceases to perceive reality. This is what we mean by mass denial."

Martin Schotz went on to say, "…our problem, the problem for people who want the truth to be known, is that despite the lack of government credibility, the public does not have the ability to think its way through the lies and discern the truth. The great shame of the 'critical community' is that rather than seizing on this as its mission, the critical community has chosen to ally itself with the government and has only fostered further public confusion." (https://ratical.org/ratville/JFK/FalseMystery/COPA1998EMS.html)

At the end of Randy Benson's documentary, *The Searchers*, the late John Judge said, "A lot of people like to play the game, even within the research community, that we'll never know. But I think that it's an empirical question and we can know. By pooling our energies together we can make changes. I mean, we've gotten to see some documents that have rewritten the whole history. And we all do pray we're wrong. We'd rather be wrong than right, you know. We'd rather not live in the world the evidence takes us to. On the other hand, if I lived in a world where I felt I couldn't know the truth, that I couldn't know anything, that would be disturbing to me." (https://youtu.be/PATLZ9z6fxE)

Many believe another lie: that the most incriminating files have long been destroyed. Do we know files have been truly destroyed? Even if they were, Oliver Stone's "stripped Mercedes" analogy still applies. When asked at a Congressional hearing what he expected to find, Stone said the JFK assassination files, like a Mercedes Benz left on the street in Harlem for years and stripped of its essentials would still be recognizable as a Mercedes.

But even with Stone's positive thinking, it is wrong to accept the lie that the most important files were destroyed. We have seen examples of the Deep State writing and keeping secret histories. It is only possible to lie to us and keep us ignorant for as long as they have if they are truthful and knowledgeable among themselves. It is more than possible to use the proof we have to force full disclosure. We can know and we will know.

As insightful as Martin Schotz was in his speech, he was not yet fully immune to helping the Deep State lie. He spoke of the "the cover-up." The American Deep State assassination conspiracies have never been cover-ups. Nothing was really covered up. The conspiracies are only denied with obvious Big Lies. Plausibility was never a requirement. Nothing shows this fluidity of physical evidence or irrelevance of plausibility better than the Single-bullet Theory.

The idea that a cover-up was a Big Lie was revealed in the Warren Commission Report, Chapter VI - Investigation of Possible Conspiracy, Conclusion, p. 374: "Based upon the investigation reviewed in this chapter, the Commission concluded that there is no credible evidence that Lee Harvey Oswald was part of a conspiracy to assassinate President Kennedy."

Now let us reread that taking out those artful qualifiers: "Based upon the investigation reviewed in this chapter, the Commission concluded that there is...evidence...of a conspiracy to assassinate President Kennedy."

The Warren Report's conspiracy conclusion goes on to say, "Review of Oswald's life and activities since 1959, although productive in illuminating the character of Lee Harvey Oswald (which is discussed in the next chapter), did not produce any meaningful evidence of a conspiracy."

The artful qualifier there being "meaningful" evidence of conspiracy. Nonetheless, evidence of conspiracy. Do you see now how thoroughly we have allowed ourselves to be duped from the beginning?

The conspirators' greatest success is their propaganda. Only the government possesses the minute history of their assassinations. We could continue to guess the details and hope for the luck to stumble across evidence for them. Or we could just make the government tell us everything, right now. We have long had enough proof of the conspiracy and conspirators. What we do not yet have is the power to force the usurpers of our government to give us the details of their conspiracy. Forcing the lies to stop forces every historian to deal with reality.

Note that even David Talbot's great book, *The Devil's Chessboard*, has changed nothing, just as with James Douglass' book, *JFK and the Unspeakable*. The Lincoln assassination is the model for the propaganda paradigm of the JFK assassination. Without a new counterpropaganda paradigm, the status quo of endless debate, discussion, and publishing will remain, as illustrated in a 2014 essay by Steven Hager.

(https://stevenhager420.wordpress.com/2014/12/12/i-was-ambushed-by-a-dogma-patrol/)

The first book proving the conspiracy behind the JFK assassination was *Who Killed Kennedy?* by Thomas G. Buchanan, published May 1964. Buchanan wrote in his preface: "The entire text of the report you are about to read--excerpts of which first appeared in l'Express of Paris--was filed in Washington in March, 1964, with the President's Commission on the Assassination of President Kennedy, headed by Chief Justice Earl Warren. This action was taken at the request of a staff member of that commission."

This first of all the books proving the conspiracy shows our folly in thinking that yet another book will change anything. We have always known the truth and it has not set us free. Our messianic fixation on the power of books to end the coup continues to be our worst delusion. That is the Gordian knot tied by the conspirators to distract us.

The one thing we have never had is an endgame.

"The Endgame" is an idea I want us all to think about. It is a chess analogy for where we stand and what we need to focus on.

By an effective endgame, I mean a strategy to stop the Deep State's ability to lie. We are in a long middle game where the Deep State controls the board, except for a fatal weakness it can only distract us from, keeping us too busy to play it to checkmate. We need to stop being distracted and find the fewest moves to victory.

If the Deep State thinks we are unaware of all this, it just lets us continue in our delusions while it plays higher priority games with others. We become a threat only when we see the endgame moves to checkmate and start playing them. But if we do find all the correct moves in advance and play them flawlessly to the end, the Deep State can't stop us.

Any previously unknown evidence that surfaces could of course be added to the endgame. But the purpose is to devise a strategy that could have been used anytime since the assassination, and still can be by using the proof we have. The idea is to stop playing the conspirators' game of trying to untie their Gordian knot, and force a resolution. Theirs is a waiting game designed not to end but just to wait; for one more book, one more scrap of evidence, one more declassified file, one more film, one more conference, one more online forum; one more debate, one more mock trial, *ad infinitum*.

As I said, we could continue to guess the details and hope for the luck to stumble across evidence for them. Or we could just make the government tell us everything, right now. We have long had enough proof of the conspiracy and conspirators. What we do not yet have is the power stop the official propaganda of denial. Forcing the lies to stop forces every historian to deal with reality.

John Judge also said in *The Searchers*, "If you want a democracy, you have to solve the Kennedy assassination." He almost nailed it but for a slip of the tongue. He failed to incorporate Vince Salandria's *False Mystery* concept. The assassination has long been solved, yet democracy is still absent, and will continue to be without an endgame. The axiom is actually, "If you want a democracy, you have to resolve the Kennedy assassination."

Can we learn anything about endgame strategy from our best and brightest assassination researchers? Yes but only a negative example.

Our best thinkers are the best example of the point I made about the folly of continuing to rely on the failed, half-century paradigm of books, journals, speeches, mass education, conferences, mock trials and file releases. If their work couldn't resolve the conspiracy, none can.

Politico's August 3, 2017 article on the July file release by Philip Shenon and Larry Sabato showed how the Deep State is prepared to continue its successful strategy of Big Lies through the new file releases and beyond:

(http://www.politico.com/magazine/story/2017/08/03/jfk-assassination-lone-gunman-cia-new-files-215449)

There were a couple of good rebuttals to the Politico article. But the Deep State continued to double down with Kurt Andersen's subsequent article, "How America Lost Its Mind," in The Atlantic Monthly's September issue. Andersen resurrected the old, debunked, gaslighting Big Lie of mass public mental retardation.
(https://www.theatlantic.com/magazine/archive/2017/09/how-america-lost-its-mind/534231/)

I did not think the Deep State was so stupid or factionalized as to spout their usual disinformation knowing the jig was up with the new file releases. If they were that stupid or factionalized, the endgame would be easy. Instead, I took their entrenched rhetoric as more evidence they knew the most damaging released files would not threaten them.

As I told Nathaniel Heidenheimer on Twitter, "They are a tiny minority and so are we. Wars are fought by tiny minorities." We are now well into the deaths of the second generation of critics. At the conferences I attended in the last couple of years, I was struck hard by the realization that the torch has already been passed. It is our turn to lead, and to learn from our mentors' successes and mistakes. As Kennedy wrote in his undelivered Dallas speech, "Learning and leadership are indispensable to each other."

How do we start thinking outside the book?

My focus since I found my own answers is to do only what is necessary to achieve justice in a *realpolitik* sense. One idea was John Judge's and COPA's pursuit of citizen-petitioned grand juries. The case has been exhausted in two of our three branches of government: executive and legislative. We have barely used the judicial branch remedies provided specifically for that purpose in the First Amendment.

A more direct pursuit has been William Pepper's attempt to get a new trial for Sirhan Sirhan. The courts tasked with the decision have stonewalled. Of course that is all they can do. The evidence and arguments are overwhelming in favor of a new trial.

New accessories after the fact reveal themselves every day by their obstruction of justice. As conspirators, they are as guilty as the ones who pulled the triggers. There are still living direct conspirators too, like Bill Moyers, who needs to be subpoenaed and asked under oath specific questions about his role in the planning of the motorcade route.

The burden of proof in a conspiracy is circumstantial. Two juries have already gotten beyond a reasonable doubt on conspiracy, Jim Garrison's (JFK) and William Pepper's (MLK). A third will too. Pepper is also the lead attorney adjudicating a new trial for Sirhan Sirhan, for which overwhelming evidence of Sirhan's innocence has been presented. The same conspirators were behind those assassinations.

Another realpolitik idea that becomes obvious once we start thinking outside the book, is the exhumation of President Kennedy's remains for forensic examination. Cyril Wecht called for such an exhumation in his keynote address to the Alexandria, VA conference in 2014. There is historical and legal precedent for the exhumation of U.S. presidents for that purpose:

"[Zachary] Taylor was apparently the first President to be exhumed for a pathological examination, but other Presidents were exhumed for different purposes.

"The coffin of Abraham Lincoln was opened four times -- most recently on Sept. 26, 1901, to confirm that it contained his remains." (http://query.nytimes.com/gst/fullpage.html?res=9E0CEFDD1F38F93B A25755C0A967958260)

The purpose of a think tank is to critically pursue such ideas and relentlessly contemplate new ones.

What is our mission?

We need a small, trusted group of experienced researchers supported and protected by a permanent endowment fund. The mission has to be a sophisticated, aggressive counterpropaganda operation.

> Vincent Salandria said it first and best: "The tyranny of power is here. Current events tell us that those who killed Kennedy can only perpetuate their power by promoting social upheaval both at home and abroad. And that will lead not to revolution but to repression. I suggest to you, my friend, that the interests of those who killed Kennedy now transcend national boundaries and national priorities. No doubt we are dealing now with an international conspiracy. We must face that fact - and not waste any more time microanalyzing the evidence. That's exactly what they want us to do. They have kept

us busy for so long. And I will bet, buddy, that is what
will happen to you. They'll keep you very, very busy
and, eventually, they'll wear you down."
— Vincent J. Salandria (1975) quoted by Gaeton
Fonzi, *The Last Investigation* (1993)

Why a think tank?

The modern game plan of using anti-democratic propaganda against
U.S. citizens began with a memo written by Supreme Court Justice
Lewis F. Powell in 1971. "Based on the ideas presented in the Powell
Memo, the Republican party created think tanks responsible for
dispersing misleading information with a false cloak of authenticity."
(http://www.addictinginfo.org/2013/12/26/powell-memo-gop-blueprint/)
It cannot be emphasized enough. As Jonathan Marshall put it in his
2016 column on the subject, "Think tanks...are prime movers of the
domestic propaganda...."
(https://consortiumnews.com/2016/09/01/us-arms-makers-invest-in-a-
new-cold-war/)
A 2014 list published in a blog entry, "The Most Popular Washington
Think Tanks," which is apparently now behind a pay wall, at
linktank.com shows the need for an opposition think tank. Studying the
Web sites listed shows how many think tanks run at a deficit. Doing a
"find" command using the text string "$1," I saw that nine of these 50
think tanks operate quite modestly. Number 34 in the list, the
International Institute for Strategic Studies takes in $1,342,151 and
operates at $694,724. That is far below "one-percenter" money. Imagine
what a deep political research think tank could do with that. As of 2014,
IISS supported 52 staffers with that budget.
Newsrooms used to run at a deficit as a matter of course. What used
to be honest journalism has been forced to show a profit the only way it
can, by marketing sensational entertainment. Propaganda has no such
restriction. Someone somewhere knows this and has more than enough
big money to fund a think tank for deep political research.

Who would staff such a think tank?

The types of people we want are not motivated by ego, or a need for
external validation, or money per se.
They are too savvy to join yet another group of well-meaning,
optimistic dreamers with no time or resources. They know the research
community and its pitfalls, and generally shun it.

Instead, they all have busy lives with all the large and small problems that go with it, giving them far less time than they would like to do the important research they have been struggling with for decades.

Despite their ability to appreciate visionary plans, adding their names to a list of researchers, even a select list of respected researchers, and little else, means nothing to them. These traits are represented by our role model Peter Dale Scott, of course, but also by the life and career of the late attorney and publisher William H. Schaap. He is an example of exactly the type we aspire to and want.

(http://mondoweiss.net/2016/03/william-h-schaap-radical-lawyer-and-publisher-dies-at-age-75/)

It is a bit of a chicken and egg problem. But imagine the response after such a think tank has the funding, structure, leadership, headquarters and mission securely established. Imagine the response if we offer such researchers a salary, benefits, staff, office and whatever other terms of employment they may need to continue their research and start new projects.

Over decades, trillions of dollars have been granted in support of the Big Lies of the American Deep State. Where is the pittance for the truth?

We cannot change the conspirators, nor can we reach an imaginary critical mass through public education, but we can change ourselves — and we must if we want to stop playing their Gordian knot games.

As Lennon and McCartney wrote, "You tell me it's the institution/ Well you know, you'd better free your mind instead." Because freeing our minds is the one true revolutionary act.

Only then will we, as Charles Drago put it, "Return the goddamn fire in Dealey Plaza!"

DIAL "P" FOR PERJURY

"...leadership and learning are indispensable to each other."
-- John F. Kennedy, undelivered speech, Dallas, November 22, 1963

Life is getting tough for the loud minority who deny the conspiracy that killed President Kennedy. Those of us who know the evidence in this case often wonder if they really believe what they are saying or if they are, at best, playing some sort of devil's advocate game. We may soon know. If they are devil's advocates, they must admit checkmate or stalemate.

Conspiracy deniers have always started their argument with "Since the rifle in question propelled two bullets into the limousine within the few seconds the car was on Elm Street; and since one of those bullets passed through both President Kennedy and Gov. Connally...blah blah blah," or words to that effect. They have been able to do that because one of the weakest arguments of authors critical of the Warren Commission, since 1978, has been their attempt to discredit the testimony of Dr. Vincent P. Guinn, who did the neutron activation analysis (NAA) tests of the ballistic evidence for the House Select Committee on Assassinations (HSCA). Those tests have been hailed as hard proof of the above-cited "facts." But the proof seems to be going poof. Dr. Vincent P. Guinn's middle name is Perry. It may soon be "Perjury."

Major authors of the critical literature have failed to note that conspiracy deniers have always spotted Guinn a credibility stipend. They have failed to note that conspiracy deniers must ignore Guinn's caveat that NAA is exclusive rather than inclusive (1 HSCA 493). Conspiracy deniers must forget that his credibility is paramount to his "opinion" and that the fragments are "most likely" from Western Cartridge Company Mannlicher Carcano bullets (ibid., 504). the deniers have had to imagine that two missing (ibid., 497; 7 HSCA 366, asterisked footnote 117) and three untestable specimens (1 HSCA 496) have no bearing on "the really interesting part" for Guinn that "there is no evidence for three bullets, four bullets, or anything more than two, but there is clear evidence that there are two." (ibid., 505). And they have had to ignore the spurious veracity of Guinn's other "opinion" that it is Dr. Cyril H. Wecht's opinions, and not his own, that "don't agree with the facts" (ibid., 506).

Conspiracy deniers have been able to get away with all of that for one simple reason: one of the worst oversights committed by Warren Commission critics appears to be our failure to see that Dr. Vincent Perry Guinn committed perjury. His HSCA testimony (1 HSCA 557) reads:

> Mr. FITHIAN. Dr. Guinn, this is not meant to be an embarrassing question, but I think I must ask it. Mr. Chairman, a recent article in the New York Times magazine stated that you had worked for the Warren Commission and therefore, your conclu-sions for this committee would be impli-citly biased. Did you ever work for the Warren Commission or work for the FBI in connection with the analysis of these evidence samples?
>
> Dr. GUINN. Neither one. I think Mr. Wolf called my attention to the existence of this article, which I haven't seen, and I don't know where they got their misinformation, but I never did anything for the Warren Commission, and although I know people in the FBI, I have never done any work for them.

Yet the New York Times (Aug.28, 1964, p. 32) reported:

RADIOACTIVE TESTS USED IN OSWALD CASE

> GLASGOW, Scotland, Aug. 27 (UPI)-- The use of radioactivity in criminology may determine whether Lee Harvey Oswald killed President Kennedy, a San Diego, Calif. [sic] chemist said today. Dr. Vincent P. Guinn, head of the activation analysis program of the General Atomic division of General Dynamics Corporation, has been working on the problem with the Federal Bureau of Investigation. In the case of murder of any crime involving a gun," Dr. Guinn said, "there is a paraffin test where a wax impression is taken of the hand and cheeks. There is a need for a better procedure and about three years ago we began working on activation analysis. We

bought a similar rifle from the same shop as Oswald and conducted two parallel tests.

He said the evidence had been given to the Warren Commission and would be included in the report soon to be published on the death of the President.

Guinn swore to tell the whole truth. He mentioned none of this even when given the perfect chance. If the 1964 United Press International report is even half right, Guinn's statement is outright perjury. It is compounded by the fact that the Warren Commission conducted additional NAA tests which they kept secret until a memo from J. Edgar Hoover surfaced in 1973 revealing their existence. It stretches our already mylar-thin credulity to the breaking point to believe that Guinn knew nothing about those tests.

He was "unaware" of too much when he testified. He developed a spurious case of amnesia about his own involvement with the Warren Commission. Some scientist! He swore to tell the whole truth. But when he talked about the FBI's 1964 NAA tests for the WC in detail, he denied the fact that he did some of them himself. Guinn was aware, however, that NAA is not destructive. He said, "the same samples I analyzed, if somebody didn't agree with the numbers, they could come back and do them all over again on the same specimens." (ibid., 557) But Guinn later said, "I would not recommend any further analytical studies at the present time." (ibid., 565) No surprise.

For readers who may be unfamiliar with this aspect of the case, here are the facts: Six of the seven items used in the 1977 NAA tests of nuclear chemist Guinn underwent emission spectrography (ES) tests in 1964. At least two of the items had also undergone NAA testing in 1964 (a fact curiously unreported by the Warren Commission).

The ES test particles were consumed. The 1964 NAA samples were not consumed and can be retested. But none of the same NAA particles were retested and are now missing--allegedly, needlessly disposed of as nuclear waste. Item Q3 (CE 569 copper right front seat base fragment), which Guinn did not test, was never fully analyzed.

In all, the Q1 and Q9 NAA 1964 test samples (from the stretcher bullet and Connally wrist fragments), and items Q14 (three CE 840 lead left jump seat rug fragments), Q15 (CE 841 lead windshield smear) and Q609 (the lead Tague curb smear) are missing in whole or in part. One of the Q14 fragments was discovered missing from the Archives in 1970. The windshield and curb smears were allegedly consumed beyond reuse.

That means less than 1 milligram remains (1 HSCA 554). Scientist Guinn, unscientifically, did not question the authenticity of these items of evidence, although authentication was a simple matter of comparing the recorded and known weights.

Researcher Anthony Marsh reportedly found a document in the Archives which shows that those irradiated samples of 1964 were disposed of as radioactive waste, something Guinn claimed he was unaware of when he testified. Guinn took his own tiny samples from the fragments and tested them.

Spotting Guinn an even more generous credibility stipend, conspiracy deniers will argue that Guinn did not know the FBI had disposed of tiny test particles from the fragments, deeming them to be radioactive waste. They will say, "Of course the weight of the fragments he tested didn't match the weight of the original samples minus what was consumed in spectrographic testing. What was missing was the 'radioactive waste.'"

We can only hope that they will share with us WHY Guinn did not know. In 1964, when the FBI did these first ever forensic studies using nuclear energy, Guinn had been doing NAA tests for eight years--a long way toward realizing his dual expertise in nuclear and forensic science. (Marquis, *Who's Who in the West*, 21st ed., 1978-1988, Willmette, IL: Macmillan. Wasserman and McLean, eds., *Who's Who in Consulting*, 2nd ed., Detroit, MI: Gale Research Company, 1973.) He did NAA tests for the WC himself. Perhaps they will grace us with another of their innocent explanations.

As for the tiny portions of fragments given the scary label, "nuclear waste," the FBI "...would have rightly considered them to be perfectly harmless," according to Guinn. (1 HSCA 563) It is odd that after Guinn discovered "quite accidentally" that the 1964 NAA tests had been done, he and Dr. John Nichols were determined to obtain the data through the Freedom of Information Act, but did not try to locate the original test samples--even after Guinn became engaged by the HSCA to replicate the tests (ibid., 557). He knew that the fragments he received from the Archives "did not include any of the specific little pieces that the FBI had analyzed." Yet despite being "...sure nobody threw them out..." he displayed a strange lack of interest in finding them. (ibid., 563)

Given Guinn's apparent willingness to deceive the HSCA, and his blind trust in the fragments he was given, new tests should be done on the original NAA samples from CE 399 and CE 842. The paper trail can be pursued further. Radioactive waste is not put at the curb on trash pickup day.

Finally, we must also come to terms with the fact that all of this seems to have fallen through the cracks of the major assassination literature. I discovered it first while combing the JFK literature on Guinn. Mark Lane mentioned him in *Rush to Judgment* (1st ed. 1966, pp. 152-153). Lane cited the New York World Telegram and Sun for Aug. 28, 1964. That amazing report contains more detailed quotes from Guinn than the New York Times article. It was then a simple matter of cross-referencing the data in DeLloyd J. Guth and David R. Wrone's excellent book, *The Assassination of John F. Kennedy: A Comprehensive Historical and Legal Bibliography, 1963-1979*. Interestingly, that incriminating article is not mentioned after Guinn's name in their index.

Nevertheless, anyone who continues to cite Guinn's opinion about the likelihood that the NAA tests support the Single Bullet and Lee Harvey Oswald's guilt is no devil's advocate. That position can now only be defined as psychological denial or poor propaganda.

[Editor's Note: Ten years after this essay, a scientific paper was published thoroughly debunking Guinn's analysis: Proper Assessment of the JFK Assassination Bullet Lead Evidence from Metallurgical and Statistical Perspectives. Journal of Forensic Sciences, July 2006, Vol. 51, No. 4. doi:10.1111/j.1556-4029.2006.00165.x. Available online at: http://www.blackwell-synergy.com.]

Z-FILM: RED FRAME, WHITE LIGHT

Red frame/white light.
There is a black lead
To a dial phone.
Red frame/white light.
Six three two
Three double-o three.
— "Red Frame/White Light" by Paul Humphreys and Andy
McCluskey, Orchestral Manoeuvres in the Dark

Zapruder film frame 227 (Z227), showing an apparent motion blur, is a composite; a false photo created by combining one or more true photos (Daryll Weatherly, "A New Look at 'the film of the Century,'" appendix to Livingstone's *Killing Kennedy and the Hoax of the Century*). Luis Alvarez noted that in Z227, "All the innumerable pointlike highlights on the irregular shiny surface of the automobile were stretched out into parallel line segments, along the '8 o'clock-2 o'clock' direction." He called this "a striking phenomenon in frame 227 (when compared with 228.)." (American Journal of Physics, Sept., 1976, Vol. 44, #9, 813-827); Josiah Thompson noted that "The Z227 blur (singled out by CBS as caused by the shot that supposedly struck both Connally and Kennedy is clearly not caused by the movement of a camera, since, although the foreground automobile is blurred, the background is in focus." (Six Seconds in Dallas, 1967, 1976, revised, p. 375.)

Photogrammetry allows only four types of natural images here: (1) When the camera follows a moving car, the car is in focus while the background and foreground are streaked. (2) When the camera is still, the background and foreground are in focus while the highlights on the car produce light streaks along the direction of the car's movement. (3) When the camera "jiggles," both the highlights on the car and the background and foreground are streaked and blurred. (4) When the camera, car, background and foreground are still or nearly so, everything is in focus. The motorcade, relative to Zapruder, was not moving in an "8 o'clock-2 o'clock" direction. Therefore, the motorcade in Z227 was copied from an example of image type 3 and superimposed into a scene from an example of image types 2 or 4.

Reliable eyewitness accounts of those who saw the shooting and those who saw unaltered copies of the Zapruder film support this scientific conclusion and explain the reason for the forgery. First, there is "Shaneyfelt's Folly." It is the portion of FBI photographic expert Lyndal L. Shaneyfelt's testimony about the motion blur (Z227) at the climax of a very unnatural movement during which Connally appears to be swatting a fly with his hat.

Six weeks before Abraham Zapurder testified to the Commission, Shaneyfelt, whose job it was to do an expert, detailed study of the film, exposed the forgery by describing this Connally sequence in two different ways: first as we see it today, then as it appeared in Zapruder's unaltered film. Shaneyfelt's folly reveals that frames after Z222 were removed, leaving the current illusion:

> "Mr. SHANEYFELT. I might say that as — in the motion picture — as the car comes out from behind the signboard, the Governor is turned slightly to his right in this manner. This would be in the first frame, in frame 222, he is turned just slightly to his right, and from there on he turns almost square, straight on with the car momentarily, and there is a jerking motion there at one point in the film about there, at which time he starts to turn this way and continues to turn.
>
> "Mr. DULLES. Jerky motion in Connally in the film.
>
> "Mr. SHANEYFELT. There is — it may be merely where he stopped turning and started turning this way. It is hard to analyze.
>
> "Mr. DULLES. What I wanted to get at — whether it was Connally who made the jerky motion or there was something in the film that was jerky. You can't tell.
>
> "Mr. SHANEYFELT. You can't tell that.
>
> "Mr. McCLOY. Certainly the film is jerky at that point. I mean there is a big blur.
>
> "Representative FORD. The President's only reaction is a motion to his throat or to his neck with his hands.
>
> "Mr. SHANEYFELT. That is correct.
>
> "Representative FORD. Whereas Governor Connally actually turns his body rather sharply?
>
> "Mr. SHANEYFELT. Yes; he turns as they go behind the signboard, he turns this way and he is turning

a little bit this way and as he comes out of the signboard he is facing slightly to the right, comes around straight on and then he turns to his left straight on and then turns to his right, continues to turn around and falls over in Mrs. Connally's lap." (5H 155-156)

It is during this missing turn to the left, with Connally's back facing the grassy knoll, that the bullet entered his back. The bullet strike was removed leaving the "jerking motion" at Z227.

From his hospital bed on November 27, 1963, Connally said, "We heard a shot. I turned to my left — I was sitting in the jump seat — I turned to my left to look in the back seat. The President had slumped. He had said nothing. Almost simultaneously, as I turned I was hit." A taped press conference shows an unidentified hospital spokesman with Dr. Shaw telling how both Connally and his wife agreed he turned to his left, and that had he not done so, he would have been struck in the heart. ("The Two Kennedys" documentary film, Italy, M.P.I., Maljack Productions, Inc.) But when the PBS TV series NOVA used Connally's bedside interview for their 1988 broadcast, "Who Shot President Kennedy?", they carefully edited out his references to the left turn: "We heard a shot. I turned [camera cuts to scene of men taking notes] to look in the [camera cuts back to Connally] back seat. The president had slumped. He had said nothing. Almost simultaneously, as I turned I was hit." S.M. Holland said, "...the President slumped over, and Governor Connally made his turn to the right and then back to the left and that's when the second shot was fired." (*"Rush to Judgment"* documentary film, Mark Lane)

Motorcycle policeman Douglas L. Jackson, at the right rear side of the limousine, said, "Mr. Connally was looking back toward me" when the bullet struck. *(Killing Kennedy, p. 144)*

By the time Dan Rather saw the Zapruder film, he was convinced that all shots had come from the Texas School Book Depository (TSBD). Describing the film on Monday, November 25, he said, "...as he turned he exposed his entire shirt front and chest because his coat was unbuttoned...at that moment a shot very clearly hit the part of the Governor. He was wounded once with a chest shot, this we now know..." And later that day Rather added, "The Governor's coat was open. He, he reached back in this fashion, back as if to, to offer aid or ask the president something. At that moment, a shot clearly hit the Governor, in the front, and he fell back in his seat." (Trask, *Pictures of the Pain*, pp. 87, 89)

Abraham Zapruder never saw his original film after Saturday,

November 23, 1963. He only saw it at full speed and never really studied it. The closest he ever came to actually studying the film was on July 22, 1964, when he viewed enlarged prints of individual frames assembled into a book (CE 885) during his Warren Commission testimony. This was primarily to identify them as being from his film. His testimony strongly indicates that had he studied his film more closely he would have been skeptical enough to discover the alteration he never imagined. The 15 frames he saw and the order in which he saw them were 185, 186, 222, 225, 227-231, 235, 249, 255, 312, and 313. Zapruder told Commission counsel Wesley Liebeler that he had seen the film "so many times," yet he had trouble orienting himself to frame 185. His authentication of them [the 15 frames he saw] was conditional on [Commission counsel Wesley] Liebeler's assurance that they were authentic.

Throughout his testimony, Mr. Zapruder searched for, but was unable to find specific Kennedy movements that had impressed him just after the first shot struck. He said they lasted "just 2 or 3 seconds." The movement, mimed by Zapruder, consisted of Kennedy leaning to his left and putting both hands on the left side of his chest as if to jokingly say, "Oh, he got me."

Liebeler, however, changed the subject to the head shot and did not return to Mr. Zapruder's "frame by frame" search for those movements. Suspiciously, the JFK movements he couldn't find coincided with the missing movements by Governor Connally at frame 227, discovered by researcher Milicent Cranor. (The Fourth Decade, July 1994, March 1995, May 1995, Sept. 1995) Note that frame 227, an apparent motion blur in which Connally's head seems to face in opposing directions, is the climax of a very odd movement during which Connally appears to be swatting a fly with his hat.

This same movement would result from an unnaturally interrupted pivoting turn to the left followed by a pivot to the right. Also note that during his testimony, frame sequence 227-231 was the uninterrupted sequence Mr. Z was shown and questioned closely about as to authenticity. Obviously it was final exam time for the film's forgers.

The $64,000 question is: What happened to the three "negatives" Zapruder thought he had in three film cans when he left the Jameison Film Company and took them back to Kodak because Kodak said that's what was required for them to make copies?

(Original publication: *JFK Deep Politics Quarterly*, Volume 2, Number 1, October 1996, pp. 22-25)

Letters to the Editors

To the Editors:

Regarding Richard Bartholomew's Z-FILM: RED FRAME, WHITE LIGHT, some who heard that I saw a less edited copy of the Z film thought that was why Mr. Bartholomew said I discovered the "missing movements at Z-227." Unfortunately, I did not focus on Connally during the one opportunity I had to view the film. My discovery was based on (1) The CBS newsreel doctored to omit Connally's quote on a left turn, (2) FBI testimony on such a turn (no longer on film), (3) witnesses who say JBC turned left as well as right. I never associated the turn with Z-227.
  --Milicent Cranor

RICHARD BARTHOLOMEW RESPONDS:
When attempting to overcome literary confusion, I have had much personal success choosing the author's cited sources over hearsay. Readers will find Ms. Cranor's writings cited following my discussion of her Zapurder testimony discoveries. A bit of legitimate clarification that is required, however, is citation of my regrettably omitted reference to the article in which she reported Mr. Zapruder's statements: "The Magic Skull," The Fourth Decade, July 1995, p. 35. As the first to attempt a rational, chronological placement of the missing movements discovered by Ms. Cranor, I look forward to her arguments, and those of others, against frame 227, in favor of another location.
  --Richard Bartholomew

SCIENCE COURT, OR:
HOW DOING THE MATH DIDN'T SOLVE THE PROBLEM

But nobody reads. Don't believe people read in this country. There will be a few professors who will read the record ... the public will read very little.
   ---Allen Dulles, Warren Commission meeting , July 9, 1964

   * * *

Opening Argument

Science is the observation, identification, description, experimental investigation, and theoretical explanation of phenomena. It is the highest standard of critical thought. Any critique of scientific literature must maintain that standard. The book reviewed here, because its authors understand and aspire to that standard, is one of the most important in the historiography of the assassination of John F. Kennedy. That murder is the most important and difficult historiographically. For those reasons, this book's successes are monumental and its failures are all the more notable and frustrating.

On the back cover of *Assassination Science: Experts Speak Out On the Death of JFK* (James H. Fetzer, Ph.D. ed., Chicago IL: Catfeet Press, 1998, pbk.: alk. paper, 463 pp.) is the blurb, "Completely lacking the wild speculations that have marred some books on the shooting of JFK, *Assassination Science* sticks to the hard facts, interpreted by medical and scientific expertise."

Dr. Fetzer's compilation of expert articles may lack some wild speculations that have marred other books on the shooting, but it is not without some of its own. Beyond the skepticism inherent to science, I have a personal reason for approaching that blurb with a high degree of skepticism.

I admit my example is a minor one, offered somewhat tongue-in-cheek. But I use it to make a fundamental point. Near the end of an article by photography researcher Jack White is the statement, "Richard Bartholomew...is a relative by marriage of the Zapruder family..." (p. 218). Since no evidence, scientific or otherwise, is presented to support that claim, let me -- the world's foremost expert on myself -- speak out on that "hard fact" as interpreted by medical and scientific expertise.

I am not related to the Zapruder family.

It might be wise for me to preface my next declaration of fact by saying I have never presumed any family would claim me. Nonetheless, I am related by marriage to Abraham Zapruder's long-time business partners (two generations). Dr. Fetzer, the editor of *Assassination Science* and a "Distinguished McKnight University Professor at the University of Minnesota, Duluth," who "has published over 100 article and 20 books on philosophy of science, artificial intelligence, computer science, and cognitive science," knew that genealogical fact. He, along with several of this book's contributors including Jack White and Dr. David Mantik, asked me and I told them on November 7, 1996, and on June 25, 1997. The book was still being revised in July, 1997 (pp. 119, 177). The error was published in late 1997.

My point? It's okay. Science is self-correcting. If you are going to make a mistake, it is best to make a scientific one because every scientific claim can be tested and proved true or false. Even without my expert anecdotal evidence, anyone can test this Zapruder-relationship claim because it is properly falsifiable and can be put to any number of conclusive tests. That is the ultimate value of science, and of this book.

One of the behaviors that gives scientists a bad reputation, however, is when one accuses others of ignoring evidence to support a theory, while the accuser is grossly guilty of the same violation. *Assassination Science* does not rise above that failing. But far more importantly, it does give definitive proof of conspiracy and illustrates that such proof is not enough to correct the official, corrupt, politically expedient "lone-assassin" definition of John F. Kennedy's murder.

Which of the book's scientific claims about Kennedy's assassination have passed this ultimate truth-test? In his preface, Dr. Fetzer lists three major findings:

Some of the autopsy X-rays "have been altered to conceal a massive blow-out to the back of the President's head, while others have been changed by the imposition of a 6.5 mm metal object."

Diagrams "in the National Archives purporting to be of JFK's brain must be of someone other than John Fitzgerald Kennedy."

The "Zapruder film of the assassination has been extensively edited using highly sophisticated techniques."

I will confine my comments mostly to that prioritized list. To support those findings, Fetzer presents his own studies and those of ten others. They are, in order of appearance: Dr. Charles Crenshaw, M.D.; Bradley Kizzia, J.D.; David W. Mantik, M.D., Ph.D.; Robert B. Livingston, M.D.; graphic arts specialist Jack White; Mike Pincher, J.D.; film development specialist Roy Schaeffer; cable engineer Ron Hepler; labor specialist Chuck Marler; and Ronald F. White, Ph.D.

The X-rays

Scientifically, how do we know the three publicly known autopsy X-rays (one taken from the front and one each of the left and right profiles) have been altered? Basically, two ways.

First, they do not appear to be consistent with the autopsy photographs or even with each other, and "The medical evidence appears to be inconsistent with reports of numerous eyewitnesses, including physicians and non-physicians, who observed the President's body at Parkland and at Bethesda" (p. 5). Appendix A (pp. 414-15) shows diagrams of Kennedy's wounds as seen by those eyewitnesses. They were approved on October 6, 1993, by Dr. Charles Crenshaw, one of the Parkland physicians who saw the wounds and who, with J. Gary Shaw, wrote a book about the experience in 1992. The head wound is diagrammed as an open hole, shaped like a wide oval, directly behind and slightly larger than the right ear. The corresponding autopsy photographs show that part of Kennedy's head to be completely intact (pp. 52, 442-44).

Is Dr. Crenshaw correct? If his critics' desperation, overreaction and failure to discredit him are any indication, yes. A non-scientific but important contribution of *Assassination Science* is its first widely published telling of the American Medical Association's bias and abuse of power, which demonstrated how "the awesome power of the media...can be employed. so irresponsibly to damage individuals in the eyes and minds of millions of people..." and "destroy the reputation of a distinguished and honorable medical professional who merely offered his opinions on a controversial subject...."

In May, 1992, the Journal of the American Medical Association, aided by massive media attention -- especially that of The Dallas Morning News -- suggested that he "should not be relied upon because Dr. Crenshaw may not have even been in Parkland Hospital's Trauma Room 1 at the time that emergency treatment was provided to President Kennedy." (p. 63) After a long defamation lawsuit, in which the Plaintiff's were represented by Dallas attorney D. Bradley Kizzia, "approximately $213,000.00 was paid to Dr. Crenshaw and Gary Shaw, on behalf of the JAMA Defendants, to partially compensate them for the damages to their reputations and reimbursement for a portion of their court costs." (p. 80) The Dallas Morning News published a "correction/clarification" followed by a rebuttal article on December 19, 1995. JAMA published "a limited and edited version of Dr. Crenshaw's rebuttal article" in its May 24-31, 1995, issue. However, "no apology or retraction was published. Rather, JAMA aggravated the situation and emphasized its irresponsibility by publishing a new smear piece about Dr. Crenshaw, Mr. Shaw, their book, and the case." Fetzer published Crenshaw's complete article (p. 37).

If Dr. Crenshaw is right -- and so far he has not been proved wrong -- the X-rays and photos are fake.

Second, replicable experimental data presented by Dr. David Mantik, "an M.D. specializing in X-ray therapy who also has a Ph.D. in physics," disproves claims that the known X-ray films are authentic.

Mantik's May, 1993, article , "The JFK Assassination: Cause for Doubt" (p. 93), concisely reviews the autopsy controversies over the skull wound and the back and throat wounds, the aberrations in the pathologists' performance, the prima facie evidence of alteration of the autopsy photographs, conflicts in the X-rays in general and Mantik's own tests of the image of a 6.5 mm bullet fragment in particular. These issues are inherently complex.

Those not already familiar with these subjects will have difficulty comprehending them. Those who are familiar with them must develop a new familiarity with radiological optical densitometry. Mantik does a good job making these subjects accessible to non-scientists. But the less experienced reader of technical and scientific texts will have the greater difficulty seeing this proof of forgery. Nonetheless, I urge all readers to struggle through it. Dr. Mantik's proof is substantial, comprehensive and compelling. Critical thinkers, regardless of prior familiarity with the material, will be astonished by the level of obfuscation made clear by this synthesis of the evidence.

In a literary disservice to readers, Fetzer gives a simplified description of Mantik's work (p. 141-42) in the chapter after Mantik's more lengthy, complex explanation. For those who have not yet read this book, I will correct that error:

"X-rays are created by projecting radiation through an object that is suitably situated in relation to a photographic plate. The object will absorb radiation proportional to its density, where denser objects absorb more than do those that are less dense. Consequently, denser objects permit less radiation to impact on the photographic plate, thereby creating a lighter image. Using an extremely sensitive device known as an optical densitometer, *it is possible to measure the amount of light an X-ray permits to pass through it.* [emphasis Fetzer's]

"Using this technique, Mantik was able to reconstruct the density of the objects that created the X-ray and detected a striking abnormality. The properties of the lateral images reveal that very dense material (possibly of a kind employed in oncology) was used to "patch" a major defect to the back of the head--not by filling in the cranium at the location where many witnesses reported having seen a gaping wound, apparently, but by superimposing X-rays to create composite fabrications. He has replicated these results many times by repeated measurements and by fabricating X-rays."

However, the discovery that some X-rays "have been altered to conceal a massive blow-out to the back of the President's head" (p. xiii) is not dealt with first as it is in Fetzer's preface. Mantik merely raised the issue in his May, 1993, article:

"The condition of the right posterior skull, based on the AP [anterior-posterior] radiograph [X-ray], was largely ignored. There appear to be surprising findings on the AP view that warrant further investigation. Were the radiologists deliberately avoiding the condition of the right occiput on the AP view? Quantitative scans of the original AP radiograph could still be done to ascertain just how much bone remains in the right occiput. So far, however, access to this material has been remarkably limited and the proper studies have never been done" (p. 111).

In the same article, Mantik presents evidence that some autopsy photographs have been altered to conceal the rear head wound. That evidence includes some history of the wild, grossly unscientific, vacillations and contradictions by the autopsy pathologists regarding both the anatomical location of the wounds and the most fundamental aspects of the case:

"To JAMA, [senior JFK autopsy pathologist James J.] Humes stated, "I believe in the single bullet theory that it struck Governor Connally immediately after exiting the President's throat." However, when queried by the Warren Commission on exactly the same point he said, "I think that is extremely unlikely." Actually he stated this twice in quick succession to the Warren Commission so there can be no possibility of misunderstanding him...Then, after all this testimony, [fellow autopsy pathologists] Boswell and Finck, who were listening to it, offered their unqualified support for it. These totally opposite statements by Humes are absolutely irreconcilable. Even more astonishing, he seems (JAMA, too, for that matter) to be oblivious to this. No questions have been asked and no explanations have been offered by him for this astounding behavior." (pp. 106-107)

Leaving the discovery of the rear head wound X-ray forgery until the next chapter, Mantik's May, 1993, article presents the discovery that other X-rays "have been changed by the imposition of a 6.5 mm metal object." Mantik's experiments demonstrate how, using a simple, standard technique of special effects cinematography, a template was used to superimpose the image of a round bullet fragment over a smaller existing image of a piece of shrapnel. This piece of shrapnel, located below the scalp but outside the skull, probably came from the bullet that caused the shallow wound near Kennedy's right shoulder blade. That existing shrapnel image was used by the forgers to register the false image in the same anatomical location on two different X-rays.

In contrast to the extensive explanation of the fake bullet-fragment image, Mantik's October, 1993, explanation of his discovery of the rear head wound forgery is succinct (pp. 154-56, and illustrations pp. 59-60):

"What I found was quite astonishing. The posterior white area transmits almost 1000 times more light than the dark area! This large difference was seen on both the left and right lateral skull X-rays...I measured these same areas for patients whom I had seen in the clinic...My measurements showed only small differences...I concluded therefore that the measured differences of about 1000 between the front and back of the JFK skull were too large to be explained by any ordinary differences as seen in typical patients. In fact, the very lucent area at the rear of the skull was almost as lucent as the densest bone in the body -- and I actually measured this on the JFK autopsy X-ray. This bone is the one which surrounds the ear canal. Not only is this bone around the ear very dense, but it is also very thick -- it extends from one side of the skull to the other. In order for the white area at the rear of the skull to match the whiteness of this very dense bone, all of the brain in this posterior area would have to be replaced by very dense bone -- and the bone would have to extend from one side of the skull to the other. No human skull is constructed in this fashion...

"If this white area really represents a normal bone fragment, it should have about the same shape on both the left and right lateral X-rays, allowing, of course, for a small differences in perspective. In fact, however, the superior border has a distinctly different shape on these two lateral views: on the left view, a small, but distinct, peninsula juts upward at one point where no similar feature is seen on the right view. The other, more normal appearing, bone fragments do not show such odd features.

"On close inspection, this remarkable white area is distinctly wider on one lateral view than on the other. This implies that it was located closer to the right side of the skull. On the frontal X-ray, such an extremely dense object should have been as visible as a tyrannosaurus rex in downtown Manhattan at noon. However, when I looked at the frontal X-ray, there was no such beast to be seen.

"The aberrations seen on these X-rays are so diverse that no explanation can accommodate such an ensemble except for the explanation of composites, i.e., they are composed of superpositions of more than one image."

If Dr. Mantik is right -- and so far he has not been proved wrong -- the X-rays and photos are fake.

The Brain Diagrams

Scientifically, how do we know that diagrams "in the National Archives purporting to be of JFK's brain must be of someone other than John Fitzgerald Kennedy"?

Robert B. Livingston, M.D., was scientific director of both the National Institute for Mental Health and the National Institute for Neurological Diseases and Blindness in both the Eisenhower and Kennedy administrations. Fetzer tells us (p. 142) that Livingston, "a world authority on the human brain, had come to the conclusion that the diagrams of the brain stored in the National Archives, which displayed an intact cerebellum, must be of the brain of someone other than JFK. He knew from observations made by competent physicians who had attended JFK, including Kemp Clark, M.D., the Director of Neurosurgery at Parkland Hospital, that cerebellum had been seen extruding from a massive wound to the back of the President's head. He had concluded that the diagrams and the observations could not have been of the same brain."

How did Dr. Livingston reach this scientific conclusion?

Livingston (p. 164): "It simply cannot be true that the cerebellum could have been seen extruding from the occipito-parietal wound--by several experienced and thoroughly competent physicians--and for the same brain to be seen in superior and lateral photographs, and depicted in a drawing (superior view) showing the cerebellum as being apparently intact. A conclusion is obligatorily forced that the photographs and drawings of the brain in the National Archives are those of some brain other than that of John Fitzgerald Kennedy."

Livingston cites Mantik as his source for the photographs in the archives, and, since he gives no other source for them, presumably also for the physicians' direct observations. Backtracking to Mantik, therefore, we read (pp. 109, 110):

"To virtually every eyewitness, these photographs are perplexing. They show a completely intact right posterior skull, which is in absolute conflict with the medical records of numerous Parkland physicians...At least six Parkland physicians saw cerebellum, usually reported as injured, through the skull defect; their reports appear for all to read in the widely available Warren Report. To make the point even clearer, Dr. Kemp Clark, the neurosurgeon, in a handwritten note described seeing both cerebral and cerebellar tissue [in the endnote for those statements, Mantik cites appendix VIII of the report]. The intact posterior skull, as seen on the posterior head photographs, however, clearly prohibits viewing a structure as inferior as the cerebellum."

Mantik had previously cited his source for one photograph as "HSCA 1978; 7, 104" [or volume seven, page 104, hearings and exhibits of the House Select Committee on Assassinations]. Presumably that photograph, not of the brain but of the intact back of Kennedy's head, is the same as the one Fetzer printed (p. 52).

Livingston's source for the superior view drawing of the brain (p. 165) is HSCA exhibit F-302, a drawing made from a photograph of the brain illustrating subcortical damage, reproduced in Joseph N. Riley's article, "The Head Wounds of John Kennedy: 1. One Bullet cannot Account for the Injuries," The Third Decade (March, 1993), p. 5.

Simple enough. If Dr. Livingston is right -- and so far he has not been proved wrong -- the drawing, X-rays and photos are fake.

Recess

With two of Fetzer's three fundamental claims proved in the first half of his book (parts I and II), readers will find a short break from all of this medical science. Part III is a 24-page section reporting on "attempts to reach out to the press to advise them that major developments were afoot." This report actually starts earlier with the story of the doctors' failed press conference and letters from Livingston to Newsweek, and from Fetzer to The New York Times.

To experienced researchers of the JFK assassination these

examples of these doctors' quaint former beliefs in a free press, investigative journalism, a virtuous government (all now oxymoronic) and the superiority of science and reason over politics may invoke melancholy amusement. Especially poignant is Professor Fetzer's attempt to show Arthur Ochs Sulzberger, publisher of The New York Times, the error of his ways by sending him an article clipped from Fetzer's college newspaper.

Fetzer also writes (p. 144): "For several days, I tried to persuade ABC that it should pursue this story, but World News Tonight thought that it was appropriate for Nightline, and Nightline would not bite." I hope Dr. Fetzer was paying close attention to the political content "between the lines," as it were, during ABC's World News Tonight broadcast of April 23, 1998, when news anchor Peter Jennings, reporting on the death of James Earl Ray, twice emphasized that conspiracy theories are "always proved wrong."

The Zapruder Film

Scientifically, how do we know the Zapruder film has been extensively edited using highly sophisticated techniques?

The fourth section of *Assassination Science* is devoted entirely to the Zapruder film. It is the largest section, comprising over a quarter of the book. In the section's introduction, Fetzer lists the fundamental discoveries presented about the film by five contributors. I will confine my comments to his prioritized list in the order introduced.

1) Jack White's "cinematic anomalies that establish a prima facie case that it has been edited in many different ways."

The anomaly in Jack's article I know best is the one attributed to me (p. 218). In the beginning of this review I addressed his misinformation regarding my relationship to the Zapruder family. However, Jack's point about my "inside information" is essentially correct. I have talked to people who knew Abraham Zapruder best, people who lived or worked with him every day, including his late wife. I am able to read his Warren Commission testimony with the knowledge that he was unhappy because he felt the Commission did not ask him the right questions. He objected to the way his questioners seemed to treat him as an unimportant eyewitness. He considered himself the only one who really saw the assassination -- through a telephoto lens.

As Jack notes, Zapruder spent much of his time before the Commission searching the film's frames for movements by Kennedy and Connally that impressed him, movements which no longer existed in the frames of his film. The climax of those movements comes at frame 227.

Following the advice of Penn Jones, Jr. to "Pick out one or two JFK subjects that really interest you, and then research the hell out of them," which Jack quoted at the beginning of his article, I compiled the available information about frame 227 and wrote a research paper about it: "Z-Film: Red Frame, White Light," JFK/Deep Politics Quarterly, (Vol. 2, No. 1, October 1996), pp. 22-25.

Here are some of the facts I compiled for that study that were repeated piecemeal and without synthesis in Jack's article and throughout Assassination Science: Jack's observation that "Connally said he turned to his left to look at the President, then turned to his right," movements which "The film does not show...", and his observation that "Unnatural jerkiness of movement or change of focus or movement is apparent in certain frame sequences" (p. 214); Ron Redmon's observation about "Dan Rather's description of the film..." (pp. 216, 299); Milicent Cranor's report that "She did an extensive study of Connally's movements from photos and witness statements, and says the Z-film does not correspond to other evidence" (p. 217); and Daryll Weatherly's "Vector Analysis blurring study" which "alone may prove tampering" (pp. 218, 315-17).

Jack White's compendium of anomalies proves the film was altered. Analyzed together, along with a few other factors, the anomalies cited above prove, simplify and pinpoint the Zapruder film's forgery at frame 227. They also reconstruct a description of what was edited from the film at that point.

2) Ron Hepler's "indications that John Connally was struck twice..."

Hepler's article, "The Wounding of Governor John Connally" (p. 239), was originally published in Fair Play Magazine (#18, Sept./Oct., 1997). For my critique, I refer the reader to my letter to the editor in the issue that followed it (#19, Nov./Dec., 1997). I will limit my comments here to some interesting background information about his article and my critique of it.

At Ron's request, I peer reviewed the article a year before its first publication. I agreed with his opening statement that "if the presence of a fact, or the lack of a necessary fact, makes a theory impossible, then that theory must be discarded and a new theory developed which includes all of the known facts," so I was compelled to use that standard in critiquing his methodology and findings.

I found that he was selectively excluding and misinterpreting evidence that does not fit his theory, something he accuses "Many highly regarded critics of the Warren Commission" of doing (p. 239). I subsequently discussed it with him via e-mail. He resisted my critique by ignoring some of my comments, ridiculing others and by attacking me personally. Ron Hepler even ridiculed the evidence that the Zapruder film had been altered! I eventually had to tell him that if he did not wish to hear my opinion, he need only cease to ask for it and stop replying to it. That is what he did.

Hopeful that Ron was a reasonable person of scientific repute, I felt he would eventually either mount a rational defense of his theory or heed my comments and revise his article. I was astonished to see it published unchanged. To prevent readers from being misled, I edited our e-mail correspondence into my letter to the editor. The comments I attributed to "true believers" in that letter are Hepler's. He did not respond to the letter.

Because of Hepler's continued resistance to scientific skepticism and his unscientific belief in the authenticity of the film, I was again astonished that his unchanged article was accepted for a book scientifically refuting the film's authenticity by an editor who is acutely aware of the pitfalls of inadequate peer review (see Fetzer's article "A Piece of My Mind: Lundberg, JFK, and JAMA," p. 27).

Referring to Hepler's article in his Zapruder film introduction, Fetzer commented that "This study by itself supplies enough evidence to refute The Warren Report--even on the basis of the edited Zapruder film!" (emphasis Fetzer's) I agree. But, as I noted in my critique:

"The Single Bullet Theory has long been demolished by the clothing holes problem, by the positions of Kennedy and Connally, and by James Tague's certainty that the first shot did not wound him. Determining the exact moment of each of their wounds will help trajectory analysis, which in turn will help identify shooters in photographs and possibly lead to reconstructing their movements into and out of Dealey Plaza. But the forgers of the Zapruder film define more of the scope of the conspiracy." (Ironically, for an excellent analysis defining that scope, see Fetzer's "The Death of JFK," pp. 366-72.)

Hepler's article was included to refute The Warren Report by way of refuting the authenticity of the Zapruder film -- something Hepler avoids doing. In light of Fetzer's documentation of a "clarification" whereby Dr. Livingston reverses himself on his opinion of Kennedy's damaged cerebellum (p. 175), Fetzer owes his readers a clarification regarding Hepler's views on the film's authenticity. Otherwise it appears, to me at least, that Hepler irrationally rejects the findings of every Zapruder film article in this book except his own.

3) Mike Pincher's and Roy Schaeffer's "reconstruction" of the film's early chain of custody which "substantiates" that on the day of the assassination, the film covertly left Dallas about 4 p.m. CST, was

counterfeited by the CIA and returned to Dallas by 7 a.m. CST.

My critique of Pincher and Schaeffer may seem harsh. But in introducing it, Fetzer chose to focus attention on their chronological reconstruction of the film's early chain of custody as substantiation of one of the most horrific -- and on-going (!) -- criminal acts in history: the CIA's theft, forgery and cover-up of the Zapruder film. Extreme allegations invite the most extreme scrutiny.

With his unqualified endorsement of this article, Fetzer lost some credibility. Ironically, over a hundred pages later in an editor's note (p. 341), he gives an excellent example of why the early chain of custody of the Zapruder film must be accurately substantiated. I consider that example important enough to repeat here in its entirety:

> "During the final production of this book, we had what appears to have been a close encounter with the CIA. In the course of ordinary events, we have become familiar with a person claiming to have been a high-ranking official of the CIA, who has told us that the Zapruder film was in the hands of the CIA almost immediately and that it was edited at Ft. Meade under the authority of the National Security Agency, part of which was done prior to the publication of selected frames in Life. He has advised us that instructions for this undertaking would have had to emanate from a level of government at least equivalent to that of Lyndon B. Johnson or of J. Edgar Hoover. We have found much of what he has to say quite fascinating and, in general, consistent with our discoveries. We are unable to confirm the specific details of his claims, which deserve further investigation. He was not personally involved in these activities, however, and his reports are not comparable in evidential significance to the scientific findings presented here. But we have found much of what he has to say quite fascinating and, in general, consistent with our discoveries. See Mike Pincher and Roy Schaeffer, Part IV."

Unfortunately, therefore, while the co-authors' conclusion of theft and extensive tampering is proved by the evidence (their blinking study of the limousine's flashing lights is one of the most monumental successes of the book), most of Pincher's and Schaeffer's chronology is unsupported by their source citations and proved wrong by the evidence.

For a more correct sequence of events, see Noel Twyman, "Chain of Possession of the Zapruder Film," *Bloody Treason*, (Rancho Santa Fe, CA: Laurel Publishing, 1997), pp. 133-49.

The co-authors miscalculated from the outset of their chronology by speculating about what happened with the film just after it was developed at the Dallas Kodak laboratory: "...after quickly reviewing the film, Zapruder and [Secret Service agent] Sorrels went to the Jamieson Film Company...to have three copies of the original [made]..." (p. 224).

Actually, Zapruder and his partner took the film back to their dress factory about 4 or 4:30 p.m. where they stayed until closing about 6 p.m. The two men then went to Jamieson, had three reversal duplicates made, then went back to Kodak to get positive prints developed from the reversal duplicates. Two of those three positive prints were delivered to the Dallas office of the Secret Service around 9:30 p.m.

In addition, other time-consuming events occurred during and after the above time interval which Twyman did not report. Pincher and Schaeffer speculate that the film was flown from Love Field to Andrews Air Force Base by a conventional-speed aircraft. When Zapruder and his partner delivered the film they were told it would be flown to Washington that night by a Navy jet waiting at Hensley Field, a.k.a. the Dallas Naval Air Station. (Twyman, pp. 138, 141; Bartholomew notes from interview of Zapruder's partner, Nov. 21, 1994.)

Pincher and Schaeffer reproduced a copy of a handwritten memo transferring an "enclosed" film copy from Secret Service Special Agent Max D. Phillips to Chief Rowley in Washington. The memo indicates it was written at "9:55 p.m." In their endnote citing that memo as proof the film was in Washington by 10 p.m. EST, Friday, November 22, 1963 (9 p.m. Dallas time), Pincher and Schaeffer wrote, "Harold Weisberg, Photographic Whitewash (1967), p. 138, prints a copy that indistinctly indicates the date of '11/22'." The cited source shows that, directly above the time notation, there is only a "2" followed by a round bottom fragment of a number, making it either a "3", "5", "6", or "8". More likely, Agent Phillips was in Dallas and enclosed the note with the film at 9:55 p.m. on Friday and mistakenly wrote the date as the 23rd.

It is also a faulty supposition by Pincher and Schaeffer that the film had to be altered before it was viewed by Zapruder and others the morning after the assassination (p. 225). As noted in several other Zapruder film articles in *Assassination Science*, eyewitness statements, including Zapruder's, indicate that they are describing the original, unaltered, film as late as Dan Rather's viewing the next Monday.

The only alteration and compositing required in a limited time would be to the nine frames published in the issue of Life magazine that went on sale on November 26th. No frame between 166 and 216 was published in that issue. Suspiciously, Life got those nine frames from the government since, by the agreement signed between Life and Zapruder on Saturday, Richard Stolley did not have the film in hand until November 26th. (Bartholomew notes from interview of Zapruder's partner, Nov. 21, 1994.)

Pincher and Schaeffer state (p. 225), "At about 9:00 a.m. CST on 23 November 1963, the film was shown once by the Secret Service at Zapruder's dress shop to a small press corps that included Dan Rather of CBS..." For this fact, the co-authors seem to cite the entry about Richard Stolley in Michael Benson's 1993 book, *Who's Who in the JFK Assassination*, pp. 431-32 (the co-authors' endnote reference numbers are transposed). There is nothing at that citation to support that statement. Not even Benson's un-cited entry on Rather supports it (Benson, p. 375).

Zapruder's partner, who ran the projector that morning, is certain Rather was not present and therefore could not have seen the film at any of the viewings the morning of November 23rd. Moreover, in his 1977 book, The Camera Never Blinks (p. 124), Rather says his first viewing was in the office of Zapruder's lawyer, Sam Passman. Zapruder's partner said Passman was not consulted until after JFK's funeral. Zapruder first met with Passman at his law office early the next week. Rather's first broadcast describing the film, which Rather claims was immediately following his first and only viewing of the film in Passman's office, was not until Monday, the 25th. (Richard B. Trask, Pictures of the Pain [Danvers, MA: Yeoman Press, 1994], pp. 86-90; Bartholomew notes from interview of Zapruder's partner, Nov. 21, 1994.)

4) Chuck Marler's study of "the Warren Commission's use of phony numbers that were changed from those established by the original surveyors of Dealey Plaza."

Some of the findings reported by Chuck Marler are the most monumental in *Assassination Science*. Others are preliminary but promising.

According to Marler (p. 250), "analysis of existing Warren Commission exhibits, along with the discovery of new documents, now establishes a clear and convincing case that the survey measurements made for the Warren Commission by Robert H. West, Dallas County Surveyor, were altered, the 24 May 1964, re-enactment was orchestrated by Arlen Specter to insure his single bullet theory would not be contradicted, and the Zapruder film was altered to conceal footage that would have proved President Kennedy was struck by multiple assassins. Initial evidence of the crime scene and the shooting sequences as established by the Zapruder film produced a different version of the assassination than depicted in the Warren Commission's final report. To understand what occurred, it is necessary to study the evidence and exhibits that had been produced prior to 24 May 1964."

If Marler's case can be proved, presidential hopeful Senator Arlen Specter, R-Pa., is guilty of obstruction of justice, which makes it even more necessary to study this evidence and these exhibits. Regrettably, Fetzer and Marler have made that task more difficult than it might have been.

The existing Warren Commission exhibits (CEs) Marler refers to are CEs 585, 882, 883 and 884. One of the "new documents" is the 1964 field notes of re-enactment surveyor Robert H. West who conducted all of the three known surveys, including the November 26, 1963 survey -- the first -- commissioned by the Time-Life Corporation. That first plat, according to Marler, presumably the second of the "new documents," has not yet been made public.

West's second survey was commissioned by the Secret Service and done on December 5, 1963. CE 585 (17H 262) is the resulting plat. West's third survey was commissioned by the Warren Commission and done on May 24, 1964. It resulted in at least two plats, CE 882 and 883 (17H 901). I say "at least" because, according to Marler (p. 251), CE 882 "came wrapped and sealed in a container--one which was never opened and to date has never been released to the public. It was Commission Counsel Arlen Specter who asked Chairman Earl Warren that the seal not be broken and the plat not be taken out of its container. Mr. Specter instead introduced what was represented as a cardboard reproduction of Mr. West's survey as CE-883. Specter also introduced as CE-884, a tabulation of elevations and angles for selected Zapruder film frames which Specter stated were also contained on the sealed survey map."

Supporting this mysterious introduction of evidence by Specter, Marler cites the testimony of Leo J. Gauthier, head of the FBI's exhibit section (5H 136-37). Sure enough, the testimony shows that Specter seems to have done exactly what Marler reported. However, unless I am confused, Marler never explained why CE 882 does not depict a container, sealed or otherwise. It depicts a survey plat. The only difference between it and its "cardboard reproduction" (CE 883) is the addition on the latter of a few more landmarks and witness position labels (Harrison E. Livingstone, *Killing Kennedy and the Hoax of the Century*, [New York: Carroll & Graf, 1995], photo no. 11, caption).

Reading Gauthier's testimony more carefully -- which, as any respectable JFK researcher knows, is mandatory whenever witnesses are questioned by the artful Mr. Specter -- may solve the "container" mystery while establishing a greater one.

Specter seemingly established only that Gauthier had a "tracing of that survey," which was already wrapped and sealed in the container. Specter asked Gauthier if he "brought a cardboard reproduction of that." To which Gauthier answered, "A copy made from the tracing; yes." Specter then established only that the printing on the cardboard copy represents an exact duplication of the tracing. He then had the pre-sealed "tracing" marked as exhibit 882. The "copy" of the "tracing" was then marked as exhibit 883.

Now the only way anything in this pre-sealed container could bear the typewritten text, "Commission Exhibit No. 882," as this exhibit does (17H 901), and "not be taken out," is if the typewriting was on it before sealing it in the container. That would mean, at minimum, that the person who labeled it knew the exhibit number well in advance of the moment it was introduced as evidence on June 4, 1964. Either that or, unless I am hopelessly confused, Marler is wrong when he says it "was never opened and to date has never been released to the public."

That mystery notwithstanding, Marler reveals more problems for the reader (p. 251): "In order to adequately study these exhibits it may be necessary to make enlargements since the plats were reduced in size to less than a half-page photo in Volume 17 of the Commission's hearings" [sic]. May be necessary? It is necessary. The reader will not find any reproductions of them, large or small, in Assassination Science, however.

The Commission's reproductions cannot be enlarged because of the loss of resolution in the halftone screens the printer used. Slightly more legible reproductions of these exhibits can be found in Harold Weisberg's 1966 book, *Whitewash II*, p. 243 (CE 585), and Livingstone's 1995 book, *Killing Kennedy*, photograph numbers 9 (CE 585), 10 (CE 882) and 11 (CE 883).

The reader of *Assassination Science* does not learn of these sources until 54 pages later in the next article, where an important related article by Daryll Weatherly is also cited: "A Comparison of the Official Reconstructions of the John F. Kennedy Assassination," The Investigator, Winter 1994-95, pp. 6-16; which, on page 11, includes the largest reproduction (8.5 by 11 inches) of the December 5th plat (CE 585).

Weatherly's article, along with research by Marler and others, was the basis of Livingstone's third chapter in *Killing Kennedy*, which also includes, on page 56, a readable detail enlargement of the bottom of CE 585, showing the legend, an "essential aid in the understanding of any survey," admits Marler (p. 251), and an important revision date ("2-7-64") mentioned by Marler (p. 252), both of which are impossible to see on any of the other reproductions.

The original exhibits are 40 inches by 72 inches, drawn to a scale of "1 inch equals 10 feet" (5H 137). Without the "necessary" and "essential" means to "adequately study these exhibits," what immediate benefit can readers get from Marler's article?

Fortunately, Marler answers that question modestly: "Hopefully, this article provides new research information and raises questions about the assumptions that have been made about the accuracy of the crime scene data used by the Warren Commission."

That it does. By using the exhibit reproductions cited above, I was able to check some of Marler's data. The location of the pairs of traffic lines in the May survey plats (CEs 882 and 883) are in error and placed too far west (downhill) on Elm Street. At the very least, as Marler notes, "This issue is of extreme importance when determining the Zapruder frames in which the oak tree blocked an assassin's view of the motorcade from the sixth floor window" (p. 253).

By using several excellent reproductions of the photograph by Associated Press photographer James Altgens showing the limousine just after the first shot sounded, I was able to verify Marler's claims about it. When the FBI re-enacted that photo (CE 900; Warren Report, p. 113), the re-enactment vehicle was placed too far west, but seemingly in correct alignment with the fifth traffic line painted on the street.

Using West's December plat (CE 585), and visual alignments seen in the Altgens photo between the fifth traffic line, the limousine and the tree in the background, and by verifying it with other landmarks, I was able to plat Altgens' position at the south curb of Elm Street (directly next to the middle of the seventh traffic line just west of the 416.5 street elevation -- he, the driver and Zapruder are aligned at Zapruder frame 343) and thus properly plat the position of the limousine (centered at street elevation 421.25). That in turn verified the correctness of the traffic lines in CE 585 and, from witness statements, the shot sequence shown on that plat. All of which disproves Arlen Specter's single bullet theory.

It is also very easy to verify Marler's observations about CE 884 (17H 902), a data block containing Zapruder film frame numbers, elevations and distances from the re-enactment. It contains data for frames 161, 166 and 210. But Robert West, according to what Marler reports about his field notes, did not make measurements for those frames. The numbers entered for those frames are the ones West entered for frames 168, 171 and 208. It is easy to see in the Warren Commission's reproduction of CE 884 that someone erased the correct frame numbers and wrote in the fake numbers. The result of this alteration was to artificially move the first two frames westward and downward, and the third slightly eastward and upward. As Marler notes, this also has a devastating impact on the authenticity of the filmed movement and speed of the limousine (p. 255).

Suspiciously, frames 208 through 211 were not published by the Warren Commission and, as noted by David Mantik in his Zapruder film article, frames 208 and 210 were among the six frames from the original film (207 through 212) destroyed by Life magazine (p. 305; Josiah Thompson, Six Seconds in Dallas [New York: Berkley, 1967, 1976], pp. 271-74).

Those are also frames in which the limousines occupants were apparently hidden behind a street sign. Supporting Marler's suspicion that "the Zapruder film was altered to increase the height of the Stemmons sign to conceal President Kennedy's reactions when struck by the first bullet," it is easy to verify his observations about the film's re-enactment photos (CEs 888 through 902). Fetzer only published three of them, CE 888 (p. 220), CE 895 (p. 248) and CE 902 (p. 262). But even with that limited information, I was able to verify Marler's observation that the re-enactment camera was at a lower elevation than Zapruder's, thus artificially raising the sign to hide the car's occupants.

Arlen Specter, Marler tells us, was in charge of the May re-enactment. He also authored the single bullet theory between the dates of the December and May re-enactments. Therefore, if possible, "Arlen Specter, who with a sleight of hand introduced altered evidence (CE-883 and CE-884) and concealed the original survey plat, should be tried for obstruction of justice at the very least" (p. 260).

5) David Mantik's "study of multiple indications that the film has been subjected to at least two kinds of editing..."; "reconstruction of the missing frames, which concludes that the driver, William Greer, actually brought the vehicle to a stop in Dealey Plaza after bullets had begun to be fired..."; finding "that JFK was hit at least twice in the head--once from behind and once from in front..."; and discovery of "a strikingly high degree of agreement among multiple witnesses about shots that hit the President's head."

Mantik's third and final contribution in *Assassination Science*, "Special Effects in the Zapruder Film: How the Film of the Century was Edited" (p. 263), is generally an outstanding overview of the first 34 years of history of the Zapruder film and the scientific investigation thereof.

The short version of Mantik's list of indications of editing is (p. 273):

Disagreements between eyewitnesses and the film.

Disagreements between early viewers of the film (November 1963) and what is currently seen.

Disagreements between the film and other photographs or movies.

Disagreements between the film and the first two reenactments.

Internal inconsistencies in the film.

Overly skeptical readers who are inclined to dismiss reports that the limousine stopped while on Elm Street -- an event contradicted by the Zapruder film -- will find themselves opposite a sizable and impressive group that includes (p. 273-75): United Press International, Newsweek magazine, Time magazine, several policemen including all four motorcycle officers riding beside both sides of the car, and Gerald Posner who is the preeminent pundit of conspiracy denial in the JFK murder.

For those still inclined to think of eyewitnesses as unreliable after reading Mantik's report of a study conducted at the University of Michigan in 1971, which was endorsed by the American Psychological Foundation and the Harvard Law Review, I have something to add. As a graduate of the first class of my local police department's Citizen Police Academy, I can report that it is common knowledge among police that most criminal investigations fail to properly solve a crime, and that 90% of those which are solved succeed as a direct result of eyewitness reports.

Mantik thus found that "the eyewitnesses merely provide the key for unlocking the door" behind which "lies a small mountain of evidence" for two successful head shots following the shot to the throat. The first was from the rear, jerking Kennedy's head slightly to the left. Mantik speculates that Zapruder may have seen him grasp his left chest at the moment of this head shot. That ignores his testimony that he saw that motion just after the first shot sounded and well before any head shot (see my article, "Z-Film: Red Frame, White Light," cited above). Next, a bloodless skull fragment fell into the limousine. Jackie then raised his head to look into his eyes. Mantik says this is the movement that was used to create the false rear head snap. At that moment, more than a second after the first shot and probably several seconds later, the other head shot hit, entering from the front right at his hairline. He fell forward a second time and into Jackie's lap. Mantik says this occurred 40 feet farther down Elm Street and produced a bloody halo. Mantik cites a Newsweek photograph that identified that location (November 22, 1993, p. 74). Indeed, the cited page shows a photograph of Dealey Plaza over which is diagrammed bullet trajectories including a "possible fourth shot from second assailant." Mantik's evidence for the above scenario is exhaustive, comprising 12 pages.

The rest of Mantik's 82-page article details the evidence for the five arguments listed above. Mantik eloquently sums up his findings:

"A strong case can be made for extensive editing of the Zapruder film. In fact, the conclusion seems inescapable--the film was deliberately altered. No other explanation is in the same league, in terms of explanatory power, for the myriad of anomalous characteristics that are seen everywhere in this case. Many frames were excised, some individual frames were extensively altered, others were changed only enough to fill in for missing frames, and others were left alone. Frames that were excised were simply too embarrassing for the official story or contained troublesome edge prints. What is perhaps most remarkable, though, is that, even in the past several years, to say nothing of the past several months, yet more evidence has accumulated--all of it pointing toward alteration. One can only wonder what still remains to be discovered."

As a researcher of the JFK assassination who long ago, and partly for personal reasons, picked the Zapruder film as one of the few subjects to "research the hell out of," and who is included in a small e-mail discussion group of Zapruder film students and experts, namely Chuck Marler, David Wimp, James Fetzer, Milicent Cranor, Michael Griffith, Russell Burr, Ron Redmon, David Mantik and Jack White, I can and do wholeheartedly endorse Dr. Mantik's summary statement.

The ultimate value of sound scientific discovery is that it is truly monumental. Governments rise and fall, as do their monuments to themselves. But competent works of art and science survive for all generations. The conspirators who killed John F. Kennedy knew that, and those who continue the cover-up know that.

It is appropriate, therefore, that *Assassination Science* ends with two facing pages showing a picture on the left of the Kennedy brothers. Its caption reads: "Bobby, Teddy, and Jack, circa 1960. Far-right conservatives not only feared that Jack would be reelected in 1964 but that Bobby would serve two terms after him and Teddy two more, indefinitely perpetuating a Kennedy dynasty."

On the right-hand page is a quote:

A whole new form of government
is going to take over the country...
--Jack Ruby

The coup plotters have always known that their time in power is limited. Their hollow denial of their conspiracies has never been more desperate, as evidenced by the embarrassing media spinning used to attacked Oliver Stone's JFK, and by ridiculous, anti-intellectual books like Case Closed. They know time is running out. What have they planned for that inevitable day when they are exposed? The more important question to keep in mind is therefore: Who is using their time more wisely, the coup plotters or we who are countering them?

Closing Arguments

It is unfortunate for readers interested in the scientific investigation of the JFK assassination that Daryll Weatherly's excellent article, "A New Look at 'the Film of the Century'," (Harrison E. Livingstone, *Killing Kennedy and the Hoax of the Century*, [New York: Carroll & Graf, 1995], pp. 371-80), was not included in *Assassination Science*. It was mentioned and discussed numerous times and in highly complimentary terms by other contributors (pp. 218, 269, 304, 315-17, 330, 333, 341, 363).

That study of the Zapruder film by Weatherly, a mathematician at the State University of New York, was the result of the physics method of adding and subtracting vectors. It is particularly missed here because, as Dr. Fetzer noted in his epilogue (p. 345), "The sense of 'proof' appropriate to empirical science, for example, is less stringent than that appropriate to pure mathematics, but more demanding than that appropriate to courts of law."

I would be remiss if I did not mention another oversight by Fetzer: his complete omission of the digital photographic photometry experiments of former U.S. Steel scientist Tom Wilson. Those experiments, completed and presented years earlier, but never published, reached many of the same conclusions as Fetzer's contributors (Harrison E. Livingstone, *High Treason 2*, [New York: Carroll & Graf, 1992], pp. 338-39).

I saw both of Wilson's initial public presentations. The first was at the Assassination Symposium on John F. Kennedy (ASK) in Dallas in 1991. It was a presentation involving charts of mathematical calculations and color slides of computer-processed images.

That debut of Wilson's work was videotaped by South by Southwest, the conference organizers, but the quality of the presentation and the video was compromised by a loud party in the next-door ballroom. The two ballrooms were separated by a non-soundproof, movable partition. In what is at best an amazing coincidence, that party was part of a reunion of U.S. Secret Service agents, some of whom had served on Kennedy's Dallas trip. That was learned about three years later by Vince Palamara while interviewing some of those former agents.

The second presentation by Wilson was his unscheduled appearance during a break-out session given by Jack White at ASK 1993, the same conference at which Doctors Fetzer, Mantik and Livingston repeated the presentation just given at their November 18th press conference in New York (pp. 17, 144). Wilson's talk was nothing more than a sketchy review of his methodology and an update of his and forensic pathologist Cyril Wecht's attempts to present Wilson's data in a way that would prevent it from being misunderstood or compromised. Those attempts led to Wilson's work as an expert witness, using his image processing technique in a federal murder trial in Clarksburg, West Virginia in 1994. That was followed by his first substantial media exposure in the sixth episode of Nigel Turner's six-hour documentary "The Men Who Killed Kennedy."

From the beginning few JFK assassination researchers have given much thought to Wilson's methods. But I have tried to approach Wilson's work scientifically, concentrating on those aspects that are precise and susceptible of some sort of check or proof.

Because he claims his method reveals photographic forgery and even exposes authentic images within and beneath the forgery, skeptics have asked, "What principle of optics would allow the image deposited on the paper to have a 'hidden' image which would not be optically visible? (other than the possibility of random or differing thicknesses/densities which could cause random 'ghost' images, or images under images like Renaissance paintings which have been refurbished). Is he talking about some non-visible light spectrum, radiation, or infrared?"

Wilson has said his studies lie within the scientific discipline of "Photonics, the science and measurement of light." I was not familiar with that term until I heard Wilson use it. The branch of science that deals with the calculation and measurement of light or of its time rate of flow is photometry. Perhaps Wilson's term is derived from the definition of "photon" as an informal unit of light energy.

Photometry is usually restricted to electromagnetic radiations of wavelengths that are capable of affecting the human eye. That makes it more closely related to Wilson's studies than anything involving the non-visible light spectrum. Photometry has, however, come to mean also the measurement of radiations in the nearby ultraviolet and infrared regions. That less common definition may be the basis for some confusion.

Wilson's work is also related to *photochromism* because it deals with differences in the way substances appear on exposure to radiant energies such as light. But what Wilson is actually talking about seems to be the digital-electronic updating of a science commonly called photographic photometry. By traditional photographic photometry, intensity of radiation, or its spectral distribution, can be measured by photography. The radiation intensity to be measured is compared with that from a standard source by matching the photographic densities produced by both. That method has a high degree of precision if the characteristics of photographic materials are accurately known and the results are interpreted intelligently.

Basically, Wilson's imaging process, developed over his 30 years of employment with U.S. Steel, digitally extends the 30 shades of light value delineated by the human eye to the 256 shades made available by using computers. The key to it is the database he has developed for interpreting the light intensity of different substances in comparison to the characteristics of different photographic materials. The accuracy of his database in identifying substances recorded on photographs has been extensively verified through decades of trials in the steel industry.

It was so accurate, a federal judge allowed the method to be admitted as evidence in a 1994 murder trial in Clarksburg, West Virginia. It was one of the first tests of Wilson's method for identifying biological or natural materials. It also involved determining bullet wounds of entry and exit. Wilson's results were verified by exhuming the corps whose photographs he studied. Re-examination of the corps completely verified Tom Wilson's results. Wecht and Wilson also established a legal precedent for the admissibility of his data as trial evidence.

According to Jack White, Tom Wilson filed suit in 1996 against the U.S. government over the Kennedy Assassination. He intended to use his studies of various photos and films of the assassination to prove not only the conspiracy to assassinate, but the conspiracy to cover up the truth through forgery of Kennedy's autopsy with the use of reconstructive mortician's techniques and direct photographic techniques.

I have not heard what, if anything, has come of the lawsuit. But as with the findings presented in *Assassination Science*, my confidence in Wilson's method lies in its basis in science. Further confidence is justified by Wilson's and Wecht's determination to present their data as legal evidence in a federal proceeding. In short, it is not paranormal pseudoscience nor is it theoretical quantum physics. The data will either be replicable and falsifiable or it won't.

As with the data James Fetzer and his contributors have presented, we need only await peer review of Tom Wilson's scientific data. So far, he has not been proved wrong.

Despite its omissions and other flaws, I highly recommend *Assassination Science*, warts and all. Readers are cautioned, however, to do their own fact-checking, research and thinking.

In his "Undelivered Speech for the Dallas Citizens Council, the Dallas Assembly and the Graduate Research Center of the Southwest in Dallas," President Kennedy wrote: "...leadership and learning are indispensable to each other." Compare that idea to the quote by former CIA Director Allen Dulles that opened this review and you will understand why the United States, and therefore the world, are in grave danger.

Fortunately, it is not against the law to learn. Not yet anyway.

CRITIQUE OF MELLEN'S
CHAPTER 17: THE FINGERPRINT

"It is a capital mistake to theorize before you have all the evidence. It biases the judgment."
    --Arthur Conan Doyle (1887), *A Study in Scarlet,* Part 1, chap. 3

When I read the parts of Joan Mellen's book, *Faustian Bargains*, regarding the fingerprints, I immediately realized that she is ignoring facts, misinterpreting evidence, taking liberties with, and misrepresenting the report of her Certified Latent Print Examiner, Robert J. Garrett.

I consulted her about our 1997-98 Wallace fingerprint investigation during three months in the spring and summer of 2012. I noted some biases and ignorance she had at that time which I tried to help her overcome. I reserved judgment about her vague claims, and the rumors circulating about her book over the years, and waited for her published findings.

I went over some of my general concerns and relevant facts in my speech in Alexandria and Dallas in 2014. But now that Mellen has published, and committed to her conclusions, I'm afraid I must raise some serious and disturbing questions about them.

Six pages into chapter 17, "The Fingerprint," where Mellen begins to give her details about J. Harrison's fingerprint investigation, the errors start piling up quickly.

She claims there was "a single fingerprint collected from the sixth floor of the Texas School Book Depository on the day of the assassination that had never been identified." (p. 252) "Yet Warren Commission Exhibit 656, which she mentions at the end of the same paragraph, and Warren Commission Exhibit 660 show several unidentified latents." Also in that paragraph, Mellen gives a different location for "Box A," from which "Print 29" had allegedly been lifted, but gives no source for this surprising claim.

It is surprising because it contradicts Warren Commission Exhibit 641 (17H292), and the testimony of Sebastian F. Latona, Supervisor of the FBI Latent Fingerprint Section. Latona testified that "Box A" was the top of three stacked boxes on which Lee Harvey Oswald allegedly rested his rifle in the alleged sniper's nest. Despite that known fact, Mellen claims "Box A" was "sitting at the edge of the entrance to the sixth floor."

Then she begins conflating two very different Wallace 10-finger inked print cards by writing, "Harrison's plan was to obtain Mac Wallace's fingerprint card from the Austin Department of Public Safety..." (p. 252), followed by, "Even with Harrison's contacts in the Austin Police Department, it was not easy for him to obtain Wallace's prints." (p. 253)

J. Harrison first obtained the Wallace card on file at the Austin Police Department. That is the one that was unusable. All ten prints were literally smudges—no lines at all—just filled-in ovals. J. rejected the Austin Police prints immediately and only showed them to anyone, including me, for their absurdity. J. then realized that the state police— the Texas Department of Public Safety (DPS)—might also have Wallace's inked prints on file. It is that excellent quality first-generation certified copy of the DPS prints that was used for all of the subsequent matches.

I have the high-resolution TIFFs of both that certified copy of the DPS card and of the certified copies of the Warren Commission latents. The details of how and when we made those scans are in my Task Report, shown in my 2014 slide presentation. I have sent those TIFF files to several researchers over the years, including Jim DiEugenio in 2009, and Joan Mellen in 2012. DiEugenio ignored them and Mellen conflated the DPS and APD inked prints which resulted in her false claim that the prints were unusable.

Her calling them the "Austin prints" (p.253) is inexact to the point of being misleading. APD, which is the Austin municipal police, and the DPS state headquarters are both in Austin, which is the state capital. Darby and Hoffmeister used only the DPS rolled prints, which were excellent quality.

Not even the flat prints at the bottom of the DPS card are smears. Any reference to smears or smudges is a conflation of the actual smeared prints on the ridiculously unusable APD print card. The DPS flat left little finger is obviously too light, due to being too dry from a lack of ink, which is the opposite of an over-inked smear. It is important therefore to counter Mellen's misinformation and restore these proper document names.

I put all of my TIFFs of these documents in a Dropbox folder. Those images show the complete DPS card and WC exhibit 656 plus detail images of both. I made them accessible to anyone with the link. *[Editor's note: Richard will be happy to be contacted about them to interested readers.]*

Those images contain no point markings, initials (D.A.N.), or signature of Darby, whose full name was Asa Nathan Darby (D.A.N. stands for Darby, Asa Nathan). They are the documents Darby used for comparison.

Any images with Darby's marks and writing, such as what Mellen gave to Garrett for comparison, are subsequent copy generations and enlargements used by Darby as working and presentation charts, and are therefore naturally distorted. Any suggestion that those marked charts were Darby's comparison documents is ignorant and absurd.

Mellen repeatedly and wrongly refers to this "one" print found on the sixth floor that was compared to the Wallace inked print provided to the "Austin police" (p. 254) and even misnames it "the Austin police print." (p. 255)

Mellen then writes, "Concluding that Hoffmeister had changed his mind out of fear, J Harrison forged ahead." (p. 256) J. did that for good reason. He was visibly upset and angry with Hoffmeister when he told me that Hoffmeister told him that both he and his wife feared for their lives if his name were connected to his print identification. He insisted to J. that his name never be used in connection with it. I respected that and never did reveal his name. I have always wondered why his name was revealed, and what he thought about it if he had ever found out.

Mellen then departs from the fingerprint to speculate about Wallace's whereabouts the day of the assassination. (p. 257) She writes that she interviewed his son, Michael, who "recalls that almost certainly Wallace was home for dinner...," does not recall what time Wallace arrived on the night of November 22, but he feels certain that he was there." Putting aside Michael Wallace's uncertainty about the time, and the fact that sunset was about six hours after the assassination in Anaheim, I want to ask a different question about this interview.

Why did Mellen go to the trouble of finding and interviewing Wallace's son, but never took the time to talk to Nathan Darby's son, a minister in Austin, before writing that Darby "had perjured himself on his affidavit"(p. 261) when he swore he was certified?

My friend Dawn Meredith, whom Mellen quotes about other matters, is a neighbor of Pastor Steve Darby. She talked to him after Mellen's book was published. In contrast to Michael's uncertainty and qualified statements, Steve, with whom his father lived, is and has always been absolutely certain that his father kept his certification up to date and was certified at the time he swore to it.

Mellen wrote that Garrett's examination was blind, that Garrett wasn't told whose prints he was examining. (p.258) Why, then, does Garrett's report call it the "Warren Commission Exhibit" and the "Wallace print"? (pp. 280-283) Darby's affidavit does not name Wallace. Hoffmeister's fearful reversal of his match after learning its context in 1998 shows the necessity of the examiner remaining blind to the identity of the prints while reporting his findings. Even if Mellen's reexamination of the Darby match had been blind, it was required to be double blind at least. One need only Google Mellen to see her JFK assassination connection, then Google "JFK assassination fingerprint" to learn about the Darby match. This lack of proper scientific blindness alone invalidates the Mellen-Garrett examination.

In August, researcher Sandy Larsen wrote on the Education Forum, "Did the Navy give Mellen authentic fingerprints?" Larsen pursued his question and discovered evidence that the Navy print Garrett used for comparison was not authentic.

On October 5th, Larsen wrote:

> "I have studied the prints and have determined that there are a few subtle (but crucial) differences between the fingerprint Darby was given and the one Garrett was given. That's right... somebody altered the Navy print.
>
> "I've also determined that Darby had to have been given pretty high quality photocopies. Because he could not have seen all fourteen of his matches on that copy floating around the internet.
>
> "And I now know (since I bought the book) that Garrett was given the low resolution copies of Darby's prints... the ones floating around the internet. The ones he said weren't good enough to read. Garrett has not seen what Darby had."

Larsen goes on to explain how he compared the Navy print to the low-resolution Darby print and found differences between them. He then reverted those changes on Garrett's (Navy) print back to what they were before the forger changed them.

After reverting the changes, Larsen said he found eleven of the Darby's fourteen matches. "So, as it turns out," Larsen writes, "the conclusions of both Darby and Garrett are correct. Garrett just had erroneous prints. I plan on documenting what I've done when I find the time."

Larsen added that "Garrett listed 8 mismatches in the lifted print compared to the Navy-provided print. All of those disappeared after reverting the alterations in the Navy-provided print." And that, "The odds of that happening because I'm seeing something in the Darby prints that were created as a result of low-resolution copying are astronomically slim."

Larsen realized something that is immediately obvious to anyone with an introductory knowledge of fingerprint science, that "Garrett wasn't given the high quality photocopies that Darby had."

He adds that "...there is nothing so mysterious about fingerprint analysis that a layman can't understand it. It's like many other skills, carpentry, for example. It takes time to become a craftsman, but understanding how things are built—using lumber, nails, and screws— takes nothing more than observation and common sense.

"If you look at the comparison of a latent print and a ten-print, and see the matches that an examiner found, you will understand right away what the examiner did. And you can do the same. Just not as well as an experienced examiner. If I didn't believe that I wouldn't be planning to present to forum members my discovery of the apparent Navy print forgery. I fully expect that members will understand my presentation."

Douglas Caddy, on October 12th posted Mellen's reply:

> "I am a firm believer in the First Amendment, which includes protection of lies. One point, however, should be corrected since there is not a shred of evidence as to its validity. That is that the US Navy fingerprints of Mac Wallace were altered or tampered with in any way. I did not request these prints of the Navy. I requested from the National Archives Mac Wallace's military file. Included in that file, along with many other documents, were the fingerprints taken when Wallace joined the U.S. Marines in 1939. (J Harrison never was able to access these prints; they were not floating around; they were not part of his files). That these prints matched the Austin prints, were of "the same person" according to Robert Garrett, is further evidence that the Navy prints were Mac Wallace's."

See how she got confused about what Larsen said? Larsen did not say that the Navy prints were the ones floating around the internet. He said the prints alleged to be what Darby used for comparison were the low resolution ones.

In reply to the point that the DPS print and the Navy print were matched by Garrett, Larsen wrote: "That's right. The prints are identical, except for the alterations." Adding, "The Austin print DOES match the WC box print. Darby failed to compare the Austin print with the high-quality WC print from the box. Had he done so he would have seen they match." Larsen concluded that "Garrett had what he needed to do the pertinent comparison. But he didn't do the pertinent comparison."

Larsen gave a more specific explanation of this by referring to Garrett's "Conclusions" paragraph:

"...note that it refers to the comparison of Austin low-quality photocopy (enlargement) which he calls D, and the WC latent low-quality photocopy (enlargement) which he calls E. Unfortunately he doesn't call the Austin photocopy by the proper designation, D, but rather by what it was copied from, B. (You'll see why when you read it.) But you can tell by reading the preceding pages that the comparison was between D and E, not B and E. (D and E are the low-quality photocopies.)

"Joan said that the Austin prints weren't usable, but that is only true of the "flat" set. According to Garrett."

Larsen is correct. There is nothing wrong with the quality of the DPS prints Darby used for comparison. In fact none of the examiners who have studied these prints, including those at the FBI, have ever rejected the materials Darby used based on quality. There is an acronym for their analysis process: ACE-V (analysis, comparison, evaluation and verification). The very first determination any CLPE makes is analysis, assessing a print to determine if it can be used for a comparison. If the print is of inadequate quality, the examination ends there.

Given Mellen's many errors and mistakes in fact and logic in this one chapter, I think Larsen is on the right track. But I have not had time duplicate all of his efforts. I have compared higher quality reproductions of Darby's matches to Garrett's mismatches and have seen Garrett making different interpretations about the location of minutia Darby matched, and have found Darby's interpretation to be more credible.

I am therefore looking forward to Larsen's published findings.

One thing is certain, however. The Mellen-Garrett reexamination is a classic case of junk science--garbage in, garbage out.

And that is a capital mistake.

[Editor's Note: On January 26, 2018, Sandy Larsen posted an update giving an innocent explanation rather than forgery, noting "...that the location of

fingerprint 'minutiae' points change over time...they merge, split, and change in other ways!" Larsen "...compared Mac Wallace's military fingerprints taken in 1939 with his DPS prints taken in 1951...and discovered many significant changes." http://educationforum.ipbhost.com/topic/4966-mac-wallace-fingerprint/?do=findComment&comment=368683]

THE DEEP POLITICAL REALITIES OF THE 2016 U.S. GENERAL ELECTION

"The forces that killed Kennedy wanted the message clear: 'We are in control and no one — not the President, nor Congress, nor any elected official — no one can do anything about it.' It was a message to the people that their Government was powerless." — Vincent J. Salandria (1975) quoted by Gaeton Fonzi, *The Last Investigation* (1993)

Vincent Salandria was right, and that message by the forces who killed Kennedy has become more clear, having been reinforced by the deep political events since Kennedy's death. Most presidents, members of Congress, and other elected and unelected officials have accepted that message and have done nothing to resist its tyranny. But not all.[1]

Some of the resisters failed to get elected. Others failed to survive in office. They were killed, or blackmailed, or bribed, or conned, or scandalized, or frightened into stopping any further attempts to do damage to the Deep State. But not all.

The next president must be a resister and a survivor who will oversee the full release of all of the files on the JFK assassination in 2017. But who among the 2016 candidates is that? It is not a matter of political advocacy, of being for or against a party or candidate in a corrupted election. We only defeat the Gordian Knot by refusing to untie it. It is a matter of explaining better the existing deep political reality using all of the evidence. In my view there is only one who meets the necessary criteria. This is my case for Hillary Rodham Clinton.

To avoid anachronistic thinking, I try to consider what a resister would do today. For the sake of survival, such a person could not repeat the careers of John or Robert Kennedy. They resisted but did not survive. The challenge for a post-1968 candidate is to survive while resisting. The electorate is trained not to talk about the politics of assassination, but it is always the elephant in the room. Such a person would spend a lifetime becoming a viable candidate, and do whatever it takes to survive.

The Kennedys, mostly Joseph P. Kennedy, knew the electoral realities in 1960. I think we have been repeating Kennedy vs. Nixon in major ways ever since. Power goes to the faction who can steal it, or foil the theft. The presidency is tough to infiltrate. But if our government's usurpers can do it repeatedly, so can its protectors and defenders. The big question is, can critical observers see the vague outlines of this battle of shadowed titans? I think so.

It is necessary to distinguish the shopkeepers from the extortionists. Because there exist resisters like Libero Grassi, the shopkeeper from Palermo who wrote an open letter to an anonymous "Dear Extortionist." It rocked the boat, and Grassi was soon dead. But there are also "shopkeepers" who both resist and survive, like "Donnie Brasco" and "Bob Musella," who successfully infiltrated organized crime families and cartels.

A modern-day Deep State resister/survivor would disingenuously act in the interest of the billion-dollar oligarchs, who finance political adventurism, in order to get into power, because it is the only way in a political system that clearly lacks legitimacy.

The Clintons know not only the deep politics of assassination, they know something important that most candidates do not: how to get elected and survive in office while doing real damage to the Deep State. Their history shows two victories against the Deep State that stand above the rest. President Clinton's greatest legacy is the Assassination Records Collection Act, which apparently would have died in its infancy if not for his intervention. First Lady Clinton's greatest legacy is Travelgate, her much misunderstood attempt to protect her husband from Deep State assassins. There is a prehistory to those victories that can be seen by connecting the dots.

During a 1992 campaign appearance with Bill Clinton in McKeesport, Pennsylvania, Clinton's running mate Albert Gore said he believed that President Kennedy was killed by a conspiracy of unknown origin and that all federal files should be opened to the public.[2]

In his acceptance speech at the Democratic convention on July 16, 1992, Clinton paid tribute to the memory of his former Georgetown professor, Carroll Quigley. What a presidential candidate says in a speech at a national party convention is always symbolically significant, and never more so when the candidate is the party's nominee. Carroll Quigley of Georgetown University was a conspiracy historian and an insider of the organizations that created the world's Deep States.[3]

I think the key to understanding Hillary Clinton is not her feelings for Wall Street or Wal-mart, but for Carl Oglesby and Sidney Blumenthal, mutual associates of the Assassination Information Bureau. From the late

1960s until his death in 2011, Clinton had a warm acquaintance with Carl Oglesby, author of the 1975 classic of JFK assassination literature, The Yankee and Cowboy War. His political writings had a life-changing effect on her as a college student. Oglesby also founded the Assassination Information Bureau (AIB). They kept their friendship quiet for obvious political reasons.[4]

Sidney Blumenthal, one of the Clintons' oldest, most trusted, most loyal friends and confidantes was also an acquaintance of Oglesby. With AIB founder Harvey Yazijian, Sidney Blumenthal co-edited Government by Gunplay: Assassination Conspiracy Theories from Dallas to Today, the classic 1976 anthology on the assassinations of JFK, RFK, MLK and Fred Hampton. Blumenthal's book, for which he wrote the forward and epilogue, and contributed two articles, includes an introduction by CIA whistleblower Philip Agee, Robert Groden's "A New Look at the Zapruder Film," and "includes the work of Peter Dale Scott, William Turner, Jeff Gerth, Carl Oglesby, Jerry Policoff...L. Fletcher Prouty and Allard Lowenstein, who himself was assassinated."[5]

In the Clinton White House, Rahm Emanuel gave Blumenthal a special nickname because he kept pointing out hidden plots. As Carl Bernstein put it in his 2007 biography of Clinton, A Woman in Charge (p. 490), "Presidential aide Rahm Emanuel had given Blumenthal the nickname 'G.K.,' for Grassy Knoll, suggesting conspiracy theories on a scale with John Kennedy's assassination." In May 2015, after their email exchanges leaked regarding Syrian intrigues, Hillary Clinton had to publicly play them down, saying it was her desire to listen to diverse opinions.

Oglesby, who stayed publicly linked to conspiracy, had to distance himself as Clinton's early political influence and acquaintance. Blumenthal, who is publicly known as her longtime close friend, has to distance himself from conspiracy analysis. As a result of these mutual acquaintances and friendships, Hillary knew exactly what she was talking about when she coined the term "Vast Right-wing Conspiracy" at the time of her husband's impeachment.[6]

In the first four days of his first term, President Clinton, or an alert aide, may have saved the Assassination Records Collection Act, and the investigative body that it mandated, from expiring prematurely. I recall pessimistic discussions at that time by researchers of deep politics that the act has a clever self-destruct clause which states, "The President shall make nominations to the Review Board not later than 90 calendar days after the date of enactment of this Act." It was suspected that President Bush's signing the act into law on October 26, 1992 set an impossible deadline for nominations on January 24, a Sunday, only four days after

Clinton was sworn into office.

Establishing the Review Board was delayed for 15 months, and Congress did not fund its operations until October 1994. Until then, it was funded solely from the Clinton White House budget. These and other delays by federal agencies threatened the completion of the Board's work by the act's mandated three-year deadline, requiring a resolution from Congress granting another year which had to be signed into law by Clinton.

Thanks largely to these necessary interventions from President Clinton, the act was saved, allowing the last major inquiry of the assassination to proceed. It succeeded in releasing nearly all of the remaining assassination documents, which further proved the conspiracy. It is easy to see how an apathetic or hostile White House could have prevented that success.[7]

President Clinton had reason to be concerned for his personal safety when he said at a 30th anniversary press conference that he thought JFK was killed by a single assassin and he (Clinton) was satisfied with his own security arrangements.[8]

The all-but-forgotten intrigues which occurred between the time of Travelgate and the death of Vince Foster are vastly important considerations in the deep politics of Clinton's public statements.

On May 19, 1993, one of Clinton's presidential helicopters crashed in the morning, followed that afternoon by Vince Foster's involvement in the firing of the White House Travel Office staff of Bush holdovers (aka Travelgate). Scott Reynolds, William Barkley, Brian Hassley and Tim Sabel, who died in the crash, reportedly had served as Clinton bodyguards. The crash site, near Quantico Virginia, was reportedly closed to the press and a video of the crash site, taken by a fire fighter, was seized by military officials.[9] [10]

I personally recall that the crash was the top story that morning on CNN, but it strangely disappeared after the travel office firings dominated the news, despite the glaring fact that the job of the White House Travel Office was to book flights on presidential aircraft. The connection between those two events remains a deafening silence.

The night of Vince Foster's "suicide," two months after the firings, it was the eve of his trip to Denver on Clinton's behalf to meet with an attorney about Travelgate. Foster's widow told Esquire magazine that Travelgate had been her husband's preoccupation since it happened.[11] In his eulogy, President Clinton called Foster "a great protector" of his friends, adding, "We could never remember a time when he ever asked us to protect him — it was always the other way around."[12]

Carl Bernstein, in *A Woman in Charge*, wrote, "The president was concerned about how Foster would react to the [July 19 Wall Street Journal] editorial [linking Foster and Hillary to the Travel Office firings], and called to invite him to a White House movie screening of In the Line of Fire (strangely, about a would-be presidential assassin and a heroic Secret Service agent) that night. Foster declined...." (p. 340) In her first meeting with Webb Hubble, one of her closest friends, after Foster's death, and after their consoling words to each other, "Hillary then changed the subject to ask for some help regarding a rumor she had heard that before his death Foster had been investigating a group of assassins who worked for the Navy and made their victims look as though they'd committed suicide. She said that the president had already been approached by a reporter about it." (p. 343) "After Vince's death, she 'found more to judge as evil,' [old friend Dick] Atkinson could see. 'There seemed to be something basic that was reinforcing her view of good and evil, an element of embitterment there, and the notion of conspiracy." (p. 346)

At her own campaign appearance at the University of Tennessee in Nashville on January 29, 2008, candidate Hillary Clinton said, when asked, that she would do everything she could as president to release the remaining classified JFK assassination files.[13]

The forces who killed President Kennedy continue to send a clear message that we are powerless to stop them. But we have never been completely powerless. We have long had enough proof of the conspiracy and conspirators. What we do not yet have is the power to force the usurpers of our government to give us the final details of their conspiracy.

Criminal science teaches that the best way to combat a conspiracy is to infiltrate it successfully. When viewed from that perspective, the Clintons appear to be doing that, and doing it well. If the Clintons retake the White House and continue to survive, the final test of this perspective will be the final deadline in the Assassination Records Collection Act: October 26, 2017. It is the day all remaining withheld records on the Kennedy assassination will be released unless the president, and only the president, decides otherwise. It is also Hillary Rodham Clinton's 70th birthday.

[Editor's Note: Needless to say, the President did not decide to release all remaining records on the Kennedy assassination.]

Notes:

1. Rex Bradford, "Whispers from the Silent Generation," Speech delivered at

November in Dallas Conference, May 2013
http://www.maryferrell.org/pages/Essay_-
_Whispers_from_the_Silent_Generation.html
     2. Los Angeles Times, July 20, 1992.
     3. Daniel Brandt, "Clinton, Quigley, and Conspiracy: What's going on
here?," NameBase NewsLine, No. 1, April-June 1993
http://www.namebase.org/news01.html
     4. James V. Grimaldi, "Clinton Quiet About Own Radical Ties," Washington
Post, May 19, 2008 http://www.washingtonpost.com/wp-
dyn/content/article/2008/05/18/AR2008051802101.html
     5. Bill Kelly, "Max the Hack is Back" JFKcountercoup, June 15, 2015.
http://jfkcountercoup.blogspot.com/2015/06/max-hack-is-back.html
     6. Carl M. Cannon, "'Far-right conspiracy' a gift from Blumenthal Clinton
adviser valued for his journalism past," Baltimore Sun, February 15, 1998.
http://articles.baltimoresun.com/1998-02-15/news/1998046033_1_aide-sidney-
blumenthal-white-house-al-gore
     Max Holland, "'Grassy Knoll' Sid: Hillary's Personal Conspiracy Theorist,"
Washington Decoded, June 11, 2015.
http://www.washingtondecoded.com/site/2015/06/blumenthal.html#fn3
     7. President John F. Kennedy Assassination Records Collection Act, 44
U.S.C. ch. 21 § 2107, Sec. 7(b)(2) http://www.gpo.gov/fdsys/pkg/STATUTE-
106/pdf/STATUTE-106-
Pg3443.pdf;https://en.wikipedia.org/wiki/President_John_F._Kennedy_Assassin
ation_Records_Collection_Act_of_1992; http://spartacus-
educational.com/JFKassboard.htm
     Final Report of the Assassinations Records Review Board, September, 1998.
ch. 2, Sec. B. http://www.fas.org/sgp/advisory/arrb98/part04.htm
     8. David E. Rosenbaum, "30-Year Commemoration In Dallas and
Arlington," New York Times Nov. 23, 1993, p. A16.
http://www.nytimes.com/1993/11/23/us/30-year-commemoration-in-dallas-and-
arlington.html
     9. Unsolved Mysteries Wiki, "US Marine Corps Helicopter Crash"
http://unsolvedmysteries.wikia.com/wiki/US_Marine_Corps_Helicopter_Crash
     10. Wikipedia, "White House travel office controversy,"
http://en.wikipedia.org/wiki/White_House_travel_office_controversy
     11. Gregory Jaynes, "The Death of Hope," Esquire, November 1993, Vol.
120 Issue 5, p. 85.http://archive.esquire.com/issue/19931101
     http://connection.ebscohost.com/c/articles/9402150567/death-hope
     12. Paul Richter, "Clinton Eulogy Recalls Friendship With Foster," Los
Angeles Times, July 24, 1993.
     http://articles.latimes.com/1993-07-24/news/mn-16379_1_white-house-aides
     13. "Hillary Clinton Called for Release of JFK Files," JFK Facts, October
28, 2015. http://jfkfacts.org/hillary-clinton-called-for-release-of-jfk-files/

ABOUT THE AUTHOR

Richard Bartholomew is a co-founder and director of the Center for Deep Political Research. His talent, education, training, and professional experience have been primarily in the visual arts, resulting in his career as an award-winning graphic designer, illustrator and editorial cartoonist.

He is syndicated internationally by Artizans, and his artwork is in the permanent collections of the University of Texas Center for American History, the Newseum in Washington, D.C., and Ohio State's Billy Ireland Cartoon Library and Museum.

Prior to syndication he was widely published by Texas Monthly Press, University of Texas Press, the Austin American-Statesman, the Austin Business Journal, The Texas Observer, The Austin Chronicle, D Magazine, The Quorum Report, the Waco Tribune-Herald, The Washington Post, The Cleveland Plain Dealer, and elsewhere. His cartoons appeared annually in Charles Brooks' Best Editorial Cartoons of the Year.

His awards include the Outstanding Entry Award in the John Fischetti Editorial Cartoon Competition, sponsored by Columbia College Chicago, and the Award of Excellence in the 10th annual International Editorial Cartoon Competition, hosted by the Canadian Committee for World Press Freedom. His animation work has appeared in two feature films, *The Quest for Camelot* (Warner Bros., 1997) and *The Prince of Egypt* (DreamWorks, 1998).

His historiography and criminal investigations of the JFK assassination were initially motivated by a civic duty to report a suspicious automobile fitting the description of a getaway car seen by several witnesses leaving Dealey Plaza in his hometown of Dallas. Bartholomew's investigative work has been more in the tradition of a self-taught Sherlock Holmes than a professional Inspector Lestrade.

His research of the JFK assassination includes his discovery of a 1959 Rambler station wagon possibly used in the conspiracy; a study co-

authored with Walter F. Graf involving a rifle clip that contaminates the
ballistic evidence; a chronological reconstruction and placement of
missing movements edited out of the Zapruder film; an in-depth
interview of Erwin Schwartz, with author Noel Twyman, regarding Mr.
Schwartz's and Mr. Zapruder's early chain of possession of Zapruder's
film; and work for author Barr McClellan resulting in Bartholomew's
monograph establishing the methods by which the FBI and the Warren
Commission concealed and obfuscated latent fingerprints from the
alleged sniper's nest.

Bartholomew's research has been presented at scholarly conferences,
and published in books and journals on the JFK assassination. In two
decades, his findings have had no serious, negative criticism in a field
rife with such.

At the JFK Historical Group conference in Washington D.C. in 2018,
he explained why 54 years of revelations about the deep political forces
who killed President Kennedy have failed to make a difference. He
argued for a new methodology aimed at using the existing knowledge of
those crimes against democracy to effectively stop the Deep State's
ability to continue its propaganda of official lies.

35947007R00237

Made in the USA
San Bernardino, CA
16 May 2019